PETERSON'S®

Master the™
SAT® 2020

 PETERSON'S®

About Peterson's®

Peterson's has been your trusted educational publisher for over 50 years. It's a milestone we're quite proud of as we continue to offer the most accurate, dependable, high-quality educational content in the field, providing you with everything you need to succeed. No matter where you are on your academic or professional path, you can rely on Peterson's for its books, online information, expert test-prep tools, the most up-to-date education exploration data, and the highest quality career success resources—everything you need to achieve your education goals. For our complete line of products, visit **www.petersons.com**.

For more information, contact Peterson's, 8740 Lucent Blvd., Suite 400, Highlands Ranch, CO 80129; 800-338-3282 Ext. 54229; or visit us online at **www.petersons.com**.

SAT® is a trademark registered and/or owned by the College Board, which was not involved in the production of, and does not endorse, this product.

SAT Subject Tests™ is a trademark registered and/or owned by the College Board, which was not involved in the production of, and does not endorse, this product.

ISBN-13: 978-0-7689-4400-6

Printed in the United States of America

10 9 8 7 6 5 4 3 2 1   22 21 20

CONTENTS

PART IV: WRITING STRATEGIES FOR THE SAT® EXAM

PART V: ESSAY WRITING STRATEGIES FOR THE SAT® EXAM

PART VI: MATH STRATEGIES FOR THE SAT® EXAM

11 Geometry

12 Functions and Intermediate Algebra

13 Data Analysis, Statistics, and Probability

PART VII: PRACTICE TESTS FOR THE SAT® EXAM

PART VIII: APPENDICES

INTRODUCTION TO PETERSON'S MASTER THE™ SAT® 2020

Whether you have three long months or just a few short weeks to go until test day, *Peterson's Master the™ SAT® 2020* can help prepare you for the SAT exam. This book not only covers the structure of the exam itself but also provides a thorough review of the topics you will encounter on the exam, hundreds of practice questions and skill builder exercises, and detailed answer explanations of why an answer is correct (and why the other answer options are incorrect).

Inside you will find a diagnostic test that, once completed and scored, will provide you with a baseline of your strengths and weaknesses. Each chapter reviews the most important topics found on the exam, and provides valuable strategies to help you navigate to the best answer choice. In addition, you'll also find that *Peterson's Master the™ SAT® 2020* discusses all of the "big picture issues" other books ignore. For example, Part 1 addresses the following questions:

- How is the SAT exam really used for college admission?
- When should you take the test?
- How many times should you plan to take the SAT exam?
- Do all SAT exam scores "count" in college admissions?

By addressing these questions, *Peterson's Master the™ SAT® 2020* debunks prevailing myths and helps you put the SAT exam into proper perspective. It also serves as your "college guidance counselor," giving you the expert advice you need to apply to college. And when you think about it, that's our number-one goal here. Our objective is to help you raise your scores so that you can maximize the likelihood of getting into the college of your choice.

How This Book Is Organized

Peterson's Master the™ SAT® 2020 is divided into eight parts to facilitate your study.

- **Part I** explains everything you need to know about the SAT exam and provides an overview with examples of the different question types you'll find on the actual test.
- **Part II** offers a diagnostic practice test to help you identify your areas of strength and those areas where you need to spend more time in your review sessions.
- **Part III** explores the Reading Test section and offers expert strategies for approaching passages and answering each type of question.
- **Part IV** goes into detail about the different types of questions you'll see on the Writing and Language Test section. You'll also find a helpful review of English conventions.
- **Part V** describes the optional Essay part of the SAT exam and provides strategies for developing a well-supported and coherent response to the essay prompt.
- **Part VI** offers a thorough review of all math topics you'll see on the Math Test—No Calculator and Math Test—Calculator sections. You'll find helpful information on multiple-choice and grid-in math strategies, plus helpful reviews of numbers and operations; basic algebra; geometry; functions and intermediate algebra; and data analysis, statistics, and probability.
- **Part VII** includes two full-length practice tests so you can simulate taking the SAT exam under timed conditions. Each of the practice tests has detailed answer explanations plus instructions on how to determine your scores for the Evidence-Based Reading and Writing section and the two Math sections. You'll also be able to calculate your subscores in the categories of Expression of Ideas, Standard English Conventions, Words in Context, Command of Evidence, Heart of Algebra,

Problem Solving and Data Analysis, and Passport to Advanced Math as well as the cross-test scores for the Analysis in History/Social Studies and Analysis in Science questions.

- **Part VIII** contains the Appendices. Appendix A is the *Parents' Guide to College Admission Testing*, offering great information to assist parents in creating a plan to help their teens prepare for college admissions tests. It discusses the various roles parents play, how to approach teens on this subject matter, and how to work with the guidance counselor. It also provides great tips on how to help teens improve their time management—essential when preparing for standardized tests like the SAT exam. Appendix B is an exhaustive list of essential math formulas to memorize for test day.

Special Study Features

You will find the following kinds of special study features scattered throughout the book:

Tips point out valuable information you need to know when taking the SAT exam. Tips provide quick and simple hints for selecting the correct answers for the most common SAT question types.

Alerts identify potential pitfalls in the testing format or question types that can cause common mistakes in selecting answers.

Notes address information about the test structure itself.

Cautions provide warnings, such as common grammatical errors or possible errors in computation or formulas that can result in choosing incorrect answers.

New to this edition are quick and simple activities designed to get your body moving and give your brain a much needed study break. These 5–10 minute **brain breaks** are strategically placed throughout to provide you with the opportunity to redirect and refresh your mind. Use and modify them as you wish. The main objective is to give your mind, and your body, a break from studying (or stressing).

Also new to this edition are **fun facts**. These tidbits of trivia are interspersed throughout and are designed to make you briefly pause in your studies to learn a random piece of information not found on the SAT exam.

At the end of every chapter (excluding Chapter 2: The Diagnostic Test), you'll find **Summing It Up**. This section provides a bulleted summary of the key ideas and strategies within a chapter. Read it in full and test yourself. Each Summing It Up is followed by three metacognitive questions that ask you to review what you learned, evaluate how well you learned it, and plan for how to address any areas of weakness. Those questions may seem like extra steps, but they're necessary for improvement. Strong learners frequently assess how well they're learning and make strategic decisions to learn better. You can too.

How to Use This Book

It's understandable that all of the information you'll be reading about the SAT exam might seem a little overwhelming. But even if you are feeling confused by everything the exam requires, take some comfort in the knowledge that you are holding a great resource to help you do well on test day. This book's job is not to make you a genius; its job is to make sure you are prepared to take the SAT exam. If you become a genius in the process, consider that a bonus.

The following four steps will help you get the most out of using this guide:

Step 1: First Things First—Get to Know the Exam

You will get the most out of *Peterson's Master the*™ *SAT*® *2020* by using this book as it is organized. You may be tempted to skip Chapter 1: All About the SAT® Exam because you're anxious to get right to the lessons. That's where the real preparation begins, right?

However, Chapter 1 is very useful for giving you a picture of the exam's content as a whole. If you skip the chapter, you'll miss out on vital information about the SAT exam: when and how many times you should take it; how to register; how the exam is scored and how scores are reported; the test format and question types, including a first look at kinds of questions on the Reading Test, the Writing and Language Test, and the Math Tests (Calculator and No Calculator); strategies for test-taking success, and much more!

Step 2: The Diagnostic Test Is Your Friend—Don't Skip It!

Once you've learned the essential information about the SAT exam in general, you will need to take the first step toward getting your scores where you want them to be by taking the diagnostic test. The diagnostic test is a full-length practice test that you take *before* you start studying or reviewing any subject material.

Understandably, taking a long diagnostic test may not seem the ideal way to get started on your test-preparation path. However, the point of a diagnostic test is to give you an idea of what your strengths and weaknesses are *before* you dive into your SAT exam preparation. By taking the diagnostic test and analyzing your answers, you will be able to pinpoint which question formats are giving you the most difficulty. You may discover that you retained more information from your English classes than you realized. You might also learn that you aren't quite the math expert you thought you were. Or maybe you will find that most of your math skills are really strong, but you need some help when it comes to quadratic equations. Your diagnostic test results will help you obtain a clearer idea of your strengths and weaknesses. This knowledge will help you identify which chapters of this book really demand your focus, and you will be better equipped to build a study plan that is best for you.

Step 3: Build Your Skills—Practice, Practice, Practice!

After evaluating your diagnostic test results, you should have a pretty good idea of where your study focus needs to be. By diligently studying the information presented within the pages of this book, you will become familiar with not only the question types that will appear on the SAT but also the language of the exam.

Throughout each review chapter (Chapters 3–13), you will find numerous practice questions that will help familiarize you with the language and presentation of the SAT exam. The practice and skill builder exercises in these review chapters are a great way to practice, and the thorough answer explanations will help you understand why an answer is right—or more importantly, why an answer is wrong. This can hopefully keep you from making a similar mistake again when you take the real test.

Step 4: See What You Have Learned—Test Yourself Again

Near the end of the book, in Part VII, you will have the opportunity to take two complete practice tests. Take these practice tests under simulated test conditions. That means finding a quiet place where you won't be interrupted and setting a timer for the required time for each section, completing each test section in the same time that will be allotted for the actual test:

- Reading Test: 65 minutes
- Writing and Language Test: 35 minutes
- Math Test—No Calculator: 25 minutes
- Math Test—Calculator: 55 minutes
- Essay: 50 minutes

Work through each test as though it were test day. Doing so will help you to get used to the time limits and to learn to pace yourself. With each practice test, you should see an improvement in your score since taking the diagnostic test.

TIP

Familiarizing yourself with the way certain questions are worded on the SAT may help you figure out the kind of question you are answering, which may help you select the best answer.

THE PETERSON'S SUITE OF SAT® EXAM PRODUCTS

As mentioned previously, one of the keys to earning the score you are aiming for is to practice, practice, practice. In addition to the information provided in *Peterson's Master the™ SAT® 2020*, Peterson's has an array of cutting-edge SAT exam preparation resources designed to give you the best test preparation possible. Our online course and interactive practice tests can be used alone or combined with other Peterson's SAT-focused products to help you succeed and get the test scores you want. Take a few minutes to discover what's available in Peterson's suite of SAT products or visit our website at **www.petersons.com/testprep/sat**.

Peterson's Master the™ SAT® 2020

Peterson's Master the™ SAT® 2020 features content and strategies that will help you master the SAT exam. It contains a full-length diagnostic test, two full-length practice tests, and access to additional practice tests online.

The expert subject review and skill-specific exercises in *Peterson's Master the™ SAT® 2020* can help familiarize you with the unique content, structure, and format of the test. Test-taking tips and advice guide you smoothly from your first day of test preparation to test day.

NOTE

You have the option to take the practice tests either in the book or online. For more information, go to www.petersons. com/testprep/sat.

In addition, taking online practice tests is desirable because you get immediate feedback and automated scoring. *Peterson's Master the™ SAT® 2020* gives you access to not only the tests in this book, but access to additional practice tests online, with detailed feedback to help you understand the concepts presented. The content in these practice tests was created by the test-prep experts at Peterson's to help you boost your test-prep confidence. You can access the practice tests at **www.petersons.com/testprep/sat**. Use coupon code **SAT2020** for complimentary access with the purchase of this book.*

* **Important:** Usage of the coupon code to access online content is intended for the original purchaser of the book and not for resellers or library patrons. Access will expire 18 months after the copyright date printed in this title.

Peterson's Online Course for the SAT® Exam

Peterson's Online Course for the SAT® Exam is a comprehensive test prep course that is customized for you. In addition to practice tests, the online course provides access to supplemental content, including additional subject-specific strategies and lessons, tips, and college search options tailored to your projected test scores and interests.

Here's how the online course works:

- An initial diagnostic pretest determines your strengths and weaknesses.
- Based on your diagnostic test results, interactive lessons teach you the subject areas you need to learn.
- Quizzes after each lesson gauge how well you have learned the materials just taught.
- Full-length practice tests allow you to apply all the skills you've learned and monitor your progress.

Peterson's Online Course for the SAT® Exam gives you the opportunity to solidify your understanding and build your confidence about any concept you may encounter on the SAT—no matter how close it is to test day!

Looking for Additional Practice? Check out Peterson's Test Prep Subscriptions

Our subscription plans allow you to study as quickly as you can, or as slowly as you'd like. How does it work? Subscribers get unlimited usage of our entire test prep catalogue for over 150 exams, including important exams for high school students like the SAT, ACT, AP Exams, and SAT Subject Tests. For more information, go to **www.petersons.com/testprep/sat**.

GIVE US YOUR FEEDBACK

Peterson's publishes a full line of books—test prep, career preparation, education exploration, and financial aid. Peterson's publications can be found at high school guidance offices, college libraries and career centers, and your local bookstore and library. Peterson's books are also available for purchase online at **petersons.com**.

We welcome any comments or suggestions you may have about this publication. Your feedback will help us make education dreams possible for you—and others like you.

Now that you know why *Peterson's Master the™ SAT® 2020* is an essential resource to prepare you to take a very important test, it's time to make the most of this powerful preparation tool. Turn the page and find out everything you need to know about the SAT!

PART I:
BASIC FACTS ABOUT THE SAT® EXAM

Chapter 1: All About the SAT® Exam

All About the SAT® Exam

OVERVIEW

- **Overview of the SAT® Exam**
- **The Current SAT® Exam Format**
- **Make an SAT® Exam Study Plan**
- **Strategies for SAT® Exam Success**
- **Top 10 Strategies to Raise Your Score**
- **Summing It Up**

OVERVIEW OF THE SAT® EXAM

For almost one hundred years, the SAT® has acted as a test of the skills and knowledge that students use every day—in class and in the world. The College Board—the maker of the SAT—claims that the SAT can predict how students will perform academically as first-year college students—indicating overall college preparedness. At the same time, college admissions officers use the test to make acceptance decisions, having access to an objective tool that assesses student skills for reading, English conventions, mathematics, and writing. On its own, that doesn't really help you. But the more you know about the test, the more you'll be prepared on test day. The following information will lay out basic details for helping you better understand the importance of the test as well as how to take your first steps toward earning your desired score. Later in the chapter are details related to test format, question types across sections, and strategies for building to scoring success.

How the SAT Exam is Used for College Admissions

When you think about it, admissions officers have a difficult job, particularly when they are asked to compare the academic records of students from different high schools in different parts of the country taking different classes. It's not easy to figure out how one student's grade point average (GPA) in New Mexico correlates with that of another student in Florida. Even though admissions officers can do a good deal of detective work to evaluate candidates fairly, they benefit a great deal from the SAT. The SAT provides a single standardized means of comparison. After all, of the roughly four million students who completed admissions testing last year, about half took the SAT, and the test was the same for everyone. It doesn't matter whether you took it in Maine, Maryland, or Montana.

So, the SAT is an important test. But it is not the be-all and end-all of admissions factors. Keep it in perspective! It is only one of several important pieces of the college admissions puzzle. Other factors that

1

weigh heavily into the admissions process include GPA, difficulty of course load, level of extracurricular involvement, and the strength of the college application itself.

When to Take the SAT Exam (and SAT Subject Tests™)

When you decide which schools you're going to apply to, find out if they require college admissions testing, the SAT and ACT. Most do! Your next step is to determine when they need your SAT scores. Write that date down. That's the one you really don't want to miss.

You do have some leeway in choosing your test date. The SAT is typically offered on one Saturday morning in August, October, November, December, March, May, and June. Check the exact dates to see which ones meet your deadlines. Tests are offered on select Sundays, usually the Sunday after each Saturday test date, for students who cannot take the test on Saturday due to religious observance. Students who wish to take the SAT exam on a Sunday must provide a letter printed on stationery from their house of worship explaining the religious reason for the request. An official religious leader must sign the letter.

You may think to yourself "What if I don't know which schools I want to apply to?" Don't panic! That's okay. Even if you take the exam in December of your senior year, you'll probably have plenty of time to send your scores to most schools. Of course, you want to make sure that your testing date will allow you enough time to receive your scores before you need to apply, whether that's for early decision, early action, or regular decision.

When you plan to take the SAT, there is something even more important than the application deadlines of particular schools. You need to select a test date that works best with your schedule. Some states—such as Colorado, Illinois, and Tennessee, among others—provide the SAT for free to high school juniors (usually in mid-April). And while your state may require you to take the exam on that test date, that doesn't have to be the only time you do so. Ideally, you should allow yourself at least two to three months to use this book to prepare. Many students like to take the test in March of their junior year, before final exams, the prom, and other end-of-the-year distractions. Taking the test in March also gives students early feedback as to how they are scoring. If they are dissatisfied with their scores, there is ample opportunity to take the test again in the spring or following fall. But your schedule might not easily accommodate a March testing. Maybe you're involved in a winter sport or school play that will take too much time away from studying. Maybe you have a family reunion planned over spring break in March. Or maybe you simply prefer to prepare during a different time of year. If that's the case, just pick another date.

If the schools you've decided on also require SAT Subject Tests™, here's one good piece of advice: Try to take SAT Subject Tests™ immediately after you finish the subject(s) in school. For most students, this means taking the SAT Subject Tests™ in June. By taking the exam then, you'll save an awful lot of review work. Remember this, too: you have to register for the SAT Subject Tests™ separately, and you can't take the Subject Tests on the same day as the SAT. So, check the dates, think ahead, and plan it out. It's worth it in the end.

How the SAT Exam Is Scored

Once you've taken the test, what's next? Off your answers go to the machines at College Board and to the high school and college teachers who have been trained to read and score the essays. The machines can scan the bubble sheets in seconds and calculate a score for most of your test. If you are taking the optional essay portion, two qualified scorers will read your essay and score it based on three criteria: reading, analysis, and writing.

1

In scoring the multiple-choice and math grid-in sections of the SAT, the machines give one point for each correct answer. Incorrect answers have no effect on your score. The result of these calculations for each part of the SAT—Math and Evidence-Based Reading and Writing—is your raw score. This is then converted to a scaled score between 400 and 1600.

Each reader of your essay uses a rubric against which he or she reads your essay. Each reader then gives your essay a score from 1 to 4 for each of the rubric categories. The two scores are then added to give you an essay subscore for each rubric category. The scores for each category will not be combined, but instead, they will be represented by three separate scores ranging from 2-8, one for Reading, Analysis, and Writing.

Scores will be reported to you and to the colleges you have chosen. Remember, if you take the SAT more than once, you can choose whether the schools you are applying to receive the scores from each test date or just some of them.

How Your Scores Are Reported

After you have taken the SAT exam, College Board scores your test and creates a score report. You and your high school receive score reports from each SAT and SAT Subject Test™ that you decide to take.

There are numerous options to choose from to send your score reports to the schools of your choice. Most schools prefer, and often list as a requirement, that scores be submitted directly from College Board either electronically or by phone. Most schools will not accept copies of online score reports or score report labels on transcripts.

At the time of registration, you can pick four colleges or universities to receive your score report. College Board will send your scores to these four schools for free. Within nine days of taking the test, you can change your school selection. If you want to send more than four reports or change your mind more than nine days after your test date, you will have to pay to do so.

Upon your approval, College Board will send *all* of your SAT scores automatically to the colleges on your list. But what if you decide to take the SAT or any SAT Subject Test™ more than once? Can you pick and choose the scores you send? The answer to this question depends upon the admissions policies of the college.

Some schools will give you the option of deciding which complete SAT exam score to send from one, several, or all test dates. Other schools will allow you to pick and choose your best scores from the Math, Evidence-Based Reading and Writing, and Essay individual sections (a process called "superscoring"), regardless of whether they are from the same test date. It is up to you to check on the individual policy of each college to which you are applying, and then decide which scores you wish to send.

To make this process a bit easier, College Board provides an optional tool to aid in helping you choose which scores to send. Score Choice™ (**https://collegereadiness. collegeboard.org/sat/scores/sending-scores/score-choice**) is a free tool that you can access from your College Board SAT online account. It allows you to search for the college or scholarship program of your choice and select which scores to send based on the

NOTE
Because the SAT can vary in format, scaled scores allow the test-maker to account for differences from one version of the SAT to another. Using scaled scores ensures that a score of 500 on one SAT is equivalent to 500 on another.

1

requirements for each specific college chosen. Keep in mind that you should also confirm with the college that the requirements have not changed.

How Often to Take the SAT Exam

Different colleges evaluate the exam in different ways. Some colleges take your highest Math, Evidence-Based Reading and Writing, and Essay scores, even if they were earned on different test days. However, other colleges may pay most attention to your highest combined score from a single day.

So what does this mean? It means that you should take the SAT exam only when you are truly prepared. There is nothing wrong with taking the SAT two or three times, as long as you are confident that your scores will improve substantially each time. Let's say that you scored an 1100 on your first SAT. If you would have been thrilled to have hit 1120, it's probably not worth taking the test again. Most colleges look at SAT scores in ranges and will not hold 20 points against you. They understand that scoring an 1100 means that you were only one or two questions away from 1120. But if you scored an 1100 and expected to score closer to 1200 or 1300 based on practice testing, then you should probably retake the exam. In other words, it is of little value to take the SAT multiple times if you expect to earn roughly the same score. But it is worthwhile if you expect to score significantly higher on a second or third try (or if you spend time preparing with the help of something like this book). For more advice about this, see your high school guidance counselor.

Registering for The SAT Exam

You should register for the SAT exam at least six weeks before your testing date. That way you will avoid late registration fees and increase your chances of taking the exam at your first-choice testing center. Late registration requires an extra fee and has the added danger of not securing you a spot for your desired date or placing you at a distant testing center, adding stress to an already stressful process.

Registering online is the probably the quickest (and preferred) method, and you will receive immediate registration confirmation. You will need to pay by credit card, and you will need to upload a photo with your registration. The photo you provide will become part of your Admission Ticket on test day. For more information, visit **https://collegereadiness.collegeboard.org/sat/register**.

In some cases, you can register through the mail by completing the SAT registration form found inside *The SAT*® and *SAT Subject Tests*™ *Student Registration Booklet*, which can be found in your guidance counselor's office or online (printable PDF) at **https://collegereadiness.collegeboard.org/pdf/sat-registration-booklet-students.pdf**.

Photo ID

The photo you provide (either uploaded with your online registration or mailed in with the printed registration) becomes part of your Admission Ticket on test day. Photos must be properly focused with a full-face view. The photo must be clearly identifiable as you, and it must match your appearance on test day.

ALERT

If you are electing to take the SAT exam during a designated SAT School Day, you will receive information from your school or school district regarding registration requirements and any fees you may need to pay. You DO NOT register for SAT School Day through the College Board. Pay careful attention to the requirements set forth by the school or district and contact your guidance counselor with any questions that you may have.

ALERT

You must provide a photo when you sign up for the SAT. The photo will be part of your Admission Ticket, and it will be checked against your photo ID on test day.

Choose a photo that:

- Shows only you—no other people in the shot
- Shows a head-and-shoulders view, with the entire face, both eyes, and hair clearly visible (head coverings are allowed if worn for religious purposes)
- Is properly focused and has no dark spots or shadows

To see examples of acceptable photos, visit **https://collegereadiness.collegeboard.org/ sat/register/policies-requirements/photo**.

In addition, you are responsible for bringing an acceptable form of identification. Some acceptable examples include:

- Government-issued driver's license
- Government-issued nondriver ID card
- Official school identification card (from the school you currently attend)
- Government-issued passport or US Global Entry identification card
- Government-issued military or national identification card
- School ID Form* prepared by your school
- Talent Search Identification Program ID/Authorization to Test Form (grades 7 and 8 only); photo not required

* Your school can prepare an ID form for you. This form must include a recognizable photo, and the school seal must overlap the photo. Sign the ID form in the presence of your counselor or principal. You will be asked to sign the ID form again at the test center. This form must be dated and is good only for one year.

Registration Fees

At the time of this book's printing, the fee for the SAT (no essay) is $49.50. If you are planning to take the SAT with the Essay section, you will need to pay $64.50. To determine if you are eligible for a fee waiver, visit **https://collegereadiness.collegeboard.org/ sat/register/fees/fee-waivers**. (Students who qualify for a fee waiver may also be eligible to apply to college, send their scores, and apply for financial aid (through CSS Profile) to as many colleges as they choose, at no cost.)

THE CURRENT SAT® EXAM FORMAT

The SAT has held its current form since 2016. The following section describes the format of the SAT, including the overall exam format and the different question forms that can be found across the test's different sections, as well as details related to the answer sheet.

Exam Format

The SAT consists of sections on math, evidence-based reading and writing, and an optional essay. The sections are timed to range from 25 to 65 minutes. The whole test takes 3 hours, plus 50 minutes for the optional essay. Don't worry. There are breaks. The following chart gives you an idea of what to expect. The test sections appear in the following order: Reading Test, Writing and Language Test, Math Test—No Calculator, Math Test—Calculator, and the Essay.

1

ALERT

If you are not easily recognizable in your photo, you will not be admitted to the test center.

FORMAT OF THE SAT TEST

Evidence-Based Reading and Writing (Score: 200–800)

Reading questions based on

- Five passages in US and world literature, history/social studies, and science (including one set of paired passages)
- Lower and higher text complexities
- Words in context, command of evidence, and analysis

Writing and Language questions based on

- Four passages in careers, history/social studies, humanities, and science
- Argument, informative/explanatory, and nonfiction narrative passages
- Words in context, standard English conventions, expression of ideas, and analysis

Total Time: 100 Minutes

- Reading Test (65 minutes)
- Writing and Language Test (35 minutes)

Question Types:

- Multiple-choice with 4 answer choices: 96 questions
  - Reading Test (52 questions)
  - Writing and Language Test (44 questions)

Math (Score: 200–800)

Real-world problem-solving using

- Algebra
- Problem solving and data analysis
- Advanced math
- Lines, triangles, and circles using theorems
- Trigonometric functions

Total Time: 80 Minutes

- Math Test—No Calculator (25 minutes)
- Math Test—Calculator (55 minutes)

Question Types

- Multiple-choice with 4 answer choices: 45 questions
  - Math Test—No Calculator (15 questions)
  - Math Test—Calculator (30 questions)
- Student-produced responses (grid-ins): 13 questions
  - Math Test—No Calculator (5 questions)
  - Math Test—Calculator (8 questions)

1

FORMAT OF THE SAT TEST	
Optional Essay	
The writing task requires you to • Read an argumentative passage written for a general audience • Analyze the passage in terms of how the writer uses evidence, reasoning, and stylistic elements to build an argument to persuade his or her audience	Total Time: 50 minutes Question Type • One prompt that emphasizes analyzing the argument presented in the passage Scoring (2 readers) • Reading: 1–4 scale per reader • Analysis: 1–4 scale per reader • Writing: 1–4 scale per reader

Exam Question Types

The question types in the SAT exam don't cover a wide variety of topics. They are very limited—no science, no world languages, no social studies. You'll find only questions testing reading comprehension, writing skills, and math skills—skills that you've been working on since kindergarten.

Most of the questions are multiple-choice. That's good because it means the correct answer is right there on the page for you. You just have to find it. That's easier said than done sometimes, but still true. Only the math grid-ins and the essay require student-produced answers. For the grid-ins, you'll need to do the calculations and then fill in circles on the answer sheet to show your answers. (More about the answer sheets later in this chapter.) The following pages provide you with a closer look at the question types and question formats that you will find in each section of the SAT.

Reading Test

The Reading Test assesses your knowledge of words in context, command of evidence, and your analysis of the passages, including graphics. All the questions are multiple-choice and based on previously published passages, covering topics in US and world literature, history/social studies, and science.

There are five passages on the Reading test, which have been presented in official practice materials in the following order: literary narrative, history/social studies, science, history/social studies, and science (again). However, there is no guarantee that passages will follow this order on test day. One passage on the test, either one of the history/social studies or science passages, will be a paired passage consisting of two shorter passages that overlap in topic. The test has 52 questions that will be divided amongst the five passages (with 10–11 questions per passage).

TIP

On the SAT, all questions count the same. You won't get any more points for answering a really difficult question than you will get for answering a very simple one. Remember that when you're moving through the test. The more time you spend wrestling with the answer to one "stumper," the less time you have to whip through several easier questions. Your goal is to answer as many questions as you can as accurately as you can. Don't let the format of the test get the better of you.

1

Words in Context

Just as the name implies, words-in-context questions assess your ability to determine the meaning of words or phrases in the context of an extended passage. If you do not recognize the meaning of the word, its meaning may be determined by context. Your job is to read the passage and the question, and then analyze the answer choices to figure out which one makes the most sense based on the words around it. That means you must look for clues in the passage.

Here is an excerpt from a passage on the opah fish, followed by three sample words-in-context questions. Read the passage excerpt and try to answer each question on your own before you read the answer explanations.

Nicholas Wegner of NOAA Fisheries' Southwest Fisheries Science Center in La Jolla, California, is lead author of a new paper on the opah, or moonfish. He and his coauthor, biologist Owyn Snodgrass, discovered that the opah has the unusual ability to keep its body warm, even in the cold depths of the ocean. An excerpt on their findings follows.

Courtesy: NOAA Fisheries

WARM BLOOD MAKES OPAH AN AGILE PREDATOR

New research by NOAA Fisheries has revealed the opah, or moonfish, as the first fully warm-blooded fish that cir-
Line
5 culates heated blood throughout its body much like mammals and birds, giving it a competitive advantage in the cold ocean depths.

The silvery fish, roughly the size of a large automobile tire, is known from
10 oceans around the world and dwells hundreds of feet beneath the surface in chilly, dimly lit waters. . . .

Fish that typically inhabit such cold depths tend to be slow and slug-
15 gish, conserving energy by ambushing prey instead of chasing it. But the opah's constant flapping of its fins heats its body, speeding its metabolism, movement and reaction times,

20 scientists report today in the journal *Science.* . . .

"Before this discovery, I was under the impression this was a slow-moving fish, like most other fish in cold envi-
25 ronments," Wegner said. "But because it can warm its body, it turns out to be a very active predator that chases down agile prey like squid and can migrate long distances."

1. As used in line 6, "competitive advantage" most nearly means

   A. a way to seek out a mate.

   B. an ability to outperform rivals.

   C. an aptitude for keeping itself moving.

   D. a capacity to conceal itself from predators.

2. As it is used in line 15, "ambushing" most nearly means

   A. pursuing for long distances.

   B. moving slowly at first.

   C. hiding and then attacking.

   D. weakening and then killing.

3. As it is used in line 28, "agile" most nearly means

   A. nimble.

   B. inactive.

   C. strong.

   D. clever.

Answer Explanations:

1. **The correct answer is B.** Clues to the meaning of the phrase don't appear until the fourth paragraph: "I was under the impression . . . like most other fish in cold environments" and "But . . . it turns out to be a very active predator." Here, you're told that the opah is *unlike* other fish in that it can swim faster and farther and catch more prey. An ability to outperform rivals is the only answer choice that makes sense in the context of the passage. Choices A, C, and D are specific traits that might help the fish in its environment.

2. **The correct answer is C.** The biggest clue to the meaning of *ambushing* is "instead of chasing it." Choice C makes sense when you consider the context clue. Because you know that the fish don't chase their prey, you can exclude choice A. Choices B and D don't make sense in the context of the sentence because neither is a method for capturing prey, as chasing is.

3. **The correct answer is A.** The phrase "very active predator" is your clue that *agile* must mean that the squid provides a challenge for the opah. *Nimble* fits the context, as it suggests that the squid is able to move quickly and easily. Choice B has the opposite meaning. Choice D can be eliminated because the context emphasizes physical, not mental, abilities. Likewise, you can eliminate choice C because the level of activity, not strength, is the focus.

Command of Evidence

The Evidence-Based Reading and Writing sections of the SAT require you to interpret information or ideas in a passage and then use evidence to support your conclusion. This element of the Reading Test makes up roughly 20 percent of the questions. You answer a multiple-choice question in which you analyze a portion of the passage or pair of passages. You then answer a second question requiring you to cite the best evidence in the text for the answer. A command of evidence question may express an implication of the text in the question and ask which set of lines provide the best evidence for such a concept.

The following is an example of how these "command of evidence" questions work. The passage is a continuation of the NOAA article cited previously, "Warm Blood Makes Opah an Agile Predator."

> **TIP**
> In SAT reading questions, the answers will always be directly stated or implied by the passage.

1

GILLS SHOW UNUSUAL DESIGN

Courtesy: NOAA Fisheries

Wegner realized the opah was unusual when a coauthor of the study, biologist Owyn Snodgrass, collected a sample
Line of its gill tissue. Wegner recognized
5 an unusual design: Blood vessels that carry warm blood into the fish's gills wind around those carrying cold blood back to the body core after absorbing oxygen from water.

10 The design is known in engineering as "counter-current heat exchange." In opah it means that warm blood leaving the body core helps heat up cold blood returning from the respiratory
15 surface of the gills, where it absorbs oxygen. Resembling a car radiator, it's a natural adaptation that conserves heat. The unique location of the heat exchange within the gills allows nearly
20 the fish's entire body to maintain an elevated temperature, known as endothermy, even in the chilly depths.

"There has never been anything like this seen in a fish's gills before,"
25 Wegner said. "This is a cool innovation by these animals that gives them a competitive edge. The concept of counter-current heat exchange was invented in fish long before we thought of it."

30 The researchers collected temperature data from opah caught during surveys off the West Coast, finding that their body temperatures were regularly warmer than the surrounding water.
35 They also attached temperature monitors to opah as they tracked the fish on dives to several hundred feet and found that their body temperatures remained steady even as the water temperature

40 dropped sharply. The 20 fish had an average muscle temperature about 5 degrees C above the surrounding water while swimming about 150 to 1,000 feet below the surface, the researchers
45 found. . . .

A few other fish . . . warm certain parts of their bodies . . . boosting their swimming performance. But internal organs, including their hearts, cool off
50 quickly and begin to slow down when they dive into cold depths, forcing them to return to shallower depths to warm up.

1. The author discusses the adaptations of some fish in the last paragraph mainly to show that

   A. opah swim faster because they are able to keep themselves warm.

   B. some fish maintain a body temperature warmer than the sea water.

   C. biologists have found evidence that some fish are warm-blooded.

   D. opah have a distinctive design that keeps them warm at greater depths.

2. Which choice provides the best evidence for the answer to the previous question?

   A. Lines 18–22 ("The unique . . . chilly depths.")

   B. Lines 27–29 ("The concept . . . of it.")

   C. Lines 30–34 ("The researchers . . . surrounding water.")

   D. Lines 40–45 ("The 20 fish . . . researchers found.")

Answer Explanations:

1. **The correct answer is D.** The author's intention is to contrast the warming ability of other fish with the warming ability of the opah to show that opah have a distinctive design that keeps them warm at greater depths. Though the passage does note that some fish maintain a body temperature warmer than seawater for a short period (choice B), this is not the reason the author includes details about other fish. Choices A and C are incorrect because neither idea is noted in the text.

2. **The correct answer is A.** This question is asking you to determine which of four segments of the passage provides the best evidence to support your answer to the first question. In this case, lines 18–22 provide the best evidence that opah have a distinctive design that keeps them warm at greater depths. Choices B, C, and D do not provide textual support for the contrast the author makes in the last paragraph.

Analysis and Graphics

Analysis questions represent the largest category of questions in the Reading section. That means they also have the greatest diversity of presentation, ranging from questions about passage details and inferences to those about a passage's purpose. Further, two passages in the SAT Reading Test include a graphic. Your job is to analyze the passage and interpret the information in the graphic as it relates to the passage. Questions based on the graphic are multiple-choice. Here is a sample reading passage with an accompanying graphic, in this case a map, and questions that require your analysis.

Questions 1–4 refer to the following passage and supplementary material.

From "About John Snow," by Professor Paul Fine, London School of Hygiene & Tropical Medicine and The John Snow Society.

JOHN SNOW (1813–1858)

John Snow is an iconic figure in epidemiology and public health, best known for his work on cholera, for a famous map, and for organizing the removal of a pump handle in Soho.

5   Less well-known are his important contributions to anesthesia and to epidemiological methods, and his engagement in public debates of the time. The breadth and depth of Snow's activities provide a model for population researchers concerned not only with sound method but also with bringing their results to public benefit.

15   Indeed, though epidemiology is often described as the study of health-related aspects of populations, its methods are applicable to studies of virtually anything in populations, and

20   disciplines which now acknowledge the methods and terminology of epidemiology range from education to crime science and economics.

Snow was born in York on 15

25   March 1813, one of eight children in a family of modest means. He apprenticed with a surgeon-apothecary in Newcastle from 1827 to 1833, and there witnessed the first epidemic of cholera

30   in the UK. He then moved to London, qualified as physician in 1843 and set up general practice in Soho. Early in his career he became interested in the physiology of respiration in recognition

35   of the major problem of asphyxia of the newborn.

These interests led him to be invited to witness one of the first applications of ether anesthesia in the UK

40   in December 1846. He immediately

1

recognized the importance of ambient temperature and within one month published tables of the vapor pressure of ether. This initiated an important
45 line of research on instruments for administering anesthetics and led to his becoming the most prominent authority on anesthesia in the UK. He administered chloroform to Queen Victoria
50 at the birth of Prince Leopold in 1853.

The second great cholera epidemic arrived in London in 1848, and many attributed its cause to an atmospheric "effluence" or "miasma." Snow's first-
55 hand experience of the disease in 1832, combined with studies of respiration, led him to question miasma theories and to publish the first edition of *On the Mode of Communication of Chol-*
60 *era* in 1849, in which he proposed that cholera was attributable to a self-replicating agent which was excreted in the cholera evacuations and inadvertently ingested, often, but not necessarily,
65 through the medium of water.

When cholera returned in 1853, Snow recognized an ideal opportunity to test his hypothesis by comparing cholera mortality rates in populations
70 of south London supplied by water drawn from sewage-contaminated versus uncontaminated regions of the Thames. He personally carried out a cohort study to make this comparison,
75 recognizing the need to confirm the water source of each case and to assure comparability of the populations concerned. On 30 August 1854 while involved in these studies, a dramatic
80 cholera epidemic began near his home in Soho, leading to more than 550 deaths within two weeks. Analysis of the addresses of the cholera deaths and interviews of residents of the area led
85 him to suspect that water from a pump

on Broad Street was responsible—and he prevailed upon the local council to remove the handle of the pump on 8 September 1854.
90 Though the epidemic was already in decline by that date, the rapidity of his action, the logic of the analysis, and the pragmatism of the response has made this a classic event in the
95 history of public health, well known to students and practitioners the world over. The combination of these studies provided overwhelming evidence for an infectious agent, known now as
100 *Vibrio cholerae.*

Snow described this work in the second edition of *On the Mode of Communication of Cholera.* He then expanded his public health interests
105 by becoming involved in debates over legislation concerning nuisance industries in London, while maintaining his research and practice in anesthesia until his death in 1858.
110 The 200th anniversary of Snow's birth provides an occasion to celebrate his achievements, to consider their original context, to discuss their place in contemporary epidemiology, and
115 consider their likely future, not only as the armamentarium of public health, but as a framework of method for science and society.

1. The primary purpose of the passage is to

   A. describe the methods used by John Snow to combat the 1853 cholera outbreak in London.

   B. examine the history of Cholera outbreaks and treatments in 19th century Europe.

   C. characterize the development of anesthesia as a landmark event in the history of modern medicine.

   D. present John Snow's contributions to the fields of public health and epidemiology.

2. It can reasonably be inferred from the passage that John Snow chose the outbreak of 1853 to conduct his study because

   A. his experiments with chloroform could be administered at a larger scale.

   B. deaths near his home in Soho motivated a desire to remove the source of the outbreak.

   C. the ideas presented in *On the Mode of Communication of Cholera* could be compared to real-world conditions.

   D. he wanted to find evidence that nuisance industries were the primary contributors to outbreaks of disease.

3. According to the passage, Snow's first key contribution to the field of medicine was

   A. his research into the effect of temperature on the administration of anesthetics.

   B. an interest in the process of respiration as related to respiratory problems in children and adults.

   C. the administration of chloroform to Queen Victoria during childbirth.

   D. witnessing the first cholera outbreak in the UK as an apprentice to a surgeon-apothecary.

4. On John Snow's map, deaths from the 1854 cholera epidemic are represented by stacks of black lines. Based on the image and the passage, what can we assume about Blenheim Street (shown magnified in the upper-left side of the map)?

   A. No one lived there.

   B. Broad Street did not supply their water.

   C. Its residents were as affected as the rest of the neighborhood.

   D. Relatives came to stay there to avoid the cholera outbreak.

1

Answer Explanations:

1. **The correct answer is D.** The passages describes the exploits of John Snow, an important figure in the history of modern medicine. The passage alludes multiple times to how Snow's contributions to medicine impacted the fields of public health and epidemiology while also providing detailed descriptions of his methods. While choice A accurately describes the topic of several paragraphs in the text, this does not reflect the overall purpose of the passage. Choice B goes beyond the scope of the passage as the outbreaks describes are limited to those in the UK during a limited period of time. Choice C draws upon an early detail that is referenced only minimally elsewhere in the passage.

2. **The correct answer is C.** The question is asking for you to form an inference based on the details provided in the passage; the sixth paragraph introduces Snow's hypothesis that describes how cholera spreads through water. The following paragraph references how Snow saw the 1853 outbreak as an opportunity to "test his hypothesis." Thus, it is reasonable to conclude that the real-world outbreak would allow Snow to determine the accuracy of his prediction. Choice A distorts a detail from earlier in the passage. Choice B misuses a detail from later in the passage, after Snow had begun his investigation. Choice D distorts the reference to Snow's later interest in combatting nuisance industries while expanding the scope beyond cholera to all disease.

3. **The correct answer is A.** This detail question requires you to find the relevant information in the passage that fits the parameters of the question. Snow's earliest achievement was spurring advances in instruments used to administer anesthetics. His research into temperature's effect on anesthesia motivated important research into medical instruments. While choice B relates an area of study that occurred prior to investigations into the effect of ambient temperature on ether, the answer distorts a key detail, applying the respiratory problems to children and adults, not newborns. Choice C selects an event that occurred later in the passage. Choice D selects an early detail but one that does not represent a key contribution to the world of medicine.

4. **The correct answer is B.** The passage explains that Snow determined that the pump on Broad Street supplied contaminated water to nearby residents. You can infer that people living on streets containing stacks of bars used the Broad Street pump. Based on the map, then, people on Blenheim Street likely did not use the Broad Street pump.

Writing and Language Test

The SAT Exam Writing and Language Test consists of 44 multiple-choice questions based on four passages of varying topics. The multiple-choice questions test how well you recognize and correct errors in standard English conventions and can optimize the expression of ideas by selecting words, phrases, and sentences (resulting in better organization, topic development, and use of language). Additionally, the passages will also present words-in-context and command of evidence questions reminiscent of the Reading test. Some passages will include graphics with related questions.

Standard English Conventions and Words in Context

The standard English conventions questions require you to act as an editor and revise text so that it conforms to the standard rules for sentence structure and formation, punctuation, and usage. In most instances, you will be given a multi-paragraph passage that includes several errors. The most common question format asks you to choose the best alternative to a potential error, identified as an underlined portion of the passage.

Here is a sample question that concerns sentence structure:

Scientists conducted a series of experiments with chimpanzees in the <u>Democratic Republic of the Congo. The results were astounding.</u> The conclusion, that chimpanzees would eventually learn to cook if provided an oven, could help explain how and when early humans began to cook their food.

1 Which choice most effectively combines the sentences at the underlined portion?

A. Democratic Republic of the Congo, and the results were astounding.

B. Democratic Republic of the Congo, the results were astounding.

C. Democratic Republic of the Congo: the results were astounding.

D. Democratic Republic of the Congo, but the results were astounding.

Explanations:

Choice B creates a comma splice, which is a form of a run-on sentence, so that's not correct. Likewise, the colon in choice C is not correct, as the clause it introduces does not really explain the first part of the sentence. Introducing *but* in choice D changes the meaning of the sentences by setting up a contrasting scenario. Only choice A maintains the two sentences' meanings and combines them without creating a grammatical error. **The correct answer is A.**

The words-in-context questions on the test measure your ability to choose appropriate words based on the context of the passage. These questions are multiple-choice and include the option to keep the word that is used.

There is a debate about whether early humans had the mental capacity to cook. Though it may not seem sophisticated, cooking requires planning, an ability to **2** <u>interrupt</u> gratification, and the complex use of tools.

2

A. NO CHANGE

B. apprehend

C. delay

D. restrain

Explanations:

Here, you must choose the word that makes the most sense in the context. The word you are looking for means "to hold off," and only *delay* conveys that sense. *Interrupt*, *apprehend*, and *restrain* don't make sense given the context of the sentence. **The correct answer is C.**

Command of Evidence

To answer the command of evidence questions in the Writing and Language Test, you need to carefully read the passage in question. Here is an example of this type of question. The excerpt comes from the passage "About John Snow."

1

The second great cholera epidemic arrived in London in 1848, and many attributed its cause to an atmospheric "effluence" or "miasma." Snow's firsthand experience of the disease in 1832, combined with studies of respiration, led him to question miasma theories and to publish the first edition of *On the Mode of Communication of Cholera* in 1849, in which he proposed that cholera was attributable to a self-replicating agent which was excreted in the cholera evacuations and inadvertently ingested, often, but not necessarily, through the medium of water. **3**

3 Which choice best summarizes the main idea of the paragraph?

A. In 1848, many people were incorrect to blame atmospheric miasma for the spread of cholera.

B. John Snow's study, *On the Mode of Communication of Cholera*, was read by scholars worldwide.

C. John Snow was curious, and he never took anything at face value.

D. Snow's questioning of the miasma theory and theories on water contamination changed the conversation about disease circulation.

Explanations:

The question asks you to determine which sentence best summarizes the main idea of the paragraph. Choices A, B, and C all contain ideas that are important in the paragraph, but this question is asking for the best choice. Choice D contains the crux of the paragraph: that Snow questioned the prevailing wisdom and then proposed his own theory about how cholera was transmitted. **The correct answer is D.**

Expression of Ideas

Some questions require you to analyze the passage's topic development, organization, and language use to make improvements for maximum impact. You may be asked to improve the wording or structure of the passage or strengthen the writer's point. Here is an excerpt from a passage about Harriet Tubman and a sample question to help illustrate this concept.

At the beginning of the Civil War, Harriet Tubman worked for the Union Army as a cook and nurse. Later in the war she shifted to a more decisive position as a spy and scout. Tubman was the first woman to lead an expedition of armed fighters, and her leadership during a raid at Combahee Ferry resulted in the liberation of 700 enslaved people. **4** Tubman was born in Dorchester County, Maryland, around 1822.

4 The writer is considering deleting the underlined sentence from the paragraph. Should the writer delete this sentence?

A. Yes, because the sentence has nothing to do with the main topic of the passage.

B. Yes, because the sentence veers from the topic of Tubman's role in the war.

C. No, because the sentence provides valuable historical information about Tubman.

D. No, because the sentence provides a strong conclusion to the paragraph.

Explanations:

Here you are being asked if the sentence in question is relevant to the paragraph. In this case, basic information about where and when Tubman was born has little to do with a paragraph about her role in the Civil War. The sentence veers from the topic of Tubman's role in the war, and should be deleted. **The correct answer is B.**

Graphics

One or two of the passages in the Writing and Language Test include graphics. You will be asked to determine how the passage needs to be revised based on the information in the graphic. Here is an excerpt from another paragraph in "About John Snow" and a sample question to help illustrate this concept.

Snow's mapping of the outbreak showed few surprising results. Little Pulteney Street is a case in point. The street is blocks from Broad Street and closer to two other water pumps. Among residents of the street, there **5** were no cases of cholera reported during the outbreak.

5 Which choice completes the sentence using accurate data based on the map?

A. NO CHANGE

B. was one new case of cholera

C. were fewer than ten new cases of cholera

D. were more than twenty new cases of cholera

1

Explanations:

Here, you are being asked to interpret the information in the passage based on the map. If you look closely at the area in question, Little Pulteney Street, you'll see that there are about six bars, and we can infer that each bar represents a case of cholera. **The correct answer is C.**

Math Test

The questions in the Math sections (Math Test—No Calculator and Math Test—Calculator) address concepts, skills, and practices that are most useful for students after they graduate from high school. There are two question formats for math questions: multiple-choice and grid-ins (student-produced responses).

Multiple-Choice Math

Multiple-choice math questions on the SAT exam look like all the other standard multiple-choice math questions you've ever seen. A problem is given for algebra, problem solving, data analysis, advanced math, or additional topics, and four choices are presented from which you must choose the correct answer. The major concepts that you might need in order to solve math problems are given in the test section. You don't need to worry about memorizing these facts, but you do need to know when to use each one. The directions are similar to the following:

DIRECTIONS: For **Questions 1–15**, solve each problem, select the best answer from the choices provided, and fill in the corresponding circle on your answer sheet. For **Questions 16–20**, solve the problem and enter your answer in the grid on the answer sheet. The directions **before Question 16** will provide information on how to enter your answers in the grid.

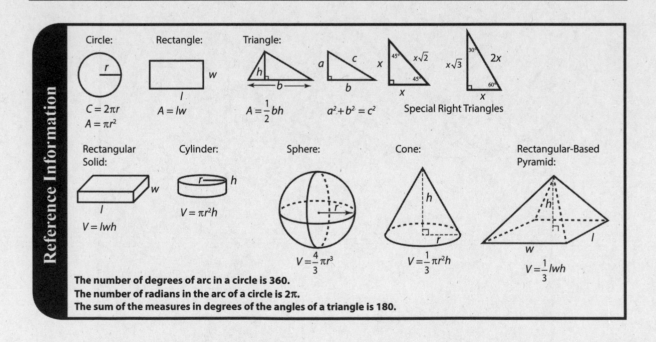

Reference Information

Circle:
$C = 2\pi r$
$A = \pi r^2$

Rectangle:
$A = lw$

Triangle:
$A = \frac{1}{2}bh$
$a^2 + b^2 = c^2$

Special Right Triangles

Rectangular Solid:
$V = lwh$

Cylinder:
$V = \pi r^2 h$

Sphere:
$V = \frac{4}{3}\pi r^3$

Cone:
$V = \frac{1}{3}\pi r^2 h$

Rectangular-Based Pyramid:
$V = \frac{1}{3}lwh$

The number of degrees of arc in a circle is 360.
The number of radians in the arc of a circle is 2π.
The sum of the measures in degrees of the angles of a triangle is 180.

ADDITIONAL INFORMATION:

1. The use of a calculator in this section is **not permitted** (**permitted** for the Math Test—Calculator section).

2. All variables and expressions used represent real numbers unless otherwise indicated.

3. Figures provided in this test are drawn to scale unless otherwise indicated.

4. All figures lie in a plane unless otherwise indicated.

5. Unless otherwise specified, the domain of a given function f is the set of all real numbers x for which $f(x)$ is a real number.

Here are some sample multiple-choice math questions. Try them yourself before looking at the solutions that are given.

TIP

A four-function, battery-powered, scientific or graphing calculator is allowed for the Math Test—Calculator section of the SAT. You may not use the following: handheld mini-computers, laptop computers, pocket organizers, calculators that print or "talk," calculators with letters on the keyboard, or calculators with internet access.

Example 1:

Michele is at the airport renting a car that costs $39.95 per day plus tax. A tax of 7% is applied to the rental rate, and an additional one-time untaxed fee of $5.00 is charged by the airport where she picks up the car. Which of the following represents Michele's total charge $c(x)$, in dollars, for renting a car for x days?

A. $c(x) = (39.95 + 0.07x) + 5$

B. $c(x) = 1.07(39.95)x + 5$

C. $c(x) = 1.07(39.95x + 5)$

D. $c(x) = 1.07(39.95 + 5)x$

Solution:

The total cost, $c(x)$, can be found by multiplying any daily charges by the number of days, x, and then adding any one-time charges. The daily charges include the $39.95 daily rate and the 7% tax. This can be computed by:

$$\$39.95 + 0.07(\$39.95) = 1(\$39.95) + 0.07(\$39.95) = 1.07(\$39.95)$$

Multiply the daily charge by x and add the one-time charge of $5 to obtain the function rule:

$$c(x) = 1.07(39.95)x + 5$$

The correct answer is B.

1

Example 2:

The graph of $y = (3x + 9)(x - 5)$ is a parabola in the xy-plane. In which of the following equivalent equations do the x- and y-coordinates of the vertex of the parabola appear as constants or coefficients?

A. $y = 3x^2 - 6x - 45$

B. $y = 3x(x - 2) - 45$

C. $y = 3(x - 1)^2 + (-48)$

D. $y = (x + 3)(3x - 15)$

Solution:

The equation $y = (3x + 9)(x - 5)$ can be written in vertex form $y = a(x - h)^2 + k$, where the vertex of the parabola is (h, k). To put the equation in vertex form, first multiply the factors, then complete the square. **The correct answer is C.**

Example 3:

The same final exam is given to two separate groups of students taking the same class. The students who took the exam on the first floor had a mean score of 84. The students who took the exam on the second floor had a mean score of 78. Which of the following represents the mean score x of both groups of students?

A. $x = 81$

B. $x < 81$

C. $x > 81$

D. $78 < x < 84$

Solution:

Many students will select choice A as the answer because 81 is the mean of 78 and 84, but there is no information about the size of the two groups that are being averaged. If the groups were equal in size, choice A would be correct. If there were more students on the second floor, then choice B would be the correct answer. Similarly, if there were more students on the first floor, then choice C would be correct. Since we don't know which floor has more students taking the exam or if the number of students is equal, we can only say that choice D is true. **The correct answer is D.**

Grid-Ins

Unlike multiple-choice math, the grid-in section of the SAT does not give you the answers. You have to compute the answer and then fill in your answer in the circles on your answer sheet. You may use the Reference Information table that appeared earlier in this chapter for these problems also.

On the SAT exam, each set of grid-in questions starts with directions that look approximately like this:

DIRECTIONS: For these questions, solve the problem and enter your answer in the grid, as described below, on the answer sheet.

---

1. Although not required, it is suggested that you write your answer in the boxes at the top of the columns to help you fill in the circles accurately. You will receive credit only if the circles are filled in correctly.

2. Mark no more than one circle in any column.

3. No question has a negative answer.

4. Some problems may have more than one correct answer. In such cases, enter only one answer.

5. Mixed numbers such as $3\frac{1}{2}$ must be entered as 3.5 or $\frac{7}{2}$.

    If $3\frac{1}{2}$ is entered into the grid as $\boxed{3\ |\ 1\ /\ 2}$, it will be interpreted as $\frac{31}{2}$, not $3\frac{1}{2}$.

6. **Decimal answers**: If you obtain a decimal answer with more digits than the grid can accommodate, it may be either rounded or truncated, but it must fill the entire grid.

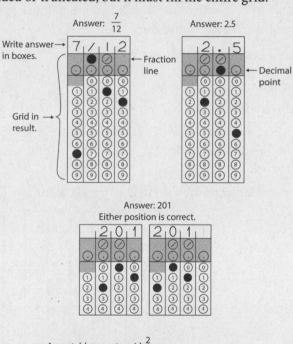

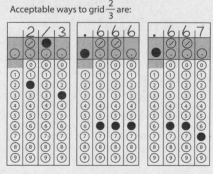

1

Once you understand the following six rules, you can concentrate on solving the math problems in this section.

1. Write your answer in the boxes at the top of the grid.

2. Mark the corresponding circles, one per column.

3. Start in any column.

4. Work with decimals or fractions.

5. Express mixed numbers as decimals or improper fractions.

Now let's look at these rules in more detail:

NOTE

Don't use a comma in a number larger than 999. Just fill in the four digits and the corresponding circles. You only have circles for numbers, decimal points, and fraction slashes; there aren't any for commas.

1. Write your answer in the boxes at the top of the grid. Technically, this isn't required by the SAT. Realistically, it gives you something to follow as you fill in the circles. Do it—it will help you.

2. Make sure to mark the circles that correspond to the answer you entered in the boxes, one per column. The machine that scores the test can only read the circles, so if you don't fill them in, you won't get credit. Just entering your answer in the boxes is not enough!

3. You can start entering your answer in any column, if space permits. Unused columns should be left blank; don't put in zeroes.

Here are some examples of these kinds of problems:

Examples:

Use the grids provided below to try the following grid-in questions.

1. There are 70 students in a school who participate in the music program. If 35% of the students participate in the music program, how many students are in the school?

2. What is one possible solution to the equation $\dfrac{1}{x} + \dfrac{3}{x-1} = -4$?

Solutions:

1. $\dfrac{35}{100} = \dfrac{70}{x}$

$35x = 7,000$

$x = 200$

2. $\dfrac{1}{x} + \dfrac{3}{x-1} = -4$

$x - 1 + 3x = -4x(x-1)$

$4x - 1 = -4x^2 + 4x$

$0 = -4x^2 + 1$

$0 = (-2x+1)(2x+1)$

$x = \pm 0.5$

Only 0.5 or $\dfrac{1}{2}$ (1/2) can be entered in the grid because, as the directions stated, no answer requires a minus sign.

OR

You will learn more about grid-ins in Chapter 8: "Grid-In Strategies."

1

SAT Exam Essay (Optional)

For the essay, you will be given a previously published passage that examines ideas in the sciences or arts, as well as civic, cultural, or political life. The passages are written for a broad-based audience, and prior knowledge of the topic is not expected. Your task in writing the essay is to read and comprehend the text sufficiently to write a thoughtful analysis of the passage.

Though the passage contents may vary from test to test, the prompt will not change. You will be asked to explain how the author of the passage builds an argument to persuade an audience. The prompt will likely look something like this:

As you read the following passage, consider how the author uses the following:

- Evidence, such as facts, statistics, or examples, to support claims.

- Reasoning to develop ideas and to connect claims and evidence.

- Stylistic or persuasive elements, such as word choice or appeals to emotion, to add power to the ideas expressed.

Your response will be evaluated based on your comprehension of the text, as well as on the quality of your analysis and writing. This means that you must show thoughtful understanding of the source text and appropriate use of textual evidence to support your arguments. You will also be expected to organize your ideas in a coherent way and to express them clearly using the conventions of standard written English. The essay does not elicit your opinion. Instead, your response should depend entirely on the source text to support your analysis of how the argument is presented, not what it is about or the quality of the ideas. You can learn more about the optional Essay in Chapter 6: "The SAT Exam Essay."

The SAT Exam Answer Sheet

On the day of the test when you are given your test booklet, you'll also be given a separate answer sheet. For each multiple-choice question, you'll see a corresponding set of answer circles. The circles are labeled A, B, C, and D. Remember the following about the answer sheet:

- Answer sheets are read by machines—and machines can't think. That means it's up to you to make sure you're in the right place on the answer sheet every time you record an answer. The machine won't know that you really meant to answer Question 25 when you marked the space for Question 26.

- If you skip a question, mark the question in your exam booklet. Don't mark the answer sheet in any way as a reminder. Erase any stray marks as they may affect how the machine scores your answer sheet.

- Always check to see that the answer space you have filled in corresponds to the question you are answering.

- Be sure to fill in the answer circles completely so that there can be no mistake about which answers you chose.

These seem like simple things, but you'd be surprised how many students fail to do them, especially keeping track of answer lines if they skip a question.

As you just read in the "Grid-Ins" section of this chapter, grid-in responses are only for questions you will see in the math sections. You'll still be filling in circles, but they will look a little different from the multiple-choice circles. Again, here's a sample of the special grid you will use.

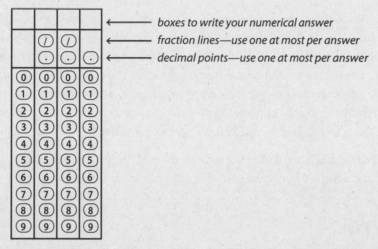

← boxes to write your numerical answer
← fraction lines—use one at most per answer
← decimal points—use one at most per answer

At the top of the grid, you'll write in the numerical answer. The slashes that appear in the second row are used for answers with fractions. If you need one of these fraction lines in your answer, darken one of the circles. The circles with the dots are for answers with decimal points—use these circles just as you do the fraction line circles. In the lower part of the grid, fill in the numbered circles that correspond to the numbers in your answer.

Here are some examples. Note that for grid-in responses, answers can begin on the left or the right.

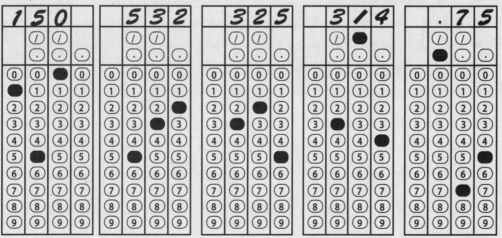

TIP

Make sure you're in the right place! Always check to see that the answer space you fill in corresponds to the question you are answering.

1

MAKE AN SAT® EXAM STUDY PLAN

Now that you know the basics of the SAT exam, it's time to create a study plan. As with almost any form of learning, preparing for the SAT is an investment of time. The more time you have, the better your chances of boosting your score significantly.

Regardless of how much time you have before the actual exam, your first step should be to take the Diagnostic Test in Part II: Chapter 2 of this book. When you are finished, compute your raw scores for Math and Evidence-Based Reading and Writing, then convert the raw scores to a scaled score. Use the scoring sheets at the end of the diagnostic test to help you compute your subscores. These scores are important starting point in identifying your relative strengths and weaknesses so that you can customize your study plan. Hang on to the scoring sheet so you know where to get started.

Next, we'll walk you through two different study plans, each tailored to a specific amount of preparation time. Choose the plan that fits your circumstances and adapt it to your needs.

The Complete Plan

If you have three or more months to prepare, you should congratulate yourself! This will give you sufficient time to familiarize yourself with the test, learn critical strategies, review grammar and math fundamentals, practice writing, and take full-length tests.

You'll get the most out of your SAT preparation if you follow these steps:

- Reread this chapter to ensure that you understand the format, structure, and scoring of the SAT.
- Take the Diagnostic Test and identify your areas that need improvement.
- Read each and every strategy and review chapter.
- Work through all the examples, exercises, and practice exams.
- Read all the answer explanations.
- Revisit the chapters where your scores show you need to still improve.

The Accelerated Plan

If you have one month or less to prepare for the SAT, or if you cannot devote a lot of time to studying for any other reason, follow the accelerated plan. You'll get the most out of this plan if you take these steps:

- Reread this chapter to ensure that you understand the format, structure, and scoring of the SAT.
- Take the Diagnostic Test and identify your areas that need improvement.
- Focus on the chapters that cover material that is most problematic for you and work through all the examples and exercises in these chapters.
- Work through as many practice exams as you can and read all the answer explanations.

> **NOTE**
>
> You may be wondering how you can possibly wade through all this information in time for the test. Don't be discouraged! We wrote this book knowing that some students would be on very condensed schedules. The information in this section will help you construct a study plan that works for you—one that will help you boost your score no matter how limited your time may be. Remember, though, that practice and targeted study are essential elements of that score boosting, so invest as much time as possible in your SAT preparation.

Measuring Your Progress

It does seem as if you're on a treadmill sometimes, doesn't it? Question after question after question—are you really getting anywhere? Is all of this studying really working?

The way to find out is to monitor your progress throughout the preparation period, whether it's three months or four weeks. By taking a diagnostic examination at the beginning, you'll establish your skill baseline, and you'll be able to craft the study plan that's right for you. Then, you can either start to read the entire book (if you are using the complete plan) or go directly to the chapters that address your weaknesses (if you are using the accelerated plan). At the end of each chapter, complete the exercises and calculate the percentage of questions you answered correctly. Compare this value to the percentage of questions you answered correctly for the corresponding section on your diagnostic test (26 out of 52 on the diagnostic test would be 50% as compared to 16 out of 22 in the Chapter 4 practice exercise—72%). How have you improved? Where do you still need work? Even if you haven't reached your ultimate performance goal, are you at least applying new test-taking methods?

Simulate Test-Taking Conditions

The two full-length practice exams at the back of this book can help you prepare for the experience of taking a timed, standardized test. Taking these tests will improve your familiarity with the SAT, reduce your number of careless errors, and increase your over-all level of confidence. To make sure that you get the most out of this practice, you should do everything in your power to simulate actual test-taking conditions.

Find a Block of Time

Because the SAT is administered in one long block of time, the best way to simulate test-taking conditions is to take an entire practice exam in one sitting. This means that you should set aside 3 and a half to 4 hours of consecutive time. You need some form of timer that will signal when you should stop working on each section of the test—preferably not your phone so you are not distracted by other notifications. Take the regularly scheduled breaks as well (10 minutes after Reading, 5 minutes after Math—No Calculator, and 2 minutes before the Essay).

If you find it difficult to find approximately 4 quiet hours at home, maybe take the test in the library. If you decide to take a test at home, take precautions. Let your friends know you are taking a practice test, put your phone in another room, and convince siblings to stay out of your room. That's easier said than done, and it's important to remember that infrequent interruptions won't completely invalidate your testing experience. Regardless, you should still try to avoid them.

Work at a Desk and Wear a Watch

Don't take a practice test while you are lounging on your bed. Not only does that not adequately simulate the test-taking experience but also your brain has been trained over the years to equate your bed with sleep. Drowsiness and comfort are not the best combination when you're trying to answer 154 questions as fast and as accurately as you can. Clear off a comfortable workspace on a desk or table. Remember to use a timer. The time

TIP

Here's an important point: You don't have to go through the book in order. You might want to start with the topic that you find most difficult, such as functions or grammar, or the question type that you're most unsure about, such as grid-ins. Then move to the next most difficult and so on down the line, saving the easiest topics or question types until the end. If you use the accelerated plan, you should definitely take this approach.

for each section is marked on the section, so check the beginning of each section and set your timer or your watch for that amount of time.

You are not allowed to explore other sections on the test while you are supposed to be working on your current section. So when you take your practice tests, don't look ahead or back. And use every last minute to complete each section.

Practice on a Weekend Morning

Since the SAT is typically administered at 8:30 a.m. on Saturday (or Sunday for religious observers), why not take the practice test at the exact same time on a weekend morning? You should be most energetic in the morning anyway. When you take the practice test, allow yourself to take some breaks. Remember, a 10-minute break after Section 1: Reading Test. Use this to run to the bathroom, eat a snack, and re-sharpen your pencils. You can take another 5-minute break after Section 4: Math Test—No Calculator. If you're going to push through with the optional Essay (you should), take a 2-minute breather before starting.

Remember that your goal is to take these practice tests in as true an environment as possible so that you're prepared to take the real SAT. You will be accustomed to sitting for a long period of time, but you will get three breaks.

The following table puts all of the SAT section times in a one-stop format, so you can refer to it often when planning your study time.

Section	Number of Questions	Time Allowed
Reading	52	65 minutes
Writing and Language	44	35 minutes
Math Test—No Calculator	20	25 minutes
Math Test—Calculator	38	55 minutes
Essay	—	50 minutes

One Third of the Way Through Your Study

When you are approximately one third of the way through your plan of study—this can be after ten days or a month—it's time to take one of the practice tests. Prior to taking the practice test, review any notes as well as the Summing It Up sections at the end of the chapters you've completed. Force yourself to recall (don't just read over) the concepts and strategies you've learned and practiced. When you have finished scoring and reading the answer explanations, compare your scores with your original diagnostic scores. You should be performing better. If you're not, don't panic. At this point in test preparation, it's not unusual to score about the same as you did at the beginning.

What's more important than *what* you scored is *how* you took the practice test. Did you really use the test-taking strategies to which you've been introduced? If you didn't, go back to the strategy chapters and either reread them, if you are doing the complete plan, or at least reread the summaries, if you are on the accelerated plan. Then continue your review. Read more review chapters and complete the relevant exercises.

CAUTION

If you're worried that you won't be able to resist the temptation to check the answer keys during the practice tests, cover them up beforehand. Don't allow yourself to become dependent upon a sneak peek now and then. You won't have answer keys available on test day, and the main purpose of the practice tests is to prepare you for the real experience.

Two Thirds of the Way Through Your Study

After you have worked through most of the review chapters (under the complete plan) or all of the material relating to your areas of weakness (under the accelerated plan), it's time to take another practice test. By now, you should be seeing some real improvement in your scores. If you are still having trouble with certain topics, review the problematic material again.

The Home Stretch

For the most part, the last phase of study should involve *less learning* and *more practice.* Take more practice tests! In addition to Peterson's practice tests (available in this book and online), the College Board offers multiple printable practice tests.

As you near the end of your study plan, you should understand how to take the exam. What you need is more practice taking the test under simulated test-day conditions to work on your pacing and test-taking strategies.

When you take additional practice exams, be sure to do so in a near-test environment. Keep analyzing your scores to ensure you're aware of and can target your remaining weaknesses. Determine which areas need additional work. If you skipped over any of the review chapters in this book, go back and use the exercises to improve your skills.

The Final Week

Here's one last piece of advice: no matter which study plan you select, you should probably take one full-length, timed practice test the week before you take the actual SAT. Before your final practice test, make sure to review section expectations for Reading, including your personalized strategies (as discussed in Chapter 3); grammar content and question goals for Writing and Language (Chapters 4 and 5); difficult math concepts (Chapters 7–13); and the advised structure and goals for your essay (Chapter 6). This will get you ready for the big day. But don't take the practice test the day before the real exam. That's a time when you should be relaxing, not cramming.

Throughout the week leading up to your official test date, there are some basic tasks you can give yourself that can optimize your physical performance for the big day. Research in the field of neuroscience from the past decade has revealed that getting regular sleep (at least 8 hours per night), staying hydrated (even mild dehydration can affect your memory and attention), and eating low-glycemic meals (a balance of healthy fats, protein, and carbohydrates) can improve (or at least maintain) cognitive performance. A student's busy schedule can often get in the way of some of these good behaviors, but you should do everything you can to treat your brain and body right each day before the test.

The Night Before and Day of the Exam

If you follow the guidelines in this book, you will be extremely well prepared. You will know the format inside and out, you will know how to approach every type of question, you will have worked hard to strengthen your weak areas, and you will have taken multiple practice tests under simulated testing conditions. The last 24 hours before the SAT exam is not the time to cram—it's actually the time to relax. Remember that the SAT is primarily a test of how you think, not what you know. So last-minute cramming can be more confusing than illuminating.

On the night before the big day, find a diversion to keep yourself from obsessing about the SAT. Maybe stay home and watch some of your favorite television shows. Or go out to an early movie. Do whatever is best for you. Just make sure you get plenty of sleep (at least 8 hours).

You should also lay out the following items before you go to bed:

- Test ticket
- Acceptable photo ID
- Sharp pencils with erasers
- Permissible calculator
- Snack and bottle of water
- Address of testing location and directions
- A sweater or sweatshirt in case of cooler test center conditions (optional)

On test day morning, take a shower to wake up and then eat a sensible breakfast. If you are a person who usually eats breakfast, you should probably eat your customary meal. If you don't usually eat breakfast, there's no need to gorge yourself. Eat something light (like a granola bar and a piece of fruit), and pack a snack. Your brain and body will thank you.

STRATEGIES FOR SAT® EXAM SUCCESS

What makes some people better test takers than others? The secret isn't just knowing the subject matter; it's knowing that specific test-taking strategies can add up to higher scores on the test. Good strategy is a combination of knowing the test and knowing your own test-taking habits and capabilities.

Higher scores on the SAT are governed by some key mindsets: you need strong content knowledge, a keen understanding of section expectations, and mastery of timing. The coming chapters are dedicated to helping you prepare those first two ingredients—and your timing will improve in conjunction. However, improved timing is not only the product of regular practice but also deliberate choices made before and during the test. The following strategies (some of which are quite detailed, so read them all the way through) will present some of those choices and help you take your first steps toward SAT success.

Set Goals

Why set a goal? The raw to scaled score conversion will be slightly different for every version of the test so that scores are comparable to one another. So, goals are rarely that precise. But you're trying to decide, before you even sit down for the test, just how you're going to use your time.

When a test taker says, "I need to get 40 questions right in Reading and 35 questions right in Writing and Language to be in the neighborhood of my goal," he or she is deciding how to spend time on the test. That student is saying there are twelve questions in Reading (maybe a whole passage) and nine questions in Writing and Language that he or she can guess on—questions the student will probably get wrong. That means the test taker will have a little extra time for all the other questions. The student can now use that scrimped time to eliminate answers and take the other steps necessary to know his or her answers are right. And, maybe, a few of the guesses will be correct too.

TIP

Make sure you plan your route and allow yourself enough time to arrive at the test site, at least 15 minutes before the 8 a.m. arrival time. You don't want to raise your level of anxiety by having to rush to get there.

The reality of the situation is this: you can always be certain about your answers on the SAT. There's a great reason why three of the four answer choices are wrong and why one is right. And the ability to know which answer is right, for a significant portion of the test, depends on how much time you have to think about it.

If you're looking for a perfect score, then you need to understand what that means. You'll need adequate time with each question on the test to know with absolute certainty that your answer choice is correct. You'll have to work quickly to apply content knowledge, recognize question traps, and exploit the expectations of the different test sections.

In the end, your goal should reflect scores needed by your desired schools, as well as your improvement as you work through this book. Adjust your scoring goals as you improve your content knowledge, practice section strategies, and develop greater comfort with the timing of the test. But, in the beginning, establish how well you want to do to so you can make the best decisions about how to approach each section of the SAT.

After you take the diagnostic test in Chapter 2, take a few minutes to work through the scoring guide and pay attention to how many questions you missed in each section. Then and there, decide how many more you need to answer correctly to approach your desired scaled score. Let those numbers guide you as you complete available practice tests.

Ignore the Test Directions

This book will give you every insight you need into how to complete each section of the current SAT. Save yourself the time and skip the directions at the beginning of each section. They're not going to tell you anything new about your objectives in each section of the test.

Pace Yourself

You need to know just how fast you must go through a section in order to meet your goal. If there are 20 questions in the Math—No Calculator section that you need to answer in 25 minutes, that means you have one minute and 15 seconds to answer each question. Just because that's what you have doesn't mean that is what you'll need. Sometimes, questions will demand less, and other times, they will require more. Your ultimate objective is to spend thoughtful time with every question. In place of that ability, however, you need to focus on your easy questions and dodge the hard.

In the Math sections in particular, this can lead to a variety of choices. Being that all questions have the same value across the test, and questions in Math typically go from simplest to most complex, you can prioritize answering easier questions first, then prioritize the harder questions—questions that you're less likely to answer correctly and that require more time. "Easy" and "hard" will be different for every student as everyone has their own personal strengths and weaknesses.

With that approach, you're investing time where you're likely to get the most points while refusing to let the test maker's choices prevent you showing off your true capabilities. In action, this means that on a first pass through a section, you'll answer some questions and skip others. You should prioritize questions you know how to do—meaning that you understand the steps and concepts required and can complete them quickly. That's true

ALERT
Don't spin your wheels by spending too much time on any one question. Give it some thought, take your best shot, mark questions you want to return to if you have time, and move along.

1

whether you're working in the Evidence-Based Reading and Writing or the Math. In the former, though, you should cycle back to any skipped questions at the end of each passage rather than the end of the section.

When you come to a question, you should perform a split-second evaluation to decide "Is this something I can answer right now because I know where to find the answer, what the problem is, or how to do the math? Or, should I come back to it later because I see that it is going to take some time?" If you're spending significant time on a question, you're often better off taking your best guess, moving on, and only returning if time allows it.

Your evaluations of where you should spend your time and when are critical. It's also important to know how proctors of the test (and a watch!) can support your pacing. In every section of the test, if the proctor is doing their job, you'll receive a verbal warning at about the halfway mark, as well as when only five minutes of total time remain in a section. At the five-minute mark, based on the standard question-to-time ratios, you should be close to the following in each section:

- Reading: 5 questions remaining
- Writing and Language: 6 questions remaining
- Math—No Calculator: 4 questions remaining
- Math—Calculator: 3 questions remaining

When you receive the five-minute warning, fill in remaining answer choices with guesses (just select the same letter for each), then take any remaining time to work through any questions for which you supplied guesses. This method can vary depending on your goals and overall pace, but it is a simple tip that can prevent any unnecessarily missed questions. You want to make sure that you have an answer for every question because a guess may be right, but a blank bubble is always wrong.

Once again, you'll understand more about your pacing once you take the diagnostic, but you always need to keep in mind just how your time is being spent. The test's design works in many ways, deliberately or not, to slow you down. You need to see that you can make choices to control your pace, not let the SAT set it for you.

Answer Every Question

You'll see this advice in a couple places in this book, but it's always worth repeating: there is no excuse for a blank bubble on your SAT answer sheet—with the exception of the Math section grid-ins. Answer every question. No matter how pressed you are for time, you need to set aside the seconds to select an answer (even the same answer) for questions you think you can't complete. You can make the effort to drill into questions if time allows it, but nothing should be unanswered when the proctor calls time.

Make Every Second Count

Some students can answer every question on the test and still have time remaining. That doesn't mean they performed poorly. Nor does it mean they performed well. But if a student chooses to relax once he or she fills in the last bubble, that student has made a critical mistake. Every second on the SAT is an opportunity to revisit a challenging question, recheck simple calculations, review personal question weaknesses, or make sure that answers were gridded correctly. The message is simple: don't stop working until the proctor tells you to.

TOP 10 STRATEGIES TO RAISE YOUR SCORE

When it comes to taking the SAT, some test-taking skills will do you more good than others. There are concepts you can learn and techniques you can follow that will help you do your best. Here are our picks for the top 10 strategies to raise your score:

1. **Create a study plan.** This plan should be complete with goals for scoring, details on your existing strengths and weaknesses, and contain a clear breakdown of how you'll spread out your study time leading up to your test date.

2. **Learn the format of the test.** This includes the directions and expectations of each section—timing, number of questions, passage types, question types, and concepts tested.

3. **Understand what your goals require.** Meeting your goals means understanding for each section when you can skip questions, when you can't, when you can guess, and when you must be certain.

4. **In Reading, use your personalized reading strategy.** Your approach should address the order in which you read passages, how you read each passage (skimming, first and last sentences, questions first, etc.), how you annotate passages, and the expectations and answer strategies for each question type. Questions tend to be arranged from general to specific and located earlier in the passage to later, allowing you to get creative with the order in which you answer questions in a passage.

5. **In Writing and Language, use a step-by-step process to work through questions.** Read the sentence with the question marker, identify if a problem exists, and eliminate answers that don't address the problem or contain errors. If it's a grammatical issue, eliminate answers that are grammatically incorrect, wordy, and irrelevant to the passage. If the question is related to organization, topic development, or use of language, you're looking for answers that create smooth logical flows, are related to the passage topic, and use language effectively.

6. **In the Math sections, try substituting in answers.** When questions use numbers for answers, you can plug in the answers for variables, effectively working backwards. Because the answers will be ordered from lowest to highest, you can substitute in a middle value. If the value is too high, you can eliminate higher answers and vice versa.

7. **For the Essay, remember that you're analyzing the ways in which the author makes his or her argument, not whether you agree with the argument.** Your essay must have an introduction and conclusion, select at least two rhetorical choices to analyze, and provide strong examples as well as analysis of how they strengthen the author's argument. Your writing must be clear, organized well, make strong use of standard English conventions, and effectively communicate your ideas.

8. **Answer every question but don't let yourself get stuck.** When you understand how to answer a question and can do so quickly, answer it. If a question is going to require more time, come back to it later. You're saving time to spend later when you can be sure you've answered all the questions you can definitely answer. If time is running out, fill in a guess for all remaining questions, then see where you can dedicate remaining time.

9. **Use every second of your testing time.** Whether you're just practicing or sitting for the real test, you need to make the most of every minute the test affords. The reality is that you can't finish the SAT early. You must wait for the time to expire. Any time left over after answering your last question should be used to review your known weaknesses (targeting quadratics or commas), revisit uncertain answers, or check grammar corrections or calculations to catch silly mistakes.

10. **Finally, regularly review and practice.** This strategy is hardly revolutionary, but even as you may consistently be working through this book and answering practice questions, you need to periodically revisit sections of the test you may have worked on earlier in your study plan. If you're focused on improvement in the Math sections of the test, that doesn't mean you should ignore the Reading and Writing and Language tests. Shake up your practice to ensure that you're retaining and consistently applying what you've learned throughout your SAT prep process.

Summing It Up

- The SAT is a mission critical part of most college application processes that you can take at any time but is best reserved for your junior year of high school and beyond.

- The SAT is scored on a scale of 400–1600, 200–800 for Evidence-Based Reading and Writing (Sections 1 and 2) and 200–800 for Math (Sections 3 and 4). The optional Essay section is not factored into the composite score but instead is evaluated in three separate categories (Reading, Writing, and Analysis) on a scale of 2–8.

- College Board offers SAT testing dates throughout the year and have a several-week turnaround on score reporting. You can register online and, in some cases, via mail. Some states offer free testing as part of their public-school systems. Some colleges' application processes will allow for the submission of the highest section scores from multiple test dates, a process called superscoring.

- Learning the test details and question types is one of the best ways to prepare for the SAT exam. You can cut down some of the stress of test day and be confident that you know exactly what to expect on test day.

  - **Reading** provides 65 minutes for 52 questions spread across five passages; the answer to every question is stated directly or implied by the passage. Often, questions are organized from general to specific and connected to information earlier in the passage to later.

  - **Writing and Language** allows 35 minutes for 44 questions spread across four passages; the questions will ask you to correct a variety of grammatical errors, usage problems, and wordiness. You'll also have to make selections to improve topic development, organization, and the effective use of language in a passage.

  - **Math—No Calculator** is 25 minutes long with 20 questions (15 multiple-choice, 5 grid-ins); the questions will cover pre-algebra and algebra topics, as well as some higher-level math, with an emphasis on algebraic thinking. Calculator use is not permitted.

  - **Math—Calculator** provides 55 minutes for 38 questions (30 multiple-choice, 8 grid-ins); the questions will cover pre-algebra, algebra, higher-level math, and problem-solving and data analysis. Select models of calculators are permitted but may sometimes be unnecessary—even detrimental.

  - The **Essay**, an optional section, allots 50 minutes to read a passage and create a written argument that identifies an author's key rhetorical choices and analyzes how those choices strengthen the purpose of the passage.

- Key strategies for success on the SAT address how you study and behave on the test. You should do the following when completing your preparation and practice:

  - Create a study plan—spread out your study time over weeks, if not months, and target your weaknesses.

  - Set goals—know what you're trying to achieve and how that impacts what you do in each section of the test.

  - Learn the test format—understand formatting, question types, and expectations for each section.

1

- Simulate test-taking conditions during practice—take the test in the morning, work under the appropriate section time constraints using a timer, sit at a desk or table, take appropriate breaks, and take your work seriously.

- Review strategies and concepts frequently—recall and remind yourself of what you've learned as you're learning it; you need to be able to recall and consistently apply strategies and exam content on test day.

- Pace yourself—move at the pace that will allow you to achieve your goals, dodging challenging and time-consuming questions so that you can spend time to be certain on the questions you need for your scores.

- Answer every question—no questions should be blank when the proctor calls time; know what to do when time is ticking down.

- Use every minute of test time—even if you think you're done, the test ends when time does; take any remaining time to review questions you usually miss, check for simple mistakes, and ensure your answers are gridded correctly.

- Take one last practice test the week of the test, but not the day before. Get adequate sleep, hydrate, and eat balanced meals in the days leading up to your test date.

- Use the day before the test to relax. Cramming increases stress levels and has little impact on performance. Plan your route to your testing location.

- Bring your test ticket, a photo ID, pencils (not mechanical), a permissible calculator, and a snack and bottle of water to your testing site. Aim to arrive at least 15 minutes before the 8:00 a.m. start time.

Take a moment to ask yourself some simple questions about your understanding of the chapter:

Review: What did I learn?

Evaluate: What do I need to learn more about?

Plan: What can I do next to keep improving?

Based on your answers to those questions, adjust your study plan to dedicate additional time to the areas of weakness that you've identified.

PART II:
THE DIAGNOSTIC TEST

Chapter 2: The Diagnostic Test

The Diagnostic Test

OVERVIEW

- **Introduction to the Diagnostic Test**
- **Diagnostic Test Answer Sheet**
- **Section 1: Reading Test**
- **Section 2: Writing and Language Test**
- **Section 3: Math Test—No Calculator**
- **Section 4: Math Test—Calculator**
- **Section 5: Essay**
- **Answer Keys and Explanations**
- **Computing Your Scores**

INTRODUCTION TO THE DIAGNOSTIC TEST

Before you begin preparing for the SAT exam, it's important to know your strengths and the areas where you need improvement. If you find the questions for the Reading Test easy, for example, it would be a mistake to spend hours practicing them. Taking the Diagnostic Test in this chapter and then working out your scores will help you determine how you should apportion your study time.

Preparing to Take the Diagnostic Test

If possible, take the Diagnostic Test in one sitting. Give yourself at least 4 hours to complete it. The actual test is 3 hours and 45 minutes, and you'll be allowed to take three short breaks—you may even want to have some healthy snacks nearby. Simulating the test this way will give you an idea of how long the sections are and how it feels to take the entire test. You will also get a sense of how long you can spend on each question in each section, so you can begin to work out a pacing schedule for yourself.

First, assemble all the things you will need to take the test, including the following items:

- No. 2 pencils, at least three
- A calculator with fresh batteries
- A timer
- The answer sheets and the lined paper for the essay—provided on the following pages

Set a timer for the time specified for each section, which is noted at the top of the first page of each test section. Stick to that time, so you are simulating the real test. At this point, it's as important to know how many questions you can answer in the time allotted as it is to answer questions correctly. Good luck!

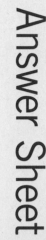

DIAGNOSTIC TEST ANSWER SHEET

Section I: Reading Test

1. Ⓐ Ⓑ Ⓒ Ⓓ
2. Ⓐ Ⓑ Ⓒ Ⓓ
3. Ⓐ Ⓑ Ⓒ Ⓓ
4. Ⓐ Ⓑ Ⓒ Ⓓ
5. Ⓐ Ⓑ Ⓒ Ⓓ
6. Ⓐ Ⓑ Ⓒ Ⓓ
7. Ⓐ Ⓑ Ⓒ Ⓓ
8. Ⓐ Ⓑ Ⓒ Ⓓ
9. Ⓐ Ⓑ Ⓒ Ⓓ
10. Ⓐ Ⓑ Ⓒ Ⓓ
11. Ⓐ Ⓑ Ⓒ Ⓓ
12. Ⓐ Ⓑ Ⓒ Ⓓ
13. Ⓐ Ⓑ Ⓒ Ⓓ

14. Ⓐ Ⓑ Ⓒ Ⓓ
15. Ⓐ Ⓑ Ⓒ Ⓓ
16. Ⓐ Ⓑ Ⓒ Ⓓ
17. Ⓐ Ⓑ Ⓒ Ⓓ
18. Ⓐ Ⓑ Ⓒ Ⓓ
19. Ⓐ Ⓑ Ⓒ Ⓓ
20. Ⓐ Ⓑ Ⓒ Ⓓ
21. Ⓐ Ⓑ Ⓒ Ⓓ
22. Ⓐ Ⓑ Ⓒ Ⓓ
23. Ⓐ Ⓑ Ⓒ Ⓓ
24. Ⓐ Ⓑ Ⓒ Ⓓ
25. Ⓐ Ⓑ Ⓒ Ⓓ
26. Ⓐ Ⓑ Ⓒ Ⓓ

27. Ⓐ Ⓑ Ⓒ Ⓓ
28. Ⓐ Ⓑ Ⓒ Ⓓ
29. Ⓐ Ⓑ Ⓒ Ⓓ
30. Ⓐ Ⓑ Ⓒ Ⓓ
31. Ⓐ Ⓑ Ⓒ Ⓓ
32. Ⓐ Ⓑ Ⓒ Ⓓ
33. Ⓐ Ⓑ Ⓒ Ⓓ
34. Ⓐ Ⓑ Ⓒ Ⓓ
35. Ⓐ Ⓑ Ⓒ Ⓓ
36. Ⓐ Ⓑ Ⓒ Ⓓ
37. Ⓐ Ⓑ Ⓒ Ⓓ
38. Ⓐ Ⓑ Ⓒ Ⓓ
39. Ⓐ Ⓑ Ⓒ Ⓓ

40. Ⓐ Ⓑ Ⓒ Ⓓ
41. Ⓐ Ⓑ Ⓒ Ⓓ
42. Ⓐ Ⓑ Ⓒ Ⓓ
43. Ⓐ Ⓑ Ⓒ Ⓓ
44. Ⓐ Ⓑ Ⓒ Ⓓ
45. Ⓐ Ⓑ Ⓒ Ⓓ
46. Ⓐ Ⓑ Ⓒ Ⓓ
47. Ⓐ Ⓑ Ⓒ Ⓓ
48. Ⓐ Ⓑ Ⓒ Ⓓ
49. Ⓐ Ⓑ Ⓒ Ⓓ
50. Ⓐ Ⓑ Ⓒ Ⓓ
51. Ⓐ Ⓑ Ⓒ Ⓓ
52. Ⓐ Ⓑ Ⓒ Ⓓ

Section II: Writing and Language Test

1. Ⓐ Ⓑ Ⓒ Ⓓ
2. Ⓐ Ⓑ Ⓒ Ⓓ
3. Ⓐ Ⓑ Ⓒ Ⓓ
4. Ⓐ Ⓑ Ⓒ Ⓓ
5. Ⓐ Ⓑ Ⓒ Ⓓ
6. Ⓐ Ⓑ Ⓒ Ⓓ
7. Ⓐ Ⓑ Ⓒ Ⓓ
8. Ⓐ Ⓑ Ⓒ Ⓓ
9. Ⓐ Ⓑ Ⓒ Ⓓ
10. Ⓐ Ⓑ Ⓒ Ⓓ
11. Ⓐ Ⓑ Ⓒ Ⓓ

12. Ⓐ Ⓑ Ⓒ Ⓓ
13. Ⓐ Ⓑ Ⓒ Ⓓ
14. Ⓐ Ⓑ Ⓒ Ⓓ
15. Ⓐ Ⓑ Ⓒ Ⓓ
16. Ⓐ Ⓑ Ⓒ Ⓓ
17. Ⓐ Ⓑ Ⓒ Ⓓ
18. Ⓐ Ⓑ Ⓒ Ⓓ
19. Ⓐ Ⓑ Ⓒ Ⓓ
20. Ⓐ Ⓑ Ⓒ Ⓓ
21. Ⓐ Ⓑ Ⓒ Ⓓ
22. Ⓐ Ⓑ Ⓒ Ⓓ

23. Ⓐ Ⓑ Ⓒ Ⓓ
24. Ⓐ Ⓑ Ⓒ Ⓓ
25. Ⓐ Ⓑ Ⓒ Ⓓ
26. Ⓐ Ⓑ Ⓒ Ⓓ
27. Ⓐ Ⓑ Ⓒ Ⓓ
28. Ⓐ Ⓑ Ⓒ Ⓓ
29. Ⓐ Ⓑ Ⓒ Ⓓ
30. Ⓐ Ⓑ Ⓒ Ⓓ
31. Ⓐ Ⓑ Ⓒ Ⓓ
32. Ⓐ Ⓑ Ⓒ Ⓓ
33. Ⓐ Ⓑ Ⓒ Ⓓ

34. Ⓐ Ⓑ Ⓒ Ⓓ
35. Ⓐ Ⓑ Ⓒ Ⓓ
36. Ⓐ Ⓑ Ⓒ Ⓓ
37. Ⓐ Ⓑ Ⓒ Ⓓ
38. Ⓐ Ⓑ Ⓒ Ⓓ
39. Ⓐ Ⓑ Ⓒ Ⓓ
40. Ⓐ Ⓑ Ⓒ Ⓓ
41. Ⓐ Ⓑ Ⓒ Ⓓ
42. Ⓐ Ⓑ Ⓒ Ⓓ
43. Ⓐ Ⓑ Ⓒ Ⓓ
44. Ⓐ Ⓑ Ⓒ Ⓓ

Section III: Math Test—NO CALCULATOR

1. Ⓐ Ⓑ Ⓒ Ⓓ

2. Ⓐ Ⓑ Ⓒ Ⓓ

3. Ⓐ Ⓑ Ⓒ Ⓓ

4. Ⓐ Ⓑ Ⓒ Ⓓ

5. Ⓐ Ⓑ Ⓒ Ⓓ

6. Ⓐ Ⓑ Ⓒ Ⓓ

7. Ⓐ Ⓑ Ⓒ Ⓓ

8. Ⓐ Ⓑ Ⓒ Ⓓ

9. Ⓐ Ⓑ Ⓒ Ⓓ

10. Ⓐ Ⓑ Ⓒ Ⓓ

11. Ⓐ Ⓑ Ⓒ Ⓓ

12. Ⓐ Ⓑ Ⓒ Ⓓ

13. Ⓐ Ⓑ Ⓒ Ⓓ

14. Ⓐ Ⓑ Ⓒ Ⓓ

15. Ⓐ Ⓑ Ⓒ Ⓓ

16.

17.

18.

19.

20.

Answer Sheet

Diagnostic Test

Section IV: Math Test—CALCULATOR

1. Ⓐ Ⓑ Ⓒ Ⓓ
2. Ⓐ Ⓑ Ⓒ Ⓓ
3. Ⓐ Ⓑ Ⓒ Ⓓ
4. Ⓐ Ⓑ Ⓒ Ⓓ
5. Ⓐ Ⓑ Ⓒ Ⓓ
6. Ⓐ Ⓑ Ⓒ Ⓓ
7. Ⓐ Ⓑ Ⓒ Ⓓ
8. Ⓐ Ⓑ Ⓒ Ⓓ

9. Ⓐ Ⓑ Ⓒ Ⓓ
10. Ⓐ Ⓑ Ⓒ Ⓓ
11. Ⓐ Ⓑ Ⓒ Ⓓ
12. Ⓐ Ⓑ Ⓒ Ⓓ
13. Ⓐ Ⓑ Ⓒ Ⓓ
14. Ⓐ Ⓑ Ⓒ Ⓓ
15. Ⓐ Ⓑ Ⓒ Ⓓ
16. Ⓐ Ⓑ Ⓒ Ⓓ

17. Ⓐ Ⓑ Ⓒ Ⓓ
18. Ⓐ Ⓑ Ⓒ Ⓓ
19. Ⓐ Ⓑ Ⓒ Ⓓ
20. Ⓐ Ⓑ Ⓒ Ⓓ
21. Ⓐ Ⓑ Ⓒ Ⓓ
22. Ⓐ Ⓑ Ⓒ Ⓓ
23. Ⓐ Ⓑ Ⓒ Ⓓ
24. Ⓐ Ⓑ Ⓒ Ⓓ

25. Ⓐ Ⓑ Ⓒ Ⓓ
26. Ⓐ Ⓑ Ⓒ Ⓓ
27. Ⓐ Ⓑ Ⓒ Ⓓ
28. Ⓐ Ⓑ Ⓒ Ⓓ
29. Ⓐ Ⓑ Ⓒ Ⓓ
30. Ⓐ Ⓑ Ⓒ Ⓓ

31. 32. 33. 34.

35. 36. 37. 38.

Section V: Essay

Diagnostic Test

Part II

Diagnostic Test

Section 1: Reading Test

65 Minutes—52 Questions

TURN TO SECTION 1 OF YOUR ANSWER SHEET TO ANSWER THE QUESTIONS IN THIS SECTION.

DIRECTIONS: Each passage (or pair of passages) in this section is followed by a number of multiple-choice questions. After reading each passage, select the best answer to each question based on what is stated or implied in the passage or passages and in any supplementary material, such as a table, graph, or chart.

Questions 1–10 are based on the following passage.

Angel De Cora was born Hinook-Mahiwi-Kalinaka on the Winnebago Reservation in Nebraska in 1871. She worked as a book illustrator, particularly on books by and about Native Americans, and lectured and wrote about Indian art. The story from which this excerpt is adapted, "The Sick Child," may be autobiographical.

It was about sunset when I, a little child, was sent with a handful of powdered tobacco leaves and red feathers to make an offering
Line to the spirit who had caused the sickness
5 of my little sister. It had been a long, hard winter, and the snow lay deep on the prairie as far as the eye could reach. The medicine-woman's directions had been that the offering must be laid upon the naked earth,
10 and that to find it I must face toward the setting sun…

But now where was a spot of earth to be found in all that white monotony? They had talked of death at the house. I hoped that
15 my little sister would live, but I was afraid of nature.

I reached a little spring. I looked down to its pebbly bottom, wondering whether I should leave my offering there, or keep
20 on in search of a spot of earth. If I put my offering in the water, would it reach the bottom and touch the earth, or would it float away, as it had always done when I made my offering to the water spirit?

25 Once more I started on in my search of the bare ground.

The surface was crusted in some places, and walking was easy; in other places I would wade through a foot or more of snow.
30 Often I paused, thinking to clear the snow away in some place and there lay my offering. But no, my faith must be in nature, and I must trust to it to lay bare the earth…

I went on and on; the reeds were waving
35 their tasselled ends in the wind. I stopped and looked at them. A reed, whirling in the wind, had formed a space round its stem, making a loose socket. I stood looking into the opening. The reed must be rooted in the
40 ground, and the hole must follow the stem to the earth. If I poured my offerings into the hole, surely they must reach the ground; so I said the prayer I had been taught, and dropped my tobacco and red feathers into
45 the opening that nature itself had created.

No sooner was the sacrifice accomplished than a feeling of doubt and fear thrilled me…

Not till I turned homeward did I real-
50 ize how cold I was. When at last I reached the house they took me in and warmed me, but did not question me, and I said nothing. Everyone was sad, for the little one had grown worse.

CONTINUE

The next day the medicine woman said my little sister was beyond hope; she could not live. Then bitter remorse was mine, for I thought I had been unfaithful, and therefore my little sister was to be called to the spirit-land. I was a silent child…

My parents would not listen to what the medicine-woman had said, but clung to hope. As soon as she had gone, they sent for a medicine-man who lived many miles away.

He arrived about dark. He was a large man, with a sad, gentle face. His presence had always filled me with awe, and that night it was especially so, for he was coming as a holy man. He entered the room where the baby….There was silence saving only for the tinkling of the little tin ornaments on his medicine-bag. He began to speak: "A soul has departed from this house, gone to the spirit-land. As I came I saw luminous vapor above the house. It ascended, it grew less, it was gone on its way to the spirit-land. It was the spirit of the little child who is sick; she still breathes, but her spirit is beyond our reach. If medicine will ease her pain, I will do what I can."

He stood up and blessed the four corners of the earth with song. Then… he began reciting the vision that had given him the right to be a medicine-man. The ruling force of the vision had been in the form of a bear. To it he addressed his prayer, saying: "Inasmuch as thou hast given me power to cure the sick… if thou seest fit, allow me to recall the spirit of this child to its body once more." He asked that the coverings be taken off the baby, and that it be brought into the middle of the room. Then, as he sang, he danced slowly around the little form. When the song was finished, he blessed the child, and then prepared the medicine…. This he took into his mouth and sprinkled it over the little body. Another mixture he gave her to drink.

Almost instantly there was a change; the little one began to breathe more easily, and as the night wore on she seemed to suffer less. Finally she opened her eyes, looked into mother's face, and smiled. The medicine-man, seeing it, said that the end was near, and though he gave her more medicine, the spirit, he said, would never return.

After saying words of comfort, he took his departure, refusing to take a pony and some blankets that were offered him, saying that he had been unable to hold the spirit back, and had no right to accept the gifts.

1. Which choice best summarizes the passage?

   A. A Native American girl recalls her experience of trying to save and losing her baby sister.

   B. A Native American child is called upon to make an offering to the spirits.

   C. A Native American family struggles with illness in the depths of winter on the Great Plains.

   D. A Native American family uses their religious beliefs to try to save their daughter.

2. Which choice best describes a major theme of the passage?

   A. The ineffectiveness of traditional medicine

   B. A community's commitment to caring for its members during a time of hardship

   C. The importance of faith and reason in overcoming tragedy

   D. The cruelty and indifference of nature

CONTINUE

3. Which choice provides the best evidence for the answer to the previous question?

   A. Lines 46–48 ("No sooner… thrilled me.")

   B. Lines 64–66 ("As soon… away.")

   C. Lines 79–83 ("It was the spirit… what I can.")

   D. Lines 112–117 ("After saying… the gifts.")

4. What evidence from the text shows the girl's dilemma in following the medicine woman's directions?

   A. Lines 8–9 ("the offering… naked earth")

   B. Lines 20–23 ("If I put… away")

   C. Lines 27–29 ("The surface… of snow. ")

   D. Lines 34–35 ("I went on… the wind.")

5. Based on the passage, the narrator most likely wants to place her offering correctly because she

   A. will have to explain her choice to her family.

   B. wants to be trusted with similar tasks in the future.

   C. thinks doing so will affect her sister's condition.

   D. is afraid of being punished for making a mistake.

6. As used in line 48, "thrilled" most nearly means

   A. inspired.

   B. refreshed.

   C. frightened.

   D. stimulated.

7. The phrase "bitter remorse was mine" (lines 57–58) mainly serves to

   A. indicate the fault of the parents in the little sister's condition.

   B. express doubt about the success of the offering.

   C. explain the actions of the narrator later in the story.

   D. justify the dismissal of the medicine woman.

8. Based on the passage, which choice best describes the narrator's relationship with her parents?

   A. The parents seem to treat the narrator as if she were an adult.

   B. The narrator wishes her parents would give her more responsibility.

   C. The parents love their youngest child, but not the narrator.

   D. The narrator receives warmth and validation from her parents.

9. It can reasonably be inferred from the passage that the girl's parents did not send for the medicine-man sooner because

   A. he was busy helping another family at the time.

   B. he had to come from an incredible distance.

   C. they thought the medicine woman would be able to help their daughter.

   D. they were directly related to the medicine woman and had to ask for her help out of respect.

10. According to the passage, the little sister's spirit has

   A. left the house as a luminous vapor.

   B. returned from the spirit-land.

   C. transformed into the form of a bear.

   D. called her elder sister to the spirit land.

Diagnostic Test

CONTINUE

Questions 11–20 are based on the following passage.

This passage is excerpted from a handbook by education pioneer Maria Montessori, who developed a special method for teaching children.

The "Children's House" is the environment which is offered to the child that he may be given the opportunity of developing his
Line activities. This kind of school is not of a
5 fixed type, but may vary according to the financial resources at disposal and to the opportunities afforded by the environment. It ought to be a real house; that is to say, a set of rooms with a garden of which the
10 children are the masters. A garden which contains shelters is ideal, because the children can play or sleep under them, and can also bring their tables out to work or dine. In this way they may live almost entirely in
15 the open air, and are protected at the same time from rain and sun.

The central and principal room of the building, often also the only room at the disposal of the children, is the room for "in-
20 tellectual work." To this central room can be added other smaller rooms according to the means and opportunities of the place: for example, a bathroom, a dining-room, a little parlor or common-room, a room for
25 manual work, a gymnasium and rest-room.

The special characteristic of the equipment of these houses is that it is adapted for children and not adults. They contain not only didactic material specially fitted for
30 the intellectual development of the child, but also a complete equipment for the management of the miniature family. The furniture is light so that the children can move it about, and it is painted in some light color
35 so that the children can wash it with soap and water. There are low tables of various sizes and shapes—square, rectangular and round, large and small. The rectangular

shape is the most common as two or more
40 children can work at it together. The seats are small wooden chairs, but there are also small wicker armchairs and sofas.

In the working-room there are two indispensable pieces of furniture. One of
45 these is a very long cupboard with large doors. It is very low so that a small child can set on the top of it small objects such as mats, flowers, etc. Inside this cupboard is kept the didactic material which is the
50 common property of all the children.

The other is a chest of drawers containing two or three columns of little drawers, each of which has a bright handle (or a handle of some color to contrast with the
55 background), and a small card with a name upon it. Every child has his own drawer, in which to put things belonging to him.

Round the walls of the room are fixed blackboards at a low level, so that the chil-
60 dren can write or draw on them, and pleasing, artistic pictures, which are changed from time to time as circumstances direct. The pictures represent children, families, landscapes, flowers and fruit, and more of-
65 ten Biblical and historical incidents. Ornamental plants and flowering plants ought always to be placed in the room where the children are at work.

Another part of the working-room's
70 equipment is seen in the pieces of carpet of various colors—red, blue, pink, green and brown. The children spread these rugs upon the floor, sit upon them and work there with the didactic material. A room of this kind is
75 larger than the customary classrooms, not only because the little tables and separate chairs take up more space, but also because a large part of the floor must be free for the children to spread their rugs and work upon
80 them.

CONTINUE

In the sitting-room, or "club-room," a kind of parlor in which the children amuse themselves by conversation, games, or music, etc., the furnishings should be
85 especially tasteful. Little tables of different sizes, little armchairs and sofas should be placed here and there. Many brackets of all kinds and sizes, upon which may be put statuettes, artistic vases or framed photo-
90 graphs, should adorn the walls; and, above all, each child should have a little flower-pot, in which he may sow the seed of some indoor plant, to tend and cultivate it as it grows. On the tables of this sitting-room
95 should be placed large albums of colored pictures, and also games of patience, or various geometric solids, with which the children can play at pleasure, constructing figures, etc. A piano, or, better, other mu-
100 sical instruments, possibly harps of small dimensions, made especially for children, completes the equipment. In this "club-room" the teacher may sometimes enter-tain the children with stories, which will
105 attract a circle of interested listeners.

The furniture of the dining-room consists, in addition to the tables, of low cupboards accessible to all the children, who can themselves put in their place and
110 take away the crockery, spoons, knives and forks, table-cloth and napkins. The plates are always of china, and the tum-blers and water-bottles of glass. Knives are always included in the table equipment.
115 In short, where the manufacture of toys has been brought to such a point of complication and perfection that children have at their disposal entire dolls' houses, complete wardrobes for the dressing and
120 undressing of dolls, kitchens where they can pretend to cook, toy animals as nearly lifelike as possible, this method seeks to give all this to the child in reality––mak-ing him an actor in a living scene.

11. The main purpose of the passage is to

A. explain the importance of play in a child's education.

B. define the qualities of the Children's House.

C. criticize traditional forms of education as unstimulating.

D. argue how children should practice adult responsibilities from an early age.

12. It can reasonably be inferred that equipment in a Children's House should be "adapted for children and not adults" (lines 27–28) because

A. adults are forbidden from entering a Children's House.

B. children are incapable of learning using adult-sized equipment.

C. it encourages children to share.

D. it helps children practice independence.

13. Which conclusion is best supported by the statements in the second paragraph (lines 17–25)?

A. Exercise is an important element of the educational method described.

B. Children require training in dining deco-rum and manners to be successful.

C. Children divide their time between manual labor and intellectual work in the Montessori school model.

D. Intellectual work is the core of the learn-ing experience but can be supported with other activities.

14. As used in line 29, "didactic" most nearly means

A. educational.

B. enjoyable.

C. pedantic.

D. distracting.

Diagnostic Test

CONTINUE

15. The sixth paragraph (lines 58–68) mainly serves to

A. communicate what decorations are appropriate for a Children's House.

B. explain the importance of color and shapes for intellectual development.

C. argue how family structure affects learning.

D. express that plants are a necessary addition to classroom spaces.

16. According to the passage, a working room must contain individual pieces of multicolored carpet because

A. colorful objects stimulate children's creativity.

B. the carpets provide spaces for children to complete work.

C. tables and chairs require too much space.

D. children must learn the importance of organizing their workspaces.

17. Which choice provides the best evidence for the author's trust in the character and abilities of children?

A. Lines 8–10 ("It ought… the masters.")

B. Lines 28–32 ("They contain… miniature family.")

C. Lines 46–50 ("It is very low… the children.")

D. Lines 106–108 ("The furniture …all the children")

18. As used in line 117, "complication" most nearly means

A. difficulty.

B. confusion.

C. simplicity.

D. intricacy.

19. Based on the passage, the author believes that

A. adults should not be involved in the education of children.

B. multiple stimuli and freedom are integral to a good education.

C. children need to live apart from adults when learning.

D. unsupervised children can be trusted to learn on their own and care for their materials.

20. Which choice provides the best evidence for the answer to the previous question?

A. Lines 1–4 ("The 'Children's House'… activities.")

B. Lines 10–16 ("A garden which… rain or sun.")

C. Lines 102–105 ("In this 'club room'… interested listeners.")

D. Lines 117–124 ("…that children… a living scene.")

CONTINUE

Questions 21–31 are based on the following passage.

This excerpt is from the article "New Link in the Food Chain? Marine Plastic Pollution and Seafood Safety," by Nate Seltenrich. It has been reproduced from the journal Environmental Health Perspectives.

World plastics production has experienced almost constant growth for more than half a century, rising from approximately 1.9
Line tons in 1950 to approximately 330 million
5 tons in 2013. The World Bank estimates that 1.4 billion tons of trash are generated globally each year, 10% of it plastic. The International Maritime Organization has banned the dumping of plastic waste (and
10 most other garbage) at sea. However, an unknown portion of the plastic produced each year escapes into the environment— instead of being landfilled, incinerated, or recycled—and at least some of it eventually
15 makes its way to sea.

Plastics that reach the ocean will gradually break down into ever-smaller pieces due to sunlight exposure, oxidation, and the physical action of waves, currents, and
20 grazing by fish and birds. So-called microplastics—variably defined in the scientific literature and popular press as smaller than 1 or 5 mm in diameter—are understood to be the most abundant type of plastic in the
25 ocean. The 5 Gyres' authors* found microplastics almost everywhere they sampled, from near-shore environments to the open ocean, in varying concentrations, and they estimated that particles 4.75 mm or
30 smaller—about the size of a lentil—made up roughly 90% of the total plastic pieces they collected.

But the degradation of larger pieces of plastic is not the only way microplastics end
35 up in the ocean. Nurdles—the plastic pellets used as a feedstock for producing plastic goods—can spill from ships or land-based sources, and "microbeads" used as scrubbing agents in personal care products such
40 as skin cleansers, toothpastes, and shampoos, can escape water-treatment facilities and pass into water-sheds with treated water. (In June 2014, Illinois became the first US state to ban the manufacture and sale
45 of products containing microbeads, which have been documented in the Great Lakes and Chicago's North Shore Channel.)

Marine organisms throughout the food chain commonly consume plastics of
50 various sizes. The tiniest microplastics are small enough to be mistaken for food by zooplankton, allowing them to enter the food chain at very low trophic levels. Some larger predators are thought to confuse
55 nurdles (which typically measure less than 5 mm in diameter) with fish eggs or other food sources.

Once plastics have been consumed, laboratory tests show that chemical addi-
60 tives and adsorbed pollutants and metals on their surface can desorb and transfer into the guts and tissues of marine organisms...

Research has shown that harmful and persistent substances can both bioac-
65 cumulate (or increase in concentration as exposures persist) and biomagnify (or increase in concentration at higher trophic levels) within organisms as they assume some of the chemical burden of their prey
70 or environment. Yet again, no research has yet demonstrated the bioaccumulation of sorbed pollutants in the environment.

Three key questions remain to be determined. To what extent do plastics trans-
75 fer pollutants and additives to organisms upon ingestion? What contribution are plastics making to the contaminant burden in organisms above and beyond their

CONTINUE

exposures through water, sediments,
80 and food? And, finally, what proportion
of humans' exposure to plastic ingredients and environmental pollutants occurs
through seafood? Researchers are moving
carefully in the direction of answers to
85 these questions...

New laws ... could require handling
plastics more responsibly at the end
of their useful life through recycling,
proper disposal, and extended producer
90 responsibility.

Rolf Halden, director of the Center
for Environmental Security at the Bio-
design Institute at Arizona State University, advocates for another solution:
95 manufacturing more sustainable plastics
from the start. "We need to design the
next generation of plastics to make them
more biodegradable so that they don't
have a long half-life, they don't accumu-
100 late in the oceans, and they don't have
the opportunity to collect chemicals long-
term," he says. "There's just no way we
can shield people from all exposures that
could occur. Let's design safer chemicals
105 and make the whole problem moot."

*The 5 Gyres Institute addresses plastic pollution in the ocean.

21. The primary purpose of the passage is to

   A. offer a theory about why the environment
      is in danger.

   B. inform the public of the problems of plas-
      tic in the ocean.

   C. start a movement to halt all plastic
      production.

   D. inspire readers to clean up the oceans
      personally.

22. Which choice provides the best evidence for
    the answer to the previous question?

   A. Lines 58–62 ("Once plastics...
      organisms.")

   B. Lines 63–66 ("Research... biomagnify")

   C. Lines 70–72 ("Yet again... environment.")

   D. Lines 73–74 ("Three key... determined.")

23. According to the passage, plastic is

   A. wasted more than any other material.

   B. produced at a significantly smaller scale
      than in the 1950s.

   C. responsible for over 100 billion tons of
      waste each year.

   D. the single most dangerous material for
      the conservation of marine ecosystems.

24. Which choice provides the best evidence for
    the answer to the previous question?

   A. Lines 1–5 ("World... 2013.")

   B. Lines 5–7 ("The World... it plastic.")

   C. Lines 7–10 ("The International... at sea.")

   D. Lines 25–32 ("The 5 Gyres'... collected.")

25. It can reasonably be inferred from the pas-
    sage that

   A. the percentage of plastic being recycled
      has increased by over 300 percent in the
      past 60 years.

   B. plastic breaks down into smaller pieces
      in the ocean, making it less dangerous to
      marine organisms.

   C. microplastics are the most common type
      of plastic found in the ocean.

   D. harmful nurdles leak into the environ-
      ment from shampoo.

26. According to the passage, Illinois banned the sale of certain personal care products because

    A. residues from the products were ending up in the ocean.

    B. the containers couldn't be recycled.

    C. ingredients were determined to be carcinogenic.

    D. the products contained microbeads that were getting into the water system.

27. As used in line 61, "desorb" most nearly means

    A. leach out.

    B. adhere.

    C. soak.

    D. multiply.

28. The use of the terms "bioaccumulate" (line 64) and "biomagnify" (line 66) and their definitions establishes a tone that is

    A. concerned and academic.

    B. emotional and persuasive.

    C. neutral and scientific.

    D. subjective and opinionated.

29. As it is used in line 67, "concentration" most nearly means

    A. absorption

    B. focus

    C. study

    D. amount

30. The main purpose of the questions asked in lines 74–83 is to

    A. establish how much plastic waste from the oceans people might be ingesting.

    B. indicate how sea creatures happen to ingest plastic waste in the oceans.

    C. suggest what kinds of plastic waste can be found in the oceans.

    D. frame the current tasks facing the community of researchers.

31. According to the passage, Rolf Halden states that the effects of pollution from plastics can be decreased by

    A. passing laws to mandate more rigorous recycling.

    B. making plastics that are safe to ingest.

    C. developing plastics that are biodegradable.

    D. banning the production of new plastic products.

CONTINUE

Diagnostic Test

Diagnostic Test

Questions 32–42 are based on the following passages and supplementary material.

Passage 1: The passage is excerpted from a speech in 1803 by young Robert Emmet who was condemned to death for treason after organizing a rebellion against the English in Ireland. He had achieved fame as an orator with speeches decrying tyranny.

Passage 2: The passage was excerpted from a speech to a Fourth of July audience in New Harmony, Indiana in 1828 by Fanny Wright, who was a reformer, author, and orator, which were unusual occupations for a woman in the early nineteenth century.

PASSAGE 1

I am charged with being an emissary of France. An emissary of France and for what end? It is alleged that I wish to sell
Line the independence of my country; and for
5 what end?...

No; I am no emissary. . . . Sell my country's independence to France and for what? Was it a change of masters? No, but for ambition. Oh, my country! Was it per-
10 sonal ambition that could influence me? Had it been the soul of my actions, could I not. . .have placed myself amongst the proudest of your oppressors? My country was my idol! To it I sacrificed every self-
15 ish, every endearing sentiment.... I acted as an Irishman, determined on delivering my country from the yoke of a foreign and unrelenting tyranny, and the more galling yoke of a domestic faction, which
20 is its joint partner. . . . It was the wish of my heart to extricate my country from this double riveted despotism—I wished to place her independence beyond the reach of any power on earth.... Connec-
25 tion with France was, indeed, intended,

but only as far as mutual interest would sanction or require...

I wished to prove to France and to the world that Irishmen deserved to be
30 assisted... I wished to procure for my country the guarantee which Washington procured for America—to procure an aid... These were my objects; not to receive new taskmasters, hilt to expel old
35 tyrants. And it was for these ends I sought aid from France; because France, even as an enemy, could not be more implacable than the enemy already in the bosom of my country.

40 Let no man dare, when I am dead, to charge me with dishonor; let no man attaint my memory by believing that I could have engaged in any cause but that of my country's liberty and independence... I
45 would not have submitted to a foreign oppressor, for the same reason that I would resist the foreign and domestic oppressor. In the dignity of freedom, I would have fought upon the threshold of my coun-
50 try, and its enemy should enter only by passing over my lifeless corpse. And am I, who lived but for my country, and who have subjected myself to the dangers of the jealous and watchful oppressor, and
55 the bondage of the grave, only to give my countrymen their rights, and my country its independence—am I to be loaded with calumny* and not suffered to resent it? No, God forbid!

* false and defamatory statements meant to damage someone's reputation

PASSAGE 2

60 In continental Europe, of late years, the words *patriotism* and *patriot* have been used in a more enlarged sense than it is usual here to attribute to them, or than is attached to them in Great Britain. Since
65 the political struggles of France, Italy, Spain, and Greece, the word *patriotism*

CONTINUE ▶

has been employed, throughout continental Europe, to express a love of the public good; a preference for the interests of the
70 many to those of the few; a desire for the emancipation of the human race from the thrall of despotism, religious and civil.... And *patriot*, in like manner, is employed to signify a lover of human liberty and human
75 improvement rather than a mere lover of the country in which he lives, or the tribe to which he belongs. Used in this sense, patriotism is a virtue, and a patriot is a virtuous man. With such an interpretation, a patriot
80 is a useful member of society capable of enlarging all minds and bettering all hearts with which he comes in contact; a useful member of the human family, capable of establishing fundamental principles and of
85 merging his own interests, those of his associates, and those of his nation in the interests of the human race. Laurels and statues are vain things, and mischievous as they are

childish; but could we imagine them of use,
90 on such a patriot alone could they be with any reason bestowed.

Is there a thought can fill the human mind more pure, more vast, more generous, more refined than that which guides
95 the enlightened patriot's toll; not he, whose view is bounded by his soil; not he, whose narrow heart can only shrine the land-the people that he calleth mine; not he, who to set up that land on high, will make whole
100 nations bleed, whole nations die; not he, who, calling that land's rights his pride trampleth the rights of all the earth beside. No: -- He it is, the just, the generous soul! Who owneth brotherhood with either pole,
105 stretches from realm to realm his spacious mind, and guards the weal of all the human kind, holds freedom's banner o'er the earth unfurl'd and stands the guardian patriot of a world!

TIMELINE

1707	Acts of Union between Scotland and England create the Kingdom of Great Britain
1776–1783	American colonies declare and win independence
1789	French storm the Bastille (prison), fight to end French monarchy
1798	Society of United Irishmen rebel unsuccessfully against British rule
1800	British Parliament passes The Act of Union, abolishing the Irish parliament
1801	United Kingdom of Great Britain and Ireland created
1803	United States purchases Louisiana Territory from France Robert Emmet leads a rebellion in Dublin against the union
1803–1815	Napoleonic Wars in Europe (France vs. European powers)
1808–1833	Spanish wars of independence
1823	France invades Spain to help restore monarchy
1828	Andrew Jackson elected president of United States

CONTINUE ➤

Diagnostic Test

32. As it is used in line 1, "emissary" most nearly means

    A. ambassador.

    B. spy.

    C. enemy.

    D. teacher.

33. Which of the following statements from Emmet's speech shows that he thinks he is a martyr?

    A. Lines 11–13 ("Had it been… your oppressors?")

    B. Lines 22–24 ("I wished to… on earth.")

    C. Lines 28–30 ("I wished to… to be assisted")

    D. Lines 40–41 ("Let no man… with dishonor;")

34. Which of the following of Emmet's statements shows that he thinks he is a patriot?

    A. Line 6 ("No… emissary.")

    B. Lines 9–10 ("Was it… influence me?")

    C. Lines 30–33 ("I wished… an aid")

    D. Lines 44–47 ("I would not. . .oppressor.")

35. The main purpose of the sentence "In the dignity of freedom, I would have fought upon the threshold of my country, and its enemy should enter only by passing over my lifeless corpse" (lines 48–51) is to

    A. persuade the judge to overturn Emmet's death sentence.

    B. remind Emmet's audience of their own patriotism.

    C. allow Emmet to admit he was a foreign agent.

    D. reaffirm Emmet's commitment to his country and his intolerance of oppression.

36. Based on information shown in the timeline, why might France have turned down Emmet's request for help?

    A. France was in the midst of trying to restore the monarchy in Spain.

    B. France was engaged in the drawn-out Napoleonic Wars.

    C. France had fought its own revolution and didn't want to get involved in that of another country.

    D. France was trying to keep the United States from taking Louisiana.

37. According to Passage 2, patriots are defined as

    A. people willing to die for their country.

    B. members of a country's armed forces.

    C. individuals who fight for improving the lives of others.

    D. people who love their country.

38. As it is used in line 103, "generous" most nearly means

    A. giving.

    B. kind.

    C. creative.

    D. noble.

39. Based on the timeline, the historical events of which year most likely influenced the concept of patriotism discouraged by Passage 2?

    A. 1707

    B. 1776

    C. 1803

    D. 1828

CONTINUE ➤

40. Which choice best describes a central difference between how Emmet (Passage 1) and Wright (Passage 2) view the concept of patriotism?

   A. Although years apart, both Wright and Emmet were advocating to rethink their country's ideas about patriotism.

   B. Emmet was focused on freedom and independence for his own country, while Wright was focused on freedom and independence for all humankind.

   C. Emmet loved his country more than Wright loved her country.

   D. Wright didn't understand tyranny because she lived in a democracy, while Emmet fought against tyranny.

41. It can be reasonably inferred that the author of Passage 2 would not call Emmet a patriot because he

   A. saw no dishonor in his actions.

   B. wanted to free his people.

   C. idolized his own country above all others.

   D. declared the court's sentence to be unjust.

42. In developing their arguments, Emmet (Passage 1) and Wright (Passage 2) both express that patriots

   A. combat oppression in various forms.

   B. must strive to protect their homeland from foreign powers.

   C. are the guardians of all peoples and nations.

   D. should respect the choices of their governments above all else.

Questions 43–52 are based on the following passage and supplementary material.

The following passage is adapted from an article about ways that spiders protect themselves.

There are, among spiders, two forms of protective modification: the first, including all cases of protective resemblance to vegetable and inorganic things—that is, all modifications of color or of color and form that tend to make them inconspicuous in their natural relations—I shall call direct protection…

…The meaning of a protective peculiarity can be determined only when the animal is seen in its natural home. The number of strangely modified forms depicted in descriptive works on spiders is enormous. Bodies are twisted, elongated, inflated, flattened, truncated, covered with tubercles or spines, enclosed within chitinous plates, colored like bark, like lichens, like flowers of every imaginable hue, like bird droppings, like sand or stones, and in every one of these modifications there is doubtless an adaptation of the spider to its surroundings which, when it is studied out of its natural relations, we can only guess at…

As a general rule the forms and colors of spiders are adapted to render them inconspicuous in their natural homes. Bright colored spiders… either keep hidden away or are found upon flowers whose tints harmonize with their own. This rule, while it has numerous exceptions, is borne out by the great majority of cases. A good illustration is found in the genus *Uloborus*, of which the members bear a deceptive resemblance to small pieces of bark or to such bits of rubbish as commonly become entangled in old deserted webs.…The spider is always found in the middle of the web, with its

CONTINUE

40 legs extended in a line with the body…
Its form and color make it like a scrap
of bark, its body being truncated and
diversified with small humps, while its
first legs are very uneven, bearing heavy
45 fringes of hair on the tibia and having the
terminal joints slender. Its color is a soft
wood-brown or gray, mottled with white.
It has the habit of hanging motionless in
the web for hours at a time, swaying in
50 the wind like an inanimate object. The
strands of its web are rough and inelastic,
so that they are frequently broken. . .

We come now to a large and interesting class in genus *Epeira*. I refer to those
55 species, mostly nocturnal, which are protected during the day, not by hiding in
crevices, nor in any way actually getting
out of sight, but by the close resemblance
which they bear to the bark of the trees
60 to which they cling. This resemblance is
brought about in two ways: through their
color, which is like that of wood or lichens,
and through their tuberculated and rugose
forms, which resemble rough bark.

65 One of the most remarkable of these
forms is *C. mitralis*, a Madagascar species, which, looked at in profile, probably
resembles a woody knot. The abdomen is
divided into two divergent cones. The en-
70 tire upper surface of the body is covered
with conical elevations, which render it
rough and uneven; the sides of the abdomen are made up of several layers, which
form stages, one above another, like the
75 ridges of bark on a woody excrescence.
The legs, formed of wide, flattened plates,
make the base. The color of the spider is
yellowish-gray, varied with white and
dark reddish-brown. It has the habit of
80 perching on a branch and clasping it like
a bird, so that the elaborate modification
of form, which would be useless if the spider hung exposed in the web, is made as
effective as possible.

43. The primary purpose of the passage is to

A. explain why direct protection is a superior adaptive strategy.

B. argue the necessity of direct observation
in scientific inquiry.

C. describe a form of protective modification that camouflages organisms.

D. discuss the behaviors and survival strategies of the spider genus *Uloborus*.

44. Which choice provides the best evidence for
the answer to the previous question?

A. Lines 1–8 ("There are. . . direct
protection.")

B. Lines 9–11 ("The meaning… natural
home.")

C. Lines 38–42 ("The spider is… scrap of
bark")

D. Lines 79–84 ("It has… as possible.")

45. It can be reasonably inferred from the passage that spiders must be viewed in their
natural habitats because

A. scientific study lacks validity when completed in a laboratory.

B. modifications are not fully understood
outside the context of their use.

C. the forms and colors of spiders resemble
human-made objects too closely.

D. several species of spiders bear strong
resemblances to one another.

46. Which choice provides the best evidence for
the answer to the previous question?

A. Lines 20–24 ("in every one… guess at.")

B. Lines 31–33 ("This rule… of cases.")

C. Lines 46–47 ("Its color is… with white.")

D. Lines 69–72 ("The entire… and uneven")

CONTINUE

47. The author uses the phrase "Bodies are... sand or stones" in lines 14–20 most likely to

   A. declare that the range of modifications common to spiders is extensive.

   B. justify the claim that when spiders are studied independently from their environmental relations adaptations remain unknown.

   C. explain that color modifications are less common than variations in bodily form.

   D. state that descriptive works have misrepresented the modified forms of spiders.

48. As used in line 27, "inconspicuous" most nearly means

   A. protected.

   B. visible.

   C. modest.

   D. imperceptible.

49. Based on the passage, spiders in the *Uloborus* genus

   A. struggle to acquire food because of poor web construction techniques.

   B. waits in the middle of its web in order to deceive passing predators and potential prey.

   C. demonstrate the rule that bright colored spiders try to hide themselves away or harmonize with similarly colored objects.

   D. simulate such a common natural occurrence as to avoid predation.

50. It can reasonably be inferred that *Epeira* are often nocturnal because

   A. protective modifications are effective when the spiders are stationary.

   B. their preferred prey appears in greater volume at night.

   C. rough protuberances increase camouflage in low light environments.

   D. changes in temperature make tree bark inhospitable after sunset.

51. The description of *C. mitralis* spiders in the last paragraph mainly serves to

   A. explain how some types of spiders are capable of more sophisticated adaptation than others.

   B. contrast with the behaviors and appearance of the Uloborus spiders.

   C. illustrate further the variety of effective modifications common to both the form and color of spiders.

   D. reinforce the idea that direct protection is unlimited within a species' specific environment.

52. As used in line 74, "stages" most nearly means

   A. phases.

   B. floors.

   C. parts.

   D. platforms.

STOP
If you finish before time is called, you may check your work on this section only.
Do not turn to any other section.

Diagnostic Test

Section 2: Writing and Language Test

35 Minutes—44 Questions

TURN TO SECTION 2 OF YOUR ANSWER SHEET TO ANSWER THE QUESTIONS IN THIS SECTION.

> **DIRECTIONS:** Each passage below is accompanied by a number of multiple-choice questions. For some questions, you will need to consider how the passage might be revised to improve the expression of ideas. Other questions will ask you to consider how the passage might be edited to correct errors in sentence structure, usage, or punctuation. A passage may be accompanied by one or more graphics—such as a chart, table, or graph—that you will need to refer to in order to best answer the question(s).
>
> Some questions will direct you to an underlined portion of a passage—it could be one word, a portion of a sentence, or the full sentence itself. Other questions will direct you to a particular paragraph or to certain sentences within a paragraph, or you'll be asked to think about the passage as a whole. Each question number refers to the corresponding number in the passage.
>
> After reading each passage, select the answer to each question that most effectively improves the quality of writing in the passage or that makes the passage follow the conventions of standard written English. Many questions include a "NO CHANGE" option. Select that option if you think the best choice is to leave that specific portion of the passage as it is.

Questions 1–11 are based on the following passage.

"DETROIT FUTURE CITY": OVERCOMING ECONOMIC DEPRESSION AND DEPOPULATION

A city of 139 square miles, with a long history of growth and middle-class success, Detroit now faces an unusual, though not entirely novel, situation for US cities: depopulation. **1** Economic transformations caused by recessions, the loss of manufacturing, and other factors have wreaked havoc on the once prosperous city, driving away its middle class and **2** it left behind vast tracts of urban blight.

1 Which choice provides the most logical introduction to the sentence?

A. NO CHANGE
B. Civic growth caused by the depression
C. The improvement in living conditions
D. The decrease in pollution

2

A. NO CHANGE
B. having left behind vast tracts of urban blight.
C. to leave behind vast tracts of urban blight.
D. leaving behind vast tracts of urban blight.

CONTINUE

The statistics **3** are staggering—since 1950, some 60 percent of the population has gone elsewhere, leaving the city with **4** 20,000 new residents. When the people left, thousands of businesses went with them.

City planners have been responding to the challenge of depopulation. Over several years, they have studied their urban spaces and used varying and innovative techniques to **5** confuse the input of some 30,000 of their residents. Planners have come up with what **6** she calls Detroit Future City, a vision that takes the long view and is projected to take some fifty years to implement. Within this plan are different strands of redevelopment, development, and—most dramatically—un-development. **7** Similarly, the strategic plan includes a concept not often seen in US city planning: downsizing, or what some prefer to call "right sizing."

3

A. NO CHANGE

B. are staggering since: 1950 some

C. are staggering since 1950 some

D. are staggering, since 1950 some

4 Which choice provides information that best supports the claim made by this sentence?

A. NO CHANGE

B. 100,000 vacant residences or lots

C. 50,000 more middle-class residents

D. 30,000 homeless people

5

A. NO CHANGE

B. belittle

C. solicit

D. return

6

A. NO CHANGE

B. they call

C. he calls

D. we call

7

A. NO CHANGE

B. In fact,

C. Nevertheless,

D. Besides,

Diagnostic Test

Diagnostic Test

[1] One of the boldest suggestions of the plan is a basic conversion of about one third of all Detroit's urban space. [2] Making the city more compact, the planners **8** <u>reasoned</u>, would save money on services and allow them to devote more resources to a smaller total area. [3] Walking paths, parks, ponds for rainwater collection and retention (the city's sewage system is overburdened), sports fields, meadows, forested areas, campgrounds, and other green space initiatives would then gradually transform the shutdown area.

9 [4] The plan contained some creative and bold suggestions. [5] Controversially, the plan suggests shutting down services in certain areas to drive current residents out of them and into neighborhoods being targeted for strengthening. [6] The plan also calls for remaining neighborhoods to be **10** <u>transformed. But not by the</u> traditional models of economic growth. [7] For example, the city, if organized carefully with viable public transportation options, hopes to create jobs right where people live. In part, the plan is predicated on the idea that within their own various redevelopment areas, or "natural economic zones," people can both live and work in fields that every city **11** <u>has, namely, healthcare, education, government, transportation, and local businesses</u> that meet core needs, such as grocery stores and eating places. The plan is also predicated on the idea that the well-planned urban space generates its own economic success, as well as on the idea that such areas will eventually draw some outside business and industry. Debt-ridden Detroit is definitely going to need the latter. A recent NPR report on Detroit posited that commercial real estate taxes can make up a substantial 70 percent of the revenue for a city.

8
A. NO CHANGE
B. insisted
C. noted
D. commented

9 To improve the flow of this paragraph, sentence 4 should be placed

A. where it is now.
B. before sentence 1.
C. after sentence 5.
D. after sentence 6.

10
A. NO CHANGE
B. transformed—but not by the
C. transformed; but not by the
D. transformed, but not by—the

11
A. NO CHANGE
B. has; namely, healthcare and education; government and transportation, local businesses
C. has, namely, healthcare; education; government; transportation; and local businesses
D. has: healthcare, education, government, transportation, and local businesses

CONTINUE ▶

Questions 12–22 are based on the following passage.

LIGHT AND SHADOW:
THE ART OF WAYANG KULIT

In a public square on the Indonesian island of Java, dusk falls. Families gather; it is a festival day. Children dart around while, on the edges of the square, vendors **12** <u>hawk</u> snacks and toys. A large screen, lit from behind, stands prominently in the square. A twenty-piece percussion orchestra, or *gamelan*, prepares to play. **13** <u>The scene is traditional Java, hundreds of years ago.</u> The performance is *wayang kulit*, or shadow puppetry, one of the world's oldest storytelling **14** <u>traditions its origins stretch</u> back to the ancient spiritual practices of Indonesia's original inhabitants, who believed that the spirits of the ancestors governed the living world. Ceremonial puppet plays addressed the spirits, asking them to help the living.

Over two thousand years ago, islands such as Java, Bali, and Sumatra saw their first **15** <u>Indian migrants, a nation to which Indonesia</u> was linked through trade relations. In the centuries that followed, Indian culture influenced every aspect of Indonesian life.

12

A. NO CHANGE

B. stock

C. advertise

D. trade

13 At this point, the author is considering deleting the underlined sentence. Should the writer do this?

A. Yes, because it inserts an irrelevant opinion.

B. Yes, because it distracts from the main ideas of the paragraph.

C. No, because it provides a transition from the previous paragraph to this one.

D. No, because it explains what *wayang kulit* is.

14

A. NO CHANGE

B. traditions and its origins stretch

C. traditions, its origins stretch

D. traditions. Its origins stretch

15

A. NO CHANGE

B. migrants from India, a nation to which Indonesia

C. Indian migrants, to which a nation Indonesia

D. Indian migrants, a nation of people to which Indonesia

CONTINUE

The puppet plays reflected these cultural changes. **16** They began to depict narratives from Hindu religious texts, including the *Mahabharata*, the *Ramayana*, and the *Serat Menak*. Traditional Indonesian stories were blended into Hindu epics or lost altogether. Later, when Islam began to spread throughout Indonesia, puppet plays again transformed.

The Islamic religion **17** prohibited the display of gods in human form, so Indonesians adapted their art by making flat, leather puppets that cast shadows on a screen. The puppets **18** themselves remain unseen during the performances; only their shadows were visible. *Wayang kulit* was born.

16 At this point, the writer is considering adding the following sentence:

A master of shadow puppetry is called a *dalang*.

Should the writer make this addition here?

A. Yes, because it provides relevant and new information about the practice of *wayang kulit*.

B. Yes, because it adds an important fact to the paragraph's focus on shadow puppetry.

C. No, because it repeats information that has already been given.

D. No, because it distracts from the paragraph's focus on cultural changes.

17

A. NO CHANGE

B. discouraged

C. hindered

D. restricted

18

A. NO CHANGE

B. themselves will remain unseen during the performances

C. themselves remained unseen during the performances

D. themselves had been remaining unseen during the performances

CONTINUE ▶

Java is particularly well-known for its continuation of the shadow puppet tradition. **(19)** _Performances are epic events, lasting all night long from sunset to sunrise with no break at all._ They take place in public spaces and are performed on holidays and at family celebrations. At the center is a large screen, backlit by a gas or electrical light. Behind this screen sits the _dalang_, or shadow master, traditionally a man. He manipulates the puppets—sometimes more than a hundred of them in one show—with rods, voicing and singing all of the roles. **(20)** _Simultaneously he directs the gamelan the large percussive orchestra which consists of percussive instruments some of which are mallets._

Each puppet is carefully crafted, a flat figure that is perforated to project a detailed shadow. Artists begin creating a puppet by tracing the outline of a paper model on leather. The leather figure is painstakingly smoothed and treated before being passed onto another craftsperson, who paints it. Then, the puppet's moving parts—the arms and hands—are added, along with the sticks used **(21)** _to manipulate their parts._ These puppets follow an established set of conventions: evil characters have grotesque faces, while noble ones have more refined features. They are highly stylized caricatures, rather **(22)** _then_ realistic figures.

(19)

A. NO CHANGE

B. Performances are epic events, lasting from sunset to sunrise with no break.

C. Performances are huge, epic events, lasting all night long from sunset to sunrise without taking a break.

D. Performances are epic events, lasting all night.

(20)

A. NO CHANGE

B. Simultaneously he directs, the _gamelan_ the large, percussive orchestra which consists of percussive, instruments some of which are mallets.

C. Simultaneously, he directs the _gamelan_— the large percussive orchestra, which consists of percussive instruments, some of which are mallets.

D. Simultaneously, he directs, the _gamelan_, the large, percussive orchestra, which consists, of percussive instruments, some of which, are mallets.

(21)

A. NO CHANGE

B. to manipulate his parts

C. to manipulate its parts

D. to manipulate her parts

(22)

A. NO CHANGE

B. that

C. than

D. this

CONTINUE ➤

Questions 23–33 are based on the following passage and supplementary material.

THE AMERICAN SOUTHWEST: SURGING POPULATIONS AND SHRINKING WATER SUPPLY

23 The arid climate and limited water resources of the American Southwest **24** has always influenced the peoples of the region. The Anasazi, ancient people of some of the most inhospitable areas of the Southwest, made a series of accommodations to **25** they're hot, arid environment by means of adaptive agricultural practices, cliff-side residences, and elaborate catchment systems.

Today, the American Southwest, simplistically defined in this document as encompassing all of Utah, Nevada, New Mexico, Arizona, and California, is the country's fastest-growing **26** region. It is home to more than 50 million people who are the source of ever-increasing water demands. Yet, the region is dependent for its water on just two river systems, the Colorado and the Rio Grande, of which the former is unequivocally the primary.

23 Which of the following sentences would make the most effective introductory sentence to this passage?

A. Consider a vacation to the American Southwest!

B. What do you know about the majestic American Southwest?

C. The Anasazi are the original people who inhabited the American Southwest.

D. There's a serious problem occurring in the American Southwest.

24

A. NO CHANGE

B. had always influence

C. have always influenced

D. is always influenced

25

A. NO CHANGE

B. their hot, arid environment

C. there hot, arid environment

D. its hot, arid environment

26 Which choice most effectively combines the sentences at the underlined portion?

A. region, but it is home

B. region; home

C. region it is home

D. region, home

CONTINUE ➡

The Colorado supplies water to some 38 million users and irrigates some 300 million acres of farmland, much of it in **27** California, however, the mighty Colorado's flow was apportioned almost one hundred years ago to include not just the southwestern United States but also Mexico. It was also apportioned according to a volume that simply does not exist in current years; for example, in the years 2001–2006, river water that had been **28** projected to flow versus river water that did flow came up a staggering 34 percent short.

In 2014, the US Department of the Interior warned that the Colorado River basin area "is in the midst of a fourteen-year drought nearly unrivaled in 1,250 years." **29** It further noted that the river's two major reservoirs, Lake Powell and Lake Mead—the once-massive backup systems for years in which drought occurs—were, alarmingly, more than 50 percent depleted. **30** Equally dire, and possibly, more alarming, predictions came out of a recent study, cited in the Proceedings of the National Academy of Science of the United States, that suggested a 50 percent chance of Lakes Powell and Mead reaching a level so low that they become inoperable by the 2020s. **31** For all intensive purposes, the Southwest's water supply is drying up.

27

A. NO CHANGE

B. California: however,

C. California; however,

D. California however,

28

A. NO CHANGE

B. hoped

C. desired

D. thought

29 At this point, the writer is considering deleting this sentence. Should the writer do this?

A. Yes, because it repeats information that has already been presented in the passage.

B. Yes, because it blurs the paragraph's focus by introducing a new idea.

C. No, because it illustrates the severity of drought conditions with a specific example.

D. No, because it introduces the argument that the Southwest's water supply is drying up.

30

A. NO CHANGE

B. Equally dire, and possibly more alarming,

C. Equally dire and possibly more alarming

D. Equally dire and, possibly more alarming,

31

A. NO CHANGE

B. For all intentional purposes,

C. For all intents and purposes,

D. For all intended purposes,

Diagnostic Test

CONTINUE ➡

32 Compounding the problems of drought, increasing population, and an overly optimistic historical assessment of water resources are problems related to climate change. For example, between 2000 and 2014, the **33** highest air temperatures in much of the Southwest rose as much as 2 degrees, increasing the negative effects of evapotranspiration, the evaporation of water from the soil. Finally, climate change and drought are leading to the greater prevalence and intensity of fires, including so-called "super fires," a result, in part, of the beetle infestations and dying trees that are weakened by the lack of water.

32

A. NO CHANGE

B. Escalating

C. Inflating

D. Exaggerating

33 Which choice makes appropriate and effective use of the data in the accompanying map?

A. NO CHANGE

B. lowest air temperatures

C. hottest water temperature

D. average air temperatures

Average Temperatures in the Southwestern United States 2000–2014 Versus Long-Term Average

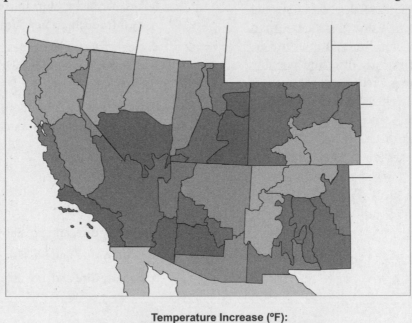

Temperature Increase (°F):

This map shows how the average air temperature from 2000 to 2014 has differed from the long-term average (1895–2014). To provide more detailed information, each state has been divided into climate divisions, which are zones that share similar climate features.

Part II

CONTINUE ➤

Questions 34–44 are based on the following passage.

WOMEN IN FILM: TROUBLING INEQUALITIES

34 In a society in which television and movies have been well documented as **35** roles of social change, current data about women in the movies are far from reassuring. **36** Women simply can't expect to play the leading roles men play or even, in general, to be on-screen for as many minutes as men are in any given film, while there seems to be no end of extraordinary acting talent among women in Hollywood. As for other categories of filmmaking, at least by Oscar standards, women seem barely to exist at all.

34 Which choice most effectively establishes the main topic of the paragraph?

A. There are many actresses in Hollywood with extraordinary talent, but they cannot seem to get the same roles as men.

B. Though women land far fewer leading roles than men, in other categories of filmmaking, they do a little better.

C. Women are not adequately represented in Hollywood, either by the roles they play or by the amount of time they appear on-screen.

D. The movie industry needs to pay female actresses more than their male counterparts, in an effort to attract new and extraordinary talent.

35

A. NO CHANGE

B. agents

C. necessities

D. relationships

36

A. NO CHANGE

B. Women simply can't expect to play the leading roles men play or even, in general, while there seems to be no end of extraordinary acting talent among women in Hollywood, to be on-screen for as many minutes as men are in any given film.

C. Women simply can't expect to play the leading roles men play or to be on-screen for as many minutes as men, and there seems to be no end of extraordinary acting talent among women in Hollywood in general.

D. While there seems to be no end of extraordinary acting talent among women in Hollywood, women simply can't expect to play the leading roles men play or even, in general, to be on-screen for as many minutes as men are in any given film.

CONTINUE

Diagnostic Test

Indeed, **37** <u>women were the protagonists</u> in only 15 percent of the top grossing films of 2013, according to a study conducted at San Diego State University. Other study findings included the fact that when women are on-screen, **38** <u>their marriage status is more identifiable than men.</u> Also, males over age 40 are much more commonly represented on-screen than women in the same age group.

Other inequities have been revealed by Cinemetrics, which strives to gather objective data on movies, and by other organizations. **39** <u>For example, in 2013, lead actresses in full-length films spent 57 minutes on-screen, while lead actors spent 85 minutes on-screen.</u> Compounding the inequity is the tendency of the camera to stay on a female actress longer in a single shot, or stare at **40** <u>them</u> passively, while the camera moves more actively when it shows a male character. In other aspects of films, women **41** <u>are treated even more outrageously.</u> Since the Oscars began in 1928, only 16 percent of all nominees have been women. In fact, there were no women nominees at all in seven categories of achievement for the 2014 Oscars. More significantly, Oscar trends do not seem to be improving over time.

37

A. NO CHANGE

B. women were the protagonist

C. a woman was the protagonists

D. the protagonists were a woman

38

A. NO CHANGE

B. their marriage status is more identifiable than a man.

C. their marriage status is more identifiable than that of men.

D. the status of their marriage is more identifiable than that of men's.

39 Which choice most effectively maintains support for claims or points in the text?

A. NO CHANGE

B. For example, women direct more documentaries than narrative films.

C. For example, the highest paid actress in 2013 made $33 million dollars.

D. For example, women buy about half of movie tickets purchased in the United States.

40

A. NO CHANGE

B. him

C. her

D. us

41

A. NO CHANGE

B. are taken advantage of.

C. are cheated.

D. fare even worse.

Part II

CONTINUE ➤

Some women, however, have managed to shine despite these inequities. Actress Meryl Streep has been nominated for 19 Oscars as of 2015, easily surpassing both male and female competitors for the record of most Academy Award nominations. She is confused for her strong, authoritative roles; she portrayed a powerful—if terrifying—boss in *The Devil Wears Prada* (2006) and a formidable leader in *The Giver* (2014). Streep has received accolades for such parts, as 15 of her 19 Academy Award nominations were in the category of Best Actress in a Leading Role. Even Streep, however, is subject to the inequities of the film industry: in *The Devil Wears Prada* her 44 characters love life was brought to the forefront and depicted as a sacrifice that she, as a woman in power, had to continually make for the good of her career.

42

A. NO CHANGE

B. famous

C. forgotten

D. lambasted

43

A. NO CHANGE

B. privileges

C. recognition

D. attention

44

A. NO CHANGE

B. character love life

C. character's love life

D. character loves life

STOP
If you finish before time is called, you may check your work on this section only.
Do not turn to any other section.

Chapter 2

Diagnostic Test

SECTION 3: Math Test—NO CALCULATOR

25 Minutes—20 Questions

TURN TO SECTION 3 OF YOUR ANSWER SHEET TO ANSWER THE QUESTIONS IN THIS SECTION.

DIRECTIONS: For **Questions 1–15**, solve each problem, select the best answer from the choices provided, and fill in the corresponding circle on your answer sheet. For **Questions 16–20**, solve the problem and enter your answer in the grid on the answer sheet. The directions **before Question 16** will provide information on how to enter your answers in the grid.

ADDITIONAL INFORMATION:

1. The use of a calculator in this section is **not permitted**.

2. All variables and expressions used represent real numbers unless otherwise indicated.

3. Figures provided in this test are drawn to scale unless otherwise indicated.

4. All figures lie in a plane unless otherwise indicated.

5. Unless otherwise specified, the domain of a given function f is the set of all real numbers x for which $f(x)$ is a real number.

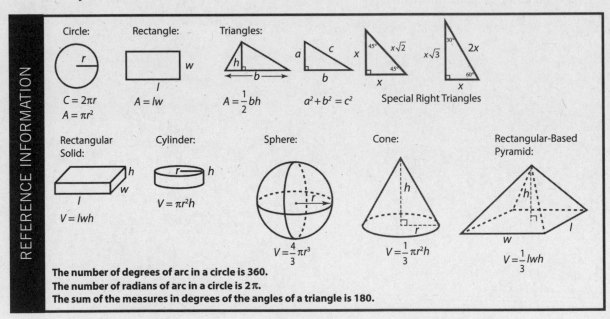

REFERENCE INFORMATION

Circle:
$C = 2\pi r$
$A = \pi r^2$

Rectangle:
$A = lw$

Triangles:
$A = \frac{1}{2}bh$
$a^2 + b^2 = c^2$
Special Right Triangles

Rectangular Solid:
$V = lwh$

Cylinder:
$V = \pi r^2 h$

Sphere:
$V = \frac{4}{3}\pi r^3$

Cone:
$V = \frac{1}{3}\pi r^2 h$

Rectangular-Based Pyramid:
$V = \frac{1}{3}lwh$

The number of degrees of arc in a circle is 360.
The number of radians of arc in a circle is 2π.
The sum of the measures in degrees of the angles of a triangle is 180.

CONTINUE ➤

1.

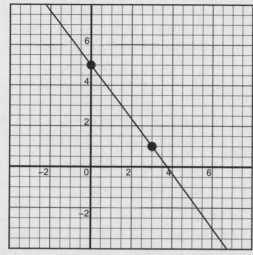

If the line drawn above is translated 3 units to the left and 6 units down, what is the slope of the new line?

A. $-\dfrac{1}{9}$

B. $-\dfrac{4}{3}$

C. $-\dfrac{7}{10}$

D. -2

2. Catherine is performing a science experiment on the distance traveled by a snail. She sets the snail on her driveway and records the time it takes the snail to crawl to the end of her driveway. She uses the equation $D = 0.4t + 12$, where D is the total distance traveled in feet, and t represents the time in minutes. Which of the following statements best interprets the meaning of 12 in Catherine's equation?

A. It would take the snail 12 minutes to reach the end of the driveway.

B. The snail began 12 feet from the beginning of the driveway.

C. The snail traveled a total distance of 12 feet.

D. The snail traveled at a rate of 12 feet per minute.

3. If $-2x + 5 = 2 - (5 - 2x)$, what is the value of x?

A. -2

B. 2

C. 3

D. 5

CONTINUE

NO CALCULATOR

4. When the expression $\dfrac{10i}{1-2i}$ is simplified to the form $a + bi$, what is the coefficient b?

 A. -5

 B. $-\dfrac{10}{3}$

 C. 2

 D. 5

5. Write $5\sqrt{-16}$ as a complex number, using $i = \sqrt{-1}$.

 A. $5 + 4i$

 B. $-20i$

 C. $20i$

 D. $80i$

6. A grain silo has a maximum capacity of 45,000 cubic feet. It currently contains 32,500 cubic feet of grain. Each week, farmers add 1,000 bushels of grain. If one cubic foot is approximately 0.8 bushel, which of the following inequalities can be used to model the number of weeks, w, until the silo reaches its maximum capacity?

 A. $32{,}500 + 1{,}250w \le 45{,}000$

 B. $32{,}500 + 800w \le 45{,}000$

 C. $32{,}500 + 1{,}250w \ge 45{,}000$

 D. $32{,}500 + 800w \ge 45{,}000$

7. The graph of $y = (3x - 4)(x + 3)$ is a parabola in the xy-plane. In which of the following equivalent equations do the x- and y-coordinates of the vertex show as constants or coefficients?

 A. $y = 3x^2 + 5x - 12$

 B. $y = 3\left(x - \dfrac{4}{3}\right)(x - (-3))$

 C. $y = 3\left(x^2 + \dfrac{5}{3}x - 4\right)$

 D. $y = 3\left(x - \left(-\dfrac{5}{6}\right)\right)^2 - \dfrac{169}{12}$

CONTINUE

Part II

8. What is the difference when $-x - y$ is subtracted from $-x^2 + 2y$?

   A. $-x^2 - x - 3y$

   B. $x^2 + 3y$

   C. $-x^2 + x + 3y$

   D. $-x^2 + x - 3y$

10. $A = \dfrac{M}{M - N}$

    Solve for M.

    A. $M = \dfrac{AN}{A - 1}$

    B. $M = \dfrac{AN}{1 - A}$

    C. $M = \dfrac{N}{A - 1}$

    D. $M = \dfrac{N}{1 - A}$

9. A semitruck has a fuel tank that holds 125 gallons of diesel fuel. When driven at 55 miles per hour, the truck can travel 6 miles on 1 gallon of fuel. If Jorge fills the tank in his truck and drives at 55 miles per hour, which of the following functions of d shows the number of gallons of diesel fuel that remains after driving h hours?

   A. $d(h) = 125 - \dfrac{6}{55h}$

   B. $d(h) = 125 - \dfrac{55h}{6}$

   C. $d(h) = \dfrac{125 - 6h}{55}$

   D. $d(h) = \dfrac{125 - 55h}{6}$

11. Donna bought a sofa with 0% interest for the first 36 months. She makes a small down payment, and then she makes equal monthly payments until she pays off the sofa. The equation $y = 90x + 75$ models the number of payments, x, that she makes to pay for a sofa that costs y dollars. What does the 90 represent in this equation?

    A. The total paid after x months.

    B. The pay-off amounts for the loan.

    C. Donna's monthly payment.

    D. Donna's down payment.

Diagnostic Test

NO CALCULATOR

12. What is the sum of all values of n that satisfy $2n^2 - 11n + 15 = 0$?

A. -11

B. -5.5

C. 5.5

D. 15

13. The Matthews family is driving to the beach, which is 480 miles away. The function that represents the distance (in miles) it takes them to get to the beach is $f(t) = 480 - 60t$, where t represents time (in hours). In this equation, t is the independent variable, and $f(t)$ is the dependent variable. At which point does the graph of the function $f(t) = 480 - 60t$ cross the x-axis?

A. $(0, 480)$

B. $(6, 0)$

C. $(0, 8)$

D. $(8, 0)$

14. The population of a small town is growing. The town currently has 500 people. Based on the growth of the population in past years, it is estimated that the population will be 650 after 1 year. Similarly, it is estimated that after 2 years, the population will be 845, and after 3 years, the population will be 1,099. Which of the following is an expression which represents the town's population growth?

A. 500×1.3^x

B. $150x + 500$

C. $500 \times (1.3)^{x-1}$

D. $650 \times (1.3)^{x-1t}$

15. The expression $\dfrac{4x+1}{x+2}$ is equivalent to which of the following?

A. $\dfrac{4+1}{2}$

B. $4 + \dfrac{1}{2}$

C. $4 + \dfrac{1}{x+2}$

D. $4 - \dfrac{7}{x+2}$

CONTINUE

NO CALCULATOR

DIRECTIONS: For **Questions 16–20**, solve the problem and enter your answer in the grid, as described below, on the answer sheet.

---

1. Although not required, it is suggested that you write your answer in the boxes at the top of the columns to help you fill in the circles accurately. You will receive credit only if the circles are filled in correctly.

2. Mark no more than one circle in any column.

3. No question has a negative answer.

4. Some problems may have more than one correct answer. In such cases, enter only one answer.

5. **Mixed numbers** such as $3\frac{1}{2}$ must be entered as 3.5 or $\frac{7}{2}$.

   If $3\frac{1}{2}$ is entered into the grid as $\boxed{3\ |\ 1\ /\ 2}$, it will be interpreted as 3.5 not $\frac{7}{2}$.

6. **Decimal answers:** If you obtain a decimal answer with more digits than the grid can accommodate, it may be either rounded or truncated, but it must fill the entire grid.

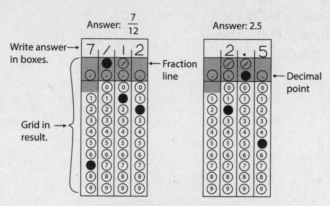

Answer: $\frac{7}{12}$ Answer: 2.5

Answer: 201
Either position is correct.

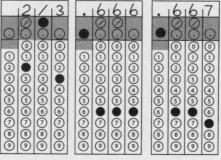

Acceptable ways to grid $\frac{2}{3}$ are:

NO CALCULATOR

16.

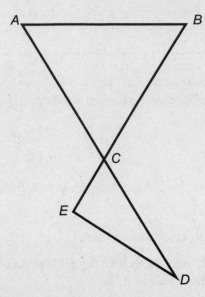

In the figure above, $AC = BC$. If $m\angle B = 50°$, what is the measure of $\angle ECD$? (Do not enter the degree symbol.)

17.
$$5x - 4y = 13$$
$$x + 2y = 4$$

If (x, y) is a solution of the system of equations above, what is the value of the ratio $\frac{x}{y}$?

CONTINUE

Diagnostic Test

NO CALCULATOR 🖩

18.

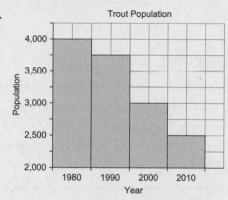

Trout Population

The bar graph above shows the population of trout in a lake from 1980 to 2010.

By what percentage did the population decline from 1980 to 2000? Round to the nearest percentage point if necessary, and enter your answer as a two-digit number. (Do not grid the percent sign.)

19. If $f(x) = 5x + 12$, what is the value of $f(p + 3) - f(p)$?

20. What is the sum of the solutions of the equation $\dfrac{9}{x-2} + \dfrac{16}{x+3} = 5$?

STOP
If you finish before time is called, you may check your work on this section only.
Do not turn to any other section.

SECTION 4: Math Test—CALCULATOR 🖩

55 Minutes—38 Questions

TURN TO SECTION 4 OF YOUR ANSWER SHEET TO ANSWER THE QUESTIONS IN THIS SECTION.

DIRECTIONS: For **Questions 1–30**, solve each problem, select the best answer from the choices provided, and fill in the corresponding circle on your answer sheet. For **Questions 31–38**, solve the problem and enter your answer in the grid on the answer sheet. The directions **before Question 31** will provide information on how to enter your answers in the grid.

ADDITIONAL INFORMATION:

1. The use of a calculator in this section **is permitted**.

2. All variables and expressions used represent real numbers unless otherwise indicated.

3. Figures provided in this test are drawn to scale unless otherwise indicated.

4. All figures lie in a plane unless otherwise indicated.

5. Unless otherwise specified, the domain of a given function f is the set of all real numbers x for which $f(x)$ is a real number.

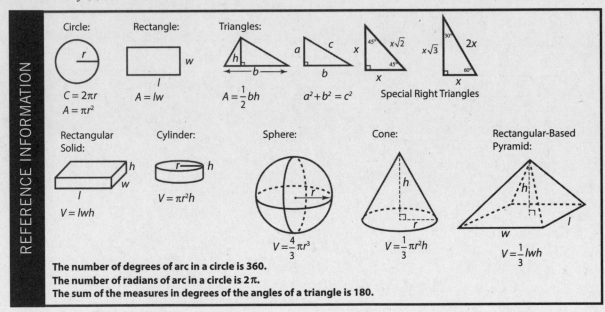

REFERENCE INFORMATION

Circle:
$C = 2\pi r$
$A = \pi r^2$

Rectangle:
$A = lw$

Triangles:
$A = \dfrac{1}{2}bh$
$a^2 + b^2 = c^2$

Special Right Triangles

Rectangular Solid:
$V = lwh$

Cylinder:
$V = \pi r^2 h$

Sphere:
$V = \dfrac{4}{3}\pi r^3$

Cone:
$V = \dfrac{1}{3}\pi r^2 h$

Rectangular-Based Pyramid:
$V = \dfrac{1}{3}lwh$

The number of degrees of arc in a circle is 360.
The number of radians of arc in a circle is 2π.
The sum of the measures in degrees of the angles of a triangle is 180.

CONTINUE ▶

1. The usual price for 10 audio singles sold by an online vendor is $12.50. During a sale, this price is reduced by 15%. What is the savings if one were to purchase 40 audio singles during such a sale?

   A. $1.88
   B. $2.50
   C. $7.50
   D. $10.00

2. If it costs $1.30 a square foot to lay linoleum, what will be the cost of laying 20 square yards of linoleum?
   (3 ft. = 1 yd.)

   A. $26
   B. $78
   C. $156
   D. $234

3. Bill averaged a score of 182 for 6 games of bowling. His scores for the first three games were 212, 181, and 160. Of the remaining three games, two scores were identical, and the third was 20 points higher than one of these two games. What was the second highest score of these 6 games?

   A. 173
   B. 181
   C. 183
   D. 193

4. A gallon of water is equal to 231 cubic inches. How many gallons of water are needed to fill a fish tank that measures 11" high, 14" long, and 9" wide?

   A. 6
   B. 9
   C. 12
   D. 14

CONTINUE ➤

📱 CALCULATOR

5. The recommended daily protein intake for an adult weighing 50 kg (approximately 110 pounds) is 40 grams. One cup of milk contains 8 grams of protein, and one egg contains 6 grams of protein. Which of the following inequalities represents the possible number of cups of milk, m, and eggs, n, an adult weighing 50 kg could consume in a day to meet or exceed the recommended daily protein intake from these alone?

   A. $8m + 6n \geq 40$

   B. $8m + 6n > 40$

   C. $\dfrac{8}{m} + \dfrac{6}{n} \geq 40$

   D. $\dfrac{8}{m} + \dfrac{6}{n} > 40$

6. Amy is renting a moving van for $19.99 per day, plus an additional $0.15 per mile. A tax of 7.5% is applied to both the daily rate and the mileage rate. Which of the following represents the total charge, y, that Amy will pay to rent the van for one day and drive it x miles?

   A. $y = 19.99 + 0.075x + 0.15$

   B. $y = 1.075(19.99) + 0.15x$

   C. $y = 1.075(19.99 + 0.15x)$

   D. $y = 1.075(19.99 + 0.15)x$

7. If nails are bought at 35 cents per dozen and sold at 3 for 10 cents, the total profit on $5\frac{1}{2}$ dozen is

   A. 25 cents.

   B. $27\frac{1}{2}$ cents.

   C. $31\frac{1}{2}$ cents.

   D. 35 cents.

8. A cubic foot of concrete weighs approximately 150 pounds. How many pounds will a similar block of concrete weigh if the edges are twice as long?

   A. 300 pounds

   B. 450 pounds

   C. 800 pounds

   D. 1,200 pounds

CONTINUE

9. Which of the following expressions is equivalent to $-2(1 - x)^2 + 2(1 - x^2)$?

   A. $-2x$

   B. $-4x^2 + 4x$

   C. $-4x^2 - 4x - 4$

   D. 0

10. An organization is giving away T-shirts for its 5-kilometer road race. The cost to produce the T-shirts is defined by the equation $C(x) = 7x + 60$, where x is the number of T-shirts produced. The organization gives away the T-shirts for free to people who sign up for the race more than one month in advance and pay the $20 sign-up fee. What is the fewest number of people who must sign up in order for the organization to profit if the only cost is manufacturing the T-shirts and the only income is the sign-up fee?

    A. 3

    B. 5

    C. 13

    D. 20

11. A small college, which has a population of 2,180 students, recently held a fundraiser in which each male student raised $20, and each female student raised $25. Together, they raised a total of $50,000. If x represents the number of male students in the college and y represents the number of female students in the college, which system of equations can be used to represent the scenario?

    A. $x + y = 50,000$
       $20x + 25y = 2,180$

    B. $x + y = 2,180$
       $20x + 25y = 50,000$

    C. $x + y = 2,180$
       $25x + 20y = 50,000$

    D. $x + y = 50,000$
       $25x + 20y = 50,000$

12. Which of the following is an expression equivalent to $\sqrt[3]{9x^3y^5z^6}$?

    A. $3y^2z^3$

    B. $3xy^2z^3$

    C. $9^{\frac{1}{3}}xy^2z^3$

    D. $9^{\frac{1}{3}}xy^{\frac{5}{3}}z^2$

CONTINUE ➤

Diagnostic Test

CALCULATOR

13.

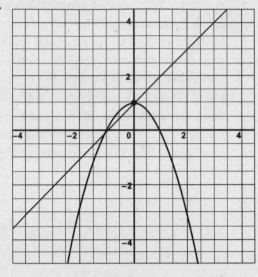

$$y = x + 1$$
$$y = -x^2 + 1$$

A system of equations and their graphs are shown above. Which of the following are solutions to the system?

I.   (0, 1)

II. (1, 0)

III. (−1, 0)

IV. (0, −1)

A. I only

B. II only

C. I and III only

D. II and IV only

14. If $\frac{x}{3} - \frac{y}{4} = 5$, what is the value of $8x - 6y$?

A. −120

B. −60

C. 60

D. 120

15. At a restaurant, the rates for meals are $7.50 for a lunch and $12 for a dinner. One weekend, the restaurant sold a total of 241 meals for $2,523. Which of the following systems of equations can be used to determine the number of lunches, x, and the number of dinners, y, that the restaurant sold?

A. $7.5x + 12y = 241$
    $x + y = 2,523$

B. $12x + 7.5y = 241$
    $x + y = 2,523$

C. $7.5x + 12y = 2,523$
    $x + y = 241$

D. $12x + 7.5y = 2,523$
    $x + y = 241$

CONTINUE

16.

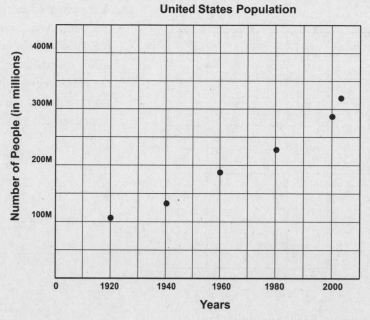

The graph above shows the relationship between the population of the United States (in millions) and the year the population was recorded. Which of the following statements is true about the data shown on the graph?

A. There is a weak correlation between the variables.

B. There is a strong correlation between the variables.

C. There is no clear correlation between the variables.

D. There is an exponential correlation between the variables.

Diagnostic Test

CONTINUE ▶

📱 **CALCULATOR**

17.

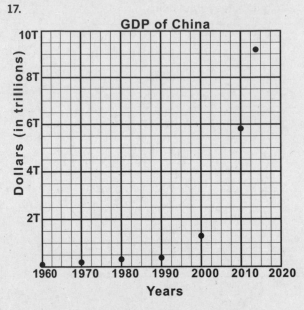

GDP of China

The graph shows data representing the gross domestic product (GDP), in trillions of dollars, of China from 1970 through 2013. Which of the following function types would best represent the data?

A. Linear

B. Logarithmic

C. Cubic

D. Exponential

18. A college graduate goes to work for x dollars per week. After several months, the company gives all the employees a 10% pay cut. A few months later, the company gives all the employees a 10% raise. Which expression is equal to the college graduate's weekly salary resulting from these changes?

A. $0.90x$

B. $.99x$

C. x

D. $1.01x$

19. Which of the following systems of inequalities has a solution set that intersects the first quadrant of the xy-plane?

A. $\begin{cases} y \leq -2x + 4 \\ y > -2x + 2 \end{cases}$

B. $\begin{cases} x \leq -2 \\ y \geq 5 \end{cases}$

C. $\begin{cases} y \geq x \\ y < -3 - x \end{cases}$

D. $\begin{cases} y > 5 + 3x \\ y \leq -3 + 3x \end{cases}$

CONTINUE ▶

20. If $\dfrac{(1-2i)^2}{2}$ is rewritten as $a + bi$, then what is the value of b? (Note: $i = \sqrt{-1}$)

   A. -2

   B. $\dfrac{-3}{2}$

   C. $\dfrac{1}{2}$

   D. 2

21. What is the original price of an item if it costs $12.60 after a 10% discount is applied to the selling price?

   A. $11.34

   B. $12.48

   C. $13.86

   D. $14

22. A recipe for a homemade weed killer calls for gallons of white vinegar and 2 cups of table salt. Miguel made a large batch of the weed killer and used 7 cups of table salt. If he followed the recipe correctly, how many gallons of white vinegar did he use?

   A. 4

   B. $4\dfrac{2}{3}$

   C. $5\dfrac{1}{3}$

   D. 6

23. Given $(1.26 + 4.52i) + (-0.89 + xi) = 0.37 + 7.4i$, what is the value of x? (Note: $i = \sqrt{-1}$)

   A. -1.64

   B. 1.64

   C. 2.88

   D. 11.92

▦ CALCULATOR

24. If $(x - 4)$ and $(x + 2)$ are factors of $f(x)$, which of the following graphs could represent the function $f(x)$?

A.

C.

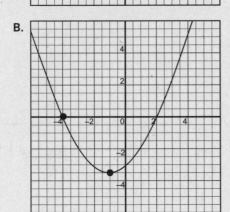

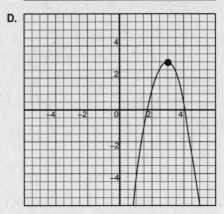

B.

D.

Part II

CONTINUE ➤

CALCULATOR 🖩

25.

	None	1 to 3	4 or more
Group A	8	23	19
Group B	14	21	5
Total	22	44	24

The table above shows data from demographic researchers studying the number of living siblings people have. If a person is chosen at random from Group A, what is the probability that the person has no living siblings?

A. $\dfrac{4}{25}$

B. $\dfrac{4}{11}$

C. $\dfrac{7}{11}$

D. $\dfrac{22}{25}$

26. During the *Apollo* 14 mission, astronaut Alan Shepard hit a golf ball on the moon. The height of the ball in meters is modeled by the function $f(t) = -0.81t^2 + 55t + 0.02$, where t is the time in seconds after the ball was hit. What does 0.02 stand for in this equation?

A. Acceleration of the ball due to gravity

B. Vertical velocity of the ball

C. Horizontal velocity of the ball

D. Height of the ball before it is hit

Diagnostic Test

CONTINUE ▶

CALCULATOR

27. If *k* is a positive constant other than 1, which of the following could be the graph of
$kx + y = c$?

A.
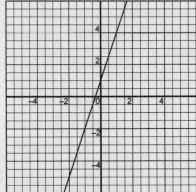

B.
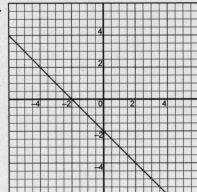

C.
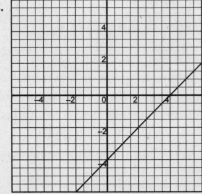

D.
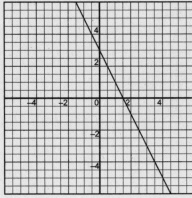

CONTINUE

28. The Cyber Corporation buys a new machine for $80,000. If the machine loses 15% of its value each year, what is its value after 4 years?

A. $41,760.50

B. $42,750.50

C. $48,000.00

D. $49,130.00

30. If the expression $\dfrac{6x}{2x+4}$ is written in the form $3+\dfrac{A}{x+2}$, what is the value of A?

A. −12

B. −6

C. 6

D. 12

29. The table below shows the total number of medals won by the United States in the Winter Olympics for the years 1994 to 2014.

Number of Medals	Year
12	1994
13	1998
31	2002
25	2006
37	2010
28	2014

How many medals would the United States have had to win in the 2018 Olympics in order for the average number of medals for the years 1994 to 2018 to be one more than the average number of medals won during the years 1994 to 2014?

A. 29

B. 31

C. 32

D. 36

📱 **CALCULATOR**

DIRECTIONS: For **Questions 31–38**, solve the problem and enter your answer in the grid, as described below, on the answer sheet.

---

1. Although not required, it is suggested that you write your answer in the boxes at the top of the columns to help you fill in the circles accurately. You will receive credit only if the circles are filled in correctly.

2. Mark no more than one circle in any column.

3. No question has a negative answer.

4. Some problems may have more than one correct answer. In such cases, enter only one answer.

5. **Mixed numbers** such as $3\frac{1}{2}$ must be entered as 3.5 or $\frac{7}{2}$.

   If $3\frac{1}{2}$ is entered into the grid as ⊡⊡⊡⊡, it will be interpreted as 3.5 not $\frac{7}{2}$.

6. **Decimal answers:** If you obtain a decimal answer with more digits than the grid can accommodate, it may be either rounded or truncated, but it must fill the entire grid.

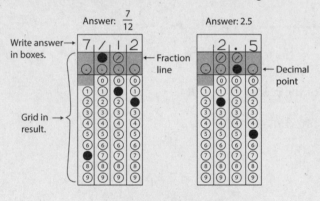

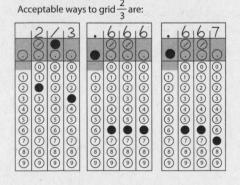

Part II

CONTINUE ➤

31. If $(ax - 1)(2x + b) = 4x^2 + 4x - 3$, what is the value of $a + b$?

32. Derek has $50 to spend on organic produce at the local farmer's market. A pint of berries costs $4, a 1-pound bag of peaches costs $3.75, and a head of lettuce costs $1.50. If he buys at least two of each item, what is the maximum number of pints of berries he could purchase?

33. In a 3-hour examination of 350 questions, there are 50 mathematical problems. If twice as much time should be allowed for each mathematical problem as for each of the other questions, how many minutes should be spent on the mathematical problems?

34. In the 1924–25 season of the National Hockey League (NHL), the Montreal Canadiens won 57% of their games. During the 1947–48 season, they won 33% of their games. If there were twice as many games played in the 1947–48 season as in the 1924–25 season, what percentage of the games did the Montreal Canadiens win in these two seasons of the league? (Do not enter the percent sign in the grid.)

35. A polling company surveys 625 randomly selected registered voters to determine whether a proposed ballot measure might pass. Of those surveyed, 400 voters were in favor of the ballot measure. The polling company reports that the poll results have a conservative margin of error of 4%. If 9,000 people actually vote, what is the minimum number of people likely to vote for the ballot measure?

🖩CALCULATOR

36. The average weight of a medium-sized bottlenose dolphin is 400 pounds. If a particular medium-sized bottlenose dolphin weighs 110% of the average, how many pounds does the dolphin weigh?

37.
$$3x + y = -4$$
$$x + y = 13$$

If (x, y) is a solution for the system of equations above, what is the value of y?

38.
$$-3x + 2y = -1$$
$$6x - by = 8$$

What is the value for b that will make the system above have no solution?

STOP
If you finish before time is called, you may check your work on this section only.
Do not turn to any other section.

Part II

Section 5: Essay

50 Minutes—1 Essay

> **DIRECTIONS:** The essay gives you an opportunity to show how effectively you can read and comprehend a passage and write an essay analyzing the passage. In your essay, you should demonstrate that you have read the passage carefully, present a clear and logical analysis, and use language precisely.
>
> Your essay will need to be written on the lines provided in your answer booklet. You will have enough space if you write on every line and keep your handwriting to an average size. Try to print or write clearly so that your writing will be legible to the readers scoring your essay.

As you read the passage below, consider how Peter Krapp uses the following:

- Evidence, such as facts, statistics, or examples, to support claims
- Reasoning to develop ideas and to connect claims and evidence
- Stylistic or persuasive elements, such as word choice or appeals to emotion, to add power to the ideas expressed

Adapted from "Penn State Hack Exposes Theft Risk of Student Personal Data" by Peter Krapp, originally published in The Conversation *on May 20, 2015. Peter Krapp is a professor of film & media studies at University of California, Irvine. (This passage was edited for length.)*

1 Pennsylvania State University's College of Engineering took its computer network offline on May 15 after disclosing two cyberattacks. The perpetrators were able to access information on 18,000 students, who are being contacted this week with the news that their personal identifying information is in hackers' hands.

2 Three days later, the computer network is back online, with new protections for its users. One of the two attacks is ascribed by a forensic cybersecurity corporation retained by Penn State to computers apparently based in China.

3 As a researcher who has published on hacking and hacktivism and serves on the board of the UC Irvine data science initiative, I believe two aspects of this news story deserve particular attention.

Compromising student data

4 Penn State announced last week that the FBI alerted it on November 21, 2014, about an attack with custom malware that started as early as September 2012.

5 Why did it take so long for Penn State to disclose the breach, despite the fact that the experience of large-scale hacks in 2013 and 2014 (against Target, Home Depot, and others) clearly demonstrated an urgent need for quick and full disclosure—both to help the victims and to preserve a modicum of trust?

6 Penn State stated only that any disclosure would have tipped off the perpetrators before their access to the College of Engineering computers could be cut off. Meanwhile, student data may have been compromised for at least six months, maybe longer.

Chapter 2

7 Another conspicuous problem with public discussion of events like this is, in fact, the lack of distinction often made in the media between actual appropriation of data (as at Penn State) and mere temporary disabling or defacement of websites (as happened to Rutgers University last month). That is like being unable to make a difference between a grand theft auto and keying a car.

8 The question is, what can universities do to limit the risk to their students?

9 The exposure of student data in higher education is not limited to Social Security numbers or email passwords. Information collected and retained by educational institutions includes full name, address, phone number, credit and debit card information, workplace information, date of birth, personal interests and of course academic performance and grade information.

Concern with data practices

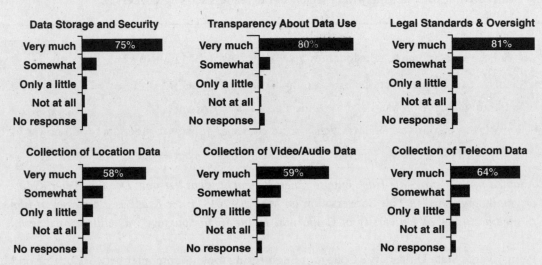

A survey conducted by the Obama administration collected responses from 24,092 individuals on how much they trusted various institutions to keep their data safe. There was a high level of concern around transparency and legal standards.

...

10 President Obama only recently called for laws covering data hacking and student privacy. "We're saying that data collected on students in the classroom should only be used for educational purposes," he stated in his speech to the Federal Trade Commission (FTC) earlier this year.

DATA PRIVACY CONCERNS

11 If students' right to privacy needs to be protected from the specter of foreign intelligence agencies poking around the Penn State Engineering School, then by the same logic it should be protected also against data-mining by for-profit actors right here in the US.

12 Until May 2014, Google, for instance, routinely mined its apps for education services for advertising and monetizing purposes. When *Education Week* reported that Google was mining student emails, it quickly led not only to lawsuits but also to landmark legislation. The California Senate Bill 1177 was enacted to prevent educational services from selling student information or mining it for advertising purposes.

13 Yet, almost a year later, students in California remain just as concerned about their data privacy as before—since the new state law was watered down to apply only to K–12 and not to higher education. And when it was disclosed earlier this spring that education publisher Pearson secretly monitored social media to discern references to their content, the legislative response was one that, according to the Electronic Privacy Information Center (EPIC) in Washington, DC, "fails to uphold President Obama's promise that the data collected in an educational context can be used only for educational purposes."

14 Students in higher education nationwide are still in a position where they cannot opt out of the computer services of their learning institutions, and so they have no expectation of privacy.

15 Despite President Obama's promises for safeguarding the privacy of consumers and families, and despite the fact that a number of technology companies concerned with growing consumer distrust recently signed a pledge to safeguard student privacy, neither Google nor Apple signed on.

16 The President's Council of Advisors on Science and Technology (PCAST) was tasked to examine current and likely future capabilities of key technologies, both those associated with the collection, analysis, and use of big data and those that can help to preserve privacy, resulting in a direct recommendation to strengthen US research in privacy-related technologies.

17 And overwhelmingly, respondents to a White House survey recently expressed severe reservations about the collection, storage, and security and use of private information.

18 Maybe it is time for higher education to heed those signals.

Write an essay in which you explain how Peter Krapp builds an argument to persuade his audience that the use of college students' personal information for anything other than educational purposes is a serious violation of privacy and a major breach of computer security. In your essay, analyze how Peter Krapp uses one or more of the features listed above (or features of your own choice) to strengthen the logic and persuasiveness of his argument. Be sure that your analysis focuses on the most relevant features of the passage. Your essay should not explain whether you agree with the writer's claims, but rather explain how he builds an argument to persuade his audience.

ANSWER KEYS AND EXPLANATIONS

Section 1: Reading Test

1. A	12. D	23. C	33. D	43. C
2. B	13. D	24. B	34. D	44. A
3. D	14. A	25. C	35. D	45. D
4. B	15. A	26. D	36. B	46. A
5. C	16. B	27. A	37. C	47. B
6. C	17. A	28. C	38. D	48. D
7. B	18. D	29. D	39. B	49. A
8. A	19. B	30. D	40. B	50. A
9. C	20. A	31. C	41. C	51. C
10. A	21. B	32. B	42. A	52. D
11. B	22. B			

READING TEST RAW SCORE ☐
(Number of correct answers)

1. **The correct answer is A.** Choice A summarizes the passage best by including its most important details: the sister's death and the narrator's efforts to save her. Choice B narrowly focuses on the girl following the instructions of the medicine woman without indicating why she was following those instructions. Choices C and D do not capture the concept of the narrative and the point of view because they both shift focus from the narrator to the entire family.

2. **The correct answer is B.** The narrator endeavors through significant trial while also observing various community members invest significant energy into saving the little sister. Choice A is incorrect as the story provides no judgement upon the methods of treatment used to remedy the sister's illness. Choice C implies that the passage is equally concerned with Native American rituals as it is with other attempts to solve the problem. Choice D indicates an extreme interpretation as no reason is provided for the cause of the little sister's illness or worsening conditions, in addition to a lack of personification of nature.

3. **The correct answer is D.** Choice D most effectively conveys the care these community members offer as, even after the loss of their daughter, the family attempts payment for services, and the medicine man, recognizing the tragedy of what has occurred, refuses to accept, allowing the family to hold on to key items after an emotional loss. Choice A speaks to the narrator's emotions after offering the sacrifice, speaking more to the self-doubt that grips people in times of crisis. Choice C establishes the inevitable outcome of the situation and speaks in some way to the character of the medicine-man and his level of care but does not adequately speak to the participation of multiple parties. Choice B mistakes the correct answer to the previous question.

4. **The correct answer is B.** Lines 20–23 show the girl having trouble analyzing how nature will affect the delivery of her offering and being unsure if she is making the right

decision. Choice A describes the instructions given by the medicine woman; it doesn't explain why they were difficult to follow. Choice C describes the variance in the terrain where she was searching for the right spot, but it does not describe any particular problem. Choice D describes the narrator's surroundings without indicating that they were causing her any particular problem.

5. **The correct answer is C.** As she places the offering, the narrator wonders whether her sister will die, so it is logical to conclude that she wants to place her offering correctly to prevent that from happening. No one at home asks her about the offering once she returns, so choices A and D can be eliminated. By worrying about her sister's potential death, the narrator indicates that she has more important things on her mind than whether she'll be trusted to make offerings again in the future, so choice B is not the best answer.

6. **The correct answer is C.** The modern meaning of *thrilled* is usually "excited," but in line 47, the author is talking about fear and doubt. Choices A, B, and D all have positive connotations that fail to capture the feelings of heightened fear the narrator was experiencing when she began thinking that her offering had failed to save her sister's life.

7. **The correct answer is B.** The narrator, due to earlier doubts about the placement of the offering, believes she has made a mistake in her actions, which is confirmed upon returning home. The narrator places no blame for her sister's condition, least of all with her parents (choice A). Once the narrator returns home, she fills a more passive role in the events that follow (choice C), but it is unclear whether her passivity is the result of her emotional state. The medicine woman elects to leave after relinquishing hope that the child would survive; she was not dismissed (choice D).

8. **The correct answer is A.** Little interaction between the parents and the narrator is described, but we know that the narrator was tasked with the important role of placing the offering. Though they give the narrator responsibility and take care of her physical needs (lines 50–53), they don't seem to offer comfort or consolation, as may be appropriate for a child. The narrator is probably given more responsibility than she wants, which makes choice B incorrect. The parents naturally focus on the child likely to die, but there is no indication they prefer the younger child, so choice C is incorrect. The narrator receives little attention from the parents, especially as they ask no questions upon her return, instead keeping focus on the little sister, making choice D incorrect.

9. **The correct answer is C.** The family didn't send for the medicine man until the medicine woman had given up hope, which makes choice C the most logical answer. What the medicine man had been doing before arriving at the family's house is never indicated, so there is no evidence for choice A. While distance is stated, it is not suggested as a reason for why the medicine-man could not come (choice B); the use of "incredible" is also extreme when compared to the passage's phrasing "many miles away." No familial relationship is stated or suggested by the passage (choice D).

10. **The correct answer is A.** In line 70, the medicine man describes seeing a "luminous vapor above the house," and clarifies that "It was the spirit of the little child who is sick" in lines 79–80. Choice B distorts details from the passage, stating the opposite of what occurs in the story. Choice C misuses the details that relate to the medicine man's vision that allowed him to have his current abilities. The narrator in no way communicates with the little sister during the narrative, making choice D incorrect.

11. **The correct answer is B.** In the second sentence of the passage, the author identifies the Children's House as a "kind of school" and uses the rest of the passage to describe the qualities that make the school unique. While play may be performed in a Children's House as part of the educational process, it is more of a place of learning than a place of play, so choice A is not the best answer. While it can be inferred that the Children's House stands in contrast to other models of education at the time, the passage does not state explicit criticism of other types of school (choice C). The passage indicates that many of the tasks bear resemblance to the activities of adults (cooking, cleaning, organizing furniture), but it does not express a direct argument for why those tasks should be prioritized over other activities.

12. **The correct answer is D.** The author refers to how equipment adapted for children will allow them to do such things as move furniture around by themselves, which implies that it fosters self-sufficiency rather than reliance on adult assistance, so choice D is the best answer. While a Children's House is specially adapted for children, the author never suggests that adults are not allowed in a Children's House (choice A) and does mention the presence of a teacher in the house. Choice B is too extreme; while the child-sized equipment in a Children's House may make it easier for children to learn, there is no suggestion that they cannot learn at all when using adult-sized equipment. Although the author does reference how the educational equipment is the common property of all the children, she never implies that the fact that it is adapted specifically for children encourages sharing (choice C).

13. **The correct answer is D.** The paragraph states that the central room is for "intellectual work" while also stating that other rooms, with a variety of purposes, can be added, implying their usefulness for the children. The paragraph mentions a gymnasium, but the paragraph does not supply a reason for its inclusion (choice A). The paragraph mentions a dining room and parlor, but, similar to choice A, choice B goes beyond the scope of what is stated to infer the reasoning for including those rooms. While elsewhere in the passage, it is clear that physical tasks are important to the Montessori model, but saying that children split their time between manual work and intellectual labor is not supported by the description of possible rooms in the Children's House (choice C).

14. **The correct answer is A.** The author uses the word *didactic* to describe materials intended to assist "the intellectual development of the child," so *educational* is the best answer. While children might enjoy the materials with which they work, the author is more concerned with children's intellectual development than their enjoyment here, so choice B can be eliminated. Choice C can be eliminated even though "pedantic" is related to learning; "pedantic" has a negative connotation, referring to something that informs unnecessarily or fixates on minor details. *Distracting* (choice D) is unrelated to the meaning of the word *didactic*.

15. **The correct answer is A.** The sixth paragraph describes a variety of decorations in a Children's House, including a blackboard for drawing, pictures, and plants, so choice A is the best answer. Choice B focuses on the description of the pictures and objects in the room but does not explicitly connect their presence to "intellectual development." Choice C makes a similar mistake as nothing is being argued, only described; it also fixates on the mention of pictures of families, jumping to an unreasonable conclusion in the circumstances. Choice D focuses on the final sentence about plants rather than on the main idea of the paragraph as a whole.

16. **The correct answer is B.** In the seventh paragraph, the author states, "The children spread these rugs upon the floor, sit upon them and work there," so choice B is the correct answer. The author never explains why the pieces of carpet should be multicolored, so choice A is not the best answer. While the author does mention that the table and chairs take up space in the working room (choice C), this does not have anything to do with why pieces of carpet are necessary in a working room. The author also states that the children are responsible for spreading out the pieces of carpet, but she does not imply that this is a necessary skill to learn, so choice D is not the best answer either.

17. **The correct answer is A.** Lines 8–10 indicate that the purpose of the Children's House is to provide a space that students have control over, implying that the author trusts the children to be responsible, as based on previous experience. Choice B indicates that the children are "managers" of the miniature family, but it implies through the presence of the equipment that those skills must be nurtured. Choice C describes the kind of equipment available to the students and how it is shared without speaking to trust in their ability to maintain it. Choice D speaks to similar details.

18. **The correct answer is D.** The context of the sentence establishes that doll houses are filled with numerous forms of small furniture, clothing items, and spaces that simulate objects in the real world; the level of detail allows a child to be an "actor in a living scene" thus making *intricacy* the best choice. Something that is complicated can be difficult (choice A), but that does not align with the following description. Similarly, a complication can cause confusion, but the author is speaking to the perfection of how the toys are designed, in that they create learning opportunities for students (choice

B). *Simplicity* (choice C) is the opposite of the meaning of the indicated word.

19. **The correct answer is B.** Throughout the passage, the author advocates a learning environment with multiple stimuli that allows children the freedom to learn in their own ways, so choice B is the best answer. Choice A is an extreme conclusion, and it ignores mention of a teacher in the passage. Even as the passage implies that the children are the masters of the house, nothing is stated regarding a child living inside the house (choice C). Choice D reaches a conclusion, and it ignores details in the text (the presence of a teacher, the presence of teaching materials, etc.).

20. **The correct answer is A.** The first lines of the passage indicate that the Children's House was designed in order to offer children the opportunities to complete multiple activities. Choice B describes how children may play or sleep at the school, connecting to the unsupported inference in choice C in the previous question. Choice C of this question describes one activity that children participate in during their day at the Children's House, but it does not speak to the "multiple stimuli" needed for a strong education. Choice D describes the doll houses available to students but does not explain the ability of the student to choose freely how they spend their time.

21. **The correct answer is B.** The article includes scientific data and explanations of the effects of plastics in the ocean and waterways, offering information to the public. The specific data in this passage contradict the idea that the author is merely theorizing that the environment could be in danger, and this conclusion is too general in any event, so choice A is not the best answer. Choices C and D are too extreme and unrealistic; it is unlikely a movement will halt all plastic production, which is not even something the author

advocates, and cleaning up the oceans is too huge a job for readers to take on personally. Choice B remains the most logical and realistic answer.

22. **The correct answer is B.** Lines 63–66: "Research has shown that harmful and persistent substances can both bioaccumulate… and biomagnify…" indicate that plastic pollution in the ocean is a problem by specifying that they are "harmful." Choice A merely states what happens when animals eat plastics without suggesting that this is or is not a problem, so it is not the best answer. Choice C describes how certain problems associated with plastic pollution are still unknown, so it fails to support the previous question's conclusion that plastic pollution is a problem. Choice D merely sets up questions to follow without providing evidence that plastic pollution in the ocean is a problem.

23. **The correct answer is C.** In the first paragraph, the author provides a number of statistics that support choice C. However, the author never compares plastic waste to the impact of other forms of waste, so choice A cannot be concluded based on information in this particular passage. The author writes that "World plastics production has experienced almost constant growth for more than half a century," which contradicts choice B. While the entire passage discusses the impact of plastic waste on the planet, the author never compares that to the impact of other forms of waste or declares any other factors that contribute to the destruction of marine ecosystems, so choice D is not the best answer.

24. **The correct answer is B.** Lines 5–7 provide specific statistics about how plastic accounts for 10 percent of the 1.4 billion tons of trash the world generates each year. Choice A indicates that plastic production continues to grow, but without specific numbers, there is no way to use this information to

conclude that plastic is responsible for a massive amount of waste. That the International Maritime Organization has had to ban dumping of plastic waste indicates it is a big enough problem to warrant such action, but choice C is simply not as specific as choice B is, so it is not the best answer choice. Choice D also refers to a problem but fails to supply specific numbers.

25. **The correct answer is C.** In lines 16–19, the author explains that microplastics are "the most abundant type of plastic in the ocean." Although it is likely that recycling has increased in the past 60 years, the passage doesn't mention it, making choice A incorrect. Although it's true that plastic breaks down into smaller pieces in the ocean, it is stated in the passage that microplastics are more dangerous to marine organisms, who mistake them for food, rather than less dangerous, making choice B incorrect. As explained in lines 35–38, nurdles are plastic pellets used in plastic production, making choice D incorrect. In lines 38–43, the passage mentions that scrubbing agents in shampoo that leak into the environment are called microbeads, not nurdles.

26. **The correct answer is D.** The author explains that a law was passed in Illinois to prevent infiltration of these tiny microbeads into local bodies the water system (lines 43–47). The microbeads were ending up in the Great Lakes and Chicago's waterways. None of the other options are offered as a reason for the law.

27. **The correct answer is A.** *Desorb* means the opposite of *absorb*, meaning to "leach out," as supported by the following verb "transfer;" it is clear that the chemical additives present in the plastics must move from the plastic to the tissues of the organisms. Choices B and C are opposites of the indicated word. Choice D indicates a physical process that fits the context of the sentence but would change its

28. **The correct answer is C.** Both terms represent specific scientific terms for biological processes and are proceeded by technical definitions; the words are not charged with emotion but aim to be precise in describing the effect the plastics have. Choice A accurately describes the academic nature of the text but also prescribes motivation to the author which is not indicated by these terms. Choice B assigns emotion to technical terminology. Choice D misunderstands the meaning of the terms as though they were judgments rather than statements following scientific observation.

29. **The correct answer is D.** *Concentration* has multiple meanings, but the context of the passage makes it clear that the "harmful and persistent substances" are increasing in amount through prolonged exposure and at higher levels of the food chain. Choice A provides a reasonable choice as based on the scientific context of the passage, as various forms of absorption and adsorption are mentioned; however, absorption is a synonym for *concentration* only when one is absorbed or focused on a task, not in the physical accumulation of substances. Similarly, the part of speech of *absorption* (a noun) would indicate that the increase is in the rate of absorption rather than the level or amount of that which is being absorbed. Choice B thus makes a similar mistake, substituting a common synonym that does not fit the context of the passage. Choice C offers another common meaning of *concentration* as related to academics, which is inappropriate for the context.

30. **The correct answer is D.** While certain pieces of information may be implied by the nature of the questions, the sentence following the question makes it clear that researchers are pursuing answers to these questions; these are the pressing tasks researchers hope to resolve. The final question of the three considers plastic consumption by humans but offers no conclusion (choice A). Choices B and C similarly draw conclusions when the paragraph makes it clear that these are subjects for further research.

31. **The correct answer is C.** In lines 96–102, Halden's quote ("We need to design the next generation of plastics to make them more biodegradable…") shows that he believes science can find a way to make plastics biodegradable, which he says will eliminate the problem. The author states that new laws may help minimize the problem ("New laws … could require handling plastics more responsibly at the end of their useful life through recycling, proper disposal, and extended producer responsibility"), not Halden, so choice A is incorrect. The author describes how some sea creatures have ingested plastic, but Halden never advocates for the invention of edible plastic in this passage, so choice B is incorrect. Banning all new plastic production is an extreme and unrealistic solution that Halden never suggests, so choice D is incorrect.

32. **The correct answer is B.** Emmet speaks of being accused of secretly selling his country out to France, which would be the actions of a spy; in this context, an emissary is a spy. The government wouldn't accuse someone of being an ambassador, an official position as a representative (choice A). While the nature of Emmet's trial has labeled him as an "enemy" of Ireland (choice C), that does not align with the use of the word. The use of "teacher" would, at best, be figurative here, but, in general, does not apply to the political nature of the situation.

33. **The correct answer is D.** In choice D, Emmet acknowledges his death sentence and declares that he is dying for a cause. Choice C explains why he asked France for

assistance, and choice B explains that he was fighting for his country's independence and freedom from tyranny. In choice A, he defends his actions by saying that he could have stood by and done nothing, but chose instead to defend liberty.

34. **The correct answer is D.** Choice D shows Emmet's investment of resisting any form of oppression, that which would have harmed Ireland. In choice A, he merely states that he is not working for France, but this alone does not prove that he feels pride in his own country. In choice B, he theorizes about the different influences that could have caused him to betray his country. Choice C makes a statement about how he feels the people in his country deserve assistance from France, but that alone does not make a strong case for the author's patriotism.

35. **The correct answer is D.** The sentence serves to establish Emmet's commitment to preserving the freedom of his fellow citizens and his country. The sentiment is not accompanied by a plea to the judge for leniency due to circumstance (choice A). Nor does Emmet directly address members of his audience to stir them to action (choice B). Emmet continually resists the charge that he was in any way operating in the interest of a foreign government (choice C).

36. **The correct answer is B.** Noting the date of Emmet's speech in his defense of his actions prior to his execution, choice A is not possible. The Louisiana Purchase by the United States (choice D) would have given France more resources to help. However, the Napoleonic Wars were draining the French treasury (choice B), leaving the country overburdened and uninterested in becoming involved elsewhere. The French Revolution had started in 1789, triggering the rise of Napoleon, but this preceded by too much time Emmet's request for assistance.

37. **The correct answer is C.** Wright says Americans' idea of a patriot is someone who loves his/her country, choice D, but that idea is too narrow. She explains that Europeans see patriotism as a more expansive concept that extends to freedom for all humans. This idea, she explains, includes working toward the best interests of all human lives, wherever they are, so that they are free from despotism. This statement suggests that she herself holds these ideas (choice C) and wants others to consider them. Physically fighting for one's country, choices A and B, are not supported by the passage.

38. **The correct answer is D.** The use of the word *generous* comes amidst multiple poetic declarations regarding the "enlightened patriot" who "stands the guardian patriot of the world," thus implying high ideals or values as embodied by the word *noble*. Choices A and B align with common definitions for generous but do not agree with the context of the passage. *Creative* (choice C) is a common pairing with the word *soul* but does not work with the passage either.

39. **The correct answer is B.** According to the timeline, American colonies declared independence in 1776, and the fact that the country needed to define itself outside of the rule of another country probably caused America's view of patriotism to focus more on the country itself, rather than a greater concern for all people. Choice A refers to events that did not concern America. Choices C and D do refer to events that concerned America, but neither had as significant an impact on the country and its views as declaring independence in 1776 did.

40. **The correct answer is B.** Although both Emmet and Wright wanted freedom from tyranny, Emmet's focus was on Ireland, and Wright had a broader objective of freedom and independence for all humankind, choice B. Choice A is incorrect because only

Wright states that her country's concept of patriotism needs to be rethought. Wright was focused on advancing an expansive concept of patriotism that included other countries, which does not mean that she did not love her country, so choice C is not the best answer. Choice D is incorrect because Wright indicates that she does understand tyranny by advocating for its opposite: freedom and concern for all people.

41. **The correct answer is C.** Emmet loved his country and declared his patriotism toward Ireland as his reason for his actions. Wright's view was more inclusive, defining it as freeing all people, whatever the country. Emmet's primary focus was on his own people (choice B), not all of humankind. He defended his actions (choice A), but this action is unrelated to Wright's concept of a patriot, as is a court that renders an unjust sentence (choice D).

42. **The correct answer is A.** As stated in the passages, both authors refuse to tolerate oppression in a variety of forms, including oppression from foreign and domestic powers and despotism from religious and civil institutions. Only Emmet makes a clear case that his patriotism would never accept the influence of foreign powers (choice B). Only Wright makes the case that patriots stand for the emancipation of all humankind (choice C). Neither author is willing to accept the directives of their own governments blindly, but especially as stated by Emmet and his resistance to "domestic" oppressors (choice D).

43. **The correct answer is C.** The majority of the passage describes the protective modification of direct protection, which sees organisms blending in with their natural environment. Choice A infers the author's opinion when none is provided. Choice B speaks to the authors repeated statement that species should be observed in their natural habitat to create opportunities for recording previously

unknown adaptations, but this occurs only in one paragraph—thus not the primary purpose. Choice D is too specific, as *Uloborus* are discussed only in one paragraph as well.

44. **The correct answer is A.** The first paragraph of the passage introduces the topic to be discussed throughout, making lines 1–8 the best choice. Choice B corresponds to the misleading answer regarding observation in the previous question. Choice C offers a detail describing the behaviors of the *Uloborus*. Choice D discusses the effectiveness of the *C. mitralis*, an attempt to suggest direct protection is a superior strategy.

45. **The correct answer is D.** The environment in which an organism is observed affects the observations that can be made. Choice A is extreme and is not addressed within the passage. Choice C does not align with the details of the passage. Choice D distorts the details of the passage related to the descriptions of color for the different spider species and has no connection to why study should occur in the spiders' habitats.

46. **The correct answer is A.** The passage states that certain adaptations would be almost impossible to understand because of their direct connection to the environment in which the spider is found. Choice B could be used to support the idea that scientific study is flawed because of the presence of exceptions to rules, but this does not support the importance of field study. Choice C provides an irrelevant detail related to *Uloborus* coloring. Choice D describes the body of the *C. mitralis*, suggesting resemblance to the other spiders described in the passage.

47. **The correct answer is B.** The topic sentence of the paragraph declares the importance of observation; as such, the list of physical traits for spiders helps express how certain adaptations may go unobserved in different contexts. Choice A speaks to the length of the list but ignores the second clause in the

sentence that restates the importance of "natural relations." Choice C observes that there are fewer descriptors of color than bodily form but overemphasizes the importance of such information. Choice D misrepresents the relationship between the indicated phrase and the previous sentence.

48. **The correct answer is D.** In the context of the passage, the author conveys that these spiders are difficult to see in their natural habitats, making *imperceptible* the best choice. While the spiders are protected by their modification that makes them inconspicuous, it cannot replace the word in question (choice A). *Visible* (choice B) means the opposite of inconspicuous. *Modest* (choice C) is a synonym for inconspicuous but does not fit the context of the passage.

49. **The correct answer is A.** The author states that members of the *Uloborus* resemble small pieces of bark that "commonly become entangled in old deserted webs." As their form of direct protection makes it so they are "always found in the middle of the web," they must benefit from the behavior. Choice A misuses the detail that strands on their webs commonly break to form an inference about hunting success. Choice B infers that the *Uloborus*' behavior works for both avoiding predators and hunting prey, which is beyond the passage's focus on direct protection. Choice C misuses details within the paragraph to imply that *Uloborus* are brightly colored, despite their later description as "wood-brown or gray, mottled with white."

50. **The correct answer is A.** The author states that *Epeira* cling to the bark of branches

and are protected during the day; the use of "cling" implies a lack of movement, especially when coupled with description of their nocturnal behavior, during the day. Choice B goes beyond the scope of the passage to discuss the spider's dietary preferences. Choice C makes an unsupported inference about the interaction between bodily forms and lighting conditions. Choice D introduces temperature as a potential factor in the spider's behaviors, unsupported by the passage.

51. **The correct answer is C.** Since introducing the idea of protective modifications and justifying the importance of observing species in their natural habitats, the author dedicates each paragraph to discussing different spiders and their specific modifications. Choice A introduces the idea of how adaptations occur, which is not alluded to in the passage. Choice B implies that there are significant differences between the *C. mitralis* and the *Uloborus* and that such a distinction is important to the discussion of protective modification. Choice D suggests that the paragraph restates an idea presented earlier in the passage; this is incorrect as no statement related to the unlimited potential of direct protection were made.

52. **The correct answer is D.** According to the description in the passage, the *C. mitralis* resembles a "woody knot" with ridges like "the bark on a woody excrescence." That description suggests different levels or platforms. Choice A uses the definition of stages as related to time. The word *floors* (choice B) is used to describe architecture. *Parts* (choice C) ignores the description in the passage.

Section 2: Writing and Language Test

1. A	10. B	19. B	28. A	37. A
2. D	11. D	20. C	29. C	38. C
3. A	12. A	21. C	30. B	39. A
4. B	13. C	22. C	31. C	40. C
5. C	14. D	23. D	32. A	41. D
6. B	15. B	24. C	33. D	42. B
7. B	16. D	25. B	34. C	43. A
8. A	17. A	26. D	35. B	44. C
9. B	18. C	27. C	36. D	

WRITING AND LANGUAGE TEST RAW SCORE
(Number of correct answers)

1. **The correct answer is A.** Choice A correctly sets up the sentence's focus on the various causes of depopulation and their negative impact. Choices B, C, and D are incorrect because they present potentially positive developments.

2. **The correct answer is D.** Choice D follows the same parallel construction as the preceding phrase, "driving away its middle class." Choices A, B, and C are incorrect because they do not demonstrate parallel construction.

3. **The correct answer is A.** Choice A is correct because the dash is being used to indicate the following explanation of what is staggering. Choice C creates a run-on sentence. Choices B moves the punctuation to the wrong part of the sentence. Choice D creates a comma splice with the initial independent clause.

4. **The correct answer is B.** Choice B correctly maintains the sentence's focus on the effects of depopulation. Choices A and C suggest a growth in residency, which contradicts the main argument of the passage. Choice D is incorrect because homelessness is unrelated to the main focus of the passage, which is Detroit's depopulation.

5. **The correct answer is C.** *Solicit* correctly establishes the implied intent of the city planners within the context of the passage—to solicit, or ask for, the input of city residents while studying their urban spaces. Choices A, B, and D do not make sense within the context of the passage, as the terms imply the opposite of the city planners' intent.

6. **The correct answer is B.** The plural pronoun *they* is required here to agree with the plural noun *planners*, so *they call* is the correct answer. Choices A and C incorrectly use singular pronouns. Choice D is incorrect because "we call" is first-person plural, not third-person plural, which is what is required here.

7. **The correct answer is B.** "In fact" properly suggests an elaboration of the previous sentence. Choice A suggests the second sentence is an equal and additional example, rather than an elaboration of the first. Choice C implies the author is drawing a conclusion despite a contradiction. Choice D implies that the second sentence is a second example supporting a contrast scenario, which is not the case.

Answers | Diagnostic Test

8. **The correct answer is A.** The sentence in choice A explains the planners' logic. Choice B implies that there was resistance to their thinking or that their thinking was absolute, which is incorrect. Choices C and D do not denote the careful calculation that the rest of the sentence implies.

9. **The correct answer is B.** This sentence would best serve as a transition between the previous and current paragraphs. The previous paragraph refers to the city planners' strategic plan, and the current paragraph begins with an example of one of the plan's boldest suggestions. A sentence that mentions that the plan contained bold suggestions would work well here. The other choices would place this notion *after* providing examples of the plan's bold suggestions, rendering it ineffective and unnecessary.

10. **The correct answer is B.** Choice B correctly places the em dash so that it separates the proceeding parenthetical thought from the independent clause. Choice A is incorrect because it treats the information after the period as an independent clause—it is a sentence fragment. Choice C is also incorrect as the semi-colon indicates the presence of two independent clauses. Choice D incorrectly places the dash.

11. **The correct answer is D.** Choice D correctly uses a colon after an independent clause to set up a list of items. Choice A is grammatically correct because items in a series should be separated by commas but it is not as concise as choice D. Choice B is unnecessarily wordy and misuses semicolons. Choice C misuses semicolons.

12. **The correct answer is A.** *Hawk* means "to call out and sell," which is what vendors at festivals do. Choice B is incorrect because, while the vendors may stock merchandise, the author's intent here is to describe *how* they sell that merchandise. Similarly, choices C and D are incorrect because the vendors are selling—not advertising or trading—goods.

13. **The correct answer is C.** Choice C correctly suggests that this sentence provides a transition between the scene depicted in the first paragraph and the ancient and modern tradition of puppetry, and the writer should not delete it. Choice A is incorrect because this sentence is not an opinion. Choice B is incorrect because this sentence does not distract from but rather helps in contextualizing the main ideas of the paragraph. Choice D is incorrect because it is the following sentence that explains what *wayang kulit* is.

14. **The correct answer is D.** Choice D correctly uses end punctuation to correct this run-on sentence. Choices A, B, and C do not employ the correct punctuation to denote two independent clauses.

15. **The correct answer is B.** Choice B is correct because the phrase, "a nation to which Indonesia was linked through trade relations" should refer to the country of India, not "migrants." Choices A and D are incorrect because the modifier is misplaced. Choice C is awkward and doesn't make sense.

16. **The correct answer is D.** Choice D is correct because this sentence is tangential to the paragraph's focus on the cultural influences of Hindu culture on the Indonesian way of life. Choice A is incorrect because this information is not relevant. Choice B is incorrect because this paragraph is not focused on the actual practice of shadow puppetry. Choice C is incorrect because this information has not been presented before this sentence.

17. **The correct answer is A.** Choice A reflects the paragraph's emphasis that depicting gods in human form was not allowed under any circumstance. Choices B, C, and D are incorrect because these words do not suggest complete proscription the way choice A does.

18. **The correct answer is C.** Choice C places the verb in the past tense. Choice A is incorrect because the present tense is an inappropriate shift from the past tense that the rest of the paragraph uses. Choices B and D are incorrect because the sentence requires the simple past tense.

19. **The correct answer is B.** Choice B conveys both the duration of the events and the lack of interruptions without being redundant or wordy. Choice A is incorrect because "all night long" is redundant. Choice C is redundant and wordy; while it is constructed better by omitting "at all," "all night long from sunset to sunrise" is still redundant, as is the use of "huge" before "epic." Choice D is incorrect because just noting that the performance lasted all night isn't as informative as noting that, from dusk to dawn, the performance had no interruptions.

20. **The correct answer is C.** As written, the sentence is a run-on and needs some added punctuation to reduce confusion. Choice C fixes the run-on by adding the appropriate commas and an em-dash. Choices B and D add commas in inappropriate places, creating additional confusion.

21. **The correct answer is C.** The pronoun *its* should refer back to the antecedent "the puppet." Choice A is incorrect because *their* is plural and *puppet* is not. Choices B and D are incorrect because "the puppet" is neither male nor female.

22. **The correct answer is C.** Comparisons require *than*, not *then*. *Then* (choice A) is an adverb that refers to time. *That* (choice B) and *this* (choice D) don't make sense in the sentence.

23. **The correct answer is D.** The intent of this passage is to bring attention to the serious water issues occurring in the American Southwest, so choice D would be the most effective introductory sentence. The passage is not an enticement to vacation in the American Southwest, so choice A is incorrect. It is also not focused on pointing out the majestic aspects of the American Southwest, so choice B is incorrect. The Anasazi people are a supporting detail about the American Southwest in the context of this passage, so choice C is also incorrect.

24. **The correct answer is C.** The sentence subject that includes "arid climate and limited water resources," is a compound subject, which means the verb must also be plural. Choice A is incorrect because "has" is singular. Choice B is incorrect because it is the past perfect instead of the present perfect tense. Choice D is present tense and changes the meaning of the sentence.

25. **The correct answer is B.** The sentence requires a possessive pronoun in order to refer back to the Anasazi people. Choice A is incorrect because *they're* is a contraction, not a possessive. Choice C is incorrect because *there* is an adverb, not a possessive. Choice D is incorrect because *its* is singular possessive, while the antecedent, *people*, is plural.

26. **The correct answer is D.** Choice D combines the sentences in a way that helps emphasize the connection between the two. Choice A is incorrect because *but* implies that the two ideas are contradictory. Choice B misuses a semicolon to connect an independent clause and what is now a dependent clause. Choice C creates a run-on sentence.

27. **The correct answer is C.** There are two independent clauses which have related topics, thus allowing for use of a semicolon. Choice A is incorrect because the comma creates a comma splice. Choice B is incorrect because a colon is not appropriate for the relationship between the sentences; while it would be preceded by an independent clause, the following information does not contain a list or explain the previous clause. Choice D creates a run-on sentence.

28. The correct answer is A. The context of the sentence suggests that a scientific forecast or prediction about water flow hàs been made. Choices B and C reflect subjective impulses and do not maintain the neutral and scientific tone of the passage. Choice D is vague and fails to suggest a basis in research.

29. The correct answer is C. This sentence adds new and relevant information by providing an example that shows the reader how severe the drought really is. Choice A is incorrect because this information has not been presented previously in the passage. Choice B is incorrect because this sentence does not blur the paragraph's focus; rather, it is relevant to the paragraph's main argument. Choice D is incorrect because this sentence does not introduce this argument; rather, it supports the argument.

30. The correct answer is B. The dependent clause "and possibly more alarming" must be set off by commas. Choice A contains one too many commas. Choice C contains no commas. Choice D is incorrect because the comma should be before *and*.

31. The correct answer is C. Although it may sound otherwise, the conventional expression is "for all intents and purposes." Choices A, B, and D are incorrect.

32. The correct answer is A. The author's intent is to suggest that there are other factors that make the problems of drought worse and more complicated. Choices B, C, and D are incorrect because each word emphasizes an increase in severity rather than an increase in the number of factors contributing to problems in the area.

33. The correct answer is D. The accompanying map measures average air temperatures. The map does not measure the highest (choice A) or lowest (choice B) air temperatures. It also doesn't measure water temperature (choice C).

34. The correct answer is C. Choice C is correct because this first paragraph establishes that women do not get as many leading roles as men nor do they spend as much time on-screen. Choice A does not stress the number of roles nor the amount of on-screen time. Choice B does not cite the amount of on-screen time, alluding to it only vaguely. Choice D is incorrect because the main idea of the passage is not a plea to pay female actresses more than their male counterparts to attract new talent.

35. The correct answer is B. Only *agents* expresses the idea that television and movies play an active role in causing social change. Choices A, C, and D don't suggest a causal relationship to social change.

36. The correct answer is D. The subordinate clause that begins with *while* is tied to the central premise of the sentence and needs to be at the beginning. Choice A is incorrect because at the end of the sentence, the relationship of the clause to the central idea is lost. Choices B and C obscure the relationship of the clause to the central idea of the sentence.

37. The correct answer is A. The noun *women* should agree in number with *protagonists*. Choice B is incorrect because *protagonist* should be plural. Choice C is incorrect because *protagonist* should be singular if it is to agree with the subject *woman*. Choice D is incorrect because "a woman" is not plural.

38. The correct answer is C. Choice C clarifies that the comparison is between women's marital status and the marital status of men. Choice A makes an illogical comparison between women's marital status and men in general. Choice B makes another illogical comparison, this time with just the singular *man*. Choice D is not as concise as choice B.

39. The correct answer is A. Choice A supports the paragraph's claim that women

Diagnostic Test

are underrepresented in the film industry. Choices B, C, and D don't support the paragraph's main focus that women are underrepresented in the film industry.

40. **The correct answer is C.** The pronoun should refer to the female actress using *her*. Choice A is incorrect because it is plural. Choice B is incorrect because it is masculine. Choice D is incorrect because it is plural and first person.

41. **The correct answer is D.** Choice D maintains the objective and neutral tone of the passage while noting unfavorable comparisons. Choices A, B, and C are incorrect because the tone of each choice is emotionally charged, which is inconsistent with the objective tone of the passage.

42. **The correct answer is B.** Given the context of the sentence and paragraph, *famous* is the most appropriate word choice. Streep is offered as an example of a woman who has achieved great acclaim as an actress, despite gender inequalities in the film industry. The

previous sentence mentions her many award nominations, so referring to her fame here makes the most sense. The other answer choices either don't make sense given the context, or we are not given enough information to determine if they are appropriate choices.

43. **The correct answer is A.** *Accolades* connotes the achievements, honor, and respect that the passage goes on to describe. Choice B is incorrect because the awards were not privileges. *Recognition* (choice C) and *attention* (choice D) do not connote the honor and respect that *accolades* does.

44. **The correct answer is C.** The word *characters* should be the possessive *character's*. Choice A is incorrect because *characters* is plural instead of possessive. Choice B is incorrect because *character* is not possessive. Choice D does not convey the appropriate meaning.

Answers | Diagnostic Test

Section 3: Math Test—NO CALCULATOR

1. B	5. C	9. B	13. D	17. 6
2. B	6. A	10. A	14. A	18. 25
3. B	7. D	11. C	15. D	19. 15
4. C	8. C	12. C	16. 80	20. 4

MATH TEST—NO CALCULATOR RAW SCORE [ ]
(Number of correct answers)

1. **The correct answer is B.** The slope of a line can be determined by finding the difference in the y-coordinates divided by the difference in the x-coordinates for any two points on the line. Using the points indicated, the slope is:

$$\frac{5-1}{0-3} = -\frac{4}{3}$$

Translating the line moves all the points on the line the same distance in the same direction, and the image will be a parallel line. Therefore, the slope of the line is $-\frac{4}{3}$.

2. **The correct answer is B.** The constant 12 represents the starting distance on the driveway. In other words, before the snail even moved, it was already 12 feet from the beginning of the driveway. Therefore, Catherine must have placed the snail 12 feet from the start of her driveway before she began recording the time it took for the snail to get to the end of her driveway.

3. **The correct answer is B.** Solve for x:

$$-2x + 5 = 2 - (5 - 2x)$$
$$-2x + 5 = 2 - 5 + 2x$$
$-2x + 5 = -3 + 2x$ Add $2x$ to both sides.
$5 = -3 + 4x$ Add $+3$ to both sides.
$8 = 4x$ Divide by 4.
$2 = x$

4. **The correct answer is C.** Multiply both the numerator and the denominator by the complex conjugate of the denominator, which is equivalent to multiplying by 1. The resulting rational expression has a real denominator and can be simplified to $-4 + 2i$.

$$\frac{10i}{1-2i}\left(\frac{1+2i}{1+2i}\right) = \frac{(10i + 20i^2)}{1 - 4i^2}$$
$$= \frac{10i - 20}{1 + 4}$$
$$= 2i - 4$$

5. **The correct answer is C.**

$$5\sqrt{-16}$$
$$= 5\left(\sqrt{16} \cdot \sqrt{-1}\right)$$
$$= 5(4i)$$
$$= 20i$$

6. **The correct answer is A.** The amount of grain added each week is 1,000 bushels. Divide 1,000 bushels by 0.8 bushels per cubic foot to obtain 1,250 cubic feet per week. So the total amount of grain in the silo is 32,500 (what is already there) plus $1{,}250w$ (the amount added each week times the number of weeks), which must be less than or equal to the volume of the silo, 45,000 cubic feet.

7. **The correct answer is D.** The vertex of a parabola is found when the equation is written in the form $y = a(x - h)^2 + k$. You don't need to perform any calculations, because only choice D is written in this form.

8. **The correct answer is C.**

$$-x^2 + 2y - (-x - y) = -x^2 + 2y + x + y$$
$$= -x^2 + x + 3y$$

9. **The correct answer is B.** Since Jorge's truck is traveling at an average speed of 55 miles per hour and the truck gets 6 miles per gallon, the number of gallons of diesel used each hour can be found by the equation

$\dfrac{55 \text{ miles}}{1 \text{ hour}} \times \dfrac{1 \text{ gallon}}{6 \text{ miles}} = \dfrac{55}{6}$. The truck uses $\dfrac{55}{6}$ gallons of diesel per hour, so it uses $\dfrac{55}{6}h$ gallons of diesel in h hours. The truck's fuel tank has 125 gallons of diesel at the beginning of the trip. Therefore, the function that models the number of gallons of diesel remaining in the tank h hours after the trip begins is $d(h) = 125 - \dfrac{55h}{6}$.

10. **The correct answer is A.**

$$A = \frac{M}{M - N}$$
$$A(M - N) = M$$
$$AM - AN = M$$
$$AM - M = AN$$
$$M(A - 1) = AN$$
$$M = \frac{AN}{A - 1}$$

11. **The correct answer is C.** The total cost of the sofa, y, is equal to the number of monthly payments multiplied by the amount of each payment, plus the down payment. The number of monthly payments is x, and x is multiplied by 90 in the given equation. So 90 represents the monthly payment. 75 represents the down payment.

12. **The correct answer is C.** The sum of the values that satisfy the equation is the sum of the solution $2.5 + 3 = 5.5$.

$$2n^2 - 11n + 15 = 0$$
$$(2n - 5)(n - 3) = 0$$
$$2n - 5 = 0, n - 3 = 0$$
$$n = 2.5, n = 3$$

13. **The correct answer is D.** The graph will cross the x-axis at the point where the function (that is, the y-coordinate) has a value of 0. As a result, the following equation needs to be solved:

$$480 - 60t = 0$$
$$-60t = -480$$
$$t = 8$$

Since t represents the independent variable, the point is $(8, 0)$.

14. **The correct answer is A.** The initial population of the town is 500. The rate of change between consecutive x values (1 year, 2 years, 3 years) is not constant. As a result, the expression cannot be linear, and choice B is eliminated. Determine the ratio of each year's population to the previous year's population to the previous year's population. Comparing the population after one year to the initial population, we have:

$$\frac{650}{500} = 1.3$$

If the population is growing exponentially, then we can calculate the population after x years by multiplying the initial population by 1.3 raised to the x power. Choice A represents that calculation. (You can eliminate choice C by substituting $x = 1$ year, and choice D doesn't make sense because it introduces the undefined quantity t.)

15. **The correct answer is D.** For questions of this type, you often can identify the correct answer by substituting values for the variable. Zero (or any value that simplifies the necessary arithmetic) is a good choice. When you substitute 0 for x, $\dfrac{4x + 1}{x + 2}$ simplifies to $\dfrac{1}{2}$. Because any equivalent expression must have the same value as the original expression for all x, look for the expression that equals $\dfrac{1}{2}$ when $x = 0$. Among the answers, only choice D is such an expression. You can also arrive at this answer using algebra, but it takes longer.

16. The correct answer is 80. If $AC = BC$, then $m\angle A = m\angle B = 50°$.

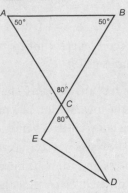

In $\triangle ABC$, $m\angle ABC = 180° - (m\angle A + m\angle B)$.

So $m\angle ABC = 80°$.

Further, $m\angle ABC = m\angle ECD$ because they are opposite angles.

Therefore, $m\angle ECD = 80°$.

17. The correct answer is 6. First, solve for x by multiplying the second equation by 2 so that the coefficient of y will be 4, the additive inverse (the opposite) of the y coefficient in the first equation. Add the two equations to eliminate y.

$$5x - 4y = 13$$
$$x + 2y = 4$$

$$5x - 4y = 13$$
$$\underline{2x + 4y = 8}$$
$$7x = 21$$
$$x = 3$$

Then, substitute $x = 3$ into the second equation to get the value of y:

$$3 + 2y = 4$$
$$2y = 1$$
$$y = \frac{1}{2}$$

Finally, substitute $x = 3$ and $y = \frac{1}{2}$ into $\frac{x}{y}$ to get the value of the ratio:

$$\frac{x}{y} = \frac{3}{\frac{1}{2}} = 6$$

18. The correct answer is 25. According to the graph, the trout population was 4,000 in the year 1980 and 3,000 in the year 2000. The decrease in number of fish is 1,000, whereas the initial trout population for the year 1980 was 4,000. So the percent decrease equals the ratio of the change in population to the original population. This relationship can be represented as $\frac{1,000}{4,000}$.

This ratio simplifies as $\frac{1}{4}$, or 25%.

19. The correct answer is 15. To begin:

$$f(p + 3) = 5(p + 3) + 12 = 5p + 15 + 12 = 5p + 27$$

Similarly:

$$f(p) = 5p + 12$$

Thus:

$$\begin{aligned} f(p + 3) - f(p) &= 5p + 27 - (5p + 12) \\ &= 5p + 27 - 5p - 12 \\ &= 15 \end{aligned}$$

20. The correct answer is 4. Solve for x:

$$\frac{9}{x - 2} + \frac{16}{x + 3} = 5$$
$$\left(\frac{9}{x - 2} + \frac{16}{x + 3}\right)(x - 2)(x + 3) = 5(x - 2)(x + 3)$$
$$9x + 27 + 16x - 32 = 5x^2 + 5x - 30$$
$$0 = 5x^2 - 20x - 25$$
$$0 = 5(x + 1)(x - 5)$$
$$x = -1 \text{ or } x = 5$$

To get the sum of the solutions, simply add -1 and 5:

$$-1 + 5 = 4$$

Part II

Section 4: Math Test—CALCULATOR 🖩

1. C	**9.** B	**17.** D	**25.** A	**33.** 45
2. D	**10.** B	**18.** B	**26.** D	**34.** 41
3. D	**11.** B	**19.** A	**27.** D	**35.** 5400
4. A	**12.** D	**20.** A	**28.** A	**36.** 440
5. A	**13.** C	**21.** D	**29.** B	**37.** 21.5
6. C	**14.** D	**22.** B	**30.** B	**38.** 4
7. B	**15.** C	**23.** C	**31.** 5	
8. D	**16.** B	**24.** A	**32.** 9	

MATH TEST—CALCULATOR RAW SCORE ☐
(Number of correct answers)

1. **The correct answer is C.** 15% of $12.50 is (0.15)($12.50) = $1.875. So the discount for every 10 audio singles purchased is $1.875. Multiply this by 4 to get the savings when purchasing 40 audio singles:

$$4(\$1.875) = \$7.50$$

2. **The correct answer is D.** When measuring length, 1 yard = 3 feet. When measuring area, 1 square yard = 9 square feet. So 20 square yards = 180 square feet. At $1.30 per square foot, it will cost 180 × $1.30 = $234.

3. **The correct answer is D.** Let x represent the score of one of the two games in which he scored identically. Then, the score of the third game is $x + 20$. Since the average of all six games is 182, solve the following equation for x:

$$\frac{212 + 181 + 160 + x + x + (x + 20)}{6} = 182$$
$$\frac{573 + 3x}{6} = 182$$
$$573 + 3x = 1,092$$
$$3x = 519$$
$$x = 173$$

So his six scores were 160, 173, 173, 181, 193, and 212. Therefore, the second highest score is 193.

4. **The correct answer is A.** The volume of the fish tank is 11(14)(9) = 1,386 cubic inches. The amount needed to fill the tank is 1,386 ÷ 231 = 6 gallons.

5. **The correct answer is A.** The amount of protein in m cups of milk is $8m$ grams, and the amount of protein in n eggs is $6n$ grams. The problem asks for the amount to meet *or* exceed the recommended daily intake, which sets up a greater-than-or-equal-to scenario.

6. **The correct answer is C.** The total charge that Amy will pay is the daily rate, the mileage rate, and the 7.5% tax on both. If Amy drove x miles, then the total charge is $(19.99 + 0.15x) + 0.075(19.99 + 0.15x)$, which can be rewritten as $1.075(19.99 + 0.15x)$.

7. **The correct answer is B.** $5\frac{1}{2}$ dozen nails are bought for $5\frac{1}{2}$ dozen × 35 cents per dozen = 192.5 cents. There are 66 nails in $5\frac{1}{2}$ dozen and 66 ÷ 3 = 22 sets sold at 10 cents per set, so 22 sets × 10 cents per set = 220 cents. The profit is 220 − 192.5 = $27\frac{1}{2}$ cents.

8. **The correct answer is D.** The weights are proportional to the volumes, and the volumes vary as the cubes of their linear dimensions. If the edges are doubled, the volume

becomes $2^3 = 8$ times as large (see the figure). Therefore, the weight is $8 \times 150 = 1,200$ pounds.

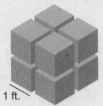

1 ft.

9. **The correct answer is B.**

$$-2(1-x)^2 + 2(1-x^2) = -2(1-2x+x^2) + 2(1-x^2)$$
$$= -2 + 4x - 2x^2 + 2 - 2x^2$$
$$= -4x^2 + 4x$$

10. **The correct answer is B.** One method of finding the correct answer is to create an inequality. The income from the sign-up fees for x people is $20x$. For the organization to profit, $20x$ must be greater than the cost of x T-shirts. Therefore, $20x > 7x + 60$ can be used to model the situation. Solving this inequality yields $x > 4.6$. Since there can't be 4.6 people, round the answer up to 5.

11. **The correct answer is B.** The total number of students, $x + y$, is equal to 2,180, so the answer must be choice B or choice C. The male students raised $20 each, and the female students raised $25 each. Since x represents the number of male students, then the amount the male students raised is represented by $20x$, and the amount the female students raised is represented by $25y$. The total amount raised is $50,000, so the sum is $20x + 25y = 50,000$. That leaves choice B as the only correct answer.

12. **The correct answer is D.** The cube root of an expression is equal to that expression raised to the $\frac{1}{3}$ power, so

$$\sqrt[3]{9x^3y^5z^6} = \left(9x^3y^5z^6\right)^{\frac{1}{3}}$$
$$= 9^{\frac{1}{3}}xy^{\frac{5}{3}}z^2$$

13. **The correct answer is C.** The two intersections of the graphs of the equations are at the points (0, 1) and (−1, 0). Substituting 0 for x and 1 for y makes both equations true. Also, substituting −1 for x and 0 for y makes both equations true.

14. **The correct answer is D.** Find the solution to this problem by using the structure of the given equation. Multiplying both sides of the equation $\frac{x}{3} - \frac{y}{4} = 5$ by 24 will clear fractions from the equation and yield $8x - 6y = 120$.

15. **The correct answer is C.** If x is the number of lunches sold and y is the number of dinners sold, then $x + y$ represents the number of meals sold during the weekend. The equation $7.5x + 12y$ represents the total amount collected in the weekend. Therefore, the correct system of equations is $x + y = 241$ and $7.5x + 12y = 2,523$.

16. **The correct answer is B.** The scatterplot shows a strong correlation between the variables. As the years increase, the population also increases.

17. **The correct answer is D.** The points on the graph display a pattern of exponential growth, as a rapidly upward-turning curve could be used to connect them; therefore, an exponential curve would best represent the data.

18. **The correct answer is B.** The graduate starts at x dollars per week. After the pay cut, the graduate receives 90% of the original salary. The 10% raise adds 9% to the salary (10% of 90%), so the new salary is $0.99x$.

19. **The correct answer is A.** The solution set is as follows. Note that it extends into all quadrants except the third.

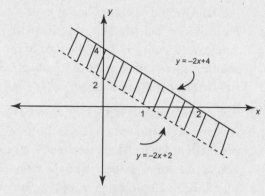

$y = -2x+4$

$y = -2x+2$

20. The correct answer is A.

$$\frac{(1-2i)^2}{2}$$

$$=\frac{1-2i-2i+4i^2}{2}$$

$$=\frac{1-4i+4i^2}{2}$$

$$=\frac{1-4i+4(-1)}{2}$$

$$=\frac{1-4i-4}{2}$$

$$=\frac{-3-4i}{2}$$

$$=-\frac{3}{2}-2i$$

$$=-\frac{3}{2}+(-2)i$$

Hence, $b=-2$.

21. The correct answer is D. If the discount is 10%, then $12.60 is 90% of $14.

22. The correct answer is B. To solve for the number of gallons of white vinegar, set up a proportion.

$$\frac{1\frac{1}{3}}{2}=\frac{x}{7}$$

$$2x=\frac{28}{3}$$

$$x=4\frac{4}{6}=4\frac{2}{3}$$

23. The correct answer is C. When adding complex numbers, we add the real parts of each number and the imaginary parts separately.

$$(1.26+4.52i)+(-0.89+xi)$$
$$=(1.26+(-0.89))+(4.52+x)i$$

We are given that this sum equals $0.37 + 7.4i$. So we know that $(4.52 + x)$, or the coefficient of i, equals 7.4. (We can disregard the real number part of the sum.) We can write:

$$4.52 + x = 7.4$$

Solving for x gives:

$$x = 7.4 - 4.52$$
$$x = 2.88$$

24. The correct answer is A. Because the function f has $(x - 4)$ and $(x + 2)$ as factors, the function should have zeros when $x - 4 = 0$ and $x + 2 = 0$. The only graph that shows a curve that has x-intercepts at -2 and 4 is choice A.

25. The correct answer is A. There are a total of $8 + 23 + 19 = 50$ people in Group A, and 8 of them have no living siblings. So the probability is:

$$\frac{8}{50}=\frac{4}{25}$$

26. The correct answer is D. When $t = 0$, the height of the ball is 0.02 meters, so 0.02 represents the height of the ball before it is hit.

27. The correct answer is D. If k is a positive constant other than 1, then the equation $kx + y = c$ can be rewritten as $y = -kx + c$. If k is positive, then $-k$ is negative, and it must be something other than -1. The only graph with a negative slope other than -1 is choice D.

28. The correct answer is A. If the machine loses 15% of its value each year, then each year its value is 85% of what it was the year before. Therefore, the value of the machine can be modeled by $V(x) = 80,000 \times (0.85)^x$, where $x =$ the number of years since the machine was purchased. After 4 years, its value is $80,000 \times (0.85)^4 = \$41,760.50$.

29. **The correct answer is B.** To find the current average, add all the medals and divide by 6:

$$\frac{12+13+31+25+37+28}{6} = \frac{146}{6}$$
$$= 24.3$$
$$\approx 24$$

The new average has to be one more than that, or 25.3. However, it will be spread over seven Winter Olympics:

$$\frac{12+13+31+25+37+28+x}{7} = \frac{146+x}{7} = 25.3$$
$$146 + x = 177.1$$
$$x = 31.1$$

30. **The correct answer is B.** Simplify the ratio by factoring out the greatest common factor (2). The result is $\frac{3x}{x+2}$. Set $\frac{3x}{x+2} = 3 + \frac{A}{x+2}$ and solve.

$$3x = 3(x+2) + A$$
$$3x = 3x + 6 + A$$
$$A = -6$$

31. **The correct answer is 5.** Expand the left side and then equate corresponding coefficients:

$$(ax-1) \cdot (2x+b) = 4x^2 + 4x - 3$$
$$2ax^2 - 2x + abx - b = 4x^2 + 4x - 3$$
$$2ax^2 + (ab-2)x - b = 4x^2 + 4x - 3$$

So:

$$2a = 4 \quad ab - 2 = 4 \quad -b = -3$$

Which means $a = 2$ and $b = 3$.
Therefore, $a + b = 5$.

32. **The correct answer is 9.** Since Derek must buy at least two of each item, first determine the cost of buying exactly 2 of each:

$$2(\$4.00 + \$3.75 + \$1.50) = \$18.50$$

Now, subtract that from $50:

$$\$50 - \$18.50 = \$31.50$$

Divide this difference by the cost of a pint of berries ($4.00) to get 7.875.

So Derek would be able to buy at most 7 more pints of berries. This, together with the 2 pints we accounted for at the start of the solution, gives a maximum of 9 pints of berries that he could purchase.

33. **The correct answer is 45.** Letting m be the time per regular question, $2m$ is the time per math problem. The total time for all the regular questions is 300m, and the total time for all the math problems is 50(2m). Since the exam is 3 hours, or 180 minutes:

$$300m + 100m = 180 \text{ minutes}$$
$$400m = 180$$
$$m = \frac{180}{400} = \frac{9}{20}$$

The time to do a math problem is:

$$2\left(\frac{9}{20}\right) = \frac{9}{10}$$

All 50 math problems can be done in $50\left(\frac{9}{10}\right) = 45$ minutes.

34. **The correct answer is 41.** The number of games that the Montreal Canadiens played is not provided, but it is given that the ratio of the number of games played in the 1947–48 season to that in the 1924–25 season is 2:1. Problems like this can be solved by plugging in real numbers. Let's say that there were 100 games in the 1924–25 season, so they won 57 of those games. In the 1947–48 season, there were twice as many games, or 200 games, so they won 33% of 200 games, or 66 games. Altogether they won 123 out of 300 games, and this fraction can be simplified to 41 out of 100, or 41%.

35. **The correct answer is 5400.** Of the number of voters polled, 400 of 625, or 64%, were in favor of the measure. If the margin of error is 4%, the likely population proportion will be between 60% and 68%:

60% of 9,000 total voters is (0.6)(9,000) = 5,400.

36. **The correct answer is 440.** If the dolphin weighs 110% of the average, it weighs 10% more than the average weight of 400 pounds, or $0.10 \times 400 = 40$ pounds. The dolphin weighs $400 + 40 = 440$ pounds.

37. **The correct answer is 21.5.** First, combine the equations by subtracting $(x + y = 13)$ from $(3x + y = -4)$:

$$3x + y = -4$$
$$\underline{-(x + y = 13)}$$
$$2x = -17$$
$$x = -8.5$$

Then solve for x and substitute into one of the equations to solve for y:

$$-8.5 + y = 13$$
$$y = 21.5$$

38. **The correct answer is 4.** In general, a system of equations that has no solution takes this form, where a, b, m, and n are constants:

$$ax + by = m$$
$$ax + by = n$$

To rewrite the given system in this form, we must multiply $-3x + 2y = -1$ by some factor so that the coefficient of x will be 6, making it equal to the coefficient in the second equation. That factor is -2. When we multiply the first equation by -2, the given system becomes this equivalent system:

$$6x - 4y = 2$$
$$6x - by = 8$$

Now the coefficients are equal, and the y coefficients would be equal if $b = 4$. So if $b = 4$, then the system has no solution.

Answers | Diagnostic Test

Section 5: Essay

Analysis of Passage

The following is an analysis of the passage by Peter Krapp, noting how the writer used evidence, reasoning, and stylistic or persuasive elements to support his claims, connect the claims and evidence, and add power to the ideas he expressed. Check to see if you evaluated the passage in a similar way.

1. Pennsylvania State University's College of Engineering took its computer network offline on May 15 after disclosing two cyberattacks. The perpetrators were able to access information on 18,000 students, who are being contacted this week with the news that their personal identifying information is in hackers' hands. Three days later, the computer network is back online, with new protections for its users.

   1. *The writer cites a specific example of a computer security breach and uses facts and statistics to show the seriousness of the problem.*

2. One of the two attacks is ascribed by a forensic cybersecurity corporation retained by Penn State to computers apparently based in China.

   2. *By mentioning that the computer hackers appear to be located in China, the writer underscores the global risks of the security breach.*

3. As a researcher who has published on hacking and hacktivism and serves on the board of the UC Irvine data science initiative, I believe two aspects of this news story deserve particular attention.

   3. *The writer establishes his credentials to write about and offer an argument on this topic.*

COMPROMISING STUDENT DATA

4. Penn State announced last week that the FBI alerted it on November 21, 2014, about an attack with custom malware that started as early as September 2012.

   4. *The writer uses facts and dates to lay the groundwork for the point he is about to make.*

5. Why did it take so long for Penn State to disclose the breach, despite the fact that the experience of large-scale hacks in 2013 and 2014 (against Target, Home Depot, and others) clearly demonstrated an urgent need for quick and full disclosure—both to help the victims and to preserve a modicum of trust?

   5. *The writer poses a rhetorical question to address one aspect of this story that he earlier said deserves "particular attention." His first point is that Penn State took too long to disclose the security breach. He cites two past breaches to support his argument about the need for quick disclosure and uses evocative words ("help the victims and to preserve a modicum of trust") to emphasize how important early disclosure is.*

Part II

Diagnostic Test

6 Penn State stated only that any disclosure would have tipped off the perpetrators before their access to the College of Engineering computers could be cut off.

6 *The writer states Penn State's justification for delaying disclosure. He uses the word* only *to imply that Penn State should have been more forthcoming, thus strengthening his own position. At the same time, he presents himself as reasonable because he offers Penn State's argument before going on with his own.*

7 Meanwhile, student data may have been compromised for at least six months, maybe longer.

7 *The writer shows why, in his opinion, Penn State's position is weak.*

8 Another conspicuous problem with public discussion of events like this is, in fact, the lack of distinction often made in the media between actual appropriation of data (as at Penn State) and mere temporary disabling or defacement of websites (as happened to Rutgers University last month). That is like being unable to make a difference between a grand theft auto and keying a car. The question is, what can universities do to limit the risk to their students?

8 *The writer now addresses the second point that he feels "deserve[s] particular attention" — The media do not treat breaches like the one at Penn State seriously, often viewing them more like nuisance problems. He supports his view that the media should be able to make a distinction between serious and non-serious security breaches by juxtaposing a significant crime (grand theft auto) with a minor infraction (keying a car).*

9 The exposure of student data in higher education is not limited to Social Security numbers or email passwords. Information collected and retained by educational institutions includes full name, address, phone number, credit and debit card information, workplace information, date of birth, personal interests and of course academic performance and grade information.

9 *The writer shows how dangerous these kinds of security breaches are, using specific examples of the kinds of information that can fall into hackers' hands.*

10 A survey conducted by the Obama administration collected responses from 24,092 individuals on how much they trusted various institutions to keep their data safe. There was a high level of concern around transparency and legal standards. (https://www.whitehouse.gov/issues/technology/big-data-review)

…

10 *The writer strengthens his viewpoint by providing statistical evidence in the form of a survey that reveals how concerned people are about the safety of their personal data.*

Answers | Diagnostic Test

11 President Obama only recently called for laws covering data hacking and student privacy. "We're saying that data collected on students in the classroom should only be used for educational purposes," he stated in his speech to the Federal Trade Commission (FTC) earlier this year.

11 *The writer supports his argument by quoting an authority no less than the president of the United States. (He also makes the point that he believes the president's concern is overdue, by saying this statement was made "only recently.")*

DATA PRIVACY CONCERNS

12 If students' right to privacy needs to be protected from the specter of foreign intelligence agencies poking around the Penn State Engineering School, then by the same logic it should be protected also against data-mining by for-profit actors right here in the US.

12 *The writer underscores the depth of the problem by pointing out that there are many entities that might access students' computer data: not only foreign intelligence agencies (as was the case with the Penn State breach), but US companies that mine computer data for profit. The writer argues that just as foreign breaches have been recognized as serious, so should domestic for-profit breaches.*

13 Until May 2014, Google, for instance, routinely mined its apps for education services for advertising and monetizing purposes. When *Education Week* reported that Google was mining student emails, it quickly led not only to lawsuits but also to landmark legislation.

13 *The writer offers a specific example of a US company mining personal data for profit to strengthen his case.*

14 The California Senate Bill 1177 was enacted to prevent educational services from selling student information or mining it for advertising purposes.

14 *The writer underscores the validity of his argument by citing legislation enacted to address the problem.*

15 Yet, almost a year later, students in California remain just as concerned about their data privacy as before—since the new state law was watered down to apply only to K–12 and not to higher education.

15 *The writer points out that the final form of the legislation to protect students' data does not extend to college students.*

16 And when it was disclosed earlier this spring that education publisher Pearson secretly monitored social media to discern references to their content, the legislative response was one that, according to the Electronic Privacy Information Center (EPIC) in Washington, DC, "fails to uphold President

16 *The writer reinforces his argument that not enough is being done to protect college students' personal data by citing another example of a US company data-mining for profit. He also quotes an authoritative source to support this claim.*

Part II

Obama's promise that the data collected in an educational context can be used only for educational purposes."

17 Students in higher education nationwide are still in a position where they cannot opt out of the computer services of their learning institutions, and so they have no expectation of privacy.

17 *The writer points out a reality that makes and keeps college students vulnerable: "they cannot opt out of the computer services of their learning institutions."*

18 Despite President Obama's promises for safeguarding the privacy of consumers and families, and despite the fact that a number of technology companies concerned with growing consumer distrust recently signed a pledge to safeguard student privacy, neither Google nor Apple signed on.

18 *The writer underscores college students' vulnerability by pointing out that two major companies (Google and Apple) have refused to sign a pledge to safeguard student privacy.*

19 The President's Council of Advisors on Science and Technology (PCAST) was tasked to examine current and likely future capabilities of key technologies, both those associated with the collection, analysis, and use of big data and those that can help to preserve privacy, resulting in a direct recommendation to strengthen US research in privacy-related technologies.

19 *The writer points out that an advisory board to the US president has recommended strengthening research on the problem.*

20 And overwhelmingly, respondents to a White House survey recently expressed severe reservations about the collection, storage, and security and use of private information.

20 *The writer cites a White House survey that reflected "severe reservations about the collection, storage, and security and use of private information." The survey shows that despite the measures that have been put in place, the public still feels its data is at risk.*

21 Maybe it is time for higher education to heed those signals.

21 *The writer concludes his argument by saying it's time for colleges (where people are particularly vulnerable) to pay attention to—and act on—the information they have, in order to remedy the situation.*

Scoring Rubric

Use the following scoring rubric as a guide to help you evaluate the sample essays that follow. Then, read and evaluate your own essay for each scoring category. Assign your essay a score between 1 and 4 for each category (Reading, Analysis, and Writing). Next, double each score to simulate that the essay was scored twice. You will now have three scores ranging from 2 to 8 for each category. These are not combined.

Score Point	Reading	Analysis	Writing
4 (Advanced)	The essay shows a comprehensive understanding of the source text, including the author's key claims, use of details and evidence, and the relationship between the two.	The essay offers an "insightful" and in-depth evaluation of the author's use of evidence and stylistic or persuasive features in building an argument. Supporting details and evidence are relevant and focus on those details that address the task.	The essay includes all of the features of a strong essay, including a precise central claim, body paragraphs, and a strong conclusion. There is a variety of sentence structures used in the essay, and it is virtually free of all convention errors.
3 (Proficient)	The essay shows an appropriate understanding of the source text, including the author's key claims and use of details in developing an argument.	The essay offers an "effective" evaluation of the author's use of evidence and stylistic or persuasive features in building an argument. Supporting details and evidence are appropriate and focus on those details that address the task.	The essay includes all of the features of an effective essay, including a precise central claim, body paragraphs, and a strong conclusion. There is a variety of sentence structures used in the essay, and it is free of significant convention errors.
2 (Partial)	The essay shows some understanding of the source text, including the author's key claims, but uses limited textual evidence and/or unimportant details.	The essay offers limited evaluation of the author's use of evidence and stylistic or persuasive features in building an argument. Supporting details and evidence are lacking and/or are not relevant to the task.	The essay does not provide a precise central claim, nor does it provide an effective introduction, body paragraphs, and conclusion. There is little variety of sentence structure used in the essay, and there are numerous errors in grammar and conventions.
1 (Inadequate)	The essay demonstrates little or no understanding of the source text or the author's use of key claims.	The essay offers no clear evaluation of the author's use of evidence and stylistic or persuasive features in building an argument. Supporting details and evidence are nonexistent or irrelevant to the task.	The essay lacks any form of cohesion or structure. There is little variety of sentence structures, and significant errors in convention make it difficult to read.

Part II

Sample Essays

The following are examples of a high-scoring and low-scoring essay, based on the passage by Peter Krapp.

High-Scoring Essay

The digital age has created incredible opportunities for every part of society but has also endangered one of our most valuable possessions—personal information—for some of our most vulnerable people—students. The villains of this story are not relegated to criminals and foreign agents but can be found just as commonly among the ranks of educational institutions and American companies. Peter Krapp, in his article "Penn State Hack Exposes Theft Risk of Student Personal Data," builds a well-structured argument emphasizing the urgent need for colleges to protect student data. Krapp strengthens his argument with effective claims to authority, precise rhetorical questioning, and keen contrast and dissections of existing laws and perspectives in order to reveal serious contradictions in policy and public and media opinions, revealing that student data is less safe than even previously thought.

Early on, Krapp begins his campaign of persuasion by establishing his ability to speak authoritatively to the issue of student data abuse. In the third paragraph, Krapp labels himself as not only a published researcher on the core issues of "hacking" (one facet of the student data quagmire) but also as a board member of a higher-ed environment, UC Irvine's data science initiative. His titles imply knowledge not only of the criminal aspects of online data privacy but also the societal concern with how citizen data is mined and used. This initial assertion of expertise allows Krapp to span the two sides of improper student data usage—a lack of rigor for protection from outside parties and improper use within institutions.

With such credentials before the audience, Krapp's launches rhetorical questions that resound loudly in the reader's mind. When he inquires as to why Penn State's disclosure of the data breach happened so long after the initial incident, the reader is assured that the delay was indeed unreasonable, rather than being a judgment from a naïve bystander unfamiliar with forensic cybersecurity. His authority allows Krapp to transition to the second half of his argument dealing with the abuse of student data (and trust) by large corporations. For Krapp to criticize some of the world's most ubiquitous companies, Apple and Google, he must offer competing authority to sway his readers.

As the passage indicates, it's easy for the public and media to gauge attacks on personal data as a solely criminal enterprise, but Krapp widens the scope of the problem by including far more surprising faces in the suspect lineup: Pearson, Apple, and Google. The selection of these companies, from all of those likely involved in the abuse of personal data, rouses the audience's attention. When companies like Apple and Google are accused of malfeasance, Krapp subverts common attitudes about data abusers and elevates the scale of the student data problem. Such a revelation is echoed by the essay structure. At the beginning of the essay, Krapp cites the theft of student data from 18,000 individuals. Krapp later returns to the victims towards the end of the essay with the White House survey data, implying significant concern among effected populations for how data is gathered—posing data abuse as a national issue well beyond the confines of Penn State's College of Engineering. Without the repeated contrast, the Penn State attack set against for-profit activities, and speaking to how students "cannot opt out of" school data policies, the audience might fail to see that students' privacy is under attack on all fronts.

Krapp creates a compelling argument with some precise rhetorical choices, choosing to build his authority early on so that he can incisively overcome common defenses of data mishandling, posing key rhetorical questions, and by laying out common misperceptions of data abuse. In effect, Krapp spreads the news that data abuse stretches far beyond foreign networks and has invaded our digital backyard.

Low-Scoring Essay

Peter Krapp tries to persuade us that students should be allowed to opt out of giving their data to colleges and companies. This would protect them from having their full name, address, phone number, credit and debit card information, workplace information, date of birth, personal interests and of course academic performance and grade information stolen by people like Chinese hackers and companies like Google and Pearson.

Peter Krapp persuades us by giving lots of examples of data being stolen, like Pennsylvania State University's College of Engineering, Target, Home Depot, Google, and Pearson. One of the examples includes a chart that shows how much 24,092 individuals trusted various institutions to keep their data safe. Most of them didn't think their data was safe.

All of this information, charts, and examples that Peter Krapp included in his essay is very convincing. I think we should pass some laws like Peter Krapp suggested. The laws would keep American companies from stealing our data and punish hackers from other countries who steal our data.

All college students should try to opt out of giving away all of their private information because we know the colleges won't protect it. The colleges actually tell students to use apps that they know companies steal data from. This makes college students more vulnerable than anyone else to losing their data.

If companies are going to use the data they take from students, they should pay the students for the data. Then, students might not mind so much if companies take their data because the students would make money from it and college is very expensive.

When I go to college, I will opt out of giving my data to colleges and companies. My information is important to me and I don't want it stolen from me.

COMPUTING YOUR SCORES

Now that you've completed this diagnostic test, it's time to compute your scores. Simply follow the instructions on the following pages, and use the conversion tables provided to calculate your scores. The formulas provided will give you as close an approximation as possible of how you might score on the actual SAT exam.

To Determine Your Practice Test Scores

1. After you go through each of the test sections (Reading, Writing and Language, Math—No Calculator, and Math—Calculator) and determine which questions you answered correctly, be sure to enter the number of correct answers in the box below the answer key for each of the sections.

2. Your total score on the practice test is the sum of your Evidence-Based Reading and Writing Section score and your Math Section score. To get your total score, convert the raw score—the number of questions you answered correctly in a particular section—into the "scaled score" for that section, and then calculate the total score. It sounds a little confusing, but we'll take you through the steps.

To Calculate Your Evidence-Based Reading and Writing Section Score

Your Evidence-Based Reading and Writing Section score is on a scale of 200–800. First determine your Reading Test score, and then determine your score on the Writing and Language Test.

1. Count the number of correct answers you got on the **Section 1: Reading Test**. Remember that there is no penalty for wrong answers. **The number of correct answers is your raw score.**

2. Go to **Raw Score Conversion Table 1: Section and Test Scores** on page 135. Look in the "Raw Score" column for your raw score, and match it to the number in the "Reading Test Score" column.

3. Do the same with **Section 2: Writing and Language Test** to determine that score.

4. Add your Reading Test score to your Writing and Language Test score.

5. Multiply that number by 10. This is your Evidence-Based Reading and Writing Section score.

To Calculate Your Math Section Score

Your Math score is also on a scale of 200–800.

1. Count the number of correct answers you got on the **Section 3: Math Test—No Calculator** and the **Section 4: Math Test—Calculator**. Again, there is no penalty for wrong answers. **The number of correct answers is your raw score.**

2. Add the number of correct answers on the Section 3: Math Test—No Calculator and the Section 4: Math Test—Calculator.

3. Use the **Raw Score Conversion Table 1: Section and Test Scores** on page 135 and convert your raw score into your Math Section score.

To Obtain Your Total Score

Add your score on the Evidence-Based Reading and Writing Section to the Math Section score. This is your total score on this SAT Diagnostic Practice Test, on a scale of 400–1600.

Subscores Provide Additional Information

Subscores offer you greater details about your strengths in certain areas within literacy and math. The subscores are reported on a scale of 1–15 and include Heart of Algebra, Problem Solving and Data Analysis, Passport to Advanced Math, Expression of Ideas, Standard English Conventions, Words in Context, and Command of Evidence.

Heart of Algebra

The **Heart of Algebra subscore** is based on questions from the **Math Test** that focus on linear equations and inequalities.

- Add up your total correct answers from these questions:
  - Math Test—No Calculator: Questions 1–3, 6, 9, 11, 17, 18
  - Math Test—Calculator: Questions 5, 6, 10, 11, 14, 15, 19, 27, 29, 37, 38
- Your Raw Score = the total number of correct answers from all of these questions
- Use the **Raw Score Conversion Table 2: Subscores** on page 137 to determine your **Heart of Algebra** subscore.

Problem Solving and Data Analysis

The **Problem Solving and Data Analysis subscore** is based on questions from the **Math Test** that focus on quantitative reasoning, the interpretation and synthesis of data, and solving problems in rich and varied contexts.

- Add up your total correct answers from these questions:

  o Math Test—No Calculator: None

  o Math Test—Calculator: Questions 1–3, 7, 8, 16–18, 21, 22, 25, 28, 32–36

- Your Raw Score = the total number of correct answers from all of these questions

- Use the **Raw Score Conversion Table 2: Subscores** on page 137 to determine your **Problem Solving and Data Analysis** subscore.

Passport to Advanced Math

The **Passport to Advanced Math subscore** is based on questions from the **Math Test** that focus on topics central to your ability to progress to more advanced math, such as understanding the structure of expressions, reasoning with more complex equations, and interpreting and building functions.

- Add up your total correct answers from these questions:

  o Math Test—No Calculator: Questions 7, 8, 10, 12–15, 19, 20

  o Math Test—Calculator: Questions 9, 12, 13, 24, 26, 30, 31

- Your Raw Score = the total number of correct answers from all of these questions

- Use the **Raw Score Conversion Table 2: Subscores** on page 137 to determine your **Passport to Advanced Math** subscore.

Expression of Ideas

The **Expression of Ideas subscore** is based on questions from the **Writing and Language Test** that focus on topic development, organization, and rhetorically effective use of language.

- Add up your total correct answers from these questions in Section 2: Writing and Language Test:

  o Questions 1, 4, 5, 7–9, 12, 13, 16, 17, 19, 20, 23, 26, 28, 29, 32–35, 39, 41–43

- Your Raw Score = the total number of correct answers from all of these questions

- Use the **Raw Score Conversion Table 2: Subscores** on page 137 to determine your **Expression of Ideas** subscore.

Standard English Conventions

The **Standard English Conventions subscore** is based on questions from the **Writing and Language Test** that focus on sentence structure, usage, and punctuation.

- Add up your total correct answers from these questions in Section 2: Writing and Language Test:

  o Questions 2, 3, 6, 10, 11, 14, 15, 18, 21, 22, 24, 25, 27, 30, 31, 36–38, 40, 44

- Your Raw Score = the total number of correct answers from all of these questions

- Use the **Raw Score Conversion Table 2: Subscores** on page 137 to determine your **Standard English Conventions** subscore.

Words in Context

The **Words in Context subscore** is based on questions from the **Reading Test** and the **Writing and Language Test** that address word/phrase meaning in context and rhetorical word choice.

- Add up your total correct answers from these questions in Sections 1 and 2:

  - Reading Test: Questions 6, 7, 14, 18, 27, 29, 32, 38, 48, 52
  - Writing and Language Test: Questions 5, 8, 12, 17, 28, 32, 35, 43

- Your Raw Score = the total number of correct answers from all of these questions
- Use the **Raw Score Conversion Table 2: Subscores** on page 137 to determine your **Words in Context** subscore.

Command of Evidence

The **Command of Evidence subscore** is based on questions from the **Reading Test** and the **Writing and Language Test** that ask you to interpret and use evidence found in a wide range of passages and informational graphics, such as graphs, tables, and charts.

- Add up your total correct answers from these questions in Sections 1 and 2:

  - Reading Test: Questions 3, 4, 17, 20, 22, 24, 33, 34, 44, 46
  - Writing and Language Test: Questions 1, 4, 13, 16, 29, 33, 34, 42

- Your Raw Score = the total number of correct answers from all of these questions
- Use the **Raw Score Conversion Table 2: Subscores** on page 137 to determine your **Command of Evidence** subscore.

Cross-Test Scores

The SAT exam also reports two cross-test scores: Analysis in History/Social Studies and Analysis in Science. These scores are based on questions in the Reading Test, Writing and Language Test, and both Math Tests that ask you to think analytically about texts and questions in these subject areas. Cross-test scores are reported on a scale of 10–40.

Analysis in History/Social Studies

- Add up your total correct answers from these questions:

  - Reading Test: Questions 11–20, 32–42
  - Writing and Language Test: Questions 12, 13, 16, 17, 19, 20
  - Math Test—No Calculator: Question 14
  - Math Test—Calculator: Questions 11, 16, 17, 25, 29, 34, 35

- Your Raw Score = the total number of correct answers from all of these questions
- Use the **Raw Score Conversion Table 3: Cross-Test Scores** on page 139 to determine your **Analysis in History/Social Studies** cross-test score.

Analysis in Science

- Add up your total correct answers from these sections:
- Reading Test: Questions 21–31, 43–52
- Writing and Language Test: Questions 23, 26, 28, 29, 32, 33

    o Math Test—No Calculator: Questions 2, 13
    o Math Test—Calculator: Questions 4, 5, 8, 22, 26, 36

- Your Raw Score = the total number of correct answers from all of these questions
- Use the **Raw Score Conversion Table 3: Cross-Test Scores** on page 139 to determine your **Analysis in Science** cross-test score.

Diagnostic Test

Raw Score Conversion Table 1: Section and Test Scores

Raw Score	Math Section Score	Reading Test Score	Writing and Language Test Score
0	200	10	10
1	200	10	10
2	210	10	10
3	230	11	10
4	240	12	11
5	260	13	12
6	280	14	13
7	290	15	13
8	310	15	14
9	320	16	15
10	330	17	16
11	340	17	16
12	360	18	17
13	370	19	18
14	380	19	19
15	390	20	19
16	410	20	20
17	420	21	21
18	430	21	21
19	440	22	22

Raw Score	Math Section Score	Reading Test Score	Writing and Language Test Score
20	450	22	23
21	460	23	23
22	470	23	24
23	480	24	25
24	480	24	25
25	490	25	26
26	500	25	26
27	510	26	27
28	520	26	28
29	520	27	28
30	530	28	29
31	540	28	30
32	550	29	30
33	560	29	31
34	560	30	32
35	570	30	32
36	580	31	33
37	590	31	34
38	600	32	34
39	600	32	35

Raw Score	Math Section Score	Reading Test Score	Writing and Language Test Score
40	610	33	36
41	620	33	37
42	630	34	38
43	640	35	39
44	650	35	40
45	660	36	
46	670	37	
47	670	37	
48	680	38	
49	690	38	
50	700	39	
51	710	40	
52	730	40	
53	740		
54	750		
55	760		
56	780		
57	790		
58	800		

Answers | Diagnostic Test

Conversion Equation 1: Section and Test Scores

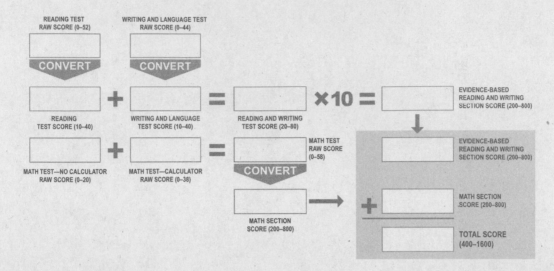

Raw Score Conversion Table 2: Subscores

Raw Score (# of correct answers)	Expression of Ideas	Standard English Conventions	Heart of Algebra	Problem Solving and Data Analysis	Passport to Advanced Math	Words in Context	Command of Evidence
0	1	1	1	1	1	1	1
1	1	1	1	1	3	1	1
2	1	1	2	2	5	2	2
3	2	2	3	3	6	3	3
4	3	2	4	4	7	4	4
5	4	3	5	5	8	5	5
6	5	4	6	6	9	6	6
7	6	5	6	7	10	6	7
8	6	6	7	8	11	7	8
9	7	6	8	8	11	8	8
10	7	7	8	9	12	8	9
11	8	7	9	10	12	9	10
12	8	8	9	10	13	9	10
13	9	8	9	11	13	10	11
14	9	9	10	12	14	11	12
15	10	10	10	13	14	12	13
16	10	10	11	14	15	13	14
17	11	11	12	15		14	15
18	11	12	13			15	15
19	12	13	15				
20	12	15					
21	13						
22	14						
23	14						
24	15						

Conversion Equation 2: Subscores

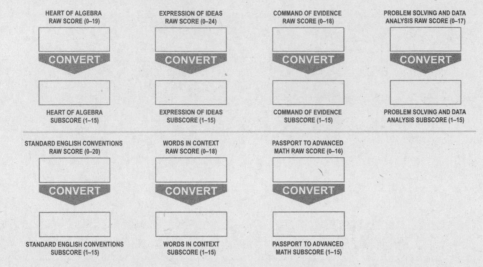

Raw Score Conversion Table 3: Cross-Test Scores

Raw Score (# of correct answers)	Analysis in History/ Social Studies Cross-Test Score	Analysis in Science Cross-Test Score	Raw Score (# of correct answers)	Analysis in History/ Social Studies Cross-Test Score	Analysis in Science Cross-Test Score
0	10	10	24	32	30
1	10	11	25	33	31
2	11	12	26	34	32
3	12	13	27	35	33
4	14	14	28	35	33
5	15	15	29	36	34
6	16	16	30	37	35
7	17	17	31	38	36
8	18	18	32	38	37
9	20	19	33	39	38
10	21	20	34	40	39
11	22	20	35	40	40
12	23	21			
13	24	22			
14	25	23			
15	26	24			
16	27	24			
17	28	25			
18	28	26			
19	29	27			
20	30	27			
21	30	28			
22	31	29			
23	32	30			

Answers | Diagnostic Test

Conversion Equation 3: Cross-Test Scores

TEST	Analysis in History/Social Studies		Analysis in Science	
	QUESTIONS	RAW SCORE	QUESTIONS	RAW SCORE
Reading Test	11–20, 32–42		21–31, 43–52	
Writing and Language Test	12, 13, 16, 17, 19, 20		25, 26, 28, 29, 32, 33	
Math Test— No Calculator	14		2, 13	
Math Test— Calculator	11, 16, 17, 25, 29, 34, 35		4, 5, 8, 22, 26, 36	
TOTAL				

ANALYSIS IN HISTORY/
SOCIAL STUDIES
RAW SCORE (0–35)

CONVERT

ANALYSIS IN HISTORY/
SOCIAL STUDIES
CROSS-TEST SCORE (10–40)

ANALYSIS IN SCIENCE
RAW SCORE (0–35)

CONVERT

ANALYSIS IN SCIENCE
CROSS-TEST SCORE (10–40)

Diagnostic Test

PART III:
READING STRATEGIES FOR THE SAT® EXAM

Chapter 3: Reading Test Strategies

Reading Test Strategies

OVERVIEW

- **A Closer Look at the Reading Test**
- **Common Problems**
- **Overall Reading Strategies**
- **Basic Steps for Answering Reading Questions**
- **Tips for Taking the Reading Test**
- **Strategies for Answering Specific Question Types**
- **Summing It Up**
- **Practice Exercise**
- **Answer Key and Explanations**

A CLOSER LOOK AT THE READING TEST

The SAT Reading Test focuses on assessing reading comprehension and reasoning skills through responses to a variety of reading passages. The passages are chosen to reflect the complexity and reading levels appropriate to college and career readiness. The questions will require you to analyze the text and use textual evidence to assess meaning and support ideas. The test emphasizes understanding of overall concepts and their development, as well as the use of textual evidence to support your answers.

Passage topics are drawn from US and world literature, social science and historical documents, and scientific writing. There will be a total of five passages, four single passages and one set of paired passages, and a total of 52 questions. Each passage has 10 to 11 questions. The official practice tests provided by College Board (six of which were used as official tests) present the passages in the following order: literary narrative, history/social studies, science, social studies/history, and science (again). However, there is no guarantee that the passages will follow that order. The single passage lengths are between 500–750 words; the paired passage divides the 500–750-word length between the two passages. If you do a little math, you'll see that you have about 13 minutes per passage (to read and answer all questions).

The reading comprehension questions are designed to assess how well you read and understand information. The questions don't test the specifics you have learned in your course work. They are based solely on explicit and implicit information contained in the passage. At least one passage will be accompanied by an informational graphic from which one or more questions will be drawn. These questions require you to analyze the data presented in such formats as tables, graphs, and charts.

Passage and Question Format

Each passage and question set starts with a direction line that looks similar to the following:

Questions 1–10 are based on the following passage.

OR

Questions 1–10 are based on the following passage[s] and supplementary material.

OR

Questions 1–10 are based on the following two passages.

The direction line is followed by a brief introduction to the text. The introduction describes the origin of the passage, and sometimes it will include additional background information. The section presents passages in two columns with line numbering appearing every five lines. If graphs, tables, or charts are present, they will be located at the end of the passage.

The questions for each passage are in standard multiple choice format with four answer choices each. These questions ask you to do one of the following:

- Determine themes and central ideas as presented in the passage.
- Determine the purpose of the passage or the point of view of the text.
- Determine the function of language in the text.
- Select evidence that best supports the answer to a previous question or support an assertion as presented in a question.
- Select and support inferences, conclusions, or arguments with textual evidence.
- Identify explicit details from the passage.
- Interpret the text to label tone or mood of the passage.
- Determine the meaning of words and phrases in the context of the passage.
- Analyze information in an accompanying graphic, such as a table, graph, or chart.

COMMON PROBLEMS

It's important to understand the common problems students like you encounter in the Reading section. You'll need to analyze your performance for a variety of factors to determine which strategies could be vital additions to your toolbox. Often, you must work to overcome one or more of the following challenges:

- Time
  - Cannot read all passages and answer all questions
  - Spend too much time on difficult passages
  - Run out of time because of how you read the passage and answer questions

NOTE

Reading questions are not arranged in order of difficulty. The questions for each passage will generally begin with broader questions about the overall ideas in the text and will then focus on specific portions of the passage.

- Technique
  - Skip a passage's introductory information
  - Misunderstand the goals of specific question types
  - Lack a personalized passage order and reading technique
- Attention
  - Read passively
  - Don't read all choices before selecting an answer
  - Search for information inefficiently or in the wrong location

To perform well on the Reading test, you need to have a set of personal strategies to help you overcome your greatest problems. You may struggle with time, technique, attention, or maybe all three issues. It's important to understand that all three problems are connected, and improvement in one area can lead to success in others. Let's look at how we can address those common problems.

OVERALL READING STRATEGIES

The Reading section feels a little different for every student, but there are a few key decisions you can make to approach the section in the way that makes the most sense for you. As you practice, you'll want to experiment with the following steps:

1. Set a goal.
2. Decide your passage order.
3. Develop your personal reading technique.
4. Read actively.
5. Answer questions strategically.
6. Be certain in your answers.
7. Keep track of your time.

These seven strategies form the first steps you can take to work through the Reading section. Let's discuss them in greater detail.

Before the Test

1. **Set a goal:** If you're taking the time to prep for the test, you should have a goal in mind for your performance. You may want a score of 1260 or even a perfect 1600, but you should also be thinking specifically about how many questions you'll allow yourself to miss in each section. You may think to yourself: "But I don't want to miss any questions." That's an important attitude, but you have to understand that there will be (almost always) questions you feel uncertain about. You need to ask yourself "How many questions can I afford to guess on?"

   For example, when you know that you can guess on five questions in the Reading section, you can pick either questions you know you struggle with (maybe overall purpose or vocab) or those you don't have time for and spend those few precious minutes tracking down answers elsewhere. If you know you can guess on 10 questions and still reach your goal, you've just eliminated an entire passage from your test time, and after filling in those bubbles with guesses, you've got 13 minutes to divide among the other passages. (For reference, missing 10 questions in Reading and another 10 questions in Writing and Language would put you in the 630–670 range for your Evidence-Based Reading and Writing score.)

2. **Decide your passage order:** On the SAT Reading Test, many students struggle with two passages in particular: literary narrative (often passage 1) and the historical document(s) (often passage 4). Those passages are organized less strictly and often prioritize different kinds of information. Those passages won't be harder for everyone, but you need to decide, either as you prepare for the test, or when you open up the section on the big day, the order in which you'll read passages and answer questions. There's no point letting something like the literary narrative passage take up your time if you tend to have poor accuracy there to begin with.

When you open the test, take a minute to identify each passage's type and then start working through your passage order. The test may make this easier some days than others, but you should have a plan. One common passage order that prioritizes the more concrete passages first is social studies, science, science, historical document, literary narrative. Remember, the purpose of a passage order is to dedicate time where time is best spent, either with the passages you like or those you scored best with during practice. Your goal is to be as accurate as you can with as many questions as you can, which usually means going outside of the test's passage order.

3. **Develop your personal reading technique:** People read in different ways and with different ability levels. That simple fact means it's hard to prescribe some super-secret reading strategy that will unlock a perfect score on the test. But there are key objectives you should have in mind. You need to read in the way that allows you to grasp the purpose of the text ("Why was this written?" "What's the main idea?"), get through the passage quickly (spending no more than three and a half minutes reading), and find the information relevant to the questions ("What's the main idea of each paragraph?").

There are a lot of ways to access those key objectives. Some students need to read the whole passage. Others can read the first and last sentence of each paragraph and know what they need to. You might be able to just work through the questions backwards (because they go from general to specific and are generally put in order of where answers can be found in the passage). You'll need to experiment to find what works for you. If your strategy doesn't allow you to find information and answer accurately (enough to meet your goal), you need to try something different (or adjust your goal). You may even use different strategies depending on what passage you're reading. If you have time to read the whole passage, you should. But you need to make the best decision for your time and accuracy.

As you work through the practice questions later in this section and the practice tests available to you, experiment with techniques and consider the following: what feels comfortable, how long does it take you, and how accurate are your answers? Here are a few suggested techniques (and keep in mind that they can be combined in a variety of ways):

- Read the whole passage and annotate key ideas and details.
- Read the first and last sentences of each paragraph and label the purpose of each paragraph.
- Read and answer the questions in reverse order, focusing on the more specific questions first and finding information in the passage as necessary.
- Read the questions first and then skim or read the passage, marking relevant details.

During the Test

4. **Read actively:** Apply your reading technique, but regardless of the exact technique you use to read the passage, you must be active. Too often, reading means quickly moving your eyes over the words on the page. On the SAT, that's only going to hurt you. To repeat, you must be active. Active reading means that you're summarizing information while you read, perhaps even asking questions, making notes, or marking on the text. That extra bit of effort is going to help when you start answering the questions. Active reading fires up your memory and your comprehension, allowing you to remember what you read (and where it was) and understand it more accurately. Once again, this must be a quick process. It needs to fit into your reading technique. Maybe you'll underline a key sentence in each paragraph before moving on to the next; maybe you'll write out a quick note in the margin that states the purpose of the paragraph. Do something that works for you.

5. **Answer questions strategically:** Consider how you approach the questions. Answer the questions that are easiest for you first. Sometimes you may be able to rattle off a perfect description of the passage's purpose (usually the first question for a passage). Other times, you'll feel more comfortable jumping to line reference questions (hunting down vocab words and key details). Often, you will learn more about the passage while searching for answers than you did while reading. After you've answered what you can, work through the other questions in reverse order, referring to the text and confirming answers as time permits.

   When tackling specific questions, you also can complete a quick checklist to sidestep several traps:

   - Read the full question.
   - Make a prediction.
   - Read all the answer choices.
   - Eliminate unsupported answers.
   - Find evidence for your choice.
   - And repeat.

6. **Be certain in your answers:** Certainty may feel like another self-explanatory tip, but you need to understand that in the Reading section there is always a reason why an answer is right and why three others are wrong. You can be certain that the answer you fill in is correct because you found evidence in the passage either to prove your choice or that proves each of the other answer choices wrong. If you have a good reason for your answer choice, you're in a great position to meet your goal. If you don't have the time to prove that you're right (by finding support in the passage), you'll have to guess. Remember that your goal will only allow you to guess on so many questions before your ideal score is in jeopardy.

7. **Keep track of your time:** For most students, time management is the greatest factor in their performance. With enough time, everyone could answer every question in the section correctly. Sadly, that's not a luxury you have. You already know that you have 13 minutes to complete each passage and how that time limit can shift when you prioritize specific passages and questions you know you're likely to do well with. But you need to be keenly aware of those constraints as you work through the section. Get an analog watch—one with hands—to track your time. While there should be a clock in your testing space, you want to make sure that you have everything you need to perform well, which means not relying on unknowns. You also need to have a plan for the five-minute warning: fill in remaining answer bubbles, answer questions with line references, and review your commonly missed question types.

3

BASIC STEPS FOR ANSWERING READING QUESTIONS

You know you need to be thinking about your plan for the entire section, but what about when you're working on a specific passage? To move through individual passages, follow these four steps:

1. **Read the passage introduction:** The introductory paragraph before each passage can give you critical insight into the topic of a passage. Some introductions will be more helpful than others—laying out the passage title and a sentence about the topic's background. Often, though, a title is enough to explain what idea you need to understand by the time you've read through the passage. The intro also may identify the source or author, the era in which the passage was written, or the event that the passage describes.

2. **Use your reading technique on the passage:** Now apply your reading technique, pushing yourself to get through the passage as quickly but actively as you can. You can't just drag your eyes over the page. Your goal is to focus on the larger ideas of the text and to identify where ideas are located in the passage. By the end of your reading, you should be able to summarize the passage and pinpoint the location of key ideas.

FUN FACT

There are no words that rhyme with orange and purple.

3. **Answer questions:** "Answer questions" may seem like it needs little explanation, but you'd be surprised at the number of students just like you who answer inattentively or who leave questions blank on their answer sheets. Remember the few basic steps that you can take for each question: read the full question, make a prediction, and read all the answer choices before making a selection. But also make sure to answer every question for the passage. You may work through passages out of order and jump between questions within a passage, but when the clock ticks down, every bubble needs to be filled on your answer sheet. Remember, there is no penalty for incorrect answers, so be sure to fill in an answer for every question on your answer sheet. There are no excuses for blank bubbles.

4. **Eliminate wrong answers and answer all questions, guessing as necessary:** You're going to answer every question, you have to, but as you're answering questions, you need to eliminate answer choices that you know are incorrect and use the better odds to guess at the remaining choices. There is always a reason why you can eliminate each of the wrong answers. The reality is, though, that sometimes you will have to guess. But a guess is always better than an empty bubble. Statistically, you're just as likely to answer correctly by guessing A as you are B, C, or D. Don't be afraid to fill in the same answer for every guess you make (if you aren't able to eliminate). The math says that if you were to fill in the same answer for every question in a single passage, you'd get two to three questions correct.

Now that you're familiar with strategies for reading passages and answering questions, let's try a few.

Sample Reading Passage 1

Questions 1–4 are based on the following passage.

The following excerpt comes from an article by José Martí, "Our America," that was published in El Partido Liberal *(Mexico City), March 5, 1892.*

The prideful villager thinks his hometown contains the whole world, and as long as he can stay on as mayor or humiliate the rival who stole his sweetheart or watch his nest egg accumulating in its strongbox he believes the universe
Line to be in good order, unaware of the giants in seven-league boots who can crush
5 him underfoot or the battling comets in the heavens that go through the air devouring the sleeping worlds. . . . It is the hour of reckoning and of marching in unison, and we must move in lines as compact as the veins of silver that lie at the roots of the Andes. . . .

Our youth go out into the world wearing Yankee- or French-colored
10 glasses and aspire to rule by guesswork a country they do not know. . . . To know is to solve. To know the country and govern it in accordance with that knowledge is the only way of freeing it from tyranny. The European university must yield to the American university. The history of America from the Incas to the present must be taught in its smallest detail, even if the Greek Archons
15 go untaught. Our own Greece is preferable to the Greece that is not ours; we need it more. Statesmen who arise from the nation must replace statesmen who are alien to it. . . .

What a vision we were: the chest of an athlete, the hands of a dandy, and the forehead of a child. We were a whole fancy dress ball, in English trousers,
20 a Parisian waistcoat, a North American overcoat, and a Spanish bullfighter's hat. The Indian circled about us, mute, and went to the mountaintop to christen his children. The black, pursued from afar, alone and unknown, sang his heart's music in the night, between waves and wild beasts. The campesinos, the men of the land, the creators, rose up in blind indignation against the
25 disdainful city, their own creation. We wore epaulets and judge's robes, in countries that came into the world wearing rope sandals and Indian head-bands. The wise thing would have been to pair, with charitable hearts and the audacity of our founders, the Indian headband and the judicial robe, to undam the Indian, make a place for the able black, and tailor liberty to the bodies of
30 those who rose up and triumphed in its name. . . . No Yankee or European book could furnish the key to the Hispanoamerican enigma. So the people tried hatred instead, and our countries amounted to less and less each year. Weary of useless hatred . . . we are beginning, almost unknowingly, to try love. The nations arise and salute one another. "What are we like?" they ask, and
35 begin telling each other what they are like. . . . The young men of America are rolling up their sleeves and plunging their hands into the dough, and making it rise with the leavening of their sweat. They understand that there is too much imitation, and that salvation lies in creating. Create is this generation's pass-word. Make wine from plantains; it may be sour, but it is our wine! . . .

NOTE

José Martí was a Cuban teacher, organizer, writer, and poet. The lyrics to the popular folk song "Guantanamera" were adapted from one of Martí's poems. Although Cuban by birth, he is considered one of the most influential writers in all of Latin America. He died in the battle for Cuba's independence from Spain, a cause to which he had devoted much of his life.

ALERT

Passages will be formatted in 2 columns on the SAT Exam. For instructional purposes, we have placed the passages across the full page throughout this chapter.

40   Anyone who promotes and disseminates opposition or hatred among races is committing a sin against humanity. . . . To think is to serve. We must not, out of a villager's antipathy, impute some lethal congenital wickedness to the continent's light-skinned nation simply because it does not speak our language or share our view of what home life should be or resemble us in its political failings, which are different from ours, or because it does not think highly of quick-
45 tempered, swarthy men or look with charity, from its still uncertain eminence, upon those less favored by history who, in heroic stages, are climbing the road that republics travel. But neither should we seek to conceal the obvious facts of the problem, which can, for the peace of the centuries, be resolved by timely study and the urgent, wordless union of the continental soul. For the unanimous hymn is already ringing forth, and the present generation is bearing industri-
50 ous America along the road sanctioned by our sublime forefathers. From the Rio Bravo to the Straits of Magellan, the Great Cemi,* seated on a condor's back, has scattered the seeds of the new America across the romantic nations of the continent and the suffering islands of the sea!

*Cemi is a deity or ancestral spirit of the Taíno people—one of the indigenous groups of the Caribbean.

1. Martí's main purpose in the passage is to

   A. appeal to fellow Latin Americans to be more like the Europeans.

   B. gain support from fellow Latin Americans to join in a fight against European invaders.

   C. rally support for himself as a leader of a revolution to free his country from tyranny.

   D. encourage fellow Latin Americans to educate themselves about their own mixed heritage.

At various points in the passage, Martí speaks to the significant European influence in Latin and South America. Martí talks about how little his fellow countrymen know of their own heritage and says that they cannot expect to govern themselves unless they understand their own history (lines 9–10). Choice D pinpoints one rationale Martí gives for education. Overall, the excerpt does not address revolution (choice B), nor does Martí present himself as revolutionary (choice C). He appeals to pride in one's heritage, not that of the Europeans (choice A). These ideas are connected because Martí believes that his fellow Latin Americans can free themselves through education (lines 11–12: "To know the country and govern it in accordance with that knowledge is the only way of freeing it from tyranny."). **The correct answer is D.**

2. Based on the passage, which statement best represents Martí's attitude toward education?

   A. Universal education is of the utmost importance.

   B. Everyone should learn about Latin American history.

   C. Education in the history of the Americas is necessary for new leadership.

   D. Education should include the study of Greek democracy as a model for freedom.

This question is asking for an overview, so you need to think about the points Martí makes and his overall message. You can eliminate choices A and B because they are general statements that are also extreme—they are not ideas that are represented in the passage (though they are related). Choice D is an incorrect interpretation of the text. Martí says that education is important for new leaders, and these leaders must be well-versed in the history of Latin America. People who are educated about their own country and heritage will rise as leaders and take over for "statesmen who are alien to it" (lines 16–17). **The correct answer is C.**

3. Which of the following best describes the overall tone of the passage?

A. Passionate and resolute

B. Angry and bitter

C. Scolding and arrogant

D. Inflammatory and rebellious

This type of question also requires you to think about the point of view and presentation, which determine the tone. Martí tries to persuade his readers, advising them to wake up to threats from those who don't understand them or hate them (lines 30–31: "No Yankee or European book could furnish the key to the Hispanoamerican enigma. So the people tried hatred instead, and our countries amounted to less and less each year."). His passion comes through in the use of flowery and emotional language (lines 6–7: "the hour of reckoning and of marching in unison"), similes (line 7: "move in lines as compact as the veins of silver"), and metaphors (lines 22–23: "sang his heart's music in the night, between waves and wild beasts"). He expresses a resolve (line 39: "Make wine from plantains; it may be sour, but it is our wine!"), not anger or bitterness, so choice B is not the best answer. Although Martí admonishes his fellow countrymen for being naïve and for ignoring dangers (lines 4–5: they are "unaware of the giants in seven-league boots who can crush him underfoot"), he does not take the position of preacher or project arrogance. Rather, he speaks as one of the people (lines 6–8: "It is the hour of reckoning and of marching in unison, and we must move in lines as compact as the veins of silver that lie at the roots of the Andes."), so choice C is not the best answer either. Martí does not use inflammatory language, nor does he call for rebellion, so you can eliminate choice D as a correct answer. Rather, he tries to persuade his fellow Latin Americans to unite in spite of their differences and to defend their lands from foreigners who do not understand them. The words *passionate* and *resolute* best describe the overall tone of the passage. **The correct answer is A.**

4. In the third paragraph, the first sentence mainly serves to

A. demonstrate how others perceive the peoples of Latin America.

B. create a picture of a unified culture.

C. explain Martí's ideals about freedom.

D. represent the opportunity to create a new beginning.

When a question refers to a specific part of the text, quickly reread the line(s) and the surrounding text. In paragraph 3, Martí offers a detailed, mocking description of the disparate parts blended to compose the peoples of Latin America. He paints a picture of a person comprising various elements of other cultures—none his or her own. This, he says, is how Europeans saw the people of Latin America. The vision is the image others have of them and how it is misunderstood and even hated by others. **The correct answer is A.**

3

Sample Reading Passage 2

Questions 1–4 are based on the following two passages.

The following passages discuss theories of how culture and language spread across Europe and Central Asia to form modern European and Asian peoples. Passage 1 is excerpted from "When modern Eurasia was born," originally published by the University of Copenhagen on June 10, 2015, by the Center for GeoGenetics and the Natural History Museum of Denmark. Passage 2 is excerpted from "European invasion: DNA reveals the origins of modern Europeans," published in March 2015, by Alan Cooper, a director at the Australian Centre for Ancient DNA at the University of Adelaide, and Wolfgang Haak, a senior research fellow at the University of Adelaide.

PASSAGE 1

With this new investigation, the researchers confirm that the changes came about as a result of migrations. The researchers think that this is interesting also because later developments in the Bronze Age are a continuation of this
Line new social perception. Things add up because the migrations can also explain
5 the origin of the northern European language families. Both language and genetics have been with us all the way up to the present. Kristian Kristiansen [professor of archaeology at the University of Gothenburg, Sweden] even thinks that it was crucial that events happened during these few centuries, as crucial as the colonization of the Americas.

10 One of the main findings from the study is how these migrations resulted in huge changes to the European gene-pool, in particular conferring a large degree of admixture on the present populations. Genetically speaking, ancient Europeans from the time post these migrations are much more similar to modern Europeans than those prior to the Bronze Age.

15 The re-writing of the genetic map began in the early Bronze Age, about 5,000 years ago. From the steppes in the Caucasus, the Yamnaya Culture migrated principally westward into North and Central Europe, and to a lesser degree, into western Siberia. Yamnaya was characterized by a new system of family and property. In northern Europe the Yamnaya mixed with the Stone
20 Age people who inhabited this region and along the way established the Corded Ware Culture, which genetically speaking resembles present-day Europeans living north of the Alps today.

Later, about 4,000 years ago, the Sintashta Culture evolved in the Caucasus. This culture's sophisticated new weapons and chariots were rapidly expand-
25 ing across Europe. The area east of the Urals and far into Central Asia was colonized around 3,800 years ago by the Andronovo Culture. The researchers' investigation shows that this culture had a European DNA background.

During the last part of the Bronze Age, and at the beginning of the Iron Age, East Asian peoples arrived in Central Asia. Here it is not genetic admixture we
30 see, but rather a replacement of genes. The European genes in the area disappear.

TIP

If you struggle to keep the information in the two paired passages straight, read just one passage and then answer the questions that are about that passage only. Repeat with the second passage, and then answer the questions about both. That sequence can keep you from mixing up the two passages in your answers.

These new results derive from DNA analyses of skeletons excavated across large areas of
Europe and Central Asia, thus enabling these crucial glimpses into the dynamics of the Bronze
Age. In addition to the population movement insights, the data also held other surprises. For
example, contrary to the research team's expectations, the data revealed that lactose tolerance
35 rose to high frequency in Europeans, in comparison to prior belief that it evolved earlier in time
(5,000–7,000 years ago).

PASSAGE 2

What we have found is that, in addition to the original European hunter-gatherers and a heavy
dose of Near Eastern farmers, we can now add a third major population: steppe pastoralists.
These nomads appear to have "invaded" central Europe in a previously unknown wave during
40 the early Bronze Age (about 4,500 years ago).

This event saw the introduction of two very significant new technologies to western Europe:
domestic horses and the wheel. It also reveals the mysterious source for the Indo-European
languages.

The genetic results have answered a number of contentious and long-standing questions
45 in European history. The first big issue was whether the first farmers in Europe were hunter-
gatherers who had learnt farming techniques from neighbours in southeast Europe, or did they
instead come from the Near East, where farming was invented.

The genetic results are clear: farming was introduced widely across Europe in one or two
rapid waves around 8,000 years ago by populations from the Near East—effectively the very
50 first skilled migrants.

At first the original hunter-gatherer populations appear to have retreated to the fringes of
Europe: to Britain, Scandinavia and Finland. But the genetics show that within a few thousand
years they had returned, and significant amounts of hunter-gatherer genomic DNA was mixed
in with the farmers 7,000 to 5,000 years ago across many parts of Europe.

55 But there was still a major outstanding mystery. Apart from these two groups, the genomic
signals clearly showed that a third—previously unsuspected—large contribution had been made
sometime before the Iron Age, around 2,000 years ago. But by whom?

We have finally been able to identify the mystery culprit, using a clever new system invented
by our colleagues at Harvard University.

60 Instead of sequencing the entire genome from a very small number of well-preserved skeletons, we analysed 400,000 small genetic markers right across the genome. This made it possible
to rapidly survey large numbers of skeletons from all across Europe and Eurasia.

This process revealed the solution to the mystery. Our survey showed that skeletons of the
Yamnaya culture from the Russian/Ukrainian grasslands north of the Black Sea, buried in large
65 mounds known as kurgans, turned out to be the genetic source we were missing.

1. Which lines from Passage 1 support the idea that migration of human populations can be tracked
through DNA testing?

A. Lines 1–2: ("With this … migrations.")

B. Lines 12–14: ("Genetically … the Bronze Age.")

C. Lines 23–25: ("Later, about 4,000… across Europe.")

D. Lines 25–26: ("The area east … the Andronovo Culture.")

3

This type of question requires that you find specific text to support an answer to a question. Although the concept given—that DNA testing was used to track population migrations—can be found in both passages, you need to review only the specific lines given in the answer choices to find the answer that best supports the concept. Choice A confirms the idea of migration, but the text does not refer to DNA as the process that tracked the migration. Choice B refers to the genetic evidence, another term for DNA, which shows a similarity between ancient and modern Europeans. This evidence illustrates that scientists have been tracking the migration patterns. Choices C and D are not directly related to DNA evidence. **The correct answer is B.**

NOTE

Paired passages have the same types of questions as the single passages. However, some of the questions may ask you to synthesize the information presented in the two passages by noting commonalities or comparing them in some way.

2. Which choice best describes the relationship between Passage 1 and Passage 2?

   A. Both passages show conflicting claims about the migrations.

   B. Both passages describe different scientific methodologies.

   C. Passage 2 provides supplementary information to Passage 1.

   D. Passage 2 is written from a different perspective than Passage 1.

When reading paired passages, you will encounter questions that ask you to examine the relationship between the passages. On your first reading, you probably noticed that the two passages do not contradict one another (choice A); nor do they show different points of view (choice D). Both passages describe scientific studies and what scientists were able to learn from them, and both describe using DNA as the methodology, so you can eliminate choice B. But notice that the second passage adds to the information in the first, which makes the information in Passage 2 supplementary to the information shown in Passage 1. **The correct answer is C.**

3. Based on information in the passages, which of the following statements could be made about scientific inquiry?

   A. DNA evidence showed why many Europeans are lactose intolerant.

   B. Genetic research can provide valid historical information.

   C. Evidence showed that the steppe pastoralists introduced horses and the wheel to Western Europe.

   D. Scientific investigation can provide evidence about human history not obtainable through other means.

This question asks you to compare the two passages and look for a topic that is not directly discussed but one that is implicit within it—the nature of scientific inquiry. While choices A and C are true, neither one answers the question. Choice B is also true, but it doesn't address the nature of scientific investigations; it is simply a general statement that could apply to many texts. Choice D, however, states a fact about scientific inquiry that can be gleaned from the text: Both passages describe how scientists were able to use DNA data to answer questions they were unable to address before the use of DNA testing was available. **The correct answer is D.**

4. How do the passages illustrate the contributions of DNA evidence to scientific inquiry?

   A. Both passages provide examples of how DNA evidence enabled scientists to fill in gaps in their knowledge about human migrations.

   B. Both passages describe how DNA analysis is used in scientific investigations.

   C. Both passages imply that DNA evidence can solve evolutionary questions.

   D. Both passages show how scientists solved the mysteries of DNA evidence.

In paired passages, you will encounter questions that ask you to compare or contrast information presented explicitly in the passages. Both passages illustrate how DNA has been used to answer questions about human migration patterns—questions that had been unresolved before the ability to use DNA as evidence for such studies. Neither passage gives details about the actual scientific methodology as both are focused on the results, so you can eliminate choice B as a possible correct answer. Choices C and D are not correct interpretations of the passages, so you can eliminate these choices as well. **The correct answer is A.**

TIPS FOR TAKING THE READING TEST

You will be allotted 65 minutes to read five passages and answer the 52 questions in the Reading section. Remember, that's 13 minutes per passage. That's a lot to do in a short period of time. However, you can use some specific strategies and techniques to help you move through this portion of the SAT exam quickly and accurately.

Start With the Passages That You're Good At

A point is a point. It doesn't matter if the point comes from answering correctly a question about a piece of fiction or a scientific experiment. If the style and subject matter appeal to you, you will probably work through a passage more quickly and answer the questions more easily. Some passages are consistently harder for students than others. Organization, language use, and purpose can be difficult to characterize depending on the passage. Practice tests are vital for the Reading section because you need to see when you do well and when you struggle. So, before you start, recall your passage order and, if you're feeling unsure, quickly check the topics by skimming the titles and introductions. Start with the topics that are most familiar, most interesting, or have the paragraphs that are shortest (usually meaning that they're easier to read). Save the hardest passages for last (usually literary narrative and the historical document(s)). Don't waste time where you know you're likely to miss more questions anyway. If you're jumping around, make a notation so you know which passages you have completed, and double check that your answers on the answer sheet correspond to the correct question numbers.

Don't Panic When You Read an Unfamiliar Passage

You know what kinds of passages the test will have. And you know that topics can vary wildly. The passages can (and likely will) be unfamiliar. To assess students' ability to apply reading skills in various subjects, the test makers purposely choose a variety of passages. This helps make sure that each test taker can demonstrate his or her reading and analysis skills. And that's good for you. This section is not about what you know. It's all about how you think. Everything you need to answer the questions is right in front of you. Every question will test your ability to do one of the following:

- Understand the author's assumptions, point of view, and theme
- Determine how the author supports the main ideas in the text
- Determine how the author uses specific language to create mood or tone
- Identify explicit details from the text
- Analyze the logical structure of the text
- Analyze overall meaning as well as specific words and phrases in context of the passage
- Interpret tables, charts, and graphs

Remember, all of those tasks may be met by using information in the passage. Everything you need to know is right there in front of you. The introductory paragraph and passage, even the questions themselves, illuminate all the information you'll need to answer the questions. Even if the passage is about the price of beans in Bulgaria or the genetic makeup of a wombat, don't worry. It's all right there on the page.

Mark Important Information as You Read the Passages

It pays to be an active reader, and making quick notes is a critical part of this process. The questions will be related to the most important information in the passage. That usually means that if you understand the purpose of each paragraph and the passage overall, you have what you need. At the same time, one strategy is to let the questions guide your notations. If you're comfortable holding the questions in your head while you read, you can preview the questions before starting the passage and use your pencil to mark the textual evidence that addresses questions about the big ideas, themes, and purpose. Use other markings to indicate places in the text that may provide evidence for other questions, for example, a specific word or phrase referred to in a question. If you've marked those pieces of information, you'll be able to find them more easily to help answer the questions. Alternatively, if reading the questions first doesn't work for you, record notes about the big ideas of a passage in the margins (a quick phrase or two) while you read so that you know what paragraph to reference for ideas stated by the questions.

Look at the Big Picture, Not the Details

Remember, you don't have to understand every bit of information. You just have to find the information you need to answer the questions. Don't waste your time trying to analyze technical details. Know where the details are, not what they are. This is not a test of your memory so much as your ability to find and use information.

BRAIN BREAK

This brain break is meant to inject a little bit of fun into your study time. Grab a pen, one that has a bit of weight to it. Place it in your dominant hand and flip it one revolution. Switch the pen to your other hand and flip it one revolution. Grab another pen, hold one in each hand, and flip the pens at the same time. For more of a challenge, try flipping both pens simultaneously and catch them in the opposite hand. Have fun with this exercise and try to do your best to avoid launching the pens into someone else's space.

Remember That the Questions Get More Specific

The SAT Reading Test often organizes the questions from broader questions about themes, purpose, point of view, and main ideas to more specific questions about explicit and implicit meaning, specific language, the structure of the text, and charts and graphs (if they're present). The order of questions may even correspond with where the answer might be found in the passage—data interpretation questions are always some of the last, and evidence and vocab questions are generally put in order of their line references. Chances are that a question towards the end of the set will have its answer later in the passage. Again, questions go from general to specific and, often, from earlier in the passage to later. If you preview questions before you read, you might find that you can answer some questions immediately without having to read the passage. The viability of that strategy depends on your judgment and comfort level.

Don't Confuse a "True" Answer for a "Correct" Answer

The fact that an answer choice is true doesn't mean it's correct. What does that mean? It means that a certain answer choice may be perfectly true—in fact, all of the answer choices may be true—but the *correct* answer is the right answer to the question that's being asked. Only one of the answer choices will be correct and, therefore, the right choice. Read carefully. Pay attention to the wording of the question and the answer choices. Just because an answer makes sense doesn't mean that it agrees fully with the information in the passage. Wrong answers were designed to play on your assumptions and inattention. Answers that go beyond the topic and context of a passage and scope of the question are wrong. Don't be fooled. As you practice, if the test regularly catches you with answers that are slightly off from what the passage actually says, try predicting the answer after reading the question. That will force you to recall (or, even better, find) the answer in the passage and avoid wording traps.

Answer All of the Questions Before You Start the Next Passage

More than likely, there won't be time to go back to reread the passages and recheck your answers, so answer every question that you can for each passage. If you don't know an answer, skip the question and return to it when you have answered the other questions in the passage. Check your time, and if you think you can answer one of the skipped questions with a quick reread of part of the passage, go ahead. Eliminate answers if you can. Otherwise, if you find it is taking too long, give it your best guess and move on. Remember, wrong answers are not penalized, so don't leave anything blank. A blank answer is always a wrong answer, while a shaded bubble might be right. Make sure you have answered every question for each passage before you move on to the next one. If you know that you normally end up with a few extra minutes after the last passage, mark questions in your test booklet that you guess on and ones that you usually miss so that you can target them for review later.

Approach Paired Passages a Little Differently

For the paired passages, you need to understand the purpose of each passage and how they're related. The passages may share a topic, but there are key differences between them. Recall your overall and question-answering strategies. Your steps will stay largely the same, but you can also break up how you read and answer questions. For paired passages, you can adjust your strategy to exploit the passage structure: read the first passage and answer questions about that passage. Next, read the second passage and answer questions about it and the questions for both passages. By working on the passages one at a time, you'll minimize the chance of confusing the two passages. Everything else is the same. You'll focus on questions you know you can support with evidence and answer. If you have to guess, you'll eliminate answers if possible, mark an answer, and move on. Make sure you have answered all the questions, and then go to the next passage.

STRATEGIES FOR ANSWERING SPECIFIC QUESTION TYPES

As you learned earlier, each Reading test question asks you to do one of the following:

- Determine themes and central ideas as presented in the passage.
- Determine the purpose of the passage or the point of view of the text.
- Determine the function of language in the text.
- Select evidence that best supports the answer to a previous question or support an assertion as presented in a question.
- Select and support inferences, conclusions, or arguments with textual evidence.
- Identify explicit details from the passage.
- Interpret the text to label tone or mood of the passage.
- Determine the meaning of words and phrases in the context of the passage.
- Analyze information in an accompanying graphic, such as a table, graph, or chart.

The following strategies can help you deal with specific types of SAT Reading questions. You should use these strategies in combination with your overall strategies and the basic steps for approaching the Reading passages. These strategies don't take the place of the basic steps but are extra tools to help you with certain types of questions. These tips work with both single and paired passages on any topic.

1. **Themes and Central Ideas:** The first questions for a passage will be broad and often require you to think about the whole passage. Keep this in mind as you read the passage, noting any references to an overview in the introduction and/or conclusion of the passage. Often, authors speak to their themes and central ideas in the first and last paragraphs of the passages (just like you would in an introduction or conclusion you wrote for one of your own essays). If you're in a hurry, you could likely answer those first questions of a passage by looking at the first and last paragraphs. Theme questions are almost exclusively reserved for the literary narrative passage. Themes are expressed through changes in circumstances or character perspectives over the course of a narrative. Consider what happens in a story and how it causes the characters to grow: what lesson does that teach the reader? Note also the positive ideas that the SAT seeks to convey with its choice of passages; the SAT wants students to leave a passage optimistic about the world, not dejected. An answer choice that presents a negative view of a situation—not just an obstacle to resolution—is likely wrong.

2. **Purpose and Point of View:** As you read, note the subject of the passage and the voice/perspective. These items can often be found in the introduction. Ask yourself if the author is providing information about a specific topic, making an argument for or against something, or telling a story. Whether fiction or nonfiction, you need to understand who is speaking and why. Similar to theme and central ideas, the purpose of the passage will be stated in some way near the first and last paragraphs as the author works to summarize their ideas and have a largely positive focus. Alternatively, if the question seeks the purpose of a paragraph, the first and last sentences can provide quick insights.

3. **Function of Language:** Function questions ask about the "why" behind an author's writing choices. When you see the phrasing "the primary function/purpose of" or "mainly serves to," consider how the meaning of the sentence, paragraph, or passage would change if the information were deleted. Think to yourself, "If I deleted this, I would lose an explanation/summary/obstacle/detail. . . ." and make a related choice.

4. **Command of Evidence:** Command of Evidence questions ask you to find evidence in a passage (or pair of passages) that directly supports the answer to a previous question or serves as the basis for a conclusion. Questions may also ask you to identify how an author uses evidence to support claims or find a relationship between a graphic and its corresponding passage. These questions rely on the language "Which choice provides the best evidence for…" The answers to these questions will have line numbers. Consider underlining or bracketing the associated lines to reduce time spent searching for the relevant text as you evaluate (and reevaluate) all answer options. While multiple choices may provide support for an answer to a previous question or conclusion, one answer will be better than the others.

5. **Inferences:** An inference requires you to come to a logical conclusion based on available evidence. When you read a question with the phrasing "supported by," "be inferred," "strongly suggests," or "implies," you must use what you know from the passage and the question to arrive at a reasonable conclusion. Make a prediction before reading the answers to these questions to avoid distortions of passage details. Keep in mind that any inference you make must support the author's ideas. Inferences that go beyond the scope of the passage (being too broad or too narrow) or don't align with the main purpose are likely wrong. If an inference question is followed by a Command of Evidence question, you can use the line references in the following question's answers to guide your search and shaping of an appropriate conclusion.

6. **Details:** When you see the question phrasing "According to the passage," you'll be able to find the answer directly in the passage. The phrasing may differ between the answer choices and the information in the passage, but the meaning should match exactly. Any answer choice that distorts the details of the passage is wrong. Just like for the inferences, some detail questions will be followed by Command of Evidence questions. The Command of Evidence answers can narrow the scope of your search if you are otherwise unsure where to look.

7. **Tone and Mood:** An author's tone is their perspective on their topic while mood describes the reader's emotional response to the topic and tone. As you read, notice the overall tone and mood of the passage and find textual evidence—specific words or phrases, imagery, point of view, and sentence structure—that contribute to these elements.

8. **Words in Context:** If a question asks about a specific word, "most nearly means," read the surrounding text to check the context in which the word is used. Always read the complete sentence as well as a little before and a little after the line reference in the question. Context can be key to answering these questions, and the test doesn't always direct you to the best information.

9. **Data Interpretation:** When passages contain graphics, the last questions will ask you to examine their information in order to answer an associated question. If it asks you to apply the illustration to the text, read that portion of the text in conjunction with the graphic illustration. Use the details in the question to guide

---

FUN FACT

Did you know that bubble wrap was originally intended to be used as 3D wallpaper? It was also marketed as insulation for greenhouses before a marketer discovered its benefits as a protective packaging material. Bubble wrap is also a popular stress-reliever. Who can resist popping the bubbles?

3

you to the correct figure and data point. The test will regularly include answers that are the result of looking at information near the correct answer, so draw on the graphic to direct your attention to the appropriate data point, table box, or label.

To help you see how these tips work, read the passage in the practice exercise located after the Summing It Up section. Then read each tip and try to answer each question before you read the answer explanation. Note, again, that on the actual SAT (and in the practice tests in this book), reading passages will appear in two columns. For instructional purposes, the passages in the practice exercise are formatted across the page.

Summing It Up

- On the Reading test, there are five passages in total—four single passages and one set of paired passages—and 52 questions. You will have 65 minutes to complete this section. That means you have 13 mins per passage.

- Passages can vary in order on the SAT, but official practice materials offered by College Board consistently use the following order: literary narrative, history/social studies, science, history/social studies, and science. Always evaluate a passage's type by reading the introductory paragraph before the first lines of the passage.

- The Reading section has a variety of different question types, each with its own strategies:

  - Determine themes and central ideas as presented in the passage.
  - Determine the purpose of the passage or the point of view of the text.
  - Determine the function of language in the text.
  - Select evidence that best supports the answer to a previous question or support an assertion as presented in a question.
  - Select and support inferences, conclusions, or arguments with textual evidence.
  - Identify explicit details from the passage.
  - Interpret the text to label tone or mood of the passage.
  - Determine the meaning of words and phrases in the context of the passage.
  - Analyze information in an accompanying graphic, such as a table, graph, or chart.

- Determine and practice your overall reading strategies:

  - Set a goal.
  - Decide your passage order.
  - Develop a personal reading technique.
  - Read actively.
  - Answer questions strategically.
  - Be certain in your answers.
  - Keep track of your time.

- Take a few basic steps with each passage:
  - Read the passage introduction.
  - Use your reading technique.
  - Answer the questions.
  - Eliminate wrong answers and answer all questions, guessing as necessary.
- Follow these key tips for the passages and questions:
  - Always work through easier passages first, leaving the hardest passage for last.
  - Remember that the answer to every question is in the passage or supported by information in the passage.
  - Mark or note important information as part of your reading technique so that you can find information when answering questions.
  - Focus on the big ideas in each passage, not the details; know where to find information, not what it is.
  - Remember that the questions are ordered from general to specific and sometimes in order of where relevant information appears in the passage.
  - Keep in mind that some answers may be true, but that doesn't mean they're correct for their question.
  - Answer every question for a passage before moving on to the next passage, even if you must guess.
  - Work through paired passages one at a time, splitting up the questions for each, then answer questions about both passages.

Take a moment to ask yourself some simple questions about your understanding of the chapter:

Review: What did I learn?

Evaluate: What do I need to learn more about?

Plan: What can I do next to keep improving?

Based on your answers to those questions, adjust your study plan to dedicate additional time to the areas of weakness that you've identified.

PRACTICE EXERCISE: READING TEST

30 Minutes—23 Questions

3

DIRECTIONS: Each passage or pair of passages is followed by a number of questions. After reading each passage or pair, choose the best answer to each question based on what is stated or implied in the passage or passages and in any accompanying graphics (such as a table or graph).

Questions 1–6 are based on the following passage.

The following is an excerpt from "The Purloined Letter," a short story by Edgar Allan Poe. Poe is best known for writing poems and stories in the horror and mystery genre.

. . . "Well, then; I have received personal information, from a very high quarter, that a certain document of the last importance, has been purloined from the royal apartments. The individual who purloined it is known; this beyond a doubt; he was seen to take it. It is known, also, that it
Line still remains in his possession."
5   "How is this known?" asked Dupin.

"It is clearly inferred," replied the Prefect, "from the nature of the document, and from the non-appearance of certain results which would at once arise from its passing out of the robber's possession; that is to say, from his employing it as he must design in the end to employ it."

"Be a little more explicit," I said.

10   "Well, I may venture so far as to say that the paper gives its holder a certain power in a certain quarter where such power is immensely valuable." The Prefect was fond of the cant of diplomacy.

"Still I do not quite understand," said Dupin.

"No? Well; the disclosure of the document to a third person, who shall be nameless, would bring in question the honor of a personage of most exalted station; and this fact gives the holder
15   of the document an ascendancy over the illustrious personage whose honor and peace are so jeopardized."

"But this ascendancy," I interposed, "would depend upon the robber's knowledge of the loser's knowledge of the robber. Who would dare—"

"The thief," said G., "is the Minister D—, who dares all things, those unbecoming as well as
20   those becoming a man. The method of the theft was not less ingenious than bold. The document in question—a letter, to be frank—had been received by the personage robbed while alone in the royal boudoir. During its perusal she was suddenly interrupted by the entrance of the other exalted personage from whom especially it was her wish to conceal it. After a hurried and vain endeavor to thrust it in a drawer, she was forced to place it, open as it was, upon a table. The
25   address, however, was uppermost, and, the contents thus unexposed, the letter escaped notice. At this juncture enters the Minister D—. His lynx eye immediately perceives the paper, recognises the handwriting of the address, observes the confusion of the personage addressed, and fathoms her secret. After some business transactions, hurried through in his ordinary manner, he produces a letter somewhat similar to the one in question, opens it, pretends to read it, and
30   then places it in close juxtaposition to the other. Again he converses, for some fifteen minutes, upon the public affairs. At length, in taking leave, he takes also from the table the letter to which he had no claim. Its rightful owner saw, but, of course, dared not call attention to the act, in the

presence of the third personage who stood at her elbow. The minister decamped; leaving his own letter—one of no importance—upon the table." …

35   "You looked among D—'s papers, of course, and into the books of the library?"

"Certainly; we opened every package and parcel; we not only opened every book, but we turned over every leaf in each volume, not contenting ourselves with a mere shake, according to the fashion of some of our police officers. We also measured the thickness of every book-cover, with the most accurate ad measurement, and applied to each the most jealous scrutiny of the
40 microscope. Had any of the bindings been recently meddled with, it would have been utterly impossible that the fact should have escaped observation. Some five or six volumes, just from the hands of the binder, we carefully probed, longitudinally, with the needles."

"You explored the floors beneath the carpets?"

"Beyond doubt. We removed every carpet, and examined the boards with the microscope."

45   "And the paper on the walls?"

"Yes."

"You looked into the cellars?"

"We did."

"Then," I said, "you have been making a miscalculation, and the letter is not upon the
50 premises, as you suppose."

"I fear you are right there," said the Prefect. "And now, Dupin, what would you advise me to do?"

"To make a thorough re-search of the premises."

"That is absolutely needless," replied G—. "I am not more sure that I breathe than I am
55 that the letter is not at the Hotel."

1. As presented in the passage, Prefect G is best described as

    A. one who delights in being obscure and frustrating to his colleagues.

    B. an individual who talks a great deal about things about which he knows nothing.

    C. a person concerned with protecting other people's privacy and honor.

    D. one who possesses investigative skills that are greater than those of anyone else.

2. As used in line 15, "ascendency" most nearly means

    A. rise.

    B. advantage.

    C. joy.

    D. weakness.

3. After the royal lady is interrupted perusing the letter (line 22), Prefect G believes that she was forced to

    A. place the letter upon a table.

    B. thrust the letter in a drawer.

    C. tuck the letter behind the wallpaper.

    D. hide the letter beneath the floorboards.

4. Based on the passage, Prefect G measured each book cover in the library in order to

A. obey Dupin's command to measure each book cover.

B. prove that the letter was not actually stolen.

C. show his fellow investigators that he was very thorough.

D. detect whether the letter was hidden in one of them.

5. Which choice provides the best evidence for the previous question?

A. Lines 40–41: ("Had any . . . escaped observation.")

B. Line 43: ("You explored . . . carpets?")

C. Line 45: ("And the paper . . . walls?")

D. Line 53: ("To make a . . . premises.")

6. It can be reasonably inferred from the passage that the royal lady did not stop Minister D from taking the letter because she

A. did not see that Minister D was stealing the letter.

B. did not want the other person in the room to know of the letter's existence.

C. had written the letter for Minister D to read.

D. knew that the letter was not very important.

Questions 7–12 are based on the following passage.

The passage below discusses how Alaska Native cultural practices and heritage are being preserved in the twenty-first century. (For more information, visit **www.nps.gov.***)*

Alaska Native cultural practices continue to be a central force in virtually all villages throughout Alaska. In order to maintain cultural knowledge and ensure its survival, Alaska Native people need to learn the best methods of recording and archiving music, dance, and oral history. Along
Line
5   with the expansion of Europeans and Americans into Alaska were accompanying hardships for the indigenous people: epidemic diseases, strong Christian missionary activities, and western educational policies such as English language-only rules. These resulted in decimated populations throughout the entire territory of Alaska, a decline in indigenous languages, and, in many cases, the abolishment of traditional religion and associated music and dance repertoires.

Native people are deeply spiritual people; historically, they had a rich ceremonial life that
10   was profoundly expressed through music and dance—core means by which people communicate their identities and beliefs. With the introduction of Christianity, traditional cultures, including aspects such as music and dance, were not viewed favorably by the missionaries. Sadly, most of the missionaries did not tolerate masked dancing and other forms of religious expressions. Dance, language, and ceremonial practices either had to be practiced in secret, or were lost.

15   In the 1960s, during the Native Solidarity Movement, as Alaska Native people became more politically active, their re-identification with their cultures, languages, music, and dance became a banner of their newfound political and social strength. One of the major outcomes of that

movement has been a renaissance in traditional music and dance practices, resulting in multiple dance festivals and younger people becoming actively involved in their village dance groups. ...

20   The Fifth Annual Kingikmiut Dance Festival featured a large Russian dance group, as well as the Tikigaq Traditional Dancers of Point Hope and dance groups from Brevig Mission and other villages on the Seward Peninsula. Kingikmiut, or Wales, was once known as the dance capital of the Seward Peninsula. Captain Henry Trollope visited Wales in 1853–54 and wrote "… the place is sort of a capital in these parts and has four dancing houses, which is a very ex-
25 pressive manner of estimating the extent and population for a place." (Ray 1975) Because of its strategic location, Kingikmiut flourished. Before the 1900 and 1917 epidemics, it consisted of two related villages and consolidated into one village once the populations had been decimated by disease. After these terrible epidemics, western educators' English-only policies forced music, dance, and other expressions of traditional Native culture to go underground.

30   Repression of Native culture by western educators and missionaries was common all over Alaska and is a major reason why many Alaska Native languages are threatened today. In the first part of the twentieth century, traditional dance and music became associated with the old ways and were looked down upon. After the 1960s, a strong revitalization movement arose. To-day there is a renaissance in traditional music and dance practices. In Wales and other Seward
35 Peninsula communities, the younger people, who make up a large percentage of the population, have a great thirst for learning to sing and dance their traditional songs.

7. Which choice best reflects the main idea of the passage?

    A. There has been a recent surge in interest in Native cultures everywhere.

    B. Native Alaskans have always tried to preserve their history and culture.

    C. Western expansion into Alaska resulted in loss of Native cultures.

    D. Native Alaskan traditions were revived in the 1960s.

8. Which choice provides the best evidence for the answer to the previous question?

    A. Lines 3–8: ("Along with the expansion . . . repertoires.")

    B. Lines 9–11: ("Native people . . . identities and beliefs.")

    C. Lines 17–19: ("One of the major . . . dance groups.")

    D. Lines 33–36 ("Today there is . . . traditional songs.")

9. According to the passage, what was the relationship between Europeans and the health of Alaska's Native people?

    A. Europeans brought newer and more effective medicines to Alaska's Native people.

    B. Europeans actively sought to wipe out Alaska's Native people with new diseases.

    C. Europeans received many medical tips from the Alaska's unusually healthy Native people.

    D. Europeans caused Alaska's Native people to fall fatally ill.

3

10. What evidence does the passage provide to suggest that Captain Henry Trollope helped introduce Kingikmuit to the rest of the world?

   A. Line 23: ("Captain Henry…and wrote…")

   B. Lines 24–25: ("…the place is…for a place.")

   C. Lines 25–28: ("Because of its…by disease.")

   D. Lines 28–29: ("After these terrible…go underground.")

11. It can be reasonably inferred from the passage that

   A. traditional Alaskan culture thrived without obstacles after the 1960s.

   B. the Native Solidarity Movement's efforts were not completely effective.

   C. music and dance are never involved in Christian ceremonies.

   D. older Alaskan Natives have no interest in Alaska's traditional culture.

12. As used in line 34, "renaissance" most nearly means

   A. repression.

   B. reconsideration.

   C. rebirth.

   D. reservation.

Questions 13–17 are based on the following passage and supplementary material.

This passage is the introduction to a report from the Office of the Chief Technologist at the US space agency NASA, entitled "Emerging Space: The Evolving Landscape of the 21st Century American Spaceflight." (The full passage can be read at www.nasa.gov/sites/default/files/files/ Emerging_Space_Report.pdf)

America stands today at the opening of a second Space Age. Innovative NASA programs and American entrepreneurs together are transforming the space industry. These initiatives—both at NASA and in the private sector—are expanding the nation's opportunities for exploration
Line and for the economic development of the solar system.
5   Today's space economy extends some 36,000 kilometers (22,369 miles) from the surface of the Earth and includes an array of evidence-based technologies—satellite communications, global positioning satellites, and imaging satellites—on which our economy depends. These technologies are now an integral part of our economy, and they would not exist if not for the over 50 years of research, development, and investment in the enabling technologies by NASA
10   and other government agencies that seeded these efforts and allowed them to bloom. As we expand our activities in the solar system over the next decades, NASA programs and investments will provide the seed and soil that encourage economic development increasingly farther from Earth. The first signs of this are already visible.
       The next era of space exploration will see governments pushing technological development
15   and the American private sector using these technologies as they expand their economic activities to new worlds. NASA's next objectives for exploration—visits to asteroids and Mars— are more complex than any previous space mission attempted. They will happen in the context of relatively smaller NASA budgets and an expanding commercial space economy. Teaming with

private-sector partners to develop keystone markets like low Earth orbit (LEO) transportation
20 and technological capabilities like asteroid mining will help NASA achieve its mission goals, help
the space economy evolve to embrace new ambitions, and provide large economic returns to the
taxpayer through the stimulation and growth of new businesses and 21st-century American jobs.

Motivated by an intrinsic desire to explore space, successful American entrepreneurs have
pledged and spent hundreds of millions of dollars to develop technologies aimed at fundamen-
25 tally improving space access. Since 2003, commercial human spaceflight has received $2.5 billion
in private investment.[1] At the same time, a new generation of space enthusiasts are engaging
directly though small-scale projects. Through cubesats, suborbital and orbital adventures, and
citizen science opportunities, the United States is transitioning from a spacefaring nation to a
nation of spacefarers.

30 In addition to executing its scientific and human spaceflight programs, NASA also has a
legislated responsibility to "encourage, to the maximum extent possible, the fullest commercial
use of space." As part of fulfilling this responsibility, this report examines how NASA has col-
laborated with American private-sector individuals and companies investing in space exploration, collectively known as "emerging space." Today, more than fifty years after the creation of
35 NASA, our goal is no longer just to reach a destination. Our goal is to develop the capabilities
that will allow the American people to explore and expand our economic sphere into the solar
system. Although when NASA was founded only a government program could undertake a voy-
age from the Earth to the Moon, this may not be true in the future. By taking full advantage of
the combined talents of government and the American private sector, our next journeys beyond
40 Earth will come sooner and we will catalyze new industries and economic growth in the process.

[1] 2013 Commercial Spaceflight Industry Indicators, Commercial Spaceflight Federation

3

NASA provides a number of resources for people willing to contribute as citizen scientists. All are available online, meaning all you need is access to the internet. Software tools are also provided. More than 1.2 million people from 80 countries have participated in NASA's citizen science projects. This table captures just a few of the projects.

Project	Citizen Scientist Role	Number of Participants
Be a Martian	Tag rover images and map craters from satellite pictures	1,230,000
HiTranslate	Help translate NASA's HiRISE project captions into different language	1,021 new in 2012
International Space Apps Challenge	Develop mobile applications, software, hardware, data visualization, and platforms to address current challenges relevant to space exploration and social need	2,083 from 17 countries in 2012
Lunar Impacts	Independent observers can monitor the rates and sizes of large meteoroids striking the far side of the moon	26 impact candidates
Rock Around the World	Help Mars scientists better understand the red planet by sending rocks to NASA for analysis	12,461 rocks received
Stardust at Home	Search for the first samples of solid matter from outside the solar system	30,649 from 2006 to 2012
Target Asteroids!	Observe asteroids, to help scientists refine orbits and determine the composition of near-Earth objects (NEOs) in support of the OSIRIS-Rex mission	104 registered users from 23 countries

13. Which choice provides the best summary of the passage?

    A. NASA is ushering in a new chapter in the Space Age that will allow the privatization of space.

    B. In the next decades, ordinary people will be able to travel in space.

    C. NASA is the US agency that is charged with developing space programs.

    D. The Second Space Age will expand the economy and increase complex technologies in space exploration.

14. According to the passage, NASA's first goal was to

    A. expand the US economy.

    B. visit asteroids and Mars.

    C. provide commercial travel.

    D. reach the moon.

15. As used in line 1, "Space Age" most nearly means

    A. an era of space exploration and exploitation.

    B. the year that space was first explored.

    C. the time it takes to travel to outer space.

    D. an advanced age in one's life.

16. Based on the information shown in the table, what is the most likely reason that the "Be a Martian" project has so many more participants than the other projects?

    A. More people are interested in exploring Mars than in other aspects of the program.

    B. Other projects require more sophisticated/complex technology skills.

    C. It is the only project that is designed for young people.

    D. The other projects all require more time as a volunteer.

17. According to the table, citizen-scientists can participate in a NASA project if they can

    A. identify different kinds of rocks.

    B. use a telescope.

    C. use software technology and the internet.

    D. locate and recognize the planets and other celestial bodies.

Questions 18–23 are based on the following two passages.

The following passages are excerpted from narratives written by two explorers. Passage 1 is by Sir Earnest Shackleton from an account he wrote entitled: South! The Story of Shackleton's Last Expedition (1914–1917). *Passage 2 is part of an account by Hiram Bingham III, from "The Discovery of Machu Picchu," first published in* Harper's Monthly *magazine in 1913.*

PASSAGE 1

Some intangible feeling of uneasiness made me leave my tent about 11 p.m. that night and glance around the quiet camp. The stars between the snow-flurries showed that the floe had swung round and was end on to the swell, a position exposing it to sudden strains. I started to
Line
5 walk across the floe in order to warn the watchman to look carefully for cracks, and as I was passing the men's tent the floe lifted on the crest of a swell and cracked right under my feet. The men were in one of the dome-shaped tents, and it began to stretch apart as the ice opened. A muffled sound, suggestive of suffocation, came from beneath the stretching tent. I rushed forward, helped some emerging men from under the canvas, and called out, "Are you all right?"

"There are two in the water," somebody answered. The crack had widened to about four
feet, and as I threw myself down at the edge, I saw a whitish object floating in the water. It was
a sleeping-bag with a man inside. I was able to grasp it, and with a heave lifted man and bag on
to the floe. A few seconds later the ice-edges came together again with tremendous force. Fortu-
nately, there had been but one man in the water, or the incident might have been a tragedy. The
rescued bag contained Holness, who was wet down to the waist but otherwise unscathed. The
crack was now opening again. The *James Caird* and my tent were on one side of the opening and
the remaining two boats and the rest of the camp on the other side. With two or three men to
help me I struck my tent; then all hands manned the painter and rushed the *James Caird* across
the opening crack. We held to the rope while, one by one, the men left on our side of the floe
jumped the channel or scrambled over by means of the boat. Finally I was left alone. The night
had swallowed all the others and the rapid movement of the ice forced me to let go the painter.
For a moment I felt that my piece of rocking floe was the loneliest place in the world. Peering
into the darkness; I could just see the dark figures on the other floe.

PASSAGE 2

Nor was I in a great hurry to move. The water was cool, the wooden bench, covered with a woolen
poncho, seemed most comfortable, and the view was marvelous. On both sides tremendous
precipices fell away to the white rapids of the Urubamba River below. In front was the solitary
peak of Huay-na Picchu, seemingly inaccessible on all sides. Behind us were rocky heights and
impassable cliffs. Down the face of one precipice the Indians had made a perilous path, which
was their only means of egress in the wet season, when the bridge over which we had come would
be washed away. Of the other precipice we had already had a taste. We were not surprised to
hear the Indians say they only went away from home about once a month.

Leaving the huts, we climbed still farther up the ridge. Around a slight promontory the
character of the stone-faced andenes began to improve, and suddenly we found ourselves in the
midst of a jungle-covered maze of small and large walls, the ruins of buildings made of blocks
of white granite, most carefully cut and beautifully fitted together without cement. Surprise
followed surprise until there came the realization that we were in the midst of as wonderful
ruins as any ever found in Peru. It seemed almost incredible that this city, only five days' journey from Cuzco, should have remained so long undescribed and comparatively unknown. Yet
so far as I have been able to discover, there is no reference in the Spanish chronicles to Machu
Picchu. It is possible that not even the conquistadors ever saw this wonderful place. From some
rude scrawls on the stones of a temple we learned that it was visited in 1902 by one Lizarraga,
a local muleteer. It must have been known long before that, because, as we said above, Wiener
[an Austrian-French explorer], who was in Ollantaytambo in the 70's, speaks of having heard
of ruins at a place named "Matcho Picchu," which he did not find.

18. What is meant by "The night had swallowed all the others" (lines 19–20)?

A. An animal swallowed some of the men.

B. Some of the men had fallen asleep.

C. Some of the men were impossible to see in the dark.

D. Some of the men had returned home.

19. What idea in Passage 1 leads to the conclusion that Shackleton shared a special connection with his men?

   A. Shackleton was concerned with rescuing them from the water.

   B. Shackleton told the watchman to look for cracks in the floe.

   C. Shackleton sensed they were in trouble before he knew it.

   D. Shackleton asked them if they were all right.

20. In Passage 2, the description of Hiram Bingham III reveals that he

   A. tends to be overwhelmed by his experiences.

   B. is a naturally mistrustful person.

   C. has a cold and calculating attitude.

   D. embraces and enjoys life.

21. How do the two passages differ in their tone?

   A. Passage 1 has a tone of surprise, and Passage 2 has a tone of fear.

   B. Passage 1 has a threatening tone, and Passage 2 has an adventurous tone.

   C. Passage 1 exhibits a tone of danger, and Passage 2, a tone of awe.

   D. Passage 1 features a gloomy tone, and Passage 2, a festive tone.

22. Based on the two passages, what can be inferred about the nature of expeditions?

   A. They are often dangerous and can't be undertaken alone.

   B. They usually add to the knowledge about a place.

   C. They are good travel destinations for people who enjoy going to little-known places.

   D. They represent undiscovered parts of the world.

23. Both passages describe stories of exploration in order to

   A. tell the world about the dangers of undeveloped places.

   B. tell the world about new and undiscovered places.

   C. persuade others to visit undeveloped places.

   D. persuade people to help develop the locales described.

ANSWER KEY AND EXPLANATIONS

3

1. C	6. B	11. B	16. B	20. D
2. B	7. C	12. C	17. C	21. C
3. A	8. A	13. D	18. C	22. B
4. D	9. D	14. D	19. C	23. B
5. A	10. B	15. A		

1. **The correct answer is C.** Prefect G's refusal to name suspects, his tendency toward "diplomacy" and his refusal to dishonor the victim illustrate his concern to protect the privacy and honor of others. While he does speak in an obscure manner that frustrates his colleagues, there is no evidence to suggest Prefect G is speaking in such a way because he enjoys it, so choice A is incorrect. Prefect G does seem to know what he is saying; he just says it unclearly, so choice B is not the best answer either. While Prefect G's investigative skills are presented in great detail in the passage, the fact that Dupin concludes that Prefect G has made a "miscalculation" casts doubt upon whether his skills are greater than those of anyone else, making choice D an extreme answer.

2. **The correct answer is B.** In line 13, Prefect G uses *ascendency* to suggest the advantage the possessor of the letter would have over the person who is the subject of the letter. *Rise* (choice A) can be a synonym of *ascendency*, but it does not match how the word is used in this particular context. *Joy* (choice C) is not usually used as a synonym for *ascendency*, and *weakness* (choice D) has the opposite meaning of *ascendency*.

3. **The correct answer is A.** According to line 24 of the passage, Prefect G believes that the royal lady was forced to leave the letter open "upon a table." Due to the suddenness of the interruption, he believes that she was not able to thrust the letter in a drawer (choice B). Later in the passage, Dupin asks if Prefect

G looked behind the wallpaper (choice C) and beneath the floorboards (choice D), and Prefect G says that he checked in all of these places (and in the cellars) and could not find the letter in any of them.

4. **The correct answer is D.** According to line 36 of the passage, Prefect G measured the cover of each book in the library, and he did so while searching for the letter. This suggests that he thought the letter could have been hidden in one of the book covers. Dupin does not command Prefect G to measure each book cover, so choice A is incorrect. Measuring the book covers would not provide proof that the letter was not stolen, so choice B is incorrect. Prefect G was very thorough, but choice C does not accurately indicate his motivation for measuring each book cover.

5. **The correct answer is A.** Lines 40–41 serve to support Prefect's motive for measuring each book cover in the library; he wanted to make sure, with the utmost certainty, that the letter was not hidden in the books. The paragraph goes into great detail regarding the lengths Prefect G went to determine that none of the books had been "meddled" with. Choices B and C are places Prefect G checked, not reasons why he measured the books in the library. Choice D is an action that Dupin advises Prefect G to do, after he has mentioned that Prefect G may have made a miscalculation in assuming that the missing letter was "upon the premises."

6. **The correct answer is B.** Her fear of a third person in the room knowing the contents of the letter prevented the royal lady from stopping Minister D's theft. Prefect G states that the royal lady saw Minister D take the letter (lines 31–32), so choice A is incorrect. The royal lady did not write the letter, so choice C is incorrect, and if the letter were not important, as choice D suggests, there would be no reason to investigate its theft.

7. **The correct answer is C.** The first paragraph in the passage provides a summary. It explicitly states the reasons that the Native Alaskan culture was almost wiped out and what needs to be done to ensure that it is not lost forever. The rest of the passage supports the concepts introduced here.

8. **The correct answer is A.** The last two sentences of the first paragraph provide the best evidence among the choices given that the western expansion into Alaska resulted in loss of native cultures. Choice B provides information that Alaskan Natives are deeply spiritual people, but this is not the main idea of the passage. Choice C provides information regarding a major outcome of the Native Solidarity Movement, which, while important, does not reflect the main idea of the passage. Choice D is a concluding sentence and not the main idea of the passage.

9. **The correct answer is D.** According to the first paragraph of the passage, Europeans brought epidemic diseases with them to Alaska, and this resulted in "decimated populations," which supports the conclusion in choice D. While it is conceivable that a new culture could bring both disease and medicine with it, there is no evidence in the passage that supports the conclusion in choice A. Choice B implies that Europeans brought epidemic diseases to Alaska intentionally, but there is no evidence in the passage that supports this conclusion. There

is no evidence that supports the conclusion in choice C either.

10. **The correct answer is B.** The fact that Captain Henry Trollope's observations regarding the Kingikmuit people are quoted in lines 24–25 indicates that they were significant and likely helped introduce Kingikmuit culture to the rest of the world. Line 23 (choice A) merely introduce Captain Henry Trollope without indicating anything about how he might have helped introduce Kingikmuit to the rest of the world. Choices C and D are unrelated to Captain Henry Trollope.

11. **The correct answer is B.** While the Native Solidarity Movement sparked a revival of traditional Alaskan culture in the 1960s, the final paragraph of the passage indicates that threats to Alaskan culture still exist today, so choice B is the best answer, and choice A cannot be correct. While Christian missionaries clearly disapproved of music and dancing in Native Alaskan ceremonies, they may have had a different attitude regarding dance and music in Christian ceremonies, so there is no clear evidence to support the inference in choice C. While the final paragraph of the passage does specify the enthusiasm of younger Alaskan Natives for traditional Alaskan culture, this does not really support the rather extreme conclusion in choice D.

12. **The correct answer is C.** The word *renaissance* is used in connection with the revitalization of traditional Alaskan music and dance, so choice C is the best choice. Choice A is incorrect because it would convey the opposite of the author's intention. While choice B might make sense in this context, it does not fit the context as strongly as choice C does. Choice D simply does not make sense in this context.

13. **The correct answer is D.** The first paragraph states that both NASA and the private sector are expanding the opportunities for exploration and for economic development, which

3

aligns with the statement provided in choice D. Privatization (choice A) is not mentioned. While choice B may be true, the ability of ordinary people travelling in space is not the main idea of the passage. Choice C simply names the US government agency in charge of developing space programs.

14. **The correct answer is D.** According to line 35, NASA's first goal was "to reach a destination," and line 38 indicates that the destination was the moon. Choice A describes one of the recent goals of NASA, not its very first goal. Choice B describes a goal of NASA beyond its first one. Choice C misinterprets the idea of reaching a destination.

15. **The correct answer is A.** "Space Age" is an idiom meaning "an era of space exploration and exploitation." Since one cannot do something first more than once, choice B does not make sense. Choice C is not an accurate definition of the idiom "Space Age," and choice D has nothing to do with the context of the idiom's use in the passage.

16. **The correct answer is B.** The table shows that the "Be a Martian" project involves tagging on the internet, and the introductory information above the table explains that participants are provided with any needed software. The other projects listed in the table require additional skills (e.g., translating text or doing more complex searches). The table does not detail how many people are interested in exploring Mars (choice A), the age the projects were designed for (choice B), or the amount of volunteer time (choice D).

17. **The correct answer is C.** Reading the descriptions, the skill required in all of the projects is how to use the internet to conduct searches. Even for projects that involve language translation, a participant would have to access the internet to get the text that needs to be translated. The ability to identify different rocks (choice A), use a telescope (choice B), and locate and recognize the

planets and other celestial bodies (choice D) are specific skills needed for specific projects.

18. **The correct answer is C.** Choice C is an accurate interpretation of lines 19–20. Evidence in the passage does not support the interpretations in choices A, B, or D.

19. **The correct answer is C.** Passage 1 opens with a line indicating that Shackleton had an "intangible feeling" that something was wrong, and his feeling was proven correct when it turned out some of his men were in trouble. One can be concerned with someone without sharing a special connection with that person, so choices A, B, and D are not the best answers.

20. **The correct answer is D.** In the second passage, Bingham speaks of how much he enjoys the sensations and sights during his exploration, which supports choice D and eliminates choice C. While he seems to be in a somewhat heightened state of enjoyment, choice A is much too extreme a conclusion. There is no evidence in the passage that Bingham is mistrustful (choice B).

21. **The correct answer is C.** The first line of Passage 1 sets the tone of danger (feeling of uneasiness) that continues after the crack in the ice. Although the men aren't killed, the path to the boat was nevertheless full of danger. Passage 2 begins with Bingham's observations that show his appreciation of the beauty of the place. He marvels at the Indians who make their way down the steep precipice on a regular basis (lines 27–29). As Bingham makes his way through the jungle and sees Machu Picchu for the first time, detailed descriptions show awe and surprise at the "wonderful ruins" (lines 36–37).

22. **The correct answer is B.** Both passages describe places about which little was known at the time. Both men undertook the trip and wrote detailed accounts of their experiences so that others could learn about them and perhaps follow their footsteps to gain even more knowledge. While expeditions are often dangerous, to infer from the passages that they can't be taken alone is extreme. Choice C implies that expedition locales are good travel destinations, but based on the passages, this may not always be the case. Choice D doesn't make sense, as the question is asking about the nature of expeditions, not what expeditions represent.

23. **The correct answer is B.** Both passages record the experiences of men who are drawn to exploring places that most people don't ever see. Both use detailed descriptions of the physical terrain of remote places that are void of other people. There is no call inviting others to join them—just descriptions that inform.

BRAIN BREAK

There are many theories as to why people yawn. Most commonly attributed to lack of sleep or a lack of oxygen in the body, yawning also occurs when someone around you yawns (or with the mere mention of yawning). Have you yawned yet? Try this technique when you feel like you need to clear your head. Massage the muscles in your jaws near where the top and bottom jaw join. Relax and let your bottom jaw drop. Open your mouth to yawn. Do this 5 or 6 times along with stretching your arms to the sky. Feel better yet? More focused?

PART IV:
WRITING STRATEGIES FOR THE SAT® EXAM

Chapter 4

Writing and Language Test Strategies

OVERVIEW

- **A Closer Look at the Writing and Language Test**
- **The Writing and Language Test Categories**
- **Basic Strategies**
- **Question-Specific Strategies: Expression of Ideas**
- **Question-Specific Strategy: Standard English Conventions**
- **Summing It Up**
- **Practice Exercise**
- **Answer Key and Explanations**

A CLOSER LOOK AT THE WRITING AND LANGUAGE TEST

The Writing and Language Test gives you opportunities to demonstrate your college and career readiness by revising and editing four passages. Each passage is 400–450 words long. There are 11 multiple-choice questions that accompany each passage for a total of 44 questions in all. You have 35 minutes to complete this section, which equates to approximately 48 seconds per question (just under 9 minutes per passage). If that doesn't sound like enough time to you, be assured that you will be able to answer many of the questions in *fewer* than 48 seconds. You can save up your extra seconds for the harder questions you'll encounter.

One passage of the four will be career-related; for example, this chapter includes a Practice Exercise passage on speech-language pathologist careers. Another passage will be humanities-related; it might be about visual art, music, theater arts, or literature. This chapter includes a short critical essay on a nineteenth-century novel by British author Jane Austen. The other two passages will be about history/social studies and science. Some of the passages will be accompanied by graphics such as tables, charts, or graphs.

The writing modes used in the passages will include argument, informative/explanatory text, and nonfiction narrative. For example, this chapter's sample passage on speech-language pathology is an informative/explanatory text. The essay on Jane Austen that appears later in this chapter includes both argument and nonfiction narrative.

Answering the multiple-choice questions on each passage will place you in an editor's role. You will revise and edit the work of an unspecified writer. You will be asked to improve each passage's development, organization, and use of language. Your tasks will include making sure that each passage conforms to standard rules of English grammar, usage, and punctuation as well as logical organization, topic relevance, and strong style. When a passage is accompanied by one or more graphics, you may need to correct the passage's inaccurate interpretation of data.

These editing and revising goals may sound overwhelming, but don't worry. Every answer is right there on your test page. All you have to do is to select one out of four possible solutions (A, B, C, or D) to choose the best use of language—what's logical and relevant or grammatically correct and concise.

FUN FACT
There are over 7,000 languages worldwide, and most of them are dialects.

THE WRITING AND LANGUAGE TEST CATEGORIES

The Writing and Language Test contains the following two primary categories of multiple-choice questions:

1. Expression of Ideas
2. Standard English Conventions

Expression of Ideas Questions

More than half of the questions fall into this category, which is further divided into three different focus areas. This category includes questions about the following:

- Development
  - Adding, deleting, revising, or retaining text in a passage to achieve clear proposition and focus and to provide support of the passage's claims
  - Relevant (or irrelevant) details
  - Consistency of the passage with informational graphics

- Organization
  - Reordering sentences so that paragraphs make better sense
  - Transitional language that smoothly and clearly takes the reader from one idea to another

- Effective Language Use
  - Words in context
  - Eliminating awkward language and wordiness
  - Consistency of style and tone
  - Combining sentences to make text more concise and flow more smoothly
  - Cohesion and precision of language

Your primary goal with Expression of Ideas questions is to select information that aligns with the topic of the passage, flows logically to create smooth transitions between and within sentences and paragraphs, and demonstrates consistent style and tone. You will learn more about how to approach Expression of Ideas questions in the sections that follow.

Standard English Conventions Questions

About 45 percent of the questions fall into this category of sentence structure, punctuation, and usage rules. The test includes questions that require you to demonstrate your knowledge of the following:

- Sentence structure and formation
- Punctuation
- Consistent (or inconsistent) verb tenses
- Consistent (or inconsistent) pronoun and verb agreement
- Correct (or incorrect) word usage

In general, Standard English Conventions questions require you to eliminate answers that are grammatically incorrect, wordier than other grammatically correct answers, and irrelevant to the passage's topic and a paragraph's purpose. The Practice Exercise section at the end of this chapter provides you with the opportunity to practice answering questions from this category. You'll learn more about some key expectations for what makes an answer the best choice for Standards of English Conventions questions later. In Chapter 5, you will also learn more about the specific grammar, punctuation, and usage concepts covered by the SAT.

BASIC STRATEGIES

Before we examine the specific question types you'll encounter on the Writing and Language Test, let's discuss some basic strategies that will help you to navigate the passages efficiently, regardless of the subject matter or genre.

Less Is More

Each question set in the Writing and Language section gives you an entire passage and an accompanying series of 11 questions. That's quite a bit of work to read through the entire passage and answer the questions. But, just like the Reading section, the test selects only parts of the passage to focus on. Because of the focused nature of the questions, much of the passage can be safely ignored. Although the test itself suggests that you read the entire passage before answering questions, you're better served by reading only what you must. In most situations, you can safely read the sentence that contains the question marker only and have enough information to answer accurately. That is true, however, until it's not. Certain question types will require you to read a little before or a little after a sentence to access the information needed to answer correctly. But you shouldn't read more of the passage unless you need to.

Pinpoint the Purpose

If you need to quickly acquire information about the purpose of a passage or a specific paragraph, the title and first and last paragraphs (or even the first and last sentences) can quickly illuminate the topic. From there, you can eliminate answers that don't align with the purpose of the passage and question and use the strategies outlined for the specific question types discussed later in this chapter to narrow your focus.

Use a Four-Step Approach

For every question, you want to apply the following basic steps to give yourself the best chance at answering correctly:

1. Read the entire sentence with the underlined information or question marker.

2. Ask yourself, "Do I see a problem?"

   ○ If yes, eliminate answers that do not address the problem.

   ○ If no, evaluate each answer choice and eliminate answers with errors.

3. Apply your question-specific strategies and knowledge to work through the remaining answer choices.

4. Reread the sentence or paragraph while substituting in your answer choice, if time allows.

Make an Educated Guess

If you're ever stuck on a question in Writing and Language, make an educated guess. Since you know the basic expectations for the different question types—the correct answer will flow logically and be grammatically correct and concise—you can eliminate usually at least one answer choice that you know is wrong (eliminating two is even better), so you won't be guessing at random. Remember that you will not be penalized for wrong answers. Educated guessing can be a secret weapon when you need to keep moving to finish the section.

QUESTION-SPECIFIC STRATEGIES: EXPRESSION OF IDEAS

The following section is designed to give you a sample of some of the Expression of Ideas question types you will encounter on the SAT Writing and Language Test. We will walk you through each example and provide strategies to help you answer each question type.

Development: Adding or Deleting Text

This Expression of Ideas question is going to ask you whether it is a good or bad idea to delete a certain sentence. Keep in mind that it is your objective to keep a strong logical flow of ideas within paragraphs and between sentences. Read the description after the question for a detailed explanation of why one answer choice is better than the others.

When I was in elementary school, I was a shy little girl. . . . The stories I made up always had the same plot: I was carried off by a prince (David) on a flying horse to his castle where I became his wife and got to live in the lap of luxury. **5** From there I would go into elaborate detail about the décor of the castle, how many horses we owned, what colors they were, and so on. It was a silly, childish fantasy, but it comforted me.

5 The writer is considering deleting the underlined sentence. Should the writer do this?

A. Yes, because it adds unnecessary technical details.

B. Yes, because it makes the grown-up writer seem silly and childish.

C. No, because it adds funny details and helps to describe the narrator's investment in her stories.

D. No, because, without this sentence, the last sentence in the paragraph would not make sense.

This question truly casts you in an editor's role. You're asked whether the paragraph would be better or worse if this sentence were deleted. Not only that, you're asked *why* your choice is the correct one. You need to decide how well the sentence before transitions into this sentence, how logical it is as related to the topic of the paragraph, and how well it connects to the next sentence in the paragraph (or the next paragraph, if it were the last sentence). You'll also be able to use the reasoning attached to each answer choice to decide whether the sentence should stay or go.

Immediately, you can also eliminate choice A. This sentence *does* contain details, but they are not technical. Then, you can eliminate choice B. The underlined sentence doesn't make the grown-up writer seem "silly and childish"—it makes her *subject* (her younger self) seem so. The writer explicitly states this in the last sentence of the paragraph—she is aware of how "childish" the fantasy was.

What about choice D? Would the paragraph's last sentence fail to make sense if the underlined sentence were deleted? Read the first two sentences and the last one *without* the middle (underlined) sentence. The last sentence still makes sense, so you can eliminate choice D.

You are left with choice C. Even if you disagree that the underlined sentence is funny, it definitely "helps to describe the narrator's investment in her stories." **The correct answer is C.**

Development: Quantitative Information

Every Writing and Language Test contains one or more passages with graphics such as tables, charts, or graphs. One or more of the questions following such a passage deals with its data representations. This type of question asks you to compare information given in the passage to similar information or data that the graphic presents. If the two sets of information are inconsistent, you will need to make editing changes to the passage.

Here is an example:

A TECHNICAL WRITING CAREER	
Quick Facts: Technical Writers	
2018 Median Pay	$71,850 per year
	$34.54 per hour
Entry-level Education	Bachelor's degree
Work Experience in a Related Occupation	Less than 5 years
On-the-job Training	Short-term on-the-job training
Number of Jobs, 2018	55,700
Job Outlook, 2018–28	8% (faster than average)
Employment Change, 2018–28	4,700

[Source: **www.bls.gov/ooh/Media-and-Communication/Technical-writers.htm**]

4

Technical communicators, better known as "technical writers," plan, write, and edit instruction manuals, print and online articles, and other documents. Requirements for this well-paid profession include **10** a bachelor's degree and five to ten years of on-the-job training in a technical field.

10 Which choice most accurately and effectively represents the information in the chart?

A. NO CHANGE

B. a bachelor's degree and less than ten years of on-the-job work experience in a related occupation.

C. a master's degree, less than five years of work experience in a related occupation, and a short period of on-the-job training.

D. a bachelor's degree, less than five years of work experience in a related occupation, and a short period of on-the-job training.

TIP

If a question seems overwhelming, circle it in your test booklet and go on to the next question. When you're done answering all of the easier questions for a passage, come back to the ones you circled. Spend time on the questions you feel certain about. Some questions, like those that ask for reordering, can absorb a lot of time with no real reward. Avoid the traps of the test by answering questions in the order you want to, not how the test delivers them.

To find the correct answer choice, you will need to pay close attention to details in the chart. In this case, carefully read the three rows beginning with "Entry-level Education" and ending with "On-the-job Training." Choice A is incorrect because the chart does not specify "five to ten years of on-the-job training in a technical field." Choice B is incorrect because the chart does not specify "less than ten years of on-the-job work experience in a related occupation." Choice C is incorrect because the chart lists a bachelor's degree, not a master's, as a prerequisite for an entry-level technical writing job. The only answer choice that matches the chart is choice D. **The correct answer is D.**

Organization: Reordering Sentences

Organization questions ask you to determine if the sequence of material in a passage could be improved or if the introductions, conclusions, and transitions of paragraphs within the passage effectively tie the passage together. Next, let's try a question that asks you to reorder sentences in a paragraph. You will reorganize sentences and paragraphs in the Writing and Language section to create smooth logical transitions between ideas. Wherever you move a sentence, it should connect logically to the sentence before and the sentence after. Concluding sentences for paragraphs should properly transition into the next paragraph when applicable.

[1] A few years ago, US government experts predicted that employment of technical writers would grow 1.5 percent from 2012 to 2022, a gain of about 7,400 jobs per year. [2] (This is faster than the average for all occupations on which the US Department of Labor gathers statistics.) [3] This causes a greater need for professionals with the talent and skills to write instructional manuals that users can easily understand and follow. **16** [4] The high-tech and electronics industries continue to change and grow.

16 For the sake of cohesion, sentence 4 should be placed

A. where it is now.

B. before sentence 1.

C. after sentence 1.

D. after sentence 2.

In this type of question, each sentence in a paragraph is numbered with a numeral in brackets. Your job is to decide whether a specific sentence should stay where it is; move to a different spot in the paragraph; and if it *should* move, where it should go. On the SAT, every paragraph should have a smooth and logical flow. Every sentence should have a clear connection to the sentence before and the sentence after. In the Basic Strategies, you learned that you should only read what you must. As soon as you see a question that references sentence placement, you know that you're going to have to read the whole paragraph. One sentence just isn't enough.

The best way to answer this question would be to read the paragraph out loud to yourself. During the SAT exam, you won't be able to do that, but if possible, try it now to see how improper organization can affect the sound of a paragraph. On the test, you'll have to focus on the topic of the indicated sentence, transitional phrases, and things like pronouns. This sentence expresses a general idea that describes the industry in which technical writers often work. It also mentions continued change and growth. Logically, it would be better placed elsewhere, but where?

Try each option one at a time. You want to place this sentence so that the sentence following it explains the importance of this general idea. You will discover that this sentence belongs right after sentence 2—before sentence 3. Sentence 3 says that "This causes a greater need . . . [for good technical writers]." *What* causes this need? The cause is the fact that "the high-tech and electronics industries continue to change and grow." If sentences 3 and 4 were to swap places, the paragraph would be "most logical"—it would make better sense than it does now, for sure. **The correct answer is D.**

> **TIP**
>
> Just like sentences within paragraphs must have a logical flow, so should introductory and concluding sentences that connect paragraphs. The SAT picks high-quality passages that have strong organization, so you need to think about where you move a sentence to and the hole that gets left behind. It should always be clear how the passage transitions from one topic to another.

Organization: Combining Sentences and Using Transitional Words and Phrases Correctly

Here is a question that asks you to complete two tasks at once: combine two shorter sentences into one longer one and choose the transitional word or phrase that makes the best sense in the new, longer sentence. On the SAT, there will be questions that only ask you to select appropriate transitional words and phrases—which you'll see in the practice exercises at the end of this chapter.

Most novel readers do not like it when story events seem artificially "rigged" by the author in order to teach a moralistic lesson. In this novel, Jane Austen rigs **7** events. Whenever Fanny is left out, we can be sure that one or some of the other characters are engaged in something sinful. This is an unrealistic (fairy-tale) element in what is otherwise a highly developed, realistic novel.

7 Which choice most effectively combines the two sentences at the underlined portion?

A. events, but whenever Fanny is left out,

B. events so that, whenever Fanny is left out,

C. events; in addition, whenever Fanny is left out,

D. events, and the cause is that, whenever Fanny is left out,

The best way to solve this editing problem is to identify what relationship the first thought ("Jane Austen rigs events") has with the second ("we can be sure"). The second thought does not contradict the first or simply add information. The second clause explains the first. The writer is saying that Jane Austen heavy-handedly rigs events in her novel such that Fanny suffers mistreatment. If you try one answer choice at a time, you will soon find the one that makes the most sense. The transitional word *but* (choice A) and the transitional phrases *in addition* (choice C) and *and the cause is that* (choice D) do not relay the correct idea. Choice A is a contrasting transition. Choice C suggests the addition of information. While choice B and D are both causative transitions, choice D says that because characters are engaged in sinful acts, Jane Austen rigged events in the novel—which reverses the reasoning. Only the transitional phrase *so that* communicates that Austen set up events in order to communicate that it was the sinfulness of other characters that caused Fanny's exclusion. **The correct answer is B.**

Effective Language Use: Words in Context

The last question type we'll explore falls under the Effective Language Use category. Effective Language Use questions challenge you to identify the best way to accomplish rhetorical goals, by improving precision and concision, ensuring consistency of style and tone, and combining sentences to make ideas flow smoothly. Words-in-Context questions are perhaps the easiest type of question among the Expression of Ideas questions, though there are few of them. Find the applicable question number reference in the passage provided, review the answer options, and choose the best response for the context of the sentence. Here are a few examples.

Jane Austen and Fanny Price

In real life, one is sometimes left out because of actual purposeful **1** <u>problems</u> on the parts of those doing the leaving out, but sometimes one is simply left out—and culpability **2** <u>was</u> beside the point. **3** <u>The second case is much less satisfying to the left-out person, but it is also much more usual.</u> **4** <u>Novels</u> such as "Cinderella" are satisfying because, in them, it is clearly the nastiness of the villains and villainesses that causes the heroes and heroines to be excluded from pleasurable activities.

4

A. NO CHANGE

B. Fairy tales

C. Autobiographies

D. Articles

You read the sentence first with the question marker, but because you need the context of the passage, you then need to read the paragraph to get a general sense of its meaning. Right now, you are answering Question 4 only, so don't worry about any errors you might spot in the rest of the paragraph—you will deal with those later in the Practice Exercise section at the end of this chapter.

Question **4** asks you to decide which word or phrase best fits the context. You have four choices:

A. NO CHANGE

B. Fairy tales

C. Autobiographies

D. Articles

Use the context clues to make the best choice. Even if you've never heard of "Cinderella," you can see that a contrast to real life is being presented ("In real life…much less satisfying" "…are satisfying because…") and that "Cinderella" is a title of a literary work. The title is enclosed in quotation marks, which signals that "Cinderella" is not a novel (choice A), but a shorter work. The fact that a contrast has been established between real life and "Cinderella" excludes both autobiographies (choice C) and articles (choice D), which are, for the most part, nonfiction genres. **The correct answer is B.**

Let's try a words-in-context question that is paired with a different passage.

A TECHNICAL WRITING CAREER

Technical communicators, better known as "technical writers," plan, write, and edit instruction manuals, print and online articles, and other documents that transform ⑫ intense technical information into simpler language that end users can understand.

11

A. NO CHANGE

B. engineers

C. manuals

D. workers

Read the entire sentence to figure out what it is mainly about. Again, focus on the question you're answering (Question 11).

Here are some clue words and phrases that will help you figure out which word belongs after the numeral ⑪: *writers; write, and edit*; and *simpler language that . . . users can understand*. To which answer choice do these clues direct you? You can eliminate *manuals* (choice C) because a manual is a thing (a set of instructions), not a person. Might *engineers* (choice B) and *workers* (choice D) be writers who write and edit text?

Maybe, but the word *communicators* is the best choice because it is most precise—a writer's main job is to communicate with others by writing understandable sentences, paragraphs, and so on.

Since the word *communicators* already appears in the paragraph after the ⑪, **the correct answer is A,** NO CHANGE.

QUESTION-SPECIFIC STRATEGY: STANDARD ENGLISH CONVENTIONS

The Standard English Conventions questions represent just under half of the total questions in the Writing and Language section of the SAT. These questions assess your understanding of English grammar and your ability to recognize and correct errors in high-level passages. The SAT has concrete expectations for what appropriate English language usage looks like, and every passage in the section has been chosen for its demonstration of strong English usage. College-level English usage requires correct grammar, concise use of language, and relevance to the topic of the passage. Unless qualified by the question, no correct answer can contain grammatical errors. From there, high-level language usage avoids redundancy and wordiness. If an answer is grammatically correct and can be made more concise while preserving the topic of the passage, paragraph, and sentence, it is correct. To answer these questions well, you need to know the conventions discussed in Chapter 5 and be able to recognize when words are unnecessary to conveying the topic of the passage.

To approach these questions, use a modified version of the four-step process discussed previously:

1. Start by reading the entire sentence that contains the underlined information or question marker.

2. Ask yourself "Do I see a problem?"

3. Eliminate answers that don't address the problem or those that contain errors. (If you see an error in the original, you can eliminate A. NO CHANGE immediately.)

4. Of the answers that are grammatically correct, choose the answer that is concise yet still relevant to the passage.

This step-by-step process can help you move through conventions questions quickly, especially after you've memorized the limited grammar rules assessed by the test.

Let's try an example of a Standard English Convention question.

The Roman Empire's water transport—or aqueduct—system was a feat of engineering it combined form and function. The aqueducts were built in Italy, Greece, Spain, France, and other regions that were within the vast reach of the Roman Empire.

19

A. NO CHANGE

B. which had been combining

C. that made a combination of

D. that combined

Follow the process: after reading the sentence carefully, ask yourself, "Do I see a problem?" As it is written, this is a run-on sentence (an error in sentence structure and punctuation), so eliminate choice A. Choice B changes the tense of the sentence and introduces a dependent clause. This corrects the initial issue with the run-on sentence, but it appears to introduce two new errors. The verb tense should be consistent in the sentence ("system *was* a feat"), and there should be a comma between *engineering* and *which*; choice B can also be eliminated. Continue checking the other choices to see if they fix the original problem or introduce new errors. Both choices C and D maintain the verb tense of the sentence and technically correct the run-on sentence. As such, they are both grammatically correct. However, in considering concision, choice C is awkward and wordy when compared to choice D. Using *that* alone makes it clear that the author is describing what the aqueduct system combined (form and function) without adding any unnecessary words to the sentence. **The correct answer is D.** It is grammatically correct, concise, and relevant to the passage.

BRAIN BREAK

Ambidexterity is the ability to use the right hand and the left hand equally well. Did you know that using your nondominant hand will help to strengthen neural connections in your brain? Challenge yourself to hold a pencil or pen in your nondominant hand and trace the outline of your other hand. Write your name. Complete a few routine tasks, such as pouring water into a glass or eating with your opposite hand. When you use your nondominant hand, you are activating both hemispheres of your brain. You are challenging your mind to consciously engage to complete what would normally be a routine task.

Summing It Up

4

- In the Writing and Language Test section of the SAT exam, there are four passages and 44 multiple-choice questions (11 questions per passage). You will have 35 minutes to complete this section, about 8 minutes and 40 seconds per passage.

- The multiple-choice questions in this section put you in an editor's role. Each question consists of an "editing problem" with four possible solutions. You'll fix issues with development of a passage's topic, organization, and various standards of English usage.

- Some passages are accompanied by informational graphics, such as graphs, charts, and tables. You'll need to refer to these supplementary graphics to answer a question or two, but no math will be required.

- There are two main categories of multiple-choice questions:

  1. **Expression of Ideas** questions cover adding, deleting, or changing text, transitional language, and relevant details; reordering sentences; combining sentences; selecting appropriate words in context; creating consistency of style and tone; and changing language for cohesion and precision.

     - Answers for Expression of Ideas questions must maintain the topic of the passage or align with data in a graphic, create a logical flow between sentences and paragraphs, and eliminate wordiness and redundancy.

  2. **Standard English Conventions** questions cover sentence structure, punctuation, and usage.

     - Answers for Standards of English Conventions must be grammatically correct, concise, and relevant to the passage.

- For every question, practice the following steps:

  o Read the entire sentence with the underlined information or question marker.

  o Ask yourself, "Do I see a problem?"

    - If yes, eliminate answers that do not address the problem.

    - If no, evaluate each answer choice and eliminate answers with errors.

  o Apply your question-specific strategies to work through the remaining answer choices.

  o Reread the sentence or paragraph while substituting in your answer choice if time allows.

Take a moment to ask yourself some simple questions about your understanding of the chapter:

Review: What did I learn?

Evaluate: What do I need to learn more about?

Plan: What can I do next to keep improving?

Based on your answers to those questions, adjust your study plan to dedicate additional time to the areas of weakness that you've identified.

PRACTICE EXERCISE: WRITING AND LANGUAGE TEST

18 Minutes—22 Questions

DIRECTIONS: Each of the following passages is accompanied by a set of questions. For some questions, you will consider how the passage might be revised to improve the expression of ideas. For other questions, you will consider how the passage might be edited to correct errors in sentence structure, usage, or punctuation. A passage or a question may be accompanied by one or more graphics (such as a table, chart, or graph) that you will consider as you make revising and editing decisions.

Some questions will direct you to an underlined portion of a passage. Other questions will direct you to a location in a passage or ask you to think about the passage as a whole.

After reading each passage, choose the answer to each question that most effectively improves the quality of writing in the passage or that makes the passage conform to the conventions of Standard Written English. Many questions include a "NO CHANGE" option. Choose that option if you think the best choice is to leave the relevant portion of the passage as it is.

Questions 1–11 are based on the following passage.

JANE AUSTEN AND FANNY PRICE

. . . In real life, one is sometimes left out because of actual purposeful **(1)** problems on the parts of those doing the leaving out, but sometimes one is simply left out—and culpability **(2)** was beside the point. **(3)** The second case is much less satisfying to the left-out person, but it is also much more usual. Fairy tales such as "Cinderella" are satisfying because, in them, it is clearly the nastiness of the villains and villainesses that causes the heroes and heroines to be excluded from pleasurable activities.

(1)

A. NO CHANGE

B. wrongdoing

C. issues

D. charity

(2)

A. NO CHANGE

B. had been

C. is

D. would have been

(3) The writer is considering deleting the underlined sentence. Should the writer do this?

A. Yes, because it does not provide a good transition between the first and third sentences in the paragraph.

B. Yes, because it fails to support the main argument of the passage: that *Mansfield Park* presents a fairytale conception of being left out.

C. No, because it identifies important distinctions among three different "cases."

D. No, because it provides a good transition between the first and third sentences in the paragraph.

[1] When I was in elementary school, I was a shy little girl not unlike Fanny Price of Jane Austen's **4** *Mansfield Park.* [2] Sometimes when I was feeling left out, I would sit on a bench at the very edge of the playground and put spit on my cheeks to simulate tears, in case David Gould, **5** <u>a boy I knew,</u> should pass by and take pity on me. **6** [3] I also had a fairytale conception of being left out (as Fanny and Jane Austen have in this novel). [4] He never did, but it didn't really **7** <u>matter. My imagination</u> would take over from that point. [5] The stories I made up always had the same **8** <u>plot I was carried off by a prince (David) on</u> a flying horse to his castle, where I became his wife and got to live in the lap of luxury. [6] (From there I would go into elaborate detail about the décor of the castle, how many horses we owned, what colors they were, and so on.)

4 The writer is considering adding the phrase "magnificent work of art" here. Should the writer do this?

A. Yes, because it identifies the genre of *Mansfield Park.*

B. Yes, because it sums up the writer's true opinion of the book.

C. No, because it is an unnecessary and possibly confusing addition.

D. No, because it contradicts the writer's previous, more critical statement.

5 Which choice provides the most relevant detail?

A. NO CHANGE

B. the shortest boy in my classroom

C. the handsomest boy in the school

D. my sister's best friend's boyfriend

6 To make this paragraph most logical, sentence 3 should be placed

A. where it is now.

B. after sentence 1.

C. after sentence 4.

D. after sentence 6.

7 Which choice most effectively combines the two sentences at the underlined portion?

A. matter because my imagination

B. matter; for example, my imagination

C. matter; in other words, my imagination

D. matter—consequently, my imagination

A. NO CHANGE

B. plot I was carried off by a prince—David—on

C. plot, I was carried off by a prince (David) on

D. plot: I was carried off by a prince (David) on

In the course of *Mansfield Park*, Fanny goes through one big suffer-and-be-**⑨** victorious cycle (her ultimate marriage to Edmund after many, many years of being left out) and many little suffer-and-be-comforted cycles:

"Edmund . . . going quietly to another table . . . brought a glass of Madeira to Fanny [who had a headache as a result of being deprived of proper exercise by the thoughtless disregard of others], and obliged her to drink the greater part. She wished to be able to decline it, but the tears which a variety of feelings created, made it easier to swallow than to speak." [*Mansfield Park*, page 513; from *The Complete Novels of Jane Austen*, Modern Library edition]

The little gush of passionate, passive gratefulness that Fanny feels when Edmund "obliges" her to drink the Madeira feels to me similar to the sweet rush of vindicated personal pathos that I felt at the moment in my David Gould fantasy when he would suddenly appear and sweep me up and away from my wrongfully left-out state into one of well-deserved bliss. This way of thinking is childish, self-pitying, and self-deluded; **⑩** accordingly, Jane Austen (who is usually far more astute) lets Fanny get away with it.

The author rigs things so that whenever Fanny is left out, we can be sure that one or some of the other characters are engaged in something sinful; this is an **⑪** unrealistic—fairy-tale—element in what is otherwise a highly developed, realistic novel.

⑨
A. NO CHANGE
B. vindicated
C. verified
D. vaulted

⑩
A. NO CHANGE
B. nevertheless,
C. predictably,
D. thus,

⑪
A. NO CHANGE
B. unrealistic fairy-tale element: in
C. unrealistic—fairy-tale element in
D. unrealistic fairy-tale, element in

4

Questions 12–22 are based on the following passage and supplementary material.

A Speech-Language Pathologist Career

Speech-language pathologists, sometimes called speech therapists, assess, diagnose, treat, and help **12** <u>encourage</u> communication and swallowing disorders resulting from a variety of causes, such as stroke, developmental delay, Parkinson's disease, a brain injury, autism, or a cleft palate.

A typical speech-language therapist evaluates difficulty levels of speech, language, or swallowing; identifies treatment options; **13** <u>creates a standardized treatment plan that addresses specific functional needs</u>; teaches an individual how to make sounds and improves his or her voice and maintains fluency; helps individuals improve vocabulary and sentence structure used in oral and written language; works with individuals to develop and strengthen the muscles used to swallow; and counsels **14** <u>individuals and families</u> on how to cope with communication and swallowing disorders.

12

A. NO CHANGE

B. facilitate

C. prevent

D. counsel

13

A. NO CHANGE

B. creates and carries out an individualized treatment plan that addresses specific functional needs

C. creates specific functional needs that are addressed in a treatment plan

D. creates and carries out an individualized treatment plan that addresses specific behavioral needs

14 Which choice provides the most relevant details?

A. NO CHANGE

B. physicians and medical staff

C. students and colleagues

D. colleagues and family members

Speech-language pathologists work with individuals who have problems with speech and language, including cognitive or social communication. Some specialize in working with certain age groups; others focus on treatment programs for specific problems. Their colleagues include physicians and surgeons, healthcare workers, social workers, occupational and physical therapists, and psychologists. Speech-language pathologists also work in the educational system, helping students, teachers, school personnel, and parents. **15** They play a vital role in the process of evaluating students and communicating with teachers, school staff, and parents to implement specific programs and support classroom activities.

15 The writer is considering deleting the underlined sentence. Should the sentence be kept or deleted?

A. Kept, because it provides details that support the main topic of the paragraph.

B. Kept, because it provides additional information to support the prior sentence.

C. Deleted, because it contradicts the main focus of the paragraph.

D. Deleted, because it repeats information that has been provided earlier in the paragraph.

4

A SPEECH-LANGUAGE PATHOLOGIST CAREER	
Quick Facts	
2018 Median Pay	$77,510 per year
	$37.26 per hour
Typical Entry-Level Education	Master's degree
Work Experience in a Related Occupation	None
On-the-job Training	Internship/residency
Number of Jobs, 2018	153,700
Job Outlook, 2018–28	27% (much faster than average)
Employment Change, 2018–28	41,900

[Source: **www.bls.gov/ooh/healthcare/speech-language-pathologists.htm**]

16 [1] Why is the speech-language pathologist field growing so quickly? [2] A few years ago, US government experts predicted that employment of speech-language pathologists would grow **17** 2.7 percent from 2018 to 2028, a gain of about 41,900 jobs per year. [3] (This is faster than the average for all occupations on which the US Department of Labor gathers statistics.) [4] As the awareness of speech and language disorders continues to **18** stall, it reflects a greater need for professionals that can treat an increasing number of speech and language disorders.

16 For the sake of cohesion, sentence 1 should be placed

A. where it is now.

B. after sentence 2.

C. after sentence 3.

D. after sentence 4.

17 Which choice most accurately and effectively represents the information shown in the chart?

A. NO CHANGE

B. 2.7 percent from 2018 to 2028, a gain of about 4,190 jobs per year.

C. 27 percent from 2018 to 2028, a gain of about 4,190 jobs per year.

D. 27 percent from 2018 to 2028, a gain of about 41,900 jobs in total.

18

A. NO CHANGE

B. evolve

C. shift

D. compress

[1] Job opportunities **19** abound. [2] This is especially true for pathologists who elect to specialize in working with a specific age group or individuals with a certain impairment. [3] The boomer generations are aging, and there is an increased need to treat speech or language impairments stemming from such health conditions as stroke or dementia. [4] Due to an increased awareness of autism and the depth of the spectrum, **20** there is a greater claim for early diagnosis and treatment to help improve communication and socialization skills. [5] **21** All of these factors are combining, joining, and uniting to create many new opportunities. **22**

19 Which choice most effectively combines the two sentences at the underlined portion?

A. abound, especially for speech-language pathologists who elect to

B. abound: especially true for pathologists who

C. abound; especially positively impacted speech-language pathologists electing to

D. abound—and especially for those lucky pathologists who have acquired

20

A. NO CHANGE

B. there is a greater demand for early diagnosis and treatment

C. there is a greater requirement for early diagnosis and treatment

D. there is a greater discrepancy for early diagnosis and treatment

21

A. NO CHANGE

B. These factors are combining to create

C. All of these factors are combining and uniting to create

D. All of these factors are combining to create

22 The writer wants to add the following sentence to the paragraph:

As a result of medical advancements, trauma victims have a greater chance of survival, and speech-language pathologists play an integral role in their rehabilitation.

The best place for the sentence is immediately

A. before sentence 1

B. after sentence 1

C. after sentence 4

D. after sentence 5

ANSWER KEY AND EXPLANATIONS

1. B	6. B	11. A	15. B	19. A
2. C	7. A	12. C	16. C	20. B
3. D	8. D	13. B	17. D	21. B
4. C	9. A	14. A	18. B	22. C
5. C	10. B			

4

1. **The correct answer is B.** In this sentence, the writer is indicating an act to deliberately do wrong to another person, so the best word choice is *wrongdoing*. While wrongdoing is a problem of sorts, the word *problems* is not specific enough, so it is not the best answer choice. *Issues* (choice C) is similarly lacking in specificity. *Charity* (choice D) has almost the opposite meaning of *wrongdoing*.

2. **The correct answer is C.** Except for this verb, *was*, the writer uses the present tense throughout the paragraph. Therefore, to be consistent, the correct answer is choice C.

3. **The correct answer is D.** The writer should not delete the sentence because it provides a good transition between the first and third sentences in the paragraph.

4. **The correct answer is C.** The writer should not add this phrase here because it is unnecessary and may confuse readers into thinking *Mansfield Park* is a work of visual art, such as a painting.

5. **The correct answer is C.** It makes sense that a girl would cast the handsomest boy in the school in the role of a prince who saves her from her unhappy state. Choices A, B, and D are incorrect because, while they are possible choices, they are not as relevant as choice C.

6. **The correct answer is B.** Sentence 3 makes the best sense when it follows sentence 1.

7. **The correct answer is A.** The linking word *because* makes sense in context: the writer is explaining *why* it did not matter that David

Gould never noticed or pitied her when she was a shy little girl.

8. **The correct answer is D.** As originally written, the sentence lacks the necessary punctuation, and choice D corrects this issue by separating an idea (the stories the writer always made up had the same plot) from its explanation with a colon. Choice B replaces the parentheses with em dashes unnecessarily and does not correct the run-on sentence. Choice C uses a comma, which creates a comma splice.

9. **The correct answer is A.** The parenthetical information in this sentence describes a situation in which someone suffers (Fanny is left out) before achieving success (she gets married), and *victorious* means "achieving success." *Vindicated* (choice B) means "being cleared of blame," and does not make much sense in this context. To be verified (choice C) is to be proven truthful or correct, so *verified* is not a strong answer either. *Vaulted* (choice D) means "domed" and makes no sense in this context.

10. **The correct answer is B.** The transitional word *nevertheless* makes sense in context: the writer is explaining that even though Jane Austen is usually astute about her characters, in this case, Austen "lets Fanny get away with" childishness, self-pity, and self-delusion. The words *predictably* and *thus* misrepresent the writer's purpose.

11. **The correct answer is A.** As originally written, the em dashes enclose an alternate and nonessential term for *unrealistic*, and

nonessential information should be enclosed in commas or em dashes. Choice B changes "fairy tale" into essential information, which could be relevant to the passage, but adds a colon before "in," which is unnecessary. Neither choice C nor D correctly encloses the nonessential phrase "fairy tale," suggesting that all the information after the em dash is nonessential (choice C) or that everything after "fairy tale" is nonessential (choice D), both of which create sentence fragments.

12. **The correct answer is C.** The first sentence lists ways that speech-language pathologists can help individuals with communication and swallowing disorders. Of the answer choices listed, *prevent*, meaning "to keep from happening or existing," makes the most sense. While a speech-language pathologist can provide encouragement during the process of treatment and help facilitate treatment, using the words *encourage* (choice A) and *facilitate* (choice B) in the underlined portion of the sentence would change the meaning of the sentence, effectively implying that the speech-language pathologist would help promote speech disorders. Similarly, a speech-language pathologist can help counsel individuals and families, but using the word *counsel* (choice D) in the underlined portion of the sentence doesn't make sense.

13. **The correct answer is B.** Only choice B offers clear and concise wording regarding creating and carrying out an individualized treatment plan that addresses specific functional needs. Choice A doesn't make sense because a standardized treatment plan typically does not address specific needs. Choice C indicates that the speech-language pathologist is creating functional needs, which doesn't make sense either. Choice D uses the word *behavioral*, which is not a need that is typically assessed or treated by a speech-language pathologist.

14. **The correct answer is A.** To answer this question, ask yourself which group of people among the choices listed will need counseling on how to cope with communication and swallowing disorders? The most relevant choice is individuals and families. A speech-language pathologist could consult with physicians, medical staff, and colleagues, but consulting is not the same as counseling.

15. **The correct answer is B.** This sentence should be kept because it clarifies information presented earlier in the paragraph.

16. **The correct answer is C.** Sentence 1 makes the most sense when it follows sentence 3.

17. **The correct answer is D.** The last two lines of the chart say that the projected job outlook for speech-language pathologists during the ten years from 2018 to 2028 is 27 percent growth and that, during those ten years, the field will gain a total of 41,900 jobs . Choices A, B, and C are incorrect because the statistics they give do not match those shown in the chart.

18. **The correct answer is B.** The sentence describes how industries change and grow, and this is what *evolve* means. *Stall* (choice A) means the opposite of *evolve*. *Shift* is not as specific a word as *evolve*, so choice C is not the best answer choice. *Compress* (choice D) means "squeeze" and does not make sense in this context.

19. **The correct answer is A.** This is the simplest, clearest way to combine the two sentences. Choice B contains incorrect punctuation, choice C is awkward, and choice D does not match the rest of the passage's style and tone.

20. **The correct answer is B.** The sentence describes an increased awareness of autism and the depth of the spectrum. This information allows you to the conclude that there is an increased need or *demand* for speech-language pathologists who specialize in early diagnosis and treatment. *Claim* (choice A),

4

meaning "a right to something," doesn't make sense. There is no requirement for early diagnosis and treatment, so choice C is incorrect. *Discrepancy* (choice D) alludes to a disagreement or being "at a variance," which has nothing to do with an increased demand for early diagnosis or treatment.

21. **The correct answer is B.** As originally written, the sentence is redundant since *combining*, *joining*, and *uniting* all share the same meaning. Choice B corrects this error by using only one of these terms. Choice C makes the mistake of eliminating only one of the redundant terms. And while choice D eliminates two terms, it does not remove the unnecessary phrasing "All of."

22. **The correct answer is C.** The additional sentence would best fit after sentence 4, right before the concluding sentence of the paragraph.

Chapter 5

Standard English Conventions

OVERVIEW

- **Sentence Structure and Formation**
- **Verb Tense, Mood, and Voice**
- **Conventions of Punctuation**
- **Conventions of Usage**
- **Agreement**
- **Frequently Confused Words and Expressions**
- **Summing It Up**

This chapter reviews Standard English Conventions as assessed by the Writing and Language section of the SAT. Chapter 4 introduced a basic set of steps for how to approach these questions. Keep those steps in mind while reviewing the following content and the practice exercises. While we're not attempting to teach you all the rules of punctuation and grammar, we do want you to review the concepts most commonly tested by the SAT and those you may need to call upon for your own writing.

Each of the three main domains covered in this chapter—sentence structure, conventions of punctuation, and conventions of usage—is broken down into smaller sections. These instructional sections are followed by exercises with answers and explanations. Be sure to read all the answer explanations, even for the questions you answered correctly. Review is an important part of your SAT exam preparation.

SENTENCE STRUCTURE AND FORMATION

There are four different kinds of sentence structures in English:

1. Simple sentences (an independent clause)
2. Compound sentences (two independent clauses joined together)
3. Complex sentences (an independent and at least one dependent clause)
4. Compound-complex sentences (at least two independent clauses and one dependent clause)

Compound, complex, and compound-complex sentences can technically have as many clauses as you want, as long as they are connected and punctuated correctly. In this section, we will review some rules about sentence structure you will need in order to be successful on the Writing and Language section of the SAT exam.

Fragments

Basic Rule

Every sentence must have a subject (something to do the action) and a verb (the action) and express a complete idea. When all those items are present, you get an **independent clause** (another way of saying "a complete sentence"). A group of words that is missing one of these elements is called a **sentence fragment** or an **incomplete sentence**. If a group of words has a subject and verb but doesn't express a complete thought, it's a **dependent clause**.

There are two ways to correct incomplete sentences:

1. Add the fragment to the sentence that precedes it or the sentence that follows.

   Incorrect: Zoologists and wildlife biologists study animals and other wildlife. Including how they interact with their ecosystems.

   Correct: Zoologists and wildlife biologists study animals and other wildlife, including how they interact with their ecosystems.

   Explanation: The fragment is added to the sentence that precedes it by inserting a comma.

   Incorrect: By studying animal behaviors. Wildlife biologists seek to understand how animals interact with their ecosystems.

   Correct: By studying animal behaviors, wildlife biologists seek to understand how animals interact with their ecosystems.

   Explanation: The fragment is added to the sentence that follows it by inserting a comma. (The fragment now serves as a prepositional phrase that modifies the rest of the sentence.)

2. Add a subject and verb to the fragment.

   Incorrect: Considerable time studying animals in their natural habitats.

   Correct: Wildlife biologists may spend considerable time studying animals in their natural habitats.

   Explanation: A subject (*wildlife biologists*) and verb (*may spend*) are added to the fragment.

Run-Ons and Comma Splices

Basic Rule

Complete sentences must be separated by a period, a comma and a coordinating conjunction, or a semicolon. A **run-on sentence** occurs when a writer fails to use either end-stop punctuation to divide complete thoughts or suitable conjunctions to join two ideas. When two independent clauses are joined only by a comma, you have an error called a **comma splice**.

The following rules will help you avoid and fix run-on sentences and comma splices:

1. Divide the sentence using periods.

   Incorrect: Zoologists need a bachelor's degree for entry-level positions a master's degree or Ph.D. is often needed for advancement.

   Correct: Zoologists need a bachelor's degree for entry-level positions. A master's degree or Ph.D. is often needed for advancement.

Explanation: Inserting a period between *positions* and *A* corrects the run-on sentence by creating two independent clauses.

2. Create a compound sentence by joining independent clauses using a coordinating conjunction (e.g., *and*, *but*, or *so*).

   Incorrect: Zoologists need a bachelor's degree for entry-level positions, a master's degree is often needed for advancement.

   Correct: Zoologists need a bachelor's degree for entry-level position, but a master's degree is often needed for advancement. (Remember that a comma is required when you use a coordinating conjunction to join two independent clauses.)

   Explanation: Adding a comma and the coordinating conjunction *but* eliminates the comma splice and connects the two independent clauses correctly.

3. Create a complex sentence by adding a subordinating conjunction (e.g., *because*, *although*, or *while*), making one of the independent clauses a dependent clause.

   Incorrect: Zoologists need only a bachelor's degree for entry-level positions a master's degree is often needed for advancement.

   Correct: Zoologists need only a bachelor's degree for entry-level positions although a master's degree is often needed for advancement.

   Explanation: Adding the conjunction *although* between the two independent clauses corrects the run-on sentence by changing the second clause to a dependent clause and creating a complex sentence (In general, commas are not required when the dependent clause follows the independent clause.)

   Also correct: Although a master's degree is often needed for advancement, zoologists need only a bachelor's degree for entry-level positions.

   Explanation: Adding the conjunction *although* before the first independent clauses corrects the run-on sentence by changing the first clause to a dependent clause and creating a complex sentence. (Commas are required when the dependent clause precedes the independent clause.)

4. Use a semicolon when ideas are closely related in meaning.

   Incorrect: Zoologists and wildlife biologists study how animals and other wildlife interact with their ecosystems, these scientists work in offices, laboratories, or outdoors.

   Correct: Zoologists and wildlife biologists study how animals and other wildlife interact with their ecosystems; these scientists work in offices, laboratories, or outdoors.

   Explanation: Inserting a semicolon between the two independent clauses corrects the comma splice and creates a compound sentence.

5

ALERT

The SAT will never ask you to choose between a semicolon and a comma with a coordinating conjunction in answer choices that connect complete sentences. If a question gives you both choices for making a compound sentence, one of them must not work for the situation either because it's not grammatically correct or it is irrelevant for the passage.

Skill Builder: Fragments and Run-ons

DIRECTIONS: Revise the following sentences to correct fragments and eliminate run-ons, while also adhering to Writing and Language section strategies laid out in Chapter 4.

5

1. Zoologists and wildlife biologists perform a variety of scientific tests and <u>experiments for example, they</u> take blood samples from animals to assess their levels of nutrition, check animals for disease and parasites, and tag animals in order to track them.

   A. NO CHANGE

   B. experiments for example. They

   C. experiments. For example, they

   D. experiments; and for example, they

2. In order to track potential threats <u>to wild-life. Wildlife biologists</u> often use computer programs.

   A. NO CHANGE

   B. to wildlife, wildlife biologists

   C. to wildlife; wildlife biologists

   D. to wildlife, yet wildlife biologists

3. Zoologists and wildlife biologists work to expand our knowledge <u>of wildlife species. Work closely</u> with public officials to develop wildlife management and conservation plans.

   A. NO CHANGE

   B. of wildlife species although they work closely

   C. of wildlife species, and work closely

   D. of wildlife species and work closely

4. Herpetologists study <u>reptiles, such as snakes. And amphibians, such as frogs.</u>

   A. NO CHANGE

   B. reptiles and amphibians, such as snakes and frogs.

   C. reptiles, such as snakes; amphibians, such as frogs.

   D. reptiles, in the case of snakes, and amphibians, such as the case of frogs.

5. Some wildlife biologists develop conservation plans and make recommendations on conservation <u>and management issues to policymakers</u> and the general public.

   A. NO CHANGE

   B. and management issues. To policymakers

   C. and management issues to various groups, including policymakers and the general public.

   D. and management issues; to policymakers

6. <u>Ecologists study ecosystems. And the relationships between organisms</u> and their surrounding environments.

   A. NO CHANGE

   B. Ecologists study ecosystems and the relationships between organisms

   C. Ecologists study ecosystems, and the relationships between organisms

   D. Ecologists study ecosystems; and the relationships between organisms

7. Evolutionary biologists study the origins <u>of species. The changes</u> in their inherited characteristics over generations.

   A. NO CHANGE

   B. of species, the changes

   C. of species. They also study the changes

   D. of species and the changes

8. Zoologists and wildlife biologists conduct <u>experimental studies, they also collect</u> biological data for analysis.

   A. NO CHANGE

   B. experimental studies while they also collect

   C. experimental studies and collect

   D. experimental, studies, and collect

Answers and Explanations

1. **The correct answer is C.** The original presents two independent clauses with no separating punctuation, thus creating a run-on sentence (choice A). Inserting a period between the two clauses solves the problem. "For example" describes the second sentence, not the first (choice B). Semicolons should not be used before coordinating conjunctions to separate two complete sentences (choice D).

2. **The correct answer is B.** Sentence fragments as presented here (choice A) must be corrected with missing sentence elements or attached to a relevant independent clause. A comma alone can be used to join the introductory phrase to the independent clause that follows it. Semicolons are used to connect two independent clauses (choice C). A comma and a coordinating conjunction (*yet*) also connect two independent clauses (choice D).

3. **The correct answer is D.** The second sentence is not an independent clause; it is missing a subject to perform the verb *work* (choice A). The best way to correct this error is to connect the incomplete clause with the conjunction *and*, creating a compound predicate ("work to expand" and "work closely") that shares the compound subject "zoologists and wildlife biologists." *Although* is a subordinating conjunction that signals the beginning of a dependent clause. While that change would be grammatically correct,

although creates a contrasting relationship between the ideas in the sentence and is thus irrelevant (choice B). The comma plus the coordinating conjunction *and* would be acceptable only if the second clause had a subject, like *they* (choice C).

4. **The correct answer is B.** "And amphibians, such as frogs" is a sentence fragment as it lacks a verb and does not express a complete thought (choice A). Combining and rephrasing the sentence and fragment to make "amphibians and reptiles" the direct object of the verb *study* and then adding the adjectival phrase "such as snakes and frogs" to provide examples creates a clear and concise sentence. A semicolon signals that the information both before and after comprises complete sentences (choice C). Choice D introduces unnecessary commas and phrases, making it awkward and wordy.

5. **The correct answer is A.** As written, the sentence is clear and grammatically correct. "To policymakers and the general public" lacks a verb and thus cannot be separated as a complete sentence (choice B). Choice D repeats the same issue as choice B, with the semicolon indicating two independent clauses. While the two phrases can be joined with a comma (choice C), the original sentence indicates no additional groups beyond policymakers and the public.

5

5

6. **The correct answer is B.** The information following "And the relationships" is a sentence fragment (choice A and D). Removing the period and combining that information changes the fragment into the direct object of the verb *study*. The sentence describes the two areas of study for ecologists: ecosystems and organisms (and their relationships), so no comma is necessary for separation (choice C).

7. **The correct answer is D.** The information after the period is a sentence fragment (choice A). Removing the period and combining that information using the conjunction *and* changes the fragment into the direct object of the verb *study*. While the information before the period and after can be joined with a comma (choice B), the comma indicates that "the changes in their inherited characteristics" is a definition for "the origin of species," while it is a distinct area of study. Choice C is grammatically correct but not as concise as choice D.

8. **The correct answer is C.** Two independent clauses cannot be joined by a comma alone (choice A). The best way to combine these clauses is to add the conjunction *and* and to remove the pronoun *they* to create a simple sentence in which *conduct* and *collect* act as the compound predicate for the subject "zoologists and wildlife biologists." Compound predicates do not require a comma between them. You can add a subordinating conjunction like *while* to an independent clause to make it a sentence fragment (choice B), but *while* changes the meaning of the original sentence, indicating that both actions, *conduct* and *collect*, occur at the same time; it is also not as concise as other options. A comma and a coordinating conjunction separate two independent clauses or are used for the last item in a list of three or more items (choice D); the information after the comma is only the second item ("experimental studies" is one item) and is also not an independent clause.

TIP

You don't always have to know why the right answer is right on the SAT. Being able to identify why other answers are wrong is just as useful a skill and often just as effective.

Coordination and Subordination

Basic Rule

Coordinating and subordinating conjunctions are used to join phrases and clauses and form compound and complex sentences.

Some common coordinating and subordinating conjunctions follow:

Coordinating conjunctions	Subordinating conjunctions
and, but, for, nor, or, so, yet	after, although, as, as if, because, before, even if, even though, if, if only, rather than, since, that, though, unless, until, when, where, whereas, wherever, whether, which, while

Basic Rule of Coordinating Conjunctions

Coordinating conjunctions are used to add items to a list and join independent clauses to make compound sentences. With items in a list, the last item in the list should be preceded by a coordinating conjunction.

> **Independent clauses:** There was a Treaty of Paris signed in 1763. There was also one signed in 1783. There was another signed in 1919.

> **Joined:** There were Treaties of Paris signed in 1763, 1783, and 1919.

When two clauses are joined, if the second remains an independent clause, a comma must be used before the coordinating conjunction. The coordinating conjunction signals that each clause carries the same weight while also creating a relationship between the ideas (additive, contrasting, or causal).

> **Independent clauses:** There was a Treaty of Paris signed in 1763. There was also one signed in 1783.

> **Joined:** There was a Treaty of Paris signed in 1763, but there was another Treaty of Paris signed in 1783.

Basic Rule of Subordinating Conjunctions

Subordinating conjunctions are added to an independent clause to make it a dependent clause.

A dependent clause establishes a place, a time, a reason, a condition, a concession, or a comparison for the independent clause—some form of extra information that clarifies the action of the independent clause. Dependent clauses have a subject and a verb but don't express a complete thought—caused by the subordinating conjunction. Because of that, the clause needs (or **depends** on) an independent clause to be grammatically correct. This also means that they are subordinate to the information in the independent clause—meaning they're less important (offering extra information) and preceded by a subordinating conjunction. Dependent clauses can come before or after an independent clause, but if they're before, they must be separated from the independent clause by a comma. Review the list of subordinating conjunctions to more quickly identify dependent clauses. Let's look at some examples of subordinating conjunctions used to create dependent clauses.

> **Independent clauses:** A tax on imported goods from another country is called a tariff. A tax on imported goods from another country to protect a home industry is called a protective tariff.

> **Joined:** A tax on imported goods from another country is called a tariff while a tax on imported goods from another country to protect a home industry is called a protective tariff.

Here, the subordinating conjunction *while* was added to the second independent clause. The resulting dependent clause is then joined to the end of the first independent clause without using any punctuation.

TIP

For coordinating conjunctions, remember the acronym **FANBOYS**. **F**or, **A**nd, **N**or, **B**ut, **O**r, **Y**et, **S**o all connect ideas together. If you're using a comma to separate two complete sentences, you also need one of the FANBOYS.

TIP

Remember that an independent clause is just a complete sentence. It has a subject and a verb and expresses a complete thought.

A subordinating conjunction can also be used at the beginning of a sentence. The resulting dependent clause must be joined to an independent clause and be separated by a comma.

Independent clauses: A tax on imported goods from another country is called a tariff. A tax on imported goods from another country to protect a home industry is called a protective tariff.

Joined: While a tax on imported goods from another country is called a tariff, a tax on imported goods from another country to protect a home industry is called a protective tariff.

Skill Builder: Subordination and Coordination

5

> **DIRECTIONS:** Join the following sentences using subordinating or coordinating conjunctions.

1. A democracy is a form of government that is run for the people. It is also run by the people.

2. A primary source is an original record of an event. A secondary source is something that was written later.

3. The Industrial Revolution ushered in a time of unparalleled human progress. People often forget the damage that this progress did, and continues to do, to the environment.

4. Elizabeth Cady Stanton became famous as an advocate of women's rights. During the Civil War, she was also an ardent abolitionist.

Answers

In some cases, there are many possible correct answers. Here are some examples:

1. A democracy is a form of government that is run for the people, and it is also run by the people.

2. Whereas a primary source is an original record of an event, a secondary source is something that was written later.

3. While the Industrial Revolution ushered in a time of unparalleled human progress, people often forget the damage that this progress did, and continues to do, to the environment.

4. Elizabeth Cady Stanton became famous as an advocate of women's rights, and during the Civil War, she was also an ardent abolitionist.

Modifier Placement

A **modifier** is a word, phrase, or clause that adds detail to a sentence. In order to avoid confusion, modifiers should be placed as close as possible to the things they modify.

Examples of different modifiers are underlined in the sentences below.

Within the field of marine biology, employment is highly competitive. (The phrase "within the field of marine biology" modifies the subject of the sentence, which is *employment*. The word *highly* modifies our understanding of the competitive nature of finding employment.)

The abundant supply of marine scientists far exceeds the demands, and the number of federal and state government jobs is limited. (*Abundant* modifies *supply*. *Marine* modifies *scientists*. *Limited* modifies our understanding of *the number of jobs*.)

When the subject of a modifier is unclear or is not included in the sentence, it is considered a dangling modifier.

Incorrect: Not realizing that the job title of marine biologist rarely exists, *marine biology* is a term recognized by most people. (What is the first phrase modifying?)

Possible revision: Not realizing that the job title of marine biologist rarely exists, most people recognize the term *marine biology*.

Misplaced modifiers occur when a modifier is poorly placed and doesn't express the writer's intent accurately.

Incorrect: The term *marine biologist* is used to almost describe all of the disciplines and jobs that deal with the study of marine life, not just those that deal with the physical properties of the sea.

Possible revision: The term *marine biologist* is used to describe almost all of the disciplines and jobs that deal with the study of marine life, not just those that deal with the physical properties of the sea.

Parallel Structure

Parallel structure is the repetition of a grammatical form within a sentence. Parallel structure is a hallmark of effective writing and is often used to emphasize ideas and present compared items in an equal light. Coordinating conjunctions are often used in parallel constructions.

Nonparallel structure: As a child, George Washington Carver enjoyed reading, learned about plants, and he made art.

Parallel structure: As a child, George Washington Carver enjoyed reading, learning about plants, and making art.

Skill Builder: Modifier Placement and Parallel Structure

DIRECTIONS: Revise the following sentences to eliminate problems with modifier placement and parallel structure.

5

1. Critical for getting a competitive edge in the job market, fishery science requires a strong background in advanced mathematics and computer skills.

2. A fishery scientist studies population dynamics of fish and marine mammals after taking course work in the animal and aquatic sciences.

3. More universities are starting to offer programs for fisheries management or to manage wildlife, increasingly important fields within marine biology.

4. As well as their interactions, biological oceanographers study both the biological and physical aspects of the sea.

5. A student in the field of physical oceanography may take course work weighted heavily in physics, the study of mathematics, and learning how to create computer models.

Answers

In some cases, there are many possible correct answers. Here are some examples:

1. A strong background in advanced mathematics and computer skills is critical for getting a competitive edge in the fishery science job market.

2. After taking course work in the animal and aquatic sciences, a fishery scientist studies fish and marine mammal population dynamics.

3. More universities are starting to offer programs in fisheries or wildlife management, another increasingly important field within marine biology.

4. Biological oceanographers study both the biological and physical aspects of the sea, as well as their interactions.

5. A student in the field of physical oceanography may take course work weighted heavily in physics, mathematics, and computer modeling.

5

BRAIN BREAK

Did you know that doodling helps some students retain more information and alleviate stress? Try it! Grab something to doodle with (a pencil, a pen, crayons, etc.) and find something to doodle on (if you own this book, you can use the margins or the NOTES pages at the back of the book). Keep in mind that you don't have to create an artistic masterpiece. The point here is to spontaneously draw anything you wish.

VERB TENSE, MOOD, AND VOICE

Verb Tense

Basic Rule

Use the same verb tense whenever possible within a sentence or paragraph. Do not shift from one tense to another unless there is a valid reason for doing so.

> **Incorrect:** The Magna Carta *was* signed in 1215 by King John of England and *has been* the first document of its kind to limit the power of the British monarchy.

> **Correct:** The Magna Carta *was* signed in 1215 by King John of England and *was* the first document of its kind to limit the power of the British monarchy.

Naturally, different verb tenses have different forms, but you will see some overlap. For example, even though the sentences "He was tall" and "He was running" both use the verb "was," the former is a simple past tense verb while the latter is called the past progressive and has a helping verb attached to the word "running." Complete verbs can be individual words or consist of a helping verb (often a form of "to be," "to have," or "to do") and a main verb or a participle. Look out for those small verbs to decide which choice is best for the passage.

When to Use the Perfect Tenses

Basic Rule

Use *present perfect* for an action begun in the past and extended to the present.

> **Example:** Scientists at NASA *have seen* an alarming increase in the accumulation of greenhouse gases.

> **Explanation:** In this case, *scientists at NASA saw* would be incorrect. What they *have seen* (present perfect) began in the past and extends to the present.

Basic Rule

Use *past perfect* for an action begun and completed in the past before some other past action.

> **Example:** Despite their preparations, Lewis and Clark *had never encountered* the kinds of challenges that awaited them before their expedition.

> **Explanation:** In this case, *never encountered* would be incorrect. The action *had never encountered* (past perfect) is used because it is referring to events prior to their expedition.

Basic Rule

Use *future perfect* for an action begun at any time and completed in the future.

> **Example:** When the American astronauts arrive, the Russian cosmonauts *will have been* on the International Space Station for six months.

> **Explanation:** In this case, although both actions occur in the future, the Russian cosmonauts *will have been* on the space station before the American astronauts *arrive.* When there are two future actions, the action completed first is expressed in the future perfect tense.

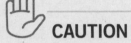

CAUTION

Different verb tenses have different forms, and there may be some overlap. It's important to choose the choice that is the best for the passage.

Knowing when to choose between the simple (past, present, and future) and perfect tenses can be challenging as those choices often depend on the author's intended meaning. Many SAT questions with verb tense issues will also include issues with agreement (discussed later in this chapter) and concision. When confronted with two grammatically correct choices, such as one in the simple past and another in the perfect past tense, concision may allow you to decide between answers if it is unclear which is better for the passage.

Tenses: Common Verbs

Refer to the following chart to familiarize yourself with some common verbs and their tenses.

Infinitive	Present	Past	Future	Present Perfect	Past Perfect	Future Perfect
to ask	ask	asked	will ask	have asked	had asked	will have asked
to be	am	was	will be	have been	had been	will have been
to become	become	became	will become	have become	had become	will have become
to begin	begin	began	will begin	have begun	had begun	will have begun
to come	come	came	will come	have come	had come	will have come
to do	do	did	will do	have done	had done	will have done
to eat	eat	ate	will eat	have eaten	had eaten	will have eaten
to feel	feel	felt	will feel	have felt	had felt	will have felt
to find	find	found	will find	have found	had found	will have found
to get	get	got	will get	have gotten	had gotten	will have gotten
to give	give	gave	will give	have given	had given	will have given
to go	go	went	will go	have gone	had gone	will have gone
to grow	grow	grew	will grow	have grown	had grown	will have grown
to have	have	had	will have	have had	had had	will have had
to hear	hear	heard	will hear	have heard	had heard	will have heard
to hide	hide	hid	will hide	have hidden	had hidden	will have hidden
to keep	keep	kept	will keep	have kept	had kept	will have kept
to know	know	knew	will know	have known	had known	will have known
to leave	leave	left	will leave	have left	had left	will have left
to like	like	liked	will like	have liked	had liked	will have liked
to look	look	looked	will look	have looked	had looked	will have looked
to make	make	made	will make	have made	had made	will have made
to meet	meet	met	will meet	have met	had met	will have met

Infinitive	Present	Past	Future	Present Perfect	Past Perfect	Future Perfect
to put	put	put	will put	have put	had put	will have put
to say	say	said	will say	have said	had said	will have said
to see	see	saw	will see	have seen	had seen	will have seen
to sleep	sleep	slept	will sleep	have slept	had slept	will have slept
to speak	speak	spoke	will speak	have spoken	had spoken	will have spoken
to study	study	studied	will study	have studied	had studied	will have studied
to take	take	took	will take	have taken	had taken	will have taken
to think	think	thought	will think	have thought	had thought	will have thought
to walk	walk	walked	will walk	have walked	had walked	will have walked
to want	want	wanted	will want	have wanted	had wanted	will have wanted
to work	work	worked	will work	have worked	had worked	will have worked
to write	write	wrote	will write	have written	had written	will have written

*Note: For consistency, all verbs are conjugated in the first-person singular.

Skill Builder: Verb Tense

DIRECTIONS: Circle the word with the correct verb tense for each sentence.

1. (was, has been) Established in Jamestown, Virginia, the House of Burgesses _____ the first representative body founded in the new world.

2. (have been, were) There _____ many great American explorers, but some scholars argue that none are as historically significant as Lewis and Clark.

3. (had never been, never was) Before 1804, Meriwether Lewis _____ on an expedition of any significance, let alone led one.

4. (will have added, has added) By the time this article is published, the United States_____ 250,000 new jobs.

5. (was, has been) Civil Disobedience, or the refusal to obey a government law or laws, _____ one of Martin Luther King, Jr.'s key tactics during the Civil Rights Movement.

Answers and Explanations

1. **The correct answer is *was*.** The past tense is used because the action occurred in the past.

2. **The correct answer is *have been*.** The present perfect tense is used because the sentence refers to action that began in the past and extended to the present.

3. **The correct answer is *had never been*.** The past perfect tense is used because the sentence contains a past tense action that occurred before another action.

4. **The correct answer is *will have added*.** The future perfect tense is used because the sentence refers to action begun at any time and completed in the future.

5. **The correct answer is *was*.** The past tense is used because the action occurred in the past.

Mood

Basic Rule

Mood, as it relates to verb forms, refers to the kind of message the writer intends to communicate.

The *indicative mood* is the most common mood and is used to state facts or opinions.

> **Example:** Zora Neale Hurston's novel *Their Eyes Were Watching God* was forgotten for many years but is now considered a literary classic.

The *imperative mood* is used when a writer wants to give a directive or make a request. Though not stated, the subject of an imperative sentence is *you.*

> **Example:** Stop pretending that it doesn't matter.

> **Example:** George Washington peered across the Potomac as the frigid wind lashed his face. "Hurry!" he exclaimed. (*Peered* is in the indicative. *Hurry* is in the imperative.)

The *subjunctive mood* expresses a condition contrary to fact, a wish, a supposition, or an indirect command. Although it is going out of use in English, the subjunctive can still be seen in the following forms:

- To express a wish not likely to be fulfilled or impossible to be realized

  > **Example:** I wish it *were* possible for us to approve his transfer at this time. (It is *not* possible.)

- In a subordinate clause after a verb that expresses a command, a request, or a suggestion

  > **Example:** It was recommended by the White House *that* the Office of Homeland Security *be* responsible for preparing the statements.

- To express a condition known or supposed to be contrary to fact

  > **Example:** If Ann were chosen to be our company's president, women would earn more than their male counterparts.

- After *as if* or *as though.* In formal writing and speech, *as if* and *as though* are followed by the subjunctive, since they introduce as supposition something not factual. In informal writing and speaking, the indicative is sometimes used.

  > **Example:** Before defecting to the British Army, Benedict Arnold talked as if he were a true American patriot. (He was not.)

5

TIP
SAT questions with verb tense issues may also include issues with agreement and concision. Eliminating redundancy without omitting important information may allow you to decide between answer choices.

Closely related to the *subjunctive mood* is the *conditional mood*. The *conditional mood* is used when making requests or statements expressing under what condition something would happen. Signaled by such words as *would*, *could*, *should*, and *might*, the *conditional mood* is often used in connection with a phrase in the *subjunctive mood* and is preceded by the word *if*:

> **Example:** Had you followed the GPS directions, we would not have been lost.

> **Example:** The door might open if I jiggle the handle.

Avoid shifts in mood. Once you have determined the mood that properly expresses the passage's message, verify that the mood is sustained throughout the sentence or the paragraph. A shift in mood is confusing to the listener or reader; it indicates that the speaker or writer has changed his or her way of looking at the conditions.

> **Incorrect:** It is requested by the White House that a report of Congressional proceedings *be* prepared and copies *should be* distributed to all citizens. (*Be* is subjunctive; *should be*, indicative.)

> **Correct:** It is requested by the White House that a report of the Congressional proceedings *be* prepared and that copies *be* distributed to all citizens.

Voice

Basic Rule

Voice tells us whether the subject of a sentence is the actor or is acted upon. In formal writing, active voice is preferred because it is more immediate and places the reader closer to the action. Passive voice can be the better choice when you want to emphasize what received the action (e.g. "I was hit by a car" vs. "A car hit me."). The SAT will almost always prefer active voice to passive construction, unless the active construction is not grammatically correct, concise, and relevant to the passage.

> **Passive voice example:** According to legend, the cherry tree was chopped down by George Washington.

> **Active voice example:** According to legend, George Washington chopped down the whole cherry tree.

5

TIP

Determine the mood that properly expresses the passage's message and verify that the same mood is sustained throughout.

Skill Builder: Mood and Voice

> **DIRECTIONS:** In the following sentences, choose the correct mood or indicate the voice being used.

1. (was, were) The team of Russian engineers _____ unable to prevent the nuclear reactor in Chernobyl from melting down.

2. (was, were) If climate change _____ not such a threat to life on this planet, the scientific community would not be making such a big deal about carbon emissions.

3. (is, were) If inflation _____ to continue to rise, the effects on the economy would be disastrous.

4. (be, should be) The president asked if the Speaker of the House _____ present when the special announcement was made.

5. (passive or active voice) The stony coral polyps were placed in a cup made of calcium carbonate by the marine biologist.

6. (passive or active voice) For over 40 years, Henry Clay played a central role on the national political stage.

Answers and Explanations

1. **The correct answer is *was*.** This sentence uses the indicative mood and requires the simple past tense.

2. **The correct answer is *were*.** The subjunctive is correct because the sentence is making a supposition.

3. **The correct answer is *were*.** The subjunctive is correct because the sentence is making a supposition.

4. **The correct answer is *should be*.** The conditional is correct because the sentence is inquiring if something should occur under a specific condition.

5. **The correct answer is *passive voice*.** This sentence is passive because the subject of the sentence is acted upon.

6. **The correct answer is *active voice*.** This sentence is active because the subject of the sentence is doing the action.

CONVENTIONS OF PUNCTUATION

The Standards of English Conventions questions will test your knowledge of several key pieces of punctuation: commas, semicolons, em dashes, parentheses, colons, and apostrophes. There will also be questions about proper end-of-sentence punctuation, but they are rare. Each punctuation mark has several uses, but not every rule is tested by the SAT. The following lists prioritize the most common conventions that the Writing and Language test assesses.

FUN FACTS

Did you know that *E* is the most common letter to appear in the English language? The letter *T* is the next most frequent letter to appear. *T* is also the most common first letter in words. (letterfrequency.org)

The Comma

Basic Rules

We use commas for a lot of things, but on the SAT, you can focus on separating the following:

- Independent clauses that are connected by a coordinating conjunction
- Introductory clauses and phrases
- Dependent and independent clauses
- Items in a series
- Nonessential and parenthetical elements
- Coordinate adjectives

Let's look at some examples:

- To separate independent clauses connected by a coordinating conjunction

   Example: Toni Morrison's first novel, *The Bluest Eye*, was published in 1970, and it received a rave review from *The New York Times*.

- To set off introductory clauses and phrases

   Example: The year after winning her Nobel Prize, Toni Morrison published the novel *Jazz*.

- To separate a leading dependent clause from an independent clause

   Example: While she was praised for her writing style and range of emotion, critics also celebrated Morrison for the attention she drew to racial tension in the past and present of the United States.

- To separates three or more items in a list

   Example: In a span of 15 years, Toni Morrison won a National Book Critics Circle Award, the Pulitzer Prize, and the Nobel Prize for Literature.

   If you pay attention to punctuation, it's likely you've noticed that not everyone puts the serial or Oxford comma before the *and* when separating three or more items in a list. In recent years, a lot of writing (especially online) has ignored the serial comma, but its absence or presence can affect what a sentence means. In 2018, a missing Oxford comma in a Maine labor law cost a dairy company in the state $5 million dollars in a lawsuit with its employees. Many standardized tests, such as the SAT and ACT, will operate with the assumption that the serial comma is essential for clear communication and will test on its use with their grammar questions.

- To separate nonessential and parenthetical elements from the main clause

   Example 1: Toni Morrison, who won the Nobel Prize in Literature in 1993, was a Professor Emeritus at Princeton University.

ALERT

The SAT considers the serial or Oxford comma as essential and will test you on its use with their grammar questions.

TIP

Nonessential and parenthetical elements (commas, parentheses, or em dashes) provide extra information that is not necessary for the meaning or grammatical correctness of a sentence. While each of these punctuation marks serves a similar purpose, the difference between them is one of emphasis.

5

Example 2: Last night, Toni Morrison began her lecture, titled "The Future of Time: Literature and Diminished Expectations," with a meditation on the nature of time and the human perception of progress.

- To separate coordinate adjectives that precede the noun they describe

Example: Toni Morrison was rumored to be a fun, entertaining speaker.

When you have at least two adjectives describing a noun (e.g., "The tall, funny man" or "The cold and windy weather"), try separating the adjectives with a comma when their order can be reversed or when the conjunction *and* can be placed between them while still preserving the meaning of the phrase. If reversing the order or adding *and* disrupts the meaning of the phrase (e.g. "The giant hockey players" as "The hockey giant players" or "The giant and hockey players"), no comma is needed.

The Semicolon

Basic Rules

A semicolon may be used to separate two complete ideas (independent clauses) in a sentence when the two ideas have a close relationship and are *not* connected with a coordinating conjunction.

Example: "Inalienable rights" are basic human rights that many believe cannot and should not be given up or taken away; life, liberty, and the pursuit of happiness are some of those rights.

The semicolon is often used between independent clauses connected by conjunctive adverbs such as *consequently, therefore, also, furthermore, for example, however, nevertheless, still, yet, moreover,* and *otherwise.*

Example: In 1867, critics thought William H. Seward foolish for buying the largely unexplored territory of Alaska for the astronomical price of $7 million; however, history has proven that it was an inspired purchase.

A word of caution. Do not use the semicolon between an independent clause and a phrase or subordinate clause.

Incorrect: While eating ice cream for dessert; Clarence and Undine discussed their next business venture.

Correct: While eating ice cream for dessert, Clarence and Undine discussed their next business venture.

Similar to serial commas, semicolons are used to separate items in a list when the items themselves contain commas.

Example: Some kinds of biologists study specific species of animals. For example, cetologists study marine mammals, such as whales and dolphins; entomologists study insects, such as beetles and butterflies; and ichthyologists study wild fish, such as sharks and lungfish.

The Em Dash

Basic Rules

Em dashes are used to set off parenthetical material that you want to emphasize. Dashes interrupt the flow of your sentence, thereby calling attention to the information they contain. An em dash always precedes the nonessential information, so the aside must start later in the sentence.

Example: Many consider Toni Morrison—winner of both the Pulitzer and Nobel Prizes in Literature—to be one of the greatest writers of her generation.

Example: Benjamin Franklin's many intellectual pursuits—from printmaking to politics—exemplify his eclectic personality.

Em dashes can also be used to rename a nearby noun. Typically, a comma would be used to set off this information, but since it includes commas already, use an em dash.

Example: Benjamin Franklin—a printer, writer, inventor, and statesman—was the son of a soap maker.

An em dash also indicates a list, a restatement, an amplification, or a dramatic shift in tone or thought.

Example: Eager to write for his brother's newspaper, young Benjamin began submitting letters to the editor under the pseudonym Silence Dogood—they were a hit!

Parentheses

Basic Rules

Just like commas and em dashes, parentheses separate nonessential (also called nonrestrictive or parenthetical) elements from the rest of the sentence. Parentheses indicate that the enclosed information is less important or more tangential to the surrounding sentence. Parentheses must always come in pairs.

Example: Toni Morrison's novel *Beloved* (1987) was made into a movie in 1998.

Example: While at Princeton, Toni Morrison (the writer) established a special creative workshop for writers and performances called the Princeton Atelier.

Skill Builder: Commas, Semicolons, Em Dashes, and Parentheses

DIRECTIONS: Select commas, semicolons, em dashes, or parentheses to correct the underlined portion(s) of each sentence.

A typical architectural program includes courses on such topics as architectural history building design computer-aided design and math. Architects must possess certain qualities: analytical skills, in order to understand the content of designs, communication skills, in order to communicate with clients, creativity, in order to develop attractive and functional structures, and organizational skills, in order to keep track of big projects.

1

A. NO CHANGE

B. as architectural history; building design; computer-aided design; and math

C. as architectural history, building design, computer-aided design, and math

D. as architectural history, building design, computer-aided design and math

2

A. NO CHANGE

B. designs; communication skills, in order to communicate with clients; creativity, in order to develop attractive and functional structures; and organizational skills, in order to keep track of big projects.

C. designs communication skills in order to communicate with clients, creativity in order to develop attractive and functional structures, and organizational skills in order to keep track of big projects.

D. designs. Communication skills, in order to communicate with clients, creativity, in order to develop attractive and functional structures, and organizational skills, in order to keep track of big projects.

In order to be hired as an architect, you typically need to; complete a professional degree in architecture; gain relevant experience through a paid internship; and pass the Architect Registration Exam. Because many have growing concerns about the environment today's architects need to understand **5** sustainable design, which emphasizes the efficient use of resources, such as energy and water conservation, waste and pollution reduction, and environmentally friendly specifications and materials.

3

A. NO CHANGE

B. need to complete a professional degree in architecture; gain relevant experience through a paid internship; and pass the Architect Registration Exam.

C. need to complete a professional degree in architecture. Gain relevant experience through a paid internship, and pass the Architect Registration Exam.

D. need to complete a professional degree in architecture, gain relevant experience through a paid internship, and pass the Architect Registration Exam.

4

A. NO CHANGE

B. the environment; today's architects

C. the environment, today's architects

D. the environment. Today's architects

5

A. NO CHANGE

B. sustainable design; which emphasizes the efficient use of resources, such as energy and water conservation, waste and pollution reduction, and environmentally friendly specifications and materials.

C. sustainable design which emphasizes the efficient use of resources. Such as energy and water conservation, waste and pollution reduction, and environmentally friendly specifications and materials.

D. sustainable design.

In addition **6** to structural plans architects often provide drawings of **7** the air-conditioning heating and ventilating systems electrical systems communications systems plumbing and possibly site and landscape plans. Mark **8** Twain the great American writer humorist and publisher was born in Florida, Missouri, to John and Jane Clemens in 1835. Mark **9** Twain whose given name was Samuel Clemens was the sixth of seven children.

6

A. NO CHANGE

B. to structural, plans, architects

C. to structural plans; architects

D. to structural plans, architects

7

A. NO CHANGE

B. the air-conditioning, heating, and ventilating systems; electrical systems; communications systems; plumbing; and possible site and landscape plans.

C. the air-conditioning, heating, and ventilating systems, electrical systems, communications systems, plumbing, and possible site and landscape plans.

D. the air-conditioning, heating, and ventilating systems. Electrical systems, communication systems, plumbing, and possible site and landscape plans

8

A. NO CHANGE

B. Twain—the great American writer, humorist, and publisher—was

C. Twain the great American writer, humorist, and publisher, was

D. Twain, the great American writer, humorist and publisher, was

9

A. NO CHANGE

B. Twain whose given name was Samuel Clemens, was

C. Twain, whose given name was Samuel Clemens, was

D. Twain, whose given name was, Samuel Clemens was

5

5

10 In 1861 when the Civil War started Sam's dreams of becoming a steamboat pilot ended abruptly. Sam's commitment to the Confederate cause was **11** short-lived he quit the army after just two weeks. Twain's "big break" came with the publication of his short story "Jim Smiley and His Jumping **12** Frog" which was picked up by papers across the country. After the success **13** of his story "Jim Smiley and His Jumping Frog," Clemens was hired by the Sacramento Union to visit and report on the Sandwich **14** Islands, known today as Hawaii.

10

A. NO CHANGE

B. In 1861—when the Civil War started, Sam's

C. In 1861 when the Civil War started, Sam's

D. In 1861, when the Civil War started, Sam's

11

A. NO CHANGE

B. short-lived, he quit the army after just two weeks.

C. short-lived—he quit the army after just two weeks.

D. short-lived—he quit the army—after just two weeks.

12

A. NO CHANGE

B. Frog"; which

C. Frog," which

D. Frog" which,

13

A. NO CHANGE

B. of his story, "Jim

C. of his story; "Jim

D. of his story. "Jim

14

A. NO CHANGE

B. Islands known today as Hawaii.

C. Islands known today, as Hawaii.

D. Islands (now Hawaii).

Clemens' writings for the Sacramento Union were wildly **15** popular upon his return he was asked to undertake a lecture tour across the United States. **16** Like many good writers, Mark Twain spent his life observing and writing about life as he saw it, with all of its joys and horrors.

15

A. NO CHANGE

B. popular—upon his return—he

C. popular; and upon his return, he

D. popular, and upon his return, he

16

A. NO CHANGE

B. Like many good writers Mark,

C. Like many, good writers, Mark

D. Like many good writers Mark

Answers and Explanations

1. **The correct answer is C.** Three or more items in a list must be separated with commas. The SAT also requires the serial comma before the *and* that precedes the final item in the list (choice D). Semicolons (choice B) are inappropriate as the items themselves do not contain commas.

2. **The correct answer is B.** When the items in a list contain commas, use semicolons to separate them. Choice C does not use semicolons, and it removes the punctuation after *designs* and from other locations in the sentence. Placing a period after *designs* (choice D) turns the information that follows into a sentence fragment.

3. **The correct answer is D.** A semicolon has two functions: to separate related independent clauses and to separate items that contain commas when listing; you do not need a semicolon after "need to." Semicolons are not necessary for separating the items in the list (choice B) as they do not contain commas. While a period after *architecture* (choice C) completes the first clause, it turns the information after the period into a sentence fragment, as the list would need a subject and verb to stand on its own.

4. **The correct answer is C.** Dependent clauses may contain a subject and verb, but they do not express a complete idea. When located at the beginning of sentences, dependent clauses must be separated from their attached independent clause by a comma. The use of a semicolon (choice B) implies that both clauses are independent; a period (choice D) is incorrect for the same reason.

5. **The correct answer is A.** Choice B inappropriately places a semicolon after "sustainable design," creating a sentence fragment, which could be corrected by altering phrasing ("That principle emphasizes. . ."), but that choice is not among those listed. Choice C also creates a sentence fragment with the period. Choice D is grammatically correct and concise; however, it eliminates information relevant to the topic; if it included the phrase "which emphasizes the efficient use of resources," it would be an acceptable answer.

6. **The correct answer is D.** Introductory phrases (which often begin with prepositions and transitional words or phrases) need to be followed by a comma. A semicolon (choice C) implies that what comes before is an independent clause, which is not the case. Placing a comma before *plans* (choice B) suggests the word is nonessential information, but if removed, it would disrupt the meaning of the sentence.

7. **The correct answer is B.** The phrase "air-conditioning, heating, and ventilating systems" represents one object in the list; as such, all items in the list must be separated with semicolons. Choice C uses only commas; in order to be grammatically correct, the word *and* should be removed before *ventilating*, and placed before *communicating*, and the word *systems* should be removed after both *ventilating* and *electrical*. Choice D creates a sentence fragment by placing a period in the middle of the list.

8. **The correct answer is B.** The phrase "the great American writer, humorist, and publisher" is nonessential information that is neither necessary for the meaning or grammar of the sentence but provides extra information; normally, you could offset it from the sentence with just commas, but because it contains commas, you should use em dashes. Choice C punctuates the list of Twain's titles but does not separate it from the main clause. Choice D uses commas for both the list and the nonessential phrase, which may be confusing for readers.

9. **The correct answer is C.** The phrase "whose given name was Samuel Clemens" is a nonessential (or parenthetical) element and should be set off from the main clause. Choice B encloses one side of the nonessential information, but not both. Choice D misplaces the closing comma within the nonessential phrase.

10. **The correct answer is D.** Introductory and nonessential phrases must be separated from the rest of the sentence using appropriate punctuation, often commas or em dashes. An em dash signals that information following is nonessential, but by not enclosing with another em dash after *started* (choice B), there is no indication of where the nonessential information ends. Choice C appropriately places a comma after *started* to separate the nonessential phrase "when the Civil War

started" but omits the necessary comma after the introductory phrase "In 1861."

11. **The correct answer is C.** Independent clauses must be separated by a comma and a coordinating conjunction, a semicolon, a period; or when the information shifts topics or explains the main idea of the first clause, they should be separated by an em dash or colon. Choice B uses only a comma to separate the two independent clauses, creating a comma splice. Choice D uses an em dash to suggest the second clause is a shift in topic or explains the main idea of the first clause; however, the em dash placed after *army* breaks up the thought and creates an awkward construction.

12. **The correct answer is C.** Nonessential information, in simplest terms, adds extra information to a sentence and should be separated from the main clause with commas—sometimes em dashes or parentheses. Choice B uses a semicolon, but the information following it is not an independent clause, nor is it a list in which the items contain commas. Choice D places the comma after the word *which*, as opposed to the title of Twain's story.

13. **The correct answer is B.** Introductory phrases, which often begin with prepositions, should be separated from the main clause of a sentence by a comma. Both choices C and D punctuate the phrase "After the success of his story" as if it were an independent clause, but it is a sentence fragment—a prepositional phrase lacking a verb and not expressing a complete idea.

14. **The correct answer is D.** Nonessential information must be separated with punctuation to offset it from the main clause; choice A does this appropriately, but information should not only be grammatically correct but also use as few words as possible. Choice B lacks a necessary comma. Choice C misplaces the comma in the middle of the

nonessential information. Both choices A and D correctly separate the phrase relating that the Sandwich Islands are now called Hawaii from the rest of the sentence, but choice D does so in a more concise way while also preserving the meaning of the sentence.

15. **The correct answer is D.** Independent clauses must be separated with some form of punctuation to prevent run-on sentences, often semicolons (if the ideas are related) or a comma and a coordinating conjunction. Em dashes (choice B) are used to separate nonessential information, but they cannot be used to separate a phrase between two complete sentences. Semicolons can separate related independent clauses; however, semicolons should not be followed by a coordinating

conjunction (choice C), as the semicolon makes the conjunction redundant. Only choice D correctly connects the two independent clauses while also separating the introductory phrase "upon his return" from the second independent clause.

16. **The correct answer is A.** Introductory phrases should be separated from the main clause (the subject, the verb, and supporting phrases) as they are neither grammatically necessary nor required by the meaning of the sentence. Choice B places the comma after "Mark," splitting the subject's name. Choice C places a comma between the adjectives "many" and "good," which are not adjectives of equal degree. Choice D lacks the necessary punctuation after the introductory phrase.

The Colon

Basic Rule

The colon is used to precede a list, a long quotation, or a statement that illustrates or clarifies the earlier information. A colon can only be used after an independent clause.

Examples:

Christopher Columbus led three ships to the New World: *La Nina*, *La Pinta*, and *La Santa Maria*.

In the United States, there are three branches of government: the Executive, the Legislative, and the Judicial.

Only use colons after independent clauses. Most commonly, that means that you won't use colons after a verb. Further, no introductory or connecting information should occur before or after a colon, such as *and* or *including*.

Incorrect: The Louisiana Purchase included territory that would become: Montana, South Dakota, Nebraska, Kansas, Oklahoma, Arkansas, Louisiana, and Missouri.

Correct: The Louisiana Purchase included territory that would become many of today's states: Montana, South Dakota, Nebraska, Kansas, Oklahoma, Arkansas, Louisiana, and Missouri.

Skill Builder: Punctuation

DIRECTIONS: Decide whether the colons and semicolons are correctly placed in the following sentences or whether another mark of punctuation would be better. Write the correct punctuation in the space provided.

5

1. He is an excellent student and a fine person; as a result, he has many friends.

2. Because he is such an industrious student; he has many friends.

3. We tried our best to purchase the books; but we were unsuccessful.

4. The students were required to pass the following exit tests: English, science, math, and social studies.

5. The rebuilt vacuum cleaner was in excellent condition; saving us a good deal of expense since we didn't have to purchase a new one.

6. Marie has a very soft voice; however, it is clear and distinct.

7. Don't open the door; the floor is still wet.

8. Don't open the door; because the floor is still wet.

9. To the campers from the city, every noise in the night sounded like a bear: a huge, ferocious, meat-eating bear.

10. We worked for three days painting the house; nevertheless, we still needed more time to complete the job.

11. The telephone rang several times, as a result; his sleep was interrupted.

12. Peter was chosen recently to be vice president of the business; and will take over his duties in a few days.

Answers

1. Correct.
2. Substitute a comma for the semicolon.
3. Substitute a comma for the semicolon.
4. Correct.
5. Substitute a comma for the semicolon.
6. Correct.
7. Correct.
8. Delete the semicolon.
9. Substitute a comma for the colon.
10. Correct.
11. The telephone rang several times; as a result, his sleep was interrupted. (Note the two punctuation changes. The semicolon is placed in front of the conjunctive adverb and the comma after it.)
12. Delete the semicolon; no punctuation is necessary in its place.

The Apostrophe

Basic Rules

Apostrophes on the SAT will serve one of two purposes:

1. To indicate the possessive case *of nouns*: If the noun does not end in *s*—whether singular or plural—add an *'s*; if the noun ends in *s*, simply add the *'*. Some writers like to add *'s* to all nouns, even those that already end in *s*, but the SAT will default to *s'*.

    Example 1: The impact of Allen Ginsberg's poem "Howl" on the cultural landscape of the United States cannot be overstated.

    Example 2: A car's headlights are typically wired in parallel so that if one burns out the other will keep functioning.

    Example 3: The women's club sponsored many charity events.

    Example 4: Charles Mingus' skill as a jazz musician is widely recognized.

2. To indicate a *contraction*—the omission of one or more letters: Place the apostrophe exactly where the missing letters occur.

    Examples:

    can't = cannot

    it's = it is

    we're = we are

CAUTION

Do not use apostrophes with possessive pronouns such as *yours*, *hers*, *ours*, *theirs*, and *whose*, which indicate possession already.

5

Skill Builder: Apostrophe Use

DIRECTIONS: For **questions 1–6**, revise the sentences to correct any apostrophe errors. For **questions 7–10**, circle the word that demonstrates the correct apostrophe usage.

1. Poet William <u>Wordsworths</u> most famous work is *The Prelude*, which was published in 1850.

2. <u>Its</u> how Wordsworth uses the language of the "common man" that strikes most readers.

3. While most of his <u>poems</u> are considered classics, *The Prelude* stands as one of the crowning <u>achievements</u> of British Romanticism.

4. <u>Wordsworths</u> poem *The Prelude* was published by his wife Mary three <u>months</u> after his death.

5. The theme of "Sonnet 18" revolves around the idea of expressing <u>ones</u> self through language.

6. What proportion of <u>humans</u> exposure to plastic ingredients and environmental <u>pollutants</u> occur through seafood?

7. According to (statistics, statistic's), 55 percent of the nursing workforce holds a (bachelors, bachelor's) degree or higher.

8. Over the past decade, the average age of (nurses, nurse's) has increased by almost two years for (RNs, RN's) and 1.75 years for (LPNs, LPN's).

9. According to the Board of Registered (Nurse's, Nurses') list of (regulations, regulation's), registered (nurses, nurse's) must have a high school diploma, appropriate pre-licensure schooling, and required certification.

10. Despite teaching similar (skills, skill's), one nursing (program, program's) (requirements, requirement's) can be very different from another (programs, program's) (requirements, requirement's).

TIP

Any question that asks you to choose *its* vs. *it's* will likely include the answer choice *its'* as well. Remember your apostrophe rules. *Its'* isn't a word. When you see it, eliminate it.

Answers

1. Poet William <u>Wordsworth's</u> most famous work is *The Prelude*, which was published in 1850.

2. <u>It's</u> how Wordsworth uses the language of the "common man" that strikes most <u>readers</u>.

3. While most of his <u>poems</u> are considered classics, *The Prelude* stands as one of the crowning <u>achievements</u> of British Romanticism.

4. <u>Wordsworth's</u> poem *The Prelude* was published by his wife Mary three <u>months</u> after his death.

5. The theme of "Sonnet 18" revolves around the idea of expressing <u>one's</u> self through language.

6. Do you know what proportion of <u>humans'</u> exposure to plastic ingredients and environmental <u>pollutants</u> occurs through seafood?

7. According to statistics, 55 percent of the nursing workforce holds a bachelor's degree or higher.

8. Over the past decade, the average age of nurses has increased by almost two years for RNs and 1.75 years for LPNs.

9. According to the Board of Registered Nurses' list of regulations, registered nurses must have a high school diploma, appropriate pre-licensure schooling, and required certification.

10. Despite teaching similar skills, one nursing program's requirements can be very different from another program's requirements.

End-of-Sentence Punctuation

There are three types of punctuation used to end a sentence: the period, the question mark, and the exclamation mark.

1. A period is used at the end of a sentence that makes a statement.

   Example: In 1620, the Pilgrims in Plymouth signed the Mayflower Compact.

2. A question mark is used after a direct question. A period is used after an indirect question.

   Direct Question: Were *The Federalist Papers* written by James Madison, John Jay, or Alexander Hamilton?

   Indirect Question: Profession Mahin wanted to know if you knew who wrote *The Federalist Papers*.

3. An exclamation mark is used after an expression that shows strong emotion or issues a command. It may follow a word, a phrase, or a sentence.

   Example: Koko the gorilla knew more than 1,000 sign-language signs and could communicate with humans. Amazing!

Unnecessary Punctuation

Unnecessary punctuation can break a sentence into confusing and illogical fragments. Here are some common mistakes to look out for.

- Don't use a comma alone to connect independent clauses. This is called a comma splice.

  Incorrect: Toni Morrison grew up in an integrated neighborhood, she did not become fully aware of racial divisions until she was in her teens.

  Possible revision: Toni Morrison grew up in an integrated neighborhood and did not become fully aware of racial divisions until she was in her teens.

- Don't use a comma between compound elements that are not independent clauses.

  Incorrect: In 1998, Oprah Winfrey, and Danny Glover starred in a film adaptation of Morrison's novel *Beloved*.

  Possible revision: In 1998, Oprah Winfrey and Danny Glover starred in a film adaptation of Morrison's novel *Beloved*.

- Do not use an apostrophe when making a noun plural.

  Incorrect: In 2006, the *New York Times Book Review* named *Beloved* the best American novel published in the last 25 year's.

  Possible revision: In 2006, the *New York Times Book Review* named *Beloved* the best American novel published in the last 25 years.

Skill Builder: Commas and Unnecessary Punctuation

> **DIRECTIONS:** Revise the following sentences to correct errors, paying special attention to unnecessary, misused, and missing punctuation marks. In some cases, there are multiple ways to fix these errors. Consider the answers a partial list of possible revisions.

1. The job of an art director is a creative one he or she is responsible for the visual style and images in magazines newspapers product packaging, and movie and television productions.

2. An art director's job includes creating the overall design of a project; and directing others who develop artwork and layouts.

3. People interested in becoming art director's often work as graphic designer's, illustrator's, copy editor's, or photographer's, or in some other types of art and design occupations.

4. Some art directors work for advertising and public relations firms and others work in print media and entertainment.

5. In order to become an art director you typically need at least a bachelor's degree in an art or design subject, and previous work experience.

6. Art direction is a management position, that oversees the work of other designers and artists.

7. An art director might choose the overall style or tone, desired for a project, and communicate this vision to the artists he or she manages.

8. In the movie industry an art director might collaborate with a director; in order to determine the look and style of a movie.

9. As of 2012: art directors held about 74,800 jobs.

10. Even though the majority of art directors are self-employed they often work under pressure to meet strict deadlines.

5

Answers

1. The job of an art director is a creative one; he or she is responsible for the visual style and images in magazines, newspapers, product packaging, and movie and television productions.

2. An art director's job includes creating the overall design of a project and directing others who develop artwork and layouts.

3. People interested in becoming art directors often work as graphic designers, illustrators, copy editors, photographers, or in some other types of art and design occupations.

4. Some art directors work for advertising and public relations firms, and others work in print media and entertainment.

5. In order to become an art director, you typically need at least a bachelor's degree in an art or design subject and previous work experience.

6. Art direction is a management position that oversees the work of other designers and artists.

7. An art director might choose the overall style or tone desired for a project and communicate this vision to the artists he or she manages.

8. In the movie industry, an art director might collaborate with a director in order to determine the look and style of a movie.

9. As of 2012, art directors held about 74,800 jobs.

10. Even though the majority of art directors are self-employed, they often work under pressure to meet strict deadlines.

Skill Builder: Punctuation

DIRECTIONS: Revise the following sentences to correct punctuation errors.

1. Architects design houses, office buildings and other structures.

2. On any given day, architects might perform the following tasks; prepare structural specifications; meet with clients to determine objectives and structural requirements; direct workers to prepare drawings and documents.

3. Architects are responsible for designing the places where we live work play learn shop and eat?

4. Architects—design both indoor and outdoor—spaces on public and private projects.

5. Architects often provide various predesign services; from environmental impact studies to cost analyses: depending on a project's needs.

6. For actual blueprints traditional paper-and-pencil drafting has been replaced by computer-aided design and drafting (CADD): however hand-drawing skills are still important during the conceptual stages of a project.

7. Did you know that BIM stands for business, information modeling?

8. Architects often collaborate with workers in related fields; civil engineers, urban planners, interior designers, and landscape architects.

9. In addition to years of schooling being a good architect requires a mix of artistic talent and mathematical ability: it's not easy!

10. The path to becoming an architect requires a college education, a five-year Bachelor of Architecture degree program is typical.

Answers

1. Architects design houses, office buildings, and other structures.

2. On any given day, architects might perform the following tasks: prepare structural specifications, meet with clients to determine objectives and structural requirements, and direct workers to prepare drawings and documents.

3. Architects are responsible for designing the places where we live, work, play, learn, shop, and eat.

4. Architects design both indoor and outdoor spaces on public and private projects.

5. Architects often provide various predesign services—from environmental impact studies to cost analyses—depending on a project's needs.

6. For actual blueprints, traditional paper-and-pencil drafting has been replaced by computer-aided design and drafting (CADD); however, hand-drawing skills are still important during the conceptual stages of a project.

7. Did you know that BIM stands for business information modeling?

8. Architects often collaborate with workers in related fields: civil engineers, urban planners, interior designers, and landscape architects.

9. In addition to years of schooling, being a good architect requires a mix of artistic talent and mathematical ability—it's not easy!

10. The path to becoming an architect requires a college education; a five-year Bachelor of Architecture degree program is typical.

BRAIN BREAK

Music facilitates multi-sensory learning. Take a break and listen to a few of your favorite songs. Close your eyes and really listen to the words. Feel the beat. Hear the harmonies. Sing along.

CONVENTIONS OF USAGE

Pronouns

Basic Rules

Pronouns substitute for nouns in sentences. Every pronoun must have a clear **antecedent** (the noun that it replaces), have the same **number** as the antecedent (singular or plural), share the same perspective or **person** (1st, 2nd, or 3rd), and be in the proper pronoun **case** for its use in the sentence (subjective, objective, possessive).

> **Examples:**
>
> George Washington was born on February 22, 1732, in Pope's Creek, Virginia; *he* was the first American president.
>
> Did you know that Besty Ross and George Washington both went to the same church? *It* was called Christ Church, and *it* was located in Philadelphia.

The following pronoun chart may prove useful:

Number	Person	Subjective Case	Objective Case	Possessive Case
Singular	1st person	I	me	mine
	2nd person	you	you	yours
	3rd person	he, she, it, who	him, her, it, whom	his, hers, whose
Plural	1st person	we	us	ours
	2nd person	you	you	yours
	3rd person	they, who	them, whom	theirs, whose

A pronoun must agree in number with its antecedent, using a singular or plural pronoun of the correct person and case.

> **Incorrect:** George Washington was among the seven figures that were key to the formation of the United States government, the Founding Fathers, because *they* shaped and served the country's executive branch. (What is the antecedent for the marked pronoun? George Washington or Founding Fathers?)
>
> **Correct:** George Washington was among the seven figures that were key to the formation of the United States government, the Founding Fathers, because *he* shaped and served the country's executive branch. (The pronoun needs to be in the third-person singular in the subjective case in order to agree with the antecedent *George Washington*.)
>
> **Incorrect:** George Washington issued two vetoes successfully during his two presidential terms. One was issued in his first term, and the other was issued after he left office. Congress was unable to overturn *it*. (What was Congress unable to overturn?)
>
> **Correct:** George Washington issued two vetoes successfully during his two presidential terms. One was issued in his first term, and the other was issued after he left office. Congress was unable to

overturn *them*. (The pronoun needs to be third-person plural in the objective case to agree with the antecedent *two vetoes* and work with the grammar of the sentence.)

A pronoun uses the *subjective* case when it is the subject of the sentence or when it renames the subject as a subject complement.

Incorrect: One story of the American flag's creation says George Ross, Robert Morris, and *him* asked Betsy Ross to sew the first flag.

Correct: One story of the American flag's creation says George Ross, Robert Morris, and *he* asked Betsy Ross to sew the first flag. (*He* is part of the compound subject of the sentence.)

Incorrect: *Him* is George Washington.

Correct: *He* is George Washington. (*He* renames the subject.)

If a pronoun is the object of a verb or preposition, it is placed in the *objective* case.

Incorrect: Washington placed a lot of trust in Benedict Arnold. In 1780, George Washington gave command of West Point to *he*.

Correct: Washington placed a lot of trust in Benedict Arnold. In 1780, George Washington gave command of West Point to *him*.

Incorrect: Despite the fact that *us* turned in our American history paper late, our teacher gave Franklin and *I* an A grade.

Correct: Despite the fact that *we* turned in our American history paper late, our teacher gave Franklin and *me* an A grade. (*We* is the subject of the dependent clause, and *me* is an object of the verb *gave*.)

Avoid ambiguity and confusion by making sure that the antecedent of the pronoun is clear. The presence of multiple nouns that share the same gender and number means that the sentence must clarify which antecedent is being referred to.

Incorrect: At the height of his career, Frank Lloyd Wright told an architectural scholar that *he* thought *his* work was improving. (Is Wright talking about his own work or the work of the scholar?)

Correct: At the height of his career, Frank Lloyd Wright told an architectural scholar that he thought *his own* work was improving.

Incorrect: Frank Lloyd Wright and his wife Olgivanna founded a school for aspiring artists in Spring Green, Wisconsin, where they could "learn by doing." (Does *they* refer to the Wrights or the artists?)

Correct: Frank Lloyd Wright and his wife Olgivanna founded a school in Spring Green, Wisconsin, where aspiring artists could "learn by doing."

Possessive Determiners

When a pronoun expresses ownership, it is placed in the possessive case. An absolute possessive pronoun can stand on its own without needing a noun to follow it to be clear. Absolute possessive pronouns are *mine*, *yours*, *his*, *hers*, *its*, *ours*, and *theirs*.

Examples:

The watch is *mine*.

That one is *his*.

Theirs are broken.

A possessive pronoun that identifies, specifies, or quantifies the noun it precedes is called a possessive determiner. Possessive determiners are *my*, *your*, *his*, *her*, *its*, *our*, and *their*.

Examples:

It's *my* watch.

That's *his* watch.

Their watches are broken.

Skill Builder: Pronouns

DIRECTIONS: In the space provided, identify, correct, and explain the pronoun error contained in each statement.

1. George Washington rejected the titles proposed by Congress for the office of the President—including "Highness," "Excellency," and "Majesty"—believing them were inappropriate for his position. So, he settled on "Mr. President."

2. The Battle of Yorktown was an important turning point in the American Revolution, and the British defeat signaled the end of it.

3. The American Bill of Rights was based on the English Bill of Rights; it protected the rights of the citizens.

4. While the Articles of Confederation is less famous than other historical documents like the Declaration of Independence and the Constitution, it's historical significance cannot be overstated.

CAUTION

Some possessive determiners (*its, your, their*) and contractions (*it's, you're, they're*) are often confused. Remember that personal pronouns that express ownership never require an apostrophe.

5. George Washington's presidential cabinet had only four original members: Thomas Jefferson, Alexander Hamilton, Henry Knox, and Edmund Randolph. It provided advice on matters of state, the economy, war, and more to the president according to their respective roles.

6. Federalists and Anti-Federalists felt differently about the division of power between national and state governments. They preferred more power be given to the states.

7. Thomas Paine was an American patriot who's pamphlets *Common Sense* and *The Crisis* helped stir the American independence movement.

8. Washington D.C. was under construction as the nation's capital during George Washington's presidency. As such, he divided our time between New York and Philadelphia.

Answers and Explanations

1. **Error:** Improper use of objective case pronoun.

   Explanation: The antecedent of the pronoun *them* is the word *titles* (a plural noun); however, the sentence structure means that the pronoun needs to be in the subjective case as the *titles were inappropriate* (subject + linking verb + adjective).

   Correction: George Washington rejected the titles proposed by Congress for the office of the President—including "Highness," "Excellency," and "Majesty"—believing *they* were inappropriate for his position. So, he settled on "Mr. President."

2. **Error:** Ambiguous pronoun.

   Explanation: It is unclear whether the *it* at the end of the sentence refers to the American Revolution or the Battle of Yorktown.

   Correction: The Battle of Yorktown was an important turning point in the American Revolution, and the British defeat signaled the end of the war.

3. **Error:** Ambiguous pronoun.

   Explanation: It is unclear whether the *it* that follows the semicolon refers to the American or English Bill of Rights or both.

   Correction: The American Bill of Rights was based on the English Bill of Rights; both Bills of Rights protected the rights of the citizens.

4. **Error:** Improper usage of contraction over possessive.

   Explanation: *It's* is a contraction; the correct word should be the possessive pronoun *its*.

   Correction: While the Articles of Confederation is less famous than other historical documents like the Declaration of Independence and the Constitution, its historical significance cannot be overstated.

5

5. **Error:** Incorrect agreement in number.

   Explanation: The antecedent for the subject of the verb *provided* is *members*, meaning the second sentence should use a third-person plural subjective case pronoun and read "They provided advice on matters of state…" Even as *cabinet* could be a logical antecedent, the rest of the sentence informs us that the antecedent is plural because of the use of *their* in the phrase "their respective roles."

   Correction: George Washington's presidential cabinet had only four original members: Thomas Jefferson, Alexander Hamilton, Henry Knox, and Edmund Randolph. *They* provided advice on matters of state, the economy, war, and more to the president according to their respective roles.

6. **Error:** Ambiguous pronoun.

   Explanation: It is unclear whether *they* refers to the Federalists or the Anti-Federalists.

   Correction: Federalists and Anti-Federalists felt differently about the division of power between national and state governments. Anti-Federalists preferred more power be given to the states.

7. **Error:** Improper usage of contraction over possessive.

   Explanation: *Who's* is a contraction; the correct word should be the possessive pronoun *whose*.

   Correction: Thomas Paine was an American patriot whose pamphlets *Common Sense* and *The Crisis* helped stir the American independence movement.

8. **Error:** Incorrect possessive determiner.

   Explanation: The possessive determiner *our* is used to signify first-person plural possession of an object. In this case, the sentence is discussing how George Washington's time was split between two different cities. The time is *his*, not *ours*.

   Correction: Washington D.C. was under construction as the nation's capital during George Washington's presidency. As such, he divided *his* time between New York and Philadelphia.

AGREEMENT

Pronoun-Antecedent Agreement

A pronoun agrees with its antecedent in both person and number.

   Example: The archaeologists examined the fossilized bone with great care to make sure they didn't damage *it*.

   Explanation: The antecedent of the pronoun *they* is *archaeologists*. The antecedent of the pronoun *it* is *bone*.

Remember to use a singular verb when you refer to indefinite pronouns such as *everyone, everybody, each, every, anyone, anybody, nobody, none, no one, one, either,* and *neither*.

FUN FACTS

Did you know that your ears aren't deceiving you and that hot and cold water really do sound different when poured? This is because cold water has a higher viscosity (is "thicker") and bubbles less, therefore creating a lower frequency of sound when poured. Hot water contains energized particles that move around more rapidly, thus producing a higher pitched sound.

Some indefinite pronouns—*any, more, most, some*—will be singular or plural as dependent on usage. The pronouns *both, many, others,* and *several* will always need a plural verb for agreement.

Examples:

Although Union High School's male lacrosse players operate as a team, each knows it's *his* (not *their*) responsibility to arrive on time and in uniform.

Despite the fact that many of the women came from wealthy families, everyone who attended the Seneca Falls conference on women's rights risked *her* (not *their*) life and reputation.

When the programmers were questioned, none could be certain if it was *his* or *her* (not *their*) mistake that caused the computer network to crash.

Subject-Verb Agreement

Basic Rule

A verb agrees in number with its subject. A singular subject takes a singular verb. A plural subject takes a plural verb.

<u>Coral reefs</u> <u>are</u> an important part of the marine ecosystem.
  [S]   [V]

My <u>teacher</u> <u>believes</u> that <u>coral reefs</u> <u>are</u> an important part of the marine ecosystem.
   [S]   [V]   [S]   [V]

Let's take a look at an example.

Example: Choose the correct verb: (is, am, are)

Booker T. Washington, Frederick Douglass, and W.E.B. DuBois _____ all important historical figures.

Explanation: Remember that the verb must agree with the subject. Since the subject is plural—subjects joined by *and* are plural—a plural verb is needed. The correct response therefore should be:

Booker T. Washington, Frederick Douglass, and W.E.B. DuBois are all important historical figures.

Sometimes the subject comes after the verb, but the rule still applies.

Example: Choose the correct verb: (is, are)

While the lecture has lasted two hours already, there _____ still three more speakers.

Explanation: The correct choice is *are* since the subject *speakers* is plural and requires a plural verb.

TIP

Increasingly, the word *their* is considered an acceptable substitute for *his* or *her* when the gender of an individual is unknown (also *them* for *him* or *her* and *they* for *he* or *she*). However, the SAT is all about formal English usage, so stick with *his* or *her, he* or *she,* or *him* or *her* when the antecedent for a pronoun is singular and gender is unclear.

5

There is one major exception to this rule. When the sentence is introduced by the word "there" and the verb is followed by a compound (double) subject, the first part of the subject dictates whether the verb should be singular or plural.

Example: There is one American astronaut in the shuttle and four Russian astronauts in the space station.

When compound subjects are joined by *either-or* or *neither-nor*, the verb agrees with the subject closest to the verb.

Examples:

Neither the violinist nor *the other musicians have had* much experience performing for an audience.

Neither you nor *I am* willing to make the sacrifices required of a professional musician.

Explanation:

In the first example, *musicians* (plural) is closest to the verb; in the second example, *I* (singular) is closest to the verb.

Sometimes a word or a group of words may come between the subject and the verb. The verb still must agree with the simple subject, and the simple subject is never part of a prepositional phrase.

Example:

Stephen King, the author of hundreds of best-selling novels, novellas, and short stories, *is* also a guitarist and singer in a band.

Explanation:

The simple subject is *Stephen King*, a singular noun. The verb must be *is*.

Example: Choose the correct verb: (was, were)

The causes of the deterioration of the coral reef _____not known until recently.

Explanation:

The simple subject is *causes*; "of the deterioration of the coral reef" is a prepositional phrase. Since the subject is plural, the plural verb *were* is required. The correct answer is were.

ALERT
The SAT test makers will often select verbs that are next to plural nouns but agree with a singular noun located earlier in the sentence. Work to identify which noun is performing the action, not just what's nearby.

Collective Nouns

Collective nouns present special problems. A collective noun names a group of people or things. Although usually singular in form, it is treated as either singular or plural according to the sense of the sentence:

- A *collective noun* is treated as singular when members of the group act, or are considered, as a unit:

  Example: The citizens' *assembly is drafting* a petition that would seek to protect local aquifers from chemical run-off and hazardous waste.

- A *collective noun* is treated as plural when the members act, or are considered, as multiple individuals:

  Example: After one of the longest and most fabled droughts in baseball history, the *Boston Red Sox have* finally overcome the "Curse of the Bambino" to win another World Series.

5

COMMON COLLECTIVE NOUNS

assembly	commission	crowd	minority
association	committee	department	number
audience	company	family	pair
band	corporation	firm	press
board	council	group	public
cabinet	counsel	jury	staff
class	couple	majority	United States

Skill Builder: Agreement

> **DIRECTIONS:** Follow the principles of agreement and choose the correct word.

1. (is, are) The president and vice president of the United States of America _____ expected to attend tomorrow's historic ceremony honoring Rosa Parks.

2. (have, has) Either the chair of the department or one of the professors _____ the necessary paperwork.

3. (was, were) In the time of the first settlers, there _____ no antibiotics to prevent outbreaks of disease.

4. (its, their) Because of _____ biodiversity, coral reefs are often called "the rainforests of the sea."

5. (her, their) After a brief introduction, each of the doctors presented _____ findings at the medical conference.

6. (is, are) Many young people are surprised to find out that the music of Verdi's operas _____ as vibrant and fun as anything on the radio.

7. (his, their) As the conductor took the podium, the musicians finished tuning _____ instruments.

8. (know, knows) Neither Sherlock Holmes nor the detectives of Scotland Yard _____ who the perpetrator is.

9. (is, are) According to preliminary market reports, either Xiaomi or Huawei _____ the biggest smartphone provider in China.

10. (is, are) However, neither the Republicans nor the Democrats _____ satisfied with the language of the new nuclear weapons treaty.

Answers and Explanations

1. **The correct answer is *are*.** The plural subject *president and vice president* requires the plural *are*.

2. **The correct answer is *has*.** The verb must agree with the subject closest to it, in this case the singular *one*.

3. **The correct answer is *were*.** The plural subject *antibiotics* requires the plural *were*.

4. **The correct answer is *their*.** The plural subject *coral reefs* requires the plural *their*.

5. **The correct answer is *her*.** The singular subject *each* requires the singular *her*.

6. **The correct answer is *is*.** The singular subject *music* requires the singular *is*.

7. **The correct answer is *their*.** The plural antecedent *musicians* requires the plural *their*.

8. **The correct answer is *know*.** In a *neither-nor* construction, the verb is governed by the closest subject, *detectives*.

9. **The correct answer is *is*.** The singular determiner *either* requires the singular verb *is*.

10. **The correct answer is *are*.** In a *neither-nor* construction, the verb is governed by the closest subject, *Democrats*.

5

TIP

The third person singular of most verbs ends in "s." For other forms, consider the following: I, we speak (first person); you speak (second person); he, she, it speaks (third person singular). Examples: He runs. She jogs. It jumps. The man sees. Mary laughs. The child walks. They run.

Skill Builder: Agreement

> **DIRECTIONS:** Revise the underlined words to eliminate agreement errors. If the underlined word is grammatically correct, write C above it. If a change is necessary, indicate the change and give a grammatical reason for it. Do not make unnecessary changes.

Joseph, one of my best friends, <u>are</u> considering becoming a medical doctor. He and I <u>believe</u> that medi-
[1]   [2]
cine, compared to other professions, <u>are</u> an exciting and fulfilling field. In order to help him decide, he
[3]
asked each of his friends to give his or her opinion about why medicine would or would not be a fulfill-

ing career choice. After that, he also asked his parents for their opinions. It seems that his friends and his

mother <u>is</u> in agreement, but his father <u>do</u> not agree.
[4]   [5]

Jacob's father feels strongly that the medical profession, unlike other professions, <u>requires</u> an excessive
[6]
amount of study and is too emotionally taxing. On the other hand, his friends and his mother <u>agree</u> that
[7]
while the schooling is rigorous, the practice itself would be very rewarding.

Jacob <u>is</u> still deciding what he wants to be, but he and I <u>has</u> learned that there <u>is</u> always many possible
[8]   [9]   [10]
answers to a question.

Answers and Explanations

1. **The correct answer is *is*.** The subject, *Joseph*, is singular.
2. **The correct answer is C.** The subject, *He and I*, is plural.
3. **The correct answer is *is*.** The subject, *medicine*, is singular.
4. **The correct answer is *are*.** The subject, *his friends and his mother*, is plural.
5. **The correct answer is *does*.** The subject, *father*, is singular.
6. **The correct answer is C.** The subject, *medical profession*, is singular.
7. **The correct answer is C.** The subject, *friends and mother*, is plural.
8. **The correct answer is C.** The subject, *Jacob*, is singular.
9. **The correct answer is *have*.** The subject, *he and I*, is plural.
10. **The correct answer is *are*.** The subject, *answers*, is plural.

FREQUENTLY CONFUSED WORDS AND EXPRESSIONS

The following pages review groups of words, phrases, and expressions that are similar in sound and/or meaning and are generally found to be confusing to students and adults alike. Misunderstanding what they mean or how they are used results in various usage problems. This section includes a brief list of some of the more commonly assessed words and phrases.

Words and Phrases

a is used before words that start with a consonant sound

an is used before words that start with a vowel sound

> Please give the baby *a* toy.

> He is *an* only child. We put up *a* united front. (*United* begins with a consonant sound—*y*.)

> We spent an hour together. (*Hour* begins with a vowel sound, since the *h* is silent.)

accept means to receive or to agree to something

except means to exclude or excluding

> I'll *accept* the gift from you.

> Everyone *except* my uncle went home.

> My uncle was *excepted* from the group of losers.

advice means counsel (noun), opinion

advise means *to* offer advice (verb)

> Let me give you some free *advice*.

> I'd *advise* you to see your doctor.

affect means to influence (verb)

effect means to cause or bring about (verb) or a result (noun)

> The pollution can *affect* your health.

> The landmark decision will *effect* a change in the law.

> The *effect* of the storm could not be measured.

all ready means everybody or everything ready

already means previously

> They were *all ready* to write when the test began.

> They had *already* written the letter.

all together means everybody or everything together

altogether means *completely*

> The boys and girls stood *all together* in line.

> His action was *altogether* strange for a person of his type.

in is used to indicate inclusion, location, or motion within limits

into is used for motion toward one place from another

> The spoons are *in* the drawer.
>
> We were walking *in* the room.
>
> I put the spoons *into* the drawer.
>
> She walked *into* the room.

it's is the contraction of *it is* or *it has*

its is a possessive pronoun meaning belonging to it

> *It's* a very difficult assignment.
>
> We tried to analyze *its* meaning.

lay means to put (a transitive verb)

lie means to recline (an intransitive verb)

Tense	To lay	To lie
(present)	I lay	I lie
(past)	I laid the gift on the table.	I lay on my blanket at the beach
(present perfect)	I have laid	I have lain

lets is third person singular present of *let*

let's is a contraction for *let us*

> He *lets* me park my car in his garage.
>
> *Let's* go home early today.

loose means not fastened or restrained, or not tight-fitting

lose means to mislay, to be unable to keep, to be defeated

> The dog got *loose* from the leash.
>
> Try not to *lose* your umbrella.

passed is the past tense of to pass

past means just preceding or an earlier time

> The week *passed* very quickly.
>
> The *past* week was a very exciting one.

principal means chief or main (adjective), or a leader, or a sum of money (noun)

principle means a fundamental truth or belief

His *principal* support comes from the real estate industry.

The *principal* of the school called a meeting of the faculty.

He earned 10 percent interest on the *principal* he invested last year.

As a matter *of principle*, he refused to register for the draft.

raise means to lift, to erect

raze means to tear down

rise means to get up, to move from a lower to a higher position, to increase in value

The neighbors helped him *raise* a new barn.

The demolition crew *razed* the old building.

The price of silver will *rise* again this month.

set means to place something down (mainly)

sit means to seat oneself (mainly)

Tense	To set	To sit
(present)	He sets	He sits
(past)	He set the lamp on the table.	He sat on the chair.
(present perfect)	He has set	He has sat

stationary means standing still

stationery means writing material

In ancient times, people thought that the earth was *stationary*.

We bought our school supplies at the *stationery* store.

than is used to express comparison

then is used to express time or a result or consequence

Jim ate more *than* we could put on the large plate.

I knocked on the door, and *then* I entered.

If you go, *then* I will go, too.

their means belonging to them

there means in that place

they're is the contraction for they are

We took *their* books home with us.

Your books are over *there* on the desk.

They're coming over for dinner.

though means although or as if

thought is the past tense of to think, or an idea (noun)

through means in one side and out another, by way of, finished

> *Though* he is my friend, I can't recommend him for this job.

> I *thought* you were serious!

> We enjoyed running *through* the snow.

to means in the direction of (preposition); it is also used before a verb to indicate the infinitive

too means very, also

two is the numeral 2

> We shall go *to* school.

> It is *too* hot today.

> We shall go, *too*.

> I ate *two* sandwiches for lunch.

weather refers to *atmospheric conditions*

whether introduces a choice; it should not be preceded by *of* or *as to*

> I don't like the *weather* in San Francisco.

> He inquired *whether* we were going to the dance.

well is an adverb (modifies a verb, adverb, or adjective) meaning in a good or proper manner

good is an adjective (modifies a noun) meaning favorable, pleasant, suitable, etc.

> I did *well* on my test.

> I received a *good* score on my test.

were is a past tense of *to be*

we're is a contraction of *we are*

where refers to place or location

> They *were* there yesterday.

> *We're* in charge of the decorations.

> *Where* are we meeting your brother?

who is a pronoun in the subjective case

whom is a pronoun in the objective case

> The man *who* stole my car was just seen at the supermarket.

> *Who* is at the door?

> For *whom* are you calling?

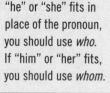
TIP
While the difference between *who* and *whom* has a minimal effect on your day-to-day life, it will more than likely come up on the SAT. Try substituting "he" or "she" and "him" or "her" for the pronoun in the sentence. You may have to rearrange the sentence a bit to make this work. If "he" or "she" fits in place of the pronoun, you should use *who*. If "him" or "her" fits, you should use *whom*.

To whom should I speak to about scheduling an appointment?

who's is the contraction for *who is* (or *who has*)

whose means of whom, implying ownership

    Who's the next batter?

    Whose notebook is on the desk?

your is a possessive, showing ownership

5

you're is a contraction for *you are*

    Please give him *your* notebook.

    You're very sweet.

Skill Builder: Usage

DIRECTIONS: Circle the correct word to complete the sentence while adhering to formal standard English conventions.

1. The patriot Samuel Adams was one of the (principal, principle) organizers of the Boston Tea Party.
2. Merchants in Boston refused to (accept, except) the taxes imposed upon them by the Tea Act of 1773.
3. Though the significance of the Tea Act of 1773 cannot be overestimated, (weather, whether) or not the Tea Act of 1773 led to the American Revolution is hard to say.
4. In late November of 1773, the ship the Dartmouth sailed (in, into) Boston Harbor.
5. Governor Hutchinson was determined to collect the taxes and (adviced, advised) the tea consignees not to back down.
6. More (than, then) 40 tons of tea were thrown into the water during the Boston Tea Party.
7. Tea smuggling was (all ready, already) a significant problem, especially in New York and Philadelphia.
8. The overall (affect, effect) of the Boston Tea Party was to bolster the revolutionary fervor that was sweeping New England.
9. The British Crown reacted swiftly and harshly in order to dispel the idea that they were (loosing, losing) control of the colonies.
10. (All together, Altogether) 342 chests of tea, weighing over 92,000 pounds, were dumped into the water.

Answers

1. principal
2. accept
3. whether
4. into
5. advised

6. than
7. already
8. effect
9. losing
10. altogether

Conventional Expressions

A conventional expression is a phrase or clause that has become a characteristic way of expressing a certain idea. Ironically, despite these expressions being conventional, they are often misused.

Here is a list of commonly misused conventional expressions and their correct usages.

Incorrect Usage	Correct Usage
It's a doggy-dog world	It's a dog-eat-dog world
For all intensive purposes	For all intents and purposes
I'm suppose to go running	...supposed to...
statue of limitations	statute of limitations
I could care less	I couldn't care less
Fall by the waste side	Fall by the wayside
Irregardless	Regardless
Escape goat	Scapegoat
I guess we'll make due	...make do...
Peak my interest	Pique my interest
The criminal got away scott free	...scot free...
I'm waiting with baited breath	...bated breath...
Without further adieu	Without further ado
The boy had free reign	...free rein...
Hunger pains	Hunger pangs
I should of called	...should have...
Don't step foot on this carpet	...set foot...
Nipped in the butt	Nipped in the bud
The waiter was at his beckon call	...beck and call...
The lawyer made a mute point	...moot point...
Case and point	Case in point
The cops were starting to hone in	...home in...
One in the same	One and the same

Logical Comparison

Basic Rule

In order for a comparison to make sense, it must be logical and complete.

In an incomplete comparison, what is being compared is unclear.

Incomplete: According to some scholars of US history, the Magna Carta is more important because it was the first document to limit the powers of the King of England.

Complete: According to some scholars of US history, the Magna Carta is more important than the Declaration of Independence because the Magna Carta was the first document to limit the powers of the King of England.

Incomplete: At 864,000 miles across, the sun is more than 100 times the size.

Complete: At 864,000 miles across, the sun is more than 100 times the size of Earth.

For a comparison to be logical, you must be comparing the same things. This can be accomplished with restatement or a demonstrative pronoun.

Illogical: The distance from the sun to the planet Neptune is 30 times greater than the sun and Earth. (This distance from the sun to Neptune is being compared to the sun and Earth, not the distance between them.)

Logical: The distance from the sun to the planet Neptune is 30 times greater than the distance from the sun to Earth.

Illogical: Despite popular opinion, many scholars believe that the political achievements of Thomas Jefferson were much more significant to American history than George Washington. (Thomas Jefferson's achievements are being compared to the person George Washington.)

Logical: Despite popular opinion, many scholars believe that the political achievements of Thomas Jefferson were much more significant to American history than those of George Washington.

Skill Builder: Logical Comparisons

DIRECTIONS: Revise the following comparisons to make sure they are logical.

1. According to scientists, the brain mass of a dolphin is actually slightly greater than a human.

2. Although they are in the same hemisphere, the average rainfall in South America differs greatly from North America.

3. In the 2015 World Happiness Report, the people of Switzerland ranked happier than America.

4. The tallest mountain in the United States is still 9,000 feet shorter than Nepal.

Answers

1. **Option 1:** According to scientists, the brain mass of a dolphin is actually slightly greater than the brain mass of a human.

   Option 2: According to scientists, the brain mass of a dolphin is actually slightly greater than that of a human.

2. **Option 1:** Although they are in the same hemisphere, the average rainfall in South America differs greatly from the average rainfall in North America.

   Option 2: Although they are in the same hemisphere, the average rainfall in South America differs greatly from that in North America.

3. **Option1:** In the 2015 World Happiness Report, the people of Switzerland ranked happier than the people of America.

   Option 2: In the 2015 World Happiness Report, the people of Switzerland ranked happier than those in America.

4. **Option 1:** The tallest mountain in the United States is still 9,000 feet shorter than the tallest mountain in Nepal.

   Option 2: The tallest mountain in the United States is still 9,000 feet shorter than that of Nepal.

Summing It Up

- The SAT Writing and Language Test is designed to test your mastery of standard English conventions.

- On the test, you will read multiple passages that may cover careers, science, history, or the humanities. The questions will require you to read the passages and select the answers that improve the writing in the passage.

- The correct answer will be the one that best follows standard English conventions (is grammatically correct), is concise (most directly and in the fewest words expresses the point), and is relevant to the topic of the passage/paragraph/sentence.

- The standard English conventions reviewed in this chapter are keys to good writing. When you utilize proper sentence structure, grammar, and punctuation, your writing is stronger, clearer, and more focused. That is why the use of standard English conventions is important for both college writing and any writing you will do in your future career.

- The following list summarizes the key conventions you need to remember to address most errors presented in the SAT's Writing and Language section:

  - **Sentence Structure and Formation**

    - **Fragments:** Every sentence must have a subject and a verb and express a complete idea.
    - **Run-Ons and Comma Splices:** Connect complete sentences with proper punctuation.
    - **Combining Independent Clauses:** Use periods, a comma + FANBOYS, or a semicolon; or make an independent clause dependent with a subordinating conjunction to link sentences.
    - **Combining Dependent and Independent Clauses:** Place a comma after a dependent clause at the beginning of a sentence.
    - **Misplaced Modifiers:** Place modifiers (adjectives, adverbs, prepositional phrases) as close to the word they're modifying as possible.
    - **Parallel Structure:** Keep verbs and phrases in the same grammatical form when writing sentences.
    - **Verb Tense and Mood:** Keep consistent verb tense and mood within sentences and paragraphs unless otherwise justified.
    - **Voice:** Shift sentences to active voice (when the subject performs the action) rather than passive voice (when the subject of the sentence receives the action).

  - **Punctuation**

    - **Commas:** Separate independent clauses with a comma and FANBOYS; add a comma after an introductory phrase or leading subordinate clause; separate items in lists of three or more (including before the *and* before the final item); place commas around nonessential information to separate it from the main clause of a sentence.
    - **Em dashes:** Indicate nonrestrictive or nonessential information with em dashes; these tangents, asides, and parenthetical statements follow em dashes and must be closed by another em dash—unless they end the sentence.

- **Semicolons:** Separate related independent clauses and items in a list with a semicolon—if the items in the list contain commas.
- **Colons:** Indicate the start of a list, a quotation, or emphasis with a colon; colons must be preceded by an independent clause.
- **Apostrophes:** Indicate possession with an *'s* (or just an apostrophe after a noun that ends in an *s*) or signal the contraction of two words into one (*they* + *are* = *they're*).
- **Parentheses:** Separate low importance nonessential information from the rest of the sentence with a pair of parentheses.
- **End-Stop Punctuation:** End statements and indirect questions with periods; use question marks to end direct questions; end statements that indicate strong emotion or commands with an exclamation point.

○ **Usage**

- **Pronouns:** Pronouns must agree in case, number, and gender (where applicable) with their antecedent (the word they replace); it must be clear to which antecedent a pronoun applies when multiple possible antecedents are present.
- **Subject-Verb Agreement:** A verb must agree with its subject in number, singular when the subject is singular, plural when the subject is plural; agreement occurs with the subject of a sentence—which may not be the word closest to the verb.
- **Confused Words and Phrases:** Select the word or phrase most appropriate to the situation, relying on common expressions and correct word choice for frequently confused words.
- **Logical Comparisons:** Make clear the objects being compared in a comparison; an object should be compared to an object of similar type.

Take a moment to ask yourself some simple questions about your understanding of the chapter:

Review: What did I learn?

Evaluate: What do I need to learn more about?

Plan: What can I do next to keep improving?

Based on your answers to those questions, adjust your study plan to dedicate additional time to the areas of weakness that you've identified.

PART V:
ESSAY WRITING STRATEGIES FOR THE SAT® EXAM

Chapter 6:   The SAT® Essay

The SAT® Essay

OVERVIEW

The SAT Essay is optional. Even so, it's still a good idea to take it and strive to perform well. Strong essay scores are just another way of sharpening your competitive edge when applying to colleges (and sometimes they're actually required). It's also important to know that much of a high-scoring essay depends on meeting the expectations of the test, not necessarily being an incredible writer—but that will be discussed more later. It's time for some basic details.

The SAT Essay is 50 minutes long and has only one "question." In that time, you need to read a short sample text (500–750 words) and plan and write a rhetorical analysis essay. It doesn't need to be—and isn't supposed to be—a final, polished version. The graduate students, high school teachers, and college instructors who will score your essay are trained to view the essays as first drafts. Two scorers will use a rubric to evaluate your essay in three categories (or domains): Reading, Analysis, and Writing. The rubric establishes expectations for each of those categories on a scale from 1–4 points; your final essay score will range between 2–8 points. Later in this chapter, you will analyze a rubric similar to the one the scorers will use.

The College Board has designed the SAT Essay to support, promote, and assess three specific skills. These three important elements will be considered in scoring an SAT essay:

1. Reading
2. Analysis
3. Writing

6

> **TIP**
> A rhetorical analysis essay describes the methods an author uses to build his or her argument. You might have heard the Greek terms *ethos*, *pathos*, and *logos* before. Those terms describe the conscious choices authors make for their word choice, sentence structure, use of statistics or facts and reasoning, appeals to emotion, and statements of authority in order to persuade their audience of their points, to name just a few. You'll need to discuss some of those traits when you write your essay for the SAT.

Essays are scored according to how well they meet these three basic criteria. To meet those criteria and improve your essay writing skills, keep the following list of questions in mind as you work your way through the essay writing process:

Reading

- Does my essay demonstrate a thorough understanding of the source text?
- Does my essay identify the author's key claims?
- Is my essay free of errors of fact or interpretation in relation to the text?
- Does my essay effectively use evidence from the source text?

Analysis

- Does my essay offer an in-depth evaluation of the author's use of evidence in building and supporting an argument?
- Does my essay offer an in-depth evaluation of the author's use of stylistic or persuasive language features to build and support his or her argument?
- Does my essay use supporting evidence from the passage that is relevant and focused on my task (analyzing the passage)?

Writing

- Does my essay include a precise central claim that is supported with body paragraphs?
- Does my essay include an effective introduction and a strong conclusion?
- Does my essay incorporate a variety of sentence structures? Is each of my sentences clearly written? Does each sentence flow well?
- Is my essay virtually error-free in spelling, grammar, usage, and mechanics?

A CLOSER LOOK AT THE ESSAY QUESTION

You will be given one essay prompt and asked to write an analytical essay in response. The essay section is made up of a prompt that directs you to read and analyze a high-quality source text. In this text, the author makes an argument or examines a current debate, idea, or trend.

Once you have closely read and analyzed the source text, you can begin your planning. You don't need any specific subject-area knowledge to write your response. The purpose of your essay is to demonstrate that you can analyze high-level writing using evidence drawn from the source text and your critical reasoning.

Familiarizing Yourself with the Prompt and the Passage

The Essay section's objectives will be consistent no matter when and where you are taking the SAT. The source text (passage) that accompanies the prompt *will* likely be new to you; however, it will share important qualities with other passages you will read and analyze as you prepare to write the SAT Essay.

All passages will meet the following criteria:

- Come from high-quality, previously published sources
- Contain arguments written for a broad audience
- Examine ideas, opinions, views, debates, or trends

- Discuss topics in the arts; the sciences; or civic, cultural, or political life
- Strive to convey nuanced views on complex subjects
- Use evidence, logical reasoning, and/or stylistic and persuasive elements to persuade their audience
- Are similarly complex: all are challenging—but not too difficult—for readers at your grade level
- Are considered to present their arguments successfully
- Do NOT require test-takers to possess prior knowledge of specific topics

The prompt that introduces the passage will be identical or very similar to the following:

> As you read the passage below, consider how [the author] uses the following:
>
> - Evidence, such as facts or examples, that supports claims
>
> - Reasoning to develop ideas and to connect claims and evidence
>
> - Stylistic or persuasive elements that add power to the ideas expressed, such as word choice, emotional appeals, logical appeals, or ethical appeals

After the passage, the prompt will continue as follows:

> Write an essay in which you explain how [the author] builds an argument to persuade [his/her] audience that [the author's claim is true or valid]. In your essay, analyze how [the author] uses one or more of the features listed above [see bullet points above] (or features of your own choice) to strengthen the logic and persuasiveness of [his/her] argument. Be sure that your analysis focuses on the most relevant aspects of the passage. Your essay should not explain whether you agree with [the author's] claims, but rather explain how [he/she] builds an argument to persuade [his/her] audience.

It is vital that you read, reread, and thoroughly understand everything the prompt asks you to do. Pay particular attention to the bullet points that tell you exactly what to look for in the passage. Also note that the prompt gives you the option of mentioning other "features of your own choice." Finally, let's take a closer look at the last sentence in the prompt (we have capitalized and underlined the word *not*):

> Your essay should NOT explain whether you agree with [the author's] claims, but rather explain how [he/she] builds an argument to persuade [his/her] audience.

In other words, your task is *not* to present your own arguments related to the topic—the passage author has already done that. Your task is to analyze the author's rhetorical strategies: "explain how the author builds an argument to persuade [his/her] audience."

ESSAY EXPECTATIONS

You know a little about your task for the essay, but let's lay out some general expectations for a strong essay so you can focus your attention as you read through this chapter. A high-scoring essay will include the following:

- An introduction that gives context for the topic and passage
- A thesis statement in the introduction that summarizes 2–3 rhetorical choices from the text that serve the author's purpose
- At least two body paragraphs, each of which discusses a rhetorical choice, offers examples (either paraphrase or quotations), and analyzes how that choice supports the author's purpose and affects his or her audience
- A conclusion that restates your thesis

The rubric requires the following objectives be met by your essay for each of the three scoring categories:

1. Reading
   - Expresses understanding of the author's purpose
   - Presents quotations appropriately
   - Paraphrases and summarizes the passage accurately

2. Analysis
   - Selects relevant rhetorical choices from the passage to discuss
   - Explains how choices support the author's purpose
   - Discusses the impact choices have on the author's audience
   - Supports every piece of evidence with analysis

3. Writing
   - Writes with an appropriate tone and vocabulary—avoiding slang and inappropriate language
   - Makes few grammatical mistakes; errors do not impede clarity of ideas
   - Presents information logically and in an organized manner, transitioning between and within paragraphs well
   - Writes with varied sentence structure

An essay that meets those objectives is likely to score well. But what are the practices that help you achieve those goals? Let's look at some more detailed information.

FUN FACTS
Did you know that the word *mogigraphia* means "writer's cramp"?

PACING YOUR ESSAY TASK

You want to use everything you've been taught about the writing process—but paced to fit within 50 minutes. Pacing yourself is important so that you are able to get your ideas down on paper in a complete, coherent, and unified essay. As you practice writing essays in this chapter and in the practice tests in this book, work out a pacing schedule for yourself. You might want to think of the essay task as a two-step process:

1. Prewriting (Reading and Analysis)
2. Writing

A general guideline would be to plan for 15–20 minutes for the first step, and 25–30 minutes for the second. If you think you might benefit from a more structured breakdown, try the following:

- Prewriting—Reading: 10–15 minutes
- Prewriting—Analysis: 5–10 minutes
- Writing—Introduction: 4–5 minutes
- Writing—Body: 15–20 minutes
- Writing—Conclusion: 3–4 minutes
- Revising: 3–5 minutes
- Proofing: 3–5 minutes

PREWRITING: READING AND ANALYSIS

You want to spend about 15–20 minutes on prewriting, as this will give you time to carefully read the prompt and then read and analyze the source text. Your goals in this planning stage are as follows:

- Identify and underline the author's key claims.
- Find and then circle or highlight specific evidence the author uses to support his or her key claims.
- Take notes on ways the author has used logic, reasoning, rhetoric (persuasive language techniques), and evidence to convince readers that his or her key claims are valid.

Reading

Before you begin to write your analysis, read the prompt and the source text. If you think time will allow, it's a good idea to read the essay prompt twice.

- Your first read-through should focus solely on the information provided. Make sure you clearly understand the author's point of view and the ideas, claims, and rhetorical devices presented that you are being asked to analyze in your essay response. Don't rush into furiously writing your essay without first knowing what it should cover!

NOTE

Remember that the readers do not take off points for specific errors in grammar, usage, and mechanics, but they will take note of errors that interfere with the clear communication of ideas. These can contribute to a lower Writing score. Check the rubric later in this chapter.

- Your second read-through should confirm that you are clear on the essay task at hand and should also be an opportunity to start preliminary brainstorming ideas that you plan to include in your essay.

Analysis

After reading the passage prompt thoroughly, gather your points for analysis by underlining the author's key claims. Then circle or highlight evidence the author uses to support these claims. Take note of the method the author uses to appeal to his or her audience—is it an appeal to logic, emotions, or authority? How do the author's claims and reasoning strengthen his or her argument?

Finally, take notes of important stylistic features or persuasive techniques the author uses in the source text. How does the use of language further advance the author's point of view? Try to recognize stylistic elements used to accomplish the goal, such as tone, repetition, or use of statistics or direct quotations from the source text. Pay attention to literary devices such as imagery, allusions, analogies, or hyperbole, that the author may use to enhance key claims.

Organizing Your Essay

Decide how many paragraphs you need to write to develop your analysis of the passage. Remember that length is not a valid substitute for strength. Your answer booklet provides a certain number of pages for your essay. You can't write more than the lines provided, but you can write less. It is more important to do a good job of analyzing the passage than it is to fill up all the lines. However, an essay of five sentences won't earn you a high score.

Five paragraphs can satisfy the demands of the prompt and rubric. Use the first paragraph for the introduction and the last one for the conclusion. That gives you three paragraphs to develop your ideas. That doesn't mean that you can't write a fourth or even fifth paragraph in the body of your essay to develop your ideas. However, you need to ensure that you have a conclusion to meet the demands of the prompt. It's more important to have a tightly written and well-developed shorter essay than a longer, rambling, repetitious one that you didn't have time to revise or proofread. There is a limit to what you can write in 50 minutes. Use the opportunity that you have for practice in this book to work on your pacing and see how much you can plan and write well in 50 minutes.

WRITING THE INTRODUCTION

Now it's time to write. You've read and analyzed the prompt and the passage in your prewriting step and identified the author's key claims, use of evidence and reasoning, and stylistic or persuasive language features. Now begin writing your introduction.

In your introduction, it is important to introduce the source text to your reader. State the author's name and the title of the passage, give a brief summary of the author's key claim, and provide a clear thesis identifying the author's choices that best support his or her argument. Two to four sentences should accomplish these tasks.

As you practice writing essays in this book, and as you write the real one on test day, keep the following five ideas in mind:

1. In writing your introduction, keep the key words and phrases of the prompt in mind. In general, your introduction should consist of three sentences.

2. Avoid being cute, funny, ironic, satiric, overly emotional, or too dramatic. Set the tone or attitude in your first sentence. You want to be sincere and clear. You should treat the task as you would an academic essay in your classes.

3. In your first paragraph, in addition to introducing the passage's author, title, topic, and the author's key claim about the topic, make it clear to your readers that you are about to analyze the passage and explain how the author accomplishes his or her persuasive purpose. This can be accomplished in a clear thesis statement.

4. Each sentence should advance your analysis, addressing the author's claims in an organized manner and using the passage content to support your observations.

5. Don't bother repeating the key claims from the source text word for word. A paraphrase in your own words is far better than just copying the words of the source text as it asserts your understanding of the passage.

Recognizing Effective Introductions

An *effective* introduction often refers to the subject of the essay, explains the value of the topic, or attracts the attention of the reader by giving a pertinent illustration. Ineffective beginnings often contain unrelated material, ramble, and lack clarity.

ALERT

Remember that you are writing an analysis of how the passage author supported his or her argument. You are NOT writing a persuasive essay describing the author's topic or whether you agree.

Skill Builder: Thesis Statements

DIRECTIONS: Identify which of the following is the best thesis or central claim.

1. I agree with the author that the use of motorized boats and watercraft should be limited in freshwater streams and lakes.

2. The author believes that the use of motorized boats and other watercraft should be limited in freshwater ecosystems in order to decrease pollution.

3. In this essay, I will examine the author's argument in favor of limiting the use of motorized boats and watercraft in freshwater streams and lakes.

4. The author introduces her argument with startling statistics on the negative effects of motorized watercraft on freshwater ecosystems; she then builds on those statistics with careful reasoning to reach the logical conclusion that we should limit the use of motorized watercraft in freshwater ecosystems.

Answer and Explanation

Of the four sentences presented, choice 4 is the best answer since it states the topic clearly, limits the scope of the essay, and presents the key points of the analysis. Sentence 4 also implies that the essay writer will expand on these key points in the body of the essay. The fourth thesis has outlined the purpose of each body paragraph, making it clear that the writer is striving to meet the essay's task.

Skill Builder: Effective Introductions

DIRECTIONS: Examine the following excerpts from five introductory paragraphs and decide whether each is effective or ineffective. Be able to defend your decision.

1. The pollution of freshwater streams and lakes has become a pretty big problem in the United States. Part of the problem is due to the unrestricted use of motorized boats and other stuff. I mostly agree with the author that something needs to be done about it, but I don't know that you should tell people where they can drive their boats. (Effective / Ineffective)

2. Freshwater lakes and streams are popular recreational destinations for many Americans. These bodies of water are also the principal ecosystems of many different animals and plants. In her essay, "Bringing Fresh Back to Freshwater Lakes and Streams," activist River Pura supports the claim that the unrestricted use of motorized watercraft is to blame for polluting these ecosystems with key statistics and emotional appeals. (Effective / Ineffective)

3. River Pura makes a very persuasive argument to persuade her audience that motorized boats should be restricted in freshwater streams and lakes. She persuades her audience with some facts and emotional appeals. (Effective / Ineffective)

4. The author makes an argument to persuade her audience about what she has thought about. It's pollution. (Effective / Ineffective)

5. Pollution in freshwater ecosystems has been growing over the past decade. Author River Pura, in her essay titled "Bringing Fresh Back to Freshwater Streams and Lakes," claims that motorized watercraft are the primary source of that pollution. Pura presents her readers with startling statistical information and emotional appeals through anecdotes that demonstrate that her argument is both a logical conclusion from the facts and interwoven with every American's personal ties to nature. (Effective / Ineffective)

Answers and Explanations

1. *Ineffective.* This paragraph is focused on the topic of the source text, not on the author's writing. Although the prompt specifically says not to present opinions on the topic, the writer states that he or she "mostly agrees" with the passage author. Also, the writer uses vague, informal expressions: "pretty big" and "mostly agree."

2. *Effective.* This paragraph effectively introduces the author, the passage title, and the topic. The paragraph also identifies the author's key claim and begins to analyze the author's work through the available rhetorical choices.

3. *Ineffective.* While this paragraph identifies the author's key claim, nonspecific phrases like "some facts" and "emotional appeal" weaken the paragraph. The author needs to add greater specificity to his or her claim while also providing greater context for the passage.

4. *Ineffective.* The paragraph does not introduce the author, the passage title, or the author's key claim. It does not explain that the writer is going to analyze the passage. The writing is poorly constructed and misuses verb tense.

5. *Effective.* This paragraph clearly introduces the source text, highlights the author's key claim, and explains how the passage author successfully builds an effective argument.

DEVELOPING YOUR IDEAS

The heart of your essay is the development, or middle paragraphs. In these paragraphs, you must use explanations, details, and examples from the source text to support the main ideas in your essay. All the sentences in the development paragraphs must explain and support your analysis of the source text and must not digress.

In the limited time you have on the SAT Essay, you can take only 15 to 20 minutes to write the body of your essay. In this time, you need to support your analysis of the author's work with careful reasoning, and back up your analysis with evidence from the source text. The rubric encourages making use of accurate quotations and paraphrases of the source text. However, an unexplained piece of evidence will impact your Analysis score. Your body paragraphs should follow a claim-evidence-reasoning structure. State the topic of the paragraph, and then take time to introduce a piece of evidence and explain not only how that evidence (a quote, an example, a paraphrase) connects to your claim (that it strengthens the author's argument) but also how it affects the author's audience. Within those objectives, your writing must be coherent, logical, unified, and organized.

Using Transitions

The successful writer uses transitional words and phrases to connect thoughts and provide a logical sequence of ideas. Become familiar with the following list of transitions and use them in your practice essays. They will help make your writing smoother:

TRANSITIONAL WORDS AND PHRASES		
also	furthermore	of course
but	however	on the other hand
consequently	in addition	second
finally	in any case	still
first of all	indeed	then
for example	moreover	therefore
for instance	nevertheless	yet

Skill Builder: Using Transitions

DIRECTIONS: In the following three samples, the transition is missing. Supply a transitional word or phrase that will allow the second sentence to follow smoothly or logically from the first.

1. Freshwater ecosystems hold only 0.01% of Earth's water supply. Over half of the people on Earth live near freshwater ecosystems.

2. Human activity comprises the primary threat to freshwater ecosystems. Damming lakes, extracting water, and filling shallow wetlands all lead to the destruction of these ecosystems.

3. Constructing dams and levees can lead to a significant loss of habitat for land animals and plant species. The restricted water flow changes natural water temperatures and impacts marine life.

Answers and Explanations

1. The sentences require a transition that indicates contrast, such as yet, but, however, still, although and either . . . or. *Although* freshwater ecosystems hold only 0.01% of Earth's water supply, over half of the people on Earth live near these ecosystems.

2. These sentences require a transition that indicates an example is to follow.

   Human activity comprises the primary threat to freshwater ecosystems; *for example*, damming lakes, extracting water, and filling shallow wetlands all lead to the destruction of these ecosystems.

3. These sentences require a transition that indicates additional information is to follow.

   The construction of dams and levees can lead to a significant loss of habitat for land animals and plant species. *Furthermore*, the restricted water flow changes natural water temperatures and impacts marine life.

WRITING THE CONCLUSION

Lewis Carroll, the author of *Alice in Wonderland*, once gave some good advice for writers: "When you come to the end, stop!"

When you come to the end of your ideas, stop writing the development—and begin writing your conclusion. You can't just end your essay with your last development paragraph. For writing in general and for the rubric, you need to draw your comments together in a strong, clear concluding paragraph.

A good concluding paragraph for your essay should be a restatement of your thesis that assures your scorers that you have successfully read, understood, and analyzed the source text. It should refer to what devices were discussed and how they support the author's primary purpose. You should be able to do this in two to six sentences.

Notice this example of a strong conclusion:

"With startling statistics, evocative imagery of troubled wetlands, and an incisive personal anecdote about the loss of a childhood watering hole, Pura persuades readers that the pollution of local waterways is a problem that affects everyone, not just life below the surface."

A good conclusion is an integral part of your essay. A missing conclusion will impact your scoring for the Writing category. Keep in mind, it may be a review or a restatement, or it may leave your readers with an intriguing question to think about (one that is closely related to your essay, of course). In any case, your conclusion must be strong, clear, and effective.

Recognizing Effective Conclusions

Remember that an *effective* concluding paragraph must restate or summarize main idea(s) in your essay, draw a logical conclusion, or offer a strong declaration on how rhetorical choices enhanced the author's work. Just as there are methods used to write effective conclusions, there are also ineffective methods that essay writers may be tempted to use in drawing a composition to a close. Try to avoid falling into the following three traps (each is followed by an example):

1. Apologizing for your inability to more thoroughly analyze the passage in the allotted time

   Example: *I wish I had more time to write a better, more in-depth analysis, but I find that in the allotted time this is all that I could do.*

2. Complaining that the source text did not interest you or that you don't think it was fair to be asked to write an analysis of the source text without giving your own opinions on the topic

   Example: *Although I have not mentioned this before, my family enjoys boating on freshwater lakes. We often pick up litter from the water in the hopes of decreasing pollution.*

3. Introducing material that you will not develop, rambling on about unimportant matters, using material that is trite or unrelated, or making a sarcastic joke that indicates your disdain for the topic you just spent 50 minutes writing about

   Example: *This passage was incredibly difficult to understand, and I felt like the author droned on and on about nothing.*

Skill Builder: Effective Conclusions

DIRECTIONS: Examine the following five excerpts from concluding paragraphs and decide whether each is effective or ineffective.

---

1. That's all I have to say about the topic. I know I'm not an expert, but at least this is an actual analysis of the work. I also used a lot of supporting details from the source text. So, I think you should give me at least a 3. (Effective / Ineffective)

2. River Pura is a passionate spokesperson for freshwater ecosystems as she forges her argument for limiting the use of motorized watercraft. In careful examination of the issue, she conveys that motorized watercraft are the main cause of pollution in freshwater ecosystems. Pura structures her impassioned pleas around valid statistical evidence, intertwining both pathos and logos to persuade her audience toward urgent action and contemplation of their responsibilities toward the natural world. (Effective / Ineffective)

3. I forgot to mention earlier that the author uses a variety of descriptive words and phrases to appeal to the emotions of readers. She also uses figurative language and makes some illusions to other articles the reader may have read. (Effective / Ineffective)

4. Protecting the biodiversity of freshwater ecosystems is a topic of importance for all of those who depend upon these ecosystems for survival. River Pura makes a solid case for the restriction of motorized watercraft in freshwater areas. Pura begins her argument with startling facts and statistics designed to capture the reader's attention. She then moves into a well-reasoned discourse that effectively negates any counter-claims opponents might make. (Effective / Ineffective)

5. In conclusion, the author makes a pretty good case for protecting freshwater ecosystems. However, most people I know aren't going to stop boating because an environmentalist says they should. (Effective / Ineffective)

Answers and Explanations

1. *Ineffective.* Do not speak directly to or "butter up" the scorers in your concluding paragraph. Maintain a formal tone.

2. *Effective.* This paragraph sums up the key points of the analysis and states the essay writer's opinion of the passage author's persuasive writing.

3. *Ineffective.* Do not introduce new ideas into a concluding paragraph. If you have more information to add that would improve or add depth to your analysis, consider adding another body paragraph. Also, the essay writer has misused the word *illusion*: he or she should have used *allusion*.

4. *Effective.* This paragraph effectively summarizes the key points of the analysis.

5. *Ineffective.* This paragraph gives only a vague summary of the analysis and offers an opinion that is irrelevant to the essay-writing task.

THE SCORING RUBRIC FOR THE SAT® ESSAY

The SAT Essay will be scored based on a 4-point rubric. Points will be awarded in three areas: Reading, Analysis, and Writing. Each essay will be scored by two graders who will give a score of 1 to 4 in each of the three areas. Those scores will be combined to yield scoring on a scale of 2-8. Scores in each area will be reported separately from the other two. For example, a test taker might earn a score of 3/4/3 (6/8/6 when doubled). This means that the test taker scored 3 out of 4 points in both reading and writing and 4 out of 4 points in analysis.

All the scorers read the essays against the same rubric developed by the College Board, which administers the SAT. This rubric guides the scorers in considering overall impression, development, organization, diction, sentence structure, grammar, usage, and mechanics. The rubric also directs scorers in evaluating essay writers' comprehension of the source text, use of relevant evidence from the passage, and their analysis of the passage author's argument. The scoring guidelines are similar to the following:

Essay Scoring 4 (Advanced)

- *Reading*: shows a comprehensive understanding of the source text, including the author's key claims, use of details and evidence, and the relationship between the two
- *Analysis*: offers an "insightful" and in-depth evaluation of the author's use of evidence and stylistic or persuasive features in building an argument; uses relevant supporting details that address the task
- *Writing*: includes all of the features of a strong essay, including a precise central claim, body paragraphs, and a strong conclusion; incorporates a variety of sentence structures; is virtually free of all convention errors

Essay Scoring 3 (Proficient)

- *Reading*: shows an appropriate understanding of the source text, including the author's key claims and use of details in developing an argument
- *Analysis*: offers an effective evaluation of the author's use of evidence and stylistic or persuasive features in building an argument; uses appropriate supporting details and evidence that are relevant and focused on the task
- *Writing*: includes all of the features of an effective essay, including a precise central claim, body paragraphs, and a strong conclusion; incorporates a variety of sentence structures and is relatively free of common grammatical errors

Essay Scoring 2 (Partial)

- *Reading*: shows some understanding of the source text, including the author's key claims; uses limited textual evidence; incorporates unimportant details
- *Analysis*: offers a limited evaluation of the author's use of evidence and stylistic or persuasive features in building an argument; supporting details are lacking and/or irrelevant to task

FUN FACTS

A pangram is a sentence that uses every letter of a given alphabet at least once. The most common pangram is, "The quick brown fox jumps over a lazy dog."

6

- *Writing*: does not provide a precise central claim, nor an effective introduction, body paragraphs, and conclusion; incorporates little variety of sentence structures and contains numerous errors in grammar and conventions

Essay Scoring 1 (Inadequate)

- *Reading*: demonstrates little or no understanding of the source text or the author's use of key claims
- *Analysis*: offers no clear evaluation of the author's use of evidence and stylistic or persuasive features in building an argument; supporting details and evidence are nonexistent or irrelevant to task
- *Writing*: lacks any form of cohesion or structure; incorporates little variety in sentence structure and includes significant errors in convention that make it difficult to read

Read the rubric several times. As you practice writing essays for the SAT, keep this rubric in mind. As you write each essay, try to focus on one or two qualities of good writing that the rubric measures. After you have finished writing your essay, come back to the rubric and see how your essay measures up.

Use the following table to help you. Give yourself anywhere from 1 to 4 points for each rubric category.

PRACTICE TEST SCORING TABLE	
Reading:	_____
Analysis:	_____
Writing:	_____
Final Score:	_____ / _____ / _____

BRAIN BREAK

Close your eyes and do nothing for 5 minutes. Let your mind wander where it will. Acknowledge any thoughts that cross your mind, but don't dwell on them. You can deal with what you need to after the mental break. Your goal for 5 minutes is to be present in the moment.

Summing It Up

- The SAT Essay is 50 minutes long. You will receive one essay prompt and be asked to write an analytical essay in response.

- SAT essays are scored based on how well they meet the following criteria:

  1. Reading—Does the essay demonstrate a thorough understanding of the source text, identify the author's key claims and explain how he or she uses evidence to support them? Does the essay use evidence from the source text effectively?

  2. Analysis—Does the essay offer in-depth evaluations of the author's use of evidence and stylistic or persuasive language features to build and support his or her argument? Does the essay include relevant supporting evidence from the passage to aid in its analysis?

  3. Writing—Does the essay include an effective introduction, a precise central claim supported by body paragraphs, and a strong conclusion? Does the essay include a variety of clearly written sentences that flow well together? Is the essay mostly error-free in grammar, usage, and mechanics?

- Your essay should not explain whether you agree with the author's claims, but, rather, it should explain how the author builds an argument to persuade his or her audience.

- Practice pacing yourself so that you are able to get your ideas down on paper in a complete, coherent, and unified essay.

- Prewriting (reading and analysis) should take 15–20 minutes. Use this time to do the following:

  o Identify and underline the author's key claims.

  o Find and then circle or highlight specific evidence the author uses to support his or her key claims.

  o Take notes on ways the author has used logic, reasoning, persuasive language techniques, and evidence to strengthen his or her key claims.

- Writing the introduction should take 4–5 minutes. Keep these five ideas in mind:

  1. Keep the key words and phrases of the prompt in mind.

  2. Be sincere, clear, and straightforward. Avoid being cute, funny, ironic, satiric, overly emotional, or too dramatic.

  3. Paraphrase key claims from the source text.

  4. Write a clear topic sentence that introduces the passage's author, title, topic and the author's key claim about the topic, and makes it clear to your readers that you are about to analyze the passage and explain how the author accomplishes his or her persuasive purpose.

  5. Write sentences that advance the topic and interest the reader.

6

- Writing the body of the essay should take 15–20 minutes. Support your analysis of the author's work with careful reasoning and back up your analysis with evidence from the source text. Explain how a rhetorical choice supports the author's purpose and how it affects the audience of the passage. Your writing must be coherent, logical, unified, and organized.

- Writing the conclusion should take 3–4 minutes. A good concluding paragraph should assure your scorers that you have successfully read, understood, and analyzed the source text. Your conclusion should contain three items:

  1. A summary of the material covered in the essay

  2. A restatement of your thesis

  3. A clear statement about the effectiveness of the passage author's work as related to the discussed rhetorical choices

- Revising (3 to 5 minutes) and proofing (3 to 5 minutes) are important steps in the writing process. Be sure to leave yourself enough time to polish your essay, even though it is considered a first draft by the test scorers.

Take a moment to ask yourself some simple questions about your understanding of the chapter:

Review: What did I learn?

Evaluate: What do I need to learn more about?

Plan: What can I do next to keep improving?

Based on your answers to those questions, adjust your study plan to dedicate additional time to the areas of weakness that you've identified.

PRACTICE EXERCISE: PRACTICING YOUR ESSAY SKILLS

DIRECTIONS: Use the following prompt to practice writing an effective essay. Carefully read the prompt and write a response. Make use of the effective writing techniques discussed in this chapter. Use the scoring rubric to evaluate your work. Then read and evaluate the three sample responses.

As you read the passage below, consider how the writer uses the following:

- Evidence, such as facts or examples, that supports claims
- Reasoning to develop ideas and to connect claims and evidence
- Stylistic or persuasive elements that add power to the ideas expressed, such as word choice, emotional appeals, logical appeals, or ethical appeals

Henry Clay (1777–1852) served several terms in Congress and was Secretary of State in 1825. In the following speech, given in 1818, he argues that the United States should support South America in gaining independence from Spain.

THE EMANCIPATION OF SOUTH AMERICA

1 Spain has undoubtedly given us abundant and just cause for war. But it is not every cause of war that should lead to war. . . . If we are to have war with Spain, I have, however, no hesitation in saying that no mode of bringing it about could be less fortunate than that of seizing, at this time, upon her adjoining province. There was a time, under certain circumstances, when we might have occupied East Florida with safety; had we then taken it, our posture in the negotiation with Spain would have been totally different from what it is.

2 But we have permitted that time, not with my consent, to pass by unimproved. If we were now to seize upon Florida after a great change in those circumstances, and after declaring our intention to acquiesce in the procrastination desired by Spain, in what light should we be viewed by foreign powers—particularly Great Britain? We have already been accused of inordinate ambition, and of seeking to aggrandize ourselves by an extension, on all sides, of our limits. Should we not, by such an act of violence, give color to the accusation? No, Mr. Chairman; if we are to be involved in a war with Spain, let us have the credit of disinterestedness. Let us put her yet more in the wrong. Let us command the respect which is never withheld from those who act a noble and generous part. I hope to communicate to the committee the conviction which I so strongly feel, that the adoption of the amendment which I intend to propose would not hazard, in the slightest degree, the peace of the country. . . .

3 In contemplating the great struggle in which Spanish America is now engaged, our attention is fixed first by the immensity and character of the country which Spain seeks again to subjugate. Stretching on the Pacific Ocean from about the fortieth degree of north latitude to about the fifty-fifth degree of south latitude, and extending from the mouth of the Rio del Norte (exclusive of East Florida), around the Gulf of Mexico and along the South Atlantic to near Cape Horn, it is nearly five thousand miles in length, and in some places nearly three thousand in breadth. . . .

4 Throughout all the extent of that great portion of the world which I have attempted thus hastily to describe, the spirit of revolt against the dominion of Spain has manifested itself. The Revolution has been attended with various degrees of success in the several parts of Spanish America. In some it has been already crowned, as I shall endeavor to show, with complete success, and in all I am persuaded that independence has struck such deep root, that the power of Spain can never eradicate it. What are the causes of this great movement?

5 Three hundred years ago, upon the ruins of the thrones of Montezuma and the Incas of Peru, Spain erected the most stupendous system of colonial despotism that the world has ever seen—the most vigorous, the most exclusive. The great principle and object of this system have been to render one of the largest portions of the world exclusively subservient, in all its faculties, to the interests of an inconsiderable spot in Europe….

6 Thus upon the ground of strict right, upon the footing of a mere legal question, governed by forensic rules, the Colonies, being absolved by the acts of the parent country from the duty of subjection to it, had an indisputable right to set up for themselves. But I take a broader and a bolder position. I maintain that an oppressed people are authorized, whenever they can, to rise and break their fetters. This was the great principle of the English Revolution. It was the great principle of our own… .

7 In the establishment of the independence of Spanish America, the United States have the deepest interest. I have no hesitation in asserting my firm belief that there is no question in the foreign policy of this country, which has ever arisen, or which I can conceive as ever occurring, in the decision of which we have had or can have so much at stake. This interest concerns our politics, our commerce, our navigation… .

8 I would invoke the spirits of our departed fathers. Was it for yourselves only that you nobly fought? No, no! It was the chains that were forging for your posterity that made you fly to arms, and, scattering the elements of these chains to the winds, you transmitted to us the rich inheritance of liberty.

Write an essay in which you explain how Henry Clay builds an argument to persuade his audience that the United States should support South America in its efforts to secure freedom from Spain. In your essay, analyze how Clay uses one or more of the features previously listed (or features of your own choice) to strengthen the logic and persuasiveness of his argument. Be sure that your analysis focuses on the most relevant aspects of the passage.

Your essay should not explain whether you agree with Clay's claims, but rather explain how he builds an argument to persuade his audience.

Use the following scoring guide to help you evaluate Sample Essay 1. Then, read our analysis of the essay, as well as suggestions for improvement.

Score Point	Reading	Analysis	Writing
4 (Advanced)	The essay shows a comprehensive understanding of the source text, including the author's key claims, use of details and evidence, and the relationship between the two.	The essay offers an "insightful" and in-depth evaluation of the author's use of evidence and stylistic or persuasive features in building an argument. Supporting details and evidence are relevant and focus on those details that address the task.	The essay includes all of the features of a strong essay, including a precise central claim, body paragraphs, and a strong conclusion. There is a variety of sentence structures used in the essay, and it is virtually free of all convention errors.
3 (Proficient)	The essay shows an appropriate understanding of the source text, including the author's key claims and use of details in developing an argument.	The essay offers an "effective" evaluation of the author's use of evidence and stylistic or persuasive features in building an argument. Supporting details and evidence are appropriate and focus on those details that address the task.	The essay includes all of the features of an effective essay, including a precise central claim, body paragraphs, and a strong conclusion. There is a variety of sentence structures used in the essay, and it is free of significant convention errors.
2 (Partial)	The essay shows some understanding of the source text, including the author's key claims, but uses limited textual evidence and/or unimportant details.	The essay offers limited evaluation of the author's use of evidence and stylistic or persuasive features in building an argument. Supporting details and evidence are lacking and/or are not relevant to the task.	The essay does not provide a precise central claim, nor does it provide an effective introduction, body paragraphs, and conclusion. There is little variety of sentence structure used in the essay, and there are numerous errors in grammar and conventions.
1 (Inadequate)	The essay demonstrates little or no understanding of the source text or the author's use of key claims.	The essay offers no clear evaluation of the author's use of evidence and stylistic or persuasive features in building an argument. Supporting details and evidence are nonexistent or irrelevant to the task.	The essay lacks any form of cohesion or structure. There is little variety of sentence structures, and significant errors in convention make it difficult to read.

The following sample essays are scored on a scale of 1–4, not doubled as would be found on the actual SAT.

Sample Essay 1

In his speech to Congress, Henry Clay emphasizes the importance of supporting South America in their revolt against Spain. Clay begins his argument by talking about the significance of the state of Florida, which isn't actually a state yet. Clay urges Congress not to invade Florida (which apparently has been captured by Spain) because it would make the US look bad. Clay's goal is for Spain to be "in the wrong" and for the US to "command the respect which is never withheld from those who act a noble and generous part."

Clay goes on to remind his listeners that the majority of South America is already involved in a Revolution against Spain. This is a key point of persuasion. Finally, Clay makes the comparison between the Revolution in South America and the Revolution against Great Britain. He even goes so far as to "invoke the spirits of our departed fathers" and uses other images like "fly to arms" and "the rich inheritance of liberty." While Clay's argument is okay, it's long-winded and focuses too much on emotional appeal.

Analysis of Sample Essay 1

This response scored a 2/2/2.

Reading—2

The writer demonstrates some comprehension of the source text. In the first paragraph, the writer conveys the basic central claim—*the importance of supporting South America in their revolt against Spain*. The writer also shows a partial understanding of Clay's position on Florida—*Clay's goal is for Spain to be "in the wrong"*—but does not effectively tie it to the central claim. In the following paragraph, the writer correctly identifies Clay's comparison of the South American Revolution to the US Revolution. However, there is little demonstration of the relationship between the central claim and the supporting details. Overall, the writer shows a partial understanding of the source text.

Analysis—2

The response offers a limited analysis of the source text, showing only partial understanding of the task. The writer mentions the *significance of the state of Florida* but then does not elaborate on this significance or explain how Florida's significance contributes to Clay's argument. In the second paragraph, the writer makes note of *a key point of persuasion*; however, there is no further discussion of why South America's revolution against Spain is a key point of persuasion. Furthermore, the writer does not develop the effect of Clay's comparison of the South American Revolution to the US Revolution. While the writer includes the use of *emotional appeal* in the analysis, there is no explanation of it. Overall, this response is only a partially successful analysis.

Writing—2

This response reflects limited cohesion and some skill in the use of language. There is no precise central claim, nor is there an effective introduction and conclusion. Phrases like *isn't actually a state yet* and *which apparently has been captured by Spain* use an informal, almost flippant tone. Calling the source text *long-winded* is subjective and inappropriate for a formal analysis. Overall, this response represents a partially developed essay.

Suggestions for Improvement

1. The response needs a clearly developed introduction that establishes the topic and presents a precise central claim. While the first paragraph makes a start, a precise central claim should briefly summarize the key points that the writer will make in his or her analysis.

2. Each body paragraph should begin with a topic sentence that summarizes the key point of the paragraph. For instance, the writer could begin the second paragraph with the sentence: *Clay begins his argument with reason rather than rhetoric, logically appealing to those who are hesitant to engage in open warfare.*

3. The use of evidence from the source text should directly support key aspects of the essay writer's analysis. Look at this sentence from paragraph 2 of Sample Essay 1: He even goes so far as to "invoke the spirits of our departed fathers" and uses other images like "fly to arms" and "the rich inheritance of liberty." The quotations here do not support the writer's analysis of the source text. A better use of quotations might be:

   Clay uses emotionally powerful language as a persuasive tool in making the correlation between the US quest for independence from Great Britain and South America's quest for independence from Spain. He wants to inspire the same passionate support for South America's struggle that most of his listeners feel about their own country's revolution, so he *uses emotional phrases like "invoke the spirits of our departed fathers," "fly to arms," and "rich inheritance of liberty."*

4. The response should include a strong conclusion that restates the thesis, recaps the most important parts of the analysis, or leaves the reader with a final thought. The conclusion should provide a sense of closure on the topic.

5. All SAT essays should maintain a formal and objective tone. The writer should limit the use of contractions and refrain from using derogatory adjectives like *long-winded* to describe the source text.

Sample Essay 2

In Henry Clay's 1818 address to Congress, he is building an argument to persuade his listeners to support South America in their revolution against Spain. He builds his argument in three different ways. Clay demonstrates an understanding of his audience, underscores the action that they need to take, and closes with an emotional appeal for liberty by referencing the Revolutionary War.

Clay begins building his argument by demonstrating an understanding of his audience. He demonstrates an understanding of his audience when he assures them at the outset of his speech that he is not calling for open warfare against Spain. This is significant because many members of Congress still remembered the bloodshed from the Revolutionary War. Clay reassures his audience and seeks to get them on his side by stating "it is not every cause of war that should lead to war." Once Congresses minds are put at ease, Clay can move onto talking about his central claim.

After Clay reassures his listeners, he then attempts to underscore the amount of involvement they would have to take in the conflict. He is seeking to minimize the nature of the conflict in order to win support for it. Clay says that, "The Revolution has been attended with various degrees of success in the several parts of Spanish America. In some it has been already crowned, as I shall endeavor to show, with complete success. . . ."

Finally, Clay seeks to draw a parallel for his listeners between the revolution they had recently won and the revolution being fought in South America. This is his emotional appeal. Clay is telling his listeners,

"Remember your fight for independence? Remember how greatly you desired freedom? This is the same thing." By getting his listeners to remember how passionately they desired freedom from Great Britain, he is hoping to sway their emotions in favor of supporting South America against Spain.

Henry Clay uses logic, minimizing, and emotional appeal to build an argument. He shows that he understands his audience and seeks to give them what they need so that they will agree with him.

Analysis of Sample Essay 2

This essay scored a 3/3/3.

Reading—3

This response demonstrates effective understanding of the source text with appropriate use of evidence through the analysis. In the second paragraph, the author discusses Clay's understanding of his audience and what the audience most fears. Although the source text does not refer explicitly to this fear, the writer infers it from a careful reading of the passage. In the next paragraph, the writer cites and discusses a claim Clay makes that supporting South America requires a minimal response. Finally, the last body paragraph paraphrases Clay's emotional call to remember the principles that guided the American Revolution. The writer shows an effective understanding of both the central idea and important details.

Analysis—3

The writer shows an effective understanding of the task by identifying three ways Clay builds his argument (*Clay demonstrates an understanding of his audience, underscores the action that they need to take, and closes with an emotional appeal . . .*) and then developing each point in the body paragraphs. Each body paragraph carefully evaluates how pieces of evidence from the source text, the author's use of reasoning, or stylistic or persuasive features are used to develop an argument. For example, in the final body paragraph the writer claims that Clay is *getting his listeners to remember how passionately they desired freedom from Great Britain* and explains that this is *to sway their emotions in favor of supporting South America against Spain*. The response could have made stronger use of evidence from the text, offering a direct quote rather than a paraphrase. However, this response shows an effective analysis of the source text using relevant support.

Writing—3

This essay includes most of the features of an effective essay, including a precise central claim and body paragraphs. The introduction and conclusion lack development, although the introduction presents the central claim and the conclusion restates it. There is appropriate variety of sentence structure, and the few errors of convention and grammar do not detract from the overall reading of the response. Overall, this analysis is proficient.

Suggestions for Improvements

1. The author should work to develop a stronger introduction and conclusion. For example, the introduction could explain the significance of the topic, and the conclusion might provide a final thought or statement related to Clay's purpose.

2. Paragraph 3 could further discuss Clay's reasons for minimizing the support needed in South America. While the writer effectively illustrates Clay's use of minimization, the importance of this technique to Clay's argument is not fully clear.

3. In paragraph 4, the writer paraphrases Clay's emotional appeal. When discussing an author's use of emotional language to persuade listeners to share his point of view or take a certain action, direct quotes from the source text are best as long as they are properly introduced.

Sample Essay 3

In 1818, South America was rising in revolt against Spain. Congressman Henry Clay believed that it was in America's best interest to support their neighbors to the south. In his speech to the 1818 Congress, Clay builds an argument tailor-made for his audience, outlining action steps Congress should take while at the same time appealing to their passionate belief in democracy. Through a combination of careful rhetoric, logic, and emotional appeal, Clay hopes to convince Congress to adopt an amendment that would put the US at war with Spain.

Clay begins his argument with careful rhetoric designed specifically for his audience. Clay understands that some may be thinking of the bloodshed of the American Revolution and have no desire to engage in another war. "It is not every cause of war that should lead to war . . . " Clay maintains. However, Clay goes on to suggest to his audience that, had they acted prior to this moment in time, war might have been avoided. In essence, Clay is telling his audience that he does not condone war; however, Congress has brought about the necessity to engage in war by previous inaction. Clay tells his audience, "There was a time . . . when . . . our posture in the negotiation with Spain would have been totally different. . . ." Yet, Clay maintains, that time has passed. Now is the time for more heavy-handed action.

Clay furthers the appeal of his argument by insisting that the action steps he proposes would not lead the country into another violent conflict. Rather, Clay maintains ". . . the adoption of the amendment which I intend to propose would not hazard, in the slightest degree, the peace of the country. . . . " He uses logic to reason that, because of the size of South America, and because of the success that some South American people have already had in their fight against Spain, the revolution in some areas is already "a complete success." Therefore, Clay is demonstrating to his audience that supporting his amendment poses no risk to them.

Finally, Clay uses an emotional appeal to ultimately convince Congress to pass the amendment. Clay draws a parallel between the ideals of freedom and democracy that underscored the fight for American independence and the ideals of freedom and democracy that are bolstering the fight in South America. His emotional appeal is summed up in the last paragraph of the speech: "I would invoke the spirits of our departed fathers. Was it for yourselves only that you nobly fought? No, no! It was the chains that were forging for your posterity that made you fly to arms. . . . "

Speaking to Congress of the imminent threat of Spain, Henry Clay seeks to persuade his listeners to pass an amendment that would essentially put the fledgling nation at war with another European nation. With careful rhetoric, logic, and emotional appeals, Clay seeks to convince his listeners that freedom is something for which one should always be willing to fight.

Analysis of Sample Essay 3

This essay scored a 4/4/4.

Reading—4

This response demonstrates thorough understanding of the source text with skillful use of paraphrases and direct quotations. The writer briefly summarizes the main idea of Clay's argument (*Clay believed that it was in America's best interest to support their neighbors to the south*) and presents many details from the text, including Clay's reflection that Congress had an opportunity to negotiate with Spain but missed it, to demonstrate why Clay's argument is significant. There are few long direct quotations from the source text. Instead, the author accurately and precisely paraphrases the key points of the speech.

Analysis—4

The writer demonstrates an insightful understanding of the task by identifying three ways Clay builds his argument (*Through a combination of careful rhetoric, logic, and emotional appeal . . .*) and expanding on each point in the body paragraphs. Each body paragraph carefully evaluates how pieces of evidence from the source text, the author's use of reasoning, or stylistic or persuasive features are used to develop an argument. For example, in the final body paragraph the writer claims that Clay "draws a parallel between the ideals of freedom and democracy that underscored the fight for American independence and the ideals of freedom and democracy that are bolstering the fight in South America." The response demonstrates a thorough understanding of both the source text and its effect on the audience.

Writing—4

This essay is cohesive and shows an effective command of language, including a precise central claim and body paragraphs. The introduction and conclusion are well developed. There is ample variety of sentence structures and no errors of convention and grammar that detract from the overall reading of the response. Overall, this analysis shows advanced writing proficiency.

ADDITIONAL ESSAY WRITING PRACTICE

DIRECTIONS: For more practice, carefully read the following prompt and source text. Then write an analysis of the passage. Score your analytical response using the rubric provided.

As you read the passage below, consider how the writer uses the following:

- Evidence, such as facts or examples, that supports claims
- Reasoning to develop ideas and to connect claims and evidence
- Stylistic or persuasive elements to add power to the ideas expressed, such as word choice, emotional appeals, logical appeals, and ethical appeals

Padre Island National Seashore separates the Gulf of Mexico from the Laguna Madre, one of a few hypersaline lagoons in the world. The park protects 70 miles of coastline, dunes, prairies, and wind tidal flats teeming with life. It is a safe nesting ground for the Kemp's Ridley sea turtle and a haven for 380 bird species. It also has a rich history, including the Spanish shipwrecks of 1554.

THE IMPORTANCE OF THE 1554 SHIPWRECKS

1 In April, 1554, three Spanish *naos* (a type of cargo and passenger ship similar to Columbus's *Santa Maria*) went aground on Padre Island following a storm that had blown them across the Gulf of Mexico from the coast of Cuba. At the time this was the greatest disaster to ever befall the Spanish fleet in the New World. Tons of treasure bound for Spain was lost in addition to the lives of approximately three hundred passengers and crew who died from hunger, thirst, and attacks by natives as they attempted to walk back to the port of Vera Cruz.

2 But the story of the 1554 shipwreck does not end there, nor does it end with the conclusion of the salvage operations that took place later that year. As with any important historical event, its effects resonate through the centuries and can still be felt today—if one looks for them.

3 First of all, the wrecks were the first documented occurrence of Europeans on the island and one of the first occurrences of Europeans in what was to become Texas. The salvage operation was the first documented instance of Europeans intentionally coming to the island and staying for an extended period.

4 Second, the three ships that wrecked (the *Santa Maria de Yciar*, the *Espiritu Santo*, and the *San Esteban*) are the oldest shipwrecks ever found in North America (excluding the Caribbean and Latin America).

5 Third, when the remains of the ships were discovered in 1967, a private company called Platoro, Ltd. began excavating them. This set off a long legal battle over ownership of the remains, as Texas had no laws governing antiquities at the time. In the long run, the state won its case and the remains were turned over to the National Park Service, which has transferred curation of the artifacts to the Corpus Christi Museum of Science and History, where they may now be viewed.

6 Historian and Marine Archeologist Dr. Donald Keith, president of the Ships of Discovery at the Corpus Christi Museum of Science and History, notes that:

7 "The 1554 shipwrecks are important for a lot of reasons. The 'mining' of them by Platoro caused the state of Texas to realize that shipwrecks and archaeological sites in general are important, and the property of the people and the state. They are cultural resources that have to be cared for. Some of the earliest experiments in the conservation of artifacts from the sea were done on the objects and hull remains that were recovered from the sites that Platoro and the State worked. . . . The Platoro conflict did lead to the establishment of the Texas Antiquities Committee, which led to the Texas Historical Commission, which led to the discovery and excavation of *La Belle* [the ship of the French explorer La Salle, found on the Texas coast within the past few years] among other accomplishments."

8 This third and last effect on our present society is undoubtedly the most important, because it resulted in new Texas laws to protect archeological resources. These laws follow the federal Antiquities Act in spirit, which gives federal agencies custody of relics found within their jurisdictions so that they may be properly protected and studied. Thus, instead of ending up in private collections where they become curiosities for a fortunate few, the knowledge derived from the artifacts goes to the public in the form of publications and exhibits in museums and on websites.

9 Bits and pieces of the 1554 wrecks and many other historical events still wash up on the island or can be found emerging from the sands. If you discover something, please remember that the right thing to do is leave it where it is and report it to us, so that we may conduct a proper archeological dig and learn more about the rich history of the island and share our findings (and yours) with the world.

Write an essay in which you explain how the writer builds an argument to persuade his or her audience of the importance of the 1554 shipwrecks. In your essay, analyze how the author uses one or more of the features listed previously (or features of your own choice) to strengthen the logic and persuasiveness of his/her argument. Be sure that your analysis focuses on the most relevant aspects of the passage.

Your essay should not explain whether you agree with the writer's claims, but rather explain how the writer builds an argument to persuade his or her audience.

PART VI:
MATH STRATEGIES FOR THE SAT® EXAM

Chapter 7

Multiple-Choice Math

OVERVIEW

- **Why Multiple-Choice Math Is Easier**
- **Question Format**
- **Solving Multiple-Choice Math Questions**
- **Know When to Use Your Calculator**
- **Learn the Most Important Multiple-Choice Math Tips**
- **Summing It Up**
- **Practice Exercises**
- **Answer Keys and Explanations**

WHY MULTIPLE-CHOICE MATH IS EASIER

How can one kind of math possibly be easier than another? Multiple-choice math questions on the SAT exam are easier than those on the math tests you take in class because the answers are right there in front of you. As you know from taking other standardized tests, multiple-choice questions always give you the answer. You just have to figure out which answer is the correct one. So even if you aren't sure and have to guess, you can use estimating to narrow your choices and improve your odds.

Of the 58 math questions on the SAT, 45 will be multiple-choice, each with four answer options. The questions in each multiple-choice math section are arranged from easiest to most difficult. The questions don't stick to one content area. They jump around from algebra to geometry to advanced math to data analysis to statistics and back to algebra in no particular pattern.

QUESTION FORMAT

On the SAT Math test, each set of multiple-choice math questions starts with directions and a reference section that look like this:

DIRECTIONS: For **Questions 1–30**, solve each problem, select the best answer from the choices provided, and fill in the corresponding circle on your answer sheet. For **Questions 31–38**, solve the problem and enter your answer in the grid on the answer sheet. The directions **before Question 31** will provide information on how to enter your answers in the grid.

ADDITIONAL INFORMATION:

- The use of a calculator **is permitted**. (In the Math Test—No Calculator section, this will say: "The use of a calculator **is not permitted**.)

- All variables and expressions used represent real numbers unless otherwise indicated.

- Figures provided in this test are drawn to scale unless otherwise indicated.

- All figures lie in a plane unless otherwise indicated.

- Unless otherwise specified, the domain of a given function f is the set of all real numbers x for which is $f(x)$ is a real number.

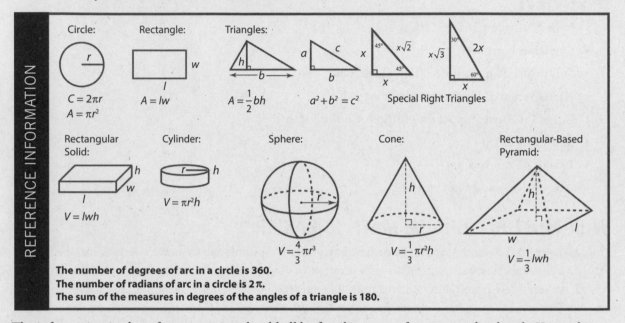

The information in the reference section should all be familiar to you from your schoolwork. Know that it's there in case you need it. But remember: the formulas themselves aren't the answers to any problems. You have to know when to use them and how to apply them.

Some multiple-choice questions ask to solve a given equation or system of equations, while others are presented in the form of word problems. Some include graphs, charts, or tables that you will be asked to interpret. All of the questions have four answer choices. These choices are arranged in order when the answers are numbers, usually from smallest to largest, but occasionally from largest to smallest.

SOLVING MULTIPLE-CHOICE MATH QUESTIONS

These five steps will help you solve multiple-choice math questions:

1. Read the question carefully and determine what's being asked.

2. Decide which math principles apply and use them to solve the problem.

3. Look for your answer among the choices. If it's there, mark it and go on.

4. If the answer you found is not there, recheck the question and your calculations.

5. If you still can't solve the problem, eliminate obviously wrong answers and take your best guess.

Now let's try out these steps on a couple of SAT-type multiple-choice math questions.

Example 1:

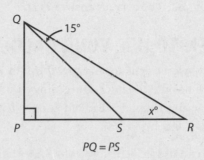

$PQ = PS$

In the figure above, $x =$

A. $15°$

B. $30°$

C. $60°$

D. $75°$

Solution:

This problem asks you to find the measure of one angle of right triangle PQR.

Two math principles apply:

1. The sum of the measures in degrees of the angles of a triangle is 180.

2. 45-45-90 right triangles have certain special properties.

Since $PQ = PS$, PQS is a 45-45-90 right triangle. This means that angle $PQS = 45°$ and angle $PQR = 45 + 15 = 60°$. So angle $x = 180 - 90 - 60 = 30°$. Now look to see if 30° is among the answer choices. Indeed, it's listed in choice B. No further steps are needed. **The correct answer is B.**

Example 2:

If x and y are negative numbers, which of the following is negative?

A. xy

B. $(xy)^2$

C. $(x - y)^2$

D. $x + y$

Solution:

This problem asks you to pick an answer choice that is a negative number. The principles that apply are those governing operations with signed numbers.

- Since x and y are negative, choice A must be positive.

- As for choices B and C, as long as x and y are not equal to each other, both expressions must be positive. (If they're equal, the expression equals zero, and any number other than zero squared gives a positive result.)

- Choice D is negative since it represents the sum of two negative numbers.

If you are having trouble working with the letters for the variables, try substituting numbers for *x* and *y* to see which answer option is negative. Pick the method that is easiest for you. **The correct answer is D.**

KNOW WHEN TO USE YOUR CALCULATOR

You are allowed to use a calculator in the SAT Math Test—Calculator section. Most calculators that you would use in class are allowed. If you can, try to use a calculator you are already comfortable using, instead of trying to learn how to use a new one on test day. This will save you valuable test time.

Even though you can use a calculator in the SAT Math Test—Calculator section, keep in mind that you don't *need* a calculator to solve any SAT math questions. A calculator can be a useful tool for simplifying expressions or graphing equations, but it can't help you solve a math problem if you don't first understand what the math question is asking you to find. In other words, if you don't understand a question in the first place, the calculator won't give you a solution.

Try making it a habit to set up your work on paper first, and then plug the information into the calculator. For example, if you have a question that deals with an equation, set up the equation first on your scratch paper. Then make your number substitutions on the calculator. This way, you always have something to refer back to without having to think, "Oh, nuts, how did I set that up?" as the seconds tick by. This is also a great way to double check your work.

When you use your calculator, check the display each time you enter numbers to make sure you entered them correctly. Make sure to hit the Clear key after each finished operation; otherwise, it could get ugly.

LEARN THE MOST IMPORTANT MULTIPLE-CHOICE MATH TIPS

You've probably heard some of the following tips before, but some may be new to you. Whatever the case, read them, learn them, and remember them. They will help you.

The Question Number Tells You How Hard the Question Is

Just as in most of the other SAT sections, the questions increase in difficulty as you work toward the end. The first third of the questions are easy, the middle third are average, and the final third are designed to be more challenging and difficult. Take a look at these three examples. Don't solve them yet (you'll be doing that in a couple of minutes); just get an idea of how the level of difficulty changes from Question 1 to Question 12 to Question 25.

ALERT

Don't automatically reach for your calculator. It is not some sort of magic eight ball that will reveal the correct answer. Use your calculator to help simplify or graph expressions, and to double check your work.

7

1. If $\dfrac{a+5}{6} = m$ and $m = 9$, what is the value of a?

   A. 24

   B. 49

   C. 59

   D. 84

12. Line a intersects the x-axis at $(3, 0)$ and the y-axis at $(0, -2)$. Line b passes through the origin and is parallel to line a. Which of the following is an equation of line b?

   A. $y = \dfrac{3}{2}x$

   B. $y = \dfrac{2}{3}x$

   C. $y = -\dfrac{3}{2}x$

   D. $y = -\dfrac{2}{3}x$

25. Yasmine owns a coffee shop and orders both coffee and tea from a wholesale supplier. The supplier will send no more than 600 kg in a shipment. Coffee beans come in packages that weigh 18.5 kg, and tea leaves come in packages that weigh 10 kg. Yasmine wants to buy at least twice as many packages of coffee as packages of tea. If c stands for the number of packages of coffee, and t stands for the number of packages of tea, which of the following systems of inequalities best represents Yasmine's order? Both c and t are nonnegative integers.

   A. $18.5c + 10t \le 600$
      $c \ge 2t$

   B. $18.5c + 10t \le 600$
      $2c \ge t$

   C. $37c + 10t \le 600$
      $c \ge 2t$

   D. $37c + 10t \le 600$
      $2c \ge t$

Can you see the difference? You can probably do Question 1 very quickly. For Question 12, you might have to think for a bit. Question 25 may cause you to wince a little and then get started on some heavy-duty thinking.

TIP
Look for shortcuts. SAT math problems test your math reasoning, not your ability to make endless calculations. If you find yourself calculating too much, you've probably missed a shortcut that would have made your work easier.

Easy Questions Have Easy Answers—Difficult Questions Don't

The easy questions are straightforward and don't have any hidden tricks. The obvious answer is almost always the correct answer. So for Question 1, the answer is indeed choice B.

When you hit the difficult stuff, you have to think harder. The information is not straightforward, and the answers aren't obvious. You can bet that the easy answer will be wrong. If you don't believe it, let's take another look at Question 25.

25. Yasmine owns a coffee shop and orders both coffee and tea from a wholesale supplier. The supplier will send no more than 600 kg in a shipment. Coffee beans come in packages that weigh 18.5 kg, and tea leaves come in packages that weigh 10 kg. Yasmine wants to buy at least twice as many packages of coffee as packages of tea. If c stands for the number of packages of coffee, and t stands for the number of packages of tea, which of the following systems of inequalities best represents Yasmine's order? Both c and t are nonnegative integers.

   A. $18.5c + 10t \leq 600$
   $$c \geq 2t$$

   B. $18.5c + 10t \leq 600$
   $$2c \geq t$$

   C. $37c + 10t \leq 600$
   $$c \geq 2t$$

   D. $37c + 10t \leq 600$
   $$2c \geq t$$

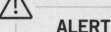

ALERT

Beware of the obvious. Don't be fooled by what look like obvious answers to difficult questions. The answers to difficult questions require some digging. They never jump out at you.

This question is difficult mostly because it takes a little longer to think through and set up the inequalities laid out in the question stem. Let's tackle this step by step.

Let's start by using the variables c for coffee beans and t for tea. The total weight, in kg, of coffee beans and tea that the wholesale supplier sends can be expressed as the weight of each package multiplied by the number of each type of package, which is $18.5c$ for coffee beans and $10t$ for tea leaves. Since the supplier will not send shipments that weigh more than 600 kg, it follows that $18.5c + 10t \leq 600$ expresses the first part of the problem.

Since Yasmine wants to buy at least twice as many packages of coffee beans as packages of tea leaves, the number of packages of coffee beans should be greater than or equal to two times the number of packages of tea leaves. This can be expressed by $c \geq 2t$.

The correct answer is A.

Why are the other answers wrong? Choice B misrepresents the relationship between the numbers of each package that Yasmine wants to buy. Choice C is incorrect because the first inequality of the system incorrectly doubles the weight per package of coffee beans. The weight of each package of coffee beans is 18.5 kg, not 37 kg. Choice D doubles the weight per package of coffee beans and transposes the relationship between the numbers of packages.

Be Certain to Answer the Question Being Asked

Suppose that you were asked to solve the following problem:

Example:

If $5x + 11 = 31$, what is the value of $x + 4$?

A. 4

B. 6

C. 8

D. 10

Solution:

The first step is to solve the equation $5x + 11 = 31$.

$$5x + 11 = 31 \quad \text{Subtract 11 from both sides.}$$
$$5x = 20 \quad \text{Divide both sides by 5.}$$
$$x = 4$$

Remember that the problem does not ask for the value of x, it asks for the value of $x + 4$, so the answer is actually 8. Make certain that the answer you select is the answer to the question that is being asked. **The correct answer is C.**

When Guessing at Hard Questions, You Can Toss Out Easy Answers

Now that you know the difficult questions won't have easy or obvious answers, use a guessing strategy. Remember, you are not penalized for incorrect answers, so guessing can't hurt. Start by scanning the answer choices and eliminating the ones that seem easy or obvious, such as any that just restate the information in the question. Then take your best guess.

Questions of Average Difficulty Won't Have Trick Answers

Let's look again at Question 12:

12. Line a intersects the x-axis at $(3, 0)$ and the y-axis at $(0, -2)$. Line b passes through the origin and is parallel to line a. Which of the following is an equation of line b?

   A. $y = \frac{3}{2}x$

   B. $y = \frac{2}{3}x$

   C. $y = -\frac{3}{2}x$

   D. $y = -\frac{2}{3}x$

This is a bit more difficult than Question 1, but it's still pretty straightforward. Since we know points on line *a*, we can calculate the slope of this line:

$$\frac{y_2 - y_1}{x_2 - x_1} = \frac{-2 - 0}{0 - 3} = \frac{2}{3}$$

Since line *b* is parallel to line *a*, the two have the same slope, that is, $\frac{2}{3}$. The problem tells us that line *b* passes through the origin, which means that it intercepts the *y*-axis at 0. Thus, line *b* can be expressed by the equation $y = \frac{2}{3}x$. **The correct answer is B.**

It's Smart to Work Backward

Every standard multiple-choice math problem includes four answer choices. One of them has to be correct; the other three are incorrect. This means that it's always possible to solve a problem by testing each of the answer choices. Just plug each choice into the problem and sooner or later you'll find the one that works! Testing answer choices can often be a much easier and surer way of solving a problem than attempting a lengthy calculation.

When Working Backward, Always Start from the Middle

When working on multiple-choice math questions, remember that all of the numeric answer choices are presented in order—either smallest to largest, or vice versa. As a result, it's always best to begin with a middle option, choice B or choice C. This way, if you start with choice C and it's too large, you'll only have to concentrate on the smaller choices. There, you've just knocked off at least two choices in a heartbeat! Now let's give it a test run.

Example 1:

If $\frac{8}{9}y = \frac{9}{4}$, what is the value of *y*?

A. $\frac{32}{81}$

B. $\frac{1}{2}$

C. 2

D. $\frac{81}{32}$

Solution:

Start with choice C, because it will be easier to compute with than choice B:

$$\frac{8}{9}(2) = \frac{16}{9} < \frac{9}{4}$$

Since choice C is too small, the only possible correct answer is choice D. Let's check:

$$\frac{8}{9}\left(\frac{81}{32}\right) = \frac{9}{4}$$

The correct answer is D.

TIP

Leave a paper trail! If you need to set up an equation, jot it down in your test booklet. That way, if you come back to recheck your work, you'll know what you were originally thinking.

Now try this process with a more difficult question.

Example 2:

In the xy-plane, the line determined by the points $(8, c)$ and $(c, 18)$ passes through the origin. Which of the following could be the value of c?

A. 10

B. 11

C. 12

D. 13

Solution:

Start with choice C because it may be easier to compute since it is an even number. The line through $(8, 12)$ and $(12, 18)$ is $y = \dfrac{18 - 12}{12 - 8} x + b$. This equation simplifies to $y = \dfrac{3}{2} x$, which is a line through the origin.

Plug $(8, 12)$ or $(12, 18)$ into $y = \dfrac{3}{2} x$, and both sides will be equal.

$$12 = \frac{3}{2}(8) \quad \text{or} \quad 18 = \frac{3}{2}(12)$$
$$12 = 12 \qquad\qquad 18 = 18$$

The other values of c will not result in an equivalent equation. **The correct answer is C.**

It's Easier to Work with Numbers Than with Letters

Because numbers are more meaningful than letters, try plugging them into equations and formulas in place of variables. This technique can make problems much easier to solve. Here are some examples:

Example 1:

If $x - 4$ is 2 greater than y, then $x + 5$ is how much greater than y?

A. 3

B. 7

C. 9

D. 11

Solution:

Choose any value for x. Let's say you decide to make $x = 4$.

Start by solving for x in the first equation. If $4 - 4 = 0$, and 0 is 2 greater than y, then $y = -2$.

In the second equation, if $x = 4$, then $4 + 5 = 9$.

Therefore, $x + 5$ is 11 more than y. **The correct answer is D.**

7

Example 2:

The cost of renting office space in a building is $2.50 per square foot per month. Which of the following represents the total cost c, in dollars, to rent p square feet of office space each year in the building?

A. $c = 2.50(12p)$

B. $c = 2.50p + 12$

C. $c = \dfrac{2.50p}{12}$

D. $c = \dfrac{12p}{2.50}$

Solution:

Let $p = 100$, then the rent for one month is $250 and the rent for one year is $3,000. The only equation that will provide that answer is $c = 2.50(12p)$. **The correct answer is A.**

If a question asks for an odd integer or an even integer, go ahead and pick any odd or even integer you like.

Solving for Variables with Restricted Values

When solving problems involving variables, you must pay careful attention to any restrictions on the possible values of the variables. Consider the following question:

Example 1:

If $x \geq 2$, which of the following is a solution to the equation $x(x-3)(x+4)(x+2)(3x-5) = 0$?

A. 2

B. 3

C. 4

D. 5

Solution:

This equation has five solutions, but the problem is looking only for a solution that is at least 2. In order for the statements left of the equals sign to be equal to zero, one of the parenthetical expressions must result in zero when a value for x is substituted. The only value that can be substituted for an x to result in zero (while also being greater than or equal to 2) is 3. Substituting in 3 for x would result in $3(0)(7)(5)(4) = 0$, which is true. **The correct answer is B.**

FUN FACTS

There is only one letter that doesn't appear in any United States state name. Can you guess which letter? It's not Z (Arizona), or X (New Mexico and Texas), or even J (New Jersey). Stumped? There is not a single letter Q in any US state name.

Now, consider this slightly different version of the same problem.

Example 2:

If $x < -2$, which of the following is a solution to the equation $x(x - 3)(x + 4)(x + 2)(3x - 5) = 0$?

A. -3

B. -4

C. -5

D. There is more than one solution.

Solution:

The solutions to the equation can be found by setting each of the factors equal to zero.

$$x = 0$$
$$x - 3 = 0$$
$$x + 4 = 0$$
$$x + 2 = 0$$
$$3x - 5 = 0$$

These lead to the solutions $x = 0, 3, -4, -2,$ and $\frac{5}{3}$ respectively. Of these five solutions, only -4 (choice B) is less than -2. **The correct answer is B.**

Solving Equations in the Three-Statement Format

You may find a three-statement format in certain questions in the multiple-choice math section. The best way to answer this kind of question is by process of elimination, tackling one statement at a time and marking it as true or false. Here is an example:

Example:

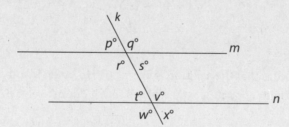

Note: Figure not drawn to scale.

In the figure above, lines k and m intersect at a point, and lines k and n intersect at a different point. If $v + s = p + q$, which of the following statements must be true?

   I. $r = w$

   II. $t = s$

   III. $q = x$

A. I only

B. II only

C. I and II only

D. I, II, and III

Solution:

Because $v + s = p + q$, we know that $p + q = 180$. Because they both make a straight line, lines m and n must be parallel. Since m and n are parallel, then statements I and II, must be true. While statement III might be true, it is only true if line k is perpendicular to lines m and n, and that does not have to be true. **The correct answer is C.**

Solving Equations Involving Square Roots or Algebraic Fractions

The procedure for solving equations involving square roots or algebraic fractions occasionally results in what are known as **extraneous solutions**. An extraneous solution is a number that is correctly obtained from the equation-solving process but doesn't actually solve the equation. Be sure to check your answer.

Example:

Solve for x: $\sqrt{x+4} + 15 = 10$

A. -29

B. -21

C. 21

D. There are no solutions.

Solution:

First, solve the equation.

$$\sqrt{x+4} + 15 = 10 \quad \text{Subtract 15 from both sides.}$$
$$\sqrt{x+4} = -5 \quad \text{Square both sides.}$$
$$\left(\sqrt{x+4}\right)^2 = \left(-5\right)^2$$
$$x + 4 = 25$$
$$x = 21$$

It appears that the solution is choice C. However, if you check the solution $x = 21$ in the original equation, you will see that it doesn't solve it.

$$\sqrt{x+4} + 15 = 10?$$
$$\sqrt{21+4} + 15 = 10?$$
$$\sqrt{25} + 15 = 10?$$
$$5 + 15 \neq 10.$$

The correct answer is D.

TIP

For multiple-choice math questions, circle what's being asked so that you don't pick a wrong answer by mistake. That way, for example, you won't pick an answer that gives perimeter when the question asks for an area.

Solving Geometry Problems of Measure

When you are asked to find the measure of a side or angle of a figure, using the measure of an angle or a side of another shape can help you find the measure you need.

Example:

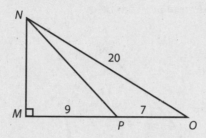

In the figure above, what is the length of *NP*?

A. 8

B. 9

C. 12

D. 15

Solution:

This figure is really two right triangles, *NMO* and *NMP*. Since *NM* is a side of both triangles, once you find its length, you can find the length of *NP*. The Pythagorean theorem is what you need:

$$NM^2 + MO^2 = NO^2$$

$$NM^2 + (16)^2 = (20)^2$$

Note that 16 and 20 are multiples of 4 and 5, respectively, so you now know that this is a 3-4-5 right triangle, which means that *NM* = 12. Since you just found out that triangle *NMP* has sides of 9 and 12, it's also a 3-4-5 right triangle, so *NP* must be 15. **The correct answer is D.**

TIP

Draw a diagram if none is supplied. Drawing a diagram is a great way to organize information. Mark it up with the information you're given, and you'll have a better idea of what you're looking for.

Solving Right Triangles Using the Pythagorean Theorem

The Pythagorean theorem is usually needed to solve problems involving a right triangle for which you are given the lengths of some of the sides. The Pythagorean theorem enables you to compute the length of the third side of a right triangle if you know the lengths of the other two sides. It is one of the most useful and common SAT exam geometry facts. Consider the problem below.

Example:

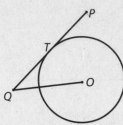

Line segment $\overline{PQ}$ is tangent to the circle with center O at point T. If T is the midpoint of $\overline{PQ}$, $OQ = 13$, and the radius of the circle is 5, what is the length of $\overline{PQ}$?

A. 10

B. 12

C. 24

D. 26

Solution:

This is a tricky question since, at the moment, it doesn't appear to involve any triangles at all. However, you are told that the radius of the circle is 5, and if you draw in radius, you will create triangle OTQ. Use the fact that a tangent line to a circle is perpendicular to the radius at the point of contact to deduce that OTQ is a right angle.

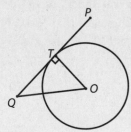

The diagram now depicts right triangle OTQ, and $OT = 5$ and $OQ = 13$. Now, use the Pythagorean theorem to determine that $TQ = 12$, as shown here:

$$OT^2 + TQ^2 = OQ^2$$
$$5^2 + TQ^2 = 13^2$$
$$25 + TQ^2 = 169$$
$$TQ^2 = 144$$
$$TQ = 12$$

Finally, since T is the midpoint of line segment $\overline{PQ}$, the entire length of the line segment is $12 + 12 = 24$. **The correct answer is C.**

Eliminate Answers That Can't Possibly Be Right

Knowing whether your calculations should produce a number that's larger or smaller than the quantity you started with can point you toward the right answer. It's also an effective way of eliminating wrong answers. Here's an example:

Example:

Daryl can set up the display for the science fair in 20 minutes. It takes Francisco 30 minutes to set it up. How long will it take the two boys to complete the setup if they work together?

A. 8 minutes

B. 12 minutes

C. 20 minutes

D. 30 minutes

Solution:

Immediately you can see that choices C and D are impossible because the two boys working together will have to complete the job in less time than either one of them working alone.

	Daryl	Francisco
$\dfrac{\text{Actual time spent}}{\text{Time needed to do entire job alone}}$	$\dfrac{x}{20}$	$\dfrac{x}{30}$

$$\frac{x}{20} + \frac{x}{30} = 1$$

Multiply by 60 to clear fractions:

$$3x + 2x = 60$$
$$5x = 60$$
$$x = 12$$

The correct answer is B.

Your Eye Is a Good Estimator

Figures in the standard multiple-choice math section are always drawn to scale unless you see the warning "Note: Figure not drawn to scale." That means you can sometimes solve a problem just by looking at the picture and estimating the answer. Here's how this works:

Example:

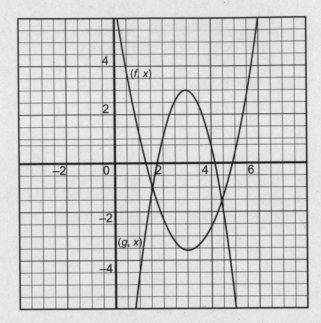

$$f(x) = (x - 3)^2 - 3$$
$$g(x) = -2(x - 3)^2 + 3$$

Graphs of the functions f and g are shown in the xy-plane above. For which of the following values of x does $f(x) + g(x) = 0$?

A. 1

B. 2

C. 3

D. 4

Solution:

The sum of the function values is 0 when the function values for f and g are opposites. That appears to be true at $x = 3$. **The correct answer is C.**

If Some Questions Always Give You Trouble, Save Them for Last

You know which little demons haunt your math skills. If you find questions that you know will give you nightmares, save them for last. They will take up a lot of your time, especially if you're panicking, and you can use that time to do more of the easier questions.

Summing It Up

- Follow the five-step plan for answering basic multiple-choice math questions:

  1. Read the question carefully and determine what's being asked.

  2. Decide which math principles apply and use them to solve the problem.

  3. Look for your answer among the choices. If it's there, mark it and go on.

  4. If the answer you found is not there, recheck the question and your calculations.

  5. If you still can't solve the problem, eliminate obviously wrong answers and take your best guess.

- In the Math Test—Calculator section, use a calculator where it can help the most: on basic arithmetic calculations, when calculating square roots and percentages, and when comparing and converting fractions.

- Set up your work on paper, then enter the numbers in your calculator. This will help you in the event your calculation goes awry. This way, you don't have to try to replicate your setup from memory.

- Math questions progress in difficulty toward the end of each Math section. The question number will clue you in as to how hard the question will be. Keep in mind that some of the difficult questions may be easier for you, and vice versa, depending upon your strengths and weaknesses.

- Work backward from the answer choices. When you do, start with choice B or choice C.

- Try to work with numbers instead of letters. This will help you avoid unnecessary algebraic calculations.

- Figures in the math section are always drawn to scale unless you see a warning. If you need to do so, use your eye as an estimator.

Take a moment to ask yourself some simple questions about your understanding of the chapter:

Review: What did I learn?

Evaluate: What do I need to learn more about?

Plan: What can I do next to keep improving?

Based on your answers to those questions, adjust your study plan to dedicate additional time to the areas of weakness that you've identified.

PRACTICE EXERCISES: MULTIPLE-CHOICE MATH

Exercise 1

18 Minutes—15 Questions

DIRECTIONS: For **Questions 1–15**, solve each problem, choose the best answer from the choices provided, and put a circle around the correct answer. You may use any available space for scratch work.

ADDITIONAL INFORMATION:

- The use of a calculator **is permitted**.

- All variables and expressions used represent real numbers unless otherwise indicated.

- Figures provided in this test are drawn to scale unless otherwise indicated.

- All figures lie in a plane unless otherwise indicated.

- Unless otherwise specified, the domain of a given function f is the set of all real numbers x for which $f(x)$ is a real number.

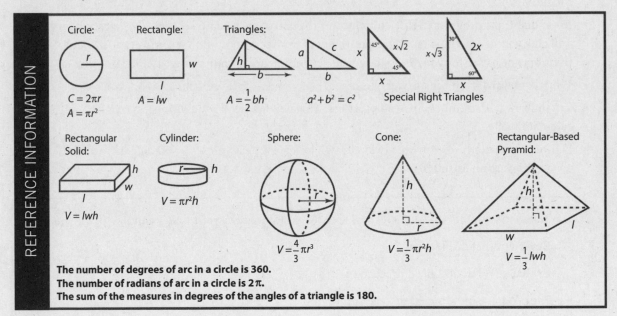

REFERENCE INFORMATION

Circle:
$C = 2\pi r$
$A = \pi r^2$

Rectangle:
$A = lw$

Triangles:
$A = \frac{1}{2}bh$
$a^2 + b^2 = c^2$

Special Right Triangles

Rectangular Solid:
$V = lwh$

Cylinder:
$V = \pi r^2 h$

Sphere:
$V = \frac{4}{3}\pi r^3$

Cone:
$V = \frac{1}{3}\pi r^2 h$

Rectangular-Based Pyramid:
$V = \frac{1}{3}lwh$

The number of degrees of arc in a circle is 360.
The number of radians of arc in a circle is 2π.
The sum of the measures in degrees of the angles of a triangle is 180.

1. A linear function $g(x)$ has x-intercept $(-3, 0)$ and y-intercept $(0, -6)$. Compute $g\left(-\dfrac{1}{2}\right)$.

   A. -7

   B. -6

   C. -5

   D. -2

2. For what values of x, if any, does the graph of $f(x) = 2 - |4 - x|$ cross the x-axis?

   A. 4

   B. 2 and 6

   C. -2

   D. No such values

3. If $H(x) = 3 - 2x^2$, compute $H(x - 1)$.

   A. $-2x^2 + 1$

   B. $-2x^2 - 2x + 4$

   C. $-2x^2 + 4x + 5$

   D. $-2x^2 + 4x + 1$

4.
$$3x - \dfrac{1}{2}y = 4$$
$$ax = 2 - y$$

   For what value of the constant a, if any, does the system shown above have infinitely many solutions?

   A. -6

   B. 0

   C. 6

   D. No such value

5. Which of these is equivalent to $(2x - 7)^2$?

   A. $4x^2 - 49$

   B. $4x^2 + 49$

   C. $4x^2 - 28x + 49$

   D. $4x^2 - 14x - 49$

6. A chiropractor charges a flat fee of \$45 plus \$15 per 10 minutes for the duration of a patient's visit. Which equation gives the cost, C, of a visit in terms of the number of hours, h?

   A. $C = 45 + 10h$

   B. $C = 45 + 60h$

   C. $C = 45 + 90h$

   D. $C = 90h$

7

SHOW YOUR WORK HERE

7.

$$\frac{R_1 - R_2}{\dfrac{1}{R_2} + \dfrac{1}{R_1}} = R_2$$

Which of the following is equivalent to the equation shown above?

A. $\dfrac{R_1 - R_2}{R_1 + R_2} = \dfrac{1}{R_1}$

B. $\dfrac{R_1}{R_2} - \dfrac{R_2}{R_1} = R_2$

C. $\dfrac{R_1^2 - R_2^2}{R_1} = R_2$

D. $\dfrac{(R_1 - R_2)(R_1 + R_2)}{2} = R_2$

8. What is the solution set of the equation $\sqrt{4x^2 + 1} = 3$?

A. $\{-2, 2\}$

B. $\left\{ -\sqrt{\dfrac{1}{2}}, \sqrt{\dfrac{1}{2}} \right\}$

C. $\{-\sqrt{5}, \sqrt{5}\}$

D. $\{-\sqrt{2}, \sqrt{2}\}$

9. The endpoints of a diameter of a circle are $(-2, -1)$ and $(0, -4)$. What is the circumference of this circle?

A. $\dfrac{\sqrt{13}}{2}\pi$

B. $\sqrt{13}\,\pi$

C. $\dfrac{13}{2}\pi$

D. 13π

10.

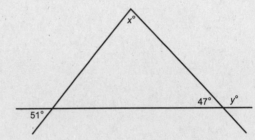

Based on the diagram above, determine the value of $x + y$.

A. 82

B. 133

C. 215

D. 266

SHOW YOUR WORK HERE

11. Find the equation of the line with x-intercept $(-4, 0)$ that is parallel to the line with equation $3x - 4y = 1$.

    A. $3x - 4y = -12$

    B. $3x - y = -12$

    C. $4x + 3y = -16$

    D. $3x - 4y = -3$

12.
$$4x + y = 0$$
$$y = 2(x - 1)^2 - 10$$

Find the solution set to the nonlinear system shown above.

    A. $\{ (-4, 16), (4, -16) \}$

    B. $\{ (-2, 8), (2, -8) \}$

    C. $\{ (-2, -8), (2, 8) \}$

    D. Empty set

13.
$$\frac{ay - 1}{a - y} = a$$

Solve the equation shown above for y, assuming a is a non-zero real number.

A. $y = \dfrac{2a + 1}{a + 1}$

B. $y = a^2 - 2a + 1$

C. $y = \dfrac{a^2 + 1}{2a}$

D. $y = \dfrac{a^2 + 1}{a + 1}$

14. Which of these is equivalent to $(3 - 2i)^2$? (Note: $i = \sqrt{-1}$)

    A. 29

    B. 8

    C. -13

    D. -22

15.
$$x(4x - 1) = -\frac{1}{16}$$

What is the solution set for the equation shown above?

    A. Empty set

    B. $\left\{ \dfrac{1}{8} \right\}$

    C. $\left\{ -\dfrac{1}{8}, \dfrac{1}{8} \right\}$

    D. $\left\{ -\dfrac{1}{16}, \dfrac{15}{64} \right\}$

SHOW YOUR WORK HERE

7

Exercise 2

12 Minutes—10 Questions

DIRECTIONS: For **Questions 1–10**, solve each problem, choose the best answer from the choices provided, and put a circle around the correct answer. You may use any available space for scratch work.

ADDITIONAL INFORMATION:

- The use of a calculator **is permitted**.
- All variables and expressions used represent real numbers unless otherwise indicated.
- Figures provided in this test are drawn to scale unless otherwise indicated.
- All figures lie in a plane unless otherwise indicated.
- Unless otherwise specified, the domain of a given function f is the set of all real numbers x for which $f(x)$ is a real number.

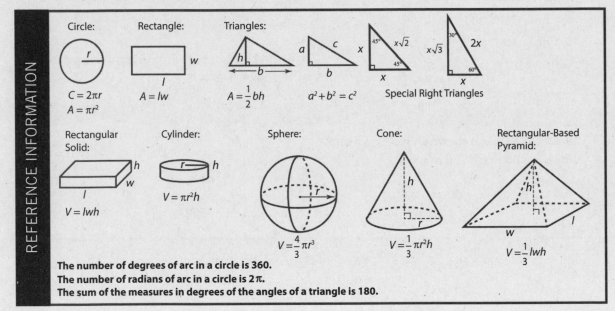

The number of degrees of arc in a circle is 360.
The number of radians of arc in a circle is 2π.
The sum of the measures in degrees of the angles of a triangle is 180.

1. Jack is training for a marathon. Currently, he runs a 5K in 29 minutes. His goal is to reduce this time by 15 seconds each week. Which of the following would be his completion time, in minutes, after w weeks?

   A. $29 - 15w$

   B. $29 \times 60 - 15w$

   C. $29 - \dfrac{1}{4}w$

   D. $29 + 15w$

2. If $\dfrac{x}{2y} = -\dfrac{1}{4}$, which of these is equal to $x - 2y$?

   A. $5x$

   B. $3x$

   C. $-\dfrac{5}{2}y$

   D. $-4y$

3. An agricultural company purchased a square plot of land for growing corn. The distance from one corner to the diagonally opposite corner is $1\dfrac{1}{4}$ miles. What is the perimeter of this plot of land?

   A. $\dfrac{25}{32}$ mile

   B. $\dfrac{5\sqrt{2}}{8}$ miles

   C. $3\dfrac{1}{8}$ miles

   D. $\dfrac{5\sqrt{2}}{2}$ miles

4. At noon, two canoes leave a dock, traveling in opposite directions. One canoe travels at 6 miles per hour, and the other at 4 miles per hour. Which equation can be used to determine the number of hours, x, it takes before the canoes are 36 miles apart?

   A. $\dfrac{x}{4} + \dfrac{x}{6} = 36$

   B. $10x = 36$

   C. $(4x)(6x) = 36$

   D. $2x = 36$

SHOW YOUR WORK HERE

5. Determine the value of a so that the points $(-a, 2)$ and $(3, 4a)$ lie on a line perpendicular to the line with the equation $x = \frac{1}{2}y - 1$.

A. $-\frac{2}{3}$

B. $\frac{1}{9}$

C. $\frac{1}{7}$

D. 4

6. Margaret is practicing her soccer goal shots. She made 23 of the last 36 shots. If she misses every shot thereafter, which of the following equations could be used to determine the number of shots, s, she missed in a row so that her "percentage of goals made" drops to 55%?

A. $\dfrac{23 - s}{36 + s} = 0.55$

B. $\dfrac{23 + s}{36 + s} = 0.55$

C. $\dfrac{23}{36 + s} = 0.55$

D. $\dfrac{23}{36} + s = 0.55$

7. The ratio of "Yes" to "No" votes at a town hall meeting regarding the installation of a new gas pipeline is 2 to 5. If there were 42 "Yes" votes, how many people, all told, voted?

A. 105

B. 126

C. 147

D. 252

8.

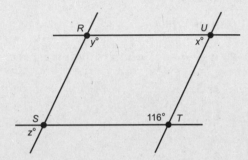

In the diagram above, assume *RSTU* is a rhombus. What is the value of $x + y + z$?

A. 64

B. 128

C. 244

D. 360

SHOW YOUR WORK HERE

9. If $-3 \le y \le 1$ and $-4 \le -x \le 2$, what is the smallest value $x - y$ can be?

   A. -7

   B. -5

   C. -3

   D. -1

10. A basketball player can spin a basketball on her finger at a rate of 100 revolutions per minute. What is the rate in revolutions per second?

   A. $\dfrac{1}{6,000}$ revolutions per second

   B. $\dfrac{3}{5}$ revolutions per second

   C. $\dfrac{5}{3}$ revolutions per second

   D. 6,000 revolutions per second

7

SHOW YOUR WORK HERE

ANSWER KEYS AND EXPLANATIONS

Exercise 1

1. C	4. D	7. A	10. C	13. C
2. B	5. C	8. D	11. A	14. A
3. D	6. C	9. B	12. B	15. B

1. **The correct answer is C.** The slope is
$m = \dfrac{0 - (-6)}{-3 - 0} = -2$. Using this in $y = mx + b$
with the y-intercept $b = -6$ yields the equation $y = -2x - 6$. This is $g(x)$. So
$$g\left(-\frac{1}{2}\right) = -2\left(-\frac{1}{2}\right) - 6 = 1 - = -5.$$

2. **The correct answer is B.** Solve the equation $2 - |4 - x| = 0$. This is the same as $|4 - x| = 2$, which breaks down into two equations, namely $4 - x = 2$ and $4 - x = -2$. Solving these for x yields the solutions $x = 2$ and $x = 6$.

3. **The correct answer is D.** Substitute the expression $x - 1$ in for x and simplify:
$$\begin{aligned} H(x-1) &= 3 - 2(x-1)^2 \\ &= 3 - 2\left(x^2 - 2x + 1\right) \\ &= 3 - 2x^2 + 4x - 2 \\ &= -2x^2 + 4x + 1 \end{aligned}$$

4. **The correct answer is D.** A system of two linear equations has infinitely many solutions when the equations are multiples of each other. If you multiply the first equation by -2, you get the equation $-6x + y = -8$, so that $-6x = -8 - y$. No matter what value of a is used, the second equation $ax = 2 - y$ can never be equivalent to this.

5. **The correct answer is C.** FOIL as follows:
$$\begin{aligned} (2x - 7)^2 &= (2x - 7)(2x - 7) \\ &= 4x^2 - 14x - 14x + 49 \\ &= 4x^2 - 28x + 49 \end{aligned}$$

6. **The correct answer is C.** There are 60 minutes in one hour. This equates to six 10-minute installments, each of which costs $15. So the hourly rate is $90. A visit of h hours costs the flat fee plus the hourly rate times h. That is, $C = 45 + 90h$.

7. **The correct answer is A.** Get a common denominator in the bottom of the left side and simplify, as follows:
$$\frac{R_1 - R_2}{\dfrac{1}{R_2} + \dfrac{1}{R_1}} = R_2$$

$$\frac{R_1 - R_2}{\dfrac{R_1 + R_2}{R_1 R_2}} = R_2$$

$$(R_1 - R_2) \cdot \frac{R_1 R_2}{R_1 + R_2} = R_2$$

$$\frac{R_1 - R_2}{R_1 + R_2} = \frac{\cancel{R_2}}{R_1 \cancel{R_2}}$$

$$\frac{R_1 - R_2}{R_1 + R_2} = \frac{1}{R_1}$$

8. **The correct answer is D.** Square both sides and then solve the resulting quadratic equation as follows:

$$\sqrt{4x^2 + 1} = 3$$
$$4x^2 + 1 = 9$$
$$4x^2 = 8$$
$$x^2 = 2$$
$$x = \pm\sqrt{2}$$

9. **The correct answer is B.** Calculate the distance between the endpoints. The length of the diameter, d, is:

$$d = \sqrt{(-2-0)^2 + (-1-(-4))^2}$$
$$= \sqrt{4+9}$$
$$= \sqrt{13}$$

The circumference of a circle is $\pi d = \sqrt{13}\pi$.

10. **The correct answer is C.** The interior angles of a triangle sum to 180. Since vertical angles are congruent, the three angles are x, 47, and 51.

$$x + 47 + 51 = 180$$
$$x = 180 - 98$$
$$x = 82$$

In addition, the angles with measures 47 and y are supplementary.

$$47 + y = 180$$
$$y = 133$$

Thus, the value of $x + y$ is $82 + 133 = 215$.

11. **The correct answer is A.** First, find the slope of the given line by putting it into slope-intercept form; solving for y yields $3x - 1 = 4y$ and so, $y = \frac{3}{4}x - \frac{1}{4}$. The slope is $\frac{3}{4}$. This is the slope of the desired line as well, since parallel lines have the same slope. Using point-slope formula for a line with the point $(-4, 0)$ yields:

$$y - 0 = \frac{3}{4}(x - (-4))$$
$$y = \frac{3}{4}x + 3$$
$$4y = 3x + 12$$
$$3x - 4y = -12$$

12. **The correct answer is B.** Solve the first equation for y so $y = -4x$. Substitute this into the second equation and solve for x:

$$-4x = 2(x - 1)^2 - 10$$
$$-4x = 2\left(x^2 - 2x + 1\right) - 10$$
$$-4x = 2x^2 - 4x + 2 - 10$$
$$-4x = 2x^2 - 4x - 8$$
$$2x^2 = 8$$
$$x^2 = 4$$
$$x = \pm 2$$

Now substitute these values back into the first equation to get the corresponding y-values. Doing so yields the solutions $(-2, 8)$ and $(2, -8)$.

13. **The correct answer is C.** Multiply both sides by the denominator of the fraction on the left; then gather the y-terms on one side:

$$\frac{ay - 1}{a - y} = a$$
$$ay - 1 = a(a - y)$$
$$ay - 1 = a^2 - ay$$
$$2ay = a^2 + 1$$
$$y = \frac{a^2 + 1}{2a}$$

14. **The correct answer is A.** FOIL and simplify:

$$(3 - 2i)^2 = (3 - 2i)(3 - 2i)$$
$$= 9 - 6i - 6i + 4i^2$$
$$= 9 - 12i - 4$$
$$= 5 - 12i$$

15. **The correct answer is B.** Gather all terms to the left side and factor the resulting quadratic expression:

$$x(4x - 1) = -\frac{1}{16}$$
$$4x^2 - x + \frac{1}{16} = 0$$
$$\left(2x - \frac{1}{4}\right)\left(2x - \frac{1}{4}\right) = 0$$
$$2x - \frac{1}{4} = 0$$
$$2x = \frac{1}{4}$$
$$x = \frac{1}{8}$$

7

Exercise 2

1. C	**3.** B	**5.** B	**7.** C	**9.** C
2. C	**4.** B	**6.** C	**8.** C	**10.** C

1. **The correct answer is C.** There are 60 seconds in one minute and 15 seconds equals $\frac{1}{4}$ minute. The number of minutes reduced after w weeks is $\frac{1}{4}w$. Subtracting this from 29 yields the number of minutes equal to Jack's completion time after w weeks.

2. **The correct answer is C.** Cross-multiply to obtain the equivalent equation $4x = -2y$. Hence, $x = -\frac{1}{2}y$. Therefore,

$$x - 2y = -\frac{1}{2}y - 2y = -\frac{5}{2}y.$$

3. **The correct answer is B.** Let x miles be the length of a side of the plot of land purchased. The following is a diagram of the plot of land:

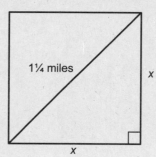

Use the Pythagorean theorem to find x:

$$x^2 + x^2 = \left(\frac{5}{4}\right)^2$$
$$2x^2 = \frac{25}{16}$$
$$x^2 = \frac{25}{32}$$
$$x = \sqrt{\frac{25}{32}}$$
$$x = \frac{5}{4\sqrt{2}} = \frac{5\sqrt{2}}{8}$$

The perimeter is $4\left(\frac{5\sqrt{2}}{8}\right) = \frac{5\sqrt{2}}{2}$ miles.

4. **The correct answer is B.** Since the canoes are traveling in the exact opposite direction, add the distances traveled after a given time to determine how far they are apart at that time. In one hour, the canoes are $6 + 4 = 10$ miles apart. The rate at which they are separating is 10 miles per hour. Let x be the number of hours it takes for the canoes to be 36 miles apart. Using distance equals rate times time yields the equation $10x = 36$.

5. **The correct answer is B.** First, find the slope of the given line by putting it into $y = mx + b$ form:

$$2x = y - 2$$
$$y = 2x + 2$$

The slope of the given line is 2. The slope of the desired line, being perpendicular to this one, is $-\frac{1}{2}$. Use the definition of slope to set up the following equation to determine the value of a:

$$\frac{4a - 2}{3 - (-a)} = -\frac{1}{2}$$
$$\frac{4a - 2}{3 + a} = -\frac{1}{2}$$
$$2(4a - 2) = -(3 + a)$$
$$8a - 4 = -3 - a$$
$$9a = 1$$
$$a = \frac{1}{9}$$

6. **The correct answer is C.** After missing s shots, the number of shots attempted is $36 + s$. Having missed all of these, Margaret has made 23 goals. The fraction made is $\frac{23}{36 + s}$. To find the value of s for which this is 55%, or 0.55, set up this equation:

$$\frac{23}{36 + s} = 0.55$$

7. **The correct answer is C.** Let x be the number of "No" votes. Set up the following proportion and solve for x:

$$\frac{2}{5} = \frac{42}{x}$$
$$2x = 42(5)$$
$$x = 105$$

The number of people who voted, all told, is the sum of "Yes" and "No" votes, namely $105 + 42 = 147$.

8. **The correct answer is C.** Since the sum of the measures of adjacent angles in a rhombus is 180, we see that $x = 64$ and $y = 116$. Since vertical angles are congruent, we have $z = 64$. Thus, $x + y + z = 64 + 116 + 64 = 244$.

9. **The correct answer is C.** Look at the values of $x - y$ for all pairs of choices of extreme values of x and y. Note that $-3 \le y \le 1$ and $-2 \le x \le 4$:

x	y	$x - y$
-2	-3	$-2 - (-3) = 1$
-2	1	$-2 - 1 = -3$
4	-3	$4 - (-3) = 7$
4	1	$4 - 1 = 3$

The smallest value of $x - y$ is -3.

10. **The correct answer is C.** Since one minute equals 60 seconds, we convert the units as follows:

$$\frac{100 \text{ revolutions}}{1 \text{ minute}} \times \frac{1 \text{ minute}}{60 \text{ seconds}} = \frac{5 \text{ revolutions}}{3 \text{ per second}}$$

In one hour, the train will cover 6(14), or 84, miles.

7

Chapter 8

Grid-In Strategies

OVERVIEW

- Why Grid-Ins Are Easier Than You Think
- How to Record Your Answers
- Guessing on Grid-Ins Can't Hurt You
- Summing It Up
- Practice Exercises
- Answer Keys and Explanations

WHY GRID-INS ARE EASIER THAN YOU THINK

Let's take a quick break from multiple-choice questions and examine the other kind of question you will see on both the Math Test—No Calculator and Math Test—Calculator sections: grid-ins. These are officially named "student-produced responses," because you have to do the calculations and find the answer on your own; there are no multiple-choice answers from which to choose.

Many students are intimidated by grid-ins. Don't be! Grid-in questions test the exact same mathematical concepts as the multiple-choice questions. The only difference is that there are no answer choices with which to work.

The grid-in questions are in a section of their own and arranged in order of difficulty from easy to hard.

Take a Look at a Grid

The special answer grid has some very different sections. There are blank boxes at the top so you can actually write in your answer. Below the boxes are some circles that have fraction slashes and decimal points. You fill these in if your answer needs them. The largest section has circles with numbers in them. You have to fill in the circles to correspond to the answer you have written in the boxes. Yes, it's a lot to think about, but once you understand how to use the grid-ins, it's not a big deal.

Here is a sample grid:

HOW TO RECORD YOUR ANSWERS

On the SAT exam, each set of grid-in questions starts with directions that look approximately like this:

> **DIRECTIONS:** For these questions, solve the problem and enter your answer in the grid, as described below, on the answer sheet.

1. Although not required, it is suggested that you write your answer in the boxes at the top of the columns to help you fill in the circles accurately. You will receive credit only if the circles are filled in correctly.

2. Mark no more than one circle in any column.

3. No question has a negative answer.

4. Some problems may have more than one correct answer. In such cases, enter only one answer.

5. Mixed numbers such as $3\frac{1}{2}$ must be entered as 3.5 or $\frac{7}{2}$.

   If $3\frac{1}{2}$ is entered into the grid as , it will be interpreted as $\frac{31}{2}$, not $3\frac{1}{2}$.

NOTE

Remember that the student-produced responses will not be negative numbers and won't be greater than 9999.

6. **Decimal answers**: If you obtain a decimal answer with more digits than the grid can accommodate, it may be either rounded or truncated, but it must fill the entire grid.

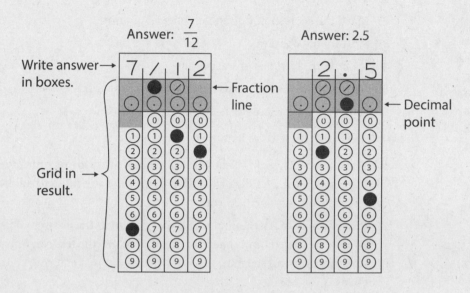

Answer: $\frac{7}{12}$

Write answer → in boxes.

← Fraction line

Grid in → result.

Answer: 2.5

← Decimal point

Answer: 201
Either position is correct.

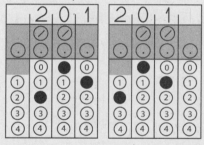

Acceptable ways to grid $\frac{2}{3}$ are:

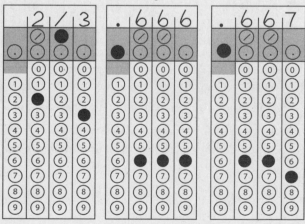

NOTE

Don't use a comma in a number larger than 999. Just fill in the four digits and the corresponding circles. You only have circles for numbers, decimal points, and fraction slashes; there aren't any for commas.

Once you understand the following six rules, you can concentrate just on solving the math problems in this section.

1. Write your answer in the boxes at the top of the grid.
2. Mark the corresponding circles, one per column.
3. Start in any column.
4. Work with decimals or fractions.
5. Express mixed numbers as decimals or improper fractions.
6. If more than one answer is possible, enter any one.

Now let's look at these rules in more detail:

1. Write your answer in the boxes at the top of the grid. Technically, this isn't required by the SAT. Realistically, it gives you something to follow as you fill in the circles. Do it—it will help you.

2. Make sure to mark the circles that correspond to the answer you entered in the boxes, one per column. The machine that scores the test can only read the circles, so if you don't fill them in, you won't get credit. Just entering your answer in the boxes is not enough!

3. You can start entering your answer in any column, if space permits. Unused columns should be left blank; don't put in zeroes. Look at this example:

Here are two ways to enter an answer of "150."

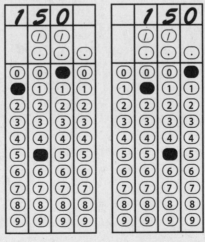

TIP

Take the time to write your answer in the spaces at the top of the grid. It will lessen your chances of filling in an incorrect circle.

4. You can write your answer as a decimal or a fraction. For example, an answer can be expressed as $\frac{3}{4}$ or as .75. You don't have to put a zero in front of a decimal that is less than 1. Just remember that you have only four spaces to work with and that a decimal point or a fraction slash uses up one of the spaces.

For decimal answers, be as accurate as possible but keep it within four spaces. Say you get an answer of .1777, here are your options:

Answers .177 and .178 would both be marked correct.

Fractions do not have to be simplified unless they don't fit in the answer grid. For example, you can enter into the grid $\frac{4}{10}$, but you can't enter $\frac{12}{16}$ because you'd need five spaces. You would simplify it and enter $\frac{3}{4}$.

5. A mixed number has to be expressed as a decimal or as an improper fraction. If you tried to enter $1\frac{3}{4}$ into the grid, it would be scored as $\frac{13}{4}$, which would give you a wrong answer. Instead, you could enter the answer as 1.75 or as $\frac{7}{4}$.

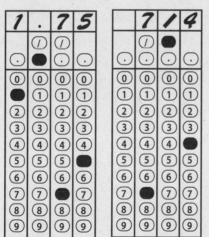

The above answers are acceptable.

The above answer is unacceptable as representing the fraction $1\frac{3}{4}$.

ALERT

If the correct answer is a mixed number such as $5\frac{1}{4}$, you must enter it as 21/4 or as 5.25 in the answer grid. If you enter it as "51/4," it will read as "fifty-one fourths," and it will be marked incorrect.

6. Sometimes, the problems in this section will have more than one correct answer. Choose one and enter it.

For example, if a question asks for a prime number between 5 and 13, the answer could be 7 or 11. Enter 7 or enter 11, but don't put in both answers.

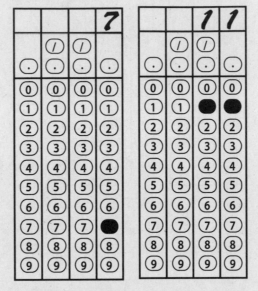

Either answer is acceptable but not both.

GUESSING ON GRID-INS CAN'T HURT YOU

Unfortunately, you cannot receive partial credit for grid-ins. Your answers are either completely correct or completely wrong. But no points are deducted for incorrect responses, so guessing is better than leaving a question blank.

Summing It Up

- When you use a grid to answer the student-produced response questions, follow these six rules:

  1. Write your answer in the boxes at the top of the grid.

  2. Mark the corresponding circles, one per column.

  3. Start in any column.

  4. Work with decimals or fractions.

  5. Express mixed numbers as decimals or improper fractions.

  6. If more than one answer is possible, enter any one.

- Remember that grid-ins test the same concepts as multiple-choice math.

- The most important advice for grid-ins? Don't be intimidated.

Take a moment to ask yourself some simple questions about your understanding of the chapter:

Review: What did I learn?

Evaluate: What do I need to learn more about?

Plan: What can I do next to keep improving?

Based on your answers to those questions, adjust your study plan to dedicate additional time to the areas of weakness that you've identified.

8

PRACTICE EXERCISES: GRID-INS

Exercise 1

15 Minutes—10 Questions

> **DIRECTIONS:** For these questions, solve the problem and enter your answer in the grid following each question, as described below.

1. Although not required, it is suggested that you write your answer in the boxes at the top of the columns to help you fill in the circles accurately. You will receive credit only if the circles are filled in correctly.

2. Mark no more than one circle in any column.

3. No question has a negative answer.

4. Some problems may have more than one correct answer. In such cases, enter only one answer.

5. Mixed numbers such as $3\frac{1}{2}$ must be entered as 3.5 or $\frac{7}{2}$.

   If $3\frac{1}{2}$ is entered into the grid as $\overline{3 \mid \mid / 2}$, it will be interpreted as $\frac{31}{2}$, not $3\frac{1}{2}$.

6. **Decimal answers:** If you obtain a decimal answer with more digits than the grid can accommodate, it may be either rounded or truncated, but it must fill the entire grid.

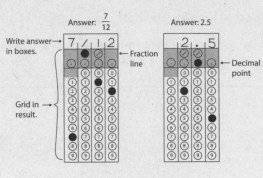

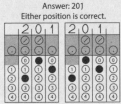

Answer: 20]
Either position is correct.

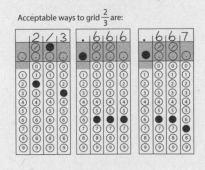

Acceptable ways to grid $\frac{2}{3}$ are:

1. What is the slope of the line parallel to the line passing through the points $(0, -4)$ and $(-2, -8)$?

2. Marion is paid \$24 for 5 hours of work in the school office. Janet works 3 hours and makes \$10.95. How much more per hour does Marion make than Janet? (Ignore the dollar sign when gridding your answer.)

SHOW YOUR WORK HERE

3. The surface area of a cubical cage is 1,176 square feet. What is the length of a diagonal of one of its faces, accurate to the tenths place?

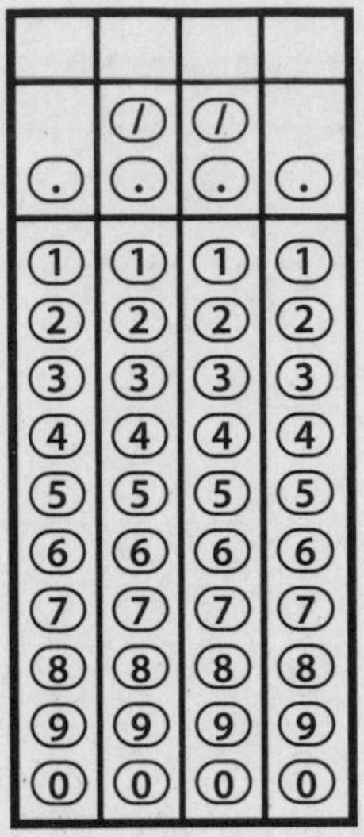

4. A car has an average mileage of 30 miles per gallon. If one gallon of gasoline costs $3.75, how many miles can the car travel on $20 worth of gasoline?

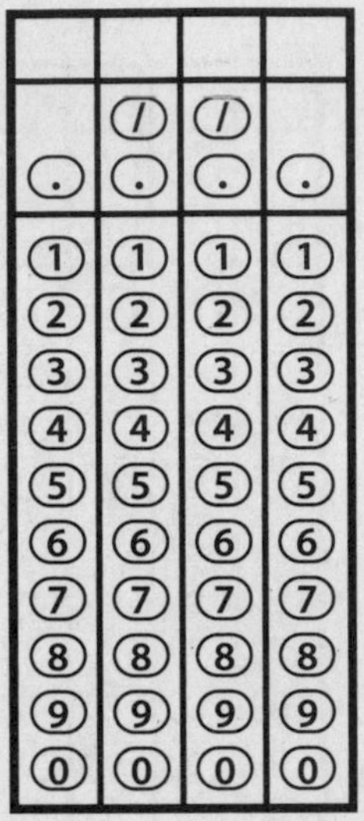

8

SHOW YOUR WORK HERE

5. If $a = \dfrac{3}{4}$, what is the value of $2a^2 - 1$?

6. Arc AB is on circle O. If the radius of circle O is 5 centimeters, and angle AOB measures 30°, what is the length of arc AB rounded to the nearest tenth of a centimeter?

SHOW YOUR WORK HERE

7. If z is a solution of the equation $\sqrt{z} - 1 = 4$, what is the value of $2z^{-1}$?

8. A cube with edges 3 centimeters long is made from solid aluminum. If the density of aluminum is approximately 2.7 grams per cubic centimeter, what is the weight of the cube to the nearest tenth of a gram?

SHOW YOUR WORK HERE

9. In May, Carter's Electronics sold 40 smart-phones. In June, because of a special promo-tion, the store sold 80 smartphones. What is the percent of increase in the number of smartphones sold?

10.

$$\sqrt{21}\left(\frac{\sqrt{7}}{\sqrt{3}} - \frac{\sqrt{3}}{\sqrt{7}}\right)$$

To what integer is the above expression equal?

SHOW YOUR WORK HERE

Exercise 2

15 Minutes—10 Questions

> **DIRECTIONS:** For these questions, solve the problem and enter your answer in the grid following each question, as described below.

1. Although not required, it is suggested that you write your answer in the boxes at the top of the columns to help you fill in the circles accurately. You will receive credit only if the circles are filled in correctly.

2. Mark no more than one circle in any column.

3. No question has a negative answer.

4. Some problems may have more than one correct answer. In such cases, enter only one answer.

5. Mixed numbers such as $3\frac{1}{2}$ must be entered as 3.5 or $\frac{7}{2}$.

   If $3\frac{1}{2}$ is entered into the grid as $\overline{3\ |\ 1\ /\ 2}$, it will be interpreted as $\frac{31}{2}$, not $3\frac{1}{2}$.

6. **Decimal answers:** If you obtain a decimal answer with more digits than the grid can accommodate, it may be either rounded or truncated, but it must fill the entire grid.

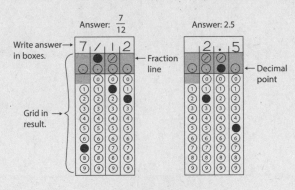

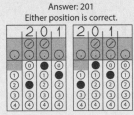

Answer: 201
Either position is correct.

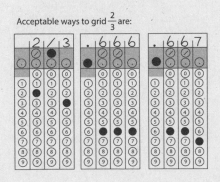

Acceptable ways to grid $\frac{2}{3}$ are:

1. A craft shop sells handmade quilts and pillows in a ratio of 2 to 6 for one week. If 8 quilts are sold at the end of this week, how many pillows and quilts were sold all together?

2.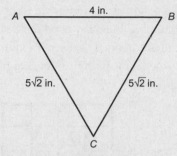

What is the height of the triangle shown? Round to the nearest hundredth.

SHOW YOUR WORK HERE

3. In a group of 40 students, 25 applied to Columbia and 30 applied to Cornell. If 3 students applied to neither Columbia nor Cornell, how many students applied to both schools?

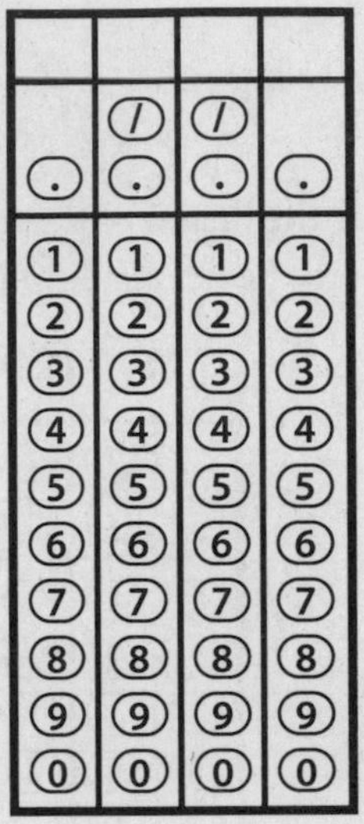

4. If $\dfrac{1}{6x^2 - 7x + 2} = \dfrac{2}{3}$ and $2 - 3x = \dfrac{1}{2}$, what is the value of $2 - 2x$?

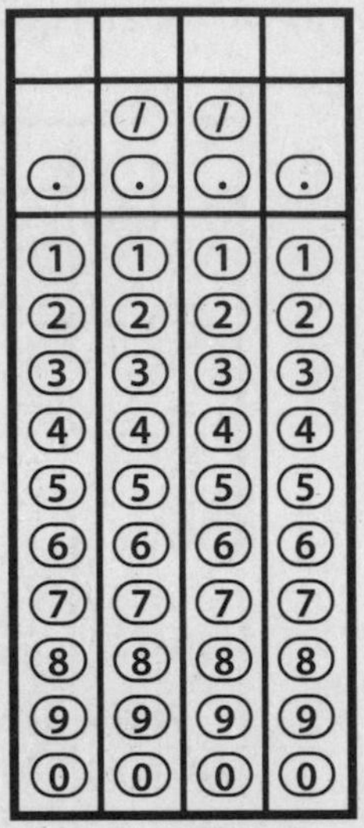

8

SHOW YOUR WORK HERE

5. A gallon of water is added to 6 quarts of a solution that is 50% acid. What percent of the new solution is acid?

6. A gasoline tank is $\frac{1}{4}$ full. After 10 gallons of gasoline are added to the tank, its gauge indicates that the tank is $\frac{2}{3}$ full. Find the capacity of the tank in gallons.

8

SHOW YOUR WORK HERE

7. A plane flies over Denver at 11:20 a.m. It passes over Coolidge, 120 miles from Denver, at 11:32 a.m. Find the rate of the plane in miles per hour.

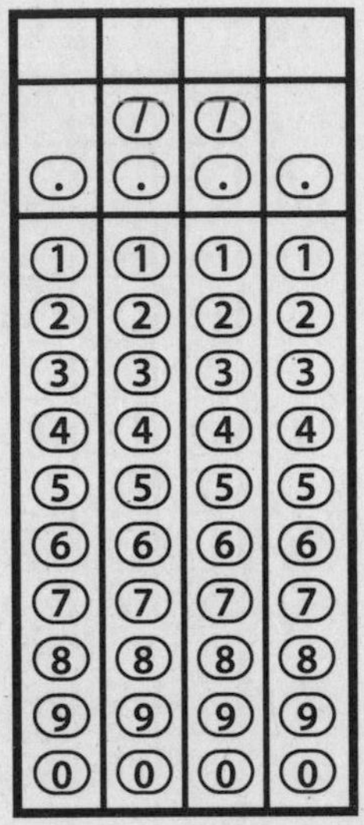

8. Solve for w: $\dfrac{4}{4-3w}=\dfrac{2}{w}$.

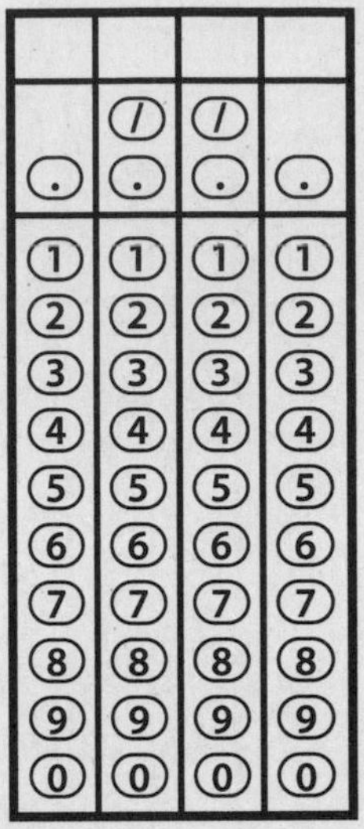

SHOW YOUR WORK HERE

Part VI

9. Find the mean of this set of numbers:

0, 0, 5, 6, 6, 10, 14, 23.

10.

$$y = x^2 - 8x + 7$$
$$y = x - 1$$

If (x, y) is a solution to the system of equations above, what is a possible value of $x + y$?

8

ANSWER KEYS AND EXPLANATIONS

Exercise 1

1. 2	3. 19.8	5. $\frac{1}{8}$	7. $\frac{2}{25}$	9. 100
2. 1.15	4. 160	6. 2.6	8. 72.9	10. 4

1. **The correct answer is 2.** The slope of the given line is $\dfrac{-8-(-4)}{-2-0} = 2$. Since parallel lines have the same slope, the slope is 2.

2. **The correct answer is 1.15.** Marion's hourly wage is $\dfrac{\$24}{5}$, or \$4.80. Janet's hourly wage is $\dfrac{\$10.95}{3}$, or \$3.65. \$4.80 − \$3.65 = \$1.15 (You do not need to enter the dollar sign in the grid.)

3. **The correct answer is 19.8.** Let e be an edge of a face of this cube. The surface area is $6e^2$. Solve the following equation for e:

$$6e^2 = 1{,}176$$
$$e^2 = 196$$
$$e = 14$$

Let d be a diagonal of an edge. Use the Pythagorean theorem to find d:

$$14^2 + 14^2 = d^2$$
$$2 \cdot 14^2 = d^2$$
$$14\sqrt{2} = d$$
$$d \approx 19.8$$

4. **The correct answer is 160.**

$$30\left(\frac{20}{3.75}\right) = 160$$

5. **The correct answer is $\frac{1}{8}$.**

$$2\left(\frac{3}{4}\right)^2 - 1 = 2\left(\frac{9}{16}\right) - 1 = \frac{9}{8} - 1 = \frac{1}{8}$$

6. **The correct answer is 2.6.** The circumference of the circle is $2(5) = 10$.

$$\frac{30}{360}\left(10\pi\right) \approx 2.6$$

7. **The correct answer is $\frac{2}{25}$.** First, solve for z:

$$\sqrt{z} = 5$$
$$z = 25$$

Then solve the equation.

$$2z^{-1} = \frac{2}{z} = \frac{2}{25}$$

8. **The correct answer is 72.9.** The formula for volume of a cube is s^3. Therefore:

$$3^3 = 27$$
$$27(2.7) = 72.9$$

9. **The correct answer is 100.** When computing the percent of increase (or decrease), use $\dfrac{\text{difference}}{\text{original}} \times 100$. In this case, the difference is $80 - 40$, which is 40. The original amount sold was 40, so $\dfrac{40}{40} \times 100 = 100\%$ increase.

10. **The correct answer is 4.**

$$\sqrt{21}\left(\frac{\sqrt{7}}{\sqrt{3}} - \frac{\sqrt{3}}{\sqrt{7}}\right) = \sqrt{21}\left(\frac{\sqrt{7} \cdot \sqrt{7} - \sqrt{3} \cdot \sqrt{3}}{\sqrt{3} \cdot \sqrt{7}}\right)$$
$$= \sqrt{21}\left(\frac{7-3}{\sqrt{21}}\right)$$
$$= 4$$

Exercise 2

1. 32	3. 18	5. 30	7. 600	9. 8
2. 6.78	4. 3	6. 24	8. $\frac{4}{5}$	10. 15 or 1

1. **The correct answer is 32.** Let x be the number of pillows sold. Set up and solve the following proportion:

$$\frac{2}{6} = \frac{8}{x}$$
$$2x = 48$$
$$x = 24$$

The number of quilts and pillows sold is $24 + 8 = 32$.

2. **The correct answer is 6.78.** Draw a perpendicular bisector from C to the opposite base, as shown:

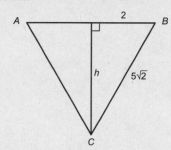

Using the Pythagorean theorem yields:

$$2^2 + h^2 = \left(5\sqrt{2}\right)^2$$
$$4 + h^2 = 50$$
$$h^2 = 46$$
$$h = \sqrt{46} \approx 6.78$$

3. **The correct answer is 18.**

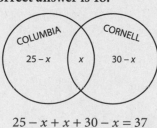

$$25 - x + x + 30 - x = 37$$
$$55 - x = 37$$
$$18 = x$$

4. **The correct answer is 3.** Solve as follows:

$$\frac{1}{6x^2 - 7x + 2} = \frac{2}{3}$$
$$\frac{1}{(2x - 1)(3x - 2)} = \frac{2}{3}$$
$$\frac{1}{(2x - 1)\left(-\frac{1}{2}\right)} = \frac{2}{3}$$
$$\frac{-2}{(2x - 1)} = \frac{2}{3}$$
$$-6 = 2(2x - 1)$$
$$-3 = 2x - 2$$
$$3 = 2 - 2x$$

5. **The correct answer is 30.**

	No. of quarts	% acid	Amount of acid
Original	6	50	3
Added	4	0	0
New	10		3

$$\frac{3}{10} = 30\%$$

Note: Ignore the percent symbol when entering your answer in the grid.

6. **The correct answer is 24.** 10 gallons is $\frac{2}{3} - \frac{1}{4}$ of the tank.

$$\frac{2}{3} - \frac{1}{4} = \frac{8 - 3}{12} = \frac{5}{12}$$
$$\frac{5}{12}x = 10$$
$$5x = 120$$
$$x = 24$$

7. **The correct answer is 600.** The plane covers 120 miles in 12 minutes, or $\frac{1}{5}$ hour. In $\frac{5}{5}$, or 1 hour, it covers 5(120), or 600 miles.

8. **The correct answer is $\frac{4}{5}$.** Cross-multiply and solve for w:

$$\frac{4}{4-3w} = \frac{2}{w}$$
$$4w = 2(4-3w)$$
$$4w = 8 - 6w$$
$$10w = 8$$
$$w = \frac{8}{10} = \frac{4}{5}$$

9. **The correct answer is 8.** Add the numbers and divide this sum by the number of values, namely 8:

$$\frac{0+0+5+6+6+10+14+23}{8} = \frac{64}{8} = 8$$

10. **The correct answer is 15 or 1 (both answers are acceptable).**

$$y = x^2 - 8x + 7$$
$$y = x - 1$$
$$x^2 - 8x + 7 = x - 1$$
$$x^2 - 9x + 8 = 0$$
$$(x-8)(x-1) = 0$$
$$x = 8 \text{ or } x = 1$$

If $x = 8$, then $y = 8 - 1 = 7$

If $x = 1$, then $y = 1 - 1 = 0$

$x + y = 15$ or $x + y = 1$

Numbers and Operations

OVERVIEW

9

OPERATIONS WITH FRACTIONS

The four basic **arithmetic** operations are addition, subtraction, multiplication, and division.

Adding and Subtracting

When adding or subtracting fractions, you must remember that the numbers must have the same (common) denominator.

> **Example:**
>
> Add $\frac{1}{3} + \frac{2}{5} + \frac{3}{4}$.
>
> **Solution:**
>
> The lowest number that is divisible by 3, 5, and 4 is 60. Therefore, use 60 as the common denominator. Convert each fraction to fractions with the common denominator, 60, by multiplying each

numerator by the same factor as you must multiply the denominator by to result in the common denominator of 60.

$$\frac{20}{60} + \frac{24}{60} + \frac{45}{60} = \frac{89}{60}$$
$$= 1\frac{29}{60}$$

Fractions should be written in the simplest form. Often, in multiple-choice questions, you may find that the answer you have correctly computed is not among the choices but an equivalent fraction is. Be careful!

In simplifying fractions involving large numbers, it is helpful to be able to tell whether a factor is common to both numerator and denominator before a lengthy trial division. Certain tests for divisibility help with this.

Test For Divisibility

To test if a number is divisible by:	Check to see:
2	if it is even
3	if the sum of the digits is divisible by 3
4	if the number formed by the last two digits is divisible by 4
5	if its last digit is a 5 or 0
6	if it is even and the sum of the digits is divisible by 3
8	if the number formed by the last three digits is divisible by 8
9	if the sum of the digits is divisible by 9
10	if its last digit is 0

Example:

Simplify: $\frac{3,525}{4,341}$

Solution:

This fraction can be simplified by dividing by 3, since the sum of the digits of the numerator is 15 and those of the denominator add up to 12, both are divisible by 3.

$$\frac{3,525}{4,341} = \frac{1,175}{1,447}$$

The resulting fraction meets no further divisibility tests and therefore has no common factor listed above. Larger divisors would be unlikely on the SAT exam.

FUN FACTS

The number 2 is the only prime number that does not have an *e* in its name. It's also the only prime number that is even.

9

To add or subtract mixed numbers, it is again important to remember common denominators. In subtraction, you must borrow in terms of the common denominator.

Addition:	Subtraction:
$43\dfrac{2}{5} = 43\dfrac{6}{15}$	$43\dfrac{2}{5} = 43\dfrac{6}{15} = 42\dfrac{21}{15}$
$+\,8\dfrac{1}{3} = +\,8\dfrac{5}{15}$	$-6\dfrac{2}{3} = -6\dfrac{10}{15} = -6\dfrac{10}{15}$
$51\dfrac{11}{15}$	$36\dfrac{11}{15}$

Multiplying

To multiply fractions, always try to divide common factors where possible before actually multiplying. In multiplying mixed numbers, always rename them as improper fractions first.

Multiply:	Multiply:
$\dfrac{\cancel{2}}{\cancel{5}} \cdot \dfrac{\cancel{10}^{\,2}}{\cancel{11}} \cdot \dfrac{\cancel{99}^{\,9}}{\cancel{110}_{\,55}} = \dfrac{18}{55}$	$4\dfrac{1}{2} \cdot 1\dfrac{2}{3} \cdot 5\dfrac{1}{5}$ $\dfrac{\cancel{9}^{\,3}}{\cancel{2}} \cdot \dfrac{\cancel{5}}{\cancel{3}} \cdot \dfrac{\cancel{26}^{\,13}}{\cancel{5}} = 39$

Dividing

To divide fractions or mixed numbers, remember to multiply by the reciprocal of the divisor (the number after the division sign).

Divide:	Divide:
$4\dfrac{1}{2} \div \dfrac{3}{4} = \dfrac{\cancel{9}^{\,3}}{\cancel{2}} \cdot \dfrac{\cancel{4}^{\,2}}{\cancel{3}} = 6$	$62\dfrac{1}{2} \div 5 = \dfrac{\cancel{125}^{\,25}}{2} \cdot \dfrac{1}{\cancel{5}} = 12\dfrac{1}{2}$

To simplify complex fractions (fractions within fractions), multiply every term by the least common multiple of all denominators in order to clear all fractions in the given numerator and denominator.

Example 1:

$$\frac{\frac{1}{2}+\frac{1}{3}}{\frac{1}{4}+\frac{1}{6}}$$

Solution:

The least number that can be used to clear all fractions is 12. Multiplying each term by 12 yields:

$$\frac{\frac{1}{2}+\frac{1}{3}}{\frac{1}{4}+\frac{1}{6}}=\frac{\frac{12}{2}+\frac{12}{3}}{\frac{12}{4}+\frac{12}{6}}=\frac{6+4}{3+2}=\frac{10}{5}=2$$

Example 2:

$$\frac{\frac{3}{4}+\frac{2}{3}}{1-\frac{1}{2}}$$

Solution:

Again, multiply by 12.

$$\frac{\frac{3}{4}+\frac{2}{3}}{1-\frac{1}{2}}=\frac{\frac{36}{4}+\frac{24}{3}}{12-\frac{12}{2}}=\frac{9+8}{12-6}=\frac{17}{6}=2\frac{5}{6}$$

PRACTICE EXERCISE: OPERATIONS WITH FRACTIONS

DIRECTIONS: Work out each problem in the space provided, then review the answer explanations that directly follow this practice exercise.

1. **Add:** $7\frac{1}{6} + 3\frac{11}{12}$

4. **Subtract:** $1\frac{7}{11}$ from $2\frac{1}{22}$.

2. **Add:** $\frac{1}{2} + \frac{1}{4} + \frac{1}{8} + \frac{1}{16}$

5. **Multiply:** $\frac{15}{8} \cdot \frac{12}{25} \cdot \frac{2}{9}$

3. **Subtract:** $5\frac{3}{4}$ from $10\frac{1}{2}$.

6. **Multiply:** $\frac{3}{4} \cdot \frac{3}{4} \cdot \frac{3}{4}$

SHOW YOUR WORK HERE

9

7. Divide: $\dfrac{1}{5} \div 5$

8. Simplify: $4\left(\dfrac{1}{6} + \dfrac{1}{12}\right)$

8. Divide: $3\dfrac{2}{3} \div 1\dfrac{5}{6}$

11. Simplify: $\left(\dfrac{1}{2} - \dfrac{1}{3}\right)\left(\dfrac{1}{2} + \dfrac{1}{3}\right)$

9. Simplify: $\dfrac{\frac{5}{6} - \frac{1}{3}}{2 + \frac{1}{5}}$

12. Simplify: $\dfrac{4}{15} \div \left(\dfrac{1}{5} + \dfrac{1}{3}\right)$

9

SHOW YOUR WORK HERE

Answer Key and Explanations

1. $11\dfrac{1}{12}$	3. $4\dfrac{3}{4}$	5. $\dfrac{1}{5}$	7. $\dfrac{1}{25}$	9. $\dfrac{5}{22}$	11. $\dfrac{5}{36}$
2. $\dfrac{15}{16}$	4. $\dfrac{9}{22}$	6. $\dfrac{27}{64}$	8. 2	10. 1	12. $\dfrac{1}{2}$

1. The correct answer is $11\dfrac{1}{12}$.

$$7\frac{1}{6} + 3\frac{11}{12} = 7\frac{2}{12} + 3\frac{11}{12}$$
$$= 10\frac{13}{12}$$
$$= 11\frac{1}{12}$$

2. The correct answer is $\dfrac{15}{16}$.

$$\frac{1}{2} + \frac{1}{4} + \frac{1}{8} + \frac{1}{16} = \frac{8}{16} + \frac{4}{16} + \frac{2}{16} + \frac{1}{16}$$
$$= \frac{8+4+2+1}{16}$$
$$= \frac{15}{16}$$

3. The correct answer is $4\dfrac{3}{4}$.

$$10\frac{1}{2} = 9\frac{3}{2} = 9\frac{6}{4}$$

$$\begin{array}{r} 9\frac{6}{4} \\ -5\frac{3}{4} \\ \hline 4\frac{3}{4} \end{array}$$

4. The correct answer is $\dfrac{9}{22}$.

$$2\frac{1}{22} - 1\frac{7}{11} = 2\frac{1}{22} - 1\frac{14}{22}$$
$$= 1\frac{23}{22} - 1\frac{14}{22}$$
$$= \frac{9}{22}$$

5. The correct answer is $\dfrac{1}{5}$.

$$\frac{15}{8} \cdot \frac{12}{25} \cdot \frac{2}{9} = \frac{\cancel{5}3}{\cancel{4}2} \cdot \frac{\cancel{4}3}{5 \cdot \cancel{5}} \cdot \frac{\cancel{2}}{3\cancel{3}} = \frac{1}{5}$$

6. The correct answer is $\dfrac{27}{64}$.

$$\frac{3}{4} \cdot \frac{3}{4} \cdot \frac{3}{4} = \frac{27}{64}$$

7. The correct answer is $\dfrac{1}{25}$.

$$\frac{1}{5} \cdot \frac{1}{5} = \frac{1}{25}$$

8. The correct answer is 2.

$$\frac{\cancel{11}}{\cancel{3}} \cdot \frac{\cancel{6}^{2}}{\cancel{11}} = 2$$

9. The correct answer is $\dfrac{5}{22}$.

$$\frac{25-10}{60+6} = \frac{15}{66} = \frac{5}{22}$$

Each term was multiplied by 30.

10. The correct answer is 1.

$$4\left(\frac{1}{6} + \frac{1}{12}\right) = 4\left(\frac{2}{12} + \frac{1}{12}\right)$$
$$= 4\left(\frac{3}{12}\right)$$
$$= \left(\frac{12}{12}\right)$$
$$= 1$$

11. The correct answer is $\dfrac{5}{36}$.

$$\left(\frac{1}{2} - \frac{1}{3}\right)\left(\frac{1}{2} + \frac{1}{3}\right) = \left(\frac{3}{6} - \frac{2}{6}\right)\left(\frac{3}{6} + \frac{2}{6}\right)$$

$$= \frac{1}{6} \cdot \frac{5}{6}$$

$$= \frac{5}{36}$$

12. The correct answer is $\dfrac{1}{2}$.

$$\frac{4}{15} \div \left(\frac{1}{5} + \frac{1}{3}\right) = \frac{4}{15} \div \left(\frac{3}{15} + \frac{5}{15}\right)$$

$$= \frac{4}{15} \div \frac{8}{15}$$

$$= \frac{4}{\cancel{15}} \cdot \frac{\cancel{15}}{8}$$

$$= \frac{4}{8}$$

$$= \frac{1}{2}$$

9

BRAIN BREAK

Let's play a 5-4-3-2-1 game. Name 5 things that you can see, 4 things that you can touch, 3 things that you can hear, 2 things that you can smell, and one thing that you can taste

WORD PROBLEMS INVOLVING FRACTIONS

Fraction problems deal with parts of a whole.

Example 1:

If a class consists of 12 boys and 18 girls, what part of the class is boys?

Solution:

The class consists of 12 boys out of 30 total students, or $\frac{12}{30} = \frac{2}{5}$. So boys represent $\frac{2}{5}$ of the class.

Notice that, to find the solution, you must add the boys and girls to find the total number of students. Problems may require more than one calculation as you can see in this example.

Example 2:

One-quarter of this year's seniors have averages above 90. One-half of the remainder have averages between 80 and 90 inclusive. What part of the senior class have averages below 80?

Solution:

We know that $\frac{1}{4}$ have averages above 90.

$\frac{1}{2}$ of $\frac{3}{4}$, or $\frac{3}{8}$, have averages between 80 and 90 inclusive.

$\frac{1}{4} + \frac{3}{8} = \frac{2}{8} + \frac{3}{8} = \frac{5}{8}$ have averages 80 and above.

Therefore, $\frac{3}{8}$ of the class have averages below 80.

Example 3:

14 is $\frac{2}{3}$ of what number?

Solution:

$$14 = \frac{2}{3}x$$

Divide each side of the equation by $\frac{2}{3}$, which is the same as multiplying the reciprocal, or $\frac{3}{2}$.

$$21 = x$$

Example 4:

If John has p hours of homework and has worked for r hours, what part of his homework is yet to be done?

Solution:

If John had 5 hours of homework and had worked for 3 hours, you would first find he had 5 minus 3 hours, or 2 hours, yet to do. This represents $\frac{2}{5}$ of his work. Using letters, his remaining work is represented by $\frac{p-r}{p}$.

9

TIP

If a problem is given with letters in place of numbers, the same reasoning must be applied as for numbers. If you are not sure how to proceed, replace the letters with numbers to determine the steps that must be taken.

PRACTICE EXERCISE: WORD PROBLEMS INVOLVING FRACTIONS

DIRECTIONS: Work out each problem. Circle the letter of your choice, then check your answers against the answer key and explanations that follow.

1. A team played 30 games, of which it won 24. What part of the games played did the team lose?

   A. $\frac{4}{5}$

   B. $\frac{1}{4}$

   C. $\frac{1}{5}$

   D. $\frac{3}{4}$

2. If Germaine earns $X a week, and he saves $Y, what part of his weekly salary does he spend?

   A. $\frac{X}{Y}$

   B. $\frac{X-Y}{X}$

   C. $\frac{X-Y}{Y}$

   D. $\frac{Y-X}{X}$

SHOW YOUR WORK HERE

3. What part of an hour elapses between 11:50 a.m. and 12:14 p.m.?

   A. $\frac{2}{5}$

   B. $\frac{7}{30}$

   C. $\frac{17}{30}$

   D. $\frac{1}{6}$

4. One half of the employees of Acme Co. earn salaries above $18,000 annually. One third of the remainder earn salaries between $15,000 and $18,000. What part of the staff earns below $15,000?

   A. $\frac{1}{6}$

   B. $\frac{2}{3}$

   C. $\frac{1}{2}$

   D. $\frac{1}{3}$

5. David received his allowance on Sunday. He spends $\frac{1}{4}$ of his allowance on Monday and $\frac{2}{3}$ of the remainder on Tuesday. What part of his allowance is left for the rest of the week?

   A. $\frac{1}{13}$

   B. $\frac{1}{9}$

   C. $\frac{1}{4}$

   D. $\frac{1}{3}$

6. A piece of fabric is cut into three sections so that the first is three times as long as the second, and the second section is three times as long as the third. What part of the entire piece is the smallest section?

   A. $\frac{1}{13}$

   B. $\frac{1}{9}$

   C. $\frac{1}{4}$

   D. $\frac{1}{3}$

7. A factory employs M men and W women. What part of its employees are women?

   A. $\frac{M}{W}$

   B. $\frac{M + W}{W}$

   C. $\frac{W}{M - W}$

   D. $\frac{W}{M + W}$

8. A motion was passed by a vote of 5:3. What part of the votes cast were in favor of the motion?

   A. $\frac{5}{8}$

   B. $\frac{5}{3}$

   C. $\frac{3}{5}$

   D. $\frac{3}{8}$

SHOW YOUR WORK HERE

9

9. In a certain class, the ratio of men to women is 3:5. If the class has 24 people in it, how many are women?

   A. 9

   B. 12

   C. 15

   D. 18

10. If a baby otter can swim at an average rate of $1\frac{3}{8}$ miles per hour, how long would it take it to swim $4\frac{1}{2}$ miles downstream with a current moving at a rate of $\frac{3}{4}$ miles per hour?

    A. $7\frac{1}{2}$ hours

    B. 6 hours

    C. $3\frac{3}{11}$ hours

    D. $2\frac{2}{17}$ hours

11. Ben's Tae Kwon Do class lasts for $1\frac{3}{4}$ hours. So far, he has been in class for $\frac{5}{6}$ of an hour. How many minutes remain until the class is finished?

    A. 50

    B. 55

    C. 65

    D. 70

12. Zain's gas tank is $\frac{1}{8}$ full. After she adds 8 gallons of gas to the tank, it is then $\frac{5}{6}$ full. Approximately how many gallons of gas can her tank hold?

    A. 9

    B. 11

    C. 13

    D. 17

9

SHOW YOUR WORK HERE

Answer Key and Explanations

1. C	3. A	5. C	7. D	9. C	11. B
2. B	4. D	6. A	8. A	10. D	12. B

1. **The correct answer is C.** The team lost 6 games out of 30.

$$\frac{6}{30} = \frac{1}{5}$$

2. **The correct answer is B.** Germaine spends X Y out of X.

$$\frac{X - Y}{X}$$

3. **The correct answer is A.** 10 minutes elapse by noon, and another 14 after noon, making a total of 24 minutes. There are 60 minutes in an hour.

$$\frac{24}{60} = \frac{2}{5}$$

4. **The correct answer is D.** One half earn over $18,000. One third of the other $\frac{1}{2}$, or $\frac{1}{6}$, earn between $15,000 and $18,000. This accounts for $\frac{1}{2} + \frac{1}{6}$, or $\frac{3}{6} + \frac{1}{6} = \frac{4}{6} = \frac{2}{3}$ of the staff, leaving $\frac{1}{3}$ to earn below $15,000.

5. **The correct answer is C.** David spends $\frac{1}{4}$ on Monday and $\frac{2}{3}$ of the other $\frac{3}{4}$, or $\frac{1}{2}$, on Tuesday, leaving only for the rest of the week.

6. **The correct answer is A.** Let the third or shortest section equal x. Then the second section equals $3x$, and the first section equals $9x$. The entire piece of fabric is then $13x$, and the shortest piece represents $\frac{x}{13x}$, or $\frac{1}{13}$, of the entire piece.

7. **The correct answer is D.** The factory employs $M + W$ people, of which W are women.

8. **The correct answer is A.** For every 5 votes in favor, 3 were cast against. Therefore, 5 out of every 8 votes cast were in favor of the motion.

9. **The correct answer is C.** The ratio of women to the total number of people is 5:8. We can set up a proportion. If $\frac{5}{8} = \frac{x}{24}$, then $x = 15$.

10. **The correct answer is D.** The otter's speed going downstream with the current is:

$$\left(1\frac{3}{8} + \frac{3}{4}\right) = 1\frac{3}{8} + \frac{6}{8}$$
$$= 1\frac{9}{8}$$
$$= 2\frac{1}{8} \text{ miles per hour}$$

Compute this quotient:

$$4\frac{1}{2} \div 2\frac{1}{8} = \frac{9}{2} \div \frac{17}{8}$$
$$= \frac{9}{2} \cdot \frac{8}{17}$$
$$= \frac{36}{17}$$
$$= 2\frac{2}{17} \text{ hours}$$

11. The correct answer is B. The time remaining in the class is

$$1\frac{3}{4} - \frac{5}{6} = \frac{7}{4} - \frac{5}{6} = \frac{21}{12} - \frac{10}{12} = \frac{11}{12}$$ of an hour.

Since there are 60 minutes in one hour, the number of minutes to which this corresponds is $\frac{11}{12}(60) = 55$.

12. The correct answer is B. Let x be the number of gallons of gas the tank can hold. Then, $\frac{1}{8}x + 8 = \frac{5}{6}x$. Solve for x:

$$\frac{1}{8}x + 8 = \frac{5}{6}x$$
$$24 \cdot \left(\frac{1}{8}x + 8\right) = 24 \cdot \left(\frac{5}{6}x\right)$$
$$3x + 192 = 20x$$
$$192 = 17x$$
$$x = \frac{192}{17} = 11\frac{5}{17}$$

The tank holds approximately 11 gallons of gas.

COMPLEX NUMBERS

A **complex number** is a number made up of a real number and an imaginary number. It can be written in standard form $a + bi$, where a and b are real numbers and i is an imaginary unit.

$$i = \sqrt{-1}, \ i^2 = -1$$

For example, in the complex number $2 + 3i$ the real number is 2 and the imaginary number is $3i$.

Complex numbers can be added, subtracted, multiplied, and divided.

Adding Complex Numbers

To add complex numbers, add the real numbers and the imaginary numbers separately.

Sum: $(a + bi) + (c + di) = (a + c) + (b + d)i$

Example:
Add: $(2 + 3i) + (8 + 4i)$

Solution:
Add the real numbers and then the imaginary numbers.

$$(2 + 8) + (3i + 4i) = 10 + 7i$$

Subtracting Complex Numbers

To subtract complex numbers, subtract the real numbers and the imaginary numbers separately.

Difference: $(a + bi) - (c + di) = (a - c) + (b - d)i$

Example:
Subtract: $(2 + 3i) - (8 + 4i)$

Solution:
Subtract the real numbers and then the imaginary numbers.

$$(2 + 3i) - (8 + 4i) = (2 - 8) + (3i - 4i) = -6 - i$$

Multiplying Complex Numbers

Multiplying complex numbers is like multiplying polynomials by using the distributive property or the FOIL method.

$$\textbf{Product: } (a + bi)(c + di) = (ac) + (adi) + (bci) + (bd)i^2$$

Example 1:

Multiply: $3i(-2 + 9i)$

Solution:

Distribute $3i$ to all of the terms in the parentheses.

Example 2:

Multiply: $(2 + 3i)(8 + 4i)$

Solution:

Find the sum of the products of the **First** terms, the **Outer** terms, the **Inner** terms, and the **Last** terms of the binomials. The acronym FOIL stands for First Outer Inner Last and will help you to remember how to multiply two binomials.

When simplifying an expression that involves complex numbers, simplify i^2 to -1.

Simplify and write in standard form $a + bi$.

$$(2 + 3i)(8 + 4i) = (2 \cdot 8) + (2 \cdot 4i) + (8 \cdot 3i) + (3i \cdot 4i)$$
$$= 16 + 8i + 24i + 12i^2$$
$$= 16 + 32i + 12(-1)$$
$$= 4 + 32i$$

Dividing Complex Numbers

Dividing complex numbers is more complicated because the denominator cannot contain a radical. This process is called **rationalizing the denominator**. In order to make the denominator rational, you must use its **complex conjugate**. The product of two complex conjugates is always a real number $a^2 + b^2$. The numbers $2 + 8i$ and $2 - 8i$ are examples of complex conjugates, and their product is the real number $2^2 + 8^2 = 4 + 64 = 68$.

$$\textbf{Complex conjugates: } (a + bi) \text{ and } (a - bi)$$

$$\textbf{Product of complex conjugates: } (a + bi)(a - bi) = a^2 + b^2$$

Example 1:

Simplify: $\dfrac{8}{7i}$

Solution:

Rationalize the denominator by multiplying the numerator and denominator by i.

$$\frac{8}{7i} = \frac{8}{7i} \cdot \frac{i}{i} = \frac{8i}{7i^2} = \frac{8i}{7(-1)} = \frac{8i}{-7}$$

Example 2:

Simplify: $\dfrac{4 + 2i}{-3 + 5i}$

Solution:

Rationalize the denominator by multiplying the numerator and denominator by the conjugate for the denominator. Then simplify by combining like terms.

$$\frac{4 + 2i}{-3 + 5i} = \frac{4 + 2i}{-3 + 5i} \cdot \frac{-3 - 5i}{-3 - 5i}$$

$$= \frac{-12 - 20i - 6i - 10i^2}{9 + 15i - 15i - 25i^2}$$

$$= \frac{-12 - 20i - 6i - 10(-1)}{9 + 15i - 15i - 25(-1)} \quad (\text{Recall that } i^2 = -1)$$

$$= \frac{-12 - 20i - 6i + 10}{9 + 15i - 15i + 25}$$

$$= \frac{-2 - 26i}{9 + 25}$$

$$= \frac{-2 - 26i}{34}$$

$$= \frac{-2}{34} - \frac{26i}{34}$$

$$= \frac{-1}{17} - \frac{13i}{17}$$

$$= -\frac{1}{17} - \frac{13}{17}i$$

PRACTICE EXERCISE: COMPLEX NUMBERS

> **DIRECTIONS:** Work out each problem in the space provided, then review the answer explanations that directly follow this exercise.

1. **Add:** $(8 + 2i) + (2 - 3i)$

    A. $15i$

    B. $5 + 4i$

    C. $6 + i$

    D. $10 - i$

2. **Add:** $\left(1 - \dfrac{1}{2}i\right) + \left(4 + 2i\right)$

    A. $5 - \dfrac{3}{2}i$

    B. $5 + \dfrac{3}{2}i$

    C. $\dfrac{7}{2}i$

    D. $\dfrac{13}{2}i$

3. **Subtract:** $(-9 + 4i) - (3 + 7i)$

    A. $-6 - 3i$

    B. $-2 + i$

    C. $-12 - 3i$

    D. $-i$

4. **Subtract:** $\left(\dfrac{3}{5} - \dfrac{1}{2}i\right) - \left(-\dfrac{3}{10} - 2i\right)$

    A. $\dfrac{9}{10} + \dfrac{3}{2}i$

    B. $\dfrac{9}{10} - \dfrac{3}{2}i$

    C. $\dfrac{3}{10} - \dfrac{3}{2}i$

    D. $\dfrac{3}{10} - \dfrac{5}{2}i$

5. **Multiply:** $(-5i)(-4i)i$

    A. $20i$

    B. $-\sqrt{20}\,i$

    C. $-20i$

    D. $\sqrt{20}\,i$

6. **Multiply:** $(-5i)(12 - 3i)$

    A. $8 + 17i$

    B. $-15 - 60i$

    C. $15 + 60i$

    D. $-8 + 17i$

SHOW YOUR WORK HERE

9

7. **Multiply:** $(4 - 6i)(1 - 2i)$

   A. $4 + 12i$

   B. $4 - 12i$

   C. $8 + 14i$

   D. $-8 - 14i$

8. **Compute:** $(2 - 3i)^2$

   A. $-5 + 12i$

   B. $-5 - 12i$

   C. 13

   D. -5

9. **Simplify:** $\dfrac{-5i}{4i + 11}$

   A. $-4 - 11i$

   B. $\dfrac{20 - 55i}{137}$

   C. $\dfrac{-20 - 55i}{137}$

   D. $4 + 11i$

10. **Simplify:** $\dfrac{17 - i}{3i}$

    A. $\dfrac{1}{3} - \dfrac{17}{3}i$

    B. $\dfrac{1}{3} + \dfrac{7}{3}i$

    C. $\dfrac{34}{5} + \dfrac{2}{5}i$

    D. $-\dfrac{1}{3} - \dfrac{17}{3}i$

11. **Simplify:** $\dfrac{3 - 5i}{3 + 5i}$

    A. $\dfrac{8}{17} + \dfrac{15}{17}i$

    B. $\dfrac{8}{17} - \dfrac{15}{17}i$

    C. $-\dfrac{8}{17} + \dfrac{15}{17}i$

    D. $-\dfrac{8}{17} - \dfrac{15}{17}i$

12. **Simplify:** $\dfrac{-3 + 5i}{-3 - 4i}$

    A. $-\dfrac{29}{5} - \dfrac{27}{5}i$

    B. $\dfrac{-11}{25} - \dfrac{27}{25}i$

    C. $\dfrac{21}{25} - \dfrac{27}{25}i$

    D. $\dfrac{11}{7} + \dfrac{27}{7}i$

9

SHOW YOUR WORK HERE

Answer Key and Explanations

1. D	3. C	5. C	7. D	9. C	11. D
2. B	4. A	6. B	8. B	10. D	12. B

1. The correct answer is D.

$(8 + 2i) + (2 - 3i) = (8 + 2) + (2i - 3i) = 10 - i$

2. The correct answer is B.

$$\left(1 - \frac{1}{2}i\right) + (4 + 2i)$$
$$= (1 + 4) + \left(-\frac{1}{2} + 2\right)i$$
$$= 5 + \frac{3}{2}i$$

3. The correct answer is C.

$$(-9 + 4i) - (3 + 7i) = (-9 - 3) + (4i - 7i)$$
$$= -12 - 3i$$

4. The correct answer is A.

$$\left(\frac{3}{5} - \frac{1}{2}i\right) - \left(-\frac{3}{10} - 2i\right)$$
$$= \left(\frac{3}{5} - \left(-\frac{3}{10}\right)\right) + \left(-\frac{1}{2} - (-2)\right)i$$
$$= \left(\frac{3}{5} + \frac{3}{10}\right) + \left(-\frac{1}{2} + 2\right)i$$
$$= \left(\frac{6}{10} + \frac{3}{10}\right) + \frac{3}{2}i$$
$$= \frac{9}{10} + \frac{3}{2}i$$

5. The correct answer is C.

$(-5i)(-4i)i = (20)(i^2)(i) = -20i$

6. The correct answer is B.

$$(-5i)(12 - 3i) = (-5i)(12) + (-5i)(-3i)$$
$$= -60i + 15i^2$$
$$= -60i + 15(-1)$$
$$= -15 - 60i$$

7. The correct answer is D.

$$(4 - 6i)(1 - 2i) = (4) + (-8i) + (-6i) + (12i^2)$$
$$= 4 + (-14i) + (-12)$$
$$= -8 - 14i$$

8. The correct answer is B.

$$(2 - 3i)^2 = (2 - 3i)(2 - 3i)$$
$$= 4 - 6i - 6i + 9i^2$$
$$= 4 - 12i - 9$$
$$= -5 - 12i$$

9. The correct answer is C.

$$\frac{-5i}{11 + 4i} = \frac{-5i}{11 + 4i} \cdot \frac{11 - 4i}{11 - 4i}$$
$$= \frac{-5i(11 - 4i)}{(11 + 4i)(11 - 4i)}$$
$$= \frac{-55i + 20i^2}{121 - 44i + 44i + 16i^2}$$
$$= \frac{-20 - 55i}{121 + 16}$$
$$= \frac{-20 - 55i}{137}$$

10. The correct answer is D.

$$\frac{17 - i}{3i} = \frac{17 - i}{3i} \cdot \frac{i}{i}$$
$$= \frac{(17 - i)(i)}{3i^2}$$
$$= \frac{17i - i^2}{3(-1)}$$
$$= \frac{1 + 17i}{-3}$$
$$= -\frac{1}{3} - \frac{17}{3}i$$

11. **The correct answer is D.** Multiply the numerator and denominator by the conjugate of the denominator. Then, simplify:

$$\frac{3-5i}{3+5i} = \frac{3-5i}{3+5i} \cdot \frac{3-5i}{3-5i}$$

$$= \frac{9-15i-15i+25i^2}{9-25i^2}$$

$$= \frac{9-30i-25}{9+25}$$

$$= \frac{-16-30i}{34}$$

$$= -\frac{8}{17} - \frac{15}{17}i$$

12. **The correct answer is B.**

$$\frac{-3+5i}{-3-4i} = \frac{-3+5i}{-3-4i} \cdot \frac{-3+4i}{-3+4i}$$

$$= \frac{\left(-3+5i\right)\left(-3+4i\right)}{\left(-3-4i\right)\left(-3+4i\right)}$$

$$= \frac{9-12i-15i+20i^2}{9-12i+12i-16i^2}$$

$$= \frac{9-12i-15i+20\left(-1\right)}{9-12i+12i-16\left(-1\right)}$$

$$= \frac{9-27i+\left(-20\right)}{9+\left(-16\right)\left(-1\right)}$$

$$= \frac{-11-27i}{25}$$

$$= \frac{-11}{25} - \frac{27}{25}i$$

DIRECT AND INVERSE VARIATION

Direct Variation

Two quantities are said to **vary directly** if as one increases, the other increases, and, as one decreases, the other decreases.

For example, the amount of sugar needed in a recipe varies directly with the amount of butter used. The number of inches between two cities on a map varies directly with the number of miles between the cities. The equation $y = ax$ represents direct variation between x and y, and y is said to vary directly with x. The variable a is called the constant of variation. By dividing each side by x, you can see that the ratio for the variable is the constant a.

Example 1:

Hooke's Law states that the distance d a spring stretches varies directly with the force F that is applied to it. Suppose a spring stretches 15 inches when a force of 9 lbs. is applied. Write an equation that relates d to F, and state the constant of variation.

Solution:

You are comparing the distance that a spring stretches with the force that is applied, so $\frac{d}{15} = \frac{F}{9}$. Solving for d in terms of F, you get $d = \frac{5}{3}F$. The constant of variation is $\frac{5}{3}$.

Example 2:

The weight of a person on the moon varies directly with the weight of a person on Earth. A person who weighs 100 lbs. on Earth weighs 16.6 lbs. on the moon. How much would a person who weighs 120 lbs. on Earth weigh on the moon?

Solution:

Start with the equation $y = ax$, where y is the weight of a person on the moon and x is the weight of a person on Earth.

$$y = ax$$
$$16.6 = a(100)$$
$$0.166 = a$$

The equation $y = 0.166x$ gives the weight y on the moon of a person who weighs x pounds on Earth. To solve the example, substitute $x = 120$ in the equation to determine the weight of the person on the moon.

$$y = 0.166x$$
$$y = 0.166(120)$$
$$y = 19.92$$

A person who weighs 120 lbs. on Earth would weigh 19.92 lbs. on the moon.

Inverse Variation

Two quantities are said to **vary inversely** if, as one increases, the other decreases.

For example, the number of workers hired to paint a house varies inversely with the number of days the job will take. A doctor's stock of flu vaccine varies inversely with the number of patients injected. The number of days a given supply of cat food lasts varies inversely with the number of cats being fed.

The equation $xy = a$, where $a \neq 0$, represents inverse variation between x and y, and y is said to vary inversely with x. The variable a is called the constant of variation.

Example:

The number of songs that can be stored on a hard drive varies inversely with the size of the song. A certain hard drive can store 3,000 songs when the average size of the song is 3.75 MB. Write an equation that gives the number of songs y that will fit on the hard drive as a function of the average song size x.

Solution:

First, write an inverse variation equation that relates x and y. Then substitute 3,000 for y and 3.75 for x.

$$xy = a$$
$$y = \frac{a}{x}$$
$$3,000 = \frac{a}{3.75}$$
$$11,250 = a$$

The inverse variation equation for this situation is $y = \dfrac{11,250}{x}$.

TIP

Whenever two quantities vary directly, you can find a missing term by setting up a proportion. However, be very careful to compare the same units, in the same order, on each side of the equal sign.

PRACTICE EXERCISE: DIRECT AND INVERSE VARIATION

DIRECTIONS: Work out each problem in the space provided, then review the answer explanations that directly follow this exercise.

1. If 60 feet of uniform wire weighs 80 pounds, what is the weight of 2 yards of the same wire?

   A. $2\frac{2}{3}$ pounds

   B. 6 pounds

   C. 8 pounds

   D. 120 pounds

2. A gear 50 inches in diameter turns a smaller gear 30 inches in diameter. If the larger gear makes 15 revolutions, how many revolutions does the smaller gear make in that time?

   A. 9

   B. 12

   C. 20

   D. 25

3. The time it takes to construct a rock concert stage varies inversely with the number of workers. If 10 people work, it takes 4 days to finish the construction. How long does the job take if 14 people work?

   A. $2\frac{1}{2}$ days

   B. $2\frac{6}{7}$ days

   C. 3 days

   D. $3\frac{2}{7}$ days

4. If a furnace uses 40 gallons of oil in a week, how many gallons, to the nearest gallon, does it use in 10 days?

   A. 4

   B. 28

   C. 57

   D. 58

SHOW YOUR WORK HERE

9

5. A recipe requires 13 ounces of sugar and 18 ounces of flour. If only 10 ounces of sugar are used, how much flour, to the nearest ounce, should be used?

   A. 13

   B. 14

   C. 15

   D. 23

6. A bottle of 20 aspirin costs $8.25. If the cost, y, varies directly with the number of aspirin, x, what is the approximate cost of a bottle of 325 aspirin?

   A. $9.50

   B. $11.25

   C. $13.40

   D. $15.30

7. A school has enough bread to feed 30 children for 4 days. If 10 more children are added, how many days will the bread last?

   A. $1\frac{1}{3}$

   B. $2\frac{2}{3}$

   C. 3

   D. $5\frac{1}{3}$

8. The intensity of a sound, I, varies inversely with the square of the distance, d, from the sound. If the distance is reduced by a factor of $\frac{1}{4}$, by what factor will the intensity of the sound increase?

   A. 4

   B. 8

   C. 12

   D. 16

9

SHOW YOUR WORK HERE

9. The number of ceramic tiles, *x*, laid on a kitchen floor varies directly with the amount of time, *y*, spent laying the tile. If it takes 20 minutes to lay 12 tiles, how long does it take to lay 190 tiles?

   A. 1 hour, 36 minutes

   B. 1 hour, 54 minutes

   C. 2 hours, 10 minutes

   D. 2 hours, 25 minutes

10. The height, *H*, and base radius, *R*, of the water in a right circular cylinder vary inversely to keep the volume of water constant. When the height is 1.2 feet, the base radius is 0.35 feet. What is the base radius when the height is 1.4 feet?

    A. 0.25 feet

    B. 0.3 feet

    C. 0.4 feet

    D. 0.55 feet

11. The price per person, *y*, for a catered event varies inversely with the number of people attending the event, *x*. It costs $20 per person if 45 people attend. What is the approximate cost per person if 65 people attend?

    A. $9

    B. $13.85

    C. $15.50

    D. $22.25

12. The profit, *P*, earned from sales of hand-crafted cheeseboards is directly proportional to the number of cheeseboards sold, *x*. What is the variation equation?

    A. $P = k + x$

    B. $P = \dfrac{1}{kx^2}$

    C. $P = kx$

    D. $P = \dfrac{k}{x}$

SHOW YOUR WORK HERE

9

Answer Key and Explanations

1. C	3. B	5. B	7. C	9. B	11. B
2. D	4. C	6. C	8. D	10. B	12. C

1. **The correct answer is C.** You are comparing feet with pounds. The more feet, the more pounds. This is DIRECT. Remember to rename yards as feet:

$$\frac{60}{80} = \frac{6}{x}$$
$$60x = 480$$
$$x = 8$$

2. **The correct answer is D.** The larger a gear, the fewer times it revolves in a given period of time. This is INVERSE.

$$50 \cdot 15 = 30 \cdot x$$
$$750 = 30x$$
$$25 = x$$

3. **The correct answer is B.** The variation equation is $P = \frac{k}{t}$. Using the given information, we can find k: $10 = \frac{k}{4}$, so that $k = 40$. So the model is $P = \frac{40}{t}$. The time is takes to complete the job if 14 people work is the solution of the equation $14 = \frac{40}{t}$. This solution is $t = \frac{40}{14} = \frac{20}{7} = 2\frac{6}{7}$ days.

4. **The correct answer is C.** The more days, the more oil. This is DIRECT. Remember to rename the week as 7 days.

$$\frac{40}{7} = \frac{x}{10}$$
$$7x = 400$$
$$x = 57\frac{1}{7}$$

5. **The correct answer is B.** The more sugar, the more flour. This is DIRECT.

$$\frac{13}{18} = \frac{10}{x}$$
$$13x = 180$$
$$x = 13\frac{11}{13}$$

6. **The correct answer is C.** The variation equation is $y = kx$. Using the given information, we can find k: $8.25 = 200k$, so that $k = \frac{8.25}{200} = 0.04125$. Hence, $y = 0.04125x$. The cost of 325 aspirin is $y = 0.04125(325) = 13.40$.

7. **The correct answer is C.** The more children, the fewer days. This is INVERSE.

$$30 \cdot 4 = 40 \cdot x$$
$$120 = 40x$$
$$3 = x$$

8. **The correct answer is D.**

$$I\left(d^2\right) = k$$
$$I\left(\frac{d}{4}\right)^2 = k$$
$$I\left(\frac{d^2}{16}\right) = k$$
$$I\left(d^2\right) = 16k$$

9. **The correct answer is B.** The variation equation is $y = kx$. Using the given information, we can find k: $12 = k(20)$ so that $k = \frac{3}{5}$. So $y = \frac{3}{5}x$. The time it takes is $\frac{3}{5}(190) = 114$ minutes, or 1 hour, 54 minutes, to lay 190 tiles.

10. **The correct answer is B.** The variation equation is $H = \frac{k}{R}$. Using the given information, we can find k: $1.2 = \frac{k}{0.35}$, so that $k = (1.2)(0.35) = 0.42$. So the model is $H = \frac{0.42}{R}$. The desired base radius R satisfies the equation $1.4 = \frac{0.42}{R}$. Solving for R yields $R = \frac{0.42}{1.4} = 0.3$.

9

11. **The correct answer is B.** The variation equation is $y = \dfrac{k}{x}$. Using the given information, we can find k:

$20 = \dfrac{k}{45}$, so that $k = (20)(45) = 900$. So the model is $y = \dfrac{900}{x}$. The cost per person if 65 people attend is

$y = \dfrac{900}{65} \approx \$13.85$.

12. **The correct answer is C.** The equation is $P = kx$, where k is the constant of proportionality.

BRAIN BREAK

Play one or two of your favorite songs. Dance to the beat or sing along. Tap on your desk. Movement breaks satisfy your need for physical activity. They also provide a burst of energy and increase your ability to focus on the next learning activity.

9

FINDING PERCENTAGES

Percent Equivalents

Percent means "out of 100." If you understand this concept, it becomes very easy to rename a percentage as an equivalent decimal or fraction.

$$5\% = \frac{5}{100} = 0.05$$

$$2.6\% = \frac{2.6}{100} = 0.026$$

$$c\% = \frac{c}{100} = \frac{1}{100} \cdot c = 0.01c$$

$$\frac{1}{2}\% = \frac{\frac{1}{2}}{100} = \frac{1}{100} \cdot \frac{1}{2} = \frac{1}{100} \cdot 0.5 = 0.005$$

Certain fractional equivalents of common percentages occur frequently enough that they should be memorized. Learning the values in the following table will make your work with percentage problems much easier.

PERCENTAGE-FRACTION EQUIVALENTS

Percentage	Fraction	Percentage	Fraction
10%	$\frac{1}{10}$	$12\frac{1}{2}\%$	$\frac{1}{8}$
20%	$\frac{1}{5}$	$16\frac{2}{3}\%$	$\frac{1}{6}$
25%	$\frac{1}{4}$	$33\frac{1}{3}\%$	$\frac{1}{3}$
30%	$\frac{3}{10}$	$37\frac{1}{2}\%$	$\frac{3}{8}$
40%	$\frac{2}{5}$	$62\frac{1}{2}\%$	$\frac{5}{8}$
50%	$\frac{1}{2}$	$83\frac{1}{3}\%$	$\frac{5}{6}$
60%	$\frac{3}{5}$	$87\frac{1}{2}\%$	$\frac{7}{8}$
70%	$\frac{7}{10}$		
75%	$\frac{3}{4}$		
80%	$\frac{4}{5}$		
90%	$\frac{9}{10}$		

Most percentage problems can be solved by using the following proportion:

$$\frac{\%}{100} = \frac{\text{part}}{\text{whole}}$$

Although this method works, it often yields unnecessarily large numbers that are difficult to compute. The following are some common ways to find equivalents:

- To change a % to a decimal, remove the % sign and divide by 100. This has the effect of moving the decimal point two places to the LEFT.

- To change a decimal to a %, add the % sign and multiply by 100. This has the effect of moving the decimal point two places to the RIGHT.

- To change a % to a fraction, remove the % sign and divide by 100. This has the effect of putting the % over 100 and simplifying the resulting fraction.

- To change a fraction to a %, add the % sign and multiply by 100.

Let's explore four basic types of percentage problems and different methods for solving them.

To Find a Percentage of a Number

Example 1:

Find 27% of 92.

Solution:

Proportional Method	Shorter Method
$\frac{27}{100} = \frac{x}{92}$ $100x = 2,428$ $x = 24.84$	Rename the percentage as its decimal or fraction equivalent and multiply. Use fractions only when they are among the familiar ones given in the previous chart. $\begin{array}{r} 92 \\ \times\,0.27 \\ \hline 644 \\ 184 \\ \hline 24.84 \end{array}$

Example 2:

Find $12\frac{1}{2}\%$ of 96.

Solution:

Proportional Method	Decimal Method	Fractional Method
$\frac{12\frac{1}{2}}{100} = \frac{x}{96}$ $100x = 1,200$ $x = 12$	$\begin{array}{r} 0.125 \\ \times\quad 96 \\ \hline 750 \\ 1125 \\ \hline 12,000 \end{array}$	$\frac{1}{8} \cdot 96 = 12$

Which method is easiest? It really pays to memorize those fractional equivalents.

To Find a Number When a Percentage of It Is Given

Example 1:

7 is 5% of what number?

Solution:

Proportional Method	Shorter Method
$\dfrac{5}{100} = \dfrac{7}{x}$ $5x = 700$ $x = 140$	Translate the problem into an algebraic equation. In doing this, the percentage must be written as a fraction or decimal. $7 = 0.05x$ $700 = 5x$ $140 = x$

Example 2:

20 is $33\dfrac{1}{2}$ of what number?

Solution:

Proportional Method	Shorter Method
$\dfrac{33\frac{1}{2}}{100} = \dfrac{20}{x}$ $33\dfrac{1}{3}x = 2,000$ $\dfrac{100}{3}x = 2,000$ $100x = 6,000$ $x = 60$	$20 = \dfrac{1}{3}x$ $60 = x$

Just think of the time you will save and the number of extra problems you will solve if you know that $33\dfrac{1}{3}\% = \dfrac{1}{3}$.

9

To Find What Percentage One Number Is of Another

Example 1:

90 is what percent of 1,500?

Solution:

Proportional Method	Shorter Method
$$\frac{x}{100} = \frac{90}{1,500}$$ $$1,500x = 9,000$$ $$15x = 90$$ $$x = 6$$	Put the part over the whole. Simplify the fraction and multiply by 100. $$\frac{90}{1,500} = \frac{9}{150} = \frac{3}{50} \cdot 100 = 6$$

Example 2:

7 is what percent of 35?

Solution:

Proportional Method	Shorter Method
$$\frac{x}{100} = \frac{7}{135}$$ $$35x = 700$$ $$x = 20$$	$$\frac{7}{35} = \frac{1}{5} = 20\%$$

Example 3:

18 is what percent of 108?

Solution:

Proportional Method	Shorter Method
$$\frac{x}{100} = \frac{18}{108}$$ $$108x = 1,800$$ Time-consuming long division is necessary to get: $$x = 16\frac{2}{3}$$	$$\frac{18}{108} = \frac{9}{54} = \frac{1}{6} = 16\frac{2}{3}\%$$ Once again, if you know the fraction equivalents of common percents, computation can be done in a few seconds.

To Find a Percentage Over 100

Example 1:

Find 125% of 64.

Solution:

Proportional Method	Decimal Method	Fractional Method
$\dfrac{125}{100} = \dfrac{x}{64}$ $100x = 8,000$ $x = 80$	$\begin{array}{r} 64 \\ \times\ 1.25 \\ \hline 320 \\ 128\ \ \\ 64\ \ \ \ \\ \hline 80.00 \end{array}$	$1\dfrac{1}{4} \cdot 64$ $\dfrac{5}{4} \cdot 64 = 80$

Example 2:

36 is 150% of what number?

Solution:

Proportional Method	Decimal Method	Fractional Method
$\dfrac{150}{100} = \dfrac{36}{x}$ $150x = 3,600$ $15x = 360$ $x = 24$	$36 = 1.50x$ $360 = 15x$ $24 = x$	$36 = 1\dfrac{1}{2}x$ $36 = \dfrac{3}{2}x$ $72 = 3x$ $24 = x$

Example 3:

60 is what percent of 50?

Solution:

Proportional Method	Shorter Method
$\dfrac{x}{100} = \dfrac{60}{50}$ $50x = 6,000$ $5x = 600$ $x = 120$	$\dfrac{60}{50} = \dfrac{6}{5} = 1\dfrac{1}{5} = 120\%$

PRACTICE EXERCISE: FINDING PERCENTAGES

DIRECTIONS: Work out each problem in the space provided, then review the answer explanations that directly follow this exercise.

1. Write 1.001% as a decimal.

   A. 0.01001

   B. 0.1001

   C. 10.1

   D. 100.1

2. Write 3.4% as a fraction.

   A. $\dfrac{34}{1,000}$

   B. $\dfrac{34}{10}$

   C. $\dfrac{34}{100}$

   D. $\dfrac{340}{100}$

3. Write $\dfrac{17}{2}\%$ as a percentage.

   A. 8.5%

   B. 85%

   C. 0.085%

   D. 850%

4. Find 60% of 70.

   A. 4,200

   B. 420

   C. 42

   D. 4.2

5. What is 175% of 16?

   A. 28

   B. 24

   C. 22

   D. 12

6. What percent of 40 is 16?

   A. 20%

   B. $2\dfrac{1}{2}\%$

   C. $33\dfrac{1}{3}\%$

   D. 40%

SHOW YOUR WORK HERE

7. What percent of 0.02 is 0.005?

   A. 4.0

   B. 2.5

   C. 25

   D. 40

8. $4 is 20% of what?

   A. $5

   B. $20

   C. $200

   D. $500

9. $\frac{9}{5}$ is $20\frac{1}{4}$% of what number?

   A. $\frac{9}{80}$

   B. $\frac{80}{9}$

   C. $\frac{81}{400}$

   D. $\frac{45}{4}$

10. What percent of 2 is 0.004?

    A. 0.02

    B. 0.2

    C. 2

    D. 20

11. Write 0.02 as a percentage.

    A. 0.0002%

    B. 0.002%

    C. 20%

    D. 2%

12. Find $5\frac{2}{5}$% of $2\frac{1}{2}$.

    A. $\frac{27}{2}$

    B. $\frac{1}{50}$

    C. $\frac{27}{200}$

    D. $\frac{1}{20}$

SHOW YOUR WORK HERE

Answer Key and Explanations

1. A	**3.** D	**5.** A	**7.** C	**9.** B	**11.** D
2. A	**4.** C	**6.** D	**8.** B	**10.** B	**12.** C

1. **The correct answer is A.** Move the decimal point to the left two places to get the equivalent decimal 0.01001.

2. **The correct answer is A.**

$$3.4\% = \frac{3.4}{100} = \frac{34}{1,000}$$

3. **The correct answer is D.**

$$\frac{17}{2} = 8\frac{1}{2} = 8.5$$

This is equivalent to 850%.

4. **The correct answer is C.**

$$60\% = \frac{3}{5} \rightarrow \frac{3}{5} \cdot 70 = 42$$

5. **The correct answer is A.**

$$175\% = 1\frac{3}{4} \rightarrow \frac{7}{4} \cdot 16 = 28$$

6. **The correct answer is D.**

$$\frac{16}{40} = \frac{2}{5} = 40\%$$

7. **The correct answer is C.** Let x denote the desired percentage. Solve the following proportion:

$$\frac{x}{100} = \frac{0.005}{0.02}$$
$$\frac{x}{100} = 0.25$$
$$x = 25$$

8. **The correct answer is B.**

$$20\% = \frac{1}{5},$$
$$\text{so } 4 = \frac{1}{5}x$$
$$20 = x$$

9. **The correct answer is B.**

$$20\frac{1}{4}\% = \frac{81}{4}\% = \frac{81}{400}.$$

Let x be the unknown number. Then, $\frac{81}{400}x = \frac{9}{5}$. Solving for x yields

$$\frac{9}{5} \cdot \frac{400}{81} = \frac{80}{9}.$$

10. **The correct answer is B.** Let x denote the desired percent. Then, $\frac{x}{100}(2) = 0.004$. Solve for x, as follows:

$$\frac{x}{100}(2) = 0.004$$
$$x = \frac{100}{2}(0.004)$$
$$x = \frac{0.4}{2} = 0.2$$

11. **The correct answer is D.**

$$0.02 = \frac{2}{100} = 2\%$$

12. **The correct answer is C.**

Change $5\frac{2}{5}\%$ to an equivalent fraction:

$$5\frac{2}{5}\% = \frac{27}{5}\% = \frac{27}{500}$$

Simplify $2\frac{1}{2} = \frac{5}{2}$ and multiply as follows:

$$\frac{27}{500} \cdot \frac{5}{2} = \frac{27}{200}$$

9

PERCENTAGE WORD PROBLEMS

Certain types of business situations are excellent applications of percentages.

Percentage of Increase or Decrease

The **percentage of increase or decrease** is found by putting the amount of increase or decrease over the original amount and renaming this fraction as a percentage.

Example 1:

Over a five-year period, the enrollment at South High dropped from 1,000 students to 800. Find the percentage of decrease.

Solution

$$\frac{1,000 - 800}{1,000} = \frac{200}{1,000} = \frac{20}{100} = 20\%$$

Example 2:

A company normally employs 100 people. During a slow spell, the company fired 20% of its employees. By what percentage must the company now increase its staff to return to full capacity?

Solution:

$$20\% = \frac{1}{5} \quad \rightarrow \quad \frac{1}{5} \cdot 100 = 20\%$$

The company now has 100 − 20 = 80 employees. If it then increases its staff by 20, the percentage of increase is $\frac{20}{80} = \frac{1}{4}$, or 25%.

Discount

A **discount** is usually expressed as a percent of the marked price that will be deducted from the marked price to determine the sale price.

Example 1:

Bill's Hardware offers a 20% discount on all appliances during a sale week. If they take advantage of the sale, how much must the Russells pay for a washing machine marked at $280?

Solution:

Long Method	Shorter Method
$20\% = \frac{1}{5}$ $\frac{1}{5} \cdot 280 = \$56$ discount $\$280 - \$56 = \$224$ sale price The danger inherent in this method is that $56 is sure to be among the multiple-choice answers.	If there is a 20% discount, the Russells will pay 80% of the marked price. $80\% = \frac{4}{5}$ $\frac{4}{5} \cdot 280 = \$224$ sale price

TIP

In word problems, *of* can usually be interpreted to mean *times* (in other words, *multiply*).

Example 2:

A store offers a television set marked at $340 less discounts of 10% and 5%. Another store offers the same television set also marked at $340 with a single discount of 15%. How much does the buyer save by buying at the better price?

Solution:

In the first store, the initial discount means the buyer pays 90%, or $\frac{9}{10}$, of $340, which is $306. The additional 5% discount means the buyer pays 95% of $306, or $290.70. Note that the second discount must be figured on the first sale price. Taking 5% off $306 is a smaller amount than taking the additional 5% off $340. The second store will therefore have a lower sale price. In the second store, the buyer will pay 85% of $340, or $289, making the price $1.70 less than in the first store.

Commission

Many salespeople earn money on a commission basis. In order to encourage sales, they are paid a percentage of the value of goods sold. This amount is called a **commission**.

Example 1:

A salesperson at Brown's Department Store is paid $80 per week in salary plus a 4% commission on all her sales. How much will that salesperson earn in a week in which she sells $4,032 worth of merchandise?

Solution:

Find 4% of $4,032 and add this amount to $80.

$$4032$$
$$\times 0.04$$
$$\overline{}$$
$$\$161.28 + \$80 = \$241.28$$

Example 2:

Bill Olson delivers frozen food for a delivery service and keeps 8% of all money collected. One month he was able to keep $16. How much did he forward to the delivery service?

Solution:

First, determine how much he collected by finding the number that 16 is 8% of.

$$16 = 0.08x$$
$$1,600 = 8x$$
$$200 = x$$

If Bill collected $200 and kept $16, he gave the delivery service $200 − $16, or $184.

Taxes

Taxes are a percentage of money spent or money earned.

Example 1:

Noname County collects a 7% sales tax on automobiles. If the price of a car is $8,532 before taxes, what will this car cost once sales tax is added in?

Solution:

Find 7% of $8,532 to determine tax and then add it to $8,532. This can be done in one step by finding 107% of $8,532.

$$
\begin{array}{r}
\$8,532 \\
\times \quad 1.07 \\
\hline
59724 \\
85320 \\
\hline
\$9,129.24
\end{array}
$$

Example 2:

If the tax rate in Anytown is $3.10 per $100, what is the annual real estate tax on a house assessed at $47,200?

Solution:

$$\text{annual tax rate} = \text{tax rate} \cdot \text{assessed value}$$

$$= \left(\frac{\$3.10}{\$100} \right)(47,200)$$
$$= (0.031)(47,200)$$
$$= \$1,463.20$$

9

BRAIN BREAK

Tired of sitting? Let's do another 5-4-3-2-1 game. Do 5 jumping jacks, hop on one foot 4 times, pat your head 3 times, spin around 2 times, and smile. Did you know that the mere act of smiling helps reduce stress and foster positive thoughts?

PRACTICE EXERCISE: PERCENTAGE WORD PROBLEMS

DIRECTIONS: Work out each problem in the space provided, then review the answer explanations that directly follow this exercise

1. What was the original price of a phone that sold for $70 during a 20%-off sale?

   A. $56

   B. $84

   C. $87.50

   D. $90

2. How many dollars does a salesperson earn on a sale of $800 at a commission of 2.5%?

   A. 20

   B. 200

   C. 2,000

   D. 20,000

3. At a selling price of $273, a refrigerator yields a 30% profit on the cost. What selling price will yield a 10% profit on the cost?

   A. $210

   B. $221

   C. $231

   D. $235

4. A store is having a sale on jeans. The manager marks the price down by 30%. A customer has a coupon that gives an additional 10% off the sale price. If the original price was $65, what is the cost of the jeans after the discounts are applied?

   A. $35.75

   B. $40.95

   C. $45.50

   D. $58.50

SHOW YOUR WORK HERE

5. The net price of a certain article is $306 after successive discounts of 15% and 10% off the marked price. What is the marked price?

A. $234.09

B. $382.50

C. $400

D. $408

6. In preparation for the holiday season, a store marks up the price of its most popular electronic toys by 15%. If such a toy was x dollars before the markup, which of these expressions represents the cost after the markup?

A. $x + 1.15$ dollars

B. $0.85x$ dollars

C. $1.15x$ dollars

D. $\dfrac{x}{0.85}$ dollars

7. A baseball team has won 40 games out of 60 played. It has 32 more games to play. How many of these must the team win to make its record 75% for the season?

A. 26

B. 28

C. 29

D. 30

8. If prices are reduced 25% and sales increase 20%, what is the net effect on gross receipts?

A. They increase by 5%.

B. They decrease by 5%.

C. They increase by 10%.

D. They decrease by 10%.

SHOW YOUR WORK HERE

9. A salesperson earns 5% on all sales between $200 and $600, and 8% on the part of the sales over $600. What is her commission in a week in which her sales total $800?

A. $20

B. $36

C. $46

D. $78

10. If the enrollment at State U. was 3,000 in 2008 and 12,000 in 2018, what was the percent of increase in enrollment?

A. 400%

B. 300%

C. 25%

D. 3%

11. Seventy percent of the members of a gym are male, and 40% of the males regularly compete in organized events. What percent of the members of the gym are males who regularly compete?

A. 25%

B. 28%

C. 30%

D. 42%

12. A salesperson receives a salary of $100 a week and a commission of 5% on all sales. What must be the amount of sales for a week in which the salesperson's total weekly income is $360?

A. $6,200

B. $5,200

C. $2,600

D. $720

9

SHOW YOUR WORK HERE

Answer Key and Explanations

1. C	3. C	5. C	7. C	9. C	11. B
2. A	4. B	6. C	8. D	10. B	12. B

1. **The correct answer is C.** $70 represents 80% of the original price.

$$70 = 0.80x$$
$$700 = 8x$$
$$\$87.50 = x$$

2. **The correct answer is A.**

$$2.5\% = \frac{2.5}{100}$$

The commission is $\frac{2.5}{100}(800) = \$20$.

3. **The correct answer is C.**

$$1.30x = 273$$
$$13x = 2,730$$
$$x = \$210 = \text{cost}$$

$273 represents 130% of the cost.

The new price will add 10% of cost, or $21, for profit.

New price = $231

4. **The correct answer is B.** The discounted price due to the markdown is $65 - 0.3($65) = $45.50. Applying the 10% coupon yields the final cost of $45.50 - $45.50(0.10) = $40.95.

5. **The correct answer is C.**

If marked price = m, first sale price = $0.85m$, and net price = $0.90(0.85m) = 0.765m$, then:

$$0.765m = 306$$
$$m = 400$$

Double check your answer against the information presented in the question.

15% of $400 is $60, making a first sale price of $340.

10% of $340 is $34, making the net price $306.

6. **The correct answer is C.** Add 15% of x to x to get the cost after the mark-up. Doing so yields $x + 0.15x = 1.15x$.

7. **The correct answer is C.** The team must win 75%, or $\frac{3}{4}$, of the games played during the entire season. With 60 games played and 32 more to play, the team must win $\frac{3}{4}$ of 92 games, and $\frac{3}{4} \cdot 92 = 69$. Since 40 games have already been won, the team must win 29 additional games.

8. **The correct answer is D.** Let original price = p, and original sales = s. Therefore, original gross receipts = ps. Let new price = $0.75p$, and new sales = $1.20s$. Therefore, new gross receipts = $0.90ps$. Gross receipts are only 90% of what they were.

9. **The correct answer is C.** Five percent of sales between $200 and $600 is $0.05(600) =$ $30. Then, 8% of sales over $600 is $0.08(200)$ = $16. Total commission = $30 + $16 = $46.

10. **The correct answer is B.** There was an increase of 9,000 students. To determine the percent of this increase in enrollment:

$$\frac{9,000}{3,000} = 3 = 300\%$$

11. **The correct answer is B.** 40% of 70% of x, the total number of members, is:

$$(0.40)(0.70)x = 0.28x$$

So 28% of members are males who regularly compete.

12. **The correct answer is B.** Let s = sales.

$$\$100 + 0.05s = 360$$
$$0.05s = 260$$
$$5s = 26,000$$
$$s = \$5,200$$

Summing It Up

- If the arithmetic looks complex, try to simplify it first.

- If a problem is given with letters in place of numbers, the same reasoning must be applied as for numbers. If you are not sure how to proceed, replace the letters with numbers to determine the steps that must be taken.

- Fractions should be written in the simplest form. Often, in multiple-choice questions, you may find that the answer you have correctly computed is not among the choices but an equivalent fraction is. Be careful!

- Whenever two quantities vary directly, you can find a missing term by setting up a proportion. However, be very careful to compare the same units, in the same order, on each side of the equal sign.

- When solving percentage problems, remember the following:

  - To change a % to a decimal, remove the % sign and divide by 100. This has the effect of moving the decimal point two places to the LEFT.

  - To change a decimal to a %, add the % sign and multiply by 100. This has the effect of moving the decimal point two places to the RIGHT.

  - To change a % to a fraction, remove the % sign and divide by 100. This has the effect of putting the % over 100 and simplifying the resulting fraction.

  - To change a fraction to a %, add the % sign and multiply by 100.

- In problems dealing with percentages, you may be presented with certain types of business situations, such as taxes or commissions. For problems asking about the percentage of increase or decrease, put the amount of increase or decrease over the original amount and rename that fraction as a percentage. A discount is usually expressed as a percentage of the marked price that will be deducted from the marked price to determine the sale price.

Take a moment to ask yourself some simple questions about your understanding of the chapter:

Review: What did I learn?

Evaluate: What do I need to learn more about?

Plan: What can I do next to keep improving?

Based on your answers to those questions, adjust your study plan to dedicate additional time to the areas of weakness that you've identified.

Chapter 10

Basic Algebra

OVERVIEW

10

SIGNED NUMBERS

To solve algebra problems, you must be able to compute accurately with signed numbers.

Addition: To add signed numbers with the same sign, add the magnitudes of the numbers (i.e., the numbers themselves) and keep the same sign. To add signed numbers with different signs, subtract the magnitudes of the numbers and use the sign of the number with the greater magnitude.

Subtraction: When subtracting a positive number from a negative number, add the magnitudes and make the difference (the answer) negative. When subtracting a negative number from a positive number, add the magnitude and make the difference positive. When asked to find the difference or a distance between a negative number and a positive number, the answer will always be positive.

Multiplication: If there is an odd number of negative signs, the product is negative. An even number of negative signs gives a positive product.

Division: If the signs are the same, the quotient is positive. If the signs are different, the quotient is negative.

Practicing these basic operations with signed numbers will help you on the more difficult problems on the SAT Exam in which these and more complex skills are tested.

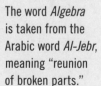

FUN FACT
The word *Algebra* is taken from the Arabic word *Al-Jebr*, meaning "reunion of broken parts."

PRACTICE EXERCISE: SIGNED NUMBERS

DIRECTIONS: Work out each problem in the space provided. Circle the letter next to your choice. Check your answers against the answer key and explanations that follow.

1. What is the sum of −6 and 8?

   A. −14

   B. 14

   C. −2

   D. 2

2. When −4 and −5 are added, what is the sum?

   A. −9

   B. 9

   C. −1

   D. 1

3. Subtract −8 from −3.

   A. −11

   B. −5

   C. 5

   D. 11

4. Subtract 8 from −2.

   A. −10

   B. −6

   C. 6

   D. 10

5. Compute the product of −9 and 3.

   A. −6

   B. 6

   C. −27

   D. 27

6. What is the product of $(-6)\left(+\dfrac{1}{2}\right)(-10)$?

   A. $-15\dfrac{1}{2}$

   B. $15\dfrac{1}{2}$

   C. −30

   D. 30

SHOW YOUR WORK HERE

10

7. Find the quotient: $\dfrac{(-6)(8)}{-12}$

   A. 36

   B. 4

   C. −36

   D. −4

8. Last winter a meteorology class recorded the daily temperatures. The coldest recorded temperature was −37 degrees Fahrenheit, and the warmest was 38 degrees Fahrenheit. How many degrees warmer was the warmest day than the coldest day?

   A. −75

   B. −1

   C. 1

   D. 75

9. The highest point in California is Mt. Whitney with an elevation of 14,494 feet. The lowest point is Death Valley with an elevation of −294 feet. How much higher is the base of a tree at the top of Mt. Whitney than a person standing at the lowest point in Death Valley?

   A. 294 feet

   B. 14,200 feet

   C. 14,494 feet

   D. 14,788 feet

10. A submarine started at an elevation of −1,250 feet, or 1,250 feet below sea level, and proceeded to submerge another 25 feet per second. It continued to submerge for 10 seconds. What was its new elevation?

   A. −1,500 feet

   B. −1,000 feet

   C. 250 feet

   D. 1,500 feet

10

SHOW YOUR WORK HERE

Answer Key and Explanations

1. D	3. C	5. C	7. B	9. D
2. A	4. A	6. D	8. D	10. A

1. **The correct answer is D.** The larger of the two whole number parts determines the sign. So $8 + (-6) = 2$.

2. **The correct answer is A.** In adding numbers with the same sign, add their magnitudes $(4 + 5 = 9)$ and keep the same sign.

3. **The correct answer is C.**

$$-3 - (-8) = -3 + 8 = 5$$

4. **The correct answer is A.**

$$-2 - 8 = -2 + (-8) = -10$$

5. **The correct answer is C.**

$$(-9)(3) = -27$$

6. **The correct answer is D.** Remember, multiplying an even number of negative terms makes the product positive.

$$(-6)\left(+\frac{1}{2}\right)(-10) = (6)\left(\frac{1}{2}\right)(10)$$

Reduce the numbers with the greatest common divisor 2, then multiply to solve:

$$(\cancel{6})\left(\frac{1}{\cancel{2}}\right)(10) = 3(10) = 30$$

7. **The correct answer is B.**

$$\frac{(-6)(8)}{-12} = \frac{-48}{-12} = 4$$

8. **The correct answer is D.** This is like a distance question. It's really asking what the distance is on the number line from −37 to +38. Try to picture the number line. Add the magnitudes:

$$-37 - 38 = -75$$

Remember, when subtracting a positive number from a negative number, you add the magnitude and make the difference positive. The difference is 75 degrees.

9. **The correct answer is D.** This question is really asking about distance between two things, so the answer will be positive. To solve, figure it is 14,494 feet from the top of Mt. Whitney to sea level, and then another 294 feet to get to the lowest point of Death Valley. Add the two numbers:

$$14,494 + 294 = 14,788$$

10. **The correct answer is A.** Find the additional distance the submarine submerged. Multiply −25 by 10. When multiplying a negative number by a positive, the product is negative.

$$-25 \times 10 = -250$$

Subtract 250 from −1,250. When subtracting a positive number from a negative number, add the magnitude and make the difference (the answer) negative:

$$1,250 + 250 = 1,500$$

The answer is −1,500.

LINEAR EQUATIONS

The next step in solving algebra problems is mastering linear equations. A **linear equation** is an equation between two variables that gives a straight line when plotted on a graph. Whether an equation involves numbers or only variables, the basic steps are the same.

Four-Step Strategy

1. If there are fractions or decimals, remove them by multiplication.

2. Collect all terms containing the unknown for which you are solving on the same side of the equation. Remember that whenever a term crosses the equal sign from one side of the equation to the other, it must "pay a toll." That is, it must change its sign.

3. Determine the coefficient of the unknown (the number used to multiply a variable) by combining similar terms or factoring when terms cannot be combined.

4. Divide both sides of the equation by this coefficient.

TIP
If you have a string of multiplications and divisions and the number of negative factors is even, the result will be positive; if the number of negative factors is odd, the result will be negative.

Example 1:

Solve for x: $5x - 3 = 3x + 5$

Solution:

Collect all like terms on the same side and solve:

$$5x - 3 = 3x + 5$$
$$5x - 3x = 5 + 3$$
$$2x = 8$$
$$x = 4$$

Example 2:

Solve for x: $\dfrac{3}{4}x + 2 = \dfrac{2}{3}x + 3$

Solution:

Multiply both sides of the equation by 12. Then move the variables to the left side and the constants to the right side (remember to change the signs), and solve:

$$\frac{3}{4}x + 2 = \frac{2}{3}x + 3$$
$$9x + 24 = 8x + 36$$
$$9x - 8x = 36 - 24$$
$$x = 12$$

10

Example 3:

Solve for x: $0.7x + 0.04 = 2.49$

Solution:

Multiply both side of the equation by 100 to eliminate the decimals. Combine like terms on the same side and solve:

$$70x + 4 = 249$$
$$70x = 245$$
$$x = 3.5$$

An equation that is true for every value of the variable is called an **identity**. It has infinitely many solutions. An equation has **no solution** if no value for the variable will make the equation true.

Example 1:

Solve for x: $0.5(6x + 4) = 3x + 2$

Solution:

First, simplify each side of the equation. Then solve for x:

$$0.5(6x + 4) = 3x + 2$$
$$3x + 2 = 3x + 2$$
$$3x = 3x$$
$$x = x$$

Since $x = x$ is always true, the original equation has infinitely many solutions and is an *identity*.

Example 2:

Solve for x: $9x + 7 = x + 2(4x + 3)$

Solution:

First, simplify each side of the equation. Then solve for x:

$$9x + 7 = x + 2(4x + 3)$$
$$9x + 7 = x + 8x + 6$$
$$9x + 7 = 9x + 6$$
$$7 = 6$$

Since $7 \neq 6$, the original equation has *no solution*.

Example 3:

In the equation $ax + 7 = 2x + 3$, for which values of a will the equation have no solutions?

Solution:

If $a = 2$, the original equation becomes $2x + 7 = 2x + 3$. Since $2x + 7 \neq 2x + 3$ there are *no solutions* that make the equation true.

TIP

If you eliminate the variable in the process of solving the equation, then you will have either infinitely many solutions or no solution.

10

Real-World Linear Equations

A **literal equation** is an equation that involves two or more variables. You can solve for one variable in terms of the others using the properties of equalities. A **formula** is a literal equation that defines a relationship among quantities. For example, the perimeter of a rectangle can be found using the formula $P = 2l + 2w$, where P = perimeter, l = length, and w = width.

Example 1:

What is the width of a rectangle with perimeter 42 and length 8?

Solution:

Using the formula $P = 2l + 2w$, where P = perimeter, l = length, and w = width, solve for the variable w.

Substitute the values that you know into the formula.

$$P = 2l + 2w$$
$$42 = 2(8) + 2w$$
$$42 = 16 + 2w$$
$$42 - 16 = 2w$$
$$26 = 2w$$
$$\frac{26}{2} = w$$
$$13 = w$$

The width of the rectangle is 13 units.

Example 2:

The drama club sold student and adult tickets to its spring play. The adult tickets cost $15 each, and the student tickets cost $10 each. Tickets sales were $4,050. If 120 adult tickets were sold, how many student tickets were sold?

Solution:

Using the formula $R = 15a + 10s$, where R = revenue from ticket sales, a = adult tickets, and s = student tickets, solve for the variable s.

Substitute the values that you know into the formula.

$$R = 15a + 10s$$
$$4,050 = 15(120) + 10s$$
$$4,050 = 1,800 + 10s$$
$$4,050 - 1,800 = 10s$$
$$2,250 = 10s$$
$$\frac{2,250}{10} = s$$
$$225 = s$$

The drama club sold 225 student tickets.

PRACTICE EXERCISE: LINEAR EQUATIONS

DIRECTIONS: Work out each problem. Circle the letter of your choice. Check your answers against the key and explanations that follow.

1. If $5x + 6 = 10$, then x equals

   A. $\dfrac{16}{5}$

   B. $\dfrac{5}{16}$

   C. $-\dfrac{5}{4}$

   D. $\dfrac{4}{5}$

2. Solve for z: $3 - 2z = 9 + 4z$

   A. 3

   B. −1

   C. 0

   D. 6

3. Solve for y: $\dfrac{3}{4}y - 2 = \dfrac{1}{6}y$

   A. $\dfrac{7}{2}$

   B. $\dfrac{24}{7}$

   C. $\dfrac{2}{7}$

   D. $\dfrac{7}{24}$

4. If $7x = 3x + 12$, then $2x + 5 =$

   A. 10

   B. 11

   C. 12

   D. 13

5. Solve for w: $-8 + 4w = -2(3 - w)$

   A. −4

   B. 0

   C. 1

   D. 4

SHOW YOUR WORK HERE

6. Solve for x: $\dfrac{2x+9}{7} = \dfrac{3x+8}{2}$

A. No solution

B. Infinitely many solutions

C. $\dfrac{17}{38}$

D. $-\dfrac{38}{17}$

7. Solve for N: $0.2(1-5N) = 0.5(1-2N)$

A. 0

B. 0.3

C. No solution

D. Infinitely many solutions

8. The formula for the area of a triangle is $A = \dfrac{1}{2}bh$. Find the base of the triangle if the area is 28 in.^{2} and its height is 7 in.

A. 2 in.

B. 8 in.

C. 98 in.

D. 196 in.

9. Membership to Iron Gym costs $40 per month plus a $30 registration fee. The monthly cost is deducted automatically from your account. If your starting balance is $350, how many months will you be able to go to the gym before you have to add money to your account?

A. 6

B. 7

C. 8

D. 9

10. Lauren started a small wreath-making business. She earns $50 per wreath that she sells. She purchased $1,500 worth of materials when she started the business. How many wreaths must she sell to break even?

A. 15

B. 30

C. 45

D. 60

10

SHOW YOUR WORK HERE

Answer Key and Explanations

1. D	3. B	5. C	7. C	9. C
2. B	4. B	6. D	8. B	10. B

1. The correct answer is D.
$$5x + 6 = 10$$
$$5x = 4$$
$$x = \frac{4}{5}$$

2. The correct answer is B.
$$3 - 2z = 9 + 4z$$
$$3 = 9 + 6z$$
$$-6 = 6z$$
$$-1 = z$$

3. The correct answer is B. Start by clearing the fractions. Solve as follows:
$$\frac{3}{4}y - 2 = \frac{1}{6}y$$
$$12 \cdot \left(\frac{3}{4}y - 2\right) = 12 \cdot \left(\frac{1}{6}y\right)$$
$$\left(3 \cdot 3y\right) - \left(12 \cdot 2\right) = 2y$$
$$9y - 24 = 2y$$
$$9y - 2y = 24$$
$$7y = 24$$
$$y = \frac{24}{7}$$

4. The correct answer is B. Solve for x in the first equation.
$$7x = 3x + 12$$
$$4x = 12$$
$$x = 3$$

Then plug in the value for x into the second equation to solve.
$$2x + 5 = 2(3) + 5 = 11$$

5. The correct answer is C.
$$-8 + 4w = -2(3 - w)$$
$$-8 + 4w = -6 + 2w$$
$$-2 + 4w = 2w$$
$$-2 = -2w$$
$$1 = w$$

6. The correct answer is D.
$$\frac{2x + 9}{7} = \frac{3x + 8}{2}$$
$$2(2x + 9) = 7(3x + 8)$$
$$4x + 18 = 21x + 56$$
$$-17x = 38$$
$$x = -\frac{38}{17}$$

7. The correct answer is C.
$$0.2(1 - 5N) = 0.5(1 - 2N)$$
$$0.2 - 0.2(5N) = 0.5 - 0.5(2N)$$
$$0.2 - N = 0.5 - N$$
$$0.2 = 0.5$$

Since the final equation is false, the equation has no solution.

8. The correct answer is B. Solve the formula for b. Then substitute in the values of the variables.
$$A = \frac{1}{2}bh$$
$$\frac{2A}{h} = b$$
$$\frac{2(28)}{7} = b$$
$$8 = b$$

9. The correct answer is C.
$$40x + 30 = 350$$
$$40x = 320$$
$$x = 8$$

10. The correct answer is B. Let x be the number of wreaths Lauren needs to sell to break even. Then $50x = 1,500$. Divide both sides by 50 to get $x = 30$.

SIMULTANEOUS EQUATIONS

In solving equations with two unknowns, you must work with two equations simultaneously. The object is to eliminate one of the two unknowns and solve for the resulting single unknown.

Example 1:

Solve for x: $2x - 4y = 2$

$\qquad\qquad 3x + 5y = 14$

Solution:

Multiply the first equation by 5:

$$10x - 20y = 10$$

Multiply the second equation by 4:

$$12x + 20y = 56$$

Since the y-terms now have the same numerical coefficients, but with opposite signs, you can eliminate them by adding the two equations. If they had the same signs, you would eliminate them by subtracting the equations.

Add the equations:

$$\begin{array}{r} 10x - 20y = 10 \\ \underline{12x + 20y = 56} \\ 22x = 66 \\ x = 3 \end{array}$$

Since you were only asked to solve for x, stop here. If you were asked to solve for both x and y, you would now substitute 3 for x in either equation and solve the resulting equation for y. Let's solve the second equation:

$$3(3) + 5y = 14$$
$$9 + 5y = 14$$
$$5y = 14$$
$$y = 1$$

In Example 1, the system of equations has exactly one solution (3, 1). It is also possible for a system of equations to have no solution or infinitely many solutions. Let's take a look at a few examples that illustrate this.

Example 2:

Solve the system: $-12x + 8y = 2$

$\qquad\qquad\qquad 3x - 2y = 7$

Solution:

Multiply the second equation by 4, so that the x-terms and y-terms have the same numerical coefficients:

$$-12x + 8y = 2$$
$$12x - 8y = 28$$

10

Now add the equations:

$$-12x + 8y = 2$$
$$\underline{12x - 8y = 28}$$
$$0 = 30$$

Since $0 \neq 30$, there is no solution to the system.

Example 3:

Solve the system: $3x - 2y = -15$

$$x - \frac{2}{3}y = -5$$

Solution:

Multiply the second equation by 3, so that the x- and y-terms have the same numerical coefficients:

$$3 \cdot \left(x - \frac{2}{3}y\right) = -15 \cdot 3$$
$$3x - 2y = -15$$

Now subtract the equations:

$$3x - 2y = -15$$
$$\underline{3x - 2y = -15}$$
$$0 = 0$$

Since $0 = 0$ is an identity, there are infinitely many solutions to the system.

Example 4:

For which value of a will the system $3x - 4y = 12$ have infinitely many solutions?

$$ax - 3y = 9$$

Solution:

Consider solving each equation for y:

$$y = \frac{3}{4}x - 3$$

$$y = \frac{a}{3x - 3}$$

To have infinitely many solutions, $\frac{3}{4} = \frac{a}{3}$. So $a = \frac{9}{4}$.

Example 5:

Solve the system: $x^2 + y = 9$

$$x - y = -3$$

Solution:

Add the equations to eliminate the y-variable:

$$x^2 + y = 9$$
$$\underline{x - y = -3}$$
$$x^2 + x = 6$$

10

Set the equation equal to 0 and solve for x:

$$x^2 + x - 6 = 0$$

Factor to solve for x:

$$(x - 2)(x + 3) = 0$$
$$x = 2 \text{ or } x = -3$$

Find the corresponding y-values by substituting each value of x into the linear equation.

$$2 - y = -3$$
$$y = 5$$

$$-3 - y = -3$$
$$y = 0$$

There are 2 possible solutions for the system: (2, 5) and (–3, 0). Check each in both equations.

1st equation: $\left(x^2\right) + y = 9$ and $\left(x\right)^2 + y = 9$
$$\left(2\right)^2 + 5 = 9 \qquad \left(-3\right)^2 + 0 = 9$$
$$9 = 9 \qquad\qquad 9 = 9$$

2nd equation: $\left(x\right) - y = -3$ and $\left(x\right) - y = -3$
$$\left(2\right) - 5 = -3 \qquad \left(-3\right) - 0 = -3$$
$$-3 = -3 \qquad\qquad -3 = -3$$

The solutions to the system are (2, 5) and (–3, 0).

Applications of Systems

Systems of equations can be used to solve many real-life problems.

Example 1:

Computer Connect, Inc. makes and sells computer parts. The material for each part costs $3.00 and sells for $12.75 each. The company spends $1,200 on additional expenses each month. How many computer parts must the company sell each month in order to break even?

Solution:

The break-even point is when the income equals the expenses. The first equation $12.75x = y$ represents the income. The second equation $3x + 1,200 = y$ represents expenses.

$$y = 12.75x$$
$$y = 3.00x + 1,200$$

Subtract the second equation from the first.

$$y = 12.75x$$
$$\underline{y = 3.00x + 1,200}$$
$$0 = 9.75x - 1,200$$

Combine similar terms and solve:

$$-9.75x = -1,200$$

$$x = \frac{-1,200}{-9.75}$$

$$x \approx 123.08$$

To break even, the company would have to sell at least 124 computer parts.

Example 2:

Jordan and Alex are planning a vacation. They plan to spend some of the time in Naples, Florida, and the rest of time in Key West. They estimate that it will cost $250 per day in Naples and $325 per day in Key West. If they plan to vacation a total of 8 days and have a budget of $2,375. How many days should they spend in each city?

Solution:

To write the equations, let $x =$ the number of days in Naples and $y =$ the number of days in Key West. The first equation $x + y = 8$ represents the total number of days on vacation. The second equation, $250x + 325y = 2,375$, represents total cost.

The system of equations is:

$$x + y = 8$$
$$250x + 325y = 2,375$$

Solve the system by multiplying the first equation by 325 and then subtract the second equation from the first.

$$
\begin{array}{r}
325x + 325y = 2,600 \\
250x + 325y = 2,375 \\
\hline
75x = 225 \\
x = 3
\end{array}
$$

Since $x + y = 8$, if $x = 3$ then $y = 5$. The couple can spend 3 days in Naples and 5 days in Key West.

Solving Systems of Inequalities by Graphing

Systems of inequalities are solved using the same methods as systems of equations. Recall that you must reverse the sign of the inequality if you multiply or divide by a negative value.

You can graph a system of linear inequalities in the coordinate plane. The solution of the system is where the graphs of the inequalities overlap. Recall, that an inequality with a < or > sign, is graphed as a dashed line, while an inequality with a ≤ or ≥ is graphed with a solid line. A solid line shows that answers along the line are included in the solution set for that inequality.

Example 1:

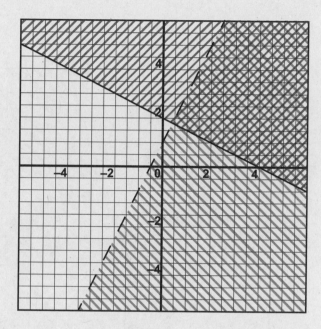

What system of inequalities is represented by the graph shown above?

Solution:

First write the inequality that represents the region bounded by the solid line, using two points along the line and the slope-intercept formula $y = mx + b$, replacing the equal sign with a comparison symbol.

$$y \geq -0.5x + 2$$

Then write the inequality that represents the region bounded by the dashed line.

$$y < 2x + 1$$

The graph shows the intersection of the system:

$$y \geq -0.5x + 2$$
$$y < 2x + 1$$

10

Chapter 10

Example 2:

Solve the system of inequalities by graphing: $x + 2y \leq 8$

$$3x - y \geq 3$$

Solution:

First solve each inequality for y to rewrite in slope-intercept form:

1st inequality: $x + 2y \leq 8$ 2nd inequality: $3x - y \geq 3$

$$2y \leq -x + 8 \qquad\qquad -y \geq -3x + 3$$

$$y \leq -\frac{1}{2}x + 4 \qquad\qquad y \leq 3x - 3$$

Then graph each inequality.

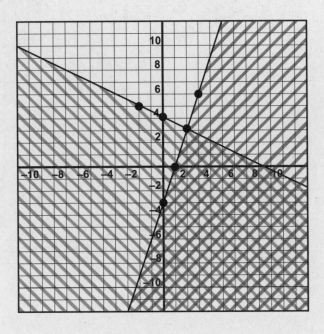

The solution is the region where the graphs overlap.

PRACTICE EXERCISE: SIMULTANEOUS EQUATIONS

DIRECTIONS: Work out each problem. Circle the letter of your choice. Check your answers against the answer key and explanations that follow.

1.
$$\begin{cases} x = 2y - 14 \\ y = 5x + 1 \end{cases}$$

What is the value of $x + y$ if the pair (x, y) satisfies the system above?

A. 3

B. 6

C. 9

D. 15

2.
$$\begin{cases} 3y + 2x = -4 \\ 2y - x = 16 \end{cases}$$

What is the value of y^2 if the pair (x, y) satisfies the system above?

A. 8

B. 16

C. 28

D. 49

3. Solve the system:
$$2y = x + 16$$
$$-\frac{1}{2}x + y = -2$$

A. No solution

B. Infinitely many solutions

C. 0

D. All positive values

4. Solve the system for y:
$$x - y^2 = 2$$
$$2x + 5y = 7$$

A. $y = 11, 2.25$

B. $y = 0.5, -3$

C. $y = 1.75, 17$

D. Infinitely many solutions

SHOW YOUR WORK HERE

5. Solve the system:

$$14y = -2x + 23$$
$$2(x + 7y) = 23$$

A. 0

B. All negative values

C. No solution

D. Infinitely many solutions

6.

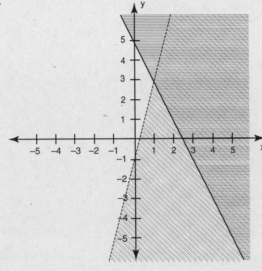

What system of inequalities is shown in the graph?

A. $y < 4x - 1$
   $2x + y \geq 5$

B. $y > 4x - 1$
   $-2x + y \geq 5$

C. $y > 4x + 1$
   $2x - y \geq 5$

D. $y \geq 4x - 1$
   $2x + y \geq -5$

7. Speedy Rent-A-Car charges $45 a day plus $0.60 per mile driven to rent a car. Zippy Rental charges $40 a day plus $0.70 per mile driven to rent a car. After how many miles would it cost the same amount to rent a car from either Speedy Rent-A-Car or Zippy Rental?

A. 25 miles

B. 50 miles

C. 75 miles

D. 100 miles

10

SHOW YOUR WORK HERE

8. Andi can work a total of no more than 35 hours per week at her two jobs. She earns $30 per hour giving music lessons and $45 per hour working as a life coach. She must earn at least $800 per week. Which system of inequalities can be used to determine the pairs of the number of hours spent at each job that would enable her to earn at least $800?

A. $\begin{cases} 35(x + y) \geq 800 \\ x + y \leq 35 \end{cases}$

B. $\begin{cases} x \leq 35 \\ y \geq 800 \end{cases}$

C. $\begin{cases} x + y \geq 35 \\ 35x + 45y \geq 800 \end{cases}$

D. $\begin{cases} x + y \leq 35 \\ 35x + 45y \geq 800 \end{cases}$

9.
$$\begin{cases} 3x + y = 1 \\ -3x + 4y = 9 \end{cases}$$

Determine the value of $\frac{y}{x}$ if the pair (x, y) satisfies the system above?

A. -6

B. $-\frac{2}{3}$

C. 2

D. $\frac{8}{3}$

10.
$$\begin{cases} y + \frac{3}{4}x = 1 \\ y = -\frac{3}{4}x - 1 \end{cases}$$

Find the solution of the system shown above.

A. $x = 0, y = -1$

B. $x = 0, y = 1$

C. Infinitely many solutions

D. No solution

10

SHOW YOUR WORK HERE

Answer Key and Explanations

1. C	3. A	5. D	7. B	9. A
2. B	4. B	6. A	8. D	10. D

1. The correct answer is C. Substitute the expression for y given by the second equation in for y in the first equation and solve the resulting for x:

$$x = 2(5x + 1) - 14$$
$$x = 10x + 2 - 14$$
$$x = 10x - 12$$
$$12 = 9x$$
$$\frac{4}{3} = x$$

Plug in this x-value into the second equation to determine the value of y:

$$y = 5\left(\frac{4}{3}\right) + 1 = \frac{23}{3}$$

Thus, $x + y = \frac{4}{3} + \frac{23}{3} = \frac{27}{3} = 9$

2. The correct answer is B. Multiply the second equation by 2:

$$2(2y - x) = 2(16)$$
$$4y - 2x = 32$$

Then add the result to the first equation to eliminate x:

$$3y + 2x = -4$$
$$\underline{4y - 2x = 32}$$
$$7y = 28$$
$$y = 4$$

Hence $4^2 = 16$.

3. The correct answer is A. Multiply the second equation by 2 and add to eliminate the variables.

$$2y = x + 16$$
$$\underline{-\frac{1}{2}x + y = -2}$$
$$-x + 2y = 16$$
$$\underline{x - 2y = 4}$$
$$0 = 20$$

Since $0 \neq 20$, there is no solution.

4. The correct answer is B. Eliminate the x-variable:

$$x - y^2 = 2$$
$$2x + 5y = 7$$
$$2x - 2y^2 = 4$$
$$\underline{2x + 5y = 7}$$
$$2y^2 + 5y = 3$$

Then solve for y:

$$2y^2 + 5y = 3$$
$$2y^2 + 5y - 3 = 0$$
$$(2y - 1)(y + 3) = 0$$
$$y = \frac{1}{2}, \; -3$$

5. The correct answer is D.

$$14y = -2x + 23$$
$$\underline{2(x + 7y) = 23}$$
$$2x + 14y = 23$$
$$\underline{2x + 14y = 23}$$
$$0 = 0$$

Since $0 = 0$ is always true, there are infinitely many solutions.

6. **The correct answer is A.** First write the inequality that represents the region bounded by the dashed line using two points and the slope intercept formula.

$$y < 4x - 1$$

Then write the inequality that represents the region bounded by the solid line.

$$y \geq -2x + 5$$

The graph shows the intersection of the system:

$$y < 4x - 1$$
$$2x + y \geq 5$$

7. **The correct answer is B.** The system of equations that represents the cost of renting a car from the places is:

$$y = 45 + 0.6x$$
$$y = 40 + 0.7x$$

Rewrite the equations so that you can eliminate the y variable.

$$-45 = 0.6x - y$$
$$40 = -0.7x + y$$

Add the second equation to the first to eliminate the y variable:

$$-45 = 0.6x - y$$
$$\underline{40 = -0.7x + y}$$
$$-5 = -0.1x$$

When simplified, $x = 50$. Therefore, 50 is the number of miles it would take for the cost (y) of both rental companies to be equal.

8. **The correct answer is D.** Let x be the number of hours spent giving music lessons and y the number of hours spent working as a life coach. Since the total number of hours worked in one week cannot exceed 35, we have the inequality $x + y \leq 35$. Next, the amount earned working x hours giving music lessons is $35x$ dollars, and the amount earned working y hours as a life coach is $45y$ dollars. The sum of these two amounts must be at least $800. This gives the inequality $35x + 45y \geq 800$. The desired system is given in choice D.

9. **The correct answer is A.** Add the two equations to eliminate x:

$$3x + y = 1$$
$$\underline{-3x + 4y = 9}$$
$$5y = 10$$
$$y = 2$$

Plug this into the first equation for y and solve for x:

$$3x + 2 = 1$$
$$3x = -1$$
$$x = -\frac{1}{3}$$

Thus $\dfrac{y}{x} = \dfrac{2}{-\dfrac{1}{3}} = 2(-3) = -6.$

10. **The correct answer is D.** Substitute the expression for y given by the second equation into y in the first equation to obtain the equation $\left(-\dfrac{3}{4}x - 1\right) + \dfrac{3}{4}x = 1$. This is equivalent to the false statement $-1 = 1$. This system has no solution.

EXPONENTS

An **exponent** is a mathematical notation indicating that a number, called the **base**, has been multiplied one or more times by itself. For example, in the term 2^3, the 2 is the base and the ^{3} is the exponent. This term means "two times two times two" and is read "two to the third power." The word *power* tells how many times the base number appears in the multiplication.

$$x^3 = x \text{ times } x \text{ times } x$$
$$x^2 = x \text{ times } x$$
$$x^1 = x$$
$$x^0 = 1$$

The Five Rules of Exponents

1. To multiply powers of the same base, add the exponents.

$$x^2 \text{ times } x^3 = x^{2+3} = x^5$$
$$x^5 \text{ times } x^4 = x^{5+4} = x^9$$

2. To divide powers of the same base, subtract the exponent of the divisor from the exponent of the dividend.

$$\frac{x^6}{x^2} = x^{6-2} = x^4$$

$$\frac{x^{10}}{x^3} = x^{10-3} = x^7$$

3. Negative powers represent reciprocals.

$$x^{-1} = \frac{1}{x}$$

$$\left(\frac{x^3}{y^5}\right)^{-2} = \left(\frac{y^5}{x^3}\right)^{2} = \frac{y^{10}}{x^6}$$

4. To find the power of a power, multiply the exponents.

$$\left(x^2\right)^3 = x^{(2)(3)} = x^6$$

$$\left(x^3 y^5\right)^2 = x^{(3)(2)} y^{(5)(2)} = x^6 y^{10}$$

- A variable base with an even exponent has two values, one positive and one negative.

  ○ $x^2 = 25$; x could be positive 5 or negative 5.

TIP

Commit to memory small powers of small numbers that come up in many questions. For example, the powers of 2: 2, 4, 8, 16, 32, . . . the powers of 3: 3, 9, 27, 81, . . . and so on.

10

- A variable base can be zero (unless otherwise stated in the problem). In that case, no matter what the exponent, the value of the term is zero.

  o Is x^4 always greater than x^2? No; if x is zero, then x^4 and x^2 are equal.

- When the base is a fraction between 0 and 1, the larger the exponent, the smaller the value of the term.

  o Which is greater, $\left(\dfrac{37}{73}\right)$ or $\left(\dfrac{37}{73}\right)^2$?

  The correct answer is $\left(\dfrac{37}{73}\right)$ because $\left(\dfrac{37}{73}\right)$ is almost $\dfrac{1}{2}$, while $\left(\dfrac{37}{73}\right)^2$ is about $\dfrac{1}{4}$.

5. Fractional exponents represent roots.

$$x^{\frac{1}{2}} = \sqrt{x}$$

$$x^{\frac{1}{3}} = \sqrt[3]{x}$$

$$x^{\frac{2}{5}} = \left(\sqrt[5]{x}\right)^2$$

$$= \sqrt[5]{x^2}$$

FUN FACTS

A **googol** is defined as 1 followed by a hundred zeros or 10^{100}. A **googolplex** is 10 to the power of a googol (10^{googol}), or 10 to the power of 10 to the power of 100 ($10^{10^{100}}$).

10

BRAIN BREAK

Blink your right eye while snapping the fingers on your left hand. Switch and blink your left eye while snapping the fingers on your right hand. Can't snap your fingers? No worries! Try opening and closing your left hand while blinking your right eye. Then switch. The object here is to simultaneously complete actions on the opposite sides of the body.

PRACTICE EXERCISE: EXPONENTS

DIRECTIONS: Work out each problem. Circle the letter of your choice. Check your answers against the answer key and explanations that follow.

1. $p^8 \times q^4 \times p^4 \times q^8 =$

   A. $p^{12}q^{12}$

   B. p^4q^4

   C. $p^{32}q^{32}$

   D. $p^{64}q^{64}$

2. $(x^2y^3)^4 =$

   A. x^6y^7

   B. x^8y^{12}

   C. $x^{12}y^8$

   D. x^2y

3. $\dfrac{x^{16}y^6}{x^4y^2} =$

   A. $x^{20}y^8$

   B. x^4y^3

   C. $x^{12}y^3$

   D. $x^{12}y^4$

4. Suppose $z^3 = -27$ and $y^2 = 16$. What is the minimum possible value for $y - z$?

   A. -7

   B. -1

   C. 1

   D. 7

5. $a^{-4} \times a^{-3} =$

   A. $\dfrac{1}{a^{12}}$

   B. $\dfrac{1}{a^7}$

   C. a^7

   D. a^{12}

SHOW YOUR WORK HERE

6. $x^{\frac{2}{3}}x^{\frac{1}{2}} =$

 A. $\sqrt[3]{x}$

 B. $\sqrt[5]{x^3}$

 C. $\left(\sqrt[6]{x}\right)^7$

 D. $\dfrac{1}{\sqrt[5]{x^2}}$

7. $\dfrac{w^{-5}}{w^{-10}} =$

 A. $\dfrac{1}{w^2}$

 B. w^5

 C. w^{15}

 D. w^2

8. $\left(x^{-3}y^2\right)^{-4} =$

 A. $\dfrac{1}{x^7 y^2}$

 B. $\dfrac{y^8}{x^{12}}$

 C. xy^6

 D. $\dfrac{x^{12}}{y^8}$

9. $\dfrac{x^{\frac{5}{6}}}{x^{\frac{2}{9}}} =$

 A. $x^{\frac{5}{27}}$

 B. $x^{\frac{11}{18}}$

 C. $\dfrac{1}{x^{\frac{11}{18}}}$

 D. $\dfrac{1}{x^{\frac{5}{27}}}$

10. $\left(\dfrac{w^2 y^{-3}}{w^{-4} y^{-5}}\right)^{-2} =$

 A. $w^6 y^2$

 B. $\dfrac{1}{w^6 y^2}$

 C. $\dfrac{1}{w^{12} y^4}$

 D. $w^{12} y^4$

SHOW YOUR WORK HERE

Answer Key and Explanations

1. A	3. D	5. B	7. B	9. B
2. B	4. B	6. C	8. D	10. C

1. **The correct answer is A.** The multiplication signs do not change the fact that this is the multiplication of terms with a common base and different exponents. Solve this kind of problem by adding the exponents.

$$p^8 \times q^4 \times p^4 \times q^8 = p^{8+4} \times q^{4+8}$$
$$= p^{12}q^{12}$$

2. **The correct answer is B.** To raise a power to a power, multiply the exponents.

$$x^{(2)(4)}y^{(3)(4)} = x^8 y^{12}$$

3. **The correct answer is D.** All fractions are implied division. When dividing terms with a common base and different exponents, subtract the exponents.

$$\frac{x^{16}y^6}{x^4 y^2} = x^{16-4}y^{6-2} = x^{12}y^4$$

4. **The correct answer is B.** First, $z = -3$ and y can be either -4 or 4. The possible values of $y - z$ are as follows:

$$-4 - (-3) = -4 + 3 = -1$$
$$4 - (-3) = 4 + 3 = 7$$

The smallest value is -1.

5. **The correct answer is B.** To multiply, add the exponents. The resulting exponent will be negative, which means you need to take the reciprocal.

$$a^{-4} \times a^{-3} = a^{-4 + (-3)}$$
$$= a^{-7}$$
$$= \frac{1}{a^7}$$

6. **The correct answer is C.** To multiply, add the exponents. Then, use the rules for rational exponents to convert to root form.

$$x^{\frac{2}{3}}x^{\frac{1}{2}} = x^{\frac{2}{3}+\frac{1}{2}}$$
$$= x^{\frac{7}{6}}$$
$$= \left(\sqrt[6]{x}\right)^7$$

7. **The correct answer is B.**

$$\frac{w^{-5}}{w^{-10}} = \frac{w^{10}}{w^5}$$
$$= w^{10-5}$$
$$= w^5$$

8. **The correct answer is D.**

$$\left(x^{-3}y^2\right)^{-4} = x^{(-3)(-4)}y^{2(-4)}$$
$$= x^{12}y^{-8}$$
$$= \frac{x^{12}}{y^8}$$

9. **The correct answer is B.**

$$\frac{x^{\frac{5}{6}}}{x^{\frac{2}{9}}} = x^{\frac{5}{6}-\frac{2}{9}}$$
$$= x^{\frac{15}{18}-\frac{4}{18}}$$
$$= x^{\frac{11}{18}}$$

10. **The correct answer is C.**

$$\left(\frac{w^2 y^{-3}}{w^{-4}y^{-5}}\right)^{-2} = \left(\frac{w^2 w^4 y^5}{y^3}\right)^{-2}$$
$$= \left(w^6 y^2\right)^{-2}$$
$$= \frac{1}{\left(w^6 y^2\right)^2}$$
$$= \frac{1}{w^{6 \cdot 2}y^{2 \cdot 2}}$$
$$= \frac{1}{w^{12}y^4}$$

10

QUADRATIC EQUATIONS

Roots and Factoring

In solving quadratic equations, remember that there will always be two roots, even though these roots may be equal. A **complete quadratic equation** is of the form $ax^2 + bx + c = 0$.

> ### Example 1:
> Factor: $x^2 + 7x + 12 = 0$
>
> $$(x + 3)(x + 4) = 0$$
>
> ### Solution:
> The last term of the equation is positive; therefore, both factors must have the same sign, since the last two terms multiply to a positive product. The middle term is also positive; therefore, both factors must be positive, since they also add to a positive sum.
>
> $$(x + 4)(x + 3) = 0$$
>
> If the product of two factors is 0, each factor may be set equal to 0, yielding the values for x of -4 or -3.
>
> ### Example 2:
> Factor: $x^2 + 7x - 18 = 0$
>
> $$(x + 9)(x - 2) = 0$$
>
> Now you are looking for two numbers with a product of -18; therefore, they must have opposite signs. To yield $+7$ as a middle coefficient, the numbers must be $+9$ and -2.
>
> $$(x + 9)(x - 2) = 0$$
>
> This equation gives the roots -9 and $+2$.

Incomplete quadratic equations are those in which b or c is equal to 0.

> ### Example 1:
> Solve for x: $x^2 - 16 = 0$
>
> ### Solution:
>
> $$x^2 = 16$$
> $$x = \pm 4$$
>
> (Remember, there must be two roots.)
>
> ### Example 2:
> Solve for x: $4x^2 - 9 = 0$

ALERT
Don't forget: In working with any equation, if you move a term from one side of the equal sign to the other, you must change its sign.

10

Solution:

$$4x^2 = 9$$

$$x^2 = \frac{9}{4}$$

$$x = \pm\frac{3}{2}$$

Example 3:

Solve for x: $x^2 + 4x = 0$

Solution:

Never divide through an equation by the unknown, as this would yield an equation of lower degree having fewer roots than the original equation. Always factor this type of equation.

$$x(x + 4) = 0$$

The roots are 0 and −4.

Example 4:

Solve for x: $4x^2 - 9x = 0$

Solution:

$$x(4x - 9) = 0$$

The roots are 0 and $\frac{9}{4}$.

The **quadratic formula** can also be used to find the solutions to quadratic equations $ax^2 + bx + c = 0$ where a, b, and c are real numbers and $a \neq 0$.

$$x = \frac{-b \pm \sqrt{b^2 - 4ac}}{2a}$$

Example:

Use the quadratic formula to solve for x: $2x^2 + 7x = 3$

Solution:

Write the equation in standard form: $2x^2 + 7x - 3 = 0$. Then, identify the values of a, b, and c and substitute them into the quadratic formula.

$$a = 2, b = 7, \text{ and } c = -3$$

$$x = \frac{-b \pm \sqrt{b^2 - 4ac}}{2a}$$

$$x = \frac{-7 \pm \sqrt{(7)^2 - 4(2)(-3)}}{2(2)}$$

$$x = \frac{-7 \pm \sqrt{73}}{4}$$

The solutions are: $x = \dfrac{-7 + \sqrt{73}}{4} \approx 0.386$ or $x = \dfrac{-7 - \sqrt{73}}{4} \approx -3.886$

PRACTICE EXERCISE: QUADRATIC EQUATIONS

DIRECTIONS: Work out each problem. Circle the letter of your choice. Check your answers against the answer key and explanations that follow.

1. Solve for x: $x^2 - 2x - 15 = 0$

   A. $+5$ or -3

   B. -5 or $+3$

   C. -5 or -3

   D. $+5$ or $+3$

2. Solve for x: $x^2 + 12 = 8x$

   A. $+6$ or -2

   B. -6 or $+2$

   C. -6 or -2

   D. $+6$ or $+2$

3. Solve for x: $4x^2 = 12$

   A. $\sqrt{3}$

   B. 3 or -3

   C. $\sqrt{3}$ or $-\sqrt{3}$

   D. $\sqrt{3}$ or $\sqrt{-3}$

4. Solve for x: $3x^2 = 4x$

   A. $\dfrac{4}{3}$

   B. $\dfrac{4}{3}$ or 0

   C. $-\dfrac{4}{3}$ or 0

   D. $\dfrac{4}{3}$ or $-\dfrac{4}{3}$

5. Solve for x: $2x^2 + 3x = 7$

   A. $x = \dfrac{3 + \sqrt{65}}{4}, x = \dfrac{3 - \sqrt{65}}{4}$

   B. $x = \dfrac{-3 + \sqrt{65}}{4}, x = \dfrac{-3 - \sqrt{65}}{4}$

   C. $x = \dfrac{3 + \sqrt{47}}{4}, x = \dfrac{3 - \sqrt{47}}{4}$

   D. $x = \dfrac{-3 + \sqrt{47}}{4}, x = \dfrac{-3 - \sqrt{47}}{4}$

10

SHOW YOUR WORK HERE

6. Solve for x: $3x^2 - 27 = 0$

   A. -3 or 3

   B. -27 or 27

   C. $-3\sqrt{3}$ or $3\sqrt{3}$

   D. $-\sqrt{3}$ or $\sqrt{3}$

7. Solve for x: $x(x - 9) = -20$

   A. -20 or -11

   B. 11 or 20

   C. 4 or 5

   D. -5 or -4

8. Solve for x: $\dfrac{1}{3}x^2 - \dfrac{7}{6}x = -1$

   A. $-\dfrac{2}{3}$ or $-\dfrac{1}{2}$

   B. $\dfrac{2}{3}$ or $\dfrac{1}{2}$

   C. $-\dfrac{3}{2}$ or -2

   D. $\dfrac{3}{2}$ or 2

9. Solve for x: $2x^2 + 3x - 1 = 0$

   A. $\dfrac{1}{2}$ or -1

   B. $\dfrac{-3 + \sqrt{17}}{4}$ or $\dfrac{-3 - \sqrt{17}}{4}$

   C. -5 or $\dfrac{7}{2}$

   D. $-\dfrac{3}{4} + \sqrt{17}$ or $-\dfrac{3}{4} - \sqrt{17}$

10. Solve for x: $4x^2 = 1$

    A. 4 or -4

    B. $\dfrac{1}{4}$ or $-\dfrac{1}{4}$

    C. $\dfrac{1}{2}$ or $-\dfrac{1}{2}$

    D. 2 or -2

10

SHOW YOUR WORK HERE

Answer Key and Explanations

1. A	3. C	5. B	7. C	9. B
2. D	4. B	6. A	8. D	10. C

1. **The correct answer is A.**

$$(x-5)(x+3) =$$
$$x = 5 \text{ or } -3$$

2. **The correct answer is D.**

$$x^2 - 8x + 12 = 0$$
$$(x-6)(x-2) = 0$$
$$x = 6 \text{ or } 2$$

3. **The correct answer is C.**

$$x^2 = 3$$
$$x = \sqrt{3} \text{ or } -\sqrt{3}$$

4. **The correct answer is B.**

$$3x^2 - 4x = 0$$
$$x(3x-4) = 0$$
$$x = 0 \text{ or } \frac{4}{3}$$

5. **The correct answer is B.** Write the equation in standard form:

$$2x^2 + 3x - 7 = 0$$
$$a = 2, b = 3, \text{ and } c = -7$$
$$x = \frac{-3 \pm \sqrt{(3)^2 - 4(2)(-7)}}{2(2)}$$

$$x = \frac{-3 \pm \sqrt{65}}{4}$$

The solutions are:

$$x = \frac{-3 + \sqrt{65}}{4} \text{ or } \frac{-3 - \sqrt{65}}{4}$$

6. **The correct answer is A.** Isolate the squared term and take the square root of both sides:

$$3x^2 - 27 = 0$$
$$3x^2 = 27$$
$$x^2 = 9$$
$$x = \pm 3$$

7. **The correct answer is C.** Bring all terms to the left side and factor:

$$x(x-9) = -20$$
$$x^2 - 9x + 20 = 0$$
$$(x-4)(x-5) = 0$$
$$x = 4, 5$$

8. **The correct answer is D.** Clear the fractions, bring all terms to the left side, and factor:

$$\frac{1}{3}x^2 - \frac{7}{6}x = -1$$
$$6\left(\frac{1}{3}x^2 - \frac{7}{6}x\right) = 6(-1)$$
$$2x^2 - 7x = -6$$
$$2x^2 - 7x + 6 = 0$$
$$(2x-3)(x-2) = 0$$
$$x = \frac{3}{2}, 2$$

9. **The correct answer is B.** Use the quadratic formula:

$$x = \frac{-3 \pm \sqrt{3^2 - 4(2)(-1)}}{2(2)} = \frac{-3 \pm \sqrt{17}}{4}$$

10. **The correct answer is C.** Divide both sides by 4 and then take the square root:

$$4x^2 = 1$$
$$x^2 = \frac{1}{4}$$
$$x = \pm\sqrt{\frac{1}{4}}$$
$$x = \pm\frac{1}{2}$$

10

LITERAL EQUATIONS

There are many equations that can be used to represent common problems, such as distance. The equation to find distance, given rate and time, is written as $d = rt$. An equation which is solved for one variable in particular, such as d in the distance formula, is called a **literal equation**. Here are some examples:

Example 1:
Solve for l in the equation $P = 2l + 2w$.

Solution:
Subtract $2w$ from both sides of the equation. This will eliminate it from the right side of the equation.

$$P - 2w = 2l$$

Divide both sides of the equation to solve for l.

$$\frac{P - 2w}{2} = l$$

$$\frac{P}{2} - w = l$$

Example 2:
Solve for c in the equation $E = mc^2$.

Solution:
Divide both sides by m. This will eliminate it from the right side of the equation.

$$\frac{E}{m} = c^2$$

Take the square root of both sides to solve for c.

$$\sqrt{\frac{E}{m}} = c$$

Example 3:
The volume of a cone can be found using the formula $V = \frac{1}{3}\pi r^2 h$. Solve for r.

Solution:
Divide both sides by h:

$$\frac{V}{h} = \frac{1}{3}\pi r^2$$

Divide both sides by pi:

$$\frac{V}{\pi h} = \frac{1}{3}r^2$$

Multiply both sides by 3:

$$3 \cdot \frac{V}{\pi h} = \frac{1}{3}r^2 \cdot 3$$

Take the square root of both sides:

$$\sqrt{3 \cdot \frac{V}{\pi h}} = r$$

FUN FACTS

Why do plants hate math? Because it gives them square roots.

PRACTICE EXERCISE: LITERAL EQUATIONS

DIRECTIONS: Work out each problem. Circle the letter of your choice. Check your answers against the answer key and explanations that follow.

1. Solve for x: $z = 5x - 25xy$

   A. $\dfrac{z}{-20y} = x$

   B. $\dfrac{z}{1 - 5y} = x$

   C. $\dfrac{z}{5 - 25y} = x$

   D. $\dfrac{z}{30y} = x$

2. A bakery orders vanilla beans at a cost of $12.45 for a package of 10. There is a shipping cost of $6 for all sizes of shipments. Which of the following shows the equation solved for p, the total number of packages purchased, where c is the total cost of the order?

   A. $p = 6c + 12.45$

   B. $p = 12.45c + 6$

   C. $p = \dfrac{c}{12.45} - 6$

   D. $p = \dfrac{c - 6}{12.45}$

3. The distance between two points is determined by the equation below, where x_1 and x_2 are the x-coordinates of two points, and y_1 and y_2 are the y-coordinates of the two points.

$$d = \sqrt{(x_2 - x_1)^2 + (y_2 - y_1)^2}$$

Which shows the equation solved for y_2?

   A. $y_2 = \sqrt{d^2 - (x_2 - x_1)^2} + y_1$

   B. $y_2 = \sqrt{d - (x_2 - x_1)} + y_1$

   C. $y_2 = \sqrt{d - (x_2 - x_1)} + y_1$

   D. $y_2 = \sqrt{d^2 - (x_2 - x_1)^2} + y_1$

10

SHOW YOUR WORK HERE

4. Solve for x_1: $y_2 - y_1 = m(x_1 - x_2)$

    A. $x_1 = \dfrac{y_2 - y_1}{m} - x_2$

    B. $x_1 = y_2 - y_1 + mx_2$

    C. $x_1 = \dfrac{y_2 - y_1 + mx_2}{m}$

    D. $x_1 = \dfrac{y_2 - y_1 + x_2}{m}$

5. The formula for converting degrees Fahrenheit to degrees Celsius is shown below.

$$C = \frac{5}{9}(F - 32)$$

    Which equation shows the formula correctly solved for F?

    A. $\dfrac{9}{5}(C + 32) = F$

    B. $\dfrac{C}{\frac{9}{5}} - 32 = F$

    C. $\dfrac{9}{5}C - 32 = F$

    D. $\dfrac{9}{5}C + 32 = F$

6. Solve for f: $\dfrac{1}{f} = \dfrac{1}{a} + \dfrac{1}{b}$

    A. $f = a + b$

    B. $f = \dfrac{ab}{a + b}$

    C. $f = ab$

    D. $f = \dfrac{ba}{b - a}$

7. Solve for A: $C = \dfrac{3B}{A}$

    A. $A = \dfrac{3B}{C}$

    B. $A = 3BC$

    C. $A = 3B - C$

    D. $A = \dfrac{C}{3B}$

8. Solve for A: $C = \dfrac{BA}{B - A}$

    A. $A = CB + (B + 1)$

    B. $A = CB - (B + C)$

    C. $A = \dfrac{CB}{B + C}$

    D. $A = \dfrac{CB}{B + 1}$

10

SHOW YOUR WORK HERE

9. Solve for b_1: $A = \frac{1}{2}h(b_1 + b_2)$

   A. $b_1 = \frac{A}{2} \cdot h - b_2$

   B. $b_1 = \frac{2A - b_2}{h}$

   C. $b_1 = \frac{2A + b_2}{h}$

   D. $b_1 = \frac{2A - hb_2}{h}$

10. Solve for t_2: $B = \dfrac{A}{M(t_1 - t_2)}$

   A. $t_2 = \frac{BMt_1}{A} - B$

   B. $t_2 = A - BMt_1$

   C. $t_2 = \frac{BMt_1 - A}{BM}$

   D. $t_2 = \frac{BMt_1 + A}{B}$

10

SHOW YOUR WORK HERE

Answer Key and Explanations

1. C	3. A	5. D	7. A	9. D
2. D	4. C	6. B	8. C	10. C

1. **The correct answer is C.** Factor out an x from both terms on the right side of the equation:

$$z = x(5 - 25y)$$

Divide both sides by $5 - 25y$:

$$\frac{z}{5 - 25y} = x$$

2. **The correct answer is D.** The total cost, c, is determined by the equation $12.45p + 6 = c$. To solve for p, subtract 6 from both sides. Divide both sides by 12.45 to isolate p.

$$12.45p + 6 = c$$
$$12.45p = c - 6$$
$$p = \frac{c - 6}{12.45}$$

3. **The correct answer is A.** Solve for y_2 by squaring both sides to remove the square root from the right side.

$$d = \sqrt{\left(x_2 - x_1\right)^2 + \left(y_2 - y_1\right)^2}$$
$$d^2 = \left(x_2 - x_1\right)^2 + \left(y_2 - y_1\right)^2$$

Subtract the term $(x_2 - x_1)^2$ from both sides.

$$d^2 - (x_2 - x_1)^2 = (y_2 - y_1)^2$$

Take the square root of both sides to eliminate the exponent on the right side.

$$\sqrt{d^2 - \left(x_2 - x_1\right)^2} = y_2 - y_1$$

Add y_1 to both sides of the equation.

$$\sqrt{d^2 - \left(x_2 - x_1\right)^2} + y_1 = y_2$$

4. **The correct answer is C.**

$$y_2 - y_1 = m\left(x_1 - x_2\right)$$
$$y_2 - y_1 = mx_1 - mx_2$$
$$y_2 - y_1 + mx_2 = mx_1$$
$$x_1 = \frac{y_2 - y_1 + mx_2}{m}$$

5. **The correct answer is D.** To solve for F, divide both sides by $\frac{5}{9}$ or multiply both sides by $\frac{9}{5}$.

$$\frac{9}{5}C = F - 32$$

Add 32 to both sides to isolate F.

$$\frac{9}{5}C + 32 = F$$

6. **The correct answer is B.** To solve for f, first multiply both sides of the equation by f to move it into the numerator.

$$1 = \frac{f}{a} + \frac{f}{b}$$

Multiply by b and then by a to write the fractions with a common denominator, ab.

$$1 = \frac{fb}{ab} + \frac{fa}{ab}$$

Add the fractions.

$$1 = \frac{fb + fa}{ab}$$

Multiply both sides of the equation by ab.

$$ab = fb + fa$$

Factor f out of the terms on the right side of the equation.

$$ab = f(b + a)$$

Divide both sides of the equation by $(b + a)$.

$$\frac{ab}{a + b} = f$$

10

7. **The correct answer is A.**

$$C = \frac{3B}{A}$$
$$AC = 3B$$
$$A = \frac{3B}{C}$$

8. **The correct answer is C.**

$$C = \frac{BA}{B - A}$$
$$C(B - A) = BA$$
$$CB - CA = BA$$
$$CB = BA + CA$$
$$CB = A(B + C)$$
$$\frac{CB}{B + C} = A$$

9. **The correct answer is D.**

$$A = \frac{1}{2}h(b_1 + b_2)$$
$$2A = h(b_1 + b_2)$$
$$2A = hb_1 + hb_2$$
$$2A - hb_2 = hb_1$$
$$\frac{2A - hb_2}{h} = b_1$$

10. **The correct answer is C.**

$$B = \frac{A}{M(t_1 - t_2)}$$
$$BM(t_1 - t_2) = A$$
$$BMt_1 - BMt_2 = A$$
$$BMt_1 - A = BMt_2$$
$$t_2 = \frac{BMt_1 - A}{BM}$$

BRAIN BREAK

Take a break to loosen your muscles. Hold each of the following stretches for 5–10 seconds:

- Reach for the sky.
- Touch your toes.
- Reach for the sky again, placing your hands in a wide V. Arch back.
- With your arms by your sides, tuck your chin to your chest. Slowly role your neck clockwise, then counterclockwise.
- Stand on your left foot and bring your right knee to your chest. Repeat for the left knee.
- Do a right and left quad stretch. Use a wall for balance if you need to.

Still feel tight? Close your eyes and pinpoint where you are holding most of your tension. Focus on stretching this area. Remember, stretching is a SLOW movement. If you feel any pain or discomfort, stop. The object here is to loosen your muscles, not injure yourself.

ROOTS AND RADICALS

Adding and Subtracting

Rules for adding and subtracting radicals are much the same as for adding and subtracting variables. Radicals must be exactly the same if they are to be added or subtracted, and they merely serve as a label that does not change.

$$4\sqrt{2} + 3\sqrt{2} = 7\sqrt{2}$$
$$\sqrt{2} + 2\sqrt{2} = 3\sqrt{2}$$
$$\sqrt{2} + \sqrt{3} \text{ cannot be added}$$

Sometimes, when radicals are not the same, simplification of one or more radicals will make them the same. Remember that radicals are simplified by factoring out any perfect square factors.

$$\sqrt{27} + \sqrt{75} = \sqrt{9 \cdot 3} + \sqrt{25 \cdot 3}$$
$$= 3\sqrt{3} + 5\sqrt{3}$$
$$= 8\sqrt{3}$$

Multiplying and Dividing

In multiplying and dividing, treat radicals in the same way as you treat variables. They are factors and must be handled as such.

$$\sqrt{2} \cdot \sqrt{3} = \sqrt{6}$$
$$2\sqrt{5} \cdot 3\sqrt{7} = 6\sqrt{35}$$
$$\left(2\sqrt{3}\right)^2 = 2\sqrt{3} \cdot 2\sqrt{3} = 4 \cdot 3 = 12$$
$$\frac{\sqrt{75}}{\sqrt{3}} = \sqrt{25} = 5$$
$$\frac{10\sqrt{3}}{5\sqrt{3}} = 2$$

Simplifying

To simplify radicals that contain a sum or difference under the radical sign, add or subtract first, then take the square root.

$$\sqrt{\frac{x^2}{9} + \frac{x^2}{16}} = \sqrt{\frac{16x^2 + 9x^2}{144}} = \sqrt{\frac{25x^2}{144}} = \frac{5|x|}{12}$$

If you take the square root of each term before combining, you would have $\frac{x}{3} + \frac{x}{4}$, or $\frac{7x}{12}$, which is clearly not the same answer. Remember that $\sqrt{25}$ is 5. However, if you write that $\sqrt{25}$ as $\sqrt{16 + 9}$, you cannot say it is 4 + 3, or 7. *Always* combine the quantities within a radical sign into a single term before taking the square root.

Radicals

In solving equations containing radicals, always get the radical alone on one side of the equation; then square both sides to remove the radical and solve. Remember that all solutions to radical equations must be checked, as squaring both sides may sometimes result in extraneous roots.

Example 1:

Solve for x: $\sqrt{x + 5} = 7$

Solution:

$$x + 5 = 49$$
$$x = 44$$

Checking, we have $\sqrt{49} = 7$, which is true.

Example 2:

Solve for x: $\sqrt{x} = -6$

Solution:

You may have written the answer: $x = 36$. Checking, we have $\sqrt{36} = 6$, which is not true, as the radical sign means the positive, or principal, square root only. This equation has no solution because $\sqrt{36} = 6$, not -6.

10

Example 3:

Solve for x: $\sqrt{x^2 + 6} - 3 = x$

Solution:

$$\sqrt{x^2 + 6} - 3 = x$$
$$\sqrt{x^2 + 6} = x + 3$$
$$x^2 + 6 = x^2 + 6x + 9$$
$$6 = 6x + 9$$
$$-3 = 6x$$
$$-\frac{1}{2} = x$$

Checking, we have:

$$\sqrt{6\frac{1}{4}} - 3 = -\frac{1}{2}$$

$$\sqrt{\frac{25}{4}} - 3 = -\frac{1}{2}$$

$$\frac{5}{2} - 3 = -\frac{1}{2}$$

$$2\frac{1}{2} - 3 = -\frac{1}{2}$$

$$-\frac{1}{2} = -\frac{1}{2}$$

This is a true statement. Therefore, $\frac{1}{2}$ is a true root.

Roots as Fractional Powers

Roots can also be written as fractional exponents to make them easier for you to work with. For example, the square root of 4 can be written as $\sqrt{4}$ or as $4^{\frac{1}{2}}$. The value of a square root includes both the positive and negative root, so $\sqrt{4} = \pm 2$ and $4^{\frac{1}{2}} = \pm 2$.

To write an nth root as a fractional exponent, use the root as the denominator of the fraction under 1 or $\sqrt[n]{x} = x^{\frac{1}{n}}$.

Use the laws of exponents to solve radical expressions and equations.

Example:

Simplify: $\sqrt{3x} \cdot \sqrt{3x}$

Solution:

$$\sqrt{3x} \cdot \sqrt{3x} = (3x)^{\frac{1}{2}} \cdot (3x)^{\frac{1}{2}}$$
$$= (3x)^{\frac{1}{2} + \frac{1}{2}}$$
$$= 3x$$

PRACTICE EXERCISE: ROOTS AND RADICALS

DIRECTIONS: Work out each problem. Circle the letter of your choice. Check your answers against the answer key and explanations that follow.

1. What is the sum of $\sqrt{12} + \sqrt{27}$?

   A. $\sqrt{29}$

   B. $3\sqrt{5}$

   C. $13\sqrt{3}$

   D. $5\sqrt{3}$

2. Compute: $\sqrt{48} - \sqrt{27}$

   A. $\sqrt{3}$

   B. $5\sqrt{3}$

   C. $\sqrt{21}$

   D. $7\sqrt{3}$

3. What is the product of $\sqrt{18x}$ and $\sqrt{2x}$, where x is greater than 0?

   A. $6x^2$

   B. $6x$

   C. $36x^2$

   D. $6\sqrt{x}$

SHOW YOUR WORK HERE

4. Solve for x: $\dfrac{\sqrt{2}}{x - \sqrt{2}} = \sqrt{6}$

   A. $\dfrac{2}{\sqrt{3}}$

   B. $\sqrt{2}$

   C. $\dfrac{1 - \sqrt{6}}{\sqrt{2}}$

   D. $\dfrac{1 + \sqrt{6}}{\sqrt{3}}$

5. Solve for x: $\sqrt{1 - 3x} = 4$

   A. 12

   B. 16

   C. -5

   D. $\dfrac{7}{2}$

6. Solve for x: $8\sqrt{x} + 7 = 3\sqrt{x} + 17$

   A. -2

   B. $\sqrt{2}$

   C. 2

   D. 4

10

7. To which of these expressions is $\sqrt[3]{81x^6y^5}$ equal?

A. $9x^3y^2\sqrt[3]{y}$

B. $3\sqrt[3]{3}\,x^3y^2$

C. $9x^2y\sqrt[3]{3y}$

D. $3x^2y\sqrt[3]{3y^2}$

8. Divide $6\sqrt{45}$ by $3\sqrt{5}$.

A. 6

B. 9

C. 15

D. 30

9. $\sqrt{\dfrac{y^2}{25}+\dfrac{y^2}{16}} =$

A. $\dfrac{2y}{9}$

B. $\dfrac{9y}{20}$

C. $\dfrac{y}{9}$

D. $\dfrac{|y|\sqrt{41}}{20}$

10. $\dfrac{\sqrt{16}-\sqrt[4]{16}}{\sqrt[3]{16}}$

To which of these expressions is the above equal to?

A. 0

B. $\dfrac{1}{\sqrt[3]{2}}$

C. 1

D. $\sqrt[3]{2}$

10

SHOW YOUR WORK HERE

Answer Key and Explanations

1. D	3. B	5. C	7. D	9. D
2. A	4. D	6. D	8. A	10. B

1. **The correct answer is D.**

$$\sqrt{12} = \sqrt{4}\sqrt{3} = 2\sqrt{3}$$
$$\sqrt{27} = \sqrt{9}\sqrt{3} = 3\sqrt{3}$$
$$2\sqrt{3} + 3\sqrt{3} = 5\sqrt{3}$$

2. **The correct answer is A.** Simplify each radical term and then combine:

$$\sqrt{48} - \sqrt{27} = \sqrt{16 \cdot 3} - \sqrt{9 \cdot 3}$$
$$= \sqrt{16}\sqrt{3} - \sqrt{9}\sqrt{3}$$
$$= 4\sqrt{3} - 3\sqrt{3}$$
$$= \sqrt{3}$$

3. **The correct answer is B.**

$$\sqrt{18x} \cdot \sqrt{2x} = \sqrt{36x^2} = 6x$$

4. **The correct answer is D.** Cross-multiply and then solve the resulting linear equation:

$$\frac{\sqrt{2}}{x - \sqrt{2}} = \sqrt{6}$$
$$\sqrt{2} = \sqrt{6}\left(x - \sqrt{2}\right)$$
$$\sqrt{2} = \sqrt{6}\,x - \sqrt{2} \cdot \sqrt{6}$$
$$\sqrt{2} + \sqrt{2} \cdot \sqrt{6} = \sqrt{6}\,x$$
$$\sqrt{2}\left(1 + \sqrt{6}\right) = \sqrt{6}\,x$$
$$x = \frac{\sqrt{2}\left(1 + \sqrt{6}\right)}{\sqrt{6}}$$
$$x = \frac{\cancel{\sqrt{2}}\left(1 + \sqrt{6}\right)}{\cancel{\sqrt{2}}\sqrt{3}}$$
$$x = \frac{1 + \sqrt{6}}{\sqrt{3}}$$

5. **The correct answer is C.** Square both sides and then solve the resulting linear equation:

$$\sqrt{1 - 3x} = 4$$
$$1 - 3x = 16$$
$$1 - 16 = 3x$$
$$-15 = 3x$$
$$x = -5$$

6. **The correct answer is D.** Subtract 7 from each side of the equation:

$$8\sqrt{x} + 7 = 3\sqrt{x} + 17$$
$$8\sqrt{x} = 3\sqrt{x} + 10$$

Subtract $3\sqrt{x}$ from each side:

$$5\sqrt{x} = 10$$

Divide each side by 5:

$$\sqrt{x} = 2$$
$$x = 4$$

7. **The correct answer is D.** Take out expressions that are cubes from the radicand:

$$\sqrt[3]{81x^6y^5} = \sqrt[3]{3^3 \cdot 3 \cdot \left(x^2\right)^3 \cdot y^3 \cdot y^2}$$
$$= 3x^2y\sqrt[3]{3y^2}$$

8. **The correct answer is A.**

$$\frac{6\sqrt{45}}{3\sqrt{5}} = 2\sqrt{9} = 2 \cdot 3 = 6$$

10

9. **The correct answer is D.**

$$\sqrt{\frac{y^2}{25} + \frac{y^2}{16}} = \frac{\sqrt{16y^2 + 25y^2}}{400}$$

$$= \frac{\sqrt{41y^2}}{400}$$

$$= \frac{|y|\sqrt{41}}{20}$$

10. **The correct answer is B.** Simplify each radical first. Then combine like terms:

$$\frac{\sqrt{16} - \sqrt[4]{16}}{\sqrt[3]{16}} = \frac{\sqrt{4^2} - \sqrt[4]{2^4}}{\sqrt[3]{2^3 \cdot 2}}$$

$$= \frac{4 - 2}{2\sqrt[3]{2}}$$

$$= \frac{\cancel{2}}{\cancel{2}\sqrt[3]{2}}$$

$$= \frac{1}{\sqrt[3]{2}}$$

MONOMIALS AND POLYNOMIALS

When we add a collection of expressions together, each expression is called a **term**. **Monomial** means "one term". For example, we might say that $2x + 3y^2 + 7$ is the sum of three terms, or three monomials. When we talk about a monomial, we generally mean a term that is just the product of constants and variables, possibly raised to various powers. Examples might be 7, $2x$, $-3y^2$, and $4x^2z^5$. The constant factor is called the **coefficient** of the variable factor. Thus, in $-3y^2$, -3 is the coefficient of y^2.

If we restrict our attention to monomials of the form Ax^n, the sums of such terms are called **polynomials** (in one variable). Expressions like $3x + 5$, $2x^2 - 5x + 8$, and $x^4 - 7x^5 - 11$ are all examples of polynomials. The highest power of the variable that appears is called the **degree** of the polynomial. The three examples just given are of degree 1, 2, and 5, respectively.

In evaluating monomials and polynomials for negative values of the variable, the greatest pitfall is keeping track of the minus signs. Always remember that in an expression like $-x^2$, the power 2 is applied to the x, and the minus sign in front should be thought of as (-1) times the expression. If you want to have the power apply to $-x$, you must write $(-x)^2$.

Combining Monomials

Monomials with identical variable factors can be added together by adding their coefficients. So $3x^2 + 4x^2 = 7x^2$. Of course, subtraction is handled the same way, thus:

$$3x^4 - 9x^4 = -6x^4$$

Monomials are multiplied by taking the product of their coefficients and taking the product of the variable part by adding exponents of factors with like bases. So $(3xy^2)(2xy^3) = 6x^2y^5$.

Monomial fractions can be simplified to simplest form by dividing out common factors of the coefficients and then using the usual rules for subtraction of exponents in division. An example might be:

$$\frac{6x^3y^5}{2x^4y^3} = \frac{3y^2}{x}$$

Example:

Combine into a single monomial: $\dfrac{8x^3}{4x^2} - 6x$

Solution:

The fraction simplifies to $2x$, and $2x - 6x = -4x$.

Combining Polynomials and Monomials

Polynomials are added or subtracted by just combining like monomial terms in the appropriate manner. For example:

$$(3x^2 - 3x - 4) + (2x^2 + 5x - 11)$$

Can be summed by removing the parentheses and combining like terms, to yield:

$$5x^2 + 2x - 15$$

In subtraction, when you remove the parentheses with a minus sign in front, be careful to change the signs of all the terms within the parentheses. So:

$$\left(3x^2 - 3x - 4\right) - \left(2x^2 + 5x - 11\right) = 3x^2 - 3x - 4 - 2x^2 - 5x + 11$$
$$= x^2 - 8x + 7$$

(Did you notice that $3x^2 - 2x^2 = 1x^2$, but the "1" is not shown?)

To multiply a polynomial by a monomial, use the distributive property to multiply each term in the polynomial by the monomial factor. For example:

$$2x(2x^2 + 5x - 11) = 4x^3 + 10x^2 - 22x$$

When multiplying a polynomial by a polynomial, you are actually repeatedly applying the distributive property to form all possible products of the terms in the first polynomial with the terms in the second polynomial. The most common use of this is in multiplying two **binomials** (polynomials with two terms), such as $(x + 3)(x - 5)$. In this case, there are four terms in the result:

$$x \cdot x = x^2$$
$$x\left(-5\right) = -5x$$
$$3 \cdot x = 3x$$
$$3 \cdot \left(-5\right) = -15$$

However, the two middle terms are added together to give $-2x$. Thus, the product is $x^2 - 2x - 15$.

This process is usually remembered as the **FOIL method**. That is, form the products of **First, Outer, Inner, Last**, as shown in the following figure.

$$(x + 3)(x - 5) = x^2 + (-5x + 3x) - 15$$

Example:

If d is an integer, and $(x + 2)(x + d) = x^2 - kx - 10$, what is the value of $k + d$?

Solution:

The product of the two last terms, $2d$, must be -10. Therefore, $d = -5$.

If $d = -5$, then the sum of the outer and inner products becomes $-5x + 2x = -3x$, which equals $-kx$.

Hence, $k = 3$, and $k + d = 3 + (-5) = -2$.

Factoring Monomials

Factoring a monomial simply involves reversing the distributive property. For example, if you are looking at $4x^2 + 12xy$, you should see that $4x$ is a factor of both terms. Hence, you could just as well write this as $4x(x + 3y)$. Multiplication using the distributive property will restore the original formulation.

Example:

If $3x - 4y = -2$, what is the value of $9x - 12y$?

Solution:

Although you seem to have one equation in two unknowns, you can still solve the problem, because you do not need to know the values of the individual variables. Just rewrite:

$$9x - 12y = 3(3x - 4y)$$

Since $3x - 4y = -2$, $9x - 12y$ is 3 times -2, or -6.

PRACTICE EXERCISE: MONOMIALS AND POLYNOMIALS

DIRECTIONS: Work out each problem. Circle the letter of your choice. Check your answers against the answer key and explanations that follow.

1. $6x^3 \left(x^2 \right)^3 =$

   A. $6x^7$

   B. $6x^8$

   C. $6x^9$

   D. $6x^{10}$

2. $(-4a^3bc^3)^3 =$

   A. $-12a^{27}b\,c^9$

   B. $64a^6b^4c^6$

   C. $-64a^9b^3c^9$

   D. $-12a^6b^4c^6$

3. $\left(-2z^3 \right)^2 \cdot \left(-3z^2 \right)^3 =$

   A. $108\,z^{17}$

   B. $-108\,z^{12}$

   C. $36\,z^{12}$

   D. $36\,z^{10}$

4. Simplify: $\dfrac{3x^3y - 9x^2}{xy^2}$

   A. $\dfrac{-6xy}{xy^2}$

   B. $\dfrac{3x\left(xy - 3 \right)}{y^2}$

   C. $\dfrac{3x^2 - 9x}{y}$

   D. $3x^2 - 9x$

5. $(a^3 + 4a^2 - 11a + 4) - (8a^2 + 2a + 4) =$

   A. $-3a^2 - 13a$

   B. $a^3 - 12a^2 - 13a - 8$

   C. $a^3 - 4a^2 - 9a + 8$

   D. $a^3 - 4a^2 - 13a$

SHOW YOUR WORK HERE

10

6. $\left(4x^3 - 2x + 5\right) + \left(8x^2 - 2x - 10\right) =$

   A. $4x^3 + 8x^2 - 4x - 5$

   B. $12x^2 - 4x - 5$

   C. $12x^3 - 5$

   D. $4x^3 + 8x^2 + 15$

7. Multiply: $\left(2 - 3x^2\right)\left(4x - 1\right)$

   A. $-12x^3 + 3x^2 + 8x - 2$

   B. $-12x^3 + 2$

   C. $12x^3 + 3x^2 - 2$

   D. $2x + 3x^2$

8. Multiply: $(x^2 - 1)(2x^3 + 5)$

   A. $2x^5 + 5x^2$

   B. $-2x^3 - 5$

   C. $2x^5 - 2x^3 + 5x^2 - 5$

   D. $2x^6 - 5x^2 - 2x^3 - 5$

9. $\left(\dfrac{9xy^3z^2}{33x^2yz^5}\right)^2 =$

   A. $\dfrac{9y^4}{121x^2z^6}$

   B. $\dfrac{3xz^3}{y^2}$

   C. $\dfrac{3y^4}{11x^3z^5}$

   D. $\dfrac{9y^2}{121xz^3}$

10. $6x(2 - 3x) - x(2x + 1) =$

   A. $16x^2 + 12x$

   B. $-20x^2 + 11x$

   C. $-6x^2 + 3x$

   D. $-2x^2 + 9x + 1$

SHOW YOUR WORK HERE

Answer Key and Explanations

1. C	3. B	5. D	7. A	9. A
2. C	4. B	6. A	8. C	10. B

1. **The correct answer is C.**

$$6x^3\left(x^2\right)^3 = \left(6 \bullet x^3\right) \bullet \left(x^2\right)^3$$
$$= 6 \bullet x^3 \bullet x^{(2 \bullet 3)}$$
$$= 6 \bullet x^3 \bullet x^6$$
$$= 6 \bullet x^9$$
$$= 6x^9$$

2. **The correct answer is C.** Apply the exponent rules, as follows:

$$\left(-4a^3bc^3\right)^3 = (-4)^3 a^9 b^3 c^9 = -64a^9 b^3 c^9$$

3. **The correct answer is B.** Apply the exponent rules, as follows:

$$\left(-2z^3\right)^2 \bullet \left(-3z^2\right)^3 = (-2)^2 z^6 \bullet (-3)^3 z^6$$
$$= 4z^6 \bullet (-27)z^6$$
$$= -108z^{12}$$

4. **4. The correct answer is B.** The variable x can be factored out of the all the terms in the numerator and denominator of the fraction:

$$\frac{3x^3y - 9x^2}{xy^2} = \frac{3x^2y - 9x^1}{(1)y^2}$$
$$= \frac{3x^2y - 9x}{y^2}$$

Factor the term $3x$ out of the expression in the numerator:

$$3x(xy - 3)$$

Because y appears in only one of the terms in the numerator, it cannot be factored out of either the numerator or the denominator. Therefore, $\dfrac{3x^3y - 9x^2}{xy^2}$ simplifies as $\dfrac{3x(xy - 3)}{y^2}$.

5. **The correct answer is D.** The term a^3 will remain because there are no other like terms to subtract. Subtract the squared terms: $4a^2 - 8a^2 = -4a^2$; the single variable terms $-11a - 2a = -13a$; and the integer terms $-4 - 4 = 0$. Combining these terms with a^3 gives us $a^3 - 4a^2 - 13a$.

6. **The correct answer is A.** The only like terms that may be combined are

$$(-2x) + (-2x) = -4x \text{ and}$$
$$+5 + (-10) = 5 - 10 = -5$$

Combine all the terms to get:

$$4x^3 + 8x^2 - 4x - 5$$

7. **The correct answer is A.** FOIL the binomials, as follows:

$$\left(2 - 3x^2\right)\left(4x - 1\right)$$
$$= 2(4x) - 2(1) - \left(3x^2\right)(4x) + \left(3x^2\right)(1)$$
$$= -12x^3 + 3x^2 + 8x - 2$$

8. **The correct answer is C.** Use the FOIL method to multiply:

First: $(x^2)(2x^3) = 2x^5$

Outer: $(x^2)(5) = 5x^2$

Inner: $(-1)(2x^3) = -2x^3$

Last: $(-1)(5) = -5$

Combine the terms to get $2x^5 - 2x^3 + 5x^2 - 5$.

9. **The correct answer is A.** Apply the exponent rules, as follows:

$$\left(\frac{9xy^3z^2}{33x^2yz^5}\right)^2 = \left(\frac{3y^2}{11xz^3}\right)^2 = \frac{9y^4}{121x^2z^6}$$

10. **The correct answer is B.** Use the distributive property and combine like terms:

$$6x(2 - 3x) - x(2x + 1) = 12x - 18x^2 - 2x^2 - x$$
$$= -20x^2 + 11x$$

10

PROBLEM SOLVING IN ALGEBRA

When you are working with algebraic word problems, remember that before you begin solving the problem you should be absolutely certain that you understand precisely what you need to answer. Once this is done, show what you are looking for algebraically. Write an equation that translates the words of the problem to the symbols of mathematics. Then solve that equation by using the techniques you just learned.

This section reviews the types of algebra problems most frequently encountered on the SAT exam. Thoroughly familiarizing yourself with the problems that follow will help you to translate and solve all kinds of word problems.

Solving Two Linear Equations in Two Unknowns

Many word problems lead to equations in two unknowns. Usually, one needs two equations to solve for both unknowns, although there are exceptions. There are two generally used methods to solve two equations in two unknowns. They are the method of **substitution** and the method of **elimination by addition and subtraction**.

We'll illustrate both methods via example. Here is one that uses the method of substitution.

Example (Substitution):

Mr. Green took his four children to the local craft fair. The total cost of their admission tickets was $14. Mr. and Mrs. Molina and their six children had to pay $23. What was the cost of an adult ticket to the craft fair, and what was the cost of a child's ticket?

Solution:

Expressing all amounts in dollars, let x = cost of an adult ticket and let y = cost of a child's ticket.

$$\text{For the Greens: } x + 4y = 14$$
$$\text{For the Molinas: } 2x + 6y = 23$$

The idea of the method of substitution is to solve one equation for one variable in terms of the other and then substitute that solution into the second equation. So we solve the first equation for x, because that is the simplest one to isolate:

$$x + 4y = 14$$
$$x = 14 - 4y$$

Then substitute into the second equation:

$$2x + 6y = 23$$
$$2(14 - 4y) + 6y = 23$$

This gives us one equation in one unknown that we can solve:

$$28 - 8y + 6y = 23$$
$$-2y = -5$$
$$y = 2.5$$

Now that we know $y = 2.5$, we substitute this into $x = 14 - 4y$ to get $x = 14 - 4(2.5) = 4$. Thus, the adult tickets were $4 each, and the children's tickets were $2.50 each.

Example (Elimination):

Paul and Denise both have after-school jobs. Two weeks ago, Paul worked 6 hours, Denise worked 3 hours, and they earned a total of $39. Last week, Paul worked 12 hours, Denise worked 5 hours, and they earned a total of $75. What is each one's hourly wage?

Solution:

Again, let us express all amounts in dollars. Let x = Paul's hourly wage, and let y = Denise's hourly wage.

$$\text{For the first week: } 6x + 3y = 39$$
$$\text{For the second week: } 12x + 5y = 75$$

The idea of the method of elimination is that adding equal quantities to equal quantities gives a true result. So we want to add some multiple of one equation to the other one so that if we add the two equations together, one variable will be eliminated. In this case, it is not hard to see that if we multiply the first equation by –2, the coefficient of x will become –12. Now when we add the two equations, x will be eliminated.

$$
\begin{array}{r}
-12x - 6y = -78 \\
\underline{12x + 5y = 75} \\
-y = -3
\end{array}
$$

Since $y = 3$, we can now substitute this into either of the two equations. Let's use the first:

$$6x + 3(3) = 39$$
$$x = 5$$

Thus, Denise makes only $3 per hour, while Paul gets $5.

Word Problems in One or Two Unknowns

Word problems can be broken down into a number of categories. To do **consecutive integer** problems, you need to remember that consecutive integers differ by 1, so a string of such numbers can be represented as $n, n + 1, n + 2$, etc. **Rate-time-distance** problems require you to know the formula $d = rt$. That is, distance equals rate times time.

Here are some examples of several types of word problems.

Example 1:

Movie tickets are $13.50 for adults and $8 for senior citizens. On Saturday night, a total of 436 adults and senior citizens attended, and the movie theater collected $4,885 from these adults and senior citizens. How many senior citizens were at the movie theater?

Solution:

To solve the problem, you must write two different equations using the data in the question. Let a be the number of adults and s represent senior citizens.

$$a + s = 436$$

You also know that $a \times \$13.50$ can be used to find the total amount the movie theater collected for adult tickets and $s \times \$8$ to find the total amount collected for senior citizen tickets. Together these dollar amounts total $4,885.

$$13.5a + 8s = 4,885$$

Solve using elimination, by multiplying the first equation by -8 to eliminate one of the variables during addition of the equations:

$$(-8)(a + s) = (-8)(436)$$
$$-8a + -8s = -3,488$$

Add the equations:

$$
\begin{aligned}
-8a - 8s &= 3,488 \\
+13.5a + 8s &= 4,885 \\
\hline
5.5a &= 1,397 \\
a &= 254
\end{aligned}
$$

If 254 adults attended, then $436 - 254 = 182$ senior citizens were at the movie theater.

10

Example 2:

A supermarket places two orders for regular and extra-large packages of paper towels. The first order had 48 regular and 120 extra-large packages and cost $644.40. The second order had 60 regular and 40 extra-large and cost $338. What is the difference in cost between a regular and extra-large package of paper towels?

Solution:

Write two equations using the data given in the question. Use r to represent a regular package of paper towels and e to represent an extra-large package.

$$48r + 120e = 644.40$$
$$60r + 40e = 338$$

Multiply the bottom equation by -3 to eliminate e:

$$(-3)(60r + 40e) = (-3)(338)$$
$$-180r - 120e = -1,014$$

Add the two equations:

$$48r + 120e = 644.4$$
$$+ -180r - 120e = -1,014$$
$$-132r = -369.6$$
$$r = 2.8$$

The price of a regular package of paper towels is $2.80. To find the price of an extra-large package, substitute 2.8 into one of the equations:

$$(48)(2.8) + 120e = 644.4$$
$$120e = 510$$
$$e = 4.25$$

The difference in cost between an extra-large package and a regular package of paper towels is:

$$\$4.25 - \$2.80 = \$1.45$$

Example 3:

It took Andrew 15 minutes to drive downtown at 28 miles per hour to get a pizza. How fast did he have to drive back in order to be home in 10 minutes?

Solution:

15 minutes is $\frac{1}{4}$ of an hour. Hence, going 28 miles per hour, the distance to the pizza parlor can be computed using the formula $d = rt$:

$$d = (28)\left(\frac{1}{4}\right)$$
$$= 7 \text{ miles}$$

Since 10 minutes is $\frac{1}{6}$ of an hour, we have the equation $7 = r\frac{1}{6}$. Multiplying by 6, $r = 42$ mph.

Fraction Problems

A fraction is a ratio between two numbers. If the value of a fraction is $\frac{2}{3}$, it does not mean the numerator must be 2 and the denominator 3. The numerator and denominator could be 4 and 6, respectively, or 1 and 1.5, or 30 and 45, or any of infinitely many combinations. All you know is that the ratio of numerator to denominator will be 2:3. Therefore, the numerator may be represented by $2x$, the denominator by $3x$, and the fraction by $\frac{2x}{3x}$.

Example:

The value of a fraction is $\frac{3}{4}$. If 3 is subtracted from the numerator and added to the denominator, the value of the fraction is $\frac{2}{5}$. Find the original fraction.

Solution:

Let the original fraction be represented by $\frac{3x}{4x}$.

If 3 is subtracted from the numerator and added to the denominator, the new fraction becomes:

$$\frac{3x - 3}{4x + 3}$$

We know that the value of the new fraction is $\frac{2}{5}$, so:

$$\frac{3x - 3}{4x + 3} = \frac{2}{5}$$

Cross-multiply to eliminate fractions:

$$15x - 15 = 8x + 6$$
$$7x = 21$$
$$x = 3$$

Therefore, the original fraction is $\frac{3x}{4x} = \frac{9}{12}$.

PRACTICE EXERCISE: PROBLEM SOLVING IN ALGEBRA

DIRECTIONS: Work out each problem. Circle the letter of your choice. Check your answers against the answer key and explanations that follow.

1. A train with a heavy load travels from Albany to Binghamton at 15 miles per hour. After unloading the load, it travels back from Binghamton to Albany at 20 miles per hour. The trip from Albany to Binghamton took 1.5 hours longer than the return trip. Which of the following equations can be used to calculate the time, t, it took for the train to go from Albany to Binghamton?

   A. $1.5t = 20t$

   B. $15t = 20t - 30$

   C. $t = 20t - 30$

   D. $15t = 20 + 30$

2. If a fleet of m buses uses g gallons of gasoline every two days, how many gallons of gasoline will be used by 4 buses every five days?

   A. $\dfrac{10g}{m}$

   B. $10gm$

   C. $\dfrac{10m}{g}$

   D. $\dfrac{20g}{m}$

10

SHOW YOUR WORK HERE

3. A faucet is dripping at a constant rate. If, at noon on Sunday, 3 ounces of water have dripped from the faucet into a holding tank and, at 5 p.m. on Sunday, a total of 7 ounces have dripped into the tank, how many ounces will have dripped into the tank by 2:00 a.m. on Monday?

   A. 10

   B. $\frac{51}{5}$

   C. 12

   D. $\frac{71}{5}$

4. Prior to the 2016 Summer Olympics, the world record in 800-meter freestyle swimming was approximately 8 minutes and 15 seconds. Marta is recording her times in seconds, *s*, for the 800-meter freestyle competition at her school. Which expression below could be used to calculate Marta's time as a percentage of that world record?

   A. $\frac{s}{8.25} \times 100$

   B. $\left(\frac{s}{60} \div 8.15 \right) \times 100$

   C. $\left(\frac{s}{60} \div 495 \right) \times 100$

   D. $\frac{s}{495} \times 100$

5. Jill is four years older than Beth. Beth's age is three years less than twice Laura's age. How old is Jill if the sum of all three ages is 43 years?

   A. 9

   B. 15

   C. 19

   D. 22

10

SHOW YOUR WORK HERE

6. Tania has nine more $5 bills than $10 bills, and three times as many $10 bills as $1 bills. If the total amount of money she has is $965, how many $10 bills does she have?

   A. 20

   B. 45

   C. 60

   D. 69

7. An experienced cashier can check out six customers in 10 minutes. A novice cashier can check out four customers in 10 minutes. How long would it take the two cashiers, working together, to check out 85 customers?

   A. 1 hour

   B. 1 hour, 10 minutes

   C. 1 hour, 25 minutes

   D. 1 hour, 45 minutes

8. The sum of four consecutive even numbers is 140. What is the second smallest of these numbers?

   A. 30

   B. 34

   C. 36

   D. 40

10

SHOW YOUR WORK HERE

9. At a yoga studio, you can either pay $130 for a monthly membership and $5 per class you attend, or you can just pay $15 per class you attend. Which of the following systems of linear equations could be used to determine how many classes, x, you would need to attend for the monthly costs to be the same?

A. $\begin{cases} C = 130(x + 5) \\ C = 15 + x \end{cases}$

B. $\begin{cases} C = 130 + 5x \\ C = 15x \end{cases}$

C. $\begin{cases} C = 5x \\ C = 15x \end{cases}$

D. $\begin{cases} C = 130 \\ C = 5x \end{cases}$

10. Nick burns 10 calories per minute rowing and 12 calories per minute lifting weights. He spends 45 minutes total rowing and lifting weights and burns 504 calories in so doing. Which of these systems of linear equations could be used to determine the number of minutes rowing, x, and the number of minutes spent lifting weights, y?

A. $\begin{cases} 22(x + y) = 504 \\ x + y = 45 \end{cases}$

B. $\begin{cases} 10 + 12 = 504x \\ y = 45 + x \end{cases}$

C. $\begin{cases} 10x + 12y = 45 \\ x + y = 504 \end{cases}$

D. $\begin{cases} 10x + 12y = 504 \\ x + y = 45 \end{cases}$

10

SHOW YOUR WORK HERE

Answer Key and Explanations

1. B	3. D	5. C	7. C	9. B
2. A	4. D	6. C	8. B	10. D

1. **The correct answer is B.** Use the distance formula $d = rt$. The train's rate from Albany to Binghamton is 15 mph. Its time can be expressed as t. The train's rate from Binghamton to Albany is 20 mph. Its time can be expressed as $t - 1.5$.

   For the trip from Albany to Binghamton:
   $$d = 15t$$

   For the trip from Binghamton to Albany:
   $$d = 20(t - 1.5) = 20t - 30$$

   Since the distance from Albany to Binghamton is equal to the distance from Binghamton to Albany, we can set these two expressions equal to each other:
   $$15t = 20t - 30$$

2. **The correct answer is A.** Running m buses for two days is the same as running one bus for $2m$ days. If we use g gallons of gasoline, each bus uses $\dfrac{g}{2m}$ gallons each day. So if you multiply the number of gallons per day used by each bus by the number of buses and the number of days, you should get total gasoline usage.
   $$\frac{g}{2m} \cdot (4)(5) = \frac{10g}{m}$$

3. **The correct answer is D.** In 5 hours, 4 ounces $(7 - 3)$ have dripped. Therefore, the drip rate is $\dfrac{4}{5}$ of an ounce per hour.

   From 5:00 p.m. on Sunday until 2:00 a.m. on Monday is 9 hours, which means the total will be:
   $$7 + \frac{4}{5} \cdot 9 = 7\frac{36}{5} = \frac{71}{5}$$

4. **The correct answer is D.** Convert the world record of 8 minutes and 15 seconds to seconds:
   $$8 \text{ minutes} \times 60 \text{ sec/min} = 480 \text{ seconds}$$
   $$480 + 15 = 495 \text{ seconds}$$

   Divide Marta's time, s, by the world record, 495, then multiply by 100 to express as a percent:
   $$\frac{s}{495} \times 100$$

5. **The correct answer is C.** Let x be Laura's age (in years). Beth's age is $2x - 3$ years and Jill's age is $(2x - 3) + 4$ years. Summing these expressions and setting them equal to 43 yields the following equation to solve for x:
   $$x + (2x - 3) + (2x - 3) + 4 = 43$$
   $$5x - 2 = 43$$
   $$5x = 45$$
   $$x = 9$$

   Jill's age is $2(9) - 3 + 4 = 19$ years.

6. **The correct answer is C.** Let x be the number of $1 bills. There are $3x$ $10 bills and $3x + 9$ $5 bills. Multiply the number of each type of bill by the dollar value of that bill, add these expressions, and set the sum equal to 965 to obtain the following equation:
   $$1x + 10(3x) + 5(3x + 9) = 965$$
   $$x + 30x + 15x + 45 = 965$$
   $$46x = 920$$
   $$x = 20$$

   There are $3(20) = 60$ $10 bills.

7. **The correct answer is C.** The number of customers checked out in 10 minutes by the pair of cashiers is $6 + 4 = 10$. The rate at which the pair checks out customers is 10 customers per 10 minutes, or 60 customers per hour (since 1 hour = 60 minutes). The time it takes the pair to check out 85 customers is:

$$\frac{85}{60} \text{ hour} = 1 \text{ hour, 25 minutes}$$

8. **The correct answer is B.** Let x be the smallest of the four consecutive even integers. The other three are $x + 2$, $x + 4$, and $x + 6$. Since the sum is 140, we get the equation:

$$x + (x + 2) + (x + 4) + (x + 6) = 140$$
$$4x + 12 = 140$$
$$4x = 128$$
$$x = 32$$

The four consecutive even integers are 32, 34, 36, and 38. The second smallest is 34.

9. **The correct answer is B.** The cost, C, of the version in which a customer pays a monthly membership is $C = 130 + 5x$, where x is the number of classes attended that month. The cost of the other option is $15x$. Since we are asked to find the number of classes for which the costs are the same, this is also equal to C. Hence the desired system is given in choice B as follows:

$$\begin{cases} C = 130 + 5x \\ C = 15x \end{cases}$$

10. **The correct answer is D.** First, the sum of the number of minutes spent rowing and the number of minutes spent lifting weights is 45 minutes; this gives the equation $x + y = 45$. To get the other equation, we account for the number of calories burned performing each exercise. The number of calories burnt for x minutes rowing is $10x$ and the number burned for y minutes of lifting weights is $12y$. The sum must be 504, which yields the equation $10x + 12y = 504$. The desired system is given in choice D as follows:

$$\begin{cases} 10x + 12y = 504 \\ x + y = 45 \end{cases}$$

10

INEQUALITIES

Algebraic inequality statements are solved just as equations are solved—by isolating the variable on one side, factoring, and canceling wherever possible. However, one important rule distinguishes inequalities from equations: whenever you multiply or divide by a negative number, the inequality symbol must be reversed.

Example 1:

Solve for x: $3 - 5x > 18$

Solution:

Add -3 to both sides:

$$3 - 5x > 18$$
$$-5x > 15$$

Divide by -5, remembering to reverse the inequality:

$$x < -3$$

Example 2:

Solve for x: $5x - 4 > 6x - 6$

Solution:

Collect all x terms on the left and numerical terms on the right. Remember that, as with equal signs in equations, if a term crosses the inequality symbol, the term changes its sign.

$$5x - 4 > 6x - 6$$
$$5x - 6x > -6 + 4$$
$$-x > -2$$

Divide (or multiply) by -1:

$$x < 2$$

Inequality Symbols

Inequalities usually have many solutions (after all, there are a lot of quantities that are not equal to each other!), and solving an inequality means finding all its solutions. The following symbols are used when solving inequalities:

Symbol	Inequality
>	greater than
≥	greater than or equal to
<	less than
≤	less than or equal to

Properties of Inequalities

In the properties in the following table, assume that a, b, and c are real numbers.

Addition Property of Inequality	Subtraction Property of Inequality
If $a > b$, then $a + c > b + c$	If $a > b$, then $a - c > b - c$
If $a < b$, then $a + c < b + c$	If $a < b$, then $a - c < b - c$
Multiplication Property of Inequality	**Division Property of Inequality**
$c > 0$:	$c > 0$:
If $a > b$, then $ac > bc$	If $a > b$, then $\dfrac{a}{c} > \dfrac{b}{c}$
If $a < b$, then $ac < bc$	If $a < b$, then $\dfrac{a}{c} < \dfrac{b}{c}$
$c < 0$:	$c < 0$:
If $a > b$, then $ac < bc$	If $a > b$, then $\dfrac{a}{c} < \dfrac{b}{c}$
If $a < b$, then $ac > bc$	If $a < b$, then $\dfrac{a}{c} > \dfrac{b}{c}$

The properties are also true for inequalities that include the $\leq$ and $\geq$ symbols.

10

Example 1:

A meeting room can hold a maximum of 250 people. If 182 people have already been admitted, how many more people can be allowed into the meeting room?

Solution:

Let x = number of people that can be admitted.

$$182 + x \leq 250$$
$$182 - 182 + x \leq 250 - 182$$
$$x \leq 68$$

There can be at most 68 more people admitted to the meeting room.

Example 2:

To stay healthy, an adult's goal should be to walk at least 10,000 steps each day. A fitness tracker showed that a person had walked 6,349 steps. What is the minimum number of steps this person can take to reach this goal?

Solution:

Let x = number of steps.

$$6,349 + x \geq 10,000$$
$$6,349 - 6,349 + x \geq 10,000 - 6,349$$
$$x \geq 3,651$$

The person must walk at least 3,651 more steps.

Example 3:

Alexander plans on mowing lawns this summer. He charges $20 per lawn. How many lawns will he have to mow in order to earn at least $575?

Solution:

Let x = number of lawns.

$$20x \geq 575$$
$$\frac{20x}{20} \geq \frac{575}{20}$$
$$x \geq 28.75$$

Alexander must mow at least 29 lawns to earn at least $575.

You can also use the properties of inequality to solve multi-step inequalities.

Example 1:

The marching band members are making a banner for the pep rally. The banner is in the shape of a rectangle that is 12 ft. long. They have no more than 32 ft. of fringe for the banner. What are the possible widths of the banner?

Solution:

Let w = width of the banner, and l = length of the banner. Use the perimeter formula $(2l + 2w \leq P)$ to find the possible allowable widths.

$$2(12) + 2w \leq 32$$
$$24 + 2w \leq 32$$
$$2w \leq 8$$
$$\frac{2w}{2} \leq \frac{8}{2}$$
$$w \leq 4$$

The width of the banner can be 4 ft. or less.

Example 2:

A prepaid cell phone has a balance of $40. Calls are $0.04 per minute, and texts are $0.07 per text. If 342 texts were used, how many minutes can be used for calls?

Solution:

Let x = number of minutes used on calls, and y = number of texts.

$$0.04x + 0.07y \leq 40$$
$$0.04x + 0.07(342) \leq 40$$
$$0.04x + 23.94 \leq 40$$
$$0.04x \leq 16.06$$
$$\frac{0.04x}{0.04} \leq \frac{16.06}{0.04}$$
$$x \leq 401.5$$

PRACTICE EXERCISE: INEQUALITIES

DIRECTIONS: Work out each problem. Circle the letter of your choice. Check your answers against the answer key and explanations that follow.

---

1. If $3x - 8 \geq 4x$, then

   A. $-8 \leq x$

   B. $-8 \geq x$

   C. $-8 < x$

   D. $-8 > x$

2. If $-9x + 7 < 43$, then

   A. $x \geq -4$

   B. $x \leq -4$

   C. $x > -4$

   D. $x < -4$

3. The admission to the local carnival is $6. You want to play games that cost $1.50 per game. If you have $30, how many games can you play?

   A. At least 24

   B. No more than 20

   C. Less than or equal to 16

   D. Greater than or equal 20

4. You want to order a bouquet of flowers that contains roses and carnations. You have only $48 to spend. Roses cost $3 each, and carnations cost $1.25 each. How many roses can be in the bouquet if there are 18 carnations in the bouquet? Let r represent the number of roses.

   A. $r \geq 8$

   B. $r \leq 9$

   C. $r \geq 9$

   D. $r \leq 8$

10

SHOW YOUR WORK HERE

5. Bike rentals cost \$15 for the first 2 hours and \$6 for any additional hours. Ali wants to bike for more than 2 hours, but she has only \$35. Which inequality represents the situation where h is the total number of hours Ali can bike?

A. $6 + 15h \leq 35$

B. $6(h - 2) + 15 \leq 35$

C. $6h + 15 \leq 35$

D. $6(h + 2) + 15 \leq 35$

6. Selena is adding trim to a rectangular tablecloth that measures 108 inches long. If she has 330 inches of trim, what is the greatest possible width of the tablecloth?

A. At most 54 inches

B. At most 57 inches

C. At most 222 inches

D. At most 114 inches

7. If $-36 \leq -3x$, then

A. $x \geq -33$

B. $x \leq 12$

C. $x \geq 12$

D. $x \leq -33$

SHOW YOUR WORK HERE

8. If $3x > -12$, then

A. $x > -4$

B. $x < -4$

C. $x > -15$

D. $x < -15$

9. Adam spent less than \$110 on a pair of gloves and four headbands. The pair of gloves cost \$45. If x is the cost (in dollars) of one headband, which inequality can be used to determine the maximum cost of one headband?

A. $4(x + 45) < 110$

B. $4x < 110 + 45$

C. $45 + 4x < 110$

D. $45(4) + x < 100$

10. The sum of two consecutive odd integers is at most 85. Which inequality could be used to find the largest pair of such integers?

A. $x + (x + 1) \geq 85$

B. $x + (x + 2) \geq 85$

C. $x + (x + 1) \leq 85$

D. $x + (x + 2) \leq 85$

10

Answer Key and Explanations

1. B	3. C	5. B	7. B	9. C
2. C	4. D	6. B	8. A	10. D

1. **The correct answer is B.** Subtract $3x$ from both sides:

$$3x - 8 \geq 4x$$
$$-8 \geq 4x - 3x$$
$$-8 \geq x$$

2. **The correct answer is C.** Subtract 7 from both sides, then divide by -9:

$$-9x + 7 < 43$$
$$-9x < 36$$
$$x > -4$$

Remember, by dividing by -9, you need to reverse the inequality sign.

3. **The correct answer is C.**

$$6 + 1.5x \leq 30$$
$$1.5x \leq 24$$
$$\frac{1.5x}{1.5} \leq \frac{24}{1.5}$$
$$x \leq 16$$

4. **The correct answer is D.**

$$3r + 1.25c \leq 48$$
$$3r + 1.25(18) \leq 48$$
$$3r + 22.5 \leq 48$$
$$3r \leq 25.5$$
$$\frac{3r}{3} \leq \frac{25.5}{3}$$
$$r \leq 8.5$$

There can only be at most 8 roses in the bouquet.

5. **The correct answer is B.** The cost for the first 2 hours is \$15. Subtract the 2 hours from the total number of hours, h, and multiply by \$6 an hour to compute the cost for the number of hours over 2. Be sure to add the initial \$15 for the first 2 hours:

$$6(h - 2) + 15 \leq 35$$

6. **The correct answer is B.**

$$2l + 2w \leq 330$$
$$2(108) + 2w \leq 330$$
$$216 + 2w \leq 330$$
$$2w \leq 114$$
$$\frac{2w}{2} \leq \frac{114}{2}$$
$$w \leq 57$$

The tablecloth can be at most 57 in. wide.

7. **The correct answer is B.** Divide both sides by -3 and reverse the inequality sign:

$$-36 \leq -3x$$
$$12 \geq x$$
$$x \leq 12$$

8. **The correct answer is A.** Divide both sides by 3. The inequality sign stays the same.

$$3x > -12$$
$$x > -4$$

9. **The correct answer is C.** To solve, you need an expression for the total cost; in other words, the cost of the pair of gloves plus the cost of 4 headbands, or $45 + 4x$. This must be less than 110, so the desired inequality is $45 + 4x < 110$.

10. **The correct answer is D.** Let x be the smaller of the two odd integers. The next consecutive odd integer is $x + 2$. Since the sum of these two integers must not exceed 85, we get the inequality $x + (x + 2) \leq 85$.

Summing It Up

- When solving algebra problems, know the basic operations with signed numbers (addition, subtraction, multiplication, and division). Understanding these operations will help with the more difficult SAT Exam problems.

- Know the four-step strategy to solving **linear equations**:

  1. If there are fractions or decimals, remove them by multiplication.
  2. Collect all terms containing the unknown for which you are solving on the same side of the equation.
  3. Determine the coefficient of the unknown by combining similar terms or factoring when terms cannot be combined.
  4. Divide both sides of the equation by this coefficient.

- An equation can have one solution, infinitely many solutions, or no solutions.

- A **literal equation** is an equation that involves two or more variables. Solve for one variable in terms of the others by using the properties of equalities.

- The five rules of **exponents** are as follows:

  1. To multiply powers of the same base, add the exponents.
  2. To divide powers of the same base, subtract the exponent of the divisor from the exponent of the dividend.
  3. Negative powers represent reciprocals.
  4. To find the power of a power, multiply the exponents.
  5. Fractional exponents represent roots.

- A **complete quadratic equation** is of the form $ax^2 + bx + c = 0$. **Incomplete quadratic equations** are those in which b or c is equal to 0.

- Always get a **radical** alone on one side of the equation; then square both sides to remove the radical and solve.

- **Roots** can be written as fractional exponents to make them easier to work with.

- When adding a collection of expressions together, each expression is called a **term**. **Monomial** means "one term." A **polynomial** is the sum of several terms that contain different powers of the same variable(s). Keep the negatives and positives straight when you're doing polynomial math.

- When solving two linear equations in two unknowns, use the method of **substitution** and the method of **elimination by addition and subtraction**.

- Algebraic **inequality statements** are solved just as equations are solved—by isolating the variable on one side, factoring, and canceling wherever possible.

10

Take a moment to ask yourself some simple questions about your understanding of the chapter:

Review: What did I learn?

Evaluate: What do I need to learn more about?

Plan: What can I do next to keep improving?

Based on your answers to those questions, adjust your study plan to dedicate additional time to the areas of weakness that you've identified.

10

Geometry

OVERVIEW

GEOMETRIC NOTATION

A **point** is represented by a dot and denoted by a capital letter.

• *P*

Point *P*

A **line** can be denoted in two different ways. First, a small letter can be placed next to the line. For example, the diagram below depicts line *l*. The arrowheads on both ends of the line indicate that lines extend infinitely in both directions.

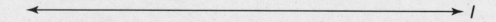

A line can also be denoted by placing a small double-headed arrow over two of its points. The diagram below depicts line $\overrightarrow{AB}$.

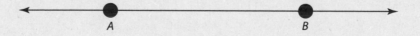

449

A **line segment** is the part of a line between two of its points, which are called the endpoints of the line segment. A line segment is denoted by placing a small line segment over the two endpoints. The diagram below depicts the line segment $\overline{AB}$.

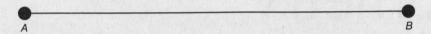

The length of a line segment is denoted by placing its two endpoints next to each other. In the diagram below, $CD = 7$.

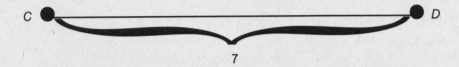

Two line segments that have the same length are said to be **congruent**. The symbol for congruence is $\cong$. Thus, if $AB = 12$ and $EF = 12$, then $\overline{AB}$ is congruent to $\overline{EF}$, or $\overline{AB} \cong \overline{EF}$.

A **ray** is the part of a line beginning at one point, called the **endpoint**, and extending infinitely in one direction. A ray is denoted by placing a small one-headed arrow over its endpoint and another point on the ray. The first diagram below depicts the ray $\overrightarrow{AB}$, and the second diagram depicts the ray $\overrightarrow{AC}$.

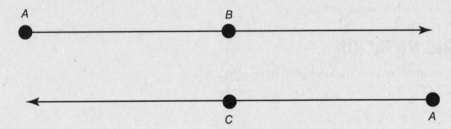

Two lines that cross each other are said to **intersect**. Two lines that do not intersect are said to be **parallel**. The symbol ∥ is used to represent parallel lines. In the diagrams below, line *k* intersects line *l* at point *P*, while lines *m* and *n* are parallel, that is, *m* ∥ *n*.

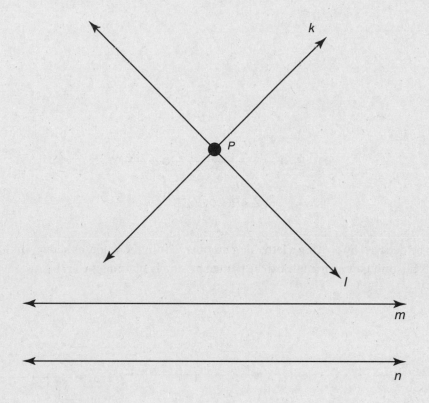

ANGLE MEASUREMENT

When two rays share a common endpoint, they form **angles**. The point at which the rays intersect is called the **vertex** of the angle, and the rays themselves are called the **sides** of the angle.

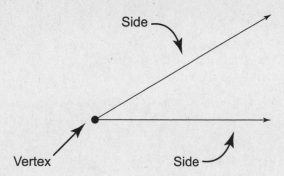

The symbol for angle is ∠. Angles can be denoted in several different ways. The most common way to denote an angle is to name a point on one side, then the vertex, and then a point on the other side as shown in the diagram below.

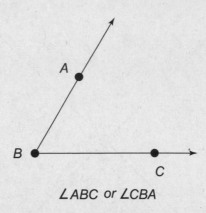

∠*ABC* or ∠*CBA*

Angles can also be denoted by writing a letter or a number within the angle, as shown in the figures that follow. If there is no ambiguity, an angle can be named by simply naming the vertex.

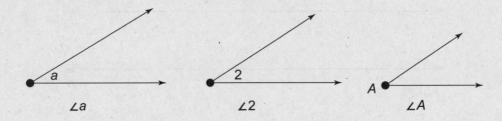

∠*a*　　　　∠*2*　　　　∠*A*

11

The size of an angle is measured in **degrees**. The symbol for degree is °. A full circle contains 360°, and all other angles can be measured as a fractional part of a full circle. Typically, the measure of an angle is written in the interior of the angle, near the vertex.

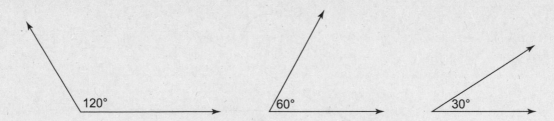

A **straight angle** is an angle that measures 180°.

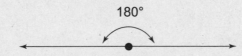

A **right angle** is an angle that measures 90°. Note, as shown in the diagram below, a "box" is used to represent a right angle.

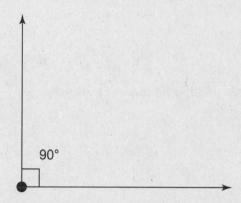

The measure of an angle is denoted by writing the letter "m" followed by the name of the angle. For example, $m\angle ABC = 45°$ denotes that angle ABC has a measure of 45°.

Two angles that have the same number of degrees are said to be **congruent**. Thus, if $m\angle P = m\angle Q$, then $\angle P \cong \angle Q$. Two angles whose measures add up to 180° are said to be **supplementary**. Two angles whose measures add up to 90° are said to be **complementary**.

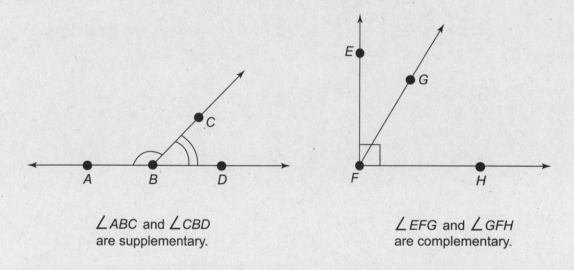

$\angle ABC$ and $\angle CBD$ are supplementary.

$\angle EFG$ and $\angle GFH$ are complementary.

A **radian** is a unit of measure used to measure angles. To convert degrees to radians, multiply the degree measure by $\dfrac{\pi \text{ radians}}{180°}$.

Example:

Convert 85° to radians

Solution:

$$85° = 85\left(\frac{\pi \text{ radians}}{180°}\right) = \frac{17\pi}{36}$$

To convert from radians to degrees, multiply the radian measure by $\frac{180°}{\pi \text{ radians}}$.

Example:

Convert $\frac{\pi}{6}$ radians to degrees:

Solution:

$$\frac{\pi}{6} = \left(\frac{\pi \text{ radians}}{6}\right)\left(\frac{180°}{\pi \text{ radians}}\right) = 30°$$

INTERSECTING LINES

When two lines intersect, four angles are formed. The angles opposite each other are congruent.

$$\angle 1 \cong \angle 3 \text{ and } \angle 2 \cong \angle 4$$

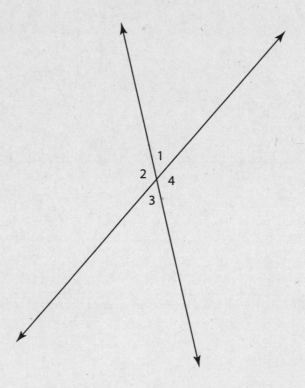

When two lines intersect, the angles adjacent to each other are supplementary.

$$m\angle5 + m\angle6 = 180°$$
$$m\angle6 + m\angle7 = 180°$$
$$m\angle7 + m\angle8 = 180°$$
$$m\angle8 + m\angle5 = 180°$$

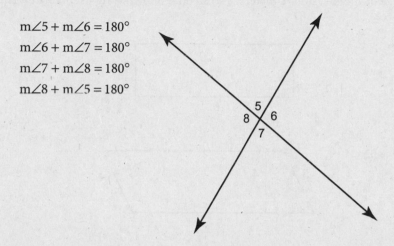

If you know the measure of any one of the four angles formed when two lines intersect, you can determine the measures of the other three.

For example, if $m\angle1 = 45°$, then $m\angle3 = 45°$, and $m\angle2 = m\angle4 = 180° - 45° = 135°$.

Two lines that intersect at right angles are said to be **perpendicular**. In the figure that follows, $\overleftrightarrow{AB}$ is perpendicular to $\overleftrightarrow{CD}$. This can be denoted as $\overleftrightarrow{AB} \perp \overleftrightarrow{CD}$.

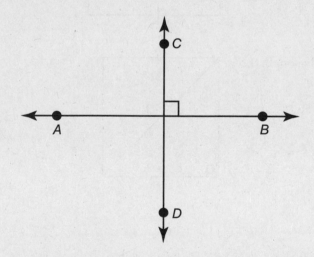

Note that all four of the angles in the diagram above are right angles.

AREA

Many of the geometry problems you will encounter on the SAT exam will ask about the **perimeter** or **area** of a polygon. A **polygon** is a closed plane figure that consists of straight line segments called **sides**. The **perimeter** of a closed plane figure is the distance around the figure and is computed by adding all the lengths of the segments/sides that form its outer boundary. The **area** of a two-dimensional plane figure is the number of unit squares needed to cover it. The units of area measure are square inches, square feet, square yards, square centimeters, square meters, and so on. Following are useful area formulas for common plane figures:

1. Rectangle $= bh$

    Area $= 6 \cdot 3 = 18$

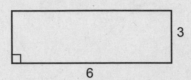

2. Parallelogram $= bh$

    Area $= 8 \cdot 4 = 32$

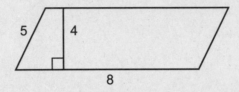

3. Square $= s^2$

    Area $= 6^2 = 36$

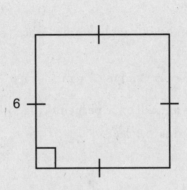

Square $= \frac{1}{2}d^2$ $(d = \text{diagonal})$

Area $= \frac{1}{2}(10)(10) = 50$

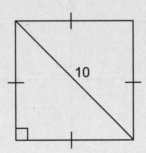

4. Triangle $= \frac{1}{2}bh$

    Area $= \frac{1}{2}(12)(4) = 24$

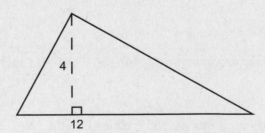

5. Trapezoid $= \frac{1}{2}h\left(b_1 + b_2\right)$

   Area $= \frac{1}{2}(5)(16) = 40$

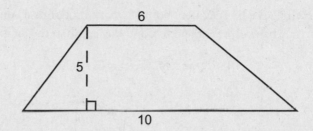

CIRCLES

A **circle** is a closed flat figure formed by a set of points all of which are the same distance from a point called the **center**. The boundary of the circle is called the **circumference**, and the distance from the center to any point on the circumference is called the **radius**. A circle is denoted by naming the point at its center—that is, the circle whose center is at point P is called circle P.

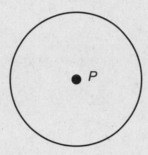

A **diameter** of a circle is a line segment that passes through the center of the circle, and whose endpoints lie on the circle. The diameter of a circle is twice as long as its radius. Typically, the letter r is used to represent the radius of a circle, and the letter d is used to represent the diameter.

$$2r = d$$

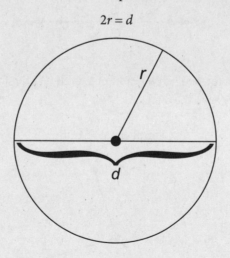

11

A **chord** of a circle is a line segment both of whose endpoints lie on the circumference of the circle. The chords of a circle have different lengths, and the length of the longest chord is equal to the diameter.

$\overline{AB}$, $\overline{CD}$, and $\overline{EF}$ are chords of circle O. $\overline{EF}$ is also a diameter.

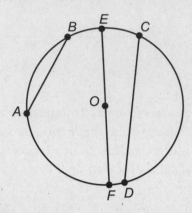

A **tangent** is a line that intersects the circle at exactly one point. A radius drawn to the point of intersection is perpendicular to the tangent line.

$$\overline{OQ} \perp \overleftrightarrow{CD}$$

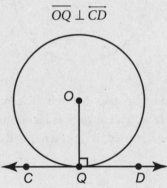

A **central angle** is an angle that is formed by two radii of a circle. As the following diagram shows, the vertex of a central angle is the center of the circle.

Central angle $\angle AOB$

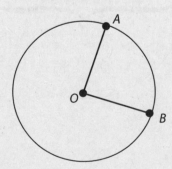

A central angle is equal in degrees to the measure of the arc that it intercepts. That is, a 40° central angle intercepts a 40° arc, and a 90° central angle intercepts a 90° arc.

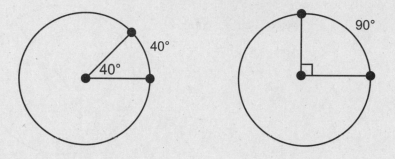

An **arc** is a piece of the circumference of a circle. The symbol ⌢ placed on top of the two endpoints is used to denote an arc. For example, $\widehat{MN}$ is indicated in the figure below.

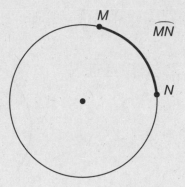

The **measure of an arc** is in degrees. The arc's length depends on the size of the circle because it represents a fraction of the circumference.

$$\text{Length of } \widehat{AB} = \frac{m\widehat{AB}}{360} \cdot 2\pi r$$

If the radius of a circle is 5 cm and the measure of the arc is 45°, then the length of the arc is

$$\frac{45°}{360°} \cdot 2\pi\left(5\right) = \frac{5\pi}{4} \text{ cm}$$
$$= 1.25\pi \text{ cm}$$
$$\approx 3.93 \text{ cm}$$

The **area of a circle** is measured using the formula πr^2. If the diameter of the circle is 12, its radius is 6:

$$\text{Area of a circle} = \pi r^2$$
$$\text{Area} = \pi(6)^2 = 36\pi$$

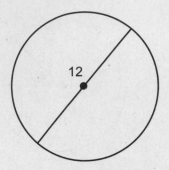

The **area of a sector** of a circle is the product of the ratio $\dfrac{\text{measure of the arc}}{360°}$ and the area of the circle. If the radius of a circle is 3 cm and the measure of the arc is 60°, then the area of the sector is $\dfrac{60°}{360°} \cdot \pi(3)^2 = \dfrac{9\pi}{6} = \dfrac{3\pi}{2}$ cm².

$$\text{Area of sector } AOB = \frac{m\widehat{AB}}{360} \cdot \pi^2$$

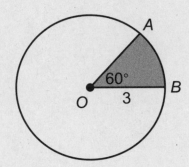

11

The **length of a chord** of a circle is the product of $2r$ and $\sin\left(\dfrac{\text{measure of the central angle}}{2}\right)$. If the radius of a circle is 4 inches and the measure of the central angle is 60°, then the length of the chord is

$$2(4)\sin\left(\frac{60°}{2}\right) = 8\sin(30°) = 4 \text{ inches.}$$

(In a right-angled triangle, the **sine** of an angle is the length of the opposite side divided by the length of the hypotenuse. The abbreviation is **sin.**)

VOLUME

The **volume of a right rectangular prism** is equal to the product of its length, width, and height.

$$V = lwh$$

$$V = (6)(2)(4) = 48$$

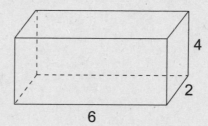

The **volume of a cube** is equal to the cube of an edge.

$$V = e^3$$

$$V = (5)^3 = 125$$

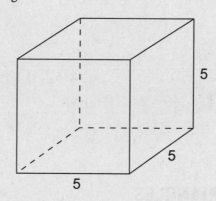

The **volume of a right circular cylinder** is equal to π times the square of the radius of the base times the height.

$$V = \pi r^2 h$$

$$V = \pi (5)^2 (3) = 75\pi$$

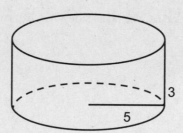

The **volume of a sphere** is equal to $\frac{4}{3}\pi$ times the cube of the radius.

$$V = \frac{4}{3}\pi r^3$$

$$V = \frac{4}{3}\pi (3)^3 = \frac{4}{3}\pi (27) = 36\pi$$

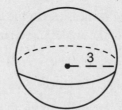

11

The **volume of a right square pyramid** is equal to $\frac{1}{3}$ times the product of the square of the side and the height.

$$V = \frac{1}{3}s^2h$$

$$V = \frac{1}{3}(2)^2(6)$$

$$V = 8$$

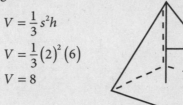

The **volume of a right circular cone** is equal to $\frac{1}{3}\pi$ times the product of the square of the radius and the height.

FUN FACT

A pizza that has a radius *z* and height *a* has volume

Pi – z – z – a

$$V = \frac{1}{3}\pi r^2h$$

$$V = \frac{1}{3}\pi(6)^2(9)$$

$$V = 108\pi$$

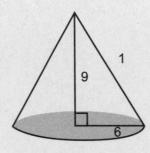

TRIANGLES

A **triangle** is a polygon with three sides. A **vertex** of a triangle is a point at which two of its sides meet. The symbol for a triangle is Δ, and a triangle can be named by writing its three vertices in any order.

ΔABC contains sides $\overline{AB}, \overline{BC},$ and $\overline{AC},$ and angles $\angle A, \angle B,$ and $\angle C.$

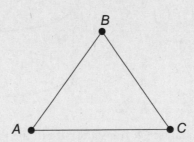

The sum of the measures of the angles in a triangle is 180°. Therefore, if the measures of any two of the angles in a triangle are known, the measure of the third angle can be determined.

In any triangle, the longest side is opposite the largest angle and the shortest side is opposite the smallest angle. In the following triangle, if $a° > b° > c°$, then $\overline{BC} > \overline{AC} > \overline{AB}.$

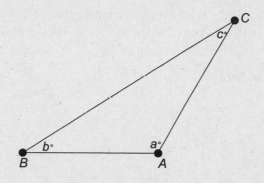

If two sides of a triangle are congruent, the angles opposite these sides are also congruent.

If $\overline{AB} \cong \overline{AC}$, then $\angle B \cong \angle C$.

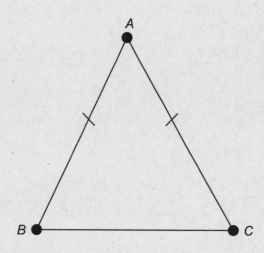

If two angles of a triangle are congruent, the sides opposite these angles are also congruent.

If $\angle B \cong \angle C$, then $\overline{AB} \cong \overline{AC}$.

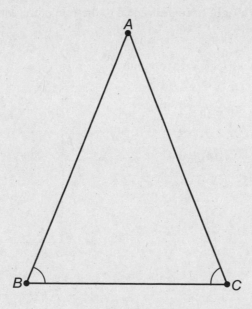

In the following diagram, $\angle 1$ is called an **exterior** angle. The measure of an exterior angle of a triangle is equal to the sum of the measures of the two **remote interior** angles—that is, the two interior angles that are the farthest away from the exterior angle.

$$m\angle 1 = 115°$$

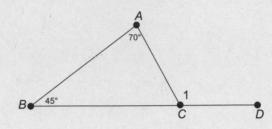

If two angles of one triangle are congruent to two angles of a second triangle, the third angles are also congruent.

$$\angle D \cong \angle A$$

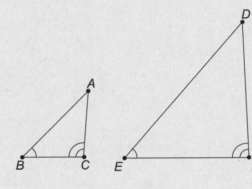

11

Right Triangles

The **Pythagorean theorem** states that the square of a hypotenuse (the leg opposite the right angle) of a right triangle is equal to the sum of the squares of the other two legs $a^2 + b^2 = c^2$.

$$(\text{leg})^2 + (\text{leg})^2 = (\text{hypotenuse})^2$$
$$4^2 + 5^2 = x^2$$
$$16 + 25 = x^2$$
$$41 = x^2$$
$$\sqrt{41} = x$$

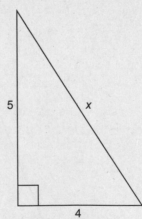

Pythagorean triples are sets of whole numbers that satisfy the Pythagorean theorem. When a given set of numbers, such as 3-4-5, forms a Pythagorean triple ($3^2 + 4^2 = 5^2$), any multiples of this set, such as 6-8-10 or 15-20-25, also form a Pythagorean triple. The most common Pythagorean triples that should be memorized are:

3-4-5

5-12-13

8-15-17

7-24-25

Let's take a look at the following right triangle:

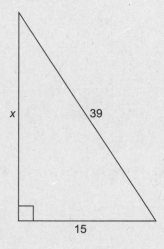

Squaring the numbers 15 and 39 in order to apply the Pythagorean theorem would take too much time. Instead, take another look and see if you can break down the given numbers into a smaller Pythagorean triple. Notice that the hypotenuse is 3(13), and the second Pythagorean triple on the list is a 5-12-13 triangle. Since the hypotenuse is 3(13) and the leg is 3(5), the missing leg must be 3(12), or 36.

> **TIP**
> Memorize the most common Pythagorean triples. On the SAT, you'll encounter right triangles with sides whose lengths correspond to these values.

11

BRAIN BREAK

Ready for some fun? Search the internet for Pythagorean theorem or hypotenuse songs. Some of the songs are silly, but studies have shown that music helps aid in retaining information.

The 30°-60°-90° triangle is a special right triangle whose sides are in the ratio of $x : \sqrt{3} : 2x$.

- The leg opposite the 30° angle is $\frac{1}{2}$ · hypotenuse.

- The leg opposite the 60° angle is $\frac{1}{2}$ · hypotenuse · $\sqrt{3}$.

- An altitude in an equilateral triangle forms a 30°-60°-90° triangle and is therefore equal to
  $\frac{1}{2}$ · hypotenuse · $\sqrt{3}$.

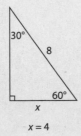

$x = 4$

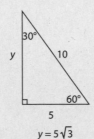

$y = 5\sqrt{3}$

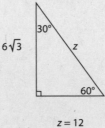

$z = 12$

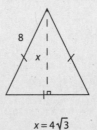

$x = 4\sqrt{3}$

The 45°-45°-90° triangle (isosceles right triangle) is a special right triangle whose sides are in the ratio of
x: $x : \sqrt{2}$

- Each leg is $\frac{1}{2}$ · hypotenuse · $\sqrt{2}$.

- The hypotenuse is eg · $\sqrt{2}$.

- The diagonal in a square forms a 45°-45°-90° triangle and is therefore equal to the length of
  one side · $\sqrt{2}$.

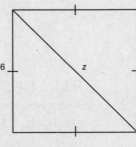

$w = 6$

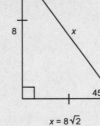

$x = 8\sqrt{2}$

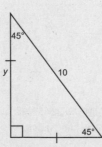

$y = 5\sqrt{2}$

$z = 6\sqrt{2}$

One way to solve SAT geometry questions that involve 30°-60°-90° triangles and 45°-45°-90° triangles is to use right triangle trigonometric relationships. In the triangle below, side $\overline{AB}$ is called the side **adjacent** to $\angle A$, side $\overline{BC}$ is called the side **opposite** $\angle A$, and side $\overline{AC}$ is the **hypotenuse**. Relative to $\angle A$, the trigonometric ratios **sine**, **cosine**, and **tangent** are defined as shown.

$$\text{sine } a° = \sin a° = \frac{\text{opposite}}{\text{hypotenuse}}$$

$$\text{cosine } a° = \cos a° = \frac{\text{adjacent}}{\text{hypotenuse}}$$

$$\text{tangent } a° = \tan a° = \frac{\text{opposite}}{\text{adjacent}}$$

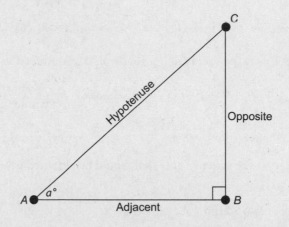

The following table shows the values of the sine, cosine, and tangent for 30°, 45°, and 60°.

Angle a	$\sin a°$	$\cos a°$	$\tan a°$
30°	$\frac{1}{2}$	$\frac{\sqrt{3}}{2}$	$\frac{\sqrt{3}}{3}$
45°	$\frac{\sqrt{2}}{2}$	$\frac{\sqrt{2}}{2}$	1
60°	$\frac{\sqrt{3}}{2}$	$\frac{1}{2}$	$\sqrt{3}$

By using the values of sine, cosine, and tangent shown in the table, problems involving 30°-60°-90° triangles and 45°-45°-90° triangles can also be solved. For example, consider the following 30°-60°-90° triangle with hypotenuse of length 8.

The computations that follow show how to determine the lengths of the other two sides.

$$\text{sine } 60° = \frac{\text{opposite}}{\text{hypotenuse}} = \frac{y}{8}$$

Since $\sin 60° = \frac{\sqrt{3}}{2}$, then $\frac{y}{8} = \frac{\sqrt{3}}{2}$. Cross-multiply to get $2y = 8\sqrt{3}$, or $y = \frac{8\sqrt{3}}{2} = 4\sqrt{3}$.

Note that this is the same answer that would be obtained using the properties of 30°-60°-90° triangles.

$$\cos 60° = \frac{\text{adjacent}}{\text{hypotenuse}} = \frac{x}{8}$$

Also, since $\cos 60° = \frac{1}{2}$, then $\frac{x}{8} = \frac{1}{2}$. Cross-multiply to get $2x = 8$, or $x = 4$.

This, again, is the same answer that would be obtained using the properties of 30°-60°-90° triangles shown.

Let's look at two additional examples.

Example 1:

Suppose a building has a handicap ramp that rises 2.5 ft. and forms a 3° angle with the ground. How far from the base of the building is the start of the ramp? Round your answer to the nearest tenth.

Solution:

$$\tan 3° = \frac{2.5}{x}$$
$$x = \frac{2.5}{\tan 3°}$$
$$x = 47.7 \text{ feet}$$

Example 2:

Suppose a 26-ft. wire is attached to the top of a pole and staked in the ground at a 40-degree angle. Estimate the height of the pole.

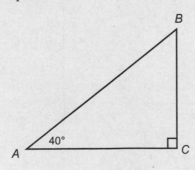

Solution:

$$\sin 40° = \frac{x}{26}$$

$$26 \sin 40° = x$$

$$16.7 \text{ ft.} \approx x$$

To find how far the stake is from the ground, you can use the Pythagorean theorem:

$$a^2 + b^2 = c^2$$

$$16.7^2 + b^2 = 26^2$$

$$19.9 \text{ ft.} \approx x$$

PARALLEL LINES

If two parallel lines are cut by a transversal, the alternate interior angles are congruent.

If $\overleftrightarrow{AB} \perp \overleftrightarrow{CD}$, then $\angle 1 \cong \angle 3$, and $\angle 2 \cong \angle 4$.

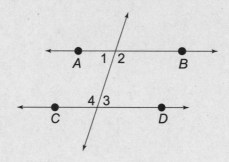

If two parallel lines are cut by a transversal, the corresponding angles are congruent.

If $\overleftrightarrow{AB} \perp \overleftrightarrow{CD}$, then

$\angle 1 \cong \angle 5$,

$\angle 2 \cong \angle 6$,

$\angle 3 \cong \angle 7$, and

$\angle 4 \cong \angle 8$.

If two parallel lines are cut by a transversal, interior angles on the same side of the transversal are supplementary.

If $\overleftrightarrow{AB} \perp \overleftrightarrow{CD}$, then

$\angle 1$ is supplementary to $\angle 4$, and

$\angle 2$ is supplementary to $\angle 3$.

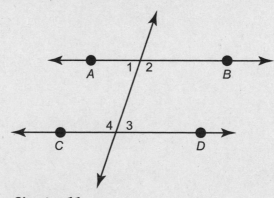

Chapter 11

COORDINATE GEOMETRY

Lines and other geometric figures can be positioned on a plane by means of the **rectangular coordinate system**. The rectangular coordinate system consists of two number lines that are perpendicular and cross each other at their **origins** (0 on each of the number lines). The horizontal number line is called the x-axis, and the vertical number line is called the y-axis.

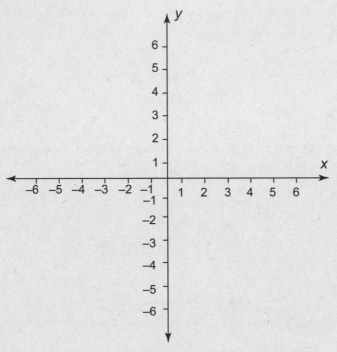

Any point on the plane can be designated by a pair of numbers. The first number is called the **x-coordinate** and indicates how far to move to the left (negative) or to the right (positive) on the **x-axis**, and the second number is called the **y-coordinate** and tells how far to move up (positive) or down (negative) on the **y-axis**. Generically, a point on the plane can be written as (x, y). When two points need to be expressed generically, they are typically written as (x_1, y_1) and (x_2, y_2).

The points (2, 3), (–4, 1), (–5, –2), and (2 –4) are graphed on a coordinate system as shown in the following figure.

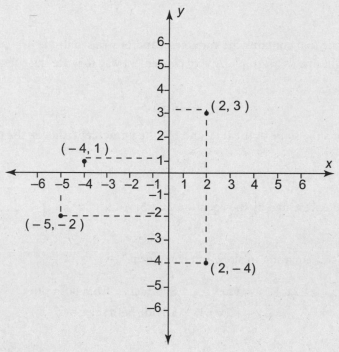

Graphing a Straight Line

The **slope** of a straight line is a number that measures how steep the line is. Traditionally, the variable m is used to stand for the slope of a line. By convention, a line that increases from left to right has a positive slope, and a line that decreases from left to right has a negative slope. A horizontal line has a slope of 0 since it is "flat," and a vertical line has an undefined slope.

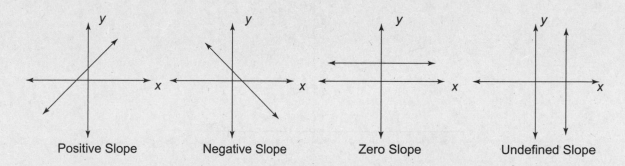

If (x_1, y_1) and (x_2, y_2) are any two points on a line, the slope is given by the formula:

$$m = \frac{(y_2 - y_1)}{(x_2 - x_1)}$$

For example, if a line contains the points (5, 7) and (3, 4), the slope would be $m = \frac{7-4}{5-3} = \frac{3}{2}$.
A slope of $\frac{3}{2}$ represents the fact that for every 2 units moved horizontally along the x-axis, the line rises vertically 3 units.

An equation of degree one that contains the variables x and/or y raised to the first power, but no higher, will always have a straight line as its graph. A very convenient way to write the equation of a line is in the **slope-intercept** form:

$$y = mx + b$$

In this form, m represents the slope of the line, and b is the **y-intercept**, that is, the point where the graph crosses the y-axis.

Example:

Consider the line represented by the equation $2x + 5y = 12$.

Solution:

Begin by writing this equation in slope-intercept form.

$$2x + 5y = 12 \qquad \text{Subtract } 2x \text{ from both sides.}$$
$$5y = -2x + 12 \qquad \text{Divide both sides by 5.}$$
$$y = -\frac{2}{5}x + \frac{12}{5}$$

Therefore, the slope of the line is $-\frac{2}{5}$, and the y-intercept is $\frac{12}{5}$. Here is the graph of this line.

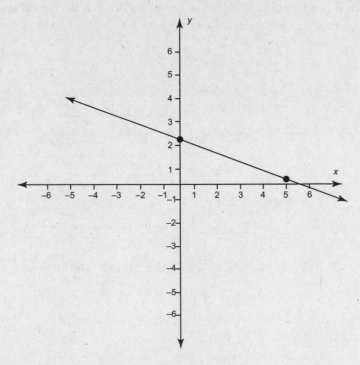

Let's look at a couple more examples.

Example 1:

Write the equation of the line containing the point (2, 1) and having slope 5.

Solution:

Begin by taking the slope-intercept form $y = mx + b$, and substituting $m = 5$ to obtain $y = 5x + b$. To determine the value of the y-intercept b, substitute the coordinates of the point (2, 1) into the equation.

$$y = 5x + b \quad \text{Substitute (2, 1).}$$
$$1 = 5(2) + b \quad \text{Solve for } b.$$
$$1 = 10 + b$$
$$-9 = b$$

Therefore, the equation of the line is $y = 5x - 9$.

Example 2:

Graph the function $f(x) = 2x + 5$.

Solution:

Begin by recognizing that the slope is 2 and the y-intercept is (0, 5). To graph this function, first graph the point (0, 5). Then move up 2 units and then to the right 1 unit. This location is (1, 7). Starting at (0, 5) again, go down 2 units and then to the left 1 unit. This location is (−1, 3). Connect these points to form the graph of the function $f(x) = 2x + 5$.

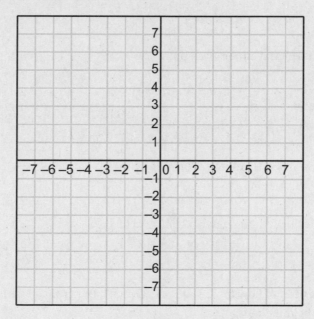

You can write an equation of a line from a graph given any two points on the line. First, use the two points to find the slope. Then use the point–slope form of an equation of a line: $y - y_1 = m(x - x_1)$. As an example, consider the following graph.

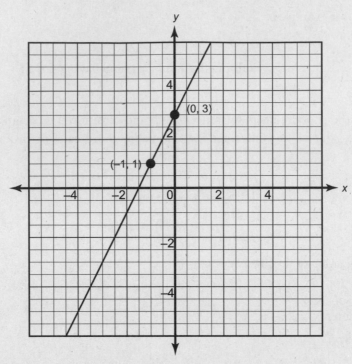

You need to first find the slope using two points on the line.

The slope formula is $m = \dfrac{y_2 - y_1}{x_2 - x_1}$. Use the points $(0, 3)$ and $(-1, 1)$ to find the slope.

$$m = \frac{y_2 - y_1}{x_2 - x_1} = \frac{1 - 3}{-1 - 0} = \frac{-2}{-1} = 2$$

Use the point-slope form and either given point.

$$y - y_1 = m(x - x_1)$$
$$y - 1 = 2(x - (-1))$$
$$y - 1 = 2(x + 1)$$

To write this equation in slope-intercept form, solve for y.

$$y - 1 = 2(x + 1)$$
$$y = 2(x + 1) + 1$$
$$y = 2x + 2 + 1$$
$$y = 2x + 3$$

Here is a sample question of how to write an equation of a line from a word problem and then graph the equation using the intercepts.

Example:

You decide to purchase holiday gift cards for your family. You have $300 to spend on the cards, and you purchase cards for either $20 or $30. What are three combinations of cards that you can purchase?

Solution:

To write an equation that represents this situation, first define your variables.

Let x = number of \$20 gift cards purchased and y = number of \$30 gift cards purchased.

Now write an equation to represent the situation.

$$20x + 30y = 300$$

Use the intercepts to draw the graph.

$$20x + 30y = 300$$
$$20(0) + 30y = 300$$
$$30y = 300$$
$$y = 10$$

$$20x + 30y = 300$$
$$20x + 30(0) = 300$$
$$20x = 300$$
$$x = 15$$

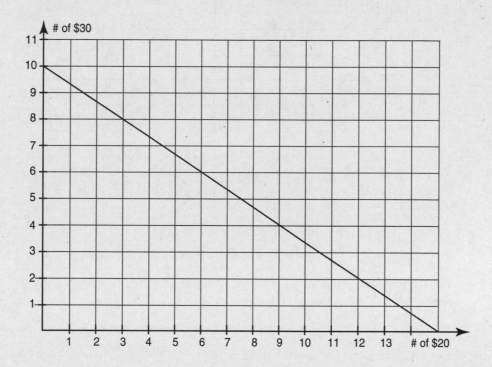

You cannot purchase a fraction of a card, so only the integer combinations can be solutions. You can purchase fifteen \$20 cards and zero \$30 cards, six \$20 cards and six \$30 cards, or zero \$20 cards and ten \$30 cards.

Although the question only asked for three answers, the other possible combinations are twelve \$20 gift cards and two \$30 gift cards, nine \$20 gift cards and four \$30 gift cards, and three \$20 gift cards and eight \$30 gift cards.

Graphing a Circle

The standard form of the equation of a circle with center at (h, k) and radius r is:

$$(x - h)^2 + (y - k)^2 = r^2$$

For example, to graph $y^2 = -x^2 + 64$, first rewrite the equation in standard form:

$$x^2 + y^2 = 64$$

Then identify the radius, $r = 8$, and the center, $(0, 0)$.

Now plot points that are on the circle:

$$(0, 8), (0, -8), (-8, 0), \text{ and } (8, 0)$$

Connect the points to draw the circle.

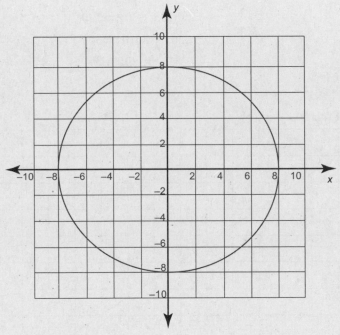

To graph $(x - 1)^2 + (y + 2)^2 = 4$, first identify the radius, $r = 2$, and the center, $(1, -2)$.

Next, plot points that are on the circle. The easiest way to do this is to find points 2 units above, below, left, and right of the center:

$$(1, 0), (1, -4), (-1, -2), \text{ and } (3, -2)$$

Connect the points to draw the circle.

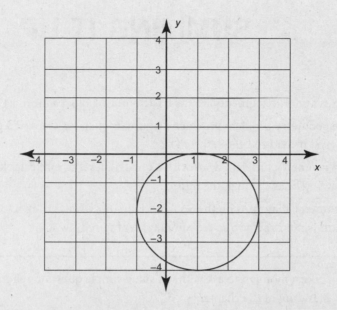

Parallel Lines

Parallel lines have the same slope. Therefore, one way to tell whether two lines are parallel or not is to write them in slope-intercept form and compare the slopes. To write the equation of the line that is parallel to the line $y = 3x + 7$ and contains the point (5, 2), begin by noting that the equation of the line we are looking for must have a slope of 3, just like the line $y = 3x + 7$. Thus, it must be of the form $y = 3x + b$.

$$y = 3x + b$$
$$y = 3x + b \quad \text{Substitute (5, 2).}$$
$$2 = 3(5) + b \quad \text{Solve for } b.$$
$$2 = 15 + b$$
$$-13 = b$$

Therefore, the equation of the line is $y = 3x - 13$.

The slopes of perpendicular lines are **negative reciprocals** of each other. That is, if a line has a slope of $\frac{a}{b}$, then the slope of the perpendicular line would be $-\frac{b}{a}$. Thus, the line perpendicular to the line with slope $\frac{2}{5}$ would have a slope of $-\frac{5}{2}$.

To write the equation of the line that is perpendicular to the line $y = \frac{1}{2}x - 7$ and contains the point (4, −3), begin by noting that the equation of the line to be determined has a slope of −2. Thus, the equation must be of the form $y = -2x + b$.

$$y = -2x + b \quad \text{Substitute (4, −3).}$$
$$-3 = -2(4) + b \quad \text{Solve for } b.$$
$$-3 = -8 + b$$
$$b = 5$$

Therefore, the equation of the line is $y = -2x + 5$.

SUMMING IT UP

- Lines and line segments are the basic building blocks for most geometry problems.

- If a geometry problem provides a figure, mine it for clues. If a geometry problem doesn't provide a figure, sketch one.

- If a geometry problem deals with a quadrilateral or circle, look to form triangles by drawing lines through the figure.

- Geometry diagrams on the SAT exam are not always drawn to scale. If the diagram is not drawn to scale, you may want to redraw it.

Take a moment to ask yourself some simple questions about your understanding of the chapter:

Review: What did I learn?

Evaluate: What do I need to learn more about?

Plan: What can I do next to keep improving?

Based on your answers to those questions, adjust your study plan to dedicate additional time to the areas of weakness that you've identified.

11

BRAIN BREAK

Acupressure is a form of massage therapy used to relieve pain, alleviate anxiety, and promote relaxation. This practice works by applying pressure or a gentle massage to specific points on the body. One of the most common pressure points is located in the webbing between the thumb and index finger. Take a moment and apply pressure to this area with the thumb and index finger of the opposite hand. If you have a headache, shoulder tension, or neck pain, you might find that the pain or tightness lessens when you apply pressure. Another pressure point is right between your eyebrows. Firm pressure in this spot can temporarily alleviate anxiety and stress. Have a knot in the area where your neck and shoulders meet? Gently press against or massage this area to relax your muscles.

PRACTICE EXERCISE: GEOMETRY

DIRECTIONS: Work out each problem in the space provided. Circle the letter of your choice. Check your answers against the answer key and explanations that follow.

1.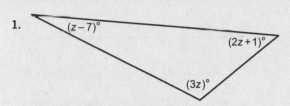

   Determine the value of z:

   A. 24

   B. 31

   C. 45

   D. 61

2. Determine the volume of a right circular cone with base diameter 8 inches and height $\dfrac{5}{2}$ inches.

   A. 20π cubic inches

   B. $\dfrac{40}{3}\pi$ cubic inches

   C. 40π cubic inches

   D. $\dfrac{20}{3}\pi$ cubic inches

3. If the radius of a circle is decreased by 10%, by what percentage is its area decreased?

   A. 10%

   B. 19%

   C. 21%

   D. 81%

4. A spotlight is mounted on the ceiling 5 feet from one wall of a room and 10 feet from the adjacent wall. How many feet is it from the intersection of the two walls?

   A. 15

   B. $5\sqrt{2}$

   C. $5\sqrt{5}$

   D. $10\sqrt{2}$

SHOW YOUR WORK HERE

11

5. A sphere has a diameter of 3 cm, and a cone has a height of 10 cm and a radius of 1.5 cm. How much bigger is the volume of the cone than the volume of the sphere?

A. $0.5\,\pi$

B. π

C. $3\,\pi$

D. $4.5\,\pi$

6.

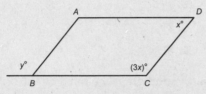

Find the value of y, assuming $ABCD$ is a parallelogram.

A. 45

B. 90

C. 135

D. 180

7.

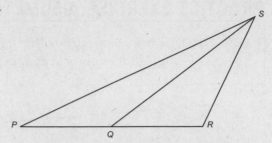

Note: Figure not drawn to scale

If $\overline{PQ} \cong \overline{QS}$, $\overline{QR} \cong \overline{RS}$ and the measure of angle $PRS = 100°$, what is the measure, in degrees, of angle QPS?

A. 10

B. 15

C. 20

D. 25

11

SHOW YOUR WORK HERE

8.

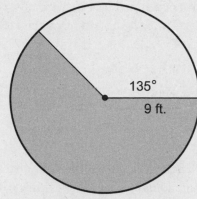

135°

9 ft.

Find the area of the shaded region.

A. 27π square feet

B. 81π square feet

C. $\dfrac{243}{8}$ square feet

D. $\dfrac{405\pi}{8}$ square feet

9. The edges of a rectangular box are in the ratio 2:3:7. If the volume of the box is 1,134 cubic meters, what is the length of the longest edge?

A. 3 meters

B. 6 meters

C. 9 meters

D. 21 meters

10. The surface area of a cube is 150 square feet. How many cubic feet are there in the volume of the cube?

A. 30

B. 50

C. 100

D. 125

11

SHOW YOUR WORK HERE

11.

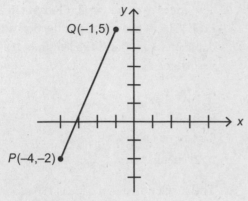

What is the length of segment *PQ*?

A. $\sqrt{10}$

B. $\sqrt{58}$

C. $2\sqrt{10}$

D. $2\sqrt{5}$

12. A square is inscribed in a circle of area 18π. Find a side of the square.

A. 3

B. 6

C. $3\sqrt{2}$

D. $6\sqrt{2}$

13. The cost of a 4-inch by 4-inch ceramic tile is *x* dollars. What is the cost of *y* square feet of such tiles?

A. $9xy$ dollars

B. $3xy$ dollars

C. xy dollars

D. $\dfrac{xy}{9}$

14. If a triangle of base 6 has the same area as a circle of radius 6, what is the altitude of the triangle?

A. 6π

B. 8π

C. 10π

D. 12π

11

15.

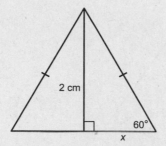

What is the value of x in the figure?

A. 1 cm

B. 2 cm

C. $\dfrac{2}{\sqrt{3}}$

D. $\dfrac{3}{\sqrt{2}}$

16. What is the circumference of a circle with an area of $\dfrac{49\pi}{4}$ square feet?

A. $\dfrac{49\pi}{2}$

B. 7π feet

C. $\dfrac{7\pi}{2}$

D. 14π feet

17. The ice compartment of a refrigerator is 8 inches long, 4 inches wide, and 5 inches high. How many ice cubes will it hold if each cube is 2 inches on an edge?

A. 8

B. 10

C. 12

D. 16

18. What is the equation of the line passing through the points $(1, -4)$ and $(-4, -1)$?

A. $5x - 3y = 17$

B. $3x - 5y = 17$

C. $5x + 3y = -17$

D. $3x + 5y = -17$

19. What is the volume of a sphere with diameter $\dfrac{1}{3}$ inch?

A. $\dfrac{4\pi}{81}$

B. $\dfrac{\pi}{162}$

C. $\dfrac{\pi}{54}$

D. $\dfrac{2\pi}{27}$

SHOW YOUR WORK HERE

11

20.

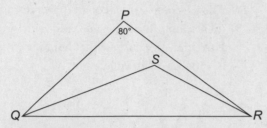

In triangle *PQR*, $\overline{QS}$ and $\overline{SR}$ are angle bisectors (meaning ∠ *PQS* is congruent to ∠ *SQR*, and ∠ *PRS* is congruent to ∠ *SRQ*), and the measure of angle *P* = 80°. How many degrees are there in angle *QSR*?

A. 115°

B. 120°

C. 125°

D. 130°

21. What is the equation of a circle with center (2, –4) and radius 9?

A. $(x + 2)^2 + (y - 4)^2 = 9$

B. $(x + 2)^2 + (y - 4)^2 = 81$

C. $(x - 2)^2 + (y + 4)^2 = 81$

D. $(x - 2)^2 + (y + 4)^2 = 3$

22.

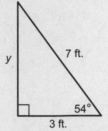

What is the value of *y* in the figure?

A. $3 \sin 54°$

B. $7 \sin 54°$

C. $\dfrac{\cos 54°}{7}$

D. $7 \cos 54°$

23. What is the equation of the line containing the points (4, 6) and (3, 8)?

A. $y = -2x + 14$

B. $y = 2x + 14$

C. $y = -2x + 2$

D. $y = 2x - 2$

11

SHOW YOUR WORK HERE

24. What is the equation of the line that runs perpendicular to the line $y - 2x = 0$ and passes through the point $(-4, 0)$?

  A. $y = 2x + 8$

  B. $y = \dfrac{1}{2}x - 4$

  C. $y = 2x - 4$

  D. $y = -\dfrac{1}{2}x - 2$

25.

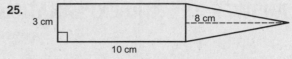

What is the area of region shown above?

  A. 24 square centimeters

  B. 30 square centimeters

  C. 42 square centimeters

  D. 54 square centimeters

SHOW YOUR WORK HERE

ANSWER KEY AND EXPLANATIONS

1. B	6. C	11. B	16. B	21. C
2. B	7. C	12. B	17. D	22. B
3. B	8. D	13. A	18. D	23. A
4. C	9. D	14. D	19. B	24. D
5. C	10. D	15. C	20. D	25. C

1. **The correct answer is B.** The sum of the three angles in a triangle is 180. This yields the equation:

$$(z-7) + (2z+1) + 3z = 180$$
$$6z - 6 = 180$$
$$6z = 186$$
$$z = 31$$

2. **The correct answer is B.** The radius, r, is one-half the diameter or 4 inches. Using this with the height $h = \frac{5}{2}$ inches in the volume formula yields the following:

$$V = \frac{1}{3}\pi r^2 h$$
$$= \frac{1}{3}\pi(4)^2\left(\frac{5}{2}\right)$$
$$= \frac{40\pi}{3} \text{ cubic inches}$$

3. **The correct answer is B.** If the radii of the two circles have a ratio of 10:9, the areas have a ratio of 100:81. Therefore, the decrease is 19 out of 100, or 19%.

4. **The correct answer is C.**

$$5^2 + 10^2 = x^2$$
$$25 + 100 = x^2$$
$$x^2 = 125$$
$$x = \sqrt{125} = \sqrt{25}\sqrt{5} = 5\sqrt{5}$$

5. **The correct answer is C.** The volume of the sphere is calculated using the formula $V = \frac{4}{3}\pi r^3$:

$$V = \frac{4}{3}\pi(1.5)^3 = 4.5\pi$$

The volume of the cone is calculated using the formula $V = \frac{4}{3}\pi r^3$:

$$V = \frac{1}{3}\pi(1.5)^2(10) = 7.5\pi$$

Since $7.5\pi - 4.5\pi = 3\pi$, the volume of the cone is 3π bigger than the volume of the sphere.

6. **The correct answer is C.** Same side angles in a parallelogram sum to 180 degrees. So $x + 3x = 180$, so that $4x = 180$ and $x = 45$. Also, opposite angles are congruent, hence the measure of angle CBA is also 45 degrees. So $y + 45 = 180$; thus $y = 135$.

7. **The correct answer is C.**

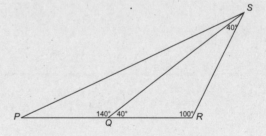

Since $\overline{QR} \cong \overline{RS}, \angle RQS \cong \angle RSQ$. There are 80° left in the triangle, so each of these angles is 40°. $\angle SQP$ is supplementary to $\angle SQR$, making it 140°. Since $\overline{QP} \cong \overline{QS}, \angle QPS \cong \angle QSP$. There are 40° left in the triangle, so each of these angles is 20°.

8. **The correct answer is D.** The central angle corresponding to the shaded region is $360 - 135 = 225$ degrees. So the area of the shaded region is $\frac{225}{360} \cdot \pi \cdot (9)^2 = \frac{405\pi}{8}$ square feet.

9. **The correct answer is D.** The width, length, and height of the rectangular box are $2x$, $3x$,

and $7x$, for some real number x. Since the volume is the product of the width, length, and height, we get the equation:

$$(2x)(3x)(7x) = 1,134$$
$$42x^3 = 1,134$$
$$x^3 = 27$$
$$x = 3$$

The longest edge is $3(7) = 21$ meters.

10. **The correct answer is D.** The surface area of a cube is made up of 6 equal squares. If each edge of the cube is x, then

$$6x^2 = 150$$
$$x^2 = 25$$
$$x = 5$$

Volume = (edge)^3 = $5^3 = 125$

11. **The correct answer is B.** Use the distance formula to solve:

$$\sqrt{\left(-4-(-1)\right)^2 + \left(-2-5\right)^2} = \sqrt{(-3)^2 + (-7)^2}$$
$$= \sqrt{9+49}$$
$$= \sqrt{58}$$

12. **The correct answer is B.**

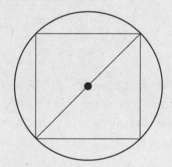

The diagonal of the square will be a diameter of the circle.

$$\pi r^2 = 18\pi$$
$$r^2 = 18$$
$$r = \sqrt{18} = \sqrt{9}\sqrt{2} = 3\sqrt{2}$$

The diameter is $6\sqrt{2}$ and, since the triangles are 45°-45°-90°, a side of the square is 6.

13. **The correct answer is A.** There are nine 4-inch by 4-inch tiles in one square-foot tile. So the cost of one square-foot tile is $9x$ dollars. Thus, the cost of y square-foot tiles is $9xy$ dollars.

14. **The correct answer is D.** The area of the circle is $(6)^2 \pi$, or 36π. In the triangle:

$$\frac{1}{2}(6)(h) = 36\pi$$
$$3h = 36\pi$$
$$h = 12\pi$$

15. **The correct answer is C.** The triangle is equilateral, so the height bisects the base. Thus, the length of the base is $2x$ cm; so all three sides have length $2x$ cm. The hypotenuse of the right triangle is $2x$. The base is x cm and height is 2 cm. Using the Pythagorean theorem yields the following:

$$x^2 = \frac{4}{3}$$

16. **The correct answer is B.** Let r be the radius of the circle. Then, $\pi r^2 = \frac{49}{4}\pi$. Solve for r:

$$\pi r^2 = \frac{49}{4}\pi$$
$$r^2 = \frac{49}{4}$$
$$r = \sqrt{\frac{49}{4}}$$
$$r = \frac{7}{2}$$

The circumference is $2\pi\left(\frac{7}{2}\right) = 7\pi$ feet.

17. **The correct answer is D.** The compartment will hold 2 layers, each of which contains 2 rows of 4 cubes each. This leaves a height of 1 inch on top empty. Therefore, the compartment can hold 16 cubes.

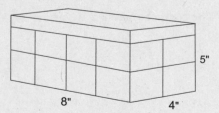

18. **The correct answer is D.** The slope of the line is $m = \dfrac{-1-(-4)}{-4-1} = -\dfrac{3}{5}$. Using the point-slope formula for the equation of a line, namely $y - y_1 = m(x - x_1)$, with the point $(1, -4)$, yields:

$$y - y_1 = m\left(x - x_1\right)$$
$$y - (-4) = -\frac{3}{5}(x - 1)$$
$$y + 4 = -\frac{3}{5}x + \frac{3}{5}$$
$$y = -\frac{3}{5}x - \frac{17}{5}$$
$$5y = -3x - 17$$
$$3x + 5y = -17$$

19. **The correct answer is B.** Let R be the radius of the sphere so that $R = \dfrac{1}{2}\left(\dfrac{1}{3}\right) = \dfrac{1}{6}$ inch. The volume is:

$$V = \frac{4}{3}\pi R^3$$
$$= \frac{4}{3}\pi\left(\frac{1}{6}\right)^3$$
$$= \frac{4\pi}{3} \cdot \frac{1}{216}$$
$$= \frac{\pi}{162} \text{ cubic inches}$$

20. **The correct answer is D.** If $m\angle P = 80°$, there are $100°$ left between $\angle PQR$ and $\angle PRQ$. If they are both bisected, there will be $50°$ between $\angle SQR$ and $\angle SRQ$, leaving $130°$ for $\angle QSR$.

21. **The correct answer is C.** The standard form for a circle is $(x - h)^2 + (y - k)^2 = r^2$, where (h, k) is the center and r is the radius. Here, $h = 2$, $k = -4$, and $r = 9$. Substituting these in and simplifying yields the equation $(x - 2)^2 + (y + 4)^2 = 81$.

22. **The correct answer is B.** $\sin 54° = \dfrac{y}{7}$ so that $y = 7 \sin 54°$.

23. **The correct answer is A.** The formula for the slope of a line is $m = \dfrac{(y_2 - y_1)}{(x_2 - x_1)}$, where (x_1, y_1) and (x_2, y_2) are any two points on the line. In this problem, the two points are $(4, 6)$ and $(3, 8)$, so

$$m = \frac{(y_2 - y_1)}{(x_2 - x_1)} = \frac{8 - 6}{3 - 4} = \frac{2}{-1} = -2.$$

Use either point and the slope to complete the equation.

$$y = mx + b$$
$$6 = (-2)(4) + b$$
$$6 = -8 + b$$
$$14 = b$$

The equation of the line is $y = -2x + 14$.

24. **The correct answer is D.** The given line's equation can be written as $y = 2x$. Its slope is 2, so the slope of the desired line, being perpendicular to this one, is $-\dfrac{1}{2}$. Using the point-slope formula for the equation of a line, namely $y - y_1 = m(x - x_1)$, with the point $(-4, 0)$, yields:

$$y - 0 = -\frac{1}{2}(x + 4)$$
$$y = -\frac{1}{2}x - 2$$

25. **The correct answer is C.** The area of the rectangular portion is $(3 \text{ cm})(10 \text{ cm}) = 30$ square centimeters. The area of the triangle portion is

$$\frac{1}{2}(3 \text{ cm})(8 \text{ cm}) = 12 \text{ square centimeters.}$$

So the area of the entire region is $30 + 12 = 42$ square centimeters.

11

Chapter 12

Functions and Intermediate Algebra

OVERVIEW

- **Functions**
- **Practice Exercise**
- **Integer and Rational Exponents**
- **Practice Exercise**
- **Solving Complex Equations**
- **Practice Exercise**
- **Linear, Quadratic, and Exponential Functions**
- **Practice Exercise**
- **Summing It Up**

FUNCTIONS

Definitions and Notation

Let D and R be any two sets of numbers. A **function** is a rule that assigns to each element of D one and only one element of R. The set D is called the **domain** of the function, and the set R is called the **range**. A function can be specified by listing all of the elements in the first set next to the corresponding elements in the second set or by giving a rule or a formula by which elements from the first set can be associated with elements from the second set.

As an example, let the set $D = \{1, 2, 3, 4\}$ and set $R = \{5, 6, 7, 8\}$. The diagram below indicates a particular function, f, by showing how each element of D is associated with an element of R.

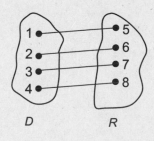

This diagram shows that the domain value of 1 is associated with the range value of 5. Similarly, 2 is associated with 6, 3 is associated with 7, and 4 is associated with 8. The function f can also be described in words by saying that f is the function that assigns to each domain value x the range value $x + 4$.

Typically, the letter x is used to represent the elements of the domain and the letter y is used to represent the elements of the range. This enables us to write the equation $y = x + 4$ to express the rule of association for the function above.

Note that as soon as a domain value x is selected, a range value y is determined by this rule. For this reason, x is referred to as the **independent variable**, and y is called the **dependent variable**.

Often, the rule of association for a function is written in **function notation**. In this notation, the symbol f (x), which is read "f of x," is used instead of y to represent the range value. Therefore, the rule for our function can be written $f(x) = x + 4$. If you were asked to determine which range value was associated with the domain value of, say, 3, you would compute $f(x) = f(3) = 3 + 4 = 7$. Note that, in this notation, the letter f is typically used to stand for "function," although any other letter could also be used. Therefore, this rule could also be written as $g(x) = x + 4$.

Example 1:

Using function notation, write the rule for a function that associates, to each number in the domain, a range value that is 7 less than 5 times the domain value.

Solution:

$$f(x) = 5x - 7$$

Example 2:

Use the function from the problem above to determine the range value that is associated with a domain value of −12.

Solution:

$$f(-12) = 5(-12) - 7 = -60 - 7 = -67$$

Example 3:

If $f(x) = 8x + 9$, determine the value of $f(5)$, $f(q)$, $f(p^2)$, and $f(r + 3)$.

Solution:

$$f(5) = 8(5) + 9 = 40 + 9 = 49$$

In the same way, to determine the value of $f(q)$, simply substitute q for the value of x in the rule for $f(x)$. Therefore, $f(q) = 8q + 9$.

Similarly, $f(p^2) = 8(p^2) + 9 = 8p^2 + 9$.

Similarly, $f(r + 3) = 8(r + 3) + 9 = 8r + 24 + 9 = 8r + 33$.

Families of Functions

A **family** of functions is a group of functions with similar characteristics. The **parent function** is the most basic function in a family.

A **linear function** is a function whose graph is a straight line. $f(x) = x$ is the parent function for all linear functions. A **quadratic function** is a function whose graph is a parabola. The graph shown, $f(x) = x^2$, is the parent function for all quadratic functions.

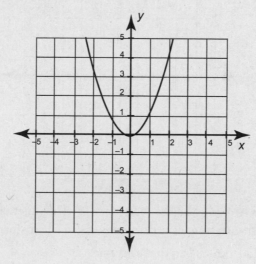

Example 1:

Compare $f(x) = 2x^2$ to $f(x) = x^2$.

Solution:

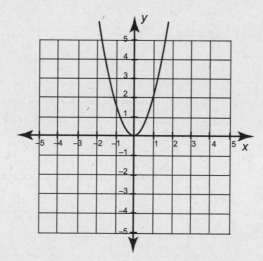

The graphs $f(x) = 2x^2$ and $f(x) = x^2$ both open up, have (0, 0) as their vertices, and have the same axis of symmetry $x = 0$. The graph $f(x) = 2x^2$ is narrower than the graph of $f(x) = x^2$.

12

Example 2:

How does the graph $f(x) = x^2 + 2$ compare to the parent function $f(x) = x^2$?

Solution:

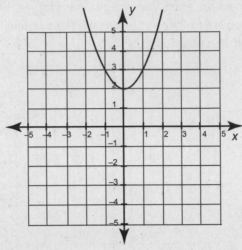

The graph $f(x) = x^2 + 2$ is two units higher than $f(x) = x^2$. The function $f(x) = x^2$ has been shifted up 2 units. The shifting, or **translating**, of a function is called a **transformation**.

To move a function up, add a value b to the function:

$$f(x) = x^2 + b$$

To move a function down, subtract a value b from the function:

$$f(x) = x^2 - b$$

The function $f(x) = (x + 2)^2$ looks like the following:

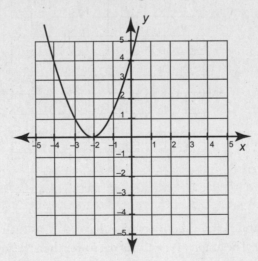

Part VI

Its graph has been shifted to the left 2 units. To shift a function to the left, add a value b to inside the function:

$$f(x) = (x + b)^2$$

To shift a function to the right, subtract a value b to inside the function:

$$f(x) = (x - b)^2$$

The function $-f(x)$ is $f(x)$ flipped upside down (across the x-axis), while $f(-x)$ is the mirror of $f(x)$ (flipped across the y-axis):

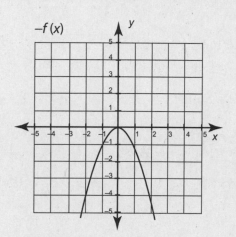
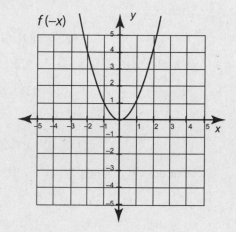

Example 3:
Describe how the function $f(x) = -2x^2 + 3$ compares with the graph $f(x) = x^2$.

Solution:
Both graphs have the same axis of symmetry but the graph $f(x) = -2x^2 + 3$ opens downward and is narrower than the graph of $f(x) = x^2$.

The vertex of $f(x) = -2x^2 + 3$ is 3 units higher than the vertex of $f(x) = x^2$.

Perform Operations on Functions and Compositions

You can add, subtract, multiply, and divide any two functions. For example, let $f(x) = 4x^2$ and $g(x) = x^2 + 9x + 6$.

Addition: $f(x) + g(x) = 4x^2 + (x^2 + 9x + 6) = 5x^2 + 9x + 6$

Subtraction: $f(x) - g(x) = 4x^2 - (x^2 + 9x + 6) = 3x^2 - 9x - 6$

Multiplication: $f(x) \cdot g(x) = 4x^2(x^2 + 9x + 6) = 4x^4 + 36x^3 + 24x^2$

Division: $\dfrac{f(x)}{g(x)} = \dfrac{4x^2}{x^2 + 9x + 6}$

FUN FACTS
The Arch in St. Louis is shaped like a parabola. So is a satellite receiver. Since the launch of Sputnik in 1957, nearly 8,400 satellites have been sent into space. According to the Index of Objects Launched into Outer Space maintained by the United Nations Office for Outer Space, 4,987 satellites are currently orbiting Earth.

The composition of functions involves applying two functions in succession. The composition of a function $g(x)$ with a function $f(x)$ is written as $g(f(x))$, read as "g of f of x."

Example:

Let $f(x) = 6x^3 + 2$ and $g(x) = 2x^2 - 8$. Find $f(g(3))$ and $g(f(3))$.

Solution:

To evaluate $f(g(3))$, first find $g(3)$.

$$g(3) = 2(3)^2 - 8 = 10$$

Then:

$$f(g(3)) = f(10) = 6(10)^3 + 2 = 6{,}002$$

To evaluate $g(f(3))$, first find $f(3)$.

$$f(3) = 6(3)^3 + 2 = 164$$

Then:

$$g(f(164)) = g(164) = 2(164)^2 - 8 = 53{,}784$$

Generally, $f(g(x)) \neq g(f(x))$.

12

BRAIN BREAK

Let's play a game of "Would You Rather?" Would you rather spend the day at the beach or in the mountains? Would you rather have the superpower of invisibility or immortality? Would you rather be reborn into the past or future? Would you rather be able to pause real-life or rewind and do-over?

PRACTICE EXERCISE: FUNCTIONS

DIRECTIONS: Work out each problem. Circle the letter of your choice. Check your answers against the answer key and explanations that follow.

1. What is the effect on the graph of the function $f(x) = 2x^2 + 5$ when it is changed to $f(x) = 2x^2 - 3$?

   A. The graph gets narrower.
   B. The graph opens down.
   C. The graph gets wider.
   D. The graph shifts down the y-axis.

2. What is the highest point on the graph of the parabola $g(x) = -(x + 4)^2 - 5$?

   A. $(4, 5)$
   B. $(-4, 5)$
   C. $(-4, -5)$
   D. $(4, -5)$

3. If $m(x) = x(x + 5)$ and $n(x) = 1 - \frac{1}{2}x^2$, compute $(m - n)(-2)$.

   A. -7
   B. -6
   C. -5
   D. -1

4. The profit from selling x number of sweatshirts can be described by the function $p(x) = 22x - 230$. What is the profit if 200 sweatshirts are sold?

   A. $4,170
   B. $4,280
   C. $4,400
   D. $4,630

SHOW YOUR WORK HERE

12

5. If $d(x) = \dfrac{9 - x^2}{16 + x^2}$ and $e(x) = \sqrt{x}$, compute $(e \circ d)(x)$.

   A. $\dfrac{\sqrt{x}\left(9 - x^2\right)}{16 + x^2}$

   B. $\dfrac{9 - x}{16 + x}$

   C. $\dfrac{3 - x}{4 + x}$

   D. $\sqrt{\dfrac{9 - x^2}{16 + x^2}}$

6. A company sells designer keychains. Its monthly revenue is modeled by $R(x) = 27x$, and its costs are modeled by $C(x) = 7x + 1,200$, where x is the number of keychains sold. Find $R(x) - C(x)$.

   A. $-34x + 1,200$

   B. $20x + 1,200$

   C. $20x - 1,200$

   D. $34x - 1,200$

7. Which of these functions is the result of shifting $f(x) = |x|$ down 5 units?

   A. $g(x) = |x - 5|$

   B. $g(x) = |x| - 5$

   C. $g(x) = |x + 5|$

   D. $g(x) = -5|x|$

8. You earn \$17.50 per hour at your job. You are given a raise of 2% after 5 months. In addition, you receive \$1 per hour for being a model employee. Find your new hourly wage if the \$1 raise is applied before the 2% raise.

   A. \$18.13

   B. \$18.15

   C. \$18.85

   D. \$18.87

12

SHOW YOUR WORK HERE

9. If $f(x) = x - \dfrac{1}{x}$ and $g(x) = x + \dfrac{1}{x}$, compute $(f \cdot g)\left(-\dfrac{1}{2}\right)$.

A. $-\dfrac{15}{4}$

B. -2

C. 0

D. $\dfrac{3}{4}$

10. If $j(x) = 2\sqrt{x} - 1$ and $k(x) = |1 - x|$, compute $(j \circ k)(-3)$.

A. 1

B. 3

C. 7

D. Not defined

SHOW YOUR WORK HERE

12

Answer Key and Explanations

1. D	3. C	5. D	7. B	9. A
2. C	4. A	6. C	8. D	10. B

1. **The correct answer is D.** The vertex of the graph changes from (0, 5) to (0, –3). The original graph is translated down the y-axis.

2. **The correct answer is C.** The standard form for a quadratic function is $f(x) = a(x - h)^2 + k$, where the vertex is (h, k); this is the highest point on the function if a is negative, as in the given function. Here, $h = -4$ and $k = -5$, so that the vertex is $(-4, -5)$.

3. **The correct answer is C.**
$(m - n)(-2) = m(-2) - n(-2)$

   Observe:
   $m(-2) = -2(3) = -6$

   $n(-2) = 1 - \frac{1}{2}(-2)^2 = 1 - \frac{1}{2}(4) = 1 - 2 = -1$

   So $(m - n)(-2) = -6 - (-1) = -6 + 1 = -5.$

4. **The correct answer is A.**

   $p(200) = 22(200) - 230 = 4{,}170.$

   The profit is $4,170.

5. **The correct answer is D.**
$$(e \circ d)(x) = e(d(x))$$

$$= e\left(\frac{9 - x^2}{16 + x^2}\right)$$

$$= \sqrt{\frac{9 - x^2}{16 + x^2}}$$

6. **The correct answer is C.**
$$R(x) - C(x) = 27x - (7x + 1{,}200)$$
$$= 27x - 7x - 1{,}200$$
$$= 20x - 1{,}200$$

7. **The correct answer is B.** Moving a function down 5 units is performed by subtracting 5 from the output, which here $|x|$. The desired function is $g(x) = |x| - 5.$

8. **The correct answer is D.** Let x be your hourly wage. The function for the 2% raise is $f(x) = x + .02x = 1.02x$. The function for the $1 raise is $g(x) = x + 1$. The composition $f(g(x))$ represents the hourly wage when the $1 raise is applied before the 2% raise.

$$f(g(x)) = f(x + 1)$$
$$= 1.02(x + 1)$$
$$= 1.02(17.5 + 1)$$
$$= 1.02(18.50)$$
$$= 18.87$$

   Your new hourly wage is $18.87.

9. **The correct answer is A.**
   First,
$$(f \cdot g)(x) = f(x) \cdot g(x)$$
$$= \left(x - \frac{1}{x}\right) \cdot \left(x + \frac{1}{x}\right)$$
$$= x^2 - \frac{1}{x^2}$$

   Then,
$$(f \cdot g)\left(-\frac{1}{2}\right) = \left(-\frac{1}{2}\right)^2 - \frac{1}{\left(-\frac{1}{2}\right)^2}$$

$$= \frac{1}{4} - \frac{1}{\frac{1}{4}}$$

$$= \frac{1}{4} - 4$$

$$= -\frac{15}{4}$$

10. **The correct answer is B**
$$(j \circ k)(-3) = f(k(-3))$$

   Since $k(-3) = |1 - (-3)| = |4| = 4,$ we see that:

$$f(k(-3)) = f(4)$$
$$= 2\sqrt{4} - 1$$
$$= 2(2) - 1$$
$$= 4 - 1$$
$$= 3$$

12

INTEGER AND RATIONAL EXPONENTS

Chapter 10: "Basic Algebra" contains the definitions and the rules for positive integer exponents. The following section extends these definitions to integer and rational exponents.

Integer Exponents

Negative exponents are defined in the following way:

$$\text{For any positive integer } n, \ x^{-n} = \frac{1}{x^n}.$$

For example, $4^{-2} = \frac{1}{4^2} = \frac{1}{16}$. Similarly, $\left(\frac{2}{3}\right)^{-4} = \left(\frac{3}{2}\right)^4 = \frac{3^4}{2^4} = \frac{81}{16}$.

All of the properties of exponents discussed in Chapter 11 apply to expressions with negative exponents as well. Thus, the expression $x^{-7} \cdot x^4$ is equal to $x^{-3} = \frac{1}{x^3}$, and $\frac{y^{-5}}{y^{-11}} = y^{-5-(-11)} = y^{-5+11} = y^6$.

Examples:

Determine the value of the following expressions:

1. $8^{-2} \cdot 8^4$

2. $x^5 \cdot x^{-5}$

3. $\dfrac{y^4}{y^{-9}}$

4. $\dfrac{x^{-2}y^9}{x^7 y^3}$

Solutions:

1. $8^{-2} \cdot 8^4 = 8^2 = 64$

2. $x^5 \cdot x^{-5} = x^0 = x$

3. $\dfrac{y^4}{y^{-9}} = y^4 y^9 = y^{13}$

4. $\dfrac{x^{-2}y^9}{x^7 y^3} = \dfrac{y^{9-3}}{x^{7-(-2)}} = \dfrac{y^6}{x^9}$

Examples:

1. If $f(x) = 5^{-x}$, what is the value of $f(-2)$?
2. If $f(x) = 5^{-x}$, what is the value of $f(2)$?

Solutions:

1. $f(-2) = 5^{-(-2)} = 5^2 = 25$
2. $f(2) = 5^{-2} = \dfrac{1}{5^2} = \dfrac{1}{25}$

12

Rational Exponents

The definition of exponents can also be extended to include rational numbers:

For a rational number, x to the power of $\frac{1}{n}$ is defined as the nth root of x. In other words, $x^{\frac{1}{n}}$ is equal to $\sqrt[n]{x}$. Therefore, $\sqrt{5}$ can be written as $5^{\frac{1}{2}}$. Similarly, $8^{\frac{1}{3}}$ represents $\sqrt[3]{8}$ and is thus equal to 2.

Next, $x^{\frac{m}{n}}$ is defined to mean $(x^{\frac{1}{n}})^m$, for $x > 0$ and $n > 0$. Therefore, when you are given a number with a rational exponent, the numerator represents the power to which the number is to be raised, and the denominator represents the root to be taken. The expression $16^{\frac{5}{4}}$ tells you to take the fourth root of 16 and then raise the result to the fifth power. This expression can be evaluated in the following way:

$$16^{\frac{5}{4}} = \left(\sqrt[4]{16}\right)^5 = (2)^5 = 32$$

In summary, all of the properties of exponents apply to expressions with rational exponents.

Examples:

Determine the value of the following expressions:

1. $27^{\frac{1}{3}}$

2. $64^{-\frac{2}{3}}$

3. $2x^{\frac{5}{6}} \cdot 3x^{-\frac{1}{3}}$

Solutions:

1. $27^{\frac{1}{3}} = \sqrt[3]{27} = 3$

2. $64^{-\frac{2}{3}} = \left(\frac{1}{64}\right)^{\frac{2}{3}} = \left(\sqrt[3]{\frac{1}{64}}\right)^2 = \left(\frac{1}{4}\right)^2 = \frac{1}{16}$

3. $2x^{\frac{5}{6}} \cdot 3x^{-\frac{1}{3}} = 6x^{\frac{5}{6} - \frac{1}{3}} = 6x^{\frac{1}{2}}$

12

Examples:

Simplify the following expressions:

1. $\left(25a^6\right)^{\frac{1}{2}}$

2. $\dfrac{b^{\frac{1}{3}}}{b^{-\frac{2}{3}}}$

3. $\left(c^{-\frac{1}{8}}d^{\frac{3}{4}}\right)^{16}$

4. $\sqrt{4x^3} \cdot \sqrt{8x^5}$

Solutions:

1. $\left(25a^6\right)^{\frac{1}{2}} = 25^{\frac{1}{2}}\left(a^6\right)^{\frac{1}{2}} = \sqrt{25}\,a^3 = 5a^3$

2. $\dfrac{b^{\frac{1}{3}}}{b^{-\frac{2}{3}}} = b^{\frac{1}{3}}b^{\frac{2}{3}} = b^{\frac{1}{3}+\frac{2}{3}} = b^1 = b$

3. $\left(c^{-\frac{1}{8}}d^{\frac{3}{4}}\right)^{16} = \left(c^{-\frac{1}{8}}\right)^{16}\left(d^{\frac{3}{4}}\right)^{16} = c^{-2}d^{12} = \dfrac{d^{12}}{c^2}$

4. $\sqrt{4x^3} \cdot \sqrt{8x^5} = 4^{\frac{1}{2}}x^{\frac{3}{2}} \cdot 8^{\frac{1}{2}}x^{\frac{5}{2}}$

$$= 4^{\frac{1}{2}} \cdot 8^{\frac{1}{2}}x^{\frac{3}{2}}x^{\frac{5}{2}}$$

$$= 2\left(2\sqrt{2}\right)x^{\frac{3}{2}+\frac{5}{2}}$$

$$= 4\sqrt{2}x^4$$

12

PRACTICE EXERCISE: INTEGER AND RATIONAL EXPONENTS

DIRECTIONS: Work out each problem. Circle the letter of your choice. Check your answers against the answer key and explanations that follow.

---

1. Simplify the expression: $\sqrt{8x} \cdot \sqrt{4x^3}$

   A. $32x^{\frac{3}{2}}$

   B. $16\sqrt{2x^4}$

   C. $4x^4$

   D. $4\sqrt{2}x^2$

2. Simplify the expression: $\sqrt{25x^4y^6} \cdot \sqrt{3x^3y^5}$

   A. $3x^{\frac{7}{2}}y^{\frac{11}{2}}$

   B. $5\sqrt{3}x^{\frac{7}{2}}y^{\frac{11}{2}}$

   C. $15x^{12}y^{11}$

   D. $75x^7y^{11}$

3. Which of these expressions is equivalent to $\left(\dfrac{4x^{-3}y^2}{3x^4y^{-1}}\right)^{-2}$?

   A. $\dfrac{4x^9y^3}{3}$

   B. $\dfrac{9x^{14}}{16y^6}$

   C. $\dfrac{16y^6}{9x^{14}}$

   D. $\dfrac{3}{4x^9y^3}$

4. Simplify the expression: $\dfrac{a^5b^{-2}c^{-3}}{a^{-2}b^4c^{-2}}$

   A. $\dfrac{a^7}{b^6c}$

   B. $\dfrac{a^7c}{b^2}$

   C. $\dfrac{a^3}{b^2c}$

   D. $\dfrac{a^3c^5}{b^2}$

12

SHOW YOUR WORK HERE

5. Which of these expressions is equivalent to

$-\left(a^2b^{-2}\right)^{-\frac{1}{2}}$?

A. $\dfrac{a}{b}$

B. $-\dfrac{a}{b}$

C. $\dfrac{b}{a}$

D. $-\dfrac{b}{a}$

6. Simplify the expression: $\left(49x^4y^8z^{-6}\right)^{\frac{1}{2}}$

A. $49x^2y^4z^6$

B. $7x^3y^4z^3$

C. $\dfrac{y^4}{7x^2z^3}$

D. $\dfrac{7x^2y^4}{z^3}$

7. Which of these expressions is equivalent to

$\dfrac{\sqrt[4]{81x^8y^{16}}}{\sqrt[4]{x^{24}y^{20}}}$?

A. $\dfrac{3}{x^4y}$

B. $\dfrac{3}{x^{15}y^4}$

C. $3x^4y$

D. $3x^{15}y^4$

8. Which of these expressions is equivalent to

$\dfrac{64x^{\frac{2}{3}}}{\left(64x^3\right)^{\frac{1}{2}}}$?

A. $\dfrac{2}{x^{\frac{5}{6}}}$

B. $\dfrac{2}{x}$

C. $\dfrac{8}{x^{\frac{5}{6}}}$

D. $2x$

9. Which of these expressions is equivalent to $\left(-\dfrac{1}{2}x^3\right)^{-3}$?

A. $\dfrac{-8}{x^9}$

B. $\dfrac{x^9}{8}$

C. $-8x^9$

D. $-\dfrac{1}{8x^6}$

10. Compute $64^{\frac{2}{3}} - 27^{\frac{1}{3}}$.

A. $\sqrt[3]{37}$

B. 5

C. 13

D. 19

SHOW YOUR WORK HERE

Answer Key and Explanations

1. D	3. B	5. D	7. A	9. A
2. B	4. A	6. D	8. C	10. C

1. The correct answer is D.

$$\sqrt{8x} \cdot \sqrt{4x^3} = (8x)^{\frac{1}{2}}\left(4x^3\right)^{\frac{1}{2}}$$
$$= \left(2\sqrt{2}x^{\frac{1}{2}}\right)\left(2x^{\frac{3}{2}}\right)$$
$$= 4\sqrt{2}x^2$$

2. The correct answer is B.

$$\sqrt{25x^4y^6} \cdot \sqrt{3x^3y^5} = \left(25x^4y^6\right)^{\frac{1}{2}}\left(3x^3y^5\right)^{\frac{1}{2}}$$
$$= 5x^2y^3 \cdot 3^{\frac{1}{2}}x^{\frac{3}{2}}y^{\frac{5}{2}}$$
$$= 5 \cdot 3^{\frac{1}{2}}x^{2+\frac{3}{2}}y^{3+\frac{5}{2}}$$
$$= 5\sqrt{3}x^{\frac{7}{2}}y^{\frac{11}{2}}$$

3. The correct answer is B. Apply the exponent rules.

$$\left(\frac{4x^{-3}y^2}{3x^4y^{-1}}\right)^{-2} = \left(\frac{4y^2y^1}{3x^4x^3}\right)^{-2}$$
$$= \left(\frac{4y^3}{3x^7}\right)^{-2}$$
$$= \left(\frac{3x^7}{4y^3}\right)^{2}$$
$$= \frac{3^2\left(x^7\right)^2}{4^2\left(y^3\right)^2}$$
$$= \frac{9x^{14}}{16y^6}$$

4. The correct answer is A.

$$\frac{a^5b^{-2}c^{-3}}{a^{-2}b^4c^{-2}} = a^{5-(-2)}b^{-2-4}c^{-3-(-2)}$$
$$= a^7b^{-6}c^{-1}$$
$$= \frac{a^7}{b^6c}$$

5. The correct answer is D.

$$-\left(a^2b^{-2}\right)^{-\frac{1}{2}} = -\left(a^2\right)^{-\frac{1}{2}}\left(b^{-2}\right)^{\frac{1}{2}}$$
$$= -a^{-1}b^1$$
$$= -\frac{b}{a}$$

6. The correct answer is D.

$$\left(49x^4y^8z^{-6}\right)^{\frac{1}{2}} = 49^{\frac{1}{2}}x^{\frac{4}{2}}y^{\frac{8}{2}}z^{\frac{-6}{2}}$$
$$= 7x^2y^4z^{-3}$$
$$= \frac{7x^2y^4}{z^3}$$

7. The correct answer is A. Compute each radical and then simplify the resulting quotient using the exponent rules:

$$\frac{\sqrt[4]{81x^8y^{16}}}{\sqrt[4]{x^{24}y^{20}}} = \frac{\sqrt[4]{81} \cdot \sqrt[4]{x^8} \cdot \sqrt[4]{y^{16}}}{\sqrt[4]{x^{24}} \cdot \sqrt[4]{y^{20}}}$$
$$= \frac{3x^2y^4}{x^6y^5}$$
$$= \frac{3}{x^4y}$$

8. The correct answer is C.

$$\frac{64x^{\frac{2}{3}}}{\left(64x^3\right)^{\frac{1}{2}}} = \frac{64x^{\frac{2}{3}}}{(64)^{\frac{1}{2}}\left(x^3\right)^{\frac{1}{2}}}$$
$$= \frac{64x^{\frac{2}{3}}}{8x^{\frac{3}{2}}}$$
$$= \frac{8}{x^{\frac{3}{2}-\frac{2}{3}}}$$
$$= \frac{8}{x^{\frac{5}{6}}}$$

12

9. The correct answer is A.

$$\left(-\frac{1}{2}x^3\right)^{-3} = \left(-\frac{1}{2}\right)^{-3}\left(x^3\right)^{-3}$$

$$= (-2)^3\left(x^3\right)^{-3}$$

$$= -8x^{-9}$$

$$= -\frac{8}{x^9}$$

10. The correct answer is C.

$$64^{\frac{2}{3}} - 27^{\frac{1}{3}} = \left(64^{\frac{1}{3}}\right)^2 - 27^{\frac{1}{3}}$$

$$= 4^2 - 3$$

$$= 16 - 3$$

$$= 13$$

BRAIN BREAK

Go outside and take a walk. Walking can help improve your mood, clear your brain, and stimulate the production of endorphins. If the weather isn't cooperating, see if you can find a place where you can breathe in fresh air. Close your eyes and focus on taking slow, deep breaths. Let the fresh air relax your body and energize your mind.

12

SOLVING COMPLEX EQUATIONS

Chapter 10: "Basic Algebra" describes how to solve linear and quadratic equations. The following section discusses how to solve some of the more complex equations and inequalities that appear on the SAT exam.

Equations Involving Rational Expressions

A **rational expression** is a fraction that contains variables in the numerator and/or the denominator. The quickest way to solve equations containing rational expressions is to determine the **least common denominator (LCD)** of all of the fractions in the equation and then eliminate the fractions by multiplying each term in the equation by this LCD. There are four steps involved in solving such an equation:

1. Find the LCD of all of the rational expressions in the equation.

2. Multiply *every* term on both sides of the equation by this LCD.

3. Solve the resulting equation using the methods previously explained.

4. Check the solution to make certain that it actually solves the equation.

Note that step 4, checking the solution, is crucial because sometimes the process produces a solution that does not actually solve the equation. Such extraneous solutions need to be eliminated.

Example 1:

Solve for x: $\dfrac{7x}{5} + \dfrac{3}{8} = 10$

Solution:

The LCD of the two fractions in the equation is 40, so every term must be multiplied by 40.

$$40\left(\frac{7x}{5}\right) + 40\left(\frac{3}{8}\right) = 40(10) \qquad \text{Perform the multiplications.}$$

$$8(7x) + 5(3) = 400$$

$$56x + 15 = 400 \qquad \text{Subtract 15 from both sides.}$$

$$56x = 385 \qquad \text{Divide both sides by 56.}$$

$$x = \frac{385}{56} = \frac{55}{8} = 6\frac{7}{8}$$

Check that the answer is correct by substituting $\dfrac{55}{8}$ into the original equation.

$$\frac{7\left(\dfrac{55}{8}\right)}{5} + \frac{3}{8} = 10$$

$$\frac{\dfrac{385}{8}}{5} + \frac{3}{8} = 10$$

$$\frac{77}{8} + \frac{3}{8} = 10$$

$$10 = 10 \quad \text{True}$$

12

Example 2:

Solve for x: $\dfrac{5}{x-4} - \dfrac{3}{x+4} = \dfrac{36}{x^2-16}$

Solution:

Begin by finding the LCD of the three fractions. Note that since $x^2 - 16 = (x - 4)(x + 4)$, the LCD is $(x - 4)(x + 4)$. Each term must be multiplied by this.

$$(x-4)(x+4)\left(\frac{5}{x-4}\right) - (x-4)(x+4)\left(\frac{3}{x+4}\right) = \left(\frac{36}{x^2-16}\right)(x-4)(x+4)$$

$$
\begin{array}{ll}
(x+4)(5)-(x-4)(3) = 36 & \text{Distribute.} \\
5x + 20 - 3x + 12 = 36 & \text{Combine like terms.} \\
2x + 32 = 36 & \text{Subtract 32 from both sides.} \\
2x = 4 & \text{Divide by 2.} \\
x = 2 &
\end{array}
$$

To check the solution, substitute 2 into the equation:

$$\frac{5}{x-4} - \frac{3}{x+4} = \frac{36}{x^2-16}$$

$$\frac{5}{2-4} - \frac{3}{2+4} = \frac{36}{2^2-16}$$

$$-\frac{5}{2} - \frac{3}{6} = -\frac{36}{12}$$

$$-3 = -3$$

Therefore, the solution is $x = 2$.

Example 3:

Solve for x: $\dfrac{1}{5} - \dfrac{1}{6} = \dfrac{1}{x}$

Solution:

The LCD is $30x$. Multiply all terms by the LCD.

$$(30x)\left(\frac{1}{5}\right) - (30x)\left(\frac{1}{6}\right) = \frac{1}{x}(30x)$$

$$6x - 5x = 30$$

$$x = 30$$

If you check the value $x = 30$ in the original equation, you will find that it works.

Radical Equations

Equations that have variables in their radicands are called **radical equations**. For example, $\sqrt{x} = 16$ is a radical equation. To solve this radical equation, square both sides:

$$\sqrt{x} = 16$$
$$\left(\sqrt{x}\right)^2 = 16^2$$
$$x = 256$$

Check $x = 256$ in the original equation.

$$\sqrt{x} = 16$$
$$\sqrt{256} = 16?$$
$$16 = 16$$

The solution works.

Extraneous solutions may occur when you raise both sides of a radical equation to an even power. For example, if you square both sides of the equation $x = 5$ you get $x^2 = 25$. This new equation has two solutions, -5 and 5, but only 5 is the solution to the original equation.

Note the four steps involved in solving a radical equation:

1. Isolate the radical on one side of the equation.
2. Raise both sides of the equation to the same power to eliminate the radical.
3. Solve the resulting equation.
4. Check the solution.

Examples:

Solve each equation.

1. $\sqrt{2x + 3} = 7$
2. $\sqrt[3]{4x - 5} = 3$
3. $\sqrt[4]{2x + 8} - 2 = 2$
4. $x + 2 = \sqrt{11x + 12}$

12

Solutions:.

1.

$$\sqrt{2x+3} = 7$$
$$\left(\sqrt{2x+3}\right)^2 = 7^2$$
$$2x+3 = 49$$
$$2x = 46$$
$$x = 23 \quad \text{Check the solution.}$$

$$\sqrt{2x+3} = 7$$
$$\sqrt{2(23)+3} = 7?$$
$$\sqrt{49} = 7?$$
$$7 = 7 \qquad \text{The solution is 23.}$$

2.

$$\sqrt[3]{4x-5} = 3$$
$$\left(\sqrt[3]{4x-5}\right)^3 = 3^3$$
$$4x-5 = 27$$
$$4x = 32$$
$$x = 8 \quad \text{Check the solution.}$$

$$\sqrt[3]{4x-5} = 3$$
$$\sqrt[3]{4(8)-5} = 3?$$
$$\sqrt[3]{27} = 3?$$
$$3 = 3 \qquad \text{The solution is 8.}$$

3.

$$\sqrt[4]{2x+8} - 2 = 2$$
$$\sqrt[4]{2x+8} = 4$$
$$\left(\sqrt[4]{2x+8}\right)^4 = \left(4\right)^4$$
$$2x+8 = 256$$
$$2x = 248$$
$$x = 124 \quad \text{Check the solution.}$$

$$\sqrt[4]{2x+8} - 2 = 2$$
$$\sqrt[4]{2(124)+8} - 2 = 2?$$
$$\sqrt[4]{256} - 2 = 2?$$
$$4 - 2 = 2?$$
$$2 = 2 \qquad \text{The solution is 124.}$$

4.

$$x+2 = \sqrt{11x+12}$$
$$\left(x+2\right)^2 = \left(\sqrt{11x+12}\right)^2$$
$$x^2+4x+4 = 11x+12$$
$$x^2-7x-8 = 0$$
$$\left(x-8\right)\left(x+1\right) = 0$$
$$x = 8, x = -1$$

$$x+2 = \sqrt{11x+12}$$
$$\left(x+2\right)^2 = \left(\sqrt{11x+12}\right)^2$$
$$x^2+4x+4 = 11x+12$$
$$x^2-7x-8 = 0$$
$$\left(x-8\right)\left(x+1\right) = 0$$
$$x = 8, x = -1$$

Check the solution $x = 8$.

$$x+2 = \sqrt{11x+12}$$
$$8+2 = \sqrt{11(8)+12}?$$
$$10 = \sqrt{100}?$$
$$10 = 10 \qquad \text{The solution is 8.}$$

Check the solution $x = -1$.

$$x+2 = \sqrt{11x+12}$$
$$-1+2 = \sqrt{11(-1)+12}?$$
$$1 = \sqrt{1}?$$
$$1 = 1 \qquad \text{The solution is } -1.$$

The solutions are $x = 8$ and $x = -1$.

PRACTICE EXERCISE: SOLVING COMPLEX EQUATIONS

DIRECTIONS: Work out each problem. Circle the letter of your choice. Check your answers against the answer key and explanations that follow.

1. Solve for x: $\dfrac{2}{x-2} - \dfrac{5}{x+2} = \dfrac{2}{x^2-4}$

   A. $x = -4$

   B. $x = -2$

   C. $x = 2$

   D. $x = 4$

2. Solve for x: $\dfrac{3x}{3x-1} + \dfrac{3}{1-3x} = -1$

   A. -2

   B. $\dfrac{2}{3}$

   C. 2

   D. No solution

3. Solve for a: $\dfrac{3}{a-7} + \dfrac{5}{a^2-13a+42} = \dfrac{7}{a-6}$

   A. $a = -18$

   B. $a = -9$

   C. $a = 9$

   D. $a = 18$

4. Solve for x: $\dfrac{x}{x+1} = \dfrac{3}{x+3}$

   A. $-\sqrt{3}$ and $\sqrt{3}$

   B. 3

   C. -1 and 3

   D. 9

5. Solve for x: $\sqrt{5-4x} - x = 0$

   A. -5 and 1

   B. -1 and 5

   C. 1

   D. 5

SHOW YOUR WORK HERE

12

6. Solve the equation: $\sqrt[4]{3x-2}+1=6$

   A. $x = 1$

   B. $x = 9$

   C. $x = 17$

   D. $x = 209$

7. Solve for x: $\sqrt[3]{4x^2-2x}=\sqrt[3]{5-10x}$

   A. 0

   B. $-\dfrac{5}{2}$ and $\dfrac{1}{2}$

   C. $-\dfrac{2}{5}$ and 2

   D. No solution

8. Solve the equation: $x = \sqrt{16x+225}$

   A. $x = 45$

   B. $x = 25$

   C. $x = -9$

   D. $x = -25$

9. Solve for t: $\dfrac{t}{4}+\dfrac{2t}{9} \geq \dfrac{3t-14}{6}$

   A. $t \leq 84$

   B. $t \leq 42$

   C. $t \geq 42$

   D. $t \geq 84$

10. Solve for x: $\sqrt[4]{\dfrac{5}{3x}}=1$

   A. $\dfrac{5}{3}$

   B. $\dfrac{3}{5}$

   C. -2

   D. $\dfrac{5}{12}$

12

SHOW YOUR WORK HERE

Answer Key and Explanations

1. D	3. C	5. C	7. B	9. A
2. B	4. A	6. D	8. B	10. A

1. **The correct answer is D.** The LCD of the fractions in the equation $\dfrac{2}{x-2} - \dfrac{5}{x+2} = \dfrac{2}{x^2-4}$ is $(x-2)(x+2)$.

   Multiply all terms by the LCD.

   $$(x-2)(x+2)\frac{2}{x-2} - (x-2)(x+2)\frac{5}{x+2} = \frac{2}{x^2-4}(x-2)(x+2)$$
   $$2(x+2) - 5(x-2) = 2$$
   $$2x + 4 - 5x + 10 = 2$$
   $$-3x + 14 = 2$$
   $$-3x = -12$$
   $$x = 4$$

   Remember that you should check the answer to make certain that it solves the equation.

2. **The correct answer is B.** Rewrite the left side so that both fractions have the same denominator. Then, combine the fractions, cross-multiply, and solve for x:

   $$\frac{3x}{3x-1} + \frac{3}{1-3x} = -1$$

   $$\frac{3x}{3x-1} - \frac{3}{3x-1} = -1$$

   $$\frac{3x-3}{3x-1} = -1$$

   $$3x - 3 = -(3x-1)$$

   $$3x - 3 = -3x + 1$$

   $$6x = 4$$

   $$x = \frac{2}{3}$$

3. **The correct answer is C.** Note that $a^2 - 13a + 42 = (a-7)(a-6)$, so the LCD of the fractions in the equation is $(a-7)(a-6)$. Now, multiply by the LCD.

$$(a-7)(a-6)\frac{3}{a-7} + (a-7)(a-6)\frac{5}{(a-7)(a-6)} = \frac{7}{a-6}(a-7)(a-6)$$
$$3a - 18 + 5 = 7(a-7)$$
$$3a - 13 = 7a - 49$$
$$4a = 36$$
$$a = 9$$

This solution checks.

4. **The correct answer is A.** Cross-multiply and then solve the resulting quadratic equation:

$$\frac{x}{x+1} = \frac{3}{x+3}$$
$$x(x+3) = 3(x+1)$$
$$x^2 + 3x = 3x + 3$$
$$x^2 = 3$$
$$x = \pm\sqrt{3}$$

5. **The correct answer is C.** Isolate the radical term on one side. Then, square both sides and solve the resulting quadratic equation:

$$\sqrt{5 - 4x} - x = 0$$
$$\sqrt{5 - 4x} = x$$
$$5 - 4x = x^2$$
$$x^2 + 4x - 5 = 0$$
$$(x+5)(x-1) = 0$$
$$x = -5, 1$$

Substituting −5 and 1 into the original equation shows that 1 is a solution, but −5 is not.

6. **The correct answer is D.** Move the constants to the right and subtract. Then raise both sides to the power of 4 and solve.

$$\sqrt[4]{3x - 2} + 1 = 6$$
$$\sqrt[4]{3x - 2} = 5$$
$$3x - 2 = 625$$
$$3x = 627$$
$$x = 209$$

7. **The correct answer is B.** Cube both sides. Then solve the resulting quadratic equation:

$$\sqrt[3]{4x^2 - 2x} = \sqrt[3]{5 - 10x}$$
$$4x^2 - 2x = 5 - 10x$$
$$4x^2 + 8x - 5 = 0$$
$$(2x - 1)(2x + 5) = 0$$
$$x = \frac{1}{2}, -\frac{5}{2}$$

8. **The correct answer is B.**

$$x = \sqrt{16x + 225}$$
$$x^2 = 16x + 225$$
$$x^2 - 16x - 225 = 0$$
$$(x - 25)(x + 9) = 0$$
$$x = 25, -9$$

Note when you substitute $x = -9$ into the equation, you get $-9 = 9$. This means that −9 is an extraneous solution. The only solution is 25.

12

9. **The correct answer is A.** To solve , multiply by the LCD of 36.

$$(36)\frac{t}{4} + (36)\ \frac{2t}{9} \ge (36)\frac{3t-14}{6}$$
$$9t + 8t \ge 6(3t - 14)$$
$$17t \ge 18t - 84$$
$$-t \ge -84$$
$$t \le 84$$

10. **The correct answer is A.** Raise both sides to the 4th power to eliminate the radical. Then solve the resulting linear equation:

$$\sqrt[4]{\frac{5}{3x}} = 1$$
$$\frac{5}{3x} = 1$$
$$5 = 3x$$
$$x = \frac{5}{3}$$

LINEAR, QUADRATIC, AND EXPONENTIAL FUNCTIONS

A **linear function** is a function of the form $f(x) = mx + b$, where m and b are real numbers. A **quadratic function** is a function of the form $g(x) = ax^2 + bx + c$, where $a \ne 0$ and a, b, and c are real numbers. An **exponential function** is a function of the form $f(x) = ab^x$ where base b is a positive integer greater than 1. These functions are important, because they can be used to model many real-world occurrences.

Applications of Linear Functions

Let's look at an example of a real-world application of a linear function.

In order to manufacture a new car model, a carmaker must initially spend \$750,000 to purchase the equipment needed to start the production process. After this, it costs \$7,500 to manufacture each car. In this case, the cost function that associates the cost of manufacturing cars to the number of cars manufactured is $C(x) = 7,500x + 750,000$, where x represents the number of cars manufactured, and $C(x)$ represents the cost of x cars. For example, the cost of making 7 cars is $C(7) = 7,500(7) + 750,000 = 52,500 + 750,000 = \$802,500$.

The above cost function is a linear function with $b = 750,000$ and $m = 7,500$. What is the domain of this function? Note that even though nothing has been said specifically about the domain, the only values that make sense as domain values are the non-negative integers, 0, 1, 2, 3, 4, 5 . . . . In such a situation, assume that the domain contains only the values that make sense.

12

Example 1:

Using the cost function for the carmaker discussed in the example above, how much would it cost to make 24 cars?

Solution:

To solve this, you need to determine the value of $C(24)$.

$$C(24) = 7,500(24) + 750,000 = 180,000 + 750,000 = \$930,000$$

Example 2:

Using the same cost function, determine how many cars could be made for \$990,000.

Solution:

In this problem, you are told that the value of $C(x)$ is \$990,000, and you need to find the value of x. To do this, solve the equation:

$$990,000 = 75,000(x) + 750,000 \quad \text{Subtract 750,000 from both sides.}$$
$$240,000 = 7,500x \quad \text{Divide by 7,500.}$$
$$32 = x$$

Therefore, for $990,000, 32 cars can be manufactured.

Example 3:

In the town of Kenmore, a taxi ride costs $2.50 plus an extra $0.50 per mile. Write a function that represents the cost of taking a taxi ride, using x to represent the number of miles traveled.

Solution:

$$C(x) = \$2.50 + 0.50x$$

If a ride costs $0.50 a mile, then the cost for x miles will be $0.50x$. Add to this the initial fee of $2.50 a ride.

Example 4:

You purchased shorts for $8 per pair, plus a shirt for $6. Write a function that represents the cost of your purchases, where x represents the number of pairs of shorts you purchase. How much did you spend if you purchased 5 pairs of shorts?

Solution:

$$f(x) = 8x + 6$$
$$\text{Let } x = 5, \text{ so } f(5) = 8(5) + 6 = 46$$

Example 5:

A bus pass has a starting value of $60. Each ride costs $2.50. Write a function that represents the remaining balance on the bus pass, where x represents the number of rides taken. How much money is left on the pass after 12 rides?

Solution:

$$f(x) = 60 - 2.5x$$
$$\text{Let } x = 12, \text{ so } f(12) = 60 - 2.5(12) = 30$$

There is $30 remaining on the pass after 12 rides.

The Graph of a Linear Function

Typically, when a function is graphed, the independent variable is graphed along the x-axis, and the dependent variable is graphed along the y-axis.

The taxi ride function from the previous problem is a linear function. In order to graph this function, you must first determine the domain. Note that the domain, once again, must consist of non-negative numbers. Next, determine a few values that satisfy the rule for the function. For example, when $x = 0$, $C(0) = \$2.50 + 0.50(0) = \$2.50$. A few additional simple computations will lead to the following table of values.

x	C(x)
0	$2.50
1	$3.00
2	$3.50
3	$4.00

If these points are plotted on a graph, you will see that they all lie on the same line. The entire graph of the taxi ride cost function follows.

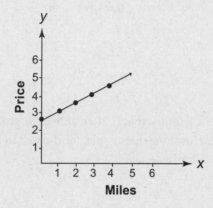

In general, the graph of any linear function is either a straight line or (depending on the domain) a portion of a straight line. The value of m represents the slope of the line, and the value of b is the y-intercept.

Applications of Quadratic Functions

Quadratic functions can also be used to model certain real-world happenings. To understand these functions better, suppose a coffee manufacturer has a revenue function given by $R(x) = 40{,}000x - 2{,}000x^2$, where x represents the amount of coffee produced in tons per week. Let's consider some of the values for this function.

- If $x = 0$, $R(x) = 40{,}000(0) - 2{,}000(0)^2 = 0$ represents the obvious fact that if no coffee is produced, there is no revenue.
- That $R(1) = 40{,}000 - 2{,}000 = 38{,}000$ tells that the revenue from 1 ton of coffee is $38,000.
- Similar computations show that $R(10) = \$200{,}000$ and $R(11) = \$198{,}000$.

Note that the revenue is smaller if 11 tons of coffee are produced than if 10 tons are produced. There are a number of possible reasons for this. Perhaps, for example, at the 11-ton level, more is produced than can be sold, and the coffee company must pay to store the overage.

The function $h(t) = -16t^2 + h_0$ models the height of an object dropped from an initial height h_0 (in feet) after t seconds. Use this function to work through the following examples.

12

Example 1:

An object is dropped from the roof of a building that is 80 ft. tall. How long will it take the object to hit the ground? Round your answer to the nearest hundredth of a second.

Solution:

$h(t) = -16t^2 + h_0$

Here $h_0 = 80$, so $h(t) = -16t^2 + 80$.

Substitute 0 in for $h(t)$ and solve the equation for t.

$$0 = -16t^2 + 80$$
$$16t^2 = 80$$
$$t^2 = 5$$
$$t \approx \pm 2.24$$

Example 2:

Suppose you drop a ball from a window that is 36 ft. above the ground and it lands on a porch that is 4 ft. above the ground. How long does it take for the ball to land on the porch? Round your answer to the nearest hundredth of a second.

Solution:

$h(t) = -16t^2 + h_0$

Here $h_0 = 36$, so $h(t) = -16t^2 + 36$.

Substitute 4 for $h(t)$, because the ball will hit the porch at 4 feet above 0, or ground level. Solve the equation for t.

$$4 = -16t^2 + 36$$
$$16t^2 = 32$$
$$t^2 = 2$$
$$t \approx \pm 1.41$$

It will take approximately 1.41 seconds for the object to land on the porch.

12

The Graph of a Quadratic Function

As you just saw, the graph of a linear function is always a straight line. To determine what the graph of a quadratic function looks like, consider the graph of the quadratic function $R(x) = 40{,}000x - 2{,}000x^2$. Negative numbers must be excluded from the domain. A few computations lead to the table here.

x	$R(x)$
0	0
3	102,000
5	150,000
9	198,000
10	200,000
11	198,000
15	150,000
17	102,000
20	0

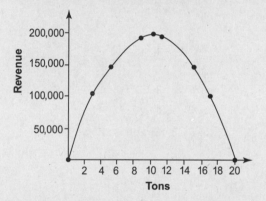

The graph of R(x) is shown above and is called a **parabola**. This parabola is said to "open down." The highest point on the parabola, (10, 200,000), is called the **extreme point**.

Recall that the general form of a quadratic function is $g(x) = ax^2 + bx + c$. In general, the graph of any quadratic function will be a parabola. If $a > 0$, the parabola will "open up," and if $a < 0$, the parabola will "open down." If the parabola opens up, its extreme point (or vertex) is the minimum value of the function, and if the parabola opens down, its vertex is the maximum value of the function.

The coordinates of the vertex of a parabola are $\left[\dfrac{-b}{2a}, f\left(\dfrac{-b}{2a} \right) \right]$.

12

Example 1:

Sketch the graph of the function $f(x) = x^2 - x - 2$.

Solution:

Since the function is quadratic, the graph will be a parabola. Note that the value of a, the number in front of the x^2-term is 1, so the parabola opens up. The x-coordinate of the minimum point is $x = \dfrac{-b}{2a} = \dfrac{-(1)}{2(1)} = \dfrac{1}{2}$, and the y-coordinate of this point is

$$f\left(\frac{1}{2}\right) = \left(\frac{1}{2}\right)^2 - \frac{1}{2} - 2$$

$$= \frac{1}{4} - \frac{1}{2} - 2$$

$$= -2\frac{1}{4}$$

In order to sketch a parabola, it is helpful to determine a few points on either side of the vertex.

x	$f(x)$
–2	4
–1	0
0	–2
1	–2
2	0
3	4

The graph is shown here.

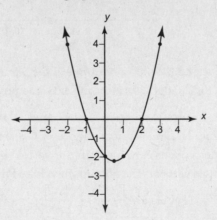

Example 2:

What is the relationship between the graph of the function $h(x) = ax^2 + bx$ and the graph of the function $j(x) = ax^2 + bx + 7$?

Solution:

If (x, y) is a point on the graph of $h(x)$, then $(x, y + 7)$ will be a point on the graph of $j(x)$. Therefore, the two graphs have exactly the same size and shape. The graph of $j(x)$ can be obtained by taking the graph of $h(x)$ and "lifting" each point 7 units, that is, increasing the y-coordinate of each point by 7.

Applications of Exponential Functions

If $a > 0$ and $b > 1$, then the function $f(x) = abx$ is an **exponential growth function** and b is called the **growth factor**. If $a > 0$ and $0 < b < 1$, then the function $f(x) = abx$ is an **exponential decay function** and b is called the **decay factor**.

An exponential growth function can model the number of students in a high school. Suppose the number of students in 2011 is given by $f(x) = 1{,}250(1.13)x$, where x is the number of years since 2011. Let's consider some of the values for this function. If $x = 0$, then $f(x) = 1{,}250(1.13)^0 = 1{,}250$ represents the student population in 2011. If $x = 1$, then $f(x) = 1{,}250(1.13)^1 = 1{,}413$ represents the student population after 1 year. Similar computations show that $f(x) = 1{,}596$ when $x = 2$ and $f(x) = 2{,}303$ when $x = 5$.

An exponential decay function can model the value of an automobile. Suppose the value of the automobile is given by $f(x) = 35{,}000(0.85)x$, where x is the number of years since the automobile was purchased. Let's consider some of the values for this function. If $x = 0$, then $f(x) = 35{,}000(0.85)^0 = 35{,}000$ represents the value of the automobile at the time of purchase. If $x = 2$, then $f(x) = 35{,}000(0.85)^2 = 25{,}287.50$ represents the value of the automobile after 2 years. Similar computations show that $f(x) = 15{,}529.69$ when $x = 5$ and $f(x) = 3{,}057.40$ when $x = 15$.

The Graph of an Exponential Function

To determine what the graph of an exponential function looks like, consider the graph of the exponential function $f(x) = 52{,}50(0.9)x$, where $f(x)$ is the value of a jet ski in dollars after x years.

The initial value of the jet ski is $5,250 and the percent of decrease per year is 10%. Some of the computations along with the graph of $f(x)$ is a curve that falls from left to right and gets less and less steep as x increases. The x-axis is a horizontal asymptote.

x	$f(x)$
0	5,250
1	4,725
5	3,100
8	2,260
12	1,482.8
15	1,080
25	339.21

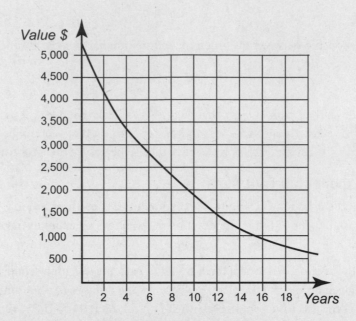

Comparing Linear and Exponential Growth Functions

Suppose you can choose how you will get your allowance. The first option is to get $5 a week every week. The second option is to get $0.50 for the first week, $1 for the second week, $2 for the third, and so on, by doubling the amount each week. Which option will pay you more?

- **Option 1:** $y = 5x$, where x is the number of weeks you were paid your allowance and y is the total amount of money you have been paid so far.

- **Option 2:** $y = (0.5)(2)x^{-1}$, where x is the number of weeks you were paid your allowance and y is the total amount of money you have been paid so far.

As you can see from the tables, Option 1 pays more until the 8th week. After that, Option 2 will always pay more since you are doubling a larger number.

Option 1: $y = 5x$

x (week)	1	2	3	4	5	6	7	8	9	10
y (total)	5	10	15	20	25	30	35	40	45	50

Option 2: $y = (0.5)(2)x^{-1}$

x (week)	1	2	3	4	5	6	7	8	9	10
y (total)	0.5	1	2	4	8	16	32	64	128	256

Option 1 is a linear function that is increasing at a constant rate, and Option 2 is an exponential function that is increasing rapidly as *x* gets bigger. You would choose Option 2 to be paid the most.

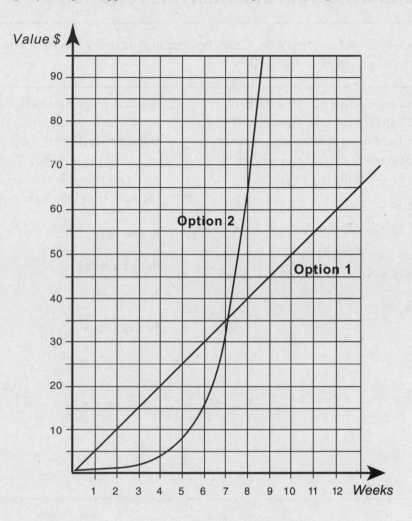

PRACTICE EXERCISE:
LINEAR, QUADRATIC, AND EXPONENTIAL FUNCTIONS

DIRECTIONS: Work out each problem. Circle the letter of your choice. Check your answers against the answer key and explanations that follow.

1. A taxi company charges $2.25 for the first mile and $0.45 for each mile thereafter. If x stands for the number of miles a passenger travels, which of the following functions relates the length of the trip to its cost?

   A. $f(x) = 2.25 + 0.45(x + 1)$

   B. $f(x) = 2.25 + 0.45(1 - x)$

   C. $f(x) = 2.25 + 0.45(x - 1)$

   D. $f(x) = 2.25 + 0.45x$

2. A soccer player kicks a ball with initial speed of 24 feet per second from the ground. The trajectory of the ball is described by the quadratic function $h(t) = -16t^2 + 24t$, where $h(t)$ is measured in feet and t is measured in seconds. How long is the ball in the air?

   A. 1 second

   B. $\dfrac{3}{2}$ seconds

   C. 2 seconds

   D. $\dfrac{5}{2}$ seconds

12

SHOW YOUR WORK HERE

3. At the Four Seasons bowling alley, it costs $1.50 to rent shoes and $2.50 for each game played. Which of the following functions relates the number of games played, x, to the cost in dollars?

   A. $f(x) = 4.00x$

   B. $f(x) = 2.50 + 1.50x$

   C. $f(x) = 1.50x - 2.50$

   D. $f(x) = 2.50x + 1.50$

4. In order to raise money for a charity, Deb makes cakes to sell at a school bake sale. Her profit function is $P(x) = \$4.50x - \$15$. How many cakes must she sell in order to earn $66 for the charity?

   A. 15

   B. 16

   C. 18

   D. 20

5. For which domain value(s) of the function $f(x) = x^2 + 3x - 10$ does $f(x) = 0$?

   A. 2

   B. -2

   C. -5

   D. 2 and -5

6. The growth in population of a small town since 1983 is described by the function $P(t) = 1880\,(1.12)^t,$ where t is the number of years since 1983 and $P(t)$ is the number of people. What is the population in the year 1983?

   A. 226

   B. 1,880

   C. 2,106

   D. 2,358

SHOW YOUR WORK HERE

12

7. What is the x-coordinate of the extreme point of the function $f(x) = 7x^2 - 28x + 16$?

A. $x = \dfrac{1}{2}$

B. $x = -\dfrac{1}{2}$

C. $x = 2$

D. $x = -2$

8. Which of the following functions can be used to model exponential growth?

A. $f(x) = \dfrac{1}{5^x}$

B. $g(x) = 2 \cdot \left(\dfrac{4}{5}\right)^{-x}$

C. $h(x) = 4 \cdot (0.9)^x$

D. $j(x) = \left(\dfrac{1}{3}\right)^{x+6}$

9. A ball is dropped from a height of 20 ft. above the ground. Given $h(t) = -16t^2 + h_0$, how long will it be before the ball hits the ground?

A. About 2.0 seconds

B. About 1.56 seconds

C. About 1.12 seconds

D. About 0.89 seconds

10. The value of a car can be modeled by the equation $f(x) = 38,000(0.89)x$, when x is the number of years since the car was purchased and $f(x)$ is the value of the car. What is the approximate value of the car after 6 years?

A. About $19,000

B. About $22,000

C. About $28,000

D. About $30,000

12

SHOW YOUR WORK HERE

Part VI

Answer Key and Explanations

1. C	**3.** D	**5.** D	**7.** C	**9.** C
2. B	**4.** C	**6.** B	**8.** B	**10.** A

1. **The correct answer is C.** The cost for the first mile on a trip of x miles is $2.25. After this, there are still $x - 1$ miles to go, and the cost for each of these miles is $0.45. Therefore, the total cost of the trip, in dollars, is $2.25 + 0.45(x - 1)$.

2. **The correct answer is B.** Solve $h(t) = 0$. The larger of the two solutions is the amount of time the ball is in the air.

$$h(t) = -16t^2 + 24t = 0$$
$$-8t(2t - 3) = 0$$
$$t = 0, \frac{3}{2}$$

   The ball is in the air for $\frac{3}{2}$ seconds.

3. **The correct answer is D.** The cost of x games, at $2.50 a game, is $2.50x$. Adding the $1.50 cost of shoe rental to this leads to the function $f(x) = 2.50x + 1.50$.

4. **The correct answer is C.** You are asked to find the value of x for which $4.50x - 15 = 66$.

$$4.50x - 15 = 66$$
$$4.50x - 15 = 66 \quad \text{Add 15 to both sides.}$$
$$4.50x = 81 \quad \text{Divide by 4.50 (or 4.5).}$$
$$x = 18$$

   Therefore, Deb must sell 18 cakes to make $66.

5. **The correct answer is D.** In order to answer this question, you need to solve the quadratic equation $x^2 + 3x - 10 = 0$.

$$x^2 + 3x - 10 = 0 \quad \text{Factor the left-hand side.}$$
$$(x + 5)(x - 2) = 0 \quad \text{Set each factor equal to 0.}$$
$$x + 5 = 0 \quad x - 2 = 0$$
$$x = -5 \quad x = 2$$

   Thus, $f(x) = x^2 + 3x - 10 = 0$ at $x = -5$ and $x = 2$.

6. **The correct answer is B.** The year 1983 corresponds to $t = 0$. So the population in 1983 is $P(0) = 1,880$.

7. **The correct answer is C.** The vertex of a quadratic function is given by the formula $x = \frac{-b}{2a}$, where a is the coefficient of the x^2-term and b is the coefficient of the x-term. In this case, then, the vertex is:

$$x = \frac{-b}{2a} = \frac{-1(-28)}{2(7)} = \frac{28}{14} = 2$$

8. **The correct answer is B.** A function that models exponential growth is of the form $y = A \cdot b^x$, where A is positive and $b > 1$. Note that $g(x) = 2 \cdot \left(\frac{4}{5}\right)^{-x} = 2 \cdot \left(\frac{5}{4}\right)^x$ is of this form.

9. **The correct answer is C.** The model giving the height h of the ball (in feet) after t seconds is $h(t) = -16t^2 + 20$. Substitute 0 in for $h(t)$ and solve the equation. The ball will hit the ground about 1.12 seconds after it is dropped.

10. **The correct answer is A.** Substitute 6 for x in the equation $f(x) = 38,000(0.89)^x$, and solve the equation. The car will be worth approximately $19,000 after 6 years.

12

SUMMING IT UP

- A **function** is a rule that assigns exactly one output to each input. In other words, each member of the domain corresponds to exactly one member of the range.

- In **function notation**, the rule of association for a function is written as $f(x)$ to represent the range value.

- For any positive integer n, $x^{-n} = \dfrac{1}{x^n}$.

- For a **rational number**, x to the power of $\dfrac{1}{n}$ is defined as the nth root of x. In other words, $x^{\frac{1}{n}}$ is equal to $\sqrt[n]{x}$.

- A **linear function** is a function of the form $f(x) = mx + b$, where m and b are real numbers.

  ○ In general, the graph of any linear function is either a straight line or depending on the domain) a portion of a straight line.

- A **quadratic function** is a function of the form $g(x) = ax^2 + bx + c$, where $a \neq 0$ and a, b, and c are real numbers.

  ○ In general, the graph of any quadratic function will be a parabola.

- An **exponential function** is a function of the form $f(x) = abx$ where base b is a positive integer greater than 1.

  ○ In general, the graph of any exponential function will curve sharply as it rapidly increases or decreases.

- There are four steps involved in solving a **rational equation**:

  1. Find the LCD of all of the rational expressions in the equation.
  2. Multiply *every* term on both sides of the equation by this LCD.
  3. Solve the resulting equation using the methods previously explained.
  4. Check the solution to make certain that it actually solves the equation.

- There are four steps involved in solving a **radical equation**:

  1. Isolate the radical on one side of the equation.
  2. Raise both sides of the equation to the same power to eliminate the radical.
  3. Solve the resulting equation.
  4. Check the solution.

Take a moment to ask yourself some simple questions about your understanding of the chapter:

Review: What did I learn?

Evaluate: What do I need to learn more about?

Plan: What can I do next to keep improving?

Based on your answers to those questions, adjust your study plan to dedicate additional time to the areas of weakness that you've identified.

Chapter 13

Data Analysis, Statistics, and Probability

OVERVIEW

CALCULATING MEASURES OF CENTER AND SPREAD

A set of data values may be summarized, using measures of center and/or measures of spread. Measures of center include mean, median, and mode and represent the center of the data. Measures of spread include range and standard deviation and represent how spread out the data values are within a data set. Standard deviation will be presented later in this chapter, when discussing ways to compare two data distributions. You will not be required to calculate standard deviation. Instead, you will need understand its meaning and how to use it to compare data sets.

The Arithmetic Mean

An **average** or **arithmetic mean** is a value that is computed by dividing the sum of a set of terms by the number of terms in the collection. To find the average (arithmetic mean) of a group of n numbers, simply add the numbers and divide by n.

Example 1:

Find the average (arithmetic mean) of 32, 50, and 47.

Solution:

$$
\begin{array}{r}
32 \\
50 \\
+\ 47 \\
\hline
129
\end{array}
\qquad
\begin{array}{r}
43 \\
3\overline{)129}
\end{array}
$$

Another type of arithmetic mean problem gives you the arithmetic mean and asks for the missing term.

Example 2:

The average (arithmetic mean) of three numbers is 43. If two of the numbers are 32 and 50, find the third number.

Solution:

Using the definition of arithmetic mean, write the equation:

$$\frac{32 + 50 + x}{3} = 43$$
$$32 + 50 + x = 129$$
$$82 + x = 129$$
$$x = 47$$

Median and Mode

In order to find the **median** of a group of numbers, list the numbers in numerical order from smallest to largest. The median is the number in the middle. For example, the median of the numbers 3, 3, 5, 9, and 10 is 5. Note that, typically, the median and the arithmetic mean are not the same. In this problem, for example, the arithmetic mean is $30 \div 5 = 6$.

If there is an even number of numbers, the median is equal to the arithmetic mean of the two numbers in the middle. For example, to find the median of 3, 3, 5, 7, 9, and 10, note that the two middle numbers are 5 and 7. The median, then, is $\frac{5 + 7}{2} = 6$.

The **mode** of a group of numbers is simply the number that occurs most frequently. Therefore, the mode of the group of numbers 3, 3, 5, 7, 9, and 10 is 3. If all of the numbers in a group only appear once, then there is no mode. A data set can have more than one mode.

Example:

What are the arithmetic mean, the median, and the mode of the following group of eight numbers?

2, 7, 8, 9, 9, 9, 10, and 10

13

Solution:

The sum of the eight numbers is 64, so the arithmetic mean is $64 \div 8 = 8$.

Since this data set has an even number of data values, the median is the arithmetic mean of the two numbers in the middle. Since these numbers are both 9, the median is $\frac{9+9}{2} = 9$.

The mode is the number that occurs most often, which is also 9.

Range

The **range**, or the spread, of a data set is the difference between the greatest and least data values. To find the range of a set of data, first write the values in ascending order to make sure that you have found the least and greatest values. Then, subtract the least data value from the greatest data value.

Example:

Celia kept track of the average price of a gallon of gas over the last 10 years. Her data is shown in the table below. What is the range in the average price of gas?

Solution:

Year	Average price/gallon in US dollars
2006	2.00
2007	2.08
2008	2.44
2009	3.40
2010	2.85
2011	2.90
2012	3.50
2013	4.20
2014	3.80
2015	3.25

Write the data in order from least to greatest:

2.00 2.08 2.44 2.85 2.90 3.25 3.40 3.50 3.80 4.20

Subtract the least value from the greatest value:

$4.20 - 2.00 = 2.20$

$2.20 is the range or spread of the data.

WEIGHTED AVERAGE

If asked to find the arithmetic mean of a group of numbers in which some of the numbers appear more than once, simplify the computation by using the **weighted average** formula. For example, suppose the question asks for the average (arithmetic mean) age of a group of 10 friends. If four of the friends are 17, and six of the friends are 19, determine the average in the usual way:

$$\text{Average age} = \frac{17+17+17+17+19+19+19+19+19+19}{10} = \frac{182}{10} = 18.2$$

However, the computation can be done more quickly by taking the *weights* of the ages into account. The age 17 is weighted four times, and the age 19 is weighted six times. The average can then be computed as follows:

$$\text{Average age} = \frac{4(17)+6(19)}{10} = \frac{182}{10} = 18.2$$

Example:

Andrea has four grades of 90 and two grades of 80 during the spring semester of calculus. What is her average (arithmetic mean) in the course for this semester?

Solution:

Calculating Using Average Formula	Calculating Using Weighted Average Formula
$\dfrac{90+90+90+90+80+80}{6} = \dfrac{520}{6} = 86\frac{2}{3}$	$\dfrac{(90\cdot 4)+(80\cdot 2)}{6} = \dfrac{520}{6} = 86\frac{2}{3}$

Be sure not to average 90 and 80, since there are four grades of 90 and only two grades of 80.

Average Rate

The **average rate** for a trip is the total distance covered, divided by the total time spent. Recall that distance can be determined by multiplying the rate by the time, that is, $d = rt$.

Example:

In driving from New York to Boston, Mr. Portney drove for 3 hours at 40 miles per hour and 1 hour at 48 miles per hour. What was his average rate for this portion of the trip?

Solution:

$$\text{Average rate} = \frac{\text{total distance}}{\text{total time}}$$

$$\text{Average rate} = \frac{3(40)+1(48)}{3+1}$$

$$\text{Average rate} = \frac{168}{4} = 42 \text{ miles per hour}$$

Since more of the trip was driven at 40 mph than at 48 mph, the average should be closer to 40 than to 48, which it is. This will help you to check your answer or to pick out the correct choice in a multiple-choice question.

WEIGHTED AVERAGE

If asked to find the arithmetic mean of a group of numbers in which some of the numbers appear more than once, simplify the computation by using the **weighted average** formula. For example, suppose the question asks for the average (arithmetic mean) age of a group of 10 friends. If four of the friends are 17, and six of the friends are 19, determine the average in the usual way:

$$\text{Average age} = \frac{17+17+17+17+19+19+19+19+19+19}{10} = \frac{182}{10} = 18.2$$

However, the computation can be done more quickly by taking the *weights* of the ages into account. The age 17 is weighted four times, and the age 19 is weighted six times. The average can then be computed as follows:

$$\text{Average age} = \frac{4(17)+6(19)}{10} = \frac{182}{10} = 18.2$$

Example:

Andrea has four grades of 90 and two grades of 80 during the spring semester of calculus. What is her average (arithmetic mean) in the course for this semester?

Solution:

Calculating Using Average Formula	Calculating Using Weighted Average Formula
$\dfrac{90+90+90+90+80+80}{6} = \dfrac{520}{6} = 86\frac{2}{3}$	$\dfrac{(90\cdot 4)+(80\cdot 2)}{6} = \dfrac{520}{6} = 86\frac{2}{3}$

Be sure not to average 90 and 80, since there are four grades of 90 and only two grades of 80.

Average Rate

The **average rate** for a trip is the total distance covered, divided by the total time spent. Recall that distance can be determined by multiplying the rate by the time, that is, $d = rt$.

Example:

In driving from New York to Boston, Mr. Portney drove for 3 hours at 40 miles per hour and 1 hour at 48 miles per hour. What was his average rate for this portion of the trip?

Solution:

$$\text{Average rate} = \frac{\text{total distance}}{\text{total time}}$$

$$\text{Average rate} = \frac{3(40)+1(48)}{3+1}$$

$$\text{Average rate} = \frac{168}{4} = 42 \text{ miles per hour}$$

Since more of the trip was driven at 40 mph than at 48 mph, the average should be closer to 40 than to 48, which it is. This will help you to check your answer or to pick out the correct choice in a multiple-choice question.

PRACTICE EXERCISE:
CALCULATING MEASURES OF CENTER AND SPREAD

DIRECTIONS: Work out each problem. Circle the letter of your choice. Check your answers against the answer key and explanations that follow.

---

1. The following are the amounts spent by nine families on purchasing gifts during the holiday season:

   $150 $325 $150 $250

   $400 $175 $150 $325 $250

   What is the mode amount spent?

   A. $150

   B. $250

   C. $325

   D. $400

2. The costs of five different airlines' tickets from Dallas to Boston are shown in the table below.

Airline	Ticket Cost
A	$356
B	$298
C	$312
D	$304
E	$283

   A sixth airline also offers flights from Dallas to Boston. The median price of the tickets from the six airlines, including those shown in the table, is $308. The range of the ticket prices is $77. What is the cost of the sixth airline's ticket?

   A. $385

   B. $360

   C. $279

   D. $231

SHOW YOUR WORK HERE

13

3. The temperatures (in degrees Fahrenheit) recorded daily in a greenhouse during the month of April are as follows:

70 72 66 70 72 71 70 70 66 68

70 68 71 72 70 78 70 66 69 78

68 66 68 70 72 68 68 70 70 72

What is the range?

A. 12

B. 20

C. 70

D. 78

4. Mike was comparison shopping for used copies of a textbook. He decided that he will purchase the book which costs the median price of the following list of prices:

$35 $52 $42 $48 $37 $48 $38

What price does he pay?

A. $37

B. $38

C. $42

D. $48

5. Seven students were asked to report the number of nights per week they work at a part-time job. Here are their responses:

0 6 3 3 5 4 0

What is the mean number of nights worked by these students?

A. 3

B. 4

C. 5

D. 6

6. Max is selling his car. He looks at the selling prices of the same type of car at five local car dealerships to determine a fair price for his car. The selling prices are listed below.

$7,505 $7,630 $7,995
$7,029 $7,135 $7,995

What is the approximate average (arithmetic mean) selling price for the type of car Max is trying to sell?

A. $7,995

B. $7,548

C. $7,512

D. $7,505

SHOW YOUR WORK HERE

13

Part VI

7. Susan has an average (arithmetic mean) of 86 on three examinations. What grade must she receive on her next test to raise her average (arithmetic mean) to 88?

A. 90

B. 94

C. 96

D. 100

8. The photography club sold calendars that were created using the best photos from their collection the previous year. Each of the 12 members sold calendars on Saturday; the number each sold is reported below:

20 5 18 18 15 12 18 14 8 10 15 3

What is the range?

A. 13

B. 15

C. 17

D. 18

9. The ages of 14 US presidents at inauguration are listed here in order of their presidencies. Which of the following correctly compares the average (arithmetic mean), median, and mode of their ages?

54 51 60 62 43 55 56
61 52 69 64 46 54 47

A. mode < mean < median

B. mode < median < mean

C. median < mode < mean

D. median < mean < mode

10. Amaya drives on two types of roads for her trip. She averages 53 miles per hour on city roads and 59 miles per hour on the highway. Amaya drives her car on a trip that has twice as many highway miles as city road miles. She drives a total of 552 miles. What is her average speed for the whole trip? Round your answer to the nearest whole.

A. 55 miles per hour

B. 56 miles per hour

C. 57 miles per hour

D. 58 miles per hour

SHOW YOUR WORK HERE

13

11. Last year, a software company paid each of its four administrative assistants $33,000, each of its two programmers $75,000, and a senior manager $140,000. How many of these employees earned less than the mean salary?

   A. 0
   B. 4
   C. 6
   D. 7

12. A statistician computes the average (arithmetic mean), median, and range of a data set consisting of 65 numbers. Because one of the numbers in the set is much greater than all the others, the statistician suspects the number is an error and recalculates the statistics after removing this largest value (called an "outlier"). Which of the following statements is true?

   A. After the greatest value is removed, the average, median, and range must decrease.
   B. After the greatest value is removed, the range must decrease, but the average and median may not be affected.
   C. After the greatest value is removed, the average and the range must decrease, but the median may not be affected.
   D. After the greatest value is removed, the median and the range will change, but the average may not be affected.

SHOW YOUR WORK HERE

13

Answer Key and Explanations

1. A	3. A	5. A	7. B	9. B	11. B
2. B	4. C	6. B	8. C	10. C	12. C

1. **The correct answer is A.** The value that occurs most often in the data set is the mode; here, it is $150.

2. **The correct answer is B.** List the given ticket costs from least to greatest:

   $283, $298, $304, $312, $356

   Add $77 to the least cost to determine if the unknown cost is also the greatest cost:

   $$283 + 77 = 360$$

   Use the value to find the median of the tickets:

   $283, $298, $304, $312, $356, $360

   Find the average (mean) of $304 and $312, which is $308. The unknown ticket cost is $360.

3. **The correct answer is A.** The range is the difference between the largest value and smallest value in a data set. Here, that difference is $78 - 66 = 12$.

4. **The correct answer is C.** First, arrange the dollar amounts in increasing order:

   $35 $37 $38 $42 $48 $48 $52

   The median is the dollar amount in the fourth place from the left, which is $42.

5. **The correct answer is A.** Add the seven values and then divide the sum by 7:

   $$\frac{0+6+3+3+5+4+0}{7} = \frac{21}{7} = 3$$

6. **The correct answer is B.**

   $$\frac{7,505 + 7,630 + 7,995 + 7,029 + 7,135 + 7,995}{6}$$

   $$= \frac{45,289}{6}$$

   $$= 7,548.167$$

   The approximate average of the cars' selling prices is $7,548.

7. **The correct answer is B.**

   $$\frac{3(86) + x}{4} = 88$$
   $$258 + x = 352$$
   $$x = 94$$

8. **The correct answer is C.** The range is the difference between the largest value and smallest value in a data set. Here, that difference is $20 - 3 = 17$.

13

9. **The correct answer is B.** First, put the ages of the presidents in order.

$$43, 46, 47, 51, 52, 54, 54, 55, 56, 60, 61, 62, 64, 69$$

The mode of their ages is 54, which is the only repeated age.

The median of their ages is the middle number, which is the average of 54 and 55, or 54.5.

The average or arithmetic mean is found by adding their ages and dividing by 14.

$$\frac{43 + 46 + 47 + 51 + 52 + 54 + 54 + 55 + 56 + 60 + 61 + 62 + 64 + 69}{14}$$

$$= \frac{774}{14}$$
$$= 55.3$$

Now order the three values: 54 < 54.5 < 55.3, which means that mode < median < mean.

10. **The correct answer is C.** Amaya drove for a time on city roads at 53 miles/hour and twice as much time on the highway at 59 miles/hour, so her average speed was as follows:

$$\frac{53x + 59(2x)}{3x} = \frac{171x}{3x} = 57$$

The average speed for the entire trip was 57 miles per hour.

11. **The correct answer is B.** Add the values and divide the sum by 7 to determine the mean salary:

$$\frac{4\left(\$33,000\right) + 2\left(\$75,000\right) + \$140,000}{7} = \frac{\$422,000}{7} \approx \$60,286$$

Four of the employees earn a salary below the mean.

12. **The correct answer is C.** Removing the greatest value from a data set will always result in reducing the arithmetic mean (unless all values in the data set are equal). The range will also decrease: after removing the outlier, the greatest value in the new data set will be a lower number, so the difference between that number and the least value will decrease.

To see that the median may or may not change, consider these two possible cases:

- When the original data set is listed from least to greatest, the 33rd value—the median—is *not* equal to the 32nd value. After removing the outlier, the data set has 64 values. The median is now the average of the 32nd and 33rd values, which will be different from the 33rd value. In this case, the median would change when the greatest value is removed.

- After listing the values from least to greatest, the 33rd and 32nd values in the original data set are equal. In that case, the median will be the same before and after the outlier is removed.

Because we do not know which of the two situations above describes the data set, we do not know whether the median will change when the largest value is removed.

> ## BRAIN BREAK
>
> Play a game of indoor basketball. Grab an empty cup and place it a few feet away from you. Look around you and find three objects that you can practice tossing into the cup (for example, a coin, a crumpled piece of paper, and a bouncy ball). Whatever is handy. Keep track of how many times you make a basket and how many times you miss. After 5 minutes, tally up your score. What are your odds of making a basket with each of the objects?

PROBABILITY

Probability is a numerical way of measuring the likelihood that a specific outcome will happen. The probability of a specific outcome is always a number between 0 and 1. An outcome with a probability of 0 cannot possibly happen, and an event with a probability of 1 will definitely happen. Therefore, the nearer the probability of an event is to 0, the less likely the event is to happen, and the nearer the probability of an event is to 1, the more likely the event is to happen.

There are two types of probability: **theoretical probability** and **experimental probability**. Theoretical probability is defined by theory, whereas experimental probability is defined by outcomes of actual trials.

Theoretical probability is calculated as the ratio of the number of favorable outcomes to the number of possible outcomes (i.e., sample space). This type of probability is independent of the outcomes of any trials. The theoretical probability of event A is represented as follows:

$$P(A) = \frac{\text{number of favorable outcomes}}{\text{number of possible outcomes}}$$

Experimental probability is calculated as the ratio of the number of times event A actually occurs to the number of trials. Outcomes in an experiment may or may not be equally likely. The experimental probability of event A is represented as follows:

$$P(A) = \frac{\text{number of times event A occurs}}{\text{number of trials}}$$

If an experiment has n possible, equally likely outcomes, the probability of each specific outcome is defined to be $\frac{1}{n}$. When tossing a coin, the theoretical probability of getting heads, written $P(H)$, is $\frac{1}{2}$, since heads is one of two equally likely outcomes, namely heads or tails. When a die is thrown, there are six possible outcomes, namely 1, 2, 3, 4, 5, or 6, so the probability of tossing an odd number is $\frac{3}{6}$ since there are 3 odd numbers (or 3 favorable outcomes), and 6 possible outcomes. This probability reduces to $\frac{1}{2}$.

Conditional Probability

The probability of an event occurring after another event has already occurred is called **conditional probability**. The notation for conditional probability is $P(B \mid A)$, which is read as "the probability of B given A."

If both events A and B are **independent**, where the result of B is not affected by the result of A, then the conditional probability of B given A is equal to the probability of B.

$$P(B \mid A) = P(B)$$

Likewise, if both events A and B are independent, where the result of A is not affected by the result of B, then the conditional probability of A given B is equal to the probability of A.

$$P(A \mid B) = P(A)$$

If both events A and B are **dependent**, where the result of B is affected by the result of A (or the result of A is affected by the result of B), then the conditional probability of B given A or A given B may be calculated using a few different methods. In probability situations involving dependent events, the way in which the question is asked will determine which equation to use.

The Multiplication Rule for dependent events states the following:

$$P(A \text{ and } B) = P(A) \cdot P(B \mid A)$$

or

$$P(A \text{ and } B) = P(B) \cdot P(A \mid B)$$

Using algebra, the following equations can be derived:

$$P(B \mid A) = \frac{P(A \text{ and } B)}{P(A)}$$

$$P(A \mid B) = \frac{P(A \text{ and } B)}{P(B)}$$

Example:

Of 100 people who work out at a gym, there are 45 people who take yoga classes, 55 people who take weightlifting classes, and 15 people who take both yoga and weightlifting. What is the probability that a randomly selected person takes weightlifting, given that the person also takes yoga?

Solution:

This question is asking you to find the probability that a person is taking weightlifting, given that he or she is also taking yoga (or $P(A \mid B)$). This probability is found by writing the following equation:

$$P(A \mid B) = \frac{P(A \text{ and } B)}{P(A)} = \frac{0.15}{0.45} = \frac{1}{3}$$

Note: It may be helpful to use letters that more closely represent the pieces of the problem. For example, you may wish to use $P(Y)$ to represent the probability of taking yoga classes and $P(W)$ to represent the probability of taking weightlifting classes. The probability of taking both would be written as $P(Y \text{ and } W)$.

The conditional probability that a person who takes weightlifting also takes yoga is $\frac{1}{3}$.

Independent Events

If events A and B are independent, then the probability of event B is not affected by the result of event A.

Example 1:

Adam tosses a coin and then tosses another coin. What is the probability that he gets heads or tails on the second toss, given that he gets heads on the first toss?

Solution:

We are going to use H to denote heads and T to denote tails. Since the events are independent, we can write the following:

$$P(H \text{ or } T \mid H) = P(H)$$

Since $P(H) = \frac{1}{2}$, we know that the probability of getting heads or tails on the second toss, given that the first toss gives heads, is also equal to $\frac{1}{2}$.

Example 2:

Again suppose that Adam tosses a coin and then tosses another coin. What is the probability that he gets heads on the first toss and tails on the second toss?

Solution:

Since the events are independent and the tosses can be distinguished, the probability can be represented as:

$$P(H \text{ and } T) = P(H) \cdot P(T) = \frac{1}{2} \cdot \frac{1}{2} = \frac{1}{4}$$

If Adam tosses two coins at the same time (and the toss that gives either result doesn't matter), the probability of getting heads and tails is $\frac{1}{2}$ because making a list would show that there are two favorite outcomes out of a sample space of four (i.e., the list HT, HH, TH, and TT shows that HT and TH have heads and tails, in some order). The ratio $\frac{2}{4}$, reduces to $\frac{1}{2}$.

Dependent Events

If events A and B are dependent, then the probability of event B is affected by the result of event A.

Example:

What is the probability of choosing a black 5, not replacing the card, and then choosing a red 5 from the same standard deck of cards?

Solution:

There are two red 5s and two black 5s in a standard deck of 52 cards. Removing a black 5 from the deck will leave only 51 cards in the deck, so the probability can be found like so:

$$P(A \text{ and } B) = \frac{2}{52} \times \frac{2}{51} = \frac{1}{663}$$

Two-Way Tables and Probability

Data on the exam is often represented in two-way tables like the one in the example below. Be careful to read the correct row or column that represents the information in the problem. These tables are often used for two or three problems in a row.

Example:

Hattie is a member of the honor society. All members of the society are polled to determine how many hours they spend studying per week and whether they prefer math or science classes. The results are shown in the table below.

	Science	Math	Total
0–3 hours per week	4	2	6
4–6 hours per week	6	7	13
Total	10	9	19

What is the probability that an honor society member selected at random prefers math, given that the member studies 4–6 hours per week?

Solution:

There are a total of 13 students who study 4–6 hours per week, and 7 of them prefer math. So the probability is $\frac{7}{13}$.

13

PRACTICE EXERCISE: PROBABILITY

DIRECTIONS: Work out each problem. Circle the letter of your choice. Check your answers against the answer key and explanations that follow.

1. Which of these pairs of events is dependent?

   A. Running a race and sweating

   B. Tossing a coin and then tossing a second coin

   C. Rolling a die and then tossing a coin

   D. Choosing a student from a math class and then choosing a student from a different math class

2. A poll asked 100 visitors at a national park the distance they hiked during their visit. The table shows the data collected based on the visitors' ages and hiking distances.

	18–25 years old	26–35 years old	Total
0–2 miles	16	22	38
2–4 miles	20	17	37
4+ miles	11	14	25
Total	47	53	100

What is the probability that a visitor hiked more than 4 miles, given that the visitor was 18–25 years old?

A. $\frac{11}{14}$

B. $\frac{11}{25}$

C. $\frac{11}{36}$

D. $\frac{11}{47}$

SHOW YOUR WORK HERE

13

3. What is the probability of selecting three black cards from a deck of 52 cards if each card is replaced before the next one is selected?

   A. $\frac{1}{256}$

   B. $\frac{1}{16}$

   C. $\frac{1}{52}$

   D. $\frac{1}{13}$

4. Slips of paper numbered 1 through 15 are placed in a bag. A student selects a slip from the bag without looking. What is the probability that the number selected is 9, given that it is known to be an odd number?

   A. $\frac{1}{10}$

   B. $\frac{1}{8}$

   C. $\frac{1}{7}$

   D. $\frac{1}{15}$

5. The two-way frequency table below shows the results of a poll regarding video game play. The poll asked 150 randomly selected people the amount of time they spend playing video games each week and the type of game they most like to play. The table shows frequencies of each category.

	1–3 hours	3–5 hours	5+ hours	Total
Role-playing	12	15	16	43
Platform	24	19	18	61
Action	33	35	28	96
Total	69	69	62	200

What is the probability that a person plays 3–5 hours of games per week, given that they prefer platform games?

   A. $\frac{19}{35}$

   B. $\frac{19}{42}$

   C. $\frac{19}{61}$

   D. $\frac{19}{69}$

SHOW YOUR WORK HERE

13

6. Which question below describes the probability of two dependent events?

   A. Two coins are flipped. What is the probability of the second coin landing heads up, if the first coin landed tails up?

   B. Two number cubes are rolled. What is the probability of rolling two even numbers?

   C. A card is selected from a deck of 52 cards. What is the probability of selecting 3 hearts in a row, if each card is replaced after being selected?

   D. A bag contains 5 red marbles and 6 blue marbles. What is the probability of selecting two marbles of different colors, without replacement of the marbles?

7. A summer camp held a fishing tournament. The participants selected the type of bait they would use. The table below shows the first type of fish caught by each participant and the bait they used.

	Perch	Bass	Trout	Catfish	Total
Live Bait	10	4	4	6	24
Artificial Bait	5	5	2	0	12
Total	15	9	6	6	36

What is the probability that a participant's first catch was a bass, given that artificial bait was used?

   A. $\dfrac{1}{4}$

   B. $\dfrac{5}{9}$

   C. $\dfrac{5}{12}$

   D. $\dfrac{5}{36}$

SHOW YOUR WORK HERE

13

8. Salena buys seven tickets in a raffle in which 50 tickets are sold. There are three prizes given: first, second, and third. What is the probability that she wins both first and second prizes?

A. $\dfrac{7}{50}$

B. $\dfrac{3}{175}$

C. $\dfrac{36}{2,401}$

D. $\dfrac{49}{2,500}$

9. During a science experiment, two studies of chemical reactions are conducted. Each experiment requires a hypothesis. Hypothesis A is correct $\dfrac{5}{7}$ of the times the experiment is conducted. Hypothesis B is correct $\dfrac{3}{4}$ of the times the experiment is conducted. If the two hypotheses do not affect each other, what is the probability that both hypotheses A and B are correct?

A. $\dfrac{5}{7}$

B. $\dfrac{3}{4}$

C. $\dfrac{15}{28}$

D. $\dfrac{5}{7}$

SHOW YOUR WORK HERE

13

10. Gustav finds that during daily marching band practice he correctly completes all steps $\frac{7}{8}$ of the time. During daily symphonic band practice he correctly plays each piece of music $\frac{11}{12}$ of the time. The probability that he completes all steps in marching band and plays each piece of music correctly in symphonic band during the same day is $\frac{3}{5}$. What is the probability that he correctly completes all steps during marching band, given that he plays each piece correctly in symphonic band?

A. $\frac{24}{35}$

B. $\frac{36}{55}$

C. $\frac{11}{20}$

D. $\frac{21}{40}$

11. A hockey team roster has 20 players on it. There are 12 forwards, 6 defensemen, and 2 goaltenders. If three players are selected at random without replacement, find the probability that all three are defensemen.

A. $\frac{1}{57}$

B. $\frac{2}{57}$

C. $\frac{27}{1,000}$

D. $\frac{3}{20}$

12. Kendra keeps loose change in a purse. If there are 8 dimes, 3 quarters, and 4 pennies in the purse and she chooses one coin without looking in the purse, what is the probability that the coin she selects is either a dime or a quarter?

A. $\frac{1}{5}$

B. $\frac{8}{15}$

C. $\frac{1}{2}$

D. $\frac{11}{15}$

SHOW YOUR WORK HERE

13

Answer Key and Explanations

1. A	3. B	5. C	7. C	9. A	11. A
2. D	4. B	6. D	8. B	10. B	12. D

1. **The correct answer is A.** Events are dependent if the occurrence of one event can affect the probability of the other. Of the pairs listed, running a race and sweating are dependent.

2. **The correct answer is D.** There are a total of 47 visitors who are 18–25 years old. In that age group, 11 of those visitors walked more than 4 miles, so the probability is $\frac{11}{47}$.

3. **The correct answer is B.** Since the card is placed back into the deck after each selection is made, you are always drawing a card from the full 52-card deck. So the selections are independent of each other. There are 26 black cards in the deck, so the probability of selecting a black card is $\frac{26}{52} = \frac{1}{2}$. The probability of selecting four black cards, one after the other, under these conditions, is $\frac{1}{2} \cdot \frac{1}{2} \cdot \frac{1}{2} \cdot \frac{1}{2} = \frac{1}{16}$.

4. **The correct answer is B.** This is a conditional probability. Since we are given that the number is odd, we reduce the sample space from 15 numbers to one including only the numbers 1, 3, 5, 7, 9, 11, 13, 15. There are 8 numbers here, each of which is equally likely to be selected. The probability of selecting the 9, given that the number is known to be odd, is $\frac{1}{8}$.

5. **The correct answer is C.** There are 61 total people who play platform games. Of those 61 people, 19 play for 3–5 hours, so the probability is $\frac{19}{61}$.

6. **The correct answer is D.** Situations that state there is no replacement have an event that is dependent on the other. In this case, the second chosen marble is dependent on the marble that was chosen first because there will be one less marble in the bag and it must be a different color.

7. **The correct answer is C.** There are 12 total fish caught using artificial bait. The number of bass caught out of those 12 is 5, so the probability is $\frac{5}{12}$.

8. **The correct answer is B.** The probability of Salena winning first prize is $\frac{7}{50}$. Once that prize is awarded, that winning ticket is discarded from the original lot of 50 tickets, and the next one is selected for second prize. The probability of Salena winning second prize is $\frac{6}{49}$. The probability that she wins both first and second prizes is the product of these two numbers:

$$\frac{7}{50} \cdot \frac{6}{49} = \frac{3}{175}$$

9. **The correct answer is A.** The probability of each hypothesis is independent of the other. The probability of both events occurring can be found by:

$$P(A \text{ and } B) = P(A) \cdot P(B)$$
$$= \frac{7}{5} \cdot \frac{3}{4}$$
$$= \frac{15}{28}$$

13

10. **The correct answer is B.** The probability of correctly completing the marching steps, given he plays each piece correctly in symphonic band, can be found by

$$\frac{P(A \text{ and } B)}{P(B)} = \frac{\frac{3}{5}}{\frac{11}{12}}$$

$$= \frac{3}{5} \cdot \frac{12}{11}$$

$$= \frac{36}{55}$$

11. **The correct answer is A.** The probability that the first selection is a defenseman is $\frac{6}{20}$. The second selection is made from a lot of 19 players, 5 of whom are defensemen; the probability that the second selection is a defenseman is $\frac{5}{19}$. Finally, the third selection is made from a lot of 18 players, 4 of whom are defensemen; the probability that the third selection is a defenseman is $\frac{4}{18}$. The probability that three defensemen are selected is the product of these probabilities:

$$\frac{6}{20} \cdot \frac{5}{19} \cdot \frac{4}{18} = \frac{1}{57}$$

12. **The correct answer is D.** The probability is $\frac{8+3}{15} = \frac{11}{15}$.

BRAIN BREAK

Are you staying hydrated? Studies have shown that if you are as little as 1% dehydrated, your cognitive function will start to decrease. At 2%, you will start to have problems focusing and will experience difficulty completing simple mental exercises such as adding or subtracting numbers. The amount of fluids you need to drink to stay hydrated varies by person and activity level. According to the National Academies of Sciences, Engineering, and Medicine, an adequate daily fluid intake should be about 15.5 cups for men and 11.5 cups for women. You know yourself best and how much you need to drink to stay focused. Get into the habit of keeping a water bottle handy, taking regular breaks, and limiting the amount of sugary or caffeinated fluids you consume throughout the day.

13

DATA INTERPRETATION

Working with Data in Tables

Some SAT exam questions ask you to solve mathematical problems based on data contained in tables. All such problems are based on problem-solving techniques that have already been reviewed. The trick when working with tables is to make certain that you select the correct data needed to solve the problem. Take your time reading each table so that you understand exactly what information the table contains. Carefully select data from the correct row and column. As you will see, things are even trickier when a problem involves more than one table.

In order to illustrate problem solving with tables, consider the two tables below. The three questions that follow are based on the data within these tables.

Paul, Mark, and Bob are computer salespeople. In addition to their regular salaries, they each receive a commission for each computer they sell. The number of computers that each salesperson sold during a particular week, as well as their commission amounts, is shown in the tables below.

NUMBER OF COMPUTERS SOLD

	Monday	Tuesday	Wednesday	Thursday	Friday
Paul	9	3	12	6	4
Mark	6	3	9	1	5
Bob	8	4	5	7	8

COMMISSION PER SALE

Paul	$15
Mark	$20
Bob	$25

Example 1:

What is the total amount of the commissions that Bob earned over the entire week?

Solution:

This problem concerns only Bob, so ignore the information for Mark and Paul. Over the course of the week, Bob sold $8 + 4 + 5 + 7 + 8 = 32$ computers. The second table tells us that Bob earns $25 per sale, so the total amount of his commission would be $25 \times 32 = \$800$.

Example 2:

What is the total amount of commission money earned by Paul, Mark, and Bob on Thursday?

Solution:

To solve this problem, focus only on what happened on Thursday. Ignore the data for the other four days. Be careful not to add the number of computers sold by the three people, since they each earn a different commission per sale.

On Thursday, Paul sold 6 computers and earned a $15 commission for each computer sold, so Paul earned $15 \times 6 = \$90$.

Mark sold 1 computer, so based on his $20 commission, he earned $20.

Bob sold 7 computers and earned a $25 commission per machine, so he made $25 × 7 = $175.

Overall, the amount of commission on Thursday is $90 + $20 + $175 = $285.

Example 3:

On what day did Paul and Mark earn the same amount in commission?

Solution:

You can save yourself a lot of time if you look at the tables before you start to compute. Note that Mark's commission is larger than Paul's, and so the only way they could have earned the same amount is if Paul sold more computers than Mark. The only days that Paul sold more computers than Mark were Monday, Wednesday, and Thursday, so those are the only days that need to be considered. By observation, you can see the following:

- On Thursday, Paul made much more in commission than Mark, so eliminate Thursday.
- On Monday, Paul earned $15 × 9 = $135 and Mark earned $20 × 6 = $120. This means that the answer must be Wednesday.

To be certain, note that on Wednesday Paul earned $15 × 12 = $180, and Mark earned $20 × 9 = $180 also.

Correlation and Scatterplots

If two variables have a relationship such that when one variable changes, the other changes in a predictable way, the two variables are **correlated**. For example, there is a correlation between the number of hours an employee works each week and the amount of money the employee earns—the more hours the employee works, the more money the employee earns. Note that in this case, as the first variable increases, the second variable increases as well. These two variables are **positively correlated**.

Sometimes, when one variable increases, a second variable decreases. For example, the more that a store charges for a particular item, the fewer of that item will be sold. In this case, these two variables are **negatively correlated**.

Sometimes, two variables are not correlated; that is, a change in one variable does not affect the other variable in any way. For example, the number of cans of soda that a person drinks each day is not correlated with the amount of money the person earns.

One way to determine whether two variables are correlated is to sketch a **scatterplot**. A scatterplot is a graph in which the x-axis represents the values of one variable and the y-axis represents the values of the other variable. Several values of one variable and the corresponding values of the other variable are measured and plotted on the graph:

- If the points appear to form a straight line, or are close to forming a straight line, then it is likely that the variables are correlated.
- If the line has a positive slope (rises up left to right), the variables are positively correlated.
- If the line has a negative slope (goes down left to right), the variables are negatively correlated.
- If the points on the scatterplot seem to be located more or less at random, then it is likely that the variables are not correlated.

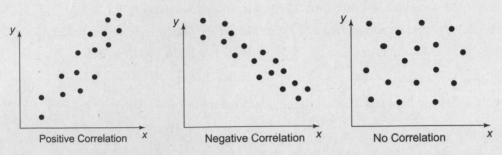

Positive Correlation   Negative Correlation   No Correlation

It is rare that the points on a scatterplot will all lie exactly on the same line. However, if there is a strong correlation, it is likely that there will be a line that could be drawn on the scatterplot that comes close to all of the points. Statisticians call the line that comes the closest to all of the points on a scatterplot the **line of best fit**. Without performing any computations, it is possible to visualize the location of the line of best fit, as the diagrams below show:

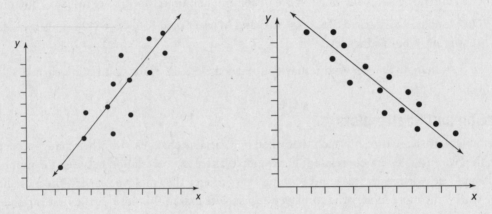

Example:

Which of the following slopes is the closest to the slope of the line of best fit for the scatterplot shown here?

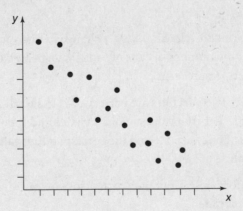

A. 3

B. 1

C. 0

D. −1

Solution:

Begin by sketching in the line of best fit in its approximate location.

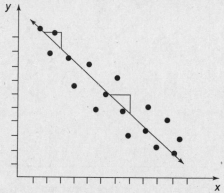

This line has a negative slope, since it decreases from left to right. In addition, the slope appears to be about −1, because if you move one unit horizontally from a point on the line, you need to move one unit vertically downward to return to the line. Since you can see that the points represent a negative correlation, the slope of the line of best fit will have to be negative, and choice D represents the only negative slope. **The correct answer is D.**

Equation of Line of Best Fit

You may see questions that ask you to create a line of best fit and give the equation for this line. Again, there is some approximation involved in determining a line of best fit. Look at the following scatterplot. Imagine a line that would come closest to all the data points and include an equal number of data points on either side of the line.

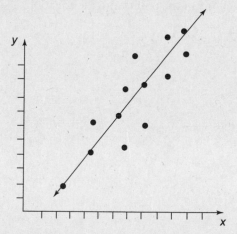

Notice the line of best fit below has 8 points above and 8 points below the line.

Note that the line of best fit does not have to cross any of the data points. In this case, the line of best fit goes through the middle of the data and does not include any of the actual data points.

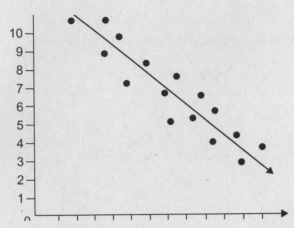

To determine the equation of the line of best fit, choose two points that lie on the line of best fit. You may have to approximate points if the line does not have points that are exactly on an intersection. The line appears to have points at (6, 8) and (12, 3). Use these two points to determine the equation of the line of best fit.

First, calculate the slope, m, using the slope formula $\dfrac{y_2 - y_1}{x_2 - x_1}$.

Plug x- and y-values into the equation: $\dfrac{3 - 8}{12 - 6} = -\dfrac{5}{6}$.

The slope-intercept formula is $y = mx + b$.

So far, we have $y = -\dfrac{5}{6}x + b$.

Substitute the x- and y-values from one of the points into the equation. Using the point (6, 8), we can write:

$$8 = \frac{-5}{6}(6) + b$$
$$8 = -5 + b$$
$$b = 13$$

The equation of the line of best fit is $y = \dfrac{-5}{6}x + 13$.

Making Predictions

The following scatterplot shows the average number of books borrowed on a weekly basis for years 2000–2009 at a local library.

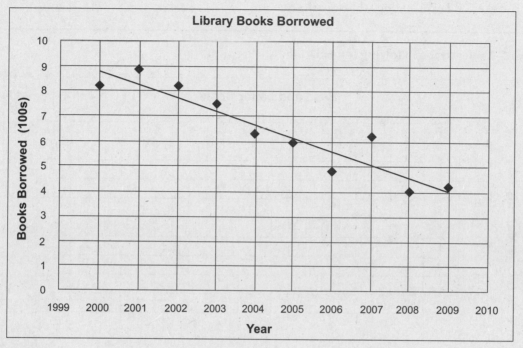

Example:

If the trend continued, about how many books were borrowed in 2010?

Solution:

Use the slope of the line to make predictions about data points that are not shown. According to the slope, the average number of books borrowed weekly goes down approximately $0.6 \times 100 = 60$ books every year. Multiply by 100 because, according to the title of the vertical axis, the numbers are in the 100s. The expected value for the number of books borrowed in 2009 was 400. The slope says we should expect that number to decrease by 60 every year, so you can predict that there were 340 books borrowed in 2010.

You have seen data that show a linear correlation, which may be represented by a line of best fit. In other cases, data may be better modeled by quadratic or exponential functions. When given a data set or plotted data, look to see if the data looks linear, parabolic, or representative of exponential growth or decay. Quadratic and exponential function models may easily be determined by entering the data into a spreadsheet or graphing calculator and selecting the appropriate function type (quadratic or exponential). The technology will provide output for the equation of the function. (The same procedure can be done with lines of best fit, as well.) Quadratic and exponential function models can also be estimated using the same sort of procedure described with the linear correlations above. Just note that not all data sets will be most appropriately modeled by a linear function.

Note that linear growth represents growth by a common difference, whereas exponential growth represents growth by a common factor. A real-world example of linear growth is simple interest, whereas a real-world example of exponential growth is compound interest.

PRACTICE EXERCISE: DATA INTERPRETATION

DIRECTIONS: Work out each problem. Circle the letter of your choice. Check your answers against the answer key and explanations that follow.

Questions 1–3 refer to the following information.

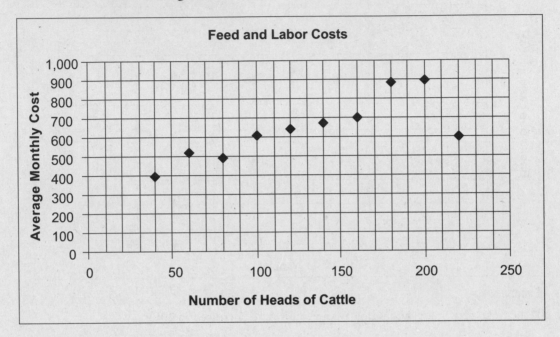

The scatterplot above shows average monthly feed and labor costs in dollars to raise different numbers of heads of beef cattle.

SHOW YOUR WORK HERE

13

1. Which of the following best represents the slope of the line of best fit for this data?

   A. 200

   B. $\dfrac{1}{2}$

   C. $\dfrac{10}{9}$

   D. 2

2. Based on the scatterplot, what is the equation of the line of best fit?

   A. $y = 200x + 400$

   B. $y = 2x + 320$

   C. $y = 2x + 380$

   D. $y = \dfrac{1}{2}x + 380$

3. If the trend continued, what would be the average monthly feed and labor costs to raise 500 heads of beef cattle?

   A. $1,380

   B. $1,000

   C. $880

   D. $600

SHOW YOUR WORK HERE

13

Questions 4–6 refer to the following information.

Geographic Area	Attended College	Did Not Attend College	No Response	Total
Northeast	72,404	68,350	29,542	170,296
Northwest	88,960	125,487	48,960	263,407
Southeast	115,488	96,541	65,880	277,909
Southwest	79,880	65,874	13,840	159,594
Total	356,732	356,252	158,222	871,206

A survey was conducted in different geographic areas of a large state, covering the entire state population, pertaining to college attendance for people over the age of 30. The table above displays a summary of the survey results.

4. According to the table, for which group did the highest percentage of people report that they had attended college?

   A. Northeast
   B. Northwest
   C. Southeast
   D. Southwest

SHOW YOUR WORK HERE

13

5. Of the people living in the northeast who reported that they did not attend college, 1,000 people were selected at random to do a follow-up survey in which they were asked if they were interested in attending adult education classes. There were 665 people who said they were interested in attending adult education classes. Using the data from both the initial survey and the follow-up survey, which of the following is most likely to be an accurate statement?

A. About 48,149 people living in the northeast who did not attend college would be interested in adult education classes.

B. About 45,453 people living in the northeast who did not attend college would be interested in adult education classes.

C. About 19,645 people living in the northeast who did not attend college would be interested in adult education classes.

D. Most people in the state are not interested in taking adult education classes.

6. What is the relative frequency of the number of people who attended college statewide, according to the survey?

A. 0.18

B. 0.41

C. 0.43

D. 0.5

SHOW YOUR WORK HERE

13

Questions 7–8 refer to the following information.

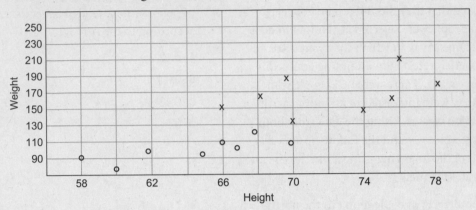

The scatterplot above shows the heights, in inches, and weights, in pounds, of 16 women and men at a health club. The women are represented by o's. The men are x's.

7. Which is a true statement about the data?

   A. The heights and weights are more strongly correlated for women than for men, and the slope of the line of best fit for women is greater than the slope for men.

   B. The heights and weights are more strongly correlated for women than for men, and the slope of the line of best fit for men is greater than the slope for women.

   C. The heights and weights are more strongly correlated for men than for women, and the slope of the line of best fit for women is greater than the slope for men.

   D. The heights and weights are more strongly correlated for men than for women, and the slope of the line of best fit for men is greater than the slope for women.

SHOW YOUR WORK HERE

13

8. Assume the 16 people whose data is plotted in the scatterplot are a random sample representing the entire health club membership. For what height would we expect a male and female club member to have roughly the same weight?

   A. 60 inches

   B. 66 inches

   C. 72 inches

   D. Based on the data, we would expect any male club member to weigh more than a female club member of the same height.

9.

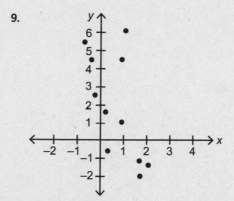

The scatterplot above shows a relationship between two variables x and y. Which of the following is the best approximation of the slope of the best fit line for this data?

   A. −3

   B. −1

   C. 1

   D. 3

SHOW YOUR WORK HERE

13

10.

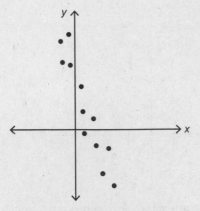

The scatterplot above shows a relationship between two variables x and y. What is true about the correlation between x and y?

A. No correlation

B. Strongly negatively correlated

C. Strongly positively correlated

D. Weakly positively correlated

Questions 11–12 refer to the following information.

A product rating site gathers data on the price, p, and quality of a product, x, (on a scale of 0 to 100, where 100 is a perfect rating). The scatterplot below shows recent data for slow cookers.

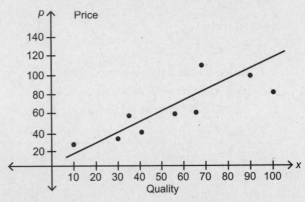

The best fit line for this data has equation $p = 0.9x + 15$.

11. What is the predicted price of a slow cooker if the quality rating is 95?

   A. $80.00

   B. $88.90

   C. $100.50

   D. $120.00

12. According to the best fit line, if you pay $51 for the slow cooker, what is its approximate expected quality rating?

   A. 36

   B. 40

   C. 45

   D. 50

SHOW YOUR WORK HERE

13

Answer Key and Explanations

1. D	3. A	5. B	7. B	9. A	11. C
2. C	4. D	6. B	8. A	10. B	12. B

1. **The correct answer is D.** First, draw an estimated line of best fit, through the points, as shown below:

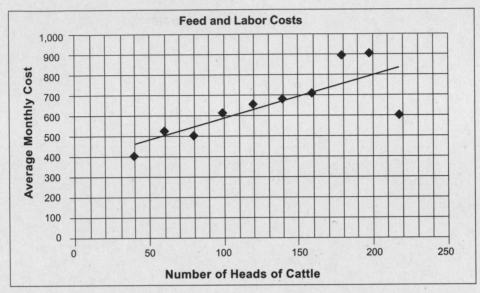

Next, choose two points that lie on, or close to, this estimated line of best fit. We can use the points, (60, 500) and (160, 700), since it looks like they lie on, or close to, the drawn line.

Use these coordinates in the slope formula:

$$\frac{y_2 - y_1}{x_2 - x_1} = \frac{700 - 500}{160 - 60} = \frac{200}{100} = 2$$

2. **The correct answer is C.** Using $m = 2$ as the slope (from Question 1), insert a set of xy-coordinates into the slope-intercept form, or $y = mx + b$. Substituting the x- and y-values from the point, (60, 500), into the equation gives $500 = 2(60) + b$, which simplifies as $500 = 120 + b$ and finally as $b = 380$. Rewriting the slope-intercept form with the slope of 2 and y-intercept of 380 gives $y = 2x + 380$.

3. **The correct answer is A.** Use the equation of the line of best fit to make predictions. Plug in 500 for the x-value:

$$y = 2(500) + 380 = 1,000 + 380 = 1,380$$

4. **The correct answer is D.** The percentage of people who attended college in the southwest region is:

$$\frac{79,880}{159,594} \approx 0.5 = 50\%$$

The percentages for the other areas are:

Northeast: $\frac{72,404}{170,296} \approx 0.425 \approx 43\%$

Northwest: $\frac{88,960}{263,407} \approx 0.337 \approx 34\%$

Southeast: $\frac{115,488}{277,909} \approx 0.415 \approx 42\%$

5. **The correct answer is B.** Extrapolating from the second survey, we can predict that $\frac{665}{1,000} = 66.5\%$ of the total population of the northeast will likely be interested in taking adult education classes. Applying this to the total northeast population who reported that they did not attend college: $68,350 \times 0.665 = 45,453$ people in this population are likely to be interested in adult education classes.

6. **The correct answer is B.** The relative frequency of college graduates in the survey is calculated by taking the total number of people who reported having attended college and dividing by the total number of people in the survey:

$$\frac{356,732}{871,206} \approx 0.41$$

7. **The correct answer is B.** See the estimated lines of best fit for women (W) and men (M):

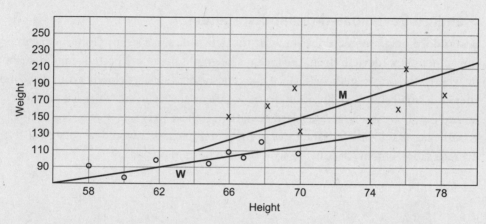

The o's generally are closer to line W than the x's are to line M, so the correlation is stronger for women. The slope of line W is about $\frac{1}{3}$; for M it is roughly $\frac{2}{3}$.

8. **The correct answer is A.** Extending line M downward, it would intersect W at roughly (60, 83). At this point of intersection, the expected height (60 inches) and weight of a man or woman would be the same.

9. **The correct answer is A.** The slope is negative since the points fall from left to right. To decide between choices A and B, notice that the points (0, 6) and (2, 0) are very close to the cluster of points in the scatterplot. Using these two points generates a line with slope −3. This steepness characterizes the pattern shown more than does a line with slope −1.

10. **The correct answer is B.** The points are closely packed together and they fall from left to right. So the data is strongly negatively correlated.

11. **The correct answer is C.** Evaluate the best line of fit when $x = 95$ to get the cost: $p = 0.9(95) + 15 = \$100.50$.

12. **The correct answer is B.** Solve the equation $51 = 0.9x + 15$ to get the expected quality rating. Doing so yields $0.9x = 36$, so that $x = \frac{36}{0.9} = 40$.

13

STATISTICS

Comparing Data Sets Using Shape, Center, and Spread

Statistics questions on the SAT exam require using measures of central tendency, meaning the mean (average), median, and mode of a data set. You will need to be familiar with the shape, center, and spread of data. The shape of the data refers to the normal distribution curve, which we examine below. The center could be the average (arithmetic mean) or the median of the data values in the set. The spread is the range of the data, or the standard deviation of the data that describes the distance between values in a data set.

Data may be presented in tables, bar graphs, and via other methods, so it is important to be familiar with different types of data presentation.

Standard Deviation—Normal Distribution

A **standard deviation** describes how far the data values in a set are from the mean or how much they "deviate" from the mean. The graphs below are both normal distribution curves. In the graph on the left, since much of the data clusters closely around the mean, there is a small standard deviation. In the graph on the right, since the data is more spread out, there is a larger standard deviation. If these were sets of test scores for Class A and Class B on a math exam, most of the scores in Class A would be very close to the average score, but, in Class B, the scores would be more varied.

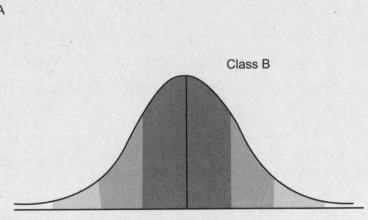

Class A

Class B

What You Really Need to Know About Standard Deviation

You won't have to calculate the standard deviation, but it is important to understand how to use it. If data has a normal distribution, the empirical rule states the following:

- Approximately 68% of the data falls within 1 standard deviation of the mean.
- Approximately 95% of the data falls within 2 standard deviations of the mean.
- Approximately 99.7% of the data falls within 3 standard deviations of the mean.

Let's see how this works with a table of data. The following table lists the number of students enrolled in six different sections of algebra, A, B, C, D, E, and F, offered by a college. First calculate the mean.

13

	A	B	C	D	E	F
Number of Students	18	23	15	19	28	11

$$\text{mean} = \frac{18 + 23 + 15 + 19 + 28 + 11}{6} = \frac{114}{6} = 19$$

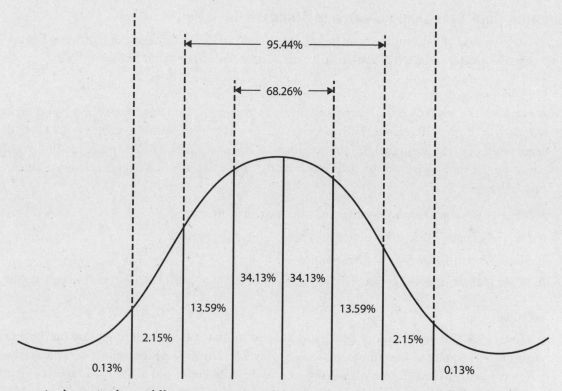

The mean is always in the middle. Here, it is 19, and the standard deviation is approximately 6.

The standard deviation of this data set is given as 6. In this example, the standard deviation of 6 means that approximately 68% of the algebra sections have between 19 – 6, or 13 students and 19 + 6, or 25 students, plus or minus 1 standard deviation.

Approximately 95% of the algebra sections lie within 2 standard deviations, meaning the sections have between 7 and 31 students.

Confidence Intervals and Measurement Errors

Measurement or sampling errors will usually occur when data cannot be collected about an entire population. If, for example, we are trying to determine the mean salary of people living in a city with 3.5 million people, we would probably use a smaller random sample of several hundred to several thousand people that was representative of the population. The difference between the mean salary of the actual population and that of the sample population is called a **measurement** or **sampling error**. The sampling error decreases as the sample size increases, since there is more data that should more accurately reflect the true population. Here's an example:

A packaging company is gathering data about how many oranges it can fit into a crate. It takes a sample of 36 crates out of a total shipment of 5,540 crates. The sample mean is 102 oranges with a sampling error of 6 oranges at a 95% confidence interval.

What does the **confidence interval** mean? A confidence interval tells you how close the sample mean is to the actual mean of the entire population. In this case, it means that based on the sample, you can be 95% confident that the true population mean for the entire shipment is between 102 − 6 and 102 + 6, or 96 and 108 oranges per crate.

Comparing Data Sets Using Mean and Standard Deviation

You may have two sets of data with similar means and ranges but different standard deviations. For the data set with the greater standard deviation, more of the data are farther from the mean.

Example:

A coach is deciding between 2 baseball players to recruit to his team. He is looking at player performance over the past 10 seasons. Both players have the same mean batting average of 0.270 and the same range of batting averages (0.080) over the past 10 seasons. However, Player A's batting averages have a higher standard deviation than Player B's batting averages. What does this indicate about each player?

A. Player A is more likely to hit better than his mean batting average.

B. Player B is more likely to hit better than his mean batting average.

C. Player A's batting average is more erratic.

D. Player B's batting average is more erratic.

Solution:

A greater standard deviation in a data set means that the data values are more spread out, or erratic, meaning performance varied more. Essentially, Player B's batting average is more dependable; he more frequently batted close to his batting average than did Player A. So, if the manager is looking for reliability, he may want to choose Player B for his team. **The correct answer is C.**

Making Inferences Using Sample Data

Frequently, a population is too large for every data value to be measured. Instead, a random sample of the population is used to make inferences about the true population.

Example:

An online retailer wants to determine the average dollar value of an order that it receives on a daily basis. Based on a random sample of 200 orders, the mean dollar value is $72 and the standard deviation is $5.

13

The normal distribution curve would look like this:

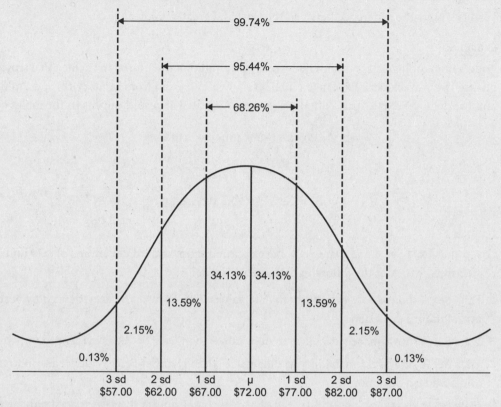

If the sample used is representative of the true population, what can be concluded about the true population of shoppers?

A. The mean of the true population is $72.

B. Most shoppers spend between $62 and $82.

C. All shoppers spend between $57 and $87.

D. The mode of the size of an order is $72.

Solution:

Shoppers who spent between $62 and $82 fall within 2 standard deviations of the mean of the sample population. Approximately 95% of the shoppers fall within 2 standard deviations of the mean. Thus, it can be concluded that most shoppers spend between $62 and $82. Though the sample is representative, it does not indicate that the mean of the true population is equal to the mean of the sample population, so choice A is incorrect. Approximately 99.7% of the population lies within 3 standard deviations of the mean, which, in this case, is between $57 and $87—but this is not all shoppers, so choice C is not fully supported. We don't know the mode of the data, so choice D is not correct. **The correct answer is B.**

Comparing Data Sets Using Spread

The spread is simply the difference between the least and greatest value in a set.

Example:

Todd's meteorology class researched weekly precipitation (measured in inches) in a tropical region during two 6-week periods. The data in Set A covers a period from January through mid-February, and the data in Set B is from July through mid-August. The results appear in the tables below.

Set A: Weeks 1–6 (January–February)					
0.43	1.73	1.93	0.28	0.08	1.18

Set B: Weeks 27–32 (July–August)					
0.20	0.01	0.00	0.08	0.04	0.00

Given that Data Set A and Data Set B have approximate standard deviations of 0.79 and 0.08, respectively, which of the following statements is true?

A. Data Set A shows more variability in data values than Data Set B, as evidenced by both the range and standard deviation.

B. Data Set A shows more variability in data values than Data Set B, as evidenced only by the range.

C. Data Set A shows less variability in data values than Data Set B, as evidenced by both the range and standard deviation.

D. Data Set A shows less variability in data values than Data Set B, as evidenced only by the standard deviation.

Solution:

To calculate range, write the data values in order from least to greatest for each set:

$$\text{Set A: } 0.08; 0.28; 0.43; 1.18; 1.73; 1.93$$
$$\text{Set B: } 0.00; 0.00; 0.01; 0.04; 0.08; 0.20$$

Find the difference between the least and greatest value for each set:

$$\text{Set A: Range} = 1.93 - 0.08 = 1.85$$
$$\text{Set B: Range} = 0.20 - 0.00 = 0.20$$

The range in Set A is greater. Since a higher standard deviation indicates more variability in data values about the mean, Data Set A has a higher level of variability than Data Set B. So, both measures of spread indicate that Data Set A shows more variability in data values. **The correct answer is A.**

13

Comparing Data Sets Using Median and Mode

Using the same data sets about tropical precipitation, let's look at problems involving median and mode.

Example:

Set A: Weeks 1–6 (January–February)					
0.43	1.73	1.93	0.28	0.08	1.18

Set B: Weeks 27–32 (July–August)					
0.20	0.01	0.00	0.08	0.04	0.00

Which is true about the two sets of data above?

A. The mode of Set A is greater than the mode of Set B.

B. The mode of Set B is greater than the mode of Set A.

C. The median of Set A is greater than the median of Set B.

D. The median of Set B is greater than the median of Set A.

Solution:

In this case, Set A does not have a mode, because there is no data value that appears more than once. So we cannot make any statements involving the mode of Set A.

Calculate the median of both sets of data. The median is the number in the middle of a data set when all the values are written in increasing order:

Set A: 0.08, 0.28, 0.43, 1.18, 1.73, 1.93

Here, the two middle numbers are 0.43 and 1.18, so we take their average:

$$\text{Median of Set A: } \frac{0.43 + 1.18}{2} = \frac{1.61}{2} = 0.805$$

We perform the same set of calculations for set B:

Set B: 0.00, 0.00, 0.01, 0.04, 0.08, 0.20

$$\text{Median of Set B: } \frac{0.01 + 0.04}{2} = \frac{0.05}{2} = 0.025$$

From this we can see that the median of Set A is greater than the median of Set B. **The correct answer is C.**

13

Evaluating Reports and Surveys

To evaluate a report about a set of data, it is important to consider the appropriateness of the data collection method. Random sampling ensures that every member of the population has an equally likely chance of being chosen. This data collection method type reduces bias and measurement error. There are different types of random sampling techniques that a researcher may use.

Example:

A local politician wants to gauge how her constituents feel about the installation of a gas pipeline that will border her district. Which of the following would allow the politician to make a valid conclusion about the opinions of her constituents?

A. Survey a random sample of local Democrats

B. Survey a sample of citizens who volunteer to provide responses

C. Survey an intact group of senior citizens at a local event

D. Survey a random sample of citizens at a local library

Solution:

Let's analyze each of these options. First is the random sample of local Democrats in Choice A. This may seem like a good choice. However, it excludes members of other parties and their opinions.

Choice B may seem okay at first, but such a sample will likely promote bias of the data, since the individuals responding will likely have strong viewpoints that may not be shared by others in the district.

Choice C also seems like an acceptable choice at first, but this sampling method excludes other age groups. Data obtained from this sampling technique cannot be generalized to the population, as a whole.

Choice D would allow for a valid conclusion (or generalization to the population), since a random sample is used and a library will likely have patrons who have varying beliefs, backgrounds, ages, and so on. Choice D does not exclude any age or party and will result in the smallest sampling error. **The correct answer is D.**

When considering whether the data in a report is representative of a population, it is important to consider the demographics of the population being studied. Their habits, behaviors, and perhaps incomes will influence their decisions and even their ability to be included in the report. The type of survey that will include the widest range of habits, behaviors, and incomes of the people being studied is likely the most representative. As discussed above, the use of random sampling reduces the sampling error and bias and results in sample data that may be used to represent the population from which the sample came.

PRACTICE EXERCISE: STATISTICS

DIRECTIONS: Work out each problem. Circle the letter of your choice. Check your answers against the answer key and explanations that follow.

1. The following tables show the number of employees in two different groups of an organization in different age ranges.

Production	
Age Range	**Number of Employees**
20–24	4
25–29	8
30–34	25
35–39	19
40–44	17

Design	
Age Range	**Number of Employees**
20–24	2
25–29	4
30–34	6
35–39	33
40–44	38

Which of the following conclusions can be made about the data shown in the tables?

A. The range of ages is greater in production than in design.

B. The range of ages is greater in design than in production.

C. The median age is greater in production than in design.

D. The median age is greater in design than in production.

SHOW YOUR WORK HERE

13

2. A nursery wants to know if a certain fertilizer is helping its rose bushes grow more roses per bush. The nursery uses the fertilizer on one plot, Plot A, of rose bushes but does not use fertilizer on another plot, Plot B. All the rose bushes in both plots were planted at the same time. The charts below show the number of flowers on each bush for the two plots.

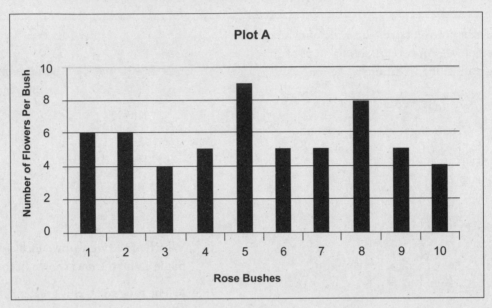

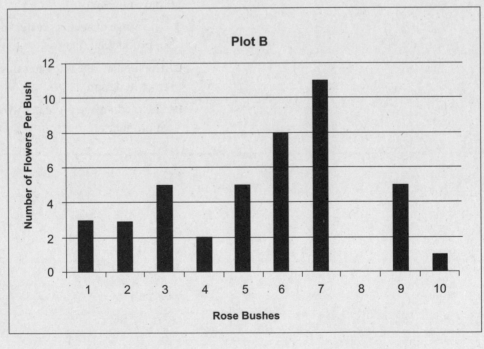

13

Which of the following conclusions could be logically drawn based on the data shown in the tables?

A. The mean number of roses in Plot A is greater, so plot A likely benefited from the fertilizer.

B. The mean number of roses in Plot B is greater, so plot B likely benefited from NOT having the fertilizer.

C. The fertilizer had no effect on the rose bushes.

D. There is not enough information to make any conclusion.

3. If the mean and standard deviation of a bell-shaped distribution are 2.0 and 0.75, respectively, what interval contains about 95% of the data?

A. (0.5, 3.5)

B. (1.25, 2.75)

C. (1.5, 2.5)

D. (1.0, 3.0)

SHOW YOUR WORK HERE

13

4. The number of donuts sold during the time-period between 6 a.m. and 8 a.m. by two local donut shops for one week is shown below:

Shop	M	T	W	Th	F	Sat	Sun
A	780	700	890	600	1,200	1,200	930
B	650	750	900	700	860	940	1,200

Which of the following statements is true?

A. The median number of donuts sold by shop A is less than the median number sold by shop B.

B. The median number of donuts sold by shop A is greater than the median number sold by shop B.

C. The mean number of donuts sold by shop A is less than the mean number sold by shop B.

D. The range of the number of donuts sold by shop A is less than the range of the number of donuts sold by shop

5. A coffee retailer kept track of the number of customers during the same 6-hour period over the course of two days and recorded her findings in the table below.

	1–2 p.m.	2–3 p.m.	3–4 p.m.	4–5 p.m.	5–6 p.m.	6–7 p.m.
Sunday	24	22	28	35	38	35
Monday	11	18	18	22	44	30

Which of the following is a valid conclusion to be drawn from the data in the table?

A. The coffee shop is busier later in the day.

B. There are probably never more than 50 customers in the coffee shop.

C. The average number of customers is higher on the weekends than during the week.

D. The range of data on the two days is equal.

SHOW YOUR WORK HERE

13

6. A sample of athletes was chosen, and the times it took them to complete an obstacle course was recorded. The mean time was 35 minutes and standard deviation was 4.25 minutes. If the sample is representative of the population of all athletes attempting the obstacle course, what conclusion can be drawn about the population of all athletes attempting the course?

A. All athletes complete the course in no more than 47.75 minutes.

B. The median completion time is 35 minutes.

C. Most athletes finish the course in between 26.5 minutes and 43.5 minutes.

D. No athlete completes the course in less than 25 minutes.

7. The data set below represents the number of hits a baseball player gets per game for 10 games.

    0   3   1   1   0   2   0   1   3   2

Which of the following statements is true?

A. The median number hits per game for this player is 2.

B. The data set is bimodal.

C. The mean number hits per game for this player is 1.

D. The range of the number of hits this player gets per game is 2.

8. The margin of error is +/− 20 points for a 95% confidence interval for a given set of data. The researcher in charge of the data wants to obtain a lower margin of error. Which of the following is the best approach for the researcher, if he wishes to decrease the margin of error?

A. Increase the confidence level to 98%.

B. Decrease the confidence level to 90%.

C. Obtain another sample of the same size.

D. Decrease the sample size.

SHOW YOUR WORK HERE

13

9. A poll was taken by the local university to determine which candidate is most likely to win the upcoming congressional race. The poll was conducted by selecting every fifth person who walked into a coffee shop in the largest city of the congressional district. Which of the following best describes the poll?

   A. The poll is a representative sample because it was done in the largest city in the district.

   B. The poll is a representative sample because it was done randomly.

   C. The poll is not a representative sample because it was done only in the largest city in the district.

   D. The poll is not a representative sample because it was done randomly.

10. The double occupancy room rates at 40 five-star hotels in Los Angeles is normally distributed with a mean of $280 and a standard deviation of $48.25. Which is the range of values, in dollars, around the mean that includes 95% of the room rates?

    A. $280.00–$328.25

    B. $231.75–$280.00

    C. $231.75–$328.25

    D. $183.50–$376.50

SHOW YOUR WORK HERE

13

11. A researcher wants to measure the opinions of university students regarding global climate change. Which of the following poll results would most likely provide reliable data about the opinions of the entire population of university students?

   A. The researcher interviewed 60 students selected at random at a political rally attended by about 16% of university students.

   B. The researcher interviewed 55 students in a physics laboratory on campus.

   C. The researcher randomly selected 100 students from the complete roster of registered students, and emailed an interview invitation. Twelve percent participated.

   D. The researcher randomly selected 100 students from the complete roster of registered students, and emailed an offer of $5 to participate in an interview. Fifty percent participated.

SHOW YOUR WORK HERE

13

12. A public health group investigates a claim that "Brand Y" cigarettes have less than 18 milligrams of tar per cigarette, and that this is less tar than "Brand X" cigarettes have. The group tests 16 randomly selected cigarettes for each brand. The findings are shown in the charts below.

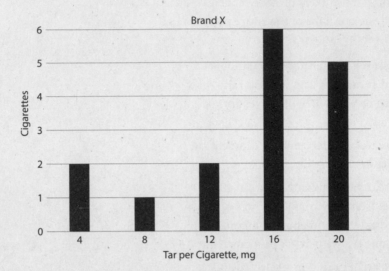

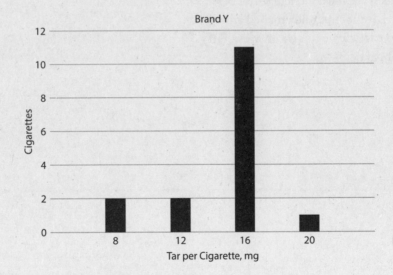

Which conclusion is supported by the data?

A. The average (arithmetic mean) tar per cigarette is higher for Brand Y than for Brand X, although the average is less than 18 milligrams for Brand Y.

B. The average (arithmetic mean) tar per cigarette is higher for Brand X than for brand Y, although the average is less than 18 milligrams for both brands.

C. The average (arithmetic mean) tar per cigarette is higher for Brand X, and it is greater than 18 milligrams.

D. The average (arithmetic mean) tar per cigarette is the same for the two brands. Brand X has greater variability, so it is more likely that a Brand X cigarette will have more than 18 grams of tar than it is that a Brand Y cigarette will exceed that amount of tar.

Answer Key and Explanations

1. D	3. A	5. A	7. B	9. C	11. D
2. A	4. B	6. C	8. B	10. D	12. D

1. **The correct answer is D.** We don't have exact ages, which is why we can't conclude anything about the range of ages and can eliminate choices A and B. There are 73 employees in the production group, so the median age is the 37th data value when the ages are written in ascending order, which would be in the 30–34 age range. There are 83 employees in the design group. The median age is the 42nd data value, which falls in the 35–39 age range. Thus the median age for the design group is higher.

2. **The correct answer is A.** First focus on the mean number of roses on the bushes in Plot A:

$$\frac{6+6+4+5+9+5+5+8+5+4}{10} = \frac{57}{10} = 5.7$$

Then, look at those in Plot B:

$$\frac{3+3+5+2+5+8+11+0+5+1}{10} = \frac{43}{10} = 4.3$$

On average, the bushes in Plot A grew more roses and so likely benefited from the fertilizer.

3. **The correct answer is A.** For a bell-shaped curve, 95% of the data occurs within two standard deviations of the mean. Here, this is 2.0: 2(0.75) = 0.5 to 2.0 + 2(0.75) = 3.5. So the interval (0.5, 3.5) is the desired answer.

4. **The correct answer is B.** The median number of donuts sold by shop A is 890, and the median number sold by shop B is 860. Statement B is true.

5. **The correct answer is A.** It is difficult to conclude that there are never more than 50 customers in the shop, as choice B says, because we don't have enough data. As for choice C, while the mean for Sunday is higher than the mean for Monday, the sample size of 2 days is not enough to make a conclusion about the weekends versus the weekdays in general. The range of the two data sets are not equal to each other, so choice D is incorrect. Sunday's range: 38 – 22 = 16 and Monday's range: 44 – 11 = 33.

6. **The correct answer is C.** The interval containing 95% of the data is 35 – 2(4.25) = 26.5 to 35 + 2(4.25) = 43.5. This is the majority of the time, so statement C is true.

7. **The correct answer is B.** There are two values that occur the same number of times, and this number exceeds the frequency of all other data values. These two data values are 0 and 1. The data set has two modes, or is bimodal.

8. **The correct answer is B.** The data has already been collected, so decreasing the sample size is not possible without redoing the study. Decreasing the sample size would increase the margin of error. Also, obtaining a new sample would not necessarily reduce the margin of error. Increasing the confidence level would increase the margin of error, while decreasing the confidence interval would decrease the margin of error. This is true because increased confidence levels have higher critical values that, when multiplied by the ratio of the population standard deviation to the square root of n, result in higher margins of error. For example, for a population standard deviation of 3

13

and sample size of 30, a 95% confidence level would give a margin of error equal to the product of $1.96 \cdot \dfrac{3}{\sqrt{n}}$, or approximately 1.07. A 90% confidence level would give a margin of error equal to the product of $1.645 \cdot \dfrac{3}{\sqrt{n}}$, or approximately 0.90. Notice the margin of error decreased with the decreased level of confidence. Decreasing the confidence level would decrease the margin of error.

9. **The correct answer is C.** A representative sample should allow for random selection within the entire population, not just random selection from one part of the population.

10. **The correct answer is D.** Ninety-five percent of the rates fall within 2 standard deviations of the mean, meaning within $\$48.25 \times 2 = \$96.50$ of the mean price of $\$280.00$ and $280.00 + 96.50 = 376.50$ and $280.00 - 96.50 = 183.50$.

11. **The correct answer is D.** Although the interview at the rally would yield the greatest number of respondents, the population of political-event attendees—only 15 percent of all students—probably differs from the general population of students in their opinions about public policy issues, including climate change. Similarly, in a chemistry lab, the students interviewed are more likely to be science students; their opinions, though possibly more authoritative, could be expected to differ from the larger population of university students. Random selection from the entire student body is most likely to provide a sample that represents the general population, and the larger sample in choice D makes it more reliable than choice C. There is no reason to think that the offer of a small incentive would bias the sample.

12. **The correct answer is D.** To calculate the mean tar per cigarette for Brand X, divide the total amount of tar in all Brand X cigarettes by the number of cigarettes, 16. Based on the bar chart we have the following (note: inside the parentheses is the amount of tar multiplied by the number of cigarettes with that much tar):

$$\frac{(4 \times 2) + (8 \times 1) + (12 \times 2) + (16 \times 6) + (20 \times 5)}{16} = \frac{236}{16} = 14.75$$

For Brand Y the corresponding calculation is:

$$\frac{(8 \times 2) + (12 \times 2) + (16 \times 11) + (20 \times 1)}{16} = \frac{236}{16} = 14.75$$

The average tar per cigarette is 14.75 milligrams for both brands. Only choice D correctly states that this average is the same for both. The statement that tar in Brand X is more variable than in Brand Y is also correct. Note as well that 5 of 16 tested Brand X cigarettes had more than 18 mg of tar, but only 1 of 16 Brand Y cigarettes exceeded that amount.

13

SUMMING IT UP

- Not all problems that deal with averages will ask you to solve for the average of a set of quantities.
- The trick when working with tables is to make sure you select the correct data needed to solve the problem.
- Take your time reading each table.
- Observe trends with scatterplots, and use lines or curves to predict unknown values.
- Read data representations carefully when comparing data sets.
- Pay attention to sampling methods when you evaluate survey data.

Take a moment to ask yourself some simple questions about your understanding of the chapter:

Review: What did I learn?

Evaluate: What do I need to learn more about?

Plan: What can I do next to keep improving?

Based on your answers to those questions, adjust your study plan to dedicate additional time to the areas of weakness that you've identified.

13

PART VII:
PRACTICE TESTS FOR THE SAT® EXAM

Practice Tests for the SAT® Exam

OVERVIEW

- **Introduction to the Practice Tests**
- **Practice Test 1**
- **Practice Test 2**

INTRODUCTION TO THE PRACTICE TESTS

The following two practice tests are provided to help you prepare for the actual SAT exam (more practice tests are available online at **www.petersons.com/testprep/sat**). Each of the practice tests contain the same sections that you will encounter on the actual SAT exam, with the same amount of questions to answer in the officially allotted test time.

- Section 1: Reading Test (65 minutes—52 questions)
- Section 2: Writing and Language Test (35 minutes—44 questions)
- Section 3: Math Test—No Calculator (25 minutes—20 questions)
- Section 4: Math Test—Calculator (55 minutes—38 questions)
- Section 5: Optional Essay (50 minutes—1 Essay)

Try to replicate the testing experience as much as possible. This means finding a quiet space, having a couple of sharpened No. 2 pencils and a calculator handy, and setting a timer for each section.

An answer sheet can be found at the beginning of each practice test. Take care to do the following:

- Mark your answer sheet properly—be sure to completely fill in the answer circle.
- Be careful to mark only one answer for each question.
- Don't make any stray marks on the answer sheet.
- If you need to erase your answer, make sure you do so completely.
- Be sure to use the answer spaces that correspond to the question numbers.

Set your timer and work on one section at a time. If you complete a section before the allotted test time for that section expires, check your work on that section only.

On test day, you are allowed to use your test booklet for scratch work. You can do the same in this book (if this book is not yours, then have some scratch paper handy). Make sure to transfer your answers properly onto your Answer Sheet.

Once you have completed all test sections, check your answers against the Answer Keys and Explanations that follow each practice test. Then score your work using the scoring section that follows.

PRACTICE TEST 1 ANSWER SHEET

Section I: Reading Test

1. Ⓐ Ⓑ Ⓒ Ⓓ   14. Ⓐ Ⓑ Ⓒ Ⓓ   27. Ⓐ Ⓑ Ⓒ Ⓓ   40. Ⓐ Ⓑ Ⓒ Ⓓ

2. Ⓐ Ⓑ Ⓒ Ⓓ   15. Ⓐ Ⓑ Ⓒ Ⓓ   28. Ⓐ Ⓑ Ⓒ Ⓓ   41. Ⓐ Ⓑ Ⓒ Ⓓ

3. Ⓐ Ⓑ Ⓒ Ⓓ   16. Ⓐ Ⓑ Ⓒ Ⓓ   29. Ⓐ Ⓑ Ⓒ Ⓓ   42. Ⓐ Ⓑ Ⓒ Ⓓ

4. Ⓐ Ⓑ Ⓒ Ⓓ   17. Ⓐ Ⓑ Ⓒ Ⓓ   30. Ⓐ Ⓑ Ⓒ Ⓓ   43. Ⓐ Ⓑ Ⓒ Ⓓ

5. Ⓐ Ⓑ Ⓒ Ⓓ   18. Ⓐ Ⓑ Ⓒ Ⓓ   31. Ⓐ Ⓑ Ⓒ Ⓓ   44. Ⓐ Ⓑ Ⓒ Ⓓ

6. Ⓐ Ⓑ Ⓒ Ⓓ   19. Ⓐ Ⓑ Ⓒ Ⓓ   32. Ⓐ Ⓑ Ⓒ Ⓓ   45. Ⓐ Ⓑ Ⓒ Ⓓ

7. Ⓐ Ⓑ Ⓒ Ⓓ   20. Ⓐ Ⓑ Ⓒ Ⓓ   33. Ⓐ Ⓑ Ⓒ Ⓓ   46. Ⓐ Ⓑ Ⓒ Ⓓ

8. Ⓐ Ⓑ Ⓒ Ⓓ   21. Ⓐ Ⓑ Ⓒ Ⓓ   34. Ⓐ Ⓑ Ⓒ Ⓓ   47. Ⓐ Ⓑ Ⓒ Ⓓ

9. Ⓐ Ⓑ Ⓒ Ⓓ   22. Ⓐ Ⓑ Ⓒ Ⓓ   35. Ⓐ Ⓑ Ⓒ Ⓓ   48. Ⓐ Ⓑ Ⓒ Ⓓ

10. Ⓐ Ⓑ Ⓒ Ⓓ   23. Ⓐ Ⓑ Ⓒ Ⓓ   36. Ⓐ Ⓑ Ⓒ Ⓓ   49. Ⓐ Ⓑ Ⓒ Ⓓ

11. Ⓐ Ⓑ Ⓒ Ⓓ   24. Ⓐ Ⓑ Ⓒ Ⓓ   37. Ⓐ Ⓑ Ⓒ Ⓓ   50. Ⓐ Ⓑ Ⓒ Ⓓ

12. Ⓐ Ⓑ Ⓒ Ⓓ   25. Ⓐ Ⓑ Ⓒ Ⓓ   38. Ⓐ Ⓑ Ⓒ Ⓓ   51. Ⓐ Ⓑ Ⓒ Ⓓ

13. Ⓐ Ⓑ Ⓒ Ⓓ   26. Ⓐ Ⓑ Ⓒ Ⓓ   39. Ⓐ Ⓑ Ⓒ Ⓓ   52. Ⓐ Ⓑ Ⓒ Ⓓ

Section II: Writing and Language Test

1. Ⓐ Ⓑ Ⓒ Ⓓ   12. Ⓐ Ⓑ Ⓒ Ⓓ   23. Ⓐ Ⓑ Ⓒ Ⓓ   34. Ⓐ Ⓑ Ⓒ Ⓓ

2. Ⓐ Ⓑ Ⓒ Ⓓ   13. Ⓐ Ⓑ Ⓒ Ⓓ   24. Ⓐ Ⓑ Ⓒ Ⓓ   35. Ⓐ Ⓑ Ⓒ Ⓓ

3. Ⓐ Ⓑ Ⓒ Ⓓ   14. Ⓐ Ⓑ Ⓒ Ⓓ   25. Ⓐ Ⓑ Ⓒ Ⓓ   36. Ⓐ Ⓑ Ⓒ Ⓓ

4. Ⓐ Ⓑ Ⓒ Ⓓ   15. Ⓐ Ⓑ Ⓒ Ⓓ   26. Ⓐ Ⓑ Ⓒ Ⓓ   37. Ⓐ Ⓑ Ⓒ Ⓓ

5. Ⓐ Ⓑ Ⓒ Ⓓ   16. Ⓐ Ⓑ Ⓒ Ⓓ   27. Ⓐ Ⓑ Ⓒ Ⓓ   38. Ⓐ Ⓑ Ⓒ Ⓓ

6. Ⓐ Ⓑ Ⓒ Ⓓ   17. Ⓐ Ⓑ Ⓒ Ⓓ   28. Ⓐ Ⓑ Ⓒ Ⓓ   39. Ⓐ Ⓑ Ⓒ Ⓓ

7. Ⓐ Ⓑ Ⓒ Ⓓ   18. Ⓐ Ⓑ Ⓒ Ⓓ   29. Ⓐ Ⓑ Ⓒ Ⓓ   40. Ⓐ Ⓑ Ⓒ Ⓓ

8. Ⓐ Ⓑ Ⓒ Ⓓ   19. Ⓐ Ⓑ Ⓒ Ⓓ   30. Ⓐ Ⓑ Ⓒ Ⓓ   41. Ⓐ Ⓑ Ⓒ Ⓓ

9. Ⓐ Ⓑ Ⓒ Ⓓ   20. Ⓐ Ⓑ Ⓒ Ⓓ   31. Ⓐ Ⓑ Ⓒ Ⓓ   42. Ⓐ Ⓑ Ⓒ Ⓓ

10. Ⓐ Ⓑ Ⓒ Ⓓ   21. Ⓐ Ⓑ Ⓒ Ⓓ   32. Ⓐ Ⓑ Ⓒ Ⓓ   43. Ⓐ Ⓑ Ⓒ Ⓓ

11. Ⓐ Ⓑ Ⓒ Ⓓ   22. Ⓐ Ⓑ Ⓒ Ⓓ   33. Ⓐ Ⓑ Ⓒ Ⓓ   44. Ⓐ Ⓑ Ⓒ Ⓓ

Section III: Math Test—NO CALCULATOR

1. Ⓐ Ⓑ Ⓒ Ⓓ
2. Ⓐ Ⓑ Ⓒ Ⓓ
3. Ⓐ Ⓑ Ⓒ Ⓓ
4. Ⓐ Ⓑ Ⓒ Ⓓ
5. Ⓐ Ⓑ Ⓒ Ⓓ

6. Ⓐ Ⓑ Ⓒ Ⓓ
7. Ⓐ Ⓑ Ⓒ Ⓓ
8. Ⓐ Ⓑ Ⓒ Ⓓ
9. Ⓐ Ⓑ Ⓒ Ⓓ
10. Ⓐ Ⓑ Ⓒ Ⓓ

11. Ⓐ Ⓑ Ⓒ Ⓓ
12. Ⓐ Ⓑ Ⓒ Ⓓ
13. Ⓐ Ⓑ Ⓒ Ⓓ
14. Ⓐ Ⓑ Ⓒ Ⓓ
15. Ⓐ Ⓑ Ⓒ Ⓓ

16.

17.

18.

19.

20.

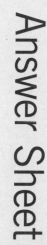

Section IV: Math Test—CALCULATOR

1. Ⓐ Ⓑ Ⓒ Ⓓ
2. Ⓐ Ⓑ Ⓒ Ⓓ
3. Ⓐ Ⓑ Ⓒ Ⓓ
4. Ⓐ Ⓑ Ⓒ Ⓓ
5. Ⓐ Ⓑ Ⓒ Ⓓ
6. Ⓐ Ⓑ Ⓒ Ⓓ
7. Ⓐ Ⓑ Ⓒ Ⓓ
8. Ⓐ Ⓑ Ⓒ Ⓓ

9. Ⓐ Ⓑ Ⓒ Ⓓ
10. Ⓐ Ⓑ Ⓒ Ⓓ
11. Ⓐ Ⓑ Ⓒ Ⓓ
12. Ⓐ Ⓑ Ⓒ Ⓓ
13. Ⓐ Ⓑ Ⓒ Ⓓ
14. Ⓐ Ⓑ Ⓒ Ⓓ
15. Ⓐ Ⓑ Ⓒ Ⓓ
16. Ⓐ Ⓑ Ⓒ Ⓓ

17. Ⓐ Ⓑ Ⓒ Ⓓ
18. Ⓐ Ⓑ Ⓒ Ⓓ
19. Ⓐ Ⓑ Ⓒ Ⓓ
20. Ⓐ Ⓑ Ⓒ Ⓓ
21. Ⓐ Ⓑ Ⓒ Ⓓ
22. Ⓐ Ⓑ Ⓒ Ⓓ
23. Ⓐ Ⓑ Ⓒ Ⓓ
24. Ⓐ Ⓑ Ⓒ Ⓓ

25. Ⓐ Ⓑ Ⓒ Ⓓ
26. Ⓐ Ⓑ Ⓒ Ⓓ
27. Ⓐ Ⓑ Ⓒ Ⓓ
28. Ⓐ Ⓑ Ⓒ Ⓓ
29. Ⓐ Ⓑ Ⓒ Ⓓ
30. Ⓐ Ⓑ Ⓒ Ⓓ

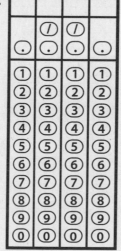

31.   32.   33.   34.

35.   36.   37.   38.

Section V: Essay

Practice Test 1

Practice Test 1

Section 1: Reading Test

65 Minutes—52 Questions

DIRECTIONS: Each passage (or pair of passages) in this section is followed by a number of multiple-choice questions. After reading each passage, select the best answer to each question based on what is stated or implied in the passage or passages and in any supplementary material, such as a table, graph, or chart.

Questions 1–10 are based on the following passage.

Pulitzer prize-winning writer Willa Cather worked as a reporter and also wrote several novels and short stories. This excerpt is from one of her more popular short stories, Paul's Case: A Study in Temperament, written in 1905.

It was Paul's afternoon to appear before the faculty of the Pittsburgh High School to account for his various misdemeanors. He
Line had been suspended a week ago, and his fa-
5 ther had called at the Principal's office and confessed his perplexity about his son. Paul entered the faculty room suave and smiling. His clothes were a trifle outgrown, and the tan velvet on the collar of his open overcoat
10 was frayed and worn; but for all that there was something of the dandy in him, and he wore an opal pin in his neatly knotted black four-in-hand, and a red carnation in his buttonhole. This latter adornment the
15 faculty somehow felt was not properly significant of the contrite spirit befitting a boy under the ban of suspension.

Paul was tall for his age and very thin, with high, cramped shoulders and a nar-
20 row chest. His eyes were remarkable for a certain hysterical brilliancy, and he continually used them in a conscious, theatrical sort of way, peculiarly offensive in a boy. The pupils were abnormally large, as
25 though he was addicted to belladonna, but there was a glassy glitter about them which that drug does not produce.

When questioned by the Principal as to why he was there Paul stated, politely
30 enough, that he wanted to come back to school. This was a lie, but Paul was quite accustomed to lying; found it, indeed, indispensable for overcoming friction. His teachers were asked to state their respective
35 charges against him, which they did with such a rancor and aggrievedness as evinced that this was not a usual case. Disorder and impertinence were among the offenses named, yet each of his instructors felt that
40 it was scarcely possible to put into words the cause of the trouble, which lay in a sort of hysterically defiant manner of the boy's; in the contempt which they all knew he felt for them, and which he seemingly made
45 not the least effort to conceal. Once, when he had been making a synopsis of a paragraph at the blackboard, his English teacher had stepped to his side and attempted to guide his hand. Paul had started back with
50 a shudder and thrust his hands violently behind him. The astonished woman could scarcely have been more hurt and embarrassed had he struck at her. The insult was so involuntary and definitely personal as to
55 be unforgettable. In one way and another he had made all of his teachers, men and women alike, conscious of the same feeling of physical aversion. In one class he habitually sat with his hand shading his eyes; in
60 another he always looked out the window during the recitation; in another he made a running commentary on the lecture, with humorous intention.

His teachers felt this afternoon that
65 his whole attitude was symbolized by his
shrug and his flippantly red carnation
flower, and they fell upon him without
mercy, his English teacher leading the
pack. He stood through it smiling, his
70 pale lips parted over his white teeth. (His
lips were constantly twitching, and he
had a habit of raising his eyebrows that
was contemptuous and irritating to the
last degree.) Older boys than Paul had
75 broken down and shed tears under that
baptism of fire, but his set smile did not
once desert him, and his only sign of discomfort was the nervous trembling of the
fingers that toyed with the buttons of his
80 overcoat, and an occasional jerking of the
other hand that held his hat. Paul was always smiling, always glancing about
him, seeming to feel that people might
be watching him and trying to detect
85 something. This conscious expression,
since it was as far as possible from boy-
ish mirthfulness, was usually attributed
to insolence or "smartness."

As the inquisition proceeded, one of
90 his instructors repeated an impertinent
remark of the boy's, and the principal
asked him whether he thought that a
courteous speech to have made a woman.
Paul shrugged his shoulders slightly and
95 his eyebrows twitched.

"I don't know," he replied. "I didn't
mean to be polite, or impolite, either. I
guess it's a sort of way I have of saying
things, regardless."
100 The principal, who was a sympathetic man, asked him whether he didn't
think that a way it would be well to get
rid of. Paul grinned and said he guessed
so. When he was told that he could go, he
105 bowed gracefully and went out. His bow
was but a repetition of the scandalous red
carnation.

1. The passage can best be summarized as

   A. a character study of a troubled student with peculiar habits and striking
   qualities.

   B. an escalation of tensions between a suspended student and his principal.

   C. an intense psychological portrait of a
   young man with a complicated past.

   D. an earnest attempt by a student to resolve
   conflict with his teachers.

2. As used in line 11, "dandy" most nearly
   means

   A. first-rate in his class.

   B. dressed with elegance and care.

   C. carefree in manner.

   D. brilliant in intellect.

3. According to the passage, Paul goes to the
   principal's office in order to

   A. explain to the teachers that he wants to
   return to school.

   B. discuss with the faculty why he has been
   misbehaving.

   C. justify his repeated tardiness and class
   interruptions to the principal.

   D. plead to the faculty of the school that he
   should not be expelled.

4. It can reasonably be inferred from the passage that Paul wears a red carnation in order
   to

   A. charm his English teacher with her favorite flower.

   B. mark the loss of a loved one whose death
   has affected him greatly.

   C. counter the faculty's view of his current
   situation.

   D. contrast with the ragged state of his
   clothes and accessories to indicate hidden
   wealth.

CONTINUE

Part VII

5. Which choice provides the best evidence for the answer to the previous question?

    A. Lines 3–6 ("He had been . . . about his son.")

    B. Lines 14–17 ("This latter . . . ban of suspension.")

    C. Lines 33–37 ("His teachers . . . not a usual case.")

    D. Lines 55–58 ("In one way . . . physical aversion.")

6. According to the author, Paul's English teacher

    A. has experience dealing with emotional students.

    B. takes Paul's dislike of being touched personally.

    C. is too impatient to allow Paul to write on his own.

    D. has to endure hearing Paul make comments on her lecture.

7. The author uses the phrase "his whole attitude was symbolized by his shrug" (lines 65–66) in order to suggest that Paul's teachers are

    A. frustrated and angry.

    B. saddened and confused.

    C. indifferent and cold.

    D. hopeful and tender.

8. The author describes Paul's physical traits and movements in great detail in order to

    A. describe how subtle signals reflect Paul's mood or disposition.

    B. compare his reactions to how others would react in similar circumstances.

    C. give details about his physical appearance and that of the teachers.

    D. provide details about his behavior and the way it is interpreted by others.

9. Which choice provides the best evidence for the answer to the previous question?

    A. Lines 69–70 ("He stood . . . white teeth.")

    B. Lines 70–74 ("His lips were . . . last degree.")

    C. Lines 74–81 ("Older boys . . . his hat.")

    D. Lines 85–88 ("This conscious . . . or 'smartness.'")

10. As used in line 93, "courteous" most nearly means

    A. courtly.

    B. mannerly.

    C. gallant.

    D. brave.

Practice Test 1

CONTINUE

Questions 11–20 are based on the following passage.

The following passage is excerpted from a biography of social reformer and activist Susan B. Anthony, who worked to ensure that women have the right to vote in the United States.

Susan B. Anthony preached militancy to women throughout the presidential campaign of 1872, urging them to claim their
Line rights under the Fourteenth and Fifteenth
5 Amendments by registering and voting in every state in the Union.

Even before Francis Minor had called her attention to the possibilities offered by these amendments, she had followed with
10 great interest a similar effort by English-women who, in 1867 and 1868, had attempted to prove that the "ancient legal rights of females" were still valid and entitled women property holders to vote for
15 representatives in Parliament, and who claimed that the word "man" in Parliamentary statutes should be interpreted to include women. In the case of the 5,346 householders of Manchester, the court held
20 that "every woman is personally incapable" in a legal sense. This legal contest had been fully reported in The Revolution, and disappointing as the verdict was, Susan looked upon this attempt to establish justice as an
25 indication of a great awakening and uprising among women.

There had also been heartening signs in her own country, which she hoped were the preparation for more successful militancy
30 to come. She had exulted in The Revolution in 1868 over the attempt of women to vote in Vineland, New Jersey. Encouraged by the enfranchisement of women in Wyoming in 1869, Mary Olney Brown and
35 Charlotte Olney French had cast their votes in Washington Territory. A young widow, Marilla Ricker, had registered and voted

in New Hampshire in 1870, claiming this right as a property holder, but her vote was
40 refused. In 1871, Nannette B. Gardner and Catherine Stebbins in Detroit, Catherine V. White in Illinois, Ellen R. Van Valkenburg in Santa Cruz, California, and Carrie S. Burnham in Philadelphia registered
45 and attempted to vote. Only Mrs. Gardner's vote was accepted. That same year, Sarah Andrews Spencer, Sarah E. Webster, and seventy other women marched to the polls to register and vote in the District of Co-
50 lumbia. Their ballots refused, they brought suit against the Board of Election Inspectors, carrying the case unsuccessfully to the Supreme Court of the United States. Another test case based on the Fourteenth
55 Amendment had also been carried to the Supreme Court by Myra Bradwell, one of the first women lawyers, who had been denied admission to the Illinois bar because she was a woman.

60 With the spotlight turned on the Fourteenth Amendment by these women, lawyers here and there throughout the country were discussing the legal points involved, many admitting that women had a good
65 case. Even the press was friendly.

Susan had looked forward to claiming her rights under the Fourteenth and Fifteenth Amendments and was ready to act. She had spent the thirty days required of
70 voters in Rochester with her family and as she glanced through the morning paper of November 1, 1872, she read these challenging words, "Now Register … If you were not permitted to vote you would fight for
75 the right, undergo all privations for it, face death for it…."

This was all the reminder she needed. She would fight for this right. She put on her bonnet and coat, telling her three

CONTINUE

80 sisters what she intended to do, asked them to join her, and with them walked briskly to the barber shop where the voters of her ward were registering. Boldly entering this stronghold of men, she

85 asked to be registered. The inspector in charge, Beverly W. Jones, tried to convince her that this was impossible under the laws of New York. She told him she claimed her right to vote not under the

90 New York constitution but under the Fourteenth Amendment, and she read him its pertinent lines. Other election inspectors now joined in the argument, but she persisted until two of them, Bev-

95 erly W. Jones and Edwin F. Marsh, both Republicans, finally consented to register the four women.

This mission accomplished, Susan rounded up twelve more women willing

100 to register. The evening papers spread the sensational news, and by the end of the registration period, fifty Rochester women had joined the ranks of the militants.

105 Election day did not bring the general uprising of women for which Susan had hoped. In Michigan, Missouri, Ohio, and Connecticut, as in Rochester, a few women tried to vote. In New York City,

110 Lillie Devereux Blake and in Fayetteville, New York, Matilda Joslyn Gage had courageously gone to the polls only to be turned away. Elizabeth Stanton did not vote on November 5, 1872, and her lack of

115 enthusiasm about a test case in the courts was very disappointing to Susan.

However, the fact that Susan B. Anthony had voted won immediate response from the press in all parts of the country.

120 Newspapers in general were friendly, the New York Times boldly declaring, "The act of Susan B. Anthony should have a place in history," and the Chicago Tribune venturing to suggest that she ought

125 to hold public office. The cartoonists, however, reveling in a new and tempting subject, caricatured her unmercifully, the New York Graphic setting the tone. Some Democratic papers condemned

130 her, following the line of the Rochester Union and Advertiser which flaunted the headline, "Female Lawlessness," and declared that Miss Anthony's lawlessness had proved women unfit for the ballot.

11. The primary purpose of the passage is to

A. describe the political victories that led to women receiving the right to vote.

B. convey the conflict plaguing the inner circles of women's suffrage.

C. critique the media response to Susan B. Anthony's goals and actions.

D. narrate part of the journey of a key historical figure in pursuing social reform.

12. It can reasonably be inferred from the passage that Susan B. Anthony would most likely promote which of the following methods to secure one's civil rights?

A. Conduct a violent revolution.

B. Complain to the press.

C. Vote for sympathetic politicians.

D. Invoke the US constitution.

13. According to the passage, when women were refused the right to vote in the District of Columbia, they

A. tried to vote anyway, but only the vote of Nannette B. Gardner was accepted.

B. sued the Board of Election Inspectors in a case heard by the US Supreme Court.

C. organized a march on Washington, D.C., to protest such unfair treatment.

D. traveled to Washington Territory to vote there instead.

CONTINUE ▶

14. Which choice provides the best evidence that Susan B. Anthony was not alone in her efforts to secure women the right to vote?

    A. Lines 32–36 ("Encouraged by . . . Washington Territory.")

    B. Lines 36–40 ("A young widow. . . vote was refused.")

    C. Lines 40–45 ("In 1871, Nannette. . . to vote.")

    D. Lines 50–53 ("Their ballots refused. . . the United States.")

15. In the third paragraph (lines 27–59), the author discusses Myra Bradwell in order to

    A. highlight the challenges women faced during Susan B. Anthony's time.

    B. emphasize how Myra Bradwell was not qualified for the Illinois bar.

    C. exaggerate the difficulties of being a woman during Susan B. Anthony's time.

    D. showcase the brightest women who lived during Susan B. Anthony's time.

16. The passage implies that social change is best enacted by

    A. the dedicated work of a single visionary.

    B. an effort to vote out the politicians currently in charge.

    C. a unified effort by many dedicated individuals.

    D. a lawsuit brought in front of the US Supreme Court.

17. Which choice provides the best evidence for the answer to the previous question?

    A. Lines 21–26 ("This legal contest. . . among women.")

    B. Lines 60–65 ("With the spotlight. . . a good case.")

    C. Lines 66–68 ("Susan had. . . ready to act.")

    D. Lines 78–83 ("She would fight. . . were registering.")

18. As used in line 92, "pertinent" most nearly means

    A. relevant.

    B. interesting.

    C. persistent.

    D. remorseful.

19. As used in line 131, "flaunted" most nearly means

    A. broadcast.

    B. printed.

    C. showcased.

    D. hid.

20. According to the passage, the news media reported on the registration of women voters in Rochester after

    A. fifty women had joined the ranks of the militants.

    B. Anthony expressed disappointment with Elizabeth Stanton.

    C. Amy Post sued the registrars who would not allow her to vote.

    D. Anthony had successfully gotten numerous women to register to vote.

Practice Test 1

CONTINUE

Questions 21–31 are based on the following passage.

The US Geological Survey (USGS) is a government agency whose goal is to provide reliable scientific information about the Earth, including minimizing loss from natural disasters. This excerpt is from the organization's website, addressing earthquakes, megaquakes, and movies. For the full passage, please visit http://earthquake.usgs.gov/learn.

Throughout the history of Hollywood, disaster films have been sure-fire winners for moviemakers. . . . With amazing special ef-
Line fects, it's easy to get caught up in the fantasy
5 disaster epic. What makes a great science fantasy film often bears no relation to real facts or the hazards people truly face. . .

Earthquakes are naturally occurring events outside the powers of humans to
10 create or stop. An earthquake is caused by a sudden slip on a fault, much like what happens when you snap your fingers. Before the snap, you push your fingers together and sideways. Because you are pushing them to-
15 gether, friction keeps them from slipping. When you apply enough stress to overcome this friction, your fingers move suddenly, releasing energy. The same "stick-slip" process goes on in the earth. Stresses in
20 the Earth's outer layer push the sides of the fault together. The friction across the surface of the fault holds the rocks together so they do not slip immediately when pushed sideways. Eventually enough stress builds
25 up and the rocks slip suddenly, releasing energy in waves that travel through the rock to cause the shaking that we feel during an earthquake.

Earthquakes typically originate several
30 to tens of miles below the surface of the Earth. It takes decades to centuries to build up enough stress to make a large earthquake, and the fault may be tens to hundreds of miles long. People cannot prevent

35 earthquakes from happening or stop them once they've started—giant nuclear explosions at shallow depths, like those in some movies, won't actually stop an earthquake.

It's well known that California, the
40 Pacific Northwest, and Alaska all have frequent earthquakes, some of which are quite damaging. Some areas of the country are more at risk than others, but, in fact, 42 of the 50 states could experience dam-
45 aging ground shaking from an earthquake in 50 years (which is the typical lifetime of a building), and 16 states have a relatively high likelihood of experiencing damaging ground shaking.

50 The two most important variables affecting earthquake damage are the intensity of ground shaking and the quality of the engineering of structures in the region. The level of shaking is controlled by
55 the proximity of the earthquake source to the affected region and the types of rocks that seismic waves pass through en route (particularly those at or near the ground surface). Generally, the bigger and closer
60 the earthquake, the stronger the shaking. But there have been large earthquakes with very little damage because they caused little shaking or because the buildings were built to withstand that shaking. In other cases,
65 moderate earthquakes have caused significant damage because the shaking was locally amplified, or because the structures were poorly engineered. . .

The idea of a "Mega-Quake"—an earth-
70 quake of magnitude 10 or larger—is very unlikely. Earthquake magnitude is based in part on the length of faults—the longer the fault, the larger the earthquake. The simple truth is that there are no known faults ca-
75 pable of generating a magnitude 10 or larger "mega-quake." The San Andreas fault is not long and deep enough to have a magnitude

CONTINUE ▶

9 or larger earthquake as depicted in the movie. The largest historical earthquake
80 on the northern San Andreas was the 1906 magnitude 7.9 earthquake. In 1857 the Fort Tejon earthquake occurred on the southern San Andreas fault; it is believed to have had a magnitude of about
85 7.9 as well. Computer models show that the San Andreas fault is capable of producing earthquakes up to about magnitude 8.3, but anything larger is extremely unlikely. Shaking from even the largest
90 possible San Andreas fault events will not be felt on the east coast.

Then there's this business of California falling off into the ocean. Not true! The ocean is not a great hole into which
95 California can fall, but is itself land at a somewhat lower elevation with water above it. It's impossible that California will be swept out to sea. Instead, southwestern California is moving slowly (2
100 inches per year) towards Alaska. 15 million years (and many earthquakes) from now, Los Angeles and San Francisco will be next-door neighbors.

Another popular cinematic and literary
105 device is a fault that opens during an earthquake to swallow up an inconvenient character. But the ground moves parallel to a fault during an earthquake, not away from it. If the fault could open, there
110 would be no friction. Without friction, there would be no earthquake. Shallow crevasses can form during earthquake-induced landslides, lateral spreads, or other types of ground failures. Faults, however,
115 do not gape open during an earthquake.

So when you see the next big disaster film, rest assured that movies are just entertainment. Enjoy them! And then go learn about the real-world science behind
120 disasters, and if you live in an area where hazards exist, take the suggested steps to protect you and your family.

21. The primary purpose of the passage is to
    A. counter the myths about earthquakes driven by fictional films.
    B. explain to people the causes and effects of earthquakes.
    C. show how Hollywood distorts science to develop engaging stories.
    D. give people advice about what to do if an earthquake strikes.

22. According to the passage, earthquakes are caused mainly by
    A. the existence of faults in the earth's crust.
    B. stresses in the earth's crust that cause a fault to slip.
    C. two faults in the earth's crust pressing against each other.
    D. the quality of the engineering of structures in the region.

23. As used in line 24, "stress" most nearly means
    A. anxiety.
    B. weight.
    C. pressure.
    D. emphasis.

24. In 1989, an earthquake caused extensive damage to San Francisco, California. Based only on information in the article, this most likely occurred because
    A. the earthquake source was very near the affected region and the buildings were poorly constructed.
    B. San Francisco has had earthquakes many times before, and they were all destructive.
    C. city officials never thought the city would experience an earthquake, so they were unprepared.
    D. the faults were deep and numerous across the country.

CONTINUE

25. Which choice provides the best evidence for the answer to the previous question?

   A. Lines 10–21 ("An earthquake is . . . the fault together.")

   B. Lines 29–34 ("Earthquakes typically . . . miles long.")

   C. Lines 50–54 ("The two most important . . . in the region.")

   D. Lines 107–110 ("But the ground . . . be no friction.")

26. In line 67, "amplified" most nearly means

   A. intensified.

   B. lifted.

   C. supplemented.

   D. made louder.

27. The author describes the earthquakes of 1857 and 1906 (lines 79–85) in order to

   A. provide examples of "mega-earthquakes."

   B. prove the depictions of earthquakes in major films as based on reality.

   C. support the assertion that the San Andreas fault is incapable of generating magnitude 10 earthquakes.

   D. demonstrate the inability of computer models to determine the size of earthquakes accurately.

28. The author of the passage counters the claim that part of California may fall off into the ocean in the future by

   A. stating that Californian government is working to prevent such a disaster.

   B. indicating that rising sea levels will counter seismic activity.

   C. building a comparison between California and Alaska.

   D. explaining how the floor of the ocean is sunken land covered by water.

29. Which choice provides the best evidence for the answer to the previous question?

   A. Lines 39–42 ("It's well known. . . quite damaging.")

   B. Lines 54–59 ("The level of shaking. . . ground surface.")

   C. Lines 94–97 ("The ocean . . . above it.")

   D. Lines 100–103 ("15 million years . . . neighbors.")

30. The author's use of the phrase "inconvenient character" (lines 106–107) affects the tone of the passage by

   A. revealing a negative attitude about unscientific data.

   B. illustrating a mocking tone toward how the storylines are written.

   C. emphasizing a scholarly attitude about science.

   D. communicating a warning about inaccurate scientific information.

31. How does the author refute the idea that an earthquake could cause the earth to open up and swallow people and things on the surface?

   A. The author points to the idea of how the earth opening up is portrayed in movies.

   B. The author notes that there are no known faults capable of producing a "mega-quake."

   C. The author explains that the ground moves parallel to a fault during an earthquake.

   D. The author suggests that subsequent landslides can cause crevasses to open.

Practice Test 1

CONTINUE

Questions 32–42 are based on the following passages.

After the Constitution was drafted, it had to be ratified by at least nine of the thirteen states. The following two passages illustrate the debate over ratification.

Passage 1 is from Patrick Henry's speech, made as governor of Virginia on June 5, 1778, at the state's convention to ratify the constitution. Passage 2 is from an essay written by James Madison, which first appeared in a New York newspaper on June 6, 1788, and later became part of what are now known as the Federalist Papers.

PASSAGE 1

If you make the citizens of this country agree to become the subjects of one great consolidated empire of America,
Line your government will not have suffi-
5 cient energy to keep them together. Such a government is incompatible with the genius of republicanism. There will be no checks, no real balances, in this government. What can avail your specious,
10 imaginary balances, your rope-dancing, chain-rattling ridiculous ideal checks and contrivances? But, sir, "we are not feared by foreigners; we do not make nations tremble." Would this constitute
15 happiness or secure liberty? I trust, sir, our political hemisphere will ever direct their operations to the security of those objects.

This Constitution is said to have
20 beautiful features; but when I come to examine these features, sir, they appear to me horribly frightful. Among other deformities, it has an awful squinting; it squints toward monarchy, and does
25 not this raise indignation in the breast of every true American? Your president may easily become king. Your Senate is so imperfectly constructed that your dearest rights may be sacrificed to what may be
30 a small minority; and a very small minority may continue for ever unchangeably this government, though horridly defective. Where are your checks in this government? Your strongholds will be in
35 the hands of your enemies. It is on a supposition that your American governors shall be honest that all the good qualities of this government are founded; but its defective and imperfect construction puts
40 it in their power to perpetrate the worst of mischiefs should they be bad men; and, sir, would not all the world, blame our distracted folly in resting our rights upon the contingency of our rulers be-
45 ing good or bad? Show me that age and country where the rights and liberties of the people were placed on the sole chance of their rulers being good men without a consequent loss of liberty! I say that the
50 loss of that dearest privilege has ever followed, with absolute certainty, every such mad attempt.

PASSAGE 2

In order to lay a due foundation for that separate and distinct exercise of the dif-
55 ferent powers of government, which to a certain extent is admitted on all hands to be essential to the preservation of liberty; it is evident that each department should have a will of its own; and con-
60 sequently should be so constituted that the members of each should have as little agency as possible in the appointment of the members of the others …. It is equally evident that the members of each de-
65 partment should be as little dependent as possible on those of the others for the emoluments annexed to their offices. Were the executive magistrate, or the judges, not independent of the legislature

CONTINUE ▶

in this particular, their independence in
every other would be merely nominal.
But the great security against a gradual
concentration of the several powers in the
same department, consists in giving to
75 those who administer each department
the necessary constitutional means and
personal motives to resist encroachments
of the others. The provision for defense
must in this, as in all other cases, be made
80 commensurate to the danger of attack.
Ambition must be made to counteract
ambition. The interest of the man must
be connected with the constitutional
rights of the place. It may be a reflec-
85 tion on human nature, that such devices
should be necessary to control the abuses
of government. But what is government
itself, but the greatest of all reflections on
human nature? If men were angels, no
90 government would be necessary. If angels
were to govern men, neither external nor
internal controls on government would
be necessary. In framing a government
which is to be administered by men over
95 men, the great difficulty lies in this: you
must first enable the government to control the governed; and in the next place
oblige it to control itself. A dependence
on the people is, no doubt, the primary
100 control on the government; but experience has taught mankind the necessity
of auxiliary precautions.

32. In lines 12–14, Henry suggests that he
believes the framers of the Constitution felt
a need to

A. display their power to Americans.

B. intimidate other countries.

C. secure happiness and liberty.

D. build strong international relationships.

33. Based on the information in this passage,
what kind of government does Henry think
is best?

A. Republic

B. Monarchy

C. Autocracy

D. Empire

34. Which choice provides the best evidence for
the answer to the previous question?

A. Lines 1–5 ("If you make . . .them
together.")

B. Lines 5–7 ("Such a government . . .
republicanism.")

C. Lines 22–26 ("Among other. . . true
American?")

D. Lines 26–27 ("Your president. . . king.")

35. Which represents the best summary of
Patrick Henry's objection to the drafted
Constitution?

A. It overemphasizes the need for checks and
balances.

B. It leaves too much power in the hands of
the people.

C. It does not centralize power enough.

D. It makes government dependent on
people who are flawed.

36. As used in line 41, "mischiefs" most nearly
means

A. pranks.

B. crimes.

C. decisions.

D. wrongdoings.

Practice Test 1

CONTINUE

37. What was Madison's strongest counterargument to those who were concerned about a strong central government?

    A. Government must reflect human nature.

    B. People are drastically flawed and can never be trusted.

    C. People would have no influence over their government.

    D. As long as the powers are separated, power will not be concentrated.

38. Which choice provides the best evidence for the answer to the previous question?

    A. Lines 72–78 ("But the great . . . of the others.")

    B. Lines 87–89 ("But what is . . . nature?")

    C. Lines 89–90 ("If men were . . . would be necessary.")

    D. Lines 98–102 ("A dependence on . . . auxiliary precautions.")

39. As it is used in line 74, "department" most nearly means

    A. executive.

    B. territory.

    C. level.

    D. branch.

40. The primary purpose of each passage is to

    A. define the roles of government for officials and citizens to align with republicanism.

    B. discuss the process by which laws are created and enforced at a national level.

    C. offer the considerations due to a system of government attempting to create a bulwark against tyranny.

    D. critique the existing constitution as affording too great of power to individual states.

41. What do these two statements show about how their authors viewed human nature?

    Henry, lines 45–49: "Show me that age and country where the rights and liberties of the people were placed on the sole chance of their rulers being good men without a consequent loss of liberty!"

    Madison, lines 90–93: "If angels were to govern men, neither external nor internal controls on government would be necessary."

    A. Henry and Madison both believed that people are too flawed to be trusted with complete control.

    B. Henry and Madison both believed rulers do not care about the rights and liberties of the people they govern.

    C. Henry didn't trust ordinary people to be rulers, and Madison believed all people could be trusted to wield complete control.

    D. Henry believed that government is unnecessary for a free people, and Madison believed that government needs to be regulated.

42. Which of the following best represents the differences in point of view of the authors of the two passages?

    A. Henry was concerned about the balance of power, and Madison was concerned about concentration of wealth.

    B. Henry worried about too much power in the hands of the government, and Madison worried about too much power in any one branch of government.

    C. Henry was focused on states' rights, and Madison was focused on adding the Bill of Rights to the Constitution.

    D. Henry was afraid of a return to monarchy, and Madison was afraid of government corruption.

CONTINUE ▶

Part VII

Questions 43–52 are based on the following passage.

This article is excerpted from the National Oceanic and Atmospheric Administration Fisheries website (NOAA). The public agency provides science news and scientific findings related to the Earth and the Earth's atmosphere. This article describes the identification of a tiny, rare shark. For the full passage, please visit www.nmfs. noaa.gov/stories.

A very small and rare species of shark is swimming its way through scientific literature. But don't worry, the chances of this
Line inches-long vertebrate biting through your
5 swimsuit is extremely slim, because if you
ever spotted one, you'd be only the third
person to ever do so.

This species' common name is the
"pocket shark," though those in the field of
10 classifying animals refer to it by its scientific name *Mollisquama* sp., according to a
new study published in the international
journal of taxonomy *Zootaxa*. While it is
small enough to, yes, fit in your pocket, it's
15 dubbed "pocket" because of the distinctive
orifice above the pectoral fin—one of many
physiological features scientists hope to better understand.

"The pocket shark we found was only
20 5 and a half inches long, and was a recently
born male," said Mark Grace of NOAA
Fisheries' Pascagoula, Miss., Laboratory,
lead author of the new study, who noted
the shark displayed an unhealed umbili-
25 cal scar. "Discovering him has us thinking
about where mom and dad may be, and how
they got to the Gulf. The only other known
specimen was found very far away, off Peru,
36 years ago."
30 Interestingly, the specimen Grace discovered wasn't found in the ocean, per se,
but rather in the holdings of NOAA's lab in
Pascagoula. It was collected in the deep sea
about 190 miles offshore Louisiana during

35 a 2010 mission by the NOAA Ship *Pisces* to
study sperm whale feeding. Grace, who was
part of that mission after the rare shark was
collected and upon uncovering the sample
at the lab years later, recruited Tulane Uni-
40 versity researchers Michael Doosey and
Henry Bart, and NOAA Ocean Service
genetics expert Gavin Naylor, to give the
specimen an up-close examination.

A tissue sample was collected, and by
45 tapping into the robust specimen collection
of Tulane University's Biodiversity Research
Institute, scientists were able to place the
specimen into the genus *Mollisquama*. Further genetic analysis from Naylor indicates
50 that pocket sharks are closely related to the
kitefin and cookie cutter species, fellow
members of the shark family *Dalatiidae*.
Like other *Dalatiidae* shark species it is possible that pocket sharks when hungry may
55 remove an oval *plug* of flesh from their prey
(various marine mammals, large fishes, and
squid).

The specimen is part of the Royal D.
Suttkus Fish Collection at Tulane Univer-
60 sity's Biodiversity Research Institute in
Belle Chasse, La., and it is hoped that further study of the specimen will lead to many
new discoveries. Already, the specimen—
when compared to the 1979 specimen
65 taxonomic description—is found to have
a series of glands along the abdomen not
previously noted. Partners at the Smithson-
ian National Museum of Natural History in
Washington, D.C., and American Natural
70 History Museum in New York City have
also contributed to the study of this shark.

"This record of such an unusual and
extremely rare fish is exciting, but it's also
an important reminder that we still have
75 much to learn about the species that inhabit
our oceans," Grace added.

CONTINUE

43. What does the passage illustrate about how scientific information is gathered?

    A. Multiple scientific institutions are needed to form any strong scientific conclusion.

    B. Luck plays an essential role whenever scientists work to gather information.

    C. All scientific research is recorded in journals.

    D. Scientists in different locations often share their findings.

44. Which statement best describes a reason for why two specimens of a shark species would be found in two distant locations such as off the coast of Peru and the Gulf of Mexico?

    A. Two separate species adapted in similar ways to similar environments.

    B. The shark species is commonly found throughout the Pacific and the Atlantic Ocean.

    C. The shark species travels from one location to another.

    D. The earlier sample was mislabeled by Tulane's Biodiversity Research Institute.

45. Which choice provides the best evidence for the answer to the previous question?

    A. Lines 8–11 ("This species'. . . name Mollisquama")

    B. Lines 19–21 ("The pocket . . . born male")

    C. Lines 25–29 ("Discovering . . . ago.")

    D. Lines 33–36 ("It was collected. . .whale feeding.")

46. According to the passage, the pocket shark got its name because of

    A. its small size.

    B. the orifice near its fin.

    C. the way it can be carried in a pocket.

    D. its pocket-like markings near its dorsal fin.

47. According to the passage, the information that was most important in determining the species of the shark was

    A. the length of the shark.

    B. the "pocket" feature that made it unique.

    C. tissue samples to provide genetic information.

    D. its position in the food chain.

48. Based on the passage, scientists determined the age of the pocket fish they found by

    A. observing the number of lines on the fins.

    B. comparing its size to other pocket fish.

    C. comparing its size to other fish found in the Gulf of Mexico.

    D. finding a scar on its body.

49. As used in line 38, "sample" most nearly means

    A. specimen.

    B. population.

    C. example.

    D. bite.

CONTINUE ▶

50. Based on its use in line 45, "robust" most nearly means

   A. typical.

   B. healthy.

   C. varied.

   D. distinguished.

51. According to the passage, scientists were so excited about finding a pocket shark because the sharks are

   A. evidence of a new family of sharks.

   B. the only known species that has pockets.

   C. proof that a single breed can live in vastly different waters.

   D. so unique and so few of them have been found.

52. Which choice provides the best evidence for the answer to the previous question?

   A. Lines 3–7 ("But don't worry . . . ever do so.")

   B. Lines 36–43 ("Grace . . . examination.")

   C. Lines 48–52 ("Further genetic . . . *Dalatiidae*.")

   D. Lines 72–76 ("'This record . . . added.'")

STOP
If you finish before time is called, you may check your work on this section only.
Do not turn to any other section.

Practice Test 1

Section 2: Writing and Language Test

35 Minutes—44 Questions

TURN TO SECTION 2 OF YOUR ANSWER SHEET TO ANSWER THE QUESTIONS IN THIS SECTION.

DIRECTIONS: Each passage below is accompanied by a number of multiple-choice questions. For some questions, you will need to consider how the passage might be revised to improve the expression of ideas. Other questions will ask you to consider how the passage might be edited to correct errors in sentence structure, usage, or punctuation. A passage may be accompanied by one or more graphics—such as a chart, table, or graph—that you will need to refer to in order to best answer the question(s).

Some questions will direct you to an underlined portion of a passage—it could be one word, a portion of a sentence, or the full sentence itself. Other questions will direct you to a particular paragraph or to certain sentences within a paragraph, or you'll be asked to think about the passage as a whole. Each question number refers to the corresponding number in the passage.

After reading each passage, select the answer to each question that most effectively improves the quality of writing in the passage or that makes the passage follow the conventions of Standard Written English. Many questions include a "NO CHANGE" option. Select that option if you think the best choice is to leave that specific portion of the passage as it is.

Questions 1–11 are based on the following passage.

ELIZABETH BLACKWELL, THE DOCTOR

On January 23, 1849, in the town of Geneva, New York, Elizabeth Blackwell stepped onto the altar of the Presbyterian church and received her medical degree from the president of Geneva Medical College. This took her place in history. Blackwell had denounced the expectations of most of her teachers and classmates to become the country's first female doctor.

1

A. NO CHANGE

B. Receiving her medical degree led to giving her a place in history.

C. She took her place in history.

D. In doing so, she took her place in history.

2

A. NO CHANGE

B. defied

C. incited

D. met

CONTINUE ➡

As a young woman, Blackwell had worked as a school teacher, but she found herself unsatisfied. Once she realized that her dream was to be a doctor, she faced tremendous obstacles. There had never before been a female physician in America. At the time, educating a boy was considered far more important than a girl. Blackwell's education did not prepare her for the challenges of medical school, and she had to work hard just to catch up. ④ To make up for the gaps in her education, the household of a physician became her home for the next several years. There, she had access to educational resources and received some medical training.

⑤ As she prepared to apply to medical school, Blackwell sought advice from physicians in New York and Philadelphia. She found that they ⑥ doubted she would be admitted to medical school; at least one advisor went so far as to suggest that she might disguise herself as a man in order to gain admittance. ⑦ Their advisors were not far from wrong in their prediction. Blackwell applied to well over a dozen medical colleges, but she received admission to only one—Geneva Medical College.

A. NO CHANGE

B. far more important than it was to a girl.

C. far more important than educating a girl.

D. far more important than opportunities for girls.

④

A. NO CHANGE

B. A physician's household, to make up for the gaps in her education, became her home for the next several years.

C. Her home for the next several years, to make up for the gaps in her education, became a physician's household.

D. To make up for the gaps in her education, she arranged to live in the household of a physician for the next several years.

⑤ Which choice provides the most logical introduction to the sentence?

A. NO CHANGE

B. After finishing medical school,

C. While attending university,

D. Before she applied to be a psychologist,

⑥

A. NO CHANGE

B. debated

C. insisted

D. supposed

⑦

A. NO CHANGE

B. Her

C. His

D. Your

Practice Test 1

 CONTINUE

Gaining admission to the college **8** <u>has become</u> the first in a long line of obstacles for Blackwell. She discovered that her fellow **9** <u>students all of whom were men had</u> elected as a joke to admit her to the medical program and were astonished when she actually showed up at the college to enroll for classes. The students were embarrassed by her presence in lectures on topics—such as human anatomy—that they considered unsuitable for mixed company.

Steadily, and with perseverance, Blackwell gained acceptance among the students and faculty. After she completed her degree, she continued **10** <u>to face prejudice and biases, which were real obstacles and challenges against her because she was a woman, and outright barriers to her career.</u> She was unable to establish the private practice she had hoped for. Nevertheless, Blackwell was successful, **11** <u>but when she went to study at a hospital in Paris, she was assigned the same duties as young girls with no education at all.</u>

8

A. NO CHANGE

B. becomes

C. became

D. will become

9

A. NO CHANGE

B. students: all of whom were men had

C. students; all of whom were men, had

D. students, all of whom were men, had

10

A. NO CHANGE

B. to face outright barriers to her career due to prejudice and biases.

C. to face a variety of significant barriers to her and her career.

D. to face barriers that obstructed her career and included bias because she was a woman.

11 Which choice most effectively maintains support for claims or points in the text?

A. NO CHANGE

B. but she is remembered for having been the first woman in America to receive a medical degree.

C. and she had a distinguished career as a promoter of preventative medicine and as a champion of medical opportunities for women.

D. but she lived an interesting life and had many opportunities to travel widely and meet new people.

CONTINUE ➡

Questions 12–22 are based on the following passage and supplementary material.

RACHEL CARSON, PROTECTOR OF THE ENVIRONMENT

Today, we can hardly imagine a world without websites, blogs, and articles that express concern for the environment. **12** Carson, a former marine biologist for the Fish and Game Service, **13** ruffled the feathers of a ton of people who had a vested interest in maintaining the status quo where the environment was concerned. Her credibility as a scientist and her personal courage enabled Carson to withstand the criticism heaped on her during her lifetime.

12 At this point, the writer is considering adding the following sentence:

But in 1962, when Rachel Carson's *Silent Spring* was published, this was not the case.

Should the writer do this?

A. Yes, because it provides the reader with a date and historical context.

B. Yes, because it informs the reader of how old Carson was when she got published.

C. No, because it inserts irrelevant information about an unimportant book.

D. No, because it divides the paragraph's focus between the book and Carson.

13

A. NO CHANGE

B. aggravated a lot of people

C. inflamed the tempers of those

D. provoked many

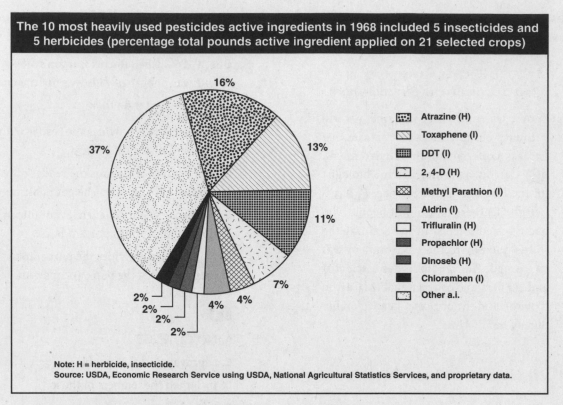

The 10 most heavily used pesticides active ingredients in 1968 included 5 insecticides and 5 herbicides (percentage total pounds active ingredient applied on 21 selected crops)

Legend:
- Atrazine (H)
- Toxaphene (I)
- DDT (I)
- 2, 4-D (H)
- Methyl Parathion (I)
- Aldrin (I)
- Trifluralin (H)
- Propachlor (H)
- Dinoseb (H)
- Chloramben (I)
- Other a.i.

Note: H = herbicide, insecticide.
Source: USDA, Economic Research Service using USDA, National Agricultural Statistics Services, and proprietary data.

And what exactly was it that Rachel Carson did that was so **14** disturbing. She pointed out the dangers of **15** pesticides—DDT in particular—to the environment. DDT was designed to contain insect pests in gardens and on farmland after World War II. Most people considered it a "wonder chemical," **16** and by 1968, they used DDT to cover approximately 11% of all farmland.

14

A. NO CHANGE

B. disturbing?

C. disturbing;

D. disturbing:

15

A. NO CHANGE

B. pesticides; DDT in particular, to

C. pesticides DDT in particular, to

D. pesticides: DDT in particular to

16 Which choice completes the sentence with accurate data based on the chart?

A. NO CHANGE

B. and in fact, by 1968, DDT accounted for 11% of all pesticides used.

C. as it was believed to contain approximately 11% of all garden pests.

D. though only about 11% of all farmers and gardeners actually used it.

CONTINUE

Rachel Carson believed, however, that the pesticides were **17** dehydrating the soil and the rivers, and adhering to tree leaves and branches that were the home for birds and beneficial insects. She contended that the levels of chemical pesticides in plants, animals, and humans had already reached alarming levels. In her view, **18** he was so potent that they were able to penetrate systems and remain there for years, **19** giving way to possible improvements in general health and well-being.

The furor caused by Carson's writing was mostly felt by the chemical companies that produced pesticides. Not willing to **20** contradict the potential hazards of their products, they resisted by seeking to discredit Carson. And despite her credentials, Carson was discredited for a period of time. However, in 1970, with the establishment of the Environmental Protection Agency, the nation became more concerned with issues that Carson had raised.

Since 2001, DDT has been banned for agricultural use worldwide except in small quantities and only as part of a plan to transition to safer alternatives. The only places in which DDT is still allowed are those countries in which it is being used to combat malaria. **21** Since malaria kills more than 800,000 people every year, most of them children in Sub-Saharan Africa, Carson has been blamed for "millions of deaths," despite the studies that show that the pesticide can contribute to cancers, male infertility, miscarriages, developmental delay in children, and damage to the liver and nervous system.

17

A. NO CHANGE

B. appropriating

C. transcending

D. permeating

18

A. NO CHANGE

B. it was

C. the pesticides were

D. everything was

19 Which choice best completes the sentence and remains consistent with Carson's argument about pesticides?

A. NO CHANGE

B. providing a definitive link between cancer and pesticides.

C. leading to an alarming decrease in local bird populations.

D. potentially leading to a breakdown in tissue and immune systems.

20

A. NO CHANGE

B. acknowledge

C. propagate

D. solicit

21

A. NO CHANGE

B. Even though

C. In addition,

D. Despite the fact

Practice Test 1

CONTINUE

615

Were it not for those like Rachel Carson, **22** DDT would probably still be seen as "wonder chemicals," and the only way to combat malaria. Though still controversial, she was a scientist of vision and determination who changed the course of history and brought environmental issues to the world's attention.

22

A. NO CHANGE

B. pesticides with DDT would probably still be seen as a "wonder chemical,"

C. DDT would probably still be seen as a "wonder chemical,"

D. DDT would probably still be seen as chemicals that are wondrous,

Questions 23–33 are based on the following passage.

A Mayan Worldview

The ancient Mayans inhabited the area that now consists of **23** Mexico; Guatemala, Belize, Honduras; and El Salvador. Their rich civilization flourished from the third through the ninth centuries. **24** Among the many notable achievements of this society were the Mayan understanding of astronomy, which was manifest not only in Mayan science but in every aspect of the culture.

23

A. NO CHANGE

B. Mexico, Guatemala, Belize, Honduras, and El Salvador.

C. Mexico, Guatemala, Belize, Honduras; El Salvador.

D. Mexico Guatemala Belize Honduras El Salvador.

24

A. NO CHANGE

B. Among the many notable achievements of this society are the Mayan understanding of astronomy,

C. Among the many notable achievements of this society will be the Mayan understanding of astronomy,

D. Among the many notable achievements of this society was the Mayan understanding of astronomy,

CONTINUE

Ancient Mayans kept meticulous records of **25** the setting Sun, the moving Moon, and the rotation of the planets that were visible to the naked eye. Based on the solar year, they created a calendar which they used to keep track of time. So **26** astute were the Mayans' observations that they could predict such events as solar and lunar eclipses, and **27** the movement of the planets.

For the ancient Mayans, astronomy was not just a science; it was a combination of science, religion, and philosophy that found **28** it's way into many aspects of their lives, including architecture. Mayan ceremonial buildings, for example, were exactly aligned with compass points, so that at the fall and spring equinoxes, light would flood the interior of the building. These buildings were designed and built as acts of worship to the **29** Mayan gods. Science, architecture, and religion, then, were all intricately and beautifully blended.

25

A. NO CHANGE

B. the setting Sun, the moving Moon, and the rotating planets

C. the set Sun, the moving Moon, and the rotated planets

D. the setting Sun, the way the moon moved, and the rotation of the planets

26

A. NO CHANGE

B. inept

C. expected

D. complicated

27 Which choice gives a supporting example that is most similar to the example already in the sentence?

A. NO CHANGE

B. the migration of birds.

C. the direction of the winds.

D. the flow of the tides.

28

A. NO CHANGE

B. its'

C. its

D. their

29 Which choice most effectively combines the two sentences at the underlined portion?

A. Mayan gods: science

B. Mayan gods; science

C. Mayan gods, science

D. Mayan gods, but science

CONTINUE

Government, too, was **30** inextrica-bly linked with astronomy. The beginning and ending of the reigns of Mayan leaders appear to have been timed to coincide with astronomical events. Ancient Mayan artwork, carvings and murals show royalty wearing **31** symbols: relating to the sun, Moon, and sky. The Mayans believed that the sun and the moon were guided across the sky by benevolent gods, and that these gods needed human help to thwart the evil gods who wanted to stop them. Human intervention took the form of different rituals, including sacrifice. It was considered an honor to die for this cause, and those who were sacrificed were believed to have gained eternal life.

The planet Venus, which can often be seen by the unaided eye, played a large role in Mayan life. The Mayans used the appearance of Venus in the sky as a means of timing when they attacked enemies. The night sky, among its other duties, could then serve as a **32** harvest calendar.

33 In short, the ancient Mayans, in looking to the night sky for guidance, discovered a natural order around which they were able to base a rich and textured civilization.

30

A. NO CHANGE

B. bafflingly

C. greedily

D. embarrassingly

31

A. NO CHANGE

B. symbols, relating to the sun, Moon, and sky.

C. symbols relating to the sun, Moon, and sky.

D. symbols; relating to the sun, Moon, and sky.

32 Which choice provides information that best supports the focus of this paragraph?

A. NO CHANGE

B. reminder of the season

C. reference point for direction

D. call to war

33

A. NO CHANGE

B. However,

C. Moreover,

D. Incidentally,

CONTINUE ➡

Questions 34–44 are based on the following passage.

THE REAL WORLD

Our college employment counseling center recommended that students have mock interviews before setting out into the world for the real thing. For reasons that I still don't understand, I **34** be-lieved that this applied to other people but not to me. Midway **35** thorough my senior year of college, I sent out resumes to several law firms in the area. I didn't consult with anybody about how to begin seeking a job. My plan was to work at a law firm for a couple of years before attending law school. I received a couple of responses and was thrilled to set up **36** mine first interview at a prestigious law firm that had offices all over the world. **37** It was exactly the type of environment in which I envisioned myself.

34

A. NO CHANGE

B. know

C. denied

D. believe

35

A. NO CHANGE

B. threw

C. though

D. through

36

A. NO CHANGE

B. our

C. my

D. their

37 Which of the following sentences, if added, would most effectively conclude this paragraph?

A. NO CHANGE

B. I couldn't imagine enjoying working in this environment.

C. I really wish college never ended!

D. I needed more time to weigh my career options.

CONTINUE

The position for which I was interviewing was a clerical job that, the interviewer made clear from the outset, would require long hours, late nights, and a great deal of filing and photocopying. I confidently announced to the interviewer that I didn't mind long hours and thankless assignments. **38** <u>And then happily informed him that I wanted to work my way up and someday be his boss.</u> I figured the surprised look on his face was because he wasn't used to seeing young men as ambitious and **39** <u>enigmatic</u> as I was. I would have kept going, had he not suggested moving on to another topic.

[1] I'm sorry to say that here I left nothing to the imagination. [2] I believed that my interviewer would value my stark honesty when I told him that my greatest **40** <u>weakness's</u> included not getting along with other people very well and a tendency to make more enemies than friends. **41** [3] <u>In the next phase of the interview, I was asked to list my strengths and weaknesses.</u> [4] The interviewer raised his eyebrows but said nothing, and I was certain that he knew he'd found his candidate. [5] After all, **42** <u>I could've cared less</u> about getting along with other people and I figured I wouldn't need to get along with people to photocopy and file, so I'd hit upon the perfect answer to a tricky question.

38

A. NO CHANGE

B. After happily informing him that I wanted to work my way up and someday be his boss.

C. Which is why I happily informed him that I wanted to work my way up and someday be his boss.

D. Then I happily informed him that I wanted to work my way up and someday be his boss.

39

A. NO CHANGE

B. articulate

C. conspicuous

D. incoherent

40

A. NO CHANGE

B. weaknesses'

C. weaknesses

D. weakness'

41 For the sake of cohesion, sentence 3 of this paragraph should be placed

A. where it is now.

B. before sentence 1.

C. before sentence 5.

D. at the beginning of the next paragraph.

42

A. NO CHANGE

B. I could have cared less

C. I could of cared less

D. I couldn't have cared less

CONTINUE

43 I did not get offered that job, nor the next several for which I interviewed at other firms. Eventually I paid a **44** deferred trip to the college job counseling office and got a few pointers on my technique. I am happy to say that while I never did end up going to law school, I have become a high school guidance counselor who specializes in helping students find internships in community businesses.

43 Which of the following would make the most effective opening sentence for this paragraph?

A. After the interview, I waited anxiously to hear back from the employer.

B. I never heard back from the employer about the job.

C. I met my friends for brunch over the following weekend.

D. I got married four years later, after dating for several years.

44

A. NO CHANGE

B. belated

C. hastened

D. disparaged

STOP
If you finish before time is called, you may check your work on this section only.
Do not turn to any other section.

SECTION 3: Math Test—NO CALCULATOR

25 Minutes—20 Questions

TURN TO SECTION 3 OF YOUR ANSWER SHEET TO ANSWER THE QUESTIONS IN THIS SECTION.

DIRECTIONS: For **Questions 1–15**, solve each problem, select the best answer from the choices provided, and fill in the corresponding circle on your answer sheet. For **Questions 16–20**, solve the problem and enter your answer in the grid on the answer sheet. The directions **before Question 16** will provide information on how to enter your answers in the grid.

ADDITIONAL INFORMATION:

1. The use of a calculator in this section **is not permitted**.

2. All variables and expressions used represent real numbers unless otherwise indicated.

3. Figures provided in this test are drawn to scale unless otherwise indicated.

4. All figures lie in a plane unless otherwise indicated.

5. Unless otherwise specified, the domain of a given function f is the set of all real numbers x for which $f(x)$ is a real number.

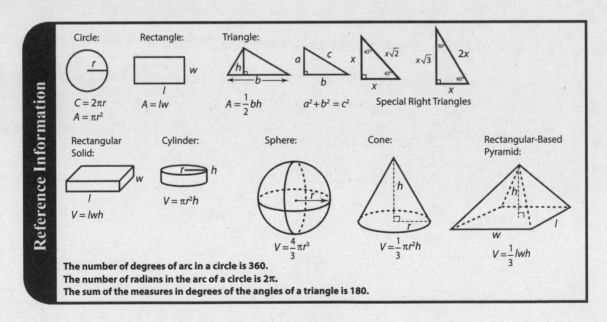

The number of degrees of arc in a circle is 360.
The number of radians in the arc of a circle is 2π.
The sum of the measures in degrees of the angles of a triangle is 180.

CONTINUE

1. Jared is beginning to track the number of steps he walks each day. Yesterday he walked 950 steps. He set a goal of increasing his steps per day by 125, with an eventual goal of walking at least 3,000 steps per day. Which of the following functions can be used to determine the number of steps Jared plans to take d days from yesterday?

    A. $f(d) = 3,000 - (950 + 125d)$

    B. $f(d) = 3,000 - 125d$

    C. $f(d) = 950 + 125d$

    D. $f(d) = 950 - 125d$

2. If $f(1) = 3, f(3) = -1, g(3) = 1$, and $g(-1) = 3$, what is the value of $f(g(3))$?

    A. -3

    B. -1

    C. 1

    D. 3

3. The amount of radioactive iodine 131 that remains in an object after d days is found using the formula $y = a(0.5)^{\frac{d}{8.02}}$. What does a represent in the formula?

    A. The number of days it takes for the object to lose half of its radioactive iodine 131

    B. The initial amount of radioactive iodine 131

    C. The amount of radioactive iodine 131 after d days

    D. The amount of radioactive iodine 131 lost each day

4. An architect is designing the roof of a house that is to be symmetric, with two equal sides meeting exactly in the middle. The house is 30 feet wide. The peak of the roof is 8 feet above the house. If the outside of the roof is separated into two parts, how long is each part from the peak of the roof to its edge?

    A. 15 ft.

    B. 17 ft.

    C. 23 ft.

    D. 31 ft.

CONTINUE

NO CALCULATOR

5. $y = 2(x - 5)^2 - 2$

Which equation, where the *x*-intercepts appear as constants, is equivalent to the equation above?

A. $y = 2x^2 - 20x + 48$

B. $y = 2(x^2 - 10x + 24)$

C. $y = 2(x - 4)(x - 6)$

D. $y = (2x - 8)(x - 6)$

6. Which of the following graphs represents the equation $3x + y = 4$?

A.

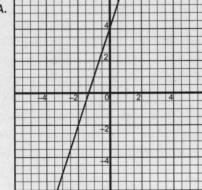

B.

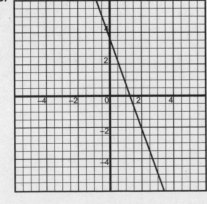

C.

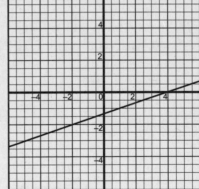

D.

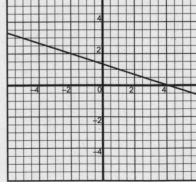

CONTINUE

Practice Test 1

NO CALCULATOR 🖩

7. Which of the following is an equation for the line through the point (2, 3) with a slope of –1?

   A. $2x + 3y = -1$

   B. $3x + 3y = 15$

   C. $3x + 2y = 10$

   D. $x + y = -5$

8.
$$3x = 6y$$
$$2x^2 - y^2 = 14$$

   If (x, y) is a solution to the system of equations above, then y^2 equals which value?

   A. $\dfrac{x^2}{2}$

   B. $\dfrac{14}{3}$

   C. 2

   D. $\sqrt{2}$

9. Which of the following is equivalent to

$$\frac{\sqrt[3]{\sqrt{z}}}{\sqrt[3]{z} \cdot \sqrt{z}}?$$

   A. z

   B. z^{-1}

   C. $z^{-\frac{2}{3}}$

   D. $z^{\frac{1}{5}}$

10. Which of the following is the equation for the graph of a parabola that has a vertex at (3, –5) and a y-intercept at 13?

   A. $y - 28 = (x - 3)(x + 5)$

   B. $y = 2(x - 3)^2 - 5$

   C. $y = (x - 3)^2 - 13$

   D. $y = x^2 - 6x + 13$

Practice Test 1

CONTINUE ➤

NO CALCULATOR

11. The admission cost for a play is $12 for adults and $7 for children. Which system of equations can be used to determine the number of adults and number of children that attended if 117 people attended the play and the total amount collected for admission was $1,079?

   A. $12x + 7y = 117$
   $x + y = 1,079$

   B. $12x + y = 117$
   $x + 7y = 1,079$

   C. $12x + 7y = 1,079$
   $x + y = 117$

   D. $x + 7y = 117$
   $12x + y = 1,079$

12. Which of the following is equivalent to $\dfrac{4 - i}{3 + i}$ that can be found by multiplying by the complex conjugate of the denominator?

   A. $\dfrac{1}{3}$

   B. $\dfrac{17}{11 + 7i}$

   C. $\dfrac{11 - 7i}{10}$

   D. $\dfrac{13 + i}{8}$

13. What is the solution to the equation $-6(t + 1) = 2(1 - 3t) - 8$?

   A. -8

   B. -6

   C. No solution

   D. Infinitely many solutions

14. A small city in Spain grows at an average rate of 1.7% a year. The population of the city in 1980 was 2,845. The equation that models the city's population in 1990 is $P = 2,845e^{(0.017)(10)}$. What does 10 represent in the equation?

   A. The city's population in 1980

   B. The number of years

   C. The city's average growth rate

   D. The factor of increase of the city's population each year

CONTINUE ▶

Practice Test 1

15. If the expression $\dfrac{9x^2}{3x-2}$ is rewritten as an equivalent expression of the form $\dfrac{4}{3x-2} + A$, then A equals:

A. $3x^2$

B. $\dfrac{5x^2}{3x-2}$

C. $(3x-2)^2$

D. $(3x+2)$

CONTINUE ➡

⊞ NO CALCULATOR

DIRECTIONS: For **Questions 16–20**, solve the problem and enter your answer in the grid, as described below, on the answer sheet.

1. Although not required, it is suggested that you write your answer in the boxes at the top of the columns to help you fill in the circles accurately. You will receive credit only if the circles are filled in correctly.

2. Mark no more than one circle in any column.

3. No question has a negative answer.

4. Some problems may have more than one correct answer. In such cases, enter only one answer.

5. **Mixed numbers** such as $3\frac{1}{2}$ must be entered as 3.5 or $\frac{7}{2}$.

   If $3\frac{1}{2}$ is entered into the grid as $\boxed{3 \mid 1 \mid / \mid 2}$, it will be interpreted as $\frac{31}{2}$, not $3\frac{1}{2}$.

6. **Decimal answers:** If you obtain a decimal answer with more digits than the grid can accommodate, it may be either rounded or truncated, but it must fill the entire grid.

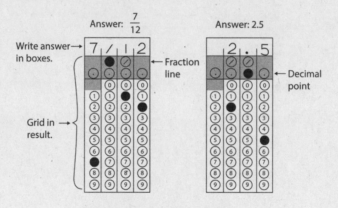

Answer: $\frac{7}{12}$ Answer: 2.5

Write answer → in boxes.

← Fraction line

← Decimal point

Grid in → result.

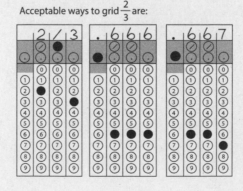

Answer: 201
Either position is correct.

Acceptable ways to grid $\frac{2}{3}$ are:

Part VII

CONTINUE ▶

NO CALCULATOR 📵

16. If $\sqrt{x+1} - 2 = 3$, what is the value of x?

17. Let b be a real number. For what value of b does the function $f(x) = x^2 - 2bx + (b^2 + 2b - 1)$ have one and only one x-intercept?

18. $\dfrac{3x^2 - 4x - 18}{x+3} = 3x - c + \dfrac{21}{x+3}$

   What is the value for c that will make the equation above true?

19. $$y = 3x + 7$$
$$4x - ty = 5$$

   According to the system of equations above, what is the value of t that makes the system of equations have no solutions?

20. A spherical scoop of ice cream is placed on top of a hollow ice cream cone. The scoop and cone have the same radius. The ice cream melts completely and it fills the cone to the top. How many times greater is the height of the cone than the radius of the cone?

Practice Test 1

STOP
If you finish before time is called, you may check your work on this section only.
Do not turn to any other section.

SECTION 4: Math Test—CALCULATOR 🖩

55 Minutes—38 Questions

TURN TO SECTION 4 OF YOUR ANSWER SHEET TO ANSWER THE QUESTIONS IN THIS SECTION.

DIRECTIONS: For **Questions 1–30**, solve each problem, select the best answer from the choices provided, and fill in the corresponding circle on your answer sheet. For **Questions 31–38**, solve the problem and enter your answer in the grid on the answer sheet. The directions **before Question 31** will provide information on how to enter your answers in the grid.

ADDITIONAL INFORMATION:

1. The use of a calculator in this section **is permitted**.

2. All variables and expressions used represent real numbers unless otherwise indicated.

3. Figures provided in this test are drawn to scale unless otherwise indicated.

4. All figures lie in a plane unless otherwise indicated.

5. Unless otherwise specified, the domain of a given function f is the set of all real numbers x for which $f(x)$ is a real number.

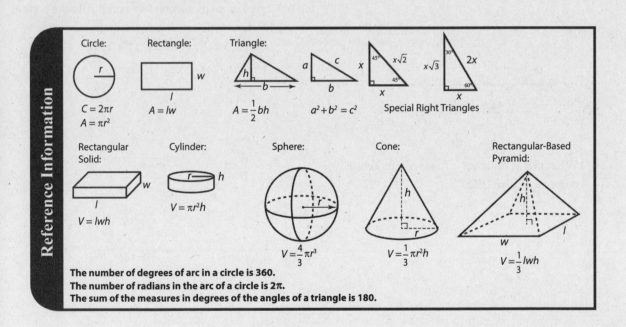

The number of degrees of arc in a circle is 360.
The number of radians in the arc of a circle is 2π.
The sum of the measures in degrees of the angles of a triangle is 180.

Part VII

CONTINUE ➡

CALCULATOR 🖩

1. A certain insect is estimated to travel 1,680 feet per year. At this rate, about how many months would it take for the insect to travel 560 feet?

   A. 0.75
   B. 3
   C. 4
   D. 5.5

2. A librarian is tracking the circulation of books at the library. Out of the books that had been loaned one day, 18 were renewed, 46 were returned on time, and 11 were returned late. At this rate, about how many books will be renewed if the library loans 25,000 books each year?

   A. 4,000
   B. 6,000
   C. 9,000
   D. 15,000

3.

	Small-town	Little-town	Total
Male	175	210	385
Female	195	205	400
Total	370	415	785

Smalltown and Littletown are two towns in Tinytown County. The table above shows the distribution of population of males and females of the towns. If a person from the county is selected at random, what is the probability that the person will be either a male from Littletown or a female from Smalltown?

   A. $\dfrac{39}{74}$
   B. $\dfrac{81}{157}$
   C. $\dfrac{42}{83}$
   D. $\dfrac{56}{157}$

CONTINUE ➤

4. Sixty incoming freshmen at a university are asked how many continents each has visited. The results are summarized in the frequency table below.

Continents Visited	Number of Students
1	12
2	18
3	14
4	8
5	6
6	2
Total Students Responding:	60

Given the data, which is a true statement about the median and mode of the data set?

A. The median is less than the mode.

B. The median is equal to the mode.

C. The median is greater than the mode.

D. The median and mode cannot be determined from the table.

5. Glen earns $10.25 per hour and pays $12.50 per day to commute to and from work on the bus. He wants to make sure that he works long enough to earn at least three times as much as he spends commuting. Which of the following inequalities best represents this situation?

A. $10.25h \geq 3(12.50)$

B. $3(10.25) \geq 12.50h$

C. $3(10.25h) \geq 12.50$

D. $h \geq 3(12.50)(10.25)$

6. Nadia spent 7 more hours on math homework last month than Peter. If they spent a total of 35 hours doing math homework last month, how many hours did Peter spend on math homework?

A. 7

B. 14

C. 21

D. 28

CONTINUE

7. If c is 22 percent of e and d is 68 percent of e, what is $d - c$ in terms of e?

A. $90e$

B. $46e$

C. $0.9e$

D. $0.46e$

9. If $n = 7$, what is $2m(16 - 6n)$ in terms of m?

A. $-52m$

B. $-15m$

C. $-14m$

D. $32m$

8.
$$2x - 9y < 12$$
$$-3x + 4y > 5$$

Which of the following is a solution to the system of inequalities shown above?

A. $(-4, -4)$

B. $(-4, 4)$

C. $(4, -4)$

D. $(4, 4)$

10. Tessa wants to raise a total of at least \$250 for her favorite charity. She has already raised \$145. Tessa asks for \$15 contributions from each person she contacts. Which inequality best represents this situation?

A. $15x \geq 250$

B. $145(15x) \geq 250$

C. $145 + 15x \geq 250$

D. $145 - 15x \geq 250$

Practice Test 1

CONTINUE ➤

CALCULATOR

Questions 11 and 12 refer to the following information.

A class raised money selling t-shirts, and then they began selling hats. The graph represents the total amount of money in the class account as the number of hats sold increases.

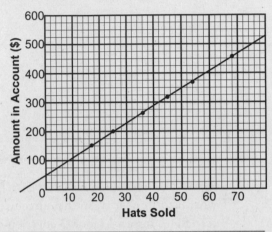

11. According to the graph, which of the following best approximates the number of hats that must be sold for the class to have raised a total of $400?

    A. 54

    B. 58

    C. 64

    D. 68

12. What does the slope of the line signify?

    A. The amount of money already raised

    B. The amount of money received per hat

    C. The number of hats that are sold

    D. The number of hats that must be sold to meet the fundraising goal

13. A survey was conducted to determine whether the voters in a city of 38,000 would support funding a new park. A sample of 18 voters randomly selected from the voting list revealed that 11 voters favored funding the park, 4 voters did not want to fund the park, and 3 voters had no preference. Which of the following makes it least likely that a reliable conclusion can be drawn from the data?

    A. The size of the sample population

    B. The size of the city's population

    C. The number of people with no preference

    D. How the sample population was selected

CONTINUE

14. In 2010, a census showed a city had a population of 22,500. The results of the census also showed that the mean income of the population was $72,350, and the median income was $65,580. Which of the following could describe the difference between the mean income and the median income of the population?

   A. Most of the income values are between the mean and median income values.

   B. There are a few income values that are much less than the other income values.

   C. There are a few income values that are much greater than the other income values.

   D. The range in income values is greater than the income value.

16. $$y = -16x^2 + 50x + 2$$

   The equation above represents the height y of a ball, in feet, x seconds after it has been thrown upward. Which of the following best describes the meaning of the coefficient 50?

   A. The height of the ball when it is thrown

   B. The height of the ball after x seconds

   C. The initial velocity of the ball when it is thrown

   D. The acceleration of the ball's upward velocity

15. A group of h neighbors has 1,230 CDs they are selling at a yard sale. If each neighbor sells on average x CDs per day for j days of the yard sale, which of the following represents the total number of CDs that will be left when the yard sale is over?

   A. $1,230 - jhx$

   B. $1,230 - hx - j$

   C. $1,230 - \dfrac{jx}{h}$

   D. $1,230 + \dfrac{jx}{h}$

Practice Test 1

CONTINUE ▶

CALCULATOR

Questions 17 and 18 refer to the following information.

Quinn is moving across the state and needs to rent a moving truck that will fit her belongings. The table below shows the mileage rate and daily rental cost for trucks from three different companies.

	Mileage rate, b, in cents per mile	Rental rate, a, in dollars per day
Company J	15	19
Company K	10	30
Company L	12	25

The total cost, y, for renting the truck for one day and driving x miles is found by using the formula $y = a + 0.01bx$.

17. For which numbers of miles x is the cost of renting from Company J less than renting from Company K?

    A. $x < 44$

    B. $x < 55$

    C. $x < 220$

    D. $x < 980$

18. If the relationship between the total cost, y, of renting the truck from Company L and driving it x miles for one day is graphed in the xy-plane, what does the slope of the line represent?

    A. The daily rental cost for the truck

    B. The cost to drive the truck each mile

    C. The total cost for the miles driven

    D. The total cost for renting and driving the truck

Part VII

CONTINUE

Questions 19 and 20 refer to the following information.

A sample of the population in two neighborhood towns, Town A and Town B, was surveyed in order to determine the most popular types of house styles. The results of the survey are shown in the table.

| House Style | | |
House Style	Town A	Town B
Ranch	75	62
Colonial	25	65
Cape Cod	53	43
Victorian	20	32

19. According to the table above, what is the probability that a randomly selected house in Town B is a colonial house?

A. $\frac{65}{202}$

B. $\frac{25}{62}$

C. $\frac{31}{45}$

D. $\frac{17}{18}$

20. What is the probability that a randomly selected house is from Town B, given that its style is either a Cape Cod or a Ranch?

A. $\frac{7}{25}$

B. $\frac{105}{233}$

C. $\frac{105}{202}$

D. $\frac{233}{375}$

21. Let a and b be positive real numbers. What is the distance between the x-coordinates of the points of intersection of the graphs of $f(x) = b^2 - (x + a)^2$ and $g(x) = (x + a)^2 - b^2$?

A. $2b$

B. $2a$

C. $a + b$

D. $2(a + b)$

CONTINUE

📟 CALCULATOR

22.

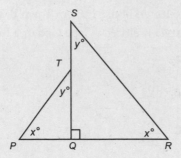

Note: Figure not drawn to scale.

In the figure above, if $QP = 11.5$, $TQ = 15$, and $QR = 46$, what is the value of SQ?

A. 65

B. 60

C. 49.5

D. 42.5

24. A certain type of weather radar, known as a Base Reflectivity Radar, has a circumference of 572π miles. The central angle of a sector of the circle that the radar makes is $\frac{3\pi}{4}$. What is the area, in square miles, of the sector of the circle?

A. 858π square miles

B. $\frac{429\pi}{4}$ square miles

C. $\frac{61,347\pi}{2}$ square miles

D. $81,796\pi$ square miles

23.

$$1 = \frac{3}{x-4} + \frac{4}{x-3}$$

Which of the following are the values of x in the equation above?

A. $7 \pm 2\sqrt{3}$

B. $7 \pm \sqrt{62}$

C. $7 \pm \sqrt{86}$

D. $1, 13$

CONTINUE ▶

25. If w is a negative constant less than -1 and v is a positive constant greater than 1, which of the following could be the graph of $y = a(x + w)(x + v)$?

A.

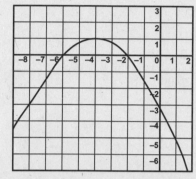

B.

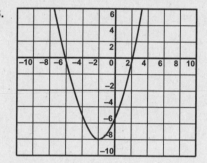

C.

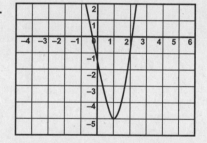

D.

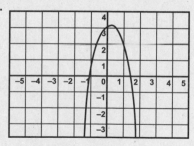

26.

$$2x - 5y < 6$$
$$x + ay < -3$$

Which of the following must be true if the system of inequalities above has solutions only in quadrants II and III?

A. $a < 0$

B. $a = 0$

C. $0 \leq a \leq 2.5$

D. $a > 2.5$

CONTINUE ➤

CALCULATOR

Questions 27 and 28 refer to the following information.

An astronomer records the luminosities (brightness) and temperatures of 19 "main sequence" stars, the most common type of star in the universe. The results are shown below with luminosity measured by comparison to the sun, and temperature in kelvins.

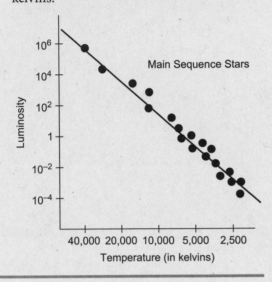

27. How many of the stars observed by the scientist were hotter than 10,000K?

    A. 3

    B. 5

    C. 6

    D. 7

28. The sun's luminosity on the scale used here is 1. Based on the line of best fit, which of the following temperatures is closest to that of the sun's?

    A. 2,500

    B. 5,000

    C. 10,000

    D. 20,000

CONTINUE

CALCULATOR 🖩

29. A recent national poll of adults in the United States found that 64% favor stricter emissions on power plants. The margin of error for the poll was ±4% with 95% confidence. Which of the following statements is a conclusion that can accurately be drawn from this poll?

A. The true percentage of people who oppose stricter emissions of power plants is definitely between 32% and 40%.

B. The true percentage of people who support stricter emissions of power plants is definitely between 60% and 68%.

C. The pollsters are 95% confident that the true percentage of people who oppose stricter emissions of power plants is between 32% and 40%.

D. The pollsters are 95% confident that the true percentage of people who support stricter emissions of power plants is between 60% and 68%.

30. The equation for the graph of a circle in the xy-plane is $x^2 + y^2 - 10x + 4y = -20$. What are the coordinates of the center of the circle?

A. $(5, -2)$

B. $(-5, 2)$

C. $(10, -4)$

D. $(-10, 4)$

Practice Test 1

CONTINUE ➡

CALCULATOR

DIRECTIONS: For **Questions 31–38**, solve the problem and enter your answer in the grid, as described below, on the answer sheet.

1. Although not required, it is suggested that you write your answer in the boxes at the top of the columns to help you fill in the circles accurately. You will receive credit only if the circles are filled in correctly.

2. Mark no more than one circle in any column.

3. No question has a negative answer.

4. Some problems may have more than one correct answer. In such cases, enter only one answer.

5. **Mixed numbers** such as $3\frac{1}{2}$ must be entered as 3.5 or $\frac{7}{2}$.

   If $3\frac{1}{2}$ is entered into the grid as 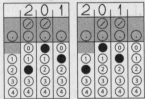, it will be interpreted as $\frac{31}{2}$, not $3\frac{1}{2}$.

6. **Decimal answers:** If you obtain a decimal answer with more digits than the grid can accommodate, it may be either rounded or truncated, but it must fill the entire grid.

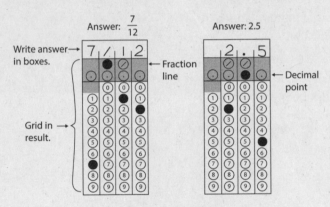

Answer: $\frac{7}{12}$ Answer: 2.5

Answer: 201
Either position is correct.

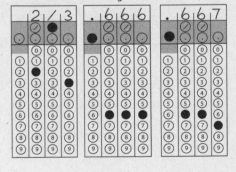

Acceptable ways to grid $\frac{2}{3}$ are:

CONTINUE ▶

31. A bowling alley charges $4.50 per hour to use a lane. They also charge $2.50 to rent a pair of bowling shoes. Miguel and his friend rent a pair of bowling shoes each. The total cost before taxes is $16.25. How many hours did they bowl?

32. If $4s - 3 < 2$ and s is an integer, what is the greatest possible value of $4s + 5$?

33. If $2a - b = 7$ and $2a + 2b = 16$, what is the value of $3a + 7b$?

34. The current population of a certain type of organism is about 100 million. The population is currently increasing at an annual rate that will make the population double in 18 years. If this pattern continues, what will the population be, in millions, 54 years from now?

Practice Test 1

CONTINUE ➤

📟 CALCULATOR

35. Sally sold pieces of her pottery for x dollars each at an art show. Paul sold pieces of his pottery for y dollars each at the same show. Paul sold four pieces of pottery for a total of $85, and Sally sold five pieces for a total of $40 more than Paul. How much more, in dollars, did Sally charge for each piece of her pottery than Paul charged for his? (Ignore the dollar sign when entering your answer in the grid.)

36. Carl knitted 4 more scarves this year than last year. If he knitted 16% more scarves this year than last year, how many did he knit this year?

37.
$$y = 2x + 5$$
$$y = -2(x + 1)^2 + 3$$

If (x, y) is a solution to the system of equations above, what is one possible value of y?

38. The average GPA for the girl's lacrosse team for each year starting in 2014 and ending in 2018 has been 3.5. What is the lowest the GPA could be in 2019 so that the average GPA for all six years is at least 3.47? Round to the nearest hundredth.

STOP
If you finish before time is called, you may check your work on this section only.
Do not turn to any other section.

Section 5: Essay

50 Minutes—1 Essay

> **DIRECTIONS:** The essay gives you an opportunity to show how effectively you can read and comprehend a passage and write an essay analyzing the passage. In your essay, you should demonstrate that you have read the passage carefully, present a clear and logical analysis, and use language precisely.
>
> Your essay will need to be written on the lines provided in your answer booklet. You will have enough space if you write on every line and keep your handwriting to an average size. Try to print or write clearly so that your writing will be legible to the readers scoring your essay.

As you read the passage below, consider how Catherine Anderson uses the following:

- Evidence, such as facts, statistics, or examples, to support claims
- Reasoning to develop ideas and to connect claims and evidence
- Stylistic or persuasive elements, such as word choice or appeals to emotion, to add power to the ideas expressed

Adapted from "Michael Graves sought to create joy through superior design" by Catherine Anderson, originally published in The Conversation on March 25, 2015. Catherine Anderson is Assistant Professor of Interior Architecture and Design at George Washington University. (This passage was edited for length.)

1 Visit the website of designer Michael Graves, and you'll be greeted with the words "Humanistic Design = Transformative Results." The mantra can double as Graves' philosophy. For Graves—who passed away at 80 earlier this month—paid no heed to architectural trends, social movements or the words of his critics. Instead, it was the everyday human being—the individual—who inspired and informed his work.

2 During a career that spanned over 50 years, Graves held firm to the belief that design could effect tremendous change in people's day-to-day lives. From small-scale kitchen products to immense buildings, a thread runs throughout his products: accessible, aesthetic forms that possess a sense of warmth and appeal.

3 Early in his career, Graves was identified as one of the New York Five, a group of influential architects who whole-heartedly embraced Modernism, the architectural movement that subscribed to the use of simple, clean lines, forms devoid of embellishments and modern materials such as steel and glass.

4 However, Graves is best described as a Post-Modernist. He eschewed the austerity of Modernism and its belief that "less is more," instead embracing history and references to the past. He rejected the notion that decoration, or ornament, was a "crime" (as Austrian architect Adolf Loos wrote in 1908); rather, he viewed it as a way for his architecture to convey meaning.

5 As the noted architectural historian Spiro Kostof explains in his book *A History of Architecture: Settings and Rituals*, "Post Modernists turn to historical memory . . . to ornament, as a way of enriching the language of architecture."

6 . . . Along these lines, Graves loathed the idea of intellectualizing his structures. Instead, he sought to make them accessible, understandable, and poignant to all passersby. . . .

7 In addition to designing buildings, Graves embarked upon a long and highly successful partnership with the Italian kitchenware company Alessi. . . . Graves' most famous Alessi design is his iconic teakettle. . . which had a cheerful red whistling bird and sky-blue handle. On sale since 1985, the best-selling product is still in production today.

8 In 1999, Minneapolis-based discount retail giant Target approached Graves with an offer to design a line of kitchen products, ranging from toasters to spatulas.

9 While some might have shied away from having their work associated with a mega-corporation like Target, Graves wholly embraced the project. . . .

10 In all, Graves' collaboration with Target would last 13 years; during this time, the designer would become a household name, with millions of units of his products appearing in American homes.

11 Many of Graves' designs for Target—his spatula, can opener, and ice cream scoop—had chunky, sky-blue handles. Other appliances that were white . . . were sprinkled with touches of color. . . . Black and beige had no place in Graves' palette.

12 The option to select a better-looking product with a slightly higher price versus the same article but with a less expensive, nondescript appearance is now the norm for most consumers: good design (and function) are part and parcel of the customer experience (nowhere is this more evident than in Apple's rise to dizzying heights as arguably one of the world's most valuable brands).

13 It's an idea that's democratic in nature, and thinking about design through this lens led Graves to create thoughtful, appealing, and affordable products for the masses. . . .

14 As Graves' popularity rose, his critics leveled blistering commentaries about what they deemed a precipitous fall from grace—from a "trend beyond compare" to a "stale trend," as architecture critic Herbert Muschamp noted in a 1999 *New York Times* article. The notion that he had commodified design—and had somehow "cheapened" it—drew the disdain of those who once lauded his works.

15 Yet Graves remained true to his beliefs even into the last phase of his life. In 2003, after an illness left him paralyzed below the waist, he realized that the design of hospitals and equipment . . . could be redesigned and made more functional, comfortable, and visually appealing. He then went on to improve ubiquitous devices such as wheelchairs and walking canes. . . .

16 Consumers may not have ever known his architecture or what the critics thought of his work (or even realized they were buying one of his products). Graves didn't seem to mind. His goal was to provide well-designed items for everyday use rather than impress his detractors.

17 As he told NPR in 2002, "It's the kind of thing where you pick something up or use it with a little bit of joy . . . it puts a smile on your face."

Write an essay in which you explain how Catherine Anderson builds an argument to persuade her audience that Michael Graves' central concern was creating designs that helped "the everyday human being." In your essay, analyze how the writer uses one or more of the features listed previously (or features of your own choice) to strengthen the logic and persuasiveness of her argument. Be sure that your analysis focuses on the most relevant aspects of the passage.

Your essay should not explain whether you agree with Catherine Anderson's claims, but rather explain how she builds an argument to persuade her audience.

Section 1: Reading Test

1. A	12. D	23. C	33. A	43. D
2. B	13. B	24. A	34. B	44. C
3. B	14. C	25. C	35. D	45. C
4. C	15. A	26. A	36. D	46. B
5. B	16. C	27. C	37. D	47. C
6. B	17. B	28. D	38. A	48. D
7. A	18. A	29. C	39. D	49. A
8. A	19. C	30. B	40. C	50. C
9. C	20. D	31. C	41. A	51. D
10. B	21. A	32. B	42. B	52. D
11. D	22. B			

READING TEST RAW SCORE ☐
(Number of correct answers)

1. **The correct answer is A.** The overall descriptions are of the character Paul. The passage describes how he looks, his actions and reactions, and his emotions. The narrator also describes how others react to Paul, giving the reader an outside perspective of the character. Thus, choice A provides the best summary of the passage. Choice B is incorrect because the principal is labeled as a sympathetic figure distant from the interactions of Paul and his teachers. Choice C is incorrect because no explicit mention is made of Paul's past. Choice D is incorrect because the reader is told that Paul is lying when expressing his interest in returning to school.

2. **The correct answer is B.** A dandy is a person who is meticulous in the way he dresses and takes extreme care in his appearance. The paragraph in which the word is used is in the context of Paul's clothing, and *dandy* suits the characterization of Paul, so choice B is the correct answer. Choices A, C, and D are incorrect because the context is a description of Paul's dress, not his personality.

3. **The correct answer is B.** The author notes in lines 1–3 that it "was Paul's afternoon to appear before the faculty of the Pittsburgh High School to account for his various misdemeanors." While the author notes that Paul does tell the principal that he wants to return to school, choice A is incorrect because this was not the reason why he was asked to appear before the faculty. Tardiness (choice C) is not mentioned as one of Paul's infractions. Choice D distorts details from the passage; Paul neither pleads nor is he at risk of expulsion.

4. **The correct answer is C.** The carnation is obvious on his coat lapel, and it is a contrast to the way Paul is dressed in shabby clothes, as if he didn't care. And yet the carnation adds a note of frivolity and mockery to the seriousness of the event. It is a way of subtly communicating that he will do as he pleases, in defiance of the wishes of the faculty, thus choice C is the best answer. There is no direct connection between the flower and the English teacher (choice A), and no information is provided to indicate mourning (choice B).

Part VII

Choice D is incorrect because nothing of the flower implies wealth.

5. **The correct answer is B.** Lines 14–17 make it clear that the faculty notice and are annoyed by the presence of the flower in the given situation. Lines 3–6 (choice A) refer to Paul's father's feelings. In lines 33–37 (choice C), the author notes that Paul's teachers stated their charges with "rancor and aggrievedness," words that suggest anger and frustration, but that do not provide insight into their response to the flower. Lines 55–58 (choice D) explain how the teachers interpreted Paul's feelings toward them.

6. **The correct answer is B.** When the English teacher took Paul's hand to guide him, he reacted by shuddering and thrusting "his hands violently behind him" (lines 50–51). His teacher reacts to this with astonishment (lines 51–53) and "could scarcely have been more hurt and embarrassed had he struck at her," which supports choice B. Her astonishment and the fact that she took his reaction so personally suggest that she may not have much experience dealing with emotional students, so choice A is not the best answer. The author merely writes that she "attempted to guide his hand" (lines 48–49); she does not suggest that the teacher took his hand because she was impatient with how slowly Paul was writing, so choice C is not the best answer either. While Paul did make "a running commentary on the lecture" (lines 61–62) in one of his classes, the author implies that incident took place in a different class from the English one, so choice D is incorrect.

7. **The correct answer is A.** In the same sentence, the author also states that Paul's teachers "fell upon him without mercy" (lines 67–68), connoting anger and frustration with the boy's attitude. While sadness and confusion can often be felt in conjunction with frustration and anger, the author's failure

to mention such emotions makes choice B incorrect. Lines 74–76 indicate extreme emotions that contradict the conclusion in choice C, and the fact that the teachers are carrying negative emotions throughout the meeting eliminates choice D.

8. **The correct answer is A.** Paul's appearance is described in great detail, and his outer appearance is often betrayed by behavior that gives away his true feelings. For example, he smiles but his fingers tremble and play with the buttons on his coat (lines 79–80). Choices B, C, and D do not describe Paul's actions and feelings; rather, they describe contrasts with others and their appearance and reactions.

9. **The correct answer is C.** Cather notes in her description of Paul playing with the buttons on his coat that it was the only outward sign of his discomfort, thus in lines 74–81, she connects his outer actions to his inner feelings, allowing the reader inside Paul's emotional state. Lines 69–70 (choice A) and lines 70–74 (choice B) do not interpret the meaning of Paul's facial expression. Lines 85–88 (choice D) are incorrect, as the interpretation noted here is made by others and not necessarily reflective of Paul's feelings.

10. **The correct answer is B.** The word *courteous* is used in the context of being polite in speech to a teacher. Choice A and C both misunderstand the meaning of *courteous* as referring to knightly and chivalrous behavior. Choice D misinterprets the context of the principal's question to imply sarcasm.

11. **The correct answer is D.** The passage describes events leading up to and proceeding Susan B. Anthony, a major figure in early women's suffrage, voting. Choice A is incorrect because the passage does not detail when women received the right to vote, almost 40 years after the events of the passage. While the passage alludes to Anthony's disappointment in Elizabeth Stanton, the passage itself

does not focus on conflict between the two figures overall (choice B). The passage ends with a discussion of how various newspapers received and spread the new of Anthony's exploits (choice C), but it does not offer judgment on the positive and negative reactions, especially those of the caricature cartoonists.

12. **The correct answer is D.** In this passage, Susan B. Anthony first successfully secures the right to vote by invoking the Fourteenth Amendment of the US Constitution. While Anthony read a publication called The Revolution and hoped for more militancy among women, such matters do not necessarily support the conclusion in choice A, since the passage never indicates Anthony took violent measures to secure voting rights for women. While Anthony did take her issue to the press, this was not the action that was most successful for her cause, so choice B is not as strong of an answer as choice D. Her actions described in this passage are to secure the right to vote; as such, voting itself is not a reasonable course of action for the situation, so choice C is not as strong of an answer as choice D.

13. **The correct answer is B.** The answer to this question can be found in the second paragraph, which states, "Sarah Andrews Spencer, Sarah E. Webster, and seventy other women marched to the polls to register and vote in the District of Columbia. Their ballots refused, they brought suit against the Board of Election Inspectors, carrying the case unsuccessfully to the Supreme Court of the United States." Choice A confuses the situation in the District of Columbia with one in Detroit. While the passage states that the women marched to the polls to register and vote, it does not say that they organized a protest march (choice C). While at least two women had voted successfully in the Washington Territory, there is no implication that the women in question were able to vote in

that area after being refused in the District of Columbia, so choice D is incorrect.

14. **The correct answer is C.** The third paragraph describes numerous other women who attempted to vote or secure the right to vote in Susan B. Anthony's time; however, the best choice will indicate a broader movement and not just a single example. Choice A discusses multiple women in two different locations, but this is not as strong as choice C, which establishes women attempting to vote across the country (from California to Michigan, Illinois, and Pennsylvania). Choice B cites a varied example of a woman attempting to vote, but it is only one example and is thus weaker than other options. Choice D cites an important moment in the women's suffrage movement, a case appearing before the Supreme Court, but it does not directly support the idea stated by the question.

15. **The correct answer is A.** While the passage is not specifically about the difficulties women faced in becoming lawyers during Susan B. Anthony's time, it is about difficulties women faced during that period, and the details about Myra Bradwell are relevant to that particular theme. Myra Bradwell was denied admission to the Illinois bar because she was a woman, not because she was unqualified, so choice B is incorrect. There is no exaggeration in this passage; women really did face major challenges during Susan B. Anthony's time, so choice C is a weak answer. While it is likely that Myra Bradwell was intelligent, choice D does not explain why the author discusses her difficulties in the third paragraph.

16. **The correct answer is C.** While Susan B. Anthony is the main focus of this passage, the passage describes the actions of many people who worked toward enacting social change, so choice C is the best answer. Choice A would be correct if the passage discussed only Anthony. The passage focuses on

securing the right to vote, but using voting as a tool to enact social change is not discussed in the passage, so there is no support for choice B. Choice D is too specific, since taking cases to the Supreme Court was just one of the numerous methods for affecting change discussed in the passage.

17. **The correct answer is B.** Lines 60–65 not only refer to lawyers taking seriously the plight of women but also allude to the number of women and their invocation of the Fourteenth Amendment as stirring attention with their actions. Choice A gestures to Anthony responding to a burgeoning movement but does not explain an element of social change. Choice C connects to an incorrect answer for the previous question (referring to a dedicated visionary). Choice D contains a detail of the event that reflected a greater moment of social change but does not speak to the broad nature of the issue.

18. **The correct answer is A.** The word *relevant* makes the most sense if used in place of the word *pertinent* in line 92. While *interesting* (choice B) would make sense, it does not fit the specific meaning of line 92 as well as choice A. *Persistent* (choice C) may be spelled similarly to *pertinent*, but the two words have very different meanings. *Remorseful* (choice D) seems to confuse *pertinent* for *penitent*, the latter of which means "sorry or remorseful."

19. **The correct answer is C.** The newspapers mentioned in the passage make a specific point of declaring Anthony's actions as "lawless." While no image is present to convey the exact nature of the headline, the word *flaunt* implies that the headline was emphasized in some way that indicated its importance or the seriousness of the opinion. As such, choice C is the best choice as *showcased* indicates that the headline received some special emphasis. Choice A is incorrect as, even though it is a synonym for *flaunted*,

broadcast does not fit the context of a newspaper and takes on a figurative meaning. *Printed* (choice B) fits the grammar of the sentence but is not an appropriate substitute for *flaunted*. *Hid* (choice D) is an antonym for *flaunted*.

20. **The correct answer is D.** According to the seventh paragraph, the news media reported on the registration of women voters in Rochester after Susan B. Anthony had successfully gotten sixteen women to register to vote. Choice A describes something that most likely happened after the news media reported Anthony's accomplishment. Choice B describes something that definitely happened after it. Choice C describes something that Anthony only says will happen in the future in this passage, so the passage does not even make clear whether Post went through with her plans to sue the registrars.

21. **The correct answer is A.** The overall main points of the passage are all meant to dispel the myths surrounding earthquakes: how and why they occur. The article provides supporting details about the science of earthquakes, which also counter the Hollywood myths. While the author does explain the causes and effects of earthquakes, it is to dispel the myths created by Hollywood, thus choice B is incorrect. Choice C is incorrect, as the passage applies to earthquakes only and not to science in general. Choice D is incorrect as safety procedures are not covered in the passage in any substantive way.

22. **The correct answer is B.** The main causes of earthquakes are described in paragraph 3, which explains that "An earthquake is caused by a sudden slip on a fault" (lines 10–11) before stating that "Stresses in the Earth's outer layer push the sides of the fault together" (lines 19–21). The mere existence of faults (choice A) is not what causes earthquakes; it is the actions to which those faults are subjected that are true causes. An

earthquake is caused by the actions on a single fault, not two faults in the earth's crust pressing against each other (choice C). The author only mentions the quality of the engineering of structures in the region (choice D) in relation to the damage earthquakes cause, not the cause of earthquakes themselves.

23. **The correct answer is C.** In the context of this passage, *stress* is pressure that builds up in rocks. Only in human interactions does the word *stress* describe the pressure that builds up in people, causing worry and/or anxiety (choice A). Stress does not imply the idea of weight (choice B) in the context of this passage. It also does not mean "emphasis" (choice D).

24. **The correct answer is A.** The passage makes it clear that the closer a region is to the earthquake source (lines 54–56), the more that region will be affected. The most likely reason that San Francisco, or any place, would experience so much damage is that it lacked buildings that could withstand the shaking from an earthquake, and the earthquake was probably very strong. Information in the passage makes it impossible to know whether or not choice B is true. The passage implies that earthquakes are a major concern in California (lines 39–42), so it is unlikely that its city officials never thought an earthquake would occur in San Francisco. So, even though the city was apparently unprepared for such a strong and damaging earthquake, choice C is not entirely correct. Faults across the country (choice D) are irrelevant to a situation in one particular city.

25. **The correct answer is C.** Lines 50–54 clearly explain that the effects of an earthquake are dependent on the proximity of the earthquake source to the affected region, as well as the quality of the engineering of the structures that are shaken by the earthquake. Lines 29–34 (choice B) discuss the creation of an earthquake but do not mention the affected region of an earthquake. Similarly, lines 10–21 (choice A) and lines 107–110 (choice D) contain information regarding attributes and causes of an earthquake but fail to address why a region is affected.

26. **The correct answer is A.** The word *amplified* is used to describe the shaking of a "moderate" earthquake that nevertheless causes "significant damage" in certain areas. It describes how in certain areas, a moderate condition is *intensified*. *Lifted* (choice B) implies an upward movement, and it would not make sense to suggest that the earthquake's shaking was lifted above the surface of the earth. *Supplemented* (choice C) means "added to," and it would not make sense for anything to be added to the shaking. While *amplified* can be used to mean "made louder" (choice D), the volume of the earthquake's noise is not significant in this context; the intensity of its shaking and how that shaking started moderately but caused significant damage is.

27. **The correct answer is C.** In order to adequately refute the myths generated by film and tv, the author needs to challenge the idea of a "mega quake;" the author does so by stating that a magnitude 10 earthquake is not possible in California, and the strongest quakes historically were well below that upper limit. Choice A is incorrect as neither earthquake has a magnitude higher than 8.0, let alone close to 10. Choice B runs contrary to the author's purpose in the passage. Choice D misuses a detail from the following sentence to inaccurately criticize the use and value of computer models in the study of earthquakes.

28. **The correct answer is D.** The article counters the myths by pointing out in lines 94–97 that the ocean isn't a hole into which a land mass can fall, as the ocean is itself just land at a lower elevation. Choice A accepts the myth as fact rather than countering it.

While the author mentions the sea, there is no implication that sea levels have any bearing on seismic activity (choice B). The author does not explain that California and Alaska are similar (choice C) but rather that southern California is moving slowly toward Alaska.

29. **The correct answer is C.** The author notes in lines 94–97 that California cannot break off, as it is part of the land that makes up the ocean floor, only at a higher elevation. Choice A does not offer an explanation as much as a declaration of common knowledge. Choices B and D merely point out features of general geology and of California; they do not clarify why California will not be swept out into the ocean.

30. **The correct answer is B.** The phrase "inconvenient character" reveals that disaster movies are made more dramatic for effect at the expense of scientific accuracy. Using the word *inconvenient* mocks the story; it implies that the earthquake is used as an easy way to write a character out of the story. Choices A, C, and D are incorrect because the use of the phrase does not directly relate to scientific information within the passages, as stated in these choices.

31. **The correct answer is C.** The passage explains that friction is required for an earthquake (lines 109–111), making the idea of a gaping fault impossible, as a fault line could only open up without friction. Choice A is incorrect because although the concept is portrayed in movies, as described in lines 104–107, that fact does not refute the myth. Choice B is incorrect because this question is about earthquakes causing the ground to open up and not "mega-quakes." While the author does state that earthquakes can cause landslides (lines 111–113), the author immediately follows this up by stating "Faults, however, do not gape open during an earthquake" (lines 114–115), so choice D is incorrect.

32. **The correct answer is B.** In lines 12–14, Henry voices his image of the framers of the Constitution with the words "we are not feared by foreigners; we do not make nations tremble," which suggest a desire to intimidate other countries. Since other countries ("foreigners . . . nations"), and not the American people, are the targets of these words, choice A is incorrect. In lines 14–15, Henry questions the idea that these intimidations would "constitute happiness or secure liberties" for Americans, so choice C is incorrect. These words of intimidation would have the opposite effect of building strong relationships with other countries (choice D).

33. **The correct answer is A.** In line 7 ("the genius of republicanism"), Henry praises a republican form of government (i.e., one that has elected representatives and is not run by a monarch). Henry indicates that such a centralized government, as outlined in the Constitution, cannot work with the goals of forming a republican government. Choices B, C, and D are incorrect because Henry is adamant about his opposition to anything similar to a monarchial government, autocracy and empire included.

34. **The correct answer is B.** Lines 5–7 ("the genius of republicanism") clearly state that Henry believes that the ideal form of government is republicanism where people select representatives. Choice A does not have to do with Henry's preference in forms of government but distorts a detail to create an answer trap for the previous question. Choices C and D both have to do with the United States becoming a monarchy.

35. **The correct answer is D.** Henry addresses the issue of concentrating power and says that it rests "on a supposition that your American governors shall be honest" (lines 35–38), which, in his view, is a dangerous and unnecessarily risky assumption to make. Choice A is incorrect because Henry actually suggests the opposite of this conclusion,

voicing concern about a lack of check and balances in lines 7–9 before speculating that a president who basically operates as a king could be the result of a lack of checks and balances in lines 26–27. Neither choice B nor choice C correlate with the views of Henry and would therefore not be an objection of his.

36. **The correct answer is D.** Henry is speaking to how the constitution as written would allow governors to act against the interest of the people, or commit wrongdoings. Choice A uses a common understanding of mischief but does not match the gravity of the situation. Choice B is inaccurate in that Henry's sentence implies that such actions would not be illegal but within the boundaries of the constitution as written. Choice C fits the structure of the sentence but is not one of the possible meanings of the word *mischiefs*.

37. **The correct answer is D.** Madison argues that a government whose powers are separated by design will act as controls, each branch on the other, and avoid concentration of power. Although Madison describes government as a reflection of human nature (choice A), this is not a counterargument to those who were concerned about a strong central government. Choice B exaggerates Madison's simple suggestion that people are not "angels" and require some monitoring from their fellow people to ensure that they always act in the people's best interests. Choice C is not the strongest counterargument because Madison does state that the people should monitor the government to a certain degree.

38. **The correct answer is A.** Lines 72–78 describe how Madison believes the government should be divided into branches that would check and balance each other. This would serve to counteract the idea that the government is too centralized because the branches would allow for the power to

be divided and would make it so that one branch would not have too much power. Choice B makes the mistake of concluding that choice A was the correct answer to the previous question. Choice C makes the mistake that choice B was the correct answer to the previous question. Choice D relates to people influencing the government, which relates to choice C in the previous question, but since that answer choice was incorrect, choice D has no bearing on the correct answer to this question.

39. **The correct answer is D.** Madison's reference to "department" refers to the branches of the government that are outlined in the Constitution (executive, legislative, judicial), which is apparent from the context. An executive may be in charge of a department, but a single person would not constitute an entire government department, so choice A does not make sense. Choice B is not the best answer since a "territory" would more likely describe an area of land rather than a segment of government. *Level* (choice C) implies a hierarchy, which does not apply to this particular context.

40. **The correct answer is C.** Both Henry and Madison wish to prevent the use of power to restrict the freedoms of a nation, even as each speaker has a different perspective for how to achieve such a goal. Choice A exaggerates the scope of Henry's speech and does not apply to Madison's topic. Choice B is irrelevant to the passage as both authors speak to the structure of government, not its inner mechanisms of legislation. Choice D discusses a common critique of the previous version of the constitution that is not addressed explicitly by Henry or Madison.

41. **The correct answer is A.** Henry and Madison's statements are both very similar, indicating that both men believed that even the most seemingly honest person was too flawed, too human, to be trusted with

complete control of the people she or he ruled. Henry says that being "good men" is not enough to earn that trust, while Madison suggests that anyone short of being a complete "angel" could not be trusted with complete control. Choice B is too extreme; one does not have to be completely disinterested in the rights and liberties of the people they rule to be undeserving of complete control. Choice C is incorrect because both men are skeptical of allowing anyone to be trusted with complete control. Even though its statement about Madison is true, choice D is incorrect because Henry does not show that he did not believe government was necessary.

42. **The correct answer is B.** Patrick Henry lashes out against concentrated power (Passage 1, lines 1–5). Madison, on the other hand, explains that power is essential, but separating the power of the government into different departments (branches) will act as a check on that power, ensuring that it cannot get out of control (Passage 2, sentence 1). The statements made in choices A, C, and D do not reflect the content of the passages.

43. **The correct answer is D.** The article mentions multiple scientists and institutions that all worked on identifying the shark and sharing their information so that it could be correctly cataloged and understood (lines 19–22, 39–43, 58–63, and 67–71). The overall conclusion about methodology, therefore, shows that science can be a collaborative endeavor. Although the passage describes multiple institutions working together, this answer choice assumes that this is necessary for all examples of scientific information gathering. This conclusion is too general and baseless for choice A to be correct. Choice B is too extreme since it assumes that the luck that led to the discovery of the pocket shark in this passage applies to all instances of scientific information gathering. Choice C also assumes that the circumstances in this

passage will be true for all other instances of scientific information gathering.

44. **The correct answer is C.** With the information from the passage, it is most likely that the specimen's close relatives traveled from one location to another from the options available. While it is possible that two different species could evolve in similar ways (choice A), nothing in the passage suggests such a relationship. Choice B is incorrect because for the species to be common to such a large area would run counter to the fact that the shark has only been found twice in nature. Choice D assumes wrongdoing on behalf of the Tulane research center, even as nothing in the article indicates a lack of credibility among their staff or in their procedures.

45. **The correct answer is C.** The quotation in lines 25–29 makes it clear that the most probable explanation for the pocket shark's presence in the Gulf of Mexico is related to the movement of its parents between the two known areas of pocket shark activity. Choice A only establishes the common and scientific names of the species and does not speak to reasoning for their presence in two distant locations. Choice B only establishes that the pocket shark was a newborn and is unrelated to the inferences in the previous question's answers. Choice D describes the method of collection but provides no insight into the possible reason for its presence in the Gulf.

46. **The correct answer is B.** Lines 13–16 state that while the shark is small enough to "fit in your pocket," it actually gets its name because of the pocket-like "orifice above the pectoral fin," which confirms that choice B is correct and eliminates choices A and C. The author never suggests that the pocket shark has markings that resemble pockets, so choice D is incorrect.

47. **The correct answer is C.** Paragraph 5 explains that tissue samples were analyzed to get genetic information that could be compared to other specimens. Using this data, scientists could then determine how to classify the pocket shark. Choice A is not the best answer since other sharks could be the same length as the pocket shark, and lines 44–48 ("A tissue . . . *Mollisquama*") explicitly explain how scientists used tissue samples to determine the shark's species. The author discusses the pocket-like orifice to explain how the shark got its name but never implies that this characteristic helped scientists determine its species (choice B). In lines 53–55, the author states that learning more about its species may provide clues to the shark's position in the food chain, not the other way around (choice D).

48. **The correct answer is D.** It is mentioned in the passage that scientists found an umbilical scar that had not healed, suggesting that the fish had been "recently born" (lines 20–21). In lines 27–29, it is mentioned that only one other pocket fish had ever been found before, giving insufficient basis for comparison to determine age, making choice B incorrect. Choices A and C are not explicitly stated in the passage, and in any case, do not make sense in relation to fish.

49. **The correct answer is A.** As used in the passage, *sample* implies an object gathered in the field, in this case a *specimen*, or individual animal. *Population* (choice B) conflates the use of *sample* from statistics with the scientific usage here. *Example* (choice C) is a common meaning of *sample* but is inappropriate for the context; even though, this sample is an example of the species, the shark's body is being used for scientific research, not only to illustrate the traits of the shark. *Bite* (choice D) is incorrect as the context does not apply to food.

50. **The correct answer is C.** *Robust* in this context describes a collection that has variety. A specimen is a sample used for testing, so it makes sense for the lab to have a large, substantial collection of marine animal samples for testing. It cannot be inferred, based on the passage, that the "robust specimen collection" is *typical* (choice A), *healthy* (choice B), or *distinguished* (choice D).

51. **The correct answer is D.** The passage explicitly states that scientists were excited to discover the pocket shark because it is unique with so few of them having been found (lines 3–7 and 27–29). Choice A is incorrect because the author actually places the pocket shark into the *Dalatiidae* shark family (lines 48–52) that existed before the pocket shark was discovered. While the pocket is "distinctive" (line 15), there is no evidence that the pocket shark is the only shark with such an orifice. Even if this is true, an explicit statement about why scientists are excited about its discovery renders choice B incorrect. The author mentions that pocket sharks were found in the Gulf and far away off the coast of Peru but does not offer this detail as the reason why scientists are so excited about its discovery, so choice C is incorrect.

52. **The correct answer is D.** Lines 72–76 explicitly state that it is "exciting" to find a shark that is so "unusual" and "rare." Choice A seems to make the mistake that the correct answer to the previous question was choice C when this is not the case. While lines 36–43 do indicate that the pocket shark is rare, they do not indicate that scientists are excited about that fact, so choice B is not the best answer. Choice C seems to make the mistake of assuming that choice A was the correct answer to the previous question when it was not.

Section 2: Writing and Language Test

1. D	10. B	19. D	28. C	37. A
2. B	11. C	20. B	29. B	38. D
3. C	12. A	21. A	30. A	39. B
4. D	13. D	22. C	31. C	40. C
5. A	14. B	23. B	32. D	41. B
6. A	15. A	24. D	33. A	42. D
7. B	16. B	25. B	34. A	43. A
8. C	17. D	26. A	35. D	44. B
9. D	18. C	27. A	36. C	

WRITING AND LANGUAGE TEST RAW SCORE
(Number of correct answers)

1. **The correct answer is D.** Choice D provides a transition between sentences and establishes the historical importance of Blackwell's accomplishment. Choice C does the latter but not the former. Choice A is awkward. Choice B unnecessarily repeats information already provided in the previous sentence.

2. **The correct answer is B.** The context of the paragraph makes clear that the expectations of those around Blackwell were that she would fail in becoming a doctor and that Blackwell had ignored or disregarded those expectations. Choice A is incorrect because her achievement was not a condemnation or criticism of the expectation that she would fail; it simply flouted it. Choice C is incorrect because *incite* means "to encourage or inspire," and the context does not support the idea that she inspired the expectation that she would fail. Choice D is incorrect because the context makes clear that in earning her degree, Blackwell did not meet the expectations of her peers. Rather, she disregarded and far surpassed them.

3. **The correct answer is C.** The comparison here is between educating a boy and educating a girl. Choice A illogically compares educating a boy to a girl, rather than to

educating a girl. Choice B illogically compares educating a boy to a girl's preference for education. Choice D illogically compares educating a boy to opportunities for girls.

4. **The correct answer is D.** The phrase, "To make up for the gaps in her education," modifies *she* or Blackwell and should directly precede a reference to Blackwell to avoid confusion. Choice A is incorrect because the phrase appears to modify household. Choices B and C are incorrect because the phrase appears awkwardly in the middle of the sentence and it is unclear what it modifies.

5. **The correct answer is A.** The first part of the sentence, "As she prepared to apply to medical school," correctly tells the reader when the events of the sentence took place. Choices B and C incorrectly state when these events take place. Choice D incorrectly suggests that Blackwell wanted to be a psychologist.

6. **The correct answer is A.** This sentence provides significant context clues to help you determine the right word to include. The latter half of the sentence is building on a specific contention, saying "at least one advisor went so far as to suggest that she might disguise herself as a man in order to gain admittance." Such a notion suggests that her advisors felt great *doubt* that she would gain

direct admittance to medical school. There is no evidence that there was any debate (choice B), insistence (choice C), or supposing going on (choice D).

7. **The correct answer is B.** The antecedent of the pronoun is Blackwell, so the pronoun should be *her*. The pronouns *their* (choice A), *his* (choice C), and *your* (choice D) do not agree with the antecedent *Blackwell*.

8. **The correct answer is C.** The sentence should be written in the simple past tense: *became* agrees with the verb tense used in the sentences that follow. *Has become* (choice A) is in the present perfect tense while the sentence that follows is in the simple past tense. *Becomes* (choice B) is in the present tense, and all of the events take place in the distant past. *Will become* (choice D) is in the future tense.

9. **The correct answer is D.** The phrase, "all of whom were men," is nonrestrictive, which means it must be set off by commas. Only choice D has the commas in the appropriate place to set off the entire phrase. Choice A is incorrect, as there are no commas to set off the nonrestrictive phrase. Choice B incorrectly uses a colon even though the information before the colon is not an independent clause—it lacks a complete idea that is formed by the information after the nonessential phrase. Choice C incorrectly uses a semicolon, implying that the information before and after the punctuation is composed of two independent clauses.

10. **The correct answer is B.** This choice reduces wordiness and redundancy, as experiencing prejudice and biases implies that obstacles and challenges were faced, something unnecessarily restated in choice A. Choice C fails to specify that the challenges faced included prejudice and biases, which is significant information that should be included. The wording in choice D is awkward and would introduce confusion to the sentence.

11. **The correct answer is C.** Only choice C supports the idea that, although she faced barriers, Blackwell was successful by distinguishing herself as a promoter of preventative medicine and medical opportunities for women. Choice A does not support the idea that she was successful, and it does not refer to her career after she graduated from medical school. Choice B does not describe anything that Blackwell went on to do after she got her degree. Choice D does not describe anything that Blackwell did in her career.

12. **The correct answer is A.** This choice provides useful historical context for when Carson's book was published, informing readers that few people in 1962 expressed concern about the environment. This helps advance the idea that Carson was brave for speaking out. Choice B is not correct, as Carson's age is not a significant factor here. Choice C is incorrect because this information is not irrelevant, and the book is indeed an important publication. Choice D is incorrect because adding this sentence does not create a division in the focus of the paragraph.

13. **The correct answer is D.** The style of the passage is formal and objective, and only choice D corresponds with this style. Choice A employs an informal style. Choices B and C are less formal and not as concise as choice D.

14. **The correct answer is B.** The sentence is a question and requires a question mark at the end. Choices A, C, and D are incorrect because the sentence is interrogative and requires a question mark.

15. **The correct answer is A.** In this sentence, the phrase "DDT in particular" represents a sharp break in thought and should be set off by em dashes. The sentence as it is written is correct. Choice B is incorrect because a semicolon would interrupt the flow of the sentence, implying that what comes after is an independent clause. Choice C is incorrect

because while commas could be used to separate the phrase, they must be used before and after the phrase to be correct. While a colon could be used for emphasis (choice D), it improperly divides the prepositional phrase after "DDT in particular" from its object earlier in the sentence.

16. **The correct answer is B.** The information above the pie chart indicates that the chart refers to the most heavily used pesticides by percentage in 1968. Only choice B accurately notes this by referencing that DDT accounted for 11% of all pesticides used in that year. The chart does not show the amount of farmland that was sprayed with DDT (choice A), does not indicate the percentage of pests contained by DDT (choice C), or show the percentage of farmers and gardeners who used DDT (choice D).

17. **The correct answer is D.** The context of the paragraph, as well as the point later in the paragraph that pesticides "were able to penetrate systems and remain there for years," indicates that the pesticides were seeping into, or permeating, the soil and rivers. There is no support for the idea that the pesticides sapped the water from soil and rivers (choice A). Pesticides cannot appropriate (choice B) the soil and rivers. *Transcending* (choice C) does not make sense in the context.

18. **The correct answer is C.** In the original text, the incorrect pronoun *he* is used, creating confusion as to what noun it's replacing. For clarity, the sentence must restate the antecedent; thus, the *pesticides were* is the correct answer. Choice B is incorrect because the pronoun *it* does not agree with any antecedent in the preceding sentence. Choice D is incorrect because *everything* is illogical in the context.

19. **The correct answer is D.** Choice D maintains Carson's argument that pesticides are dangerous. Choice A incorrectly suggests that pesticides are beneficial to health.

Choice B is incorrect because Carson is not making an argument about cancer specifically, nor does she definitively link the two. Choice C is incorrect because Carson is not talking about only bird populations.

20. **The correct answer is B.** The context of the paragraph suggests that the chemical companies were not willing to accept or admit the potential hazards of their product; thus, choice B is the correct answer. *Contradict* (choice A) suggests that they agreed with Carson, an idea not supported by the context. While it is likely true that chemical companies were not willing to "propagate" (choice C) or communicate the potential hazards of their product, the fact that they discredited Carson suggests that they were even stronger in their reaction to her claims. *Solicit* (choice D), or try to obtain, doesn't make sense in the context.

21. **The correct answer is A.** The first part of the sentence is a subordinating clause, and the subordinating conjunction *since* helps establish the clause's connection to the rest of the sentence. It explains why Carson is blamed for the deaths. Choices B, C, and D deploy incorrect subordinating conjunctions and introductory phrases that introduce confusion and awkwardness into the sentences.

22. **The correct answer is C.** The noun DDT must agree in number with "wonder chemical"; thus, choice C is the correct answer. Choice A is incorrect because DDT does not agree in number with "wonder chemicals." Likewise, choice B is incorrect because "pesticides" does not agree in number with "wonder chemical." Choice D is also incorrect because DDT does not agree in number with *chemicals*.

23. **The correct answer is B.** Because this is a simple list of countries, the items in the series should be set off by commas. The items shown in choices A and C are incorrectly set off by both commas and semicolons. The

lack of internal punctuation in choice D creates a grammatically incorrect sentence.

24. **The correct answer is D.** The subject and verb in a sentence must agree in number. In this case, only choice D reflects agreement of the subject and verb as well as appropriate verb tense. Choice A is incorrect because the subject of the sentence, "the Mayan understanding of astronomy," is singular and requires a singular verb, and *were* is plural. Choice B is incorrect because *are* is plural and is in the present tense rather than the past tense. Choice C is incorrect because the verb form *will be* is in the future tense, while the notable achievements of the Mayans occurred in the past.

25. **The correct answer is B.** All of the items in the list should be in the same form, or parallel. Only choice B reflects a parallel structure for all of the verbs: *setting, moving,* and *rotating.* The verbs in the other answer choices do not have parallel structure and are incorrect.

26. **The correct answer is A.** The context of the sentence suggests that the Mayans' observations were accurate, as they could predict eclipses and the movement of the planets. Only *astute* reflects this level of accuracy. *Inept* (choice B) suggests the Mayans weren't skilled at making observations. Choice C is incorrect, as the observations were not "expected," given the time period in which they were made. There's no evidence or support within the sentence that refers to the complexity of the Mayan's observations (choice D).

27. **The correct answer is A.** This answer ("the movement of the planets") provides an example that is related to astronomy, which is the main focus of the paragraph and sentence. The migration of birds (choice B), the direction of the winds (choice C), and the flow of the tides (choice D) are examples that are inconsistent with the topic of astronomy.

28. **The correct answer is C.** *Its* is a possessive determiner and does not require an apostrophe. *It's* (choice A) is a contraction of *it is. Its'* (choice B) is not a word (you can't have plural possession for a word, *it,* that's singular by definition). *Their* (choice D) is a possessive pronoun that is incorrect in number for its antecedent.

29. **The correct answer is B.** A semicolon is used to join two related sentences that can stand on their own. Choice A is incorrect because a colon is not used to join two independent clauses. Choice C is incorrect because a comma may only be used to join two independent clauses if it is followed by a conjunction. Choice D is incorrect because, while it is followed by a conjunction, *but* indicates that the second clause is somehow at odds with the first.

30. **The correct answer is A.** The paragraph suggests that the link between government and astronomy was so complete that the two were inseparable, so choice A is the correct answer, as the word *inextricably* means in a manner that is impossible to separate. There's nothing in the passage to suggest that the link was baffling (choice B) or embarrassing (choice D), or that an element of greed was involved (choice C).

31. **The correct answer is C.** No punctuation is required after the word *symbols* because the phrase that follows it is restrictive, or necessary for identifying which symbols. Only choice C contains no punctuation after *symbols.* Choice A incorrectly uses a colon. Choice B incorrectly uses a comma to set the restrictive phrase off from *symbols.* Choice D is incorrect because a semicolon is used only to separate two independent clauses, and "relating to the sun, Moon, and sky" is not an independent clause.

32. **The correct answer is D.** "Call to war" is correct because it supports the paragraph's focus on when the Mayans would attack

their enemies. Choices A, B, and C provide information that is inconsistent with the paragraph's focus.

33. **The correct answer is A.** The last paragraph is a short summary of the rest of the passage, as the phrase "in short," suggests. Thus, choice A is the correct answer. *However* (choice B) indicates a contrast with information that preceded it. *Moreover* (choice C) suggests that the paragraph will include new information, which it does not. *Incidentally* (choice D) suggests that a digression or side topic will follow.

34. **The correct answer is A.** In college, the narrator believed that the employment counselor's advice did not apply to him. Throughout the story, it was made apparent that the narrator was mistaken and should have taken the advice and done a mock interview. Choices B and D are incorrect because *know* and *believe* are in present tense, while the rest of the paragraph is past tense. Choice C goes against the premise of the story. If the narrator denied that it applied to other people but not to him, he would have known it applied to him and would have done the mock interview. This does not make sense as an introduction to the rest of the story, which shows the narrator did not know how to properly behave and answer questions in a job interview.

35. **The correct answer is D.** The narrator has intended to use the preposition *through* here, and only choice D reflects the correct spelling. *Thorough* (choice A) is an adjective that means complete or exhaustive. *Threw* (choice B) is the past tense of *throw*. *Though* (choice C) functions as either an adverb meaning "however" or a conjunction meaning "while."

36. **The correct answer is C.** Because it is clear that the narrator is seeking a job, the correct possessive modifier before a noun must be *my*, as the passage is written in the first person and the narrator is referring to himself

and no one else. Choice A incorrectly uses the incorrect first person singular possessive pronoun. Choice B is incorrect because *our* is plural in number and refers to the narrator and others, an incorrect reference. Choice D is also incorrect because there is no antecedent for *their*.

37. **The correct answer is A.** The sentence that currently concludes the paragraph provides an effective summation of the ideas in the paragraph, that the law firm that will be the location of the narrator's first interview is the ideal working environment. It also provides context for the paragraph that follows, letting readers know that this job is one that the narrator really wants to get. Choice B is the opposite of the narrator's actual thoughts about the law firm, and there's no evidence to suggest that choices C and D represent the narrator's actual beliefs.

38. **The correct answer is D.** A complete sentence contains both a subject and a predicate. The sentence as it stands is a fragment, as it does not contain a subject. Only choice D contains both a subject (*I*) and a predicate (*informed*). Choice A does not contain a subject. Choice B is a dependent clause, containing neither a subject nor a predicate. Choice C is incorrect because it, too, is a dependent clause.

39. **The correct answer is B.** The context of the paragraph suggests that the narrator thinks that he is ambitious and well-spoken, as he has articulated his goals to the interviewer. Only *articulate* fits with the context. *Enigmatic* (choice A) means "mysterious," and there is nothing mysterious about the narrator. Further, the narrator wouldn't assume that the interviewer thought he was mysterious. *Conspicuous* (choice C) means "noticeable." While this could potentially work, it is not usually considered an admirable trait in a job interview. In this case, *articulate* is a better fit. *Incoherent* (choice D) means

"unable to be understood," and the narrator clearly thinks he has made a good impression on the interviewer.

40. **The correct answer is C.** The context requires the plural form of *weakness*, which is *weaknesses*. *Weakness's* (choice A) is a possessive form of *weakness*. *Weaknesses'* (choice B) is the possessive form of the plural *weaknesses*, rather than just the plural. *Weakness'* (choice D) neither accurately reflects the plural of *weakness* nor the possessive of the word.

41. **The correct answer is B.** Sentence 3 introduces the topic of the paragraph, which is the narrator's listing of his strengths and weaknesses. Because the sentence clearly introduces the main point of the paragraph, it belongs at the beginning of the paragraph. Choice B, then, is the correct answer, which makes choice A incorrect. Choice C is incorrect because it makes no sense to place the sentence after the sentences that tell the narrator's response to the interviewer's question. Choice D is incorrect, as the existing paragraph is where information regarding the phases of the interview fits best.

42. **The correct answer is D.** The conventional phrase, "I couldn't have cared less," expresses apathy, as the speaker cannot care any less. Only choice D reflects the correct usage. Choice A is incorrect because the narrator is suggesting that he actually *could* have cared

less than he already does—the degree of care can be reduced. Choices B and C are incorrect for the same reason, though choice C also incorrectly uses "of" instead of "have."

43. **The correct answer is A.** The previous paragraph ends following the job interview, and this paragraph begins with the narrator not getting the job. An effective transition sentence would chronicle the waiting period between the interview and the hiring decision. Choice B is incorrect because the narrator did hear back about the job. Choices C and D are outside the scope and context of the paragraph.

44. **The correct answer is B.** The word *eventually*, along with the narrator's admission in the first paragraph that he did not go to the college job counseling office when first advised to, suggests that the correct term here is *belated*, or overdue. *Deferred* (choice A) implies that he put off the trip with the intention of going at a later time, and there is no indication that the narrator did this. *Hastened* (choice C) suggests that the narrator made a speedy trip. *Disparaged* (choice D), meaning "belittled or criticized," is an adjective that doesn't make sense in the context of describing his trip to the college job counseling office.

Practice Test 1

Section 3: Math Test—NO CALCULATOR

1. C	5. C	9. C	13. D	17. $\frac{1}{2}$ (0.5)
2. D	6. B	10. B	14. B	18. 13
3. B	7. B	11. C	15. D	19. $\frac{4}{3}$ (1.33)
4. B	8. C	12. C	16. 24	20. 4

MATH TEST—NO CALCULATOR RAW SCORE
(Number of correct answers)

1. **The correct answer is C.** The question asks for Jared's goal in steps per day after d days. He increases his goal by 125 steps each day, so after 1 day it will go up 125(1), after 2 days it will go up by 125(2), and after d days it will go up by 125d from his original amount of 950.

2. **The correct answer is D.** Use the correct order of evaluating functions. First evaluate $g(3) = 1$, then substitute in $f(g(3))$ as $f(1)$ to find that $f(g(3)) = 3$.

3. **The correct answer is B.** The formula for exponential decay is $y = a(1 - r)^n$, where r is the rate of change, n is the number of times the rate is applied, a is the initial amount, and y is the amount remaining.

4. **The correct answer is B.** First, find half the length of the horizontal distance, which is 15 ft. Then, use the Pythagorean theorem to find the length of each of the slanted sides.

$$a^2 + b^2 = c^2$$
$$8^2 + 15^2 = c^2$$
$$64 + 225 = c^2$$
$$289 = c^2$$
$$17 = c$$

5. **The correct answer is C.** Distribute, combine like terms, and factor to identify the x-intercepts (4 and 6) as:

$$y = 2(x - 5)^2 - 2$$
$$= 2(x^2 - 10x + 25) - 2$$
$$= 2x^2 - 20x + 48$$
$$= 2(x^2 - 10x - 24)$$
$$= 2(x - 4)(x - 6)$$

Answer choices A, B, and D are equivalent to the given equation, but they do not directly reveal that 4 and 6 are the x-intercepts.

6. **The correct answer is B.** Find the x- and y-intercepts of the given equation.

$$3x + y = 4$$
$$3(0) + y = 4$$
$$y = 4$$
$$3x + 0 = 4$$
$$x = \frac{4}{3}$$

Check the intercepts on the graph of each line to see if they match the intercepts of the equation in the problem. Only choice B has intercepts at (0, 4) and $\left(\frac{4}{3}, 0\right)$.

7. **The correct answer is B.** Use the point slope form of a linear equation to write the slope-intercept form of the equation:

$$y - y_1 = m(x - x_1)$$
$$y - 3 = -1(x - 2)$$
$$y - 3 = -x + 2$$
$$y = -x + 5$$

Then find the equation that is equivalent to the slope-intercept form:

$$3x + 3y = 15$$
$$3y = -3x + 15$$
$$y = -x + 5$$

8. **The correct answer is C.** The first equation simplifies to $x = 2y$. Substituting $2y$ for x into the second equation gives:

$$2(2y)^2 - y^2 = 14$$
$$2 \cdot 4y^2 - y^2 = 14$$
$$7y^2 = 14$$
$$y^2 = 2$$

9. **The correct answer is C.** Simplify the expression using the exponent rules:

$$\sqrt[3]{\sqrt{z}} = \left(z^{\frac{1}{2}}\right)^{\frac{1}{3}} = z^{\frac{1}{6}}$$

$$\sqrt[3]{z} \cdot \sqrt{z} = z^{\frac{1}{3}} \cdot z^{\frac{1}{2}} = z^{\frac{5}{6}}$$

$$\frac{\sqrt[3]{\sqrt{z}}}{\sqrt[3]{z} \cdot \sqrt{z}} = \frac{z^{\frac{1}{6}}}{z^{\frac{5}{6}}} = z^{\frac{1}{6} - \frac{5}{6}} = z^{-\frac{2}{3}}$$

10. **The correct answer is B.** The equation for a parabola with a vertex at (h, k) is $y = a(x - h)^2 + k$, and if the y-intercept is 13, then $(0, 13)$ is a point on the parabola, and $13 = a(0 - h)^2 - k$. Since $13 = 2(0 - 3)^2 - 5$, the equation shown in choice B is correct.

11. **The correct answer is C.** The amount per each type of admission is $12 and $17, so the total admission of $1,079 based upon number of adults and children is $12x + 7y$. The total number of people, 117, is represented by $x + y$.

12. **The correct answer is C.**

$$\frac{4 - i}{3 + i} \cdot \frac{3 - i}{3 - i} = \frac{11 - 7i}{10}$$

13. **The correct answer is D.** Solve the equation:

$$-6(t + 1) = 2(1 - 3t) - 8$$
$$-6t - 6 = 2 - 6t - 8$$
$$-6 = -6$$

The equation has infinitely many solutions.

14. **The correct answer is B.** The formula for population growth is $P = P_o e^{rt}$, where P represents the total population, P_o represents the initial population, e represents the constant value, r represents the rate of growth, and t represents the time. The "10" in the problem represents the time, in years, between the two years of interest—the initial year 1980 and the city's population in 1990. There are 10 years between 1980 and 1990.

15. **The correct answer is D.** Long division reveals that 4 is the remainder when we divide $9x^2$ by $3x - 2$.

$$
\begin{array}{r}
3x + 2 \\
3x - 2 \overline{)9x^2} \\
\underline{9x^2 - 6x} \\
6x - 4 \\
\underline{4}
\end{array}
$$

In general, when we divide F by G and obtain quotient Q and remainder R, then $\dfrac{F}{G} = Q + \dfrac{R}{G}$. In this case:

$$\frac{9x^2}{3x - 2} = (3x + 2) + \frac{4}{3x - 2}$$

16. **The correct answer is 24.** To solve this problem, first isolate $\sqrt{x + 1}$ on one side of the equation. Then, square both sides:

$$\sqrt{x + 1} - 2 = 3$$
$$\sqrt{x + 1} = 5$$
$$x + 1 = 25$$
$$x = 24$$

17. **The correct answer is $\dfrac{1}{2}$ (0.5).** Complete the square on the function so that the vertex is readily identifiable:

$$f(x) = x^2 - 2bx + \left(b^2 + 2b - 1\right)$$
$$= \left(x^2 - 2bx + b^2\right) + \left(b^2 + 2b - 1\right) - b^2$$
$$= (x - b)^2 + (2b - 1)$$

The vertex is $(b, 2b - 1)$, and the parabola opens upward. The graph will have one x-intercept, which coincides with the vertex, if and only if $2b - 1 = 0$. That is, when $b = \frac{1}{2}$.

18. **The correct answer is 13.** To find the value of c, divide the numerator by the denominator using either long division or synthetic division. Remember that the remainder can be written as a fraction, with the remainder as the numerator and the divisor as the denominator.

$$
\begin{array}{r}
3x - 13 \\
x + 3 \overline{\smash{)}\, 3x^2 - 4x - 18} \\
\underline{3x^2 + 9x} \\
-13x \\
\underline{-13x - 39} \\
21
\end{array}
$$

Here, the remainder is 21, so the fraction is equal to $3x - 13 + \frac{21}{x + 3}$. Set this equal to the expression in the equation to find that $c = 13$.

$$\frac{3x^2 - 4x - 18}{x + 3} = 3x - 13 + \frac{21}{x + 3}$$
$$c = 13$$

19. **The correct answer is $\frac{4}{3}$ (1.33).** The equations need to have the same slope but different y-intercepts. The first equation is already written in slope-intercept form. First, rewrite the second equation so that it is in slope-intercept form, then find the value for t that makes the slope 3. This should make the y-intercept different than 7.

$$4x - ty = 5$$
$$-ty = -4x + 5$$
$$y = \frac{-4x + 5}{-t}$$
$$y = \frac{-4x}{-t} + \frac{5}{-t}$$

So:

$$\frac{-4}{-t} = 3$$
$$4 = 3t$$
$$t = \frac{4}{3}$$

To check that the y-intercept is not 7:

$$\frac{5}{-t} = \frac{5}{-\frac{4}{3}}$$
$$= 5\left(-\frac{3}{4}\right)$$
$$= -\frac{15}{4}$$

20. **The correct answer is 4.** Use the formulas for the volume of a sphere and volume of a cone. Set the formulas equal to each other since their volumes are equal. In the formulas, r represents the radius of the cone or the radius of the circle, which are equal. The height of the cone is h. Solve for the value of $\frac{h}{r}$.

$$V_{cone} = V_{scoop}$$
$$\frac{1}{3}\pi r^2 h = \frac{4}{3}\pi r^3$$
$$h = \frac{\cancel{3}\left(\frac{4}{\cancel{3}}\cancel{\pi} r^{\cancel{3}^1}\right)}{\cancel{\pi} \, \cancel{r}^{\cancel{2}}}$$
$$h = 4r$$
$$\frac{h}{r} = 4$$

Section 4: Math Test—CALCULATOR ▦

1. C	**9.** A	**17.** C	**25.** B	**33.** 36
2. B	**10.** C	**18.** B	**26.** C	**34.** 800
3. B	**11.** B	**19.** A	**27.** B	**35.** 3.75
4. C	**12.** B	**20.** B	**28.** B	**36.** 29
5. A	**13.** A	**21.** A	**29.** D	**37.** 1 or 3
6. B	**14.** C	**22.** B	**30.** A	**38.** 3.32
7. D	**15.** A	**23.** A	**31.** 2.5	
8. B	**16.** C	**24.** C	**32.** 9	

MATH TEST—CALCULATOR RAW SCORE ☐
(Number of correct answers)

1. **The correct answer is C.** We must first determine how many feet the insect travels in an average month. Then we can determine how many months it will take for the insect to travel 560 feet. To determine the number of feet the insect travels per month, we divide the yearly total by 12:

$$\frac{1,680}{12} = 140$$

The insect travels 140 feet each month. To determine how many months it would take the insect to travel 560 feet, we divide the total number of feet (560) by the number of feet that the insect travels in a month (140):

$$\frac{560}{140} = 4$$

Traveling at a rate of 140 feet per month, it would take the insect 4 months to travel 560 feet.

2. **The correct answer is B.** The question asks for the number of books that will be renewed if the library loans 25,000 books. Use a proportion to solve. Note that 18 of 75 (= 18 + 46 + 11) books were renewed in one day.

$$\frac{18}{75} = \frac{x}{25,000}$$

$$75x = 18(25,000)$$

$$x = \frac{18(25,000)}{75}$$

$$x = 6,000$$

3. **The correct answer is B.** The number of males in Littletown is 210, and the number of females in Smalltown is 195. The probability of choosing a male who lives in Littletown is $\frac{210}{785}$, and the probability of choosing a woman who lives in Smalltown is $\frac{195}{785}$. The probability of choosing one or the other is the sum of the individual probabilities:

$$\frac{210}{785} + \frac{195}{785} = \frac{405}{785} = \frac{81}{157}$$

4. **The correct answer is C.** The median is 2.5. When, as in this case, there is an even number of values in a data set, we average the two middle values after listing all of the values from smallest to largest. In the case of the sixty students, the thirtieth number in the list will be 2, because there are 12 *1*'s and

18 2's. The next value on the list, the thirty-first, is 3. So, the median is $\frac{2+3}{2} = 2.5.$ The mode is 2, the most frequent value. We know this because 18 is the largest number in the column on the right. Hence, the median, 2.5, is greater than the mode, 2.

5. **The correct answer is A.** The total amount that Glen earns in one day is 10.25h where h is the number of hours Glen works, and 3(12.50) is three times what he spends commuting. If he wants to earn at least three times what he spends commuting, then the inequality in choice A is the only answer that represents the situation.

6. **The correct answer is B.** If Peter spent x hours, then Nadia spent $x + 7$ hours on math homework, and together they spent $x + (x + 7) = 35$ hours. Solve for x:

$$x + (x + 7) = 35$$
$$2x + 7 = 35$$
$$2x = 28$$
$$x = 14$$

7. **The correct answer is D.** Since c is 22 percent of e, c equals ($e \times 0.22$), or $c = 0.22e$. Likewise, because d is 68 percent of e, d equals ($e \times 0.68$), or $d = 0.68e$. To find the value of $d - c$ in terms of e, we can set up an equation:

$$d - c = (0.68e - 0.22e)$$
$$d - c = 0.46e$$

8. **The correct answer is B.** Graph the inequalities and look for where they overlap, or substitute each point into both inequalities to determine which point satisfies both inequalities.

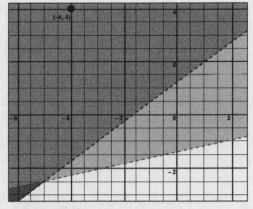

Only choice B is correct:

$$2x - 9y < 12 \qquad -3x + 4y > 5$$
$$2(-4) - 9(4) < 12 \qquad -3(-4) + 4(4) > 5$$
$$-8 - 36 < 12 \qquad 12 + 16 > 5$$

9. **The correct answer is A.** The question is just asking us to substitute the value that we are given for n and then to simplify the expression. We're asked to provide an answer in terms of m or, in other words, an answer that contains the variable m. Let's see what we get when we substitute 7 for n:

$$2m(16 - 6n) = 2m\left[16 - 6(7)\right]$$
$$= 2m(16 - 42)$$
$$= 2m(-26)$$
$$= -52m$$

10. **The correct answer is C.** The total amount that she has raised is $145. If she gets $15 from each additional donor, then the total contributions will be equal to 145 + 15x, where x is the number of contributions she gets from this point forward.

11. **The correct answer is B.** Read the graph and look for where the line has a vertical coordinate of $400. The closest approximation is 58 hats.

12. **The correct answer is B.** The x-axis of the graph shows the number of hats sold, and the y-axis shows the amount of money raised. Consequently, the slope of the line shows the amount of money received per hat.

Answers | Practice Test 1

13. The correct answer is A. A sample size of 18 people is not large enough to make a conclusion for a city of 38,000. The sample population was randomly selected, the size of the city population alone doesn't affect the reliability, and the number of people with no preference does not affect the reliability.

14. The correct answer is C. When the mean and median of a set of data are not the same, outliers tend to affect the mean more than the median. If some income values are much greater than the others, the mean will be greater than the median.

15. The correct answer is A. The amount of CDs sold would be equal to the number of days in the sale (j) times the number of neighbors (h) times the average number of CDs sold by each neighbor each day (x), or jhx. To determine the number of CDs that will be left after the total number of CDs, (jhx), are sold, we subtract jhx from 1,230. This value can be expressed as $1,230 - jhx$.

16. The correct answer is C. The formula that is useful for this problem is the formula for projectile motion: $y = 0.5at^2 + vt + h$, where a is the acceleration, v is the upward velocity, h is the initial height, t is the time in seconds, and y is the height after t seconds. Here, the coefficient, v, equals 50, so the correct answer must be choice C.

17. The correct answer is C. First, write equations that represent the price for each company. Then let the price from Company J be less than the price for Company K and solve the inequality.

$$\text{Company J} = 0.15x + 19$$
$$\text{Company K} = 0.10x + 30$$

$$0.15x + 19 < 0.1x + 30$$
$$0.05x < 11$$
$$x < 220$$

18. The correct answer is B. The daily rental cost for the truck is the y-intercept. The slope of the graph of this relationship is the per-mile cost. The total cost for the miles driven is $0.12x$. The total cost for driving the truck the entire distance is $0.12x + 25$.

19. The correct answer is A. To find the conditional probability that a randomly chosen house in Town B is a colonial house, first find the total number of houses that are in Town B:

$$62 + 65 + 43 + 32 = 202$$

Then write and simplify a ratio of colonial houses in Town B to the total number of houses in Town B in the survey:

$$\frac{65}{202}$$

20. The correct answer is B. Reduce the set of outcomes under consideration to only those houses that are either Cape Cod or Ranch; this gives a total of $53 + 43 + 75 + 62 = 233$ outcomes. Of these, $62 + 43 = 105$ are from Town B. So the probability is $\frac{105}{233}$.

21. The correct answer is A. Set $f(x)$ equal to $g(x)$ and solve the equation that results to get the x-coordinates of the points of intersection:

$$b^2 - (x + a)^2 = (x + a)^2 - b^2$$
$$2b^2 = 2(x + a)^2$$
$$b^2 = (x + a)^2$$
$$\pm b = x + a$$
$$x = -a \pm b$$

So the x-coordinates are $-a - b$ and $-a + b$. The difference between these two numbers is:

$$(-a + b) - (-a - b) = -a + b + a + b = 2b$$

22. The correct answer is B. The key to solving this geometry problem is to recognize that the figure contains two similar triangles. We know that the triangles are similar because their corresponding angles are equal ($x = x$,

$y = y$) and the two right angles at point Q are equal. Since the triangles have equal corresponding angles, we know that the sides are in proportion to one another.

We want to determine the ratio between the corresponding sides in the larger triangle, SQR, and the smaller triangle, TQP. We can do this by comparing the two corresponding sides for which we have measures. We're given the length of QP in the smaller triangle as 11.5. We're also given the length of its corresponding leg from the larger triangle, QR, as 46. How many times larger is QR than QP? If we divide 46 by 11.5, we see that QR is 4 times larger than QP.

The question asks us to determine the length of SQ, which is a side of the larger triangle, SQR. We know that the measure of its corresponding side in the smaller triangle, TQP, is TQ, which measures 15. We also know that all corresponding sides in the larger triangle, SQR, are 4 times longer than the ones in the smaller triangle, TQP, so SQ measures 4 times longer than TQ, or $4 \times 15 = 60$.

23. **The correct answer is A.** First, rewrite the equation as a quadratic one:

$$1 = \frac{3}{x-4} + \frac{4}{x-3}$$
$$(x-3)(x-4) = (x-3)(x-4)\left[\frac{3}{x-4} + \frac{4}{x-3}\right]$$
$$x^2 - 7x + 12 = 3x - 9 + 4x - 16$$
$$x^2 - 14x + 37 = 0$$

Now use the quadratic formula with $a = 1$, $b = -14$, and $c = 37$ to simplify:

$$x = \frac{14 \pm \sqrt{(-14)^2 - 4(37)}}{2}$$

$$x = \frac{14 \pm \sqrt{196 - 148}}{2}$$

$$x = 7 \pm 2\sqrt{3}$$

24. **The correct answer is C.** Use the circumference of the circle to find the radius.

$$C = 2\pi r$$
$$572\pi = 2\pi r$$
$$286 = r$$

Then use the measure of the central angle and the radius to find the area of the sector. The area of a sector is the product of the ratio

$$\frac{\text{measure of the central angle in radians}}{2\pi}$$

and the area of the circle:

$$A = \frac{\frac{3\pi}{4}}{2\pi}\pi\left(r\right)^2$$
$$A = \frac{3}{8}\pi\left(286\right)^2$$
$$A = \frac{61,347\pi}{2}$$

25. **The correct answer is B.** If $w < -1$ and $v > 1$, then the x-intercepts of the graph must be greater than 1 and less than -1. Choice D is incorrect because the graph shows an x-intercept exactly at $(-1, 0)$.

26. **The correct answer is C.** If you try values of a that are (1) less than zero, (2) greater than zero but less than 2.5, and (3) greater than 2.5, then you will be able to select the correct answer from among the choices provided. To graph more easily, note that the line corresponding to the first inequality is $y = \left(\frac{2}{5}\right)x - \frac{6}{5}$, and the line corresponding to the second inequality is $y = \left(-\frac{1}{a}\right)x - \frac{3}{a}$. The cases where $a = -1$, $a = 1$, and $a = 6$ are shown at the end of this explanation. Only in the second graph, where $a = 1$, is the dark-gray solution completely within quadrants II and III (left of the y-axis). So among the choices, $0 \leq a \leq 2.5$ must be correct.

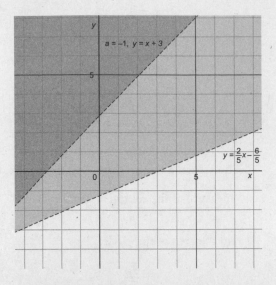

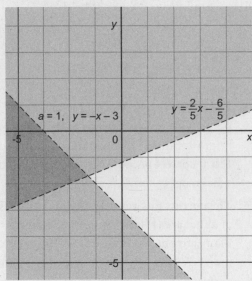

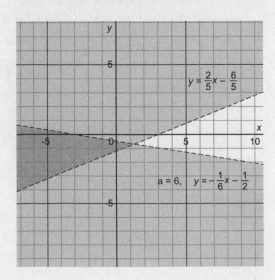

27. **The correct answer is B.** There are five dots to the left of a vertical line drawn upward from the 10,000K mark on the horizontal axis. Notice that the scale increases from right to left.

28. **The correct answer is B.** A horizontal line drawn through the mark at 1 on the vertical scale meets the line of best fit at a point closest to 5,000 on the horizontal axis. (The actual surface temperature of the sun is about 5,800K.)

29. **The correct answer is D.** The 95% confidence that the margin of error is ± 4% is important, and choices A and B ignore the confidence interval. Choice C is not correct because there are likely people who don't know or have no opinion on whether there should be stricter emissions standards for power plants. Only choice D accurately uses the confidence interval and the data given in the problem.

30. **The correct answer is A.** Use completing the square to find the coordinates of the center of the circle. Separate the equation x- and y-terms:

$$x^2 + y^2 - 10x + 4y = -20$$
$$x^2 - 10x + y^2 + 4y = -20$$
$$\left(x^2 - 10x + 25\right) + \left(y^2 + 4y + 4\right) = -20 + 25 + 4$$
$$\left(x - 5\right)^2 + \left(y + 2\right)^2 = 9$$

The center is (5, –2) because the standard form of the circle is $(x - h)^2 + (y - k)^2 = r^2$.

31. **The correct answer is 2.5.** Write an equation to represent the situation, and then solve:

$$16.25 = 2.5\left(2\right) + 4.5x$$
$$11.25 = 4.5x$$
$$2.5 = x$$

32. **The correct answer is 9.** Solve for the expression requested in the inequality, then interpret the answer in the context of the question asked:

$$4s - 3 < 2$$
$$4s < 5$$
$$s < \frac{5}{4}$$

We want an integer value for s that will maximize the value of $4s + 5$. The greatest integer less than $\frac{5}{4}$ is 1. Substitute 1 for s:

$$4s + 5 = 4(1) + 5 = 9$$

33. **The correct answer is 36.** Use the method of combination to determine the values of a and b. Start by subtracting the first equation from the second equation:

$$2a + 2b = 16$$
$$-\left(2a - b\right) = -\left(7\right)$$
$$\overline{\qquad\qquad\qquad}$$
$$3b = 9$$
$$b = 3$$

Insert $b = 3$ into the first equation:

$$2a - \left(3\right) = 7$$
$$2a = 10$$
$$a = 5$$

Now you are ready to plug both values into the expression in question:

$$3a + 7b = 3\left(5\right) + 7\left(3\right)$$
$$= 15 + 21$$
$$= 36$$

34. **The correct answer is 800.** The formula for population growth is given in terms of n, the number of years. In order to solve this problem, plug the value of n, in this case 54,

into the formula and calculate the value of the expression $100(2)^{\frac{n}{18}}$:

$$\text{Population (in millions) after } n \text{ years} = 100(2)^{\frac{n}{18}}$$
$$= 100(2)^{\frac{54}{18}}$$
$$= 100(2)^{3}$$
$$= 800$$

35. **The correct answer is 3.75.** Read the question carefully; it asks for the difference in the prices of one object, not the difference between the amounts of money they made, or any other quantity.

Since Paul sold four pieces of pottery for $85, he made $y = \frac{85}{4} = \$21.25$ per piece. Sally made $40 more than Paul did for all of her pieces, so she made $85 + $40 = $125 in total. Since she sold five pieces, she made $x = \frac{125}{5} = \$25.00$ per piece. Per piece, Sally made $x - y = \$25 - \$21.25 = \$3.75$ more than Paul did. The correct answer is 3.75.

36. **The correct answer is 29.** First, find the number of scarves knitted last year using a percent proportion. Then add 4 to find this year's new total.

$$\frac{16}{100} = \frac{4}{x}$$
$$16x = 400$$
$$x = \frac{400}{16}$$
$$x = 25$$
$$25 + 4 = 29$$

37. The correct answer is 1 or 3. First, combine the equations by substituting $2x + 5$ for y in the second equation. Then solve for x. Next, substitute the x-values back in and solve for y:

$$2x + 5 = -2(x + 1)^2 + 3$$
$$2x + 5 = -2x^2 - 4x - 2 + 3$$
$$0 = -2x^2 - 6x - 4$$
$$0 = -2(x + 2)(x + 1)$$
$$x = -1, -2$$
$$y = 2(-1) + 5 = 3$$
$$\text{or}$$
$$y = 2(-2) + 5 = 1$$

38. The correct answer is 3.32. Let x be the GPA for the year 2019. Compute the average of 3.5, 3.5, 3.5, 3.5, 3.5, and x:

$$\frac{3.5(5) + x}{6} = 3.47$$
$$17.5 + x = 20.82$$
$$x = 3.32$$

Practice Test 1

Section 5: Essay

Analysis of Passage

The following is an analysis of the passage by Catherine Anderson, noting how the writer used evidence, reasoning, and stylistic or persuasive elements to support her claims, connect the claims and evidence, and add power to the ideas she expressed. Check to see if you evaluated the passage in a similar way.

1. Visit the website of designer Michael Graves, and you'll be greeted with the words "Humanistic Design = Transformative Results."

   1. *Anderson lays the groundwork for the validity of her argument by referring the reader to an authoritative source on this subject—the website of Michael Graves.*

2. The mantra can double as Graves' philosophy. For Graves—who passed away at 80 earlier this month—paid no heed to architectural trends, social movements or the words of his critics.

   2. *The writer uses evocative words and phrases such as "mantra," "double as," "philosophy," "paid no heed," and "trends."*

3. Instead, it was the everyday human being—the individual—who inspired and informed his work.

   3. *The writer clearly states her central argument.*

4. During a career that spanned over 50 years, Graves held firm to the belief that design could effect tremendous change in people's day-to-day lives. From small-scale kitchen products to immense buildings, a thread runs throughout his products: accessible, aesthetic forms that possess a sense of warmth and appeal.

   4. *Anderson continues using evocative phrases: "held firm," "effect tremendous change," "immense buildings," "a thread runs throughout," a "sense of warmth and appeal."*

5. Early in his career, Graves was identified as one of the New York Five, a group of influential architects who whole-heartedly embraced Modernism, the architectural movement that subscribed to the use of simple, clean lines, forms devoid of embellishments and modern materials such as steel and glass.

   5. *She provides historical context by discussing Graves' early career and establishing his status as a Modernist architect. She also defines Modernism for the reader.*

6. However, Graves is best described as a Post-Modernist.

   6. *The writer expands her historical context by claiming that Graves was really a Post-Modernist. She then explains exactly what this means.*

7. He eschewed the austerity of Modernism and its belief that "less is more," instead embracing history and references to the past.

   7. *The writer uses evocative phrases to paint pictures for the reader: "eschewed the austerity," "embracing history," "rejected the notion."*

8   He rejected the notion that decoration, or ornament, was a "crime" (as Austrian architect Adolf Loos wrote in 1908); rather, he viewed it as a way for his architecture to convey meaning.

8   *Anderson enlivens her writing with a vivid word (crime) used by an authority and cites her source.*

9   As the noted architectural historian Spiro Kostof explains in his book *A History of Architecture: Settings and Rituals*, "Post Modernists turn to historical memory …to ornament, as a way of enriching the language of architecture."

9   *Anderson quotes an authoritative source to support her claim that Graves was a Post-Modernist.*

10 …Along these lines, Graves

10 *The writer builds on this quotation to advance her argument that Graves was a Post-Modernist.*

11 loathed the idea of intellectualizing his structures. Instead, he sought to make them accessible, understandable and poignant to all passersby. …

11 *The writer uses evocative phrases to make her argument vivid: "loathed the idea," "intellectualizing his structures," "poignant to all passersby."*

12 In addition to designing buildings, Graves embarked upon a long and highly successful partnership with the Italian kitchenware company Alessi …

12 *Anderson points out that Graves did more than design buildings, mentioning his partnership with the Italian kitchenware company Alessi.*

13 Graves' most famous Alessi design is his iconic teakettle … which had a cheerful red whistling bird and sky-blue handle. On sale since 1985, the best-selling product is still in production today.

13 *She also mentions one of Graves' famous creations for Alessi and points out that it sold extremely well.*

14 In 1999, Minneapolis-based discount retail giant Target approached Graves with an offer to design a line of kitchen products, ranging from toasters to spatulas.

14 *Continuing her discussion of Graves' non-architectural creations, the writer refers to his work designing kitchen products for Target.*

15 While some might have shied away from having their work associated with a mega-corporation like Target, Graves wholly embraced the project….

15 *The writer anticipates a possible negative reaction to this work, pointing out that Graves "embraced" it.*

16 In all, Graves' collaboration with Target would last 13 years; during this time, the designer would become a household name, with millions of units of his products appearing in American homes.

16 *Anderson legitimizes Graves' work with Target, saying his creations sold millions of units and that he became "a household name."*

Practice Test 1

17 Many of Graves' designs for Target—his spatula, can opener and ice cream scoop—had chunky, sky-blue handles. Other appliances that were white . . . were sprinkled with touches of color. ... Black and beige had no place in Graves' palette.

18 The option to select a better-looking product with a slightly higher price versus the same article but with a less expensive, nondescript appearance is now the norm for most consumers: good design (and function) are part and parcel of the customer experience

19 (nowhere is this more evident than in Apple's rise to dizzying heights as arguably one of the world's most valuable brands).

20 It's an idea that's democratic in nature, and thinking about design through this lens led Graves to create thoughtful, appealing and affordable products for the masses. …

21 As Graves' popularity rose, his critics leveled

22 blistering commentaries about what they deemed a precipitous fall from grace—from a "trend beyond compare" to a "stale trend," as

23 architecture critic Herbert Muschamp noted in a 1999 *New York Times* article. The notion that he had commodified design—and had somehow "cheapened" it—drew the disdain of those who once lauded his works.

17 *She gives the reader a strong sense of Graves' practical, everyday Target creations, naming specific products and describing what they looked like.*

18 *Anderson cites the significance of Graves' work with Target, pointing out that better design in everyday products has become the norm.*

19 *She supports this claim by citing Apple as an example of a company that routinely offers customers good design in its products.*

20 *The writer reasserts the importance of Graves' place in the movement to create "affordable products for the masses."*

21 *The writer provides historical context to trace the negative reaction to Graves' work with Target.*

22 *She brings this reaction to life using evocative phrases: "blistering commentaries, precipitous fall from grace, commodified design, drew the disdain of those who once lauded his works."*

23 *The writer cites a source to support her claim that there was a negative reaction to Graves' Target products.*

24 Yet Graves remained true to his beliefs even into the last phase of his life. In 2003, after an illness left him paralyzed below the waist, he realized that the design of hospitals and equipment . . . could be redesigned and made more functional, comfortable and visually appealing. He then went on to improve ubiquitous devices such as wheelchairs and walking canes. . . .

24 *Anderson provides additional historical context for Graves' later designs for common things and gives specific examples.*

25 Consumers may not have ever known his architecture or what the critics thought of his work (or even realized they were buying one of his products). Graves didn't seem to mind. His goal was to provide well-designed items for everyday use rather than impress his detractors.

25 *The writer provides psychological insight into Graves' personality and reasserts his primary goal: "to provide well-designed items for everyday use."*

26 As he told NPR in 2002, "It's the kind of thing where you pick something up or use it with a little bit of joy … it puts a smile on your

26 *The writer concludes her argument with a quotation from Graves that supports her claim that his primary concern was quality design for the everyday human being.*

Scoring Rubric

Use the following scoring rubric as a guide to help you evaluate the sample essays that follow. Then, read and evaluate your own essay for each scoring category. Assign your essay a score between 1 and 4 for each category (Reading, Analysis, and Writing). Next, double each score to simulate that the essay was scored twice. You will now have three scores ranging from 2 to 8 for each category. These are not combined.

Score Point	Reading	Analysis	Writing
4 (Advanced)	The essay shows a comprehensnjive understanding of the source text, including the author's key claims, use of details and evidence, and the relationship between the two.	The essay offers an "insightful" and in-depth evaluation of the author's use of evidence and stylistic or persuasive features in building an argument. Supporting details and evidence are relevant and focus on those details that address the task.	The essay includes all of the features of a strong essay, including a precise central claim, body paragraphs, and a strong conclusion. There is a variety of sentence structures used in the essay, and it is virtually free of all convention errors.
3 (Proficient)	The essay shows an appropriate understanding of the source text, including the author's key claims and use of details in developing an argument.	The essay offers an "effective" evaluation of the author's use of evidence and stylistic or persuasive features in building an argument. Supporting details and evidence are appropriate and focus on those details that address the task.	The essay includes all of the features of an effective essay, including a precise central claim, body paragraphs, and a strong conclusion. There is a variety of sentence structures used in the essay, and it is free of significant convention errors.
2 (Partial)	The essay shows some understanding of the source text, including the author's key claims, but uses limited textual evidence and/or unimportant details.	The essay offers limited evaluation of the author's use of evidence and stylistic or persuasive features in building an argument. Supporting details and evidence are lacking and/or are not relevant to the task.	The essay does not provide a precise central claim, nor does it provide an effective introduction, body paragraphs, and conclusion. There is little variety of sentence structure used in the essay, and there are numerous errors in grammar and conventions.
1 (Inadequate)	The essay demonstrates little or no understanding of the source text or the author's use of key claims.	The essay offers no clear evaluation of the author's use of evidence and stylistic or persuasive features in building an argument. Supporting details and evidence are nonexistent or irrelevant to the task.	The essay lacks any form of cohesion or structure. There is little variety of sentence structures, and significant errors in convention make it difficult to read.

Sample Essays

The following are examples of a high-scoring and low-scoring essay, based on the passage by Catherine Anderson.

High-Scoring Essay

Catherine Anderson is clearly a fan of Michael Graves's architecture and product design. Anderson identifies the everyday human being as Graves's inspiration. She gives a history of Graves' work, explaining how his focus on people inspired him. Anderson's word choices and descriptions bring Graves's products to life. Anderson's words are as warm and appealing as the products she describes. Supporting her descriptions with a history of Graves's designs and biographical details convinces readers to admire the products he designed and, perhaps, to buy one that fits in their own kitchens.

Anderson tells readers that Graves's career started as an architect in New York 50 years ago. She provides historical context by identifying Graves as one of an elite group of Modernist architects who designed simple, plain buildings constructed of the modern materials steel and glass. Because her description of Modernist architecture sounds cold and empty, Anderson hastens to say that Graves was actually a Post-Modernist architect whose creations were less plain and more inviting. He used embellishments in his architectural designs to convey meaning, which sounds more warm and comforting than the Modernist architectural style she described with the words *plain*, *steel and glass*, and *austerity*.

To support her statements, Anderson cites a well-known architectural expert who describes Post-Modernist architecture as enriched by ornamentation. She then uses appealing words to attract readers to Graves's work—*accessible*, *understandable*, and *poignant*.

Graves didn't design architecture only. He also designed common items, such as teakettles and spatulas, for common people. His most famous design is a quirky teakettle that has a sky-blue handle and a bright red bird that whistles when the water is hot enough to make tea. Just the image Anderson created of the whistling bird on the teakettle makes Graves's work sound fun and appealing. The kitchen products Graves designed are sold by Target, a store where the people who inspired Graves could afford to shop. They must be buying his products because millions of them have been purchased at Target and are still selling today.

While Graves's popularity rose among Target shoppers, it dropped among architecture critics. Anderson informs readers of the critics' changing attitudes by quoting their comments such as "stale trend" and "cheapened." Graves, however, heroically "remained true to his beliefs" by continuing to design attractive products that could be bought by average people.

In 2003 an illness made Graves a paraplegic. Instead of becoming bitter, like many people would have in the same situation, Graves looked around at the poorly designed medical products and decided that he could make improvements. Even a hospital environment benefited from his design abilities. He created products, such as wheelchairs and canes, that Anderson said were "more functional, comfortable and visually attractive."

Anderson closed the article by quoting Graves's comment that he hoped his products would make people smile. Anderson showed that throughout his life, Graves's main concern was creating designs for the average person. Just as he had hoped, his products have inspired, and continue to inspire, joy in the people who inspired him—especially when making tea.

Low-Scoring Essay

Catherine Anderson started the article by focusing on Michael Graves's mantra of "Humanistic Design = Transformative Results." This means that focusing on people can make things better.

Michael Graves focused on people to design buildings and things they could use like teakettles and wheelchairs. Because Michael Graves likes people, he designed things that they would like, things that would make them happy.

Catherine Anderson says his products are warm and appealing. She describes a teakettle that's fun to use because it whistles. The buildings he designed have historical meaning because he added a lot of decorations. He said it's not a crime to build decorated buildings.

Michael Graves worked with Alessi to design attractive kitchen products that people liked a lot, like the whistling teakettle. He used warm colors like red to make it more appealing. Catherine Anderson describes his kitchen products as "chunky" and colorful. This makes them sound like things everyone would want to have. Because millions were sold at Target, he probably made a lot of money on them. That's a good reason to ignore the critics who didn't like his designs. The critics said his kitchen products were "stale," which is a clever food-related way to say they were old and boring. Regardless of the critics, his stuff is popular.

Michael Graves was pretty old when he got sick and couldn't walk. Because he couldn't walk, he designed wheelchairs and canes that he and other people could use. Catherine Anderson says they're "functional, comfortable and visually appealing." If Target sold them, they would probably be as popular as his teakettle.

Michael Graves died in 2015 when he was 80 years old. His buildings and products followed his mantra of "Humanistic Design = Transformative Results." He made things better by focusing on people. He improved a lot of things that he designed and made a lot of people happy. Catherine Anderson proved that the things he made were attractive and made people happy.

COMPUTING YOUR SCORES

Now that you've completed this practice test, it's time to compute your scores. Simply follow the instructions on the following pages, and use the conversion tables provided to calculate your scores. The formulas provided will give you as close an approximation as possible of how you might score on the actual SAT exam.

To Determine Your Practice Test Scores

1. After you go through each of the test sections (Reading, Writing and Language, Math—No Calculator, and Math—Calculator) and determine which answers you got right, be sure to enter the number of correct answers in the box below the answer key for each of the sections.

2. Your total score on the practice test is the sum of your Evidence-Based Reading and Writing Section score and your Math Section score. To get your total score, convert the raw score—the number of questions you got right in a particular section—into the "scaled score" for that section, and then you'll calculate the total score. It sounds a little confusing, but we'll take you through the steps.

To Calculate Your Evidence-Based Reading and Writing Section Score

Your Evidence-Based Reading and Writing Section score is on a scale of 200–800. First determine your Reading Test score, and then determine your score on the Writing and Language Test.

1. Count the number of correct answers you got on the **Section 1: Reading Test.** Remember that there is no penalty for wrong answers. **The number of correct answers is your raw score.**

2. Go to **Raw Score Conversion Table 1: Section and Test Scores** on page 684. Look in the "Raw Score" column for your raw score, and match it to the number in the "Reading Test Score" column.

3. Do the same with **Section 2: Writing and Language Test** to determine that score.

4. Add your Reading Test score to your Writing and Language Test score.

5. Multiply that number by 10. This is your Evidence-Based Reading and Writing Section score.

To Calculate Your Math Section Score

Your Math score is also on a scale of 200–800.

1. Count the number of correct answers you got on the questions in **Section 3: Math Test—No Calculator** and **Section 4: Math Test—No Calculator**. Again, there is no penalty for wrong answers. **The number of correct answers is your raw score.**

2. Add the number of correct answers on the Section 3: Math Test—No Calculator and the Section 4: Math Test—No Calculator.

3. Use the **Raw Score Conversion Table 1: Section and Test Scores** on page 684 and convert your raw score into your Math Section score.

To Obtain Your Total Score

Add your score on the Evidence-Based Reading and Writing Section to the Math Section score. This is your total score on this Practice Test, on a scale of 400–1600.

Subscores Provide Additional Information

Subscores offer you greater details about your strengths in certain areas within literacy and math. The subscores are reported on a scale of 1–15 and include Heart of Algebra, Problem Solving and Data Analysis, Passport to Advanced Math, Expression of Ideas, Standard English Conventions, Words in Context, and Command of Evidence.

Heart of Algebra

The **Heart of Algebra subscore** is based on questions from the **Math Test** sections that focus on linear equations and inequalities.

- Add up your total correct answers from these sections:
  - Math Test—No Calculator: Questions 1, 6, 7, 11, 13, 14, 17, 19
  - Math Test—Calculator: Questions 6–8, 10, 15, 17, 18, 26, 31–33
- Your Raw Score = the total number of correct answers from all of these questions.
- Use the **Raw Score Conversion Table 2: Subscores** on page 686 to determine your **Heart of Algebra** subscore.

Problem Solving and Data Analysis

The **Problem Solving and Data Analysis subscore** is based on questions from the **Math Test** that focus on quantitative reasoning, interpretation and synthesis of data, and solving problems in rich and varied contexts.

- Add up your total correct answers from these questions:
  - Math Test—No Calculator: None
  - Math Test—Calculator: Questions 1–5, 11–14, 19, 20, 27–29, 35, 36, 38
- Your Raw Score = the total number of correct answers from all of these questions.
- Use the **Raw Score Conversion Table 2: Subscores** on page 686 to determine your **Problem Solving and Data Analysis** subscore.

Passport to Advanced Math

The **Passport to Advanced Math subscore** is based on questions from the **Math Test** that focus on topics central to your ability to progress to more advanced math, such as understanding the structure of expressions, reasoning with more complex equations, and interpreting and building functions.

- Add up your total correct answers from these questions:
  - Math Test—No Calculator: 2, 3, 5, 8–10, 15, 16, 18
  - Math Test—Calculator: Questions 9, 16, 21, 23, 25, 34, 37
- Your Raw Score = the total number of correct answers from all of these questions.
- Use the **Raw Score Conversion Table 2: Subscores** on page 686 to determine your **Passport to Advanced Math** subscore.

Expression of Ideas

The **Expression of Ideas subscore** is based on questions from the **Writing and Language Test** that focus on topic development, organization, and rhetorically effective use of language.

- Add up your total correct answers from these questions in Section 2: Writing and Language Test:

  - Questions 1, 2, 5, 6, 10–13, 16, 17, 19, 20, 26, 27, 29, 30, 32, 33, 37, 39, 41, 43, 44

- Your Raw Score = the total number of correct answers from all of these questions.

- Use the **Raw Score Conversion Table 2: Subscores** on page 686 to determine your **Expression of Ideas** subscore.

Standard English Conventions

The **Standard English Conventions subscore** is based on questions from the **Writing and Language Test** that focus on sentence structure, **usage**, and punctuation.

- Add up your total correct answers from these questions in Section 2: Writing and Language Test:

  - Questions 3, 4, 7–9, 14, 15, 18, 21–25, 28, 31, 35, 36, 38, 40, 42

- Your Raw Score = the total number of correct answers from all of these questions.

- Use the **Raw Score Conversion Table 2: Subscores** on page 686 to determine your **Standard English Conventions** subscore.

Words in Context

The **Words in Context subscore** is based on questions from the **Reading Test** and the **Writing and Language Test** that address word/phrase meaning in context and rhetorical word choice.

- Add up your total correct answers from these questions in Sections 1 and 2:

  - Reading Test: Questions 2, 10, 18, 19, 23, 26, 36, 39, 49, 50

  - Writing and Language Test: Questions 2, 6, 17, 20, 26, 30, 39, 44

- Your Raw Score = the total number of correct answers from all of these questions.

- Use the **Raw Score Conversion Table 2: Subscores** on page 686 to determine your **Words in Context** subscore.

Command of Evidence

The **Command of Evidence subscore** is based on questions from the **Reading Test** and the **Writing and Language Test** that ask you to interpret and use evidence found in a wide range of passages and informational graphics, such as graphs, tables, and charts.

- Add up your total correct answers from Sections 1 and 2:

  - Reading Test: Questions 5, 9, 14, 17, 25, 29, 34, 38, 45, 52

  - Writing and Language Test: Questions 5, 11, 12, 19, 27, 32, 37, 43

- Your Raw Score = the total number of correct answers from all of these questions.

- Use the **Raw Score Conversion Table 2: Subscores** on page 686 to determine your **Command of Evidence** subscore.

Practice Test 1

Cross-Test Scores

The SAT exam also reports two cross-test scores: Analysis in History/Social Studies and Analysis in Science. These scores are based on questions in the Reading Test, Writing and Language Test, and both Math Tests that ask you to think analytically about texts and questions in these subject areas. Cross-test scores are reported on a scale of 10–40.

Analysis in History/Social Studies

- Add up your total correct answers from these questions:

  ○ Reading Test: Questions 11–20, 32–42

  ○ Writing and Language Test: Questions 26, 27, 29, 30, 32, 33

  ○ Math Test—No Calculator: Question 14

  ○ Math Test—Calculator: Questions 4, 13, 14, 19, 20, 29, 38

- Your Raw Score = the total number of correct answers from all of these questions.

- Use the **Raw Score Conversion Table 3: Cross-Test Scores** on page 688 to determine your **Analysis in History/Social Studies** cross-test score.

Analysis in Science

- Add up your total correct answers from these questions:

  ○ Reading Test: Questions 21–31, 43–52

  ○ Writing and Language Test: Questions 12, 13, 16, 17, 19, 20

  ○ Math Test—No Calculator: Question 3

  ○ Math Test—Calculator: Questions 1, 3, 16, 24, 27, 28, 34

- Your Raw Score = the total number of correct answers from all of these questions.

- Use the **Raw Score Conversion Table 3: Cross-Test Scores** on page 688 to determine your **Analysis in Science** cross-test score.

Answers

Practice Test 1

Raw Score Conversion Table 1: Section and Test Scores

Raw Score	Math Section Score	Reading Test Score	Writing and Language Test Score	Raw Score	Math Section Score	Reading Test Score	Writing and Language Test Score	Raw Score	Math Section Score	Reading Test Score	Writing and Language Test Score
0	200	10	10	20	450	22	23	40	610	33	36
1	200	10	10	21	460	23	23	41	620	33	37
2	210	10	10	22	470	23	24	42	630	34	38
3	230	11	10	23	480	24	25	43	640	35	39
4	240	12	11	24	480	24	25	44	650	35	40
5	260	13	12	25	490	25	26	45	660	36	
6	280	14	13	26	500	25	26	46	670	37	
7	290	15	13	27	510	26	27	47	670	37	
8	310	15	14	28	520	26	28	48	680	38	
9	320	16	15	29	520	27	28	49	690	38	
10	330	17	16	30	530	28	29	50	700	39	
11	340	17	16	31	540	28	30	51	710	40	
12	360	18	17	32	550	29	30	52	730	40	
13	370	19	18	33	560	29	31	53	740		
14	380	19	19	34	560	30	32	54	750		
15	390	20	19	35	570	30	32	55	760		
16	410	20	20	36	580	31	33	56	780		
17	420	21	21	37	590	31	34	57	790		
18	430	21	21	38	600	32	34	58	800		
19	440	22	22	39	600	32	35				

Part VII

Conversion Equation 1: Section and Test Scores

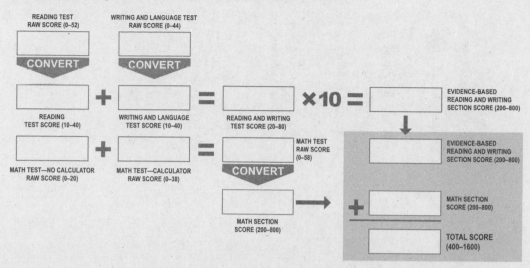

Raw Score Conversion Table 2: Subscores

Raw Score (# of correct answers)	Expression of Ideas	Standard English Conventions	Heart of Algebra	Problem Solving and Data Analysis	Passport to Advanced Math	Words in Context	Command of Evidence
0	1	1	1	1	1	1	1
1	1	1	1	1	3	1	1
2	1	1	2	2	5	2	2
3	2	2	3	3	6	3	3
4	3	2	4	4	7	4	4
5	4	3	5	5	8	5	5
6	5	4	6	6	9	6	6
7	6	5	6	7	10	6	7
8	6	6	7	8	11	7	8
9	7	6	8	8	11	8	8
10	7	7	8	9	12	8	9
11	8	7	9	10	12	9	10
12	8	8	9	10	13	9	10
13	9	8	9	11	13	10	11
14	9	9	10	12	14	11	12
15	10	10	10	13	14	12	13
16	10	10	11	14	15	13	14
17	11	11	12	15		14	15
18	11	12	13			15	15
19	12	13	15				
20	12	15					
21	13						
22	14						
23	14						
24	15						

Conversion Equation 2: Subscores

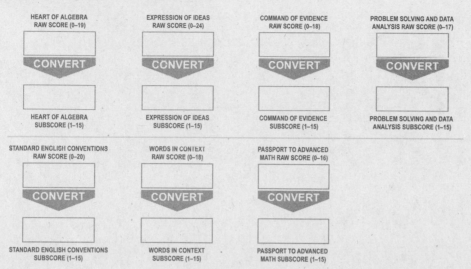

Raw Score Conversion Table 3: Cross-Test Scores

Raw Score (# of correct answers)	Analysis in History/ Social Studies Cross-Test Score	Analysis in Science Cross-Test Score	Raw Score (# of correct answers)	Analysis in History/ Social Studies Cross-Test Score	Analysis in Science Cross-Test Score
0	10	10	24	32	30
1	10	11	25	33	31
2	11	12	26	34	32
3	12	13	27	35	33
4	14	14	28	35	33
5	15	15	29	36	34
6	16	16	30	37	35
7	17	17	31	38	36
8	18	18	32	38	37
9	20	19	33	39	38
10	21	20	34	40	39
11	22	20	35	40	40
12	23	21			
13	24	22			
14	25	23			
15	26	24			
16	27	24			
17	28	25			
18	28	26			
19	29	27			
20	30	27			
21	30	28			
22	31	29			
23	32	30			

Practice Test 1

Conversion Equation 3: Cross-Test Scores

TEST	Analysis in History/Social Studies		Analysis in Science	
	QUESTIONS	RAW SCORE	QUESTIONS	RAW SCORE
Reading Test	11–20, 32–42		21–31, 43–52	
Writing and Language Test	26, 27–30, 32, 33		12, 13, 16, 17, 25, 19, 20	
Math Test— No Calculator	14		3	
Math Test— Calculator	3, 13, 14, 19, 20, 29, 38		1, 4, 16, 24, 27, 28, 34	
TOTAL				

ANALYSIS IN HISTORY/
SOCIAL STUDIES
RAW SCORE (0–35)

CONVERT

ANALYSIS IN HISTORY/
SOCIAL STUDIES
CROSS-TEST SCORE (10–40)

ANALYSIS IN SCIENCE
RAW SCORE (0–35)

CONVERT

ANALYSIS IN SCIENCE
CROSS-TEST SCORE (10–40)

Answers | Practice Test 1

PRACTICE TEST 2 ANSWER SHEET

Section I: Reading Test

1. Ⓐ Ⓑ Ⓒ Ⓓ
2. Ⓐ Ⓑ Ⓒ Ⓓ
3. Ⓐ Ⓑ Ⓒ Ⓓ
4. Ⓐ Ⓑ Ⓒ Ⓓ
5. Ⓐ Ⓑ Ⓒ Ⓓ
6. Ⓐ Ⓑ Ⓒ Ⓓ
7. Ⓐ Ⓑ Ⓒ Ⓓ
8. Ⓐ Ⓑ Ⓒ Ⓓ
9. Ⓐ Ⓑ Ⓒ Ⓓ
10. Ⓐ Ⓑ Ⓒ Ⓓ
11. Ⓐ Ⓑ Ⓒ Ⓓ
12. Ⓐ Ⓑ Ⓒ Ⓓ
13. Ⓐ Ⓑ Ⓒ Ⓓ

14. Ⓐ Ⓑ Ⓒ Ⓓ
15. Ⓐ Ⓑ Ⓒ Ⓓ
16. Ⓐ Ⓑ Ⓒ Ⓓ
17. Ⓐ Ⓑ Ⓒ Ⓓ
18. Ⓐ Ⓑ Ⓒ Ⓓ
19. Ⓐ Ⓑ Ⓒ Ⓓ
20. Ⓐ Ⓑ Ⓒ Ⓓ
21. Ⓐ Ⓑ Ⓒ Ⓓ
22. Ⓐ Ⓑ Ⓒ Ⓓ
23. Ⓐ Ⓑ Ⓒ Ⓓ
24. Ⓐ Ⓑ Ⓒ Ⓓ
25. Ⓐ Ⓑ Ⓒ Ⓓ
26. Ⓐ Ⓑ Ⓒ Ⓓ

27. Ⓐ Ⓑ Ⓒ Ⓓ
28. Ⓐ Ⓑ Ⓒ Ⓓ
29. Ⓐ Ⓑ Ⓒ Ⓓ
30. Ⓐ Ⓑ Ⓒ Ⓓ
31. Ⓐ Ⓑ Ⓒ Ⓓ
32. Ⓐ Ⓑ Ⓒ Ⓓ
33. Ⓐ Ⓑ Ⓒ Ⓓ
34. Ⓐ Ⓑ Ⓒ Ⓓ
35. Ⓐ Ⓑ Ⓒ Ⓓ
36. Ⓐ Ⓑ Ⓒ Ⓓ
37. Ⓐ Ⓑ Ⓒ Ⓓ
38. Ⓐ Ⓑ Ⓒ Ⓓ
39. Ⓐ Ⓑ Ⓒ Ⓓ

40. Ⓐ Ⓑ Ⓒ Ⓓ
41. Ⓐ Ⓑ Ⓒ Ⓓ
42. Ⓐ Ⓑ Ⓒ Ⓓ
43. Ⓐ Ⓑ Ⓒ Ⓓ
44. Ⓐ Ⓑ Ⓒ Ⓓ
45. Ⓐ Ⓑ Ⓒ Ⓓ
46. Ⓐ Ⓑ Ⓒ Ⓓ
47. Ⓐ Ⓑ Ⓒ Ⓓ
48. Ⓐ Ⓑ Ⓒ Ⓓ
49. Ⓐ Ⓑ Ⓒ Ⓓ
50. Ⓐ Ⓑ Ⓒ Ⓓ
51. Ⓐ Ⓑ Ⓒ Ⓓ
52. Ⓐ Ⓑ Ⓒ Ⓓ

Section II: Writing and Language Test

1. Ⓐ Ⓑ Ⓒ Ⓓ
2. Ⓐ Ⓑ Ⓒ Ⓓ
3. Ⓐ Ⓑ Ⓒ Ⓓ
4. Ⓐ Ⓑ Ⓒ Ⓓ
5. Ⓐ Ⓑ Ⓒ Ⓓ
6. Ⓐ Ⓑ Ⓒ Ⓓ
7. Ⓐ Ⓑ Ⓒ Ⓓ
8. Ⓐ Ⓑ Ⓒ Ⓓ
9. Ⓐ Ⓑ Ⓒ Ⓓ
10. Ⓐ Ⓑ Ⓒ Ⓓ
11. Ⓐ Ⓑ Ⓒ Ⓓ

12. Ⓐ Ⓑ Ⓒ Ⓓ
13. Ⓐ Ⓑ Ⓒ Ⓓ
14. Ⓐ Ⓑ Ⓒ Ⓓ
15. Ⓐ Ⓑ Ⓒ Ⓓ
16. Ⓐ Ⓑ Ⓒ Ⓓ
17. Ⓐ Ⓑ Ⓒ Ⓓ
18. Ⓐ Ⓑ Ⓒ Ⓓ
19. Ⓐ Ⓑ Ⓒ Ⓓ
20. Ⓐ Ⓑ Ⓒ Ⓓ
21. Ⓐ Ⓑ Ⓒ Ⓓ
22. Ⓐ Ⓑ Ⓒ Ⓓ

23. Ⓐ Ⓑ Ⓒ Ⓓ
24. Ⓐ Ⓑ Ⓒ Ⓓ
25. Ⓐ Ⓑ Ⓒ Ⓓ
26. Ⓐ Ⓑ Ⓒ Ⓓ
27. Ⓐ Ⓑ Ⓒ Ⓓ
28. Ⓐ Ⓑ Ⓒ Ⓓ
29. Ⓐ Ⓑ Ⓒ Ⓓ
30. Ⓐ Ⓑ Ⓒ Ⓓ
31. Ⓐ Ⓑ Ⓒ Ⓓ
32. Ⓐ Ⓑ Ⓒ Ⓓ
33. Ⓐ Ⓑ Ⓒ Ⓓ

34. Ⓐ Ⓑ Ⓒ Ⓓ
35. Ⓐ Ⓑ Ⓒ Ⓓ
36. Ⓐ Ⓑ Ⓒ Ⓓ
37. Ⓐ Ⓑ Ⓒ Ⓓ
38. Ⓐ Ⓑ Ⓒ Ⓓ
39. Ⓐ Ⓑ Ⓒ Ⓓ
40. Ⓐ Ⓑ Ⓒ Ⓓ
41. Ⓐ Ⓑ Ⓒ Ⓓ
42. Ⓐ Ⓑ Ⓒ Ⓓ
43. Ⓐ Ⓑ Ⓒ Ⓓ
44. Ⓐ Ⓑ Ⓒ Ⓓ

Section III: Math Test—NO CALCULATOR

1. Ⓐ Ⓑ Ⓒ Ⓓ
2. Ⓐ Ⓑ Ⓒ Ⓓ
3. Ⓐ Ⓑ Ⓒ Ⓓ
4. Ⓐ Ⓑ Ⓒ Ⓓ
5. Ⓐ Ⓑ Ⓒ Ⓓ

6. Ⓐ Ⓑ Ⓒ Ⓓ
7. Ⓐ Ⓑ Ⓒ Ⓓ
8. Ⓐ Ⓑ Ⓒ Ⓓ
9. Ⓐ Ⓑ Ⓒ Ⓓ
10. Ⓐ Ⓑ Ⓒ Ⓓ

11. Ⓐ Ⓑ Ⓒ Ⓓ
12. Ⓐ Ⓑ Ⓒ Ⓓ
13. Ⓐ Ⓑ Ⓒ Ⓓ
14. Ⓐ Ⓑ Ⓒ Ⓓ
15. Ⓐ Ⓑ Ⓒ Ⓓ

16.
17.
18.
19.
20.

Part VII

Practice Test 2

Section IV: Math Test—CALCULATOR

1. Ⓐ Ⓑ Ⓒ Ⓓ
2. Ⓐ Ⓑ Ⓒ Ⓓ
3. Ⓐ Ⓑ Ⓒ Ⓓ
4. Ⓐ Ⓑ Ⓒ Ⓓ
5. Ⓐ Ⓑ Ⓒ Ⓓ
6. Ⓐ Ⓑ Ⓒ Ⓓ
7. Ⓐ Ⓑ Ⓒ Ⓓ
8. Ⓐ Ⓑ Ⓒ Ⓓ

9. Ⓐ Ⓑ Ⓒ Ⓓ
10. Ⓐ Ⓑ Ⓒ Ⓓ
11. Ⓐ Ⓑ Ⓒ Ⓓ
12. Ⓐ Ⓑ Ⓒ Ⓓ
13. Ⓐ Ⓑ Ⓒ Ⓓ
14. Ⓐ Ⓑ Ⓒ Ⓓ
15. Ⓐ Ⓑ Ⓒ Ⓓ
16. Ⓐ Ⓑ Ⓒ Ⓓ

17. Ⓐ Ⓑ Ⓒ Ⓓ
18. Ⓐ Ⓑ Ⓒ Ⓓ
19. Ⓐ Ⓑ Ⓒ Ⓓ
20. Ⓐ Ⓑ Ⓒ Ⓓ
21. Ⓐ Ⓑ Ⓒ Ⓓ
22. Ⓐ Ⓑ Ⓒ Ⓓ
23. Ⓐ Ⓑ Ⓒ Ⓓ
24. Ⓐ Ⓑ Ⓒ Ⓓ

25. Ⓐ Ⓑ Ⓒ Ⓓ
26. Ⓐ Ⓑ Ⓒ Ⓓ
27. Ⓐ Ⓑ Ⓒ Ⓓ
28. Ⓐ Ⓑ Ⓒ Ⓓ
29. Ⓐ Ⓑ Ⓒ Ⓓ
30. Ⓐ Ⓑ Ⓒ Ⓓ

31.
32.
33.
34.

35.
36.
37.
38.

Section V: Essay

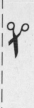

Practice Test 2

Section 1: Reading Test

65 Minutes—52 Questions

DIRECTIONS: Each passage (or pair of passages) in this section is followed by a number of multiple-choice questions. After reading each passage, select the best answer to each question based on what is stated or implied in the passage or passages and in any supplementary material, such as a table, graph, or chart.

Questions 1–10 are based on the following passage.

Rudyard Kipling (1865–1936) was one of the most popular English writers of his era, authoring stories, novels, and poems, many of which take place in colonial India, where he was born and lived as a young child and returned to as a young adult. "The Arrest of Lieutenant Golightly," one of his earliest stories, was first published in an English-language newspaper in India where Kipling worked as a journalist. The following is an excerpt from that story.

If there was one thing on which Golightly prided himself more than another, it was looking like "an Officer and a gentleman."
Line He said it was for the honor of the Service
5 that he attired himself so elaborately; but those who knew him best said that it was just personal vanity. There was no harm about Golightly. ... He recognized a horse when he saw one, ... he played a very fair
10 game at billiards, and was a sound man at the whist-table. Everyone liked him; and nobody ever dreamed of seeing him handcuffed on a station platform as a deserter. But this sad thing happened.
15   He was going down from Dalhousie,[1] at the end of his leave—riding down. He had cut his leave as fine as he dared, and wanted to come down in a hurry.

It was fairly warm at Dalhousie and
20 knowing what to expect below, he descended in a new khaki suit—tight fitting—of a delicate olive-green; a peacock-blue tie, white collar, and a snowy white solah[2] helmet. He prided himself on looking neat even when
25 he was riding post. He did look neat, and he was so deeply concerned about his appearance before he started that he quite forgot to take anything but some small change with him. He left all his notes at the hotel. His
30 servants had gone down the road before him, to be ready in waiting at Pathankote with a change of gear.

    Twenty-two miles out of Dalhousie it began to rain—not a mere hill-shower,
35 but a good, tepid monsoonish downpour. Golightly bustled on, wishing that he had brought an umbrella. The dust on the roads turned into mud, and the pony mired a good deal. So did Golightly's khaki gaiters.
40 But he kept on steadily and tried to think how pleasant the coolth was.

    His next pony was rather a brute at starting, and Golightly's hands being slippery with the rain, contrived to get rid of
45 Golightly at a corner. He chased the animal, caught it, and went ahead briskly. The spill had not improved his clothes or his temper, and he had lost one spur. He kept the other one employed. By the time that stage

CONTINUE ▶

was ended, the pony had had as much
exercise as he wanted, and, in spite of the
rain, Golightly was sweating freely. At the
end of another miserable half-hour, Golightly found the world disappear before
55 his eyes in clammy pulp. The rain had
turned the pith of his huge and snowy
solah-topee into an evil-smelling dough,
and it had closed on his head like a half-
opened mushroom. Also the green lining
60 was beginning to run.

Golightly did not say anything worth
recording here. He tore off and squeezed
up as much of the brim as was in his eyes
and ploughed on. The back of the helmet
65 was flapping on his neck and the sides
stuck to his ears, but the leather band and
green lining kept things roughly together,
so that the hat did not actually melt away
where it flapped.

70 Presently, the pulp and the green
stuff made a sort of slimy mildew which
ran over Golightly in several directions—
down his back and bosom for choice.
The khaki color ran too … and sections
75 of Golightly were brown, and patches
were violet, and contours were ochre,
and streaks were ruddy red, and blotches
were nearly white, according to the nature and peculiarities of the dye. When
80 he took out his handkerchief to wipe his
face and the green of the hat-lining and
the purple stuff that had soaked through
on to his neck from the tie became thoroughly mixed, the effect was amazing.

85 He went to the Station-Master to negotiate for a first-class ticket to Khasa,
where he was stationed. The booking-
clerk said something to the Station-Master, the Station-Master said something
90 to the Telegraph Clerk, and the three
looked at him with curiosity. They asked
him to wait for half-an-hour, while they
telegraphed to Umritsar for authority. So
he waited, and four constables came and

95 grouped themselves picturesquely round
him. Just as he was preparing to ask them
to go away, the Station-Master said that he
would give the Sahib[3] a ticket to Umritsar,
if the Sahib would kindly come inside the
100 booking-office. Golightly stepped inside,
and the next thing he knew was that a
constable was attached to each of his legs
and arms, while the Station-Master was
trying to cram a mailbag over his head.

1. A town in India in the hills, used as a summer retreat for
British personnel
2. A plant made into fabric used in hat-making
3. A term of respect; like calling someone "sir" in English

1. The tone of the story can best be described
as

A. surreal.

B. prideful.

C. ironic.

D. mocking.

2. Which choice provides the best evidence for
the answer to the previous question?

A. Lines 1–3 ("If there . . . gentleman.'")

B. Lines 7–11 ("There was . . . whist-table.")

C. Lines 19–23 ("It was fairly warm . . .
helmet.")

D. Lines 33–35 ("Twenty-two miles . . .
downpour.")

3. Which of the following best explains the
identity and actions of the main character?

A. He's a proper military man on leave from
his post.

B. He's a British soldier trying to escape
capture by the Indian government.

C. He's an outlaw trying to escape capture.

D. He's a British businessman on a trip
overseas.

CONTINUE

4. Which choice provides the best evidence for the answer to the previous question?

   A. Lines 11–14 ("Everyone liked him . . . happened.")

   B. Lines 16–18 ("He had cut. . . down in a hurry.")

   C. Lines 23–25 ("He prided . . . riding post.")

   D. Lines 42–45 ("His next pony . . .at a corner.")

5. The author ridicules Golightly by

   A. explaining the satirical nature of Golightly's vanity.

   B. describing how Golightly's experience demonstrates that he has trouble coping with India's severe rainstorms.

   C. providing detailed descriptions of Golightly's looks.

   D. proving that Golightly has incredible difficulty riding horses.

6. What is the meaning of the sentence "He had cut his leave as fine as he dared" (lines 16–17)?

   A. He dared to take leave without telling the authorities.

   B. He arranged to take as much time as he could without getting in trouble.

   C. He was daring in leaving the military post because it was dangerous.

   D. He wanted to leave but was afraid he'd get caught.

7. Kipling frequently provides details on Golightly's looks in order to

   A. imply that Golightly only physically resembles an officer.

   B. show how intense the climate is in India.

   C. help the reader understand the setting.

   D. describe the problems of the British military in India.

8. As used in line 38, "mired" most nearly means

   A. sped.

   B. slowed.

   C. pooled.

   D. ate.

9. Even though the author says "this sad thing happened," which detail from the passage shows the narrator considers Golightly to be responsible for what happened to him?

   A. Golightly is so concerned with looking neat that he neglects to take anything but small change with him.

   B. Golightly intends to dress well even when riding a horse.

   C. Golightly wishes that he had thought to bring an umbrella for his ride.

   D. Golightly struggles with his next horse, which manages to throw him when traversing a corner.

10. How are lines 61–62 ("Golightly did. . . recording here.") distinguished from the rest of the text in the passage?

   A. Kipling describes the character's verbal response to the situation.

   B. The narrator describes Golightly's thoughts rather than Golightly's appearance.

   C. It adds internal dialogue to the story where previously the perspective had been limited to more objective description.

   D. The narrator interjects his own viewpoint.

CONTINUE

Practice Test 2

Questions 11–21 are based on the following passage.

The following passage is adapted from a history of England written in 1890. This passage discusses the origin of towns.

As in the case of the manor, which was the Norman name for the Saxon "townships," the town, in the modern sense of the word, had its origin from the primitive settlement known as the mark. The only difference between a town and a manor originally lay in the number of its population, and in the fact that the town was a more defensible place than the "township," or rural manor, probably having a mound or moat surrounding it, instead of the hedges which ran round the villages. In itself it was merely a manor or group of manors; as Professor Freeman puts it, "one part of the district where men lived closer together than elsewhere." The town had at first a constitution like that of a primitive village in the mark, but its inhabitants had gradually gained certain rights and functions of a special nature. These rights and privileges had been received from the lord of the manor on which the town had grown up; for towns, especially provincial towns, were at first only dependent manors, which gained safety and solidity under the protection of some great noble, prelate, or the king himself, who finally would grant the town thus formed a charter.

Towns first became important in England towards the end of the Saxon period. Saxon England had never been a settlement of towns, but of villages and townships, or manors. But gradually towns did grow up, though differing widely in the circumstances and manner of their rise. Some grew up in the fortified camps of the invaders themselves, as being in a secure position; some arose from a later occupation of the once sacked and deserted Roman towns. Many grew silently in the shadow of a great abbey or monastery. Others clustered round the country houses of some Saxon king or earl. Several important boroughs owed their rise to the convenience of their site as a port or a trading center. . . . But all the English towns were far less flourishing before the arrival of the Normans than they afterwards became.

If, now, we once more go back to our great authority, the survey made by William the Norman, we find that the status of these towns or boroughs is clearly recognized, though they are regarded as held by the lord of the manor "in demesne," or in default of a lord, as part of the king's demesne. . . . It was possible, too, that one town might belong to several lords, because it spread over, or was an aggregate of, several manors or townships. . . .

London was a town apart, as it had always been, and was the only town which had a civic constitution, being regulated by a port-reeve and a bishop, and having a kind of charter, though afterwards the privileges of this charter were much increased. London was of course a great port and trading centre, and had many foreign merchants in it. It was then, as well as in subsequent centuries, the centre of English national life, and the voice of its citizens counted for something in national affairs. The other great ports of England at that time were Bristol, Southampton, and Norwich, and as trade grew and prospered, many other ports rose into prominence.

Even at the time of the Conquest most towns, though small, were of sufficient importance to have a certain status of their own, with definite privileges. The most important of these was the right of composition for taxation, *i.e.* the right of paying a fixed sum, or rent, to the Crown, instead

Part VII

CONTINUE

of the various tallages, taxes, and imposts that might be required of other places. This fixed sum, or composition, was
85 called the *firma burgi*, and by the time of the Conquest was nearly always paid in money. Previously it had been paid both in money and kind, for we find Oxford paying to Edward the Confessor six
90 sectaries of honey as well as £20 in coin; while to William the Norman it paid £60 as an inclusive lump sum. By the end of the Norman period all the towns had secured the *firma burgi*, and the right of
95 assessing it themselves, instead of being assessed by the sheriff; they had the right also of choosing a mayor of their own, instead of the king's bailiff or *reeve*. They had, moreover, their own tribunals,
100 a charter for their customs, and special rules of local administration, and, generally speaking, gained entire judicial and commercial freedom.

11. The primary purpose of the passage is to

   A. compare life in English towns to life in manors.

   B. provide a history of the development of English towns.

   C. prove that the English town evolved from the mark.

   D. describe the qualities that define a town.

12. The author would most likely agree with which of the following statements regarding London?

   A. London was flourishing even before the Normans arrived there.

   B. Most people know of London's status as a great port and trading center.

   C. People are too cramped and crammed together to be comfortable in London.

   D. Living in London is preferable to rural living because of the privileges town life affords.

13. According to the passage, a manor is best described as

   A. a rural township.

   B. far more defensible place than a town.

   C. a Norman settlement named by the Saxons.

   D. a group of townships.

14. As it is used in line 10, "mound" most nearly means

   A. human-made body of water.

   B. protective wall.

   C. small heap of dirt.

   D. scenic hill.

15. According to the passage, one place towns arose in England was

   A. in the camps of Saxon invaders.

   B. near shops and stores.

   C. within the vicinity of monasteries.

   D. near Bristol, Southhampton, and Norwich.

16. The passage implies that the most valuable source of information regarding English towns has been

   A. records from the deserted Roman towns.

   B. William the Norman's survey.

   C. the writings of Professor Freeman.

   D. town charters.

17. According to the passage, anyone who holds a town "in demesne"

   A. rules the town but does not own it.

   B. understands that the town really belongs to the king.

   C. is the owner of that town.

   D. shares the town with other lords.

CONTINUE

18. Which choice provides the best evidence for the answer to the previous question?

    A. Lines 40–42 ("Others clustered . . . king or earl.")

    B. Lines 50–54 ("we find . . . default of a lord")

    C. Lines 55–58 ("It was possible, too. . . or townships.")

    D. Lines 87–92 ("Previously it had been . . . lump sum.")

19. According to the passage, a town's influence on national matters was most significantly impacted by

    A. the town's success as a trading center.

    B. the town's ability to distinguish itself from other towns.

    C. the influence of the town's civic constitution.

    D. the town's ability to draw in people from other areas.

20. Which choice provides the best evidence for the answer to the previous question?

    A. Lines 59–64 ("London was . . . much increased.")

    B. Lines 64–67 ("London was . . . merchants in it.")

    C. Lines 70–74 ("The other great . . . into prominence.")

    D. Lines 75–78 ("Even at the time . . . definite privileges.")

21. As it is used in line 96, "assessed" most nearly means

    A. tested.

    B. examined.

    C. arrested.

    D. estimated.

Questions 22–32 are based on the following passage.

The Galapagos Islands, which belong to Ecuador, are located approximately 906 km (563 mi.) west of the mainland. Because of their isolation, these volcanic islands are home to a variety of unique species. The following text has been adapted from Ecosystem Restoration: Invasive Snail Detection Dogs, which was originally published by Galapagos Conservancy (www.galapagos.org). (For the complete article, see http://galapagos.org/conservation.)

In Galapagos, native species are threatened by introduced, invasive species such as goats, rats, pigs, and cats, among many
Line others. While much has been accom-
5 plished in the management of existing invasive species, the islands are constantly at risk of new unwanted species arriving each day. The Giant African Land Snail (GALS)—the largest species of snail found
10 on land, growing to nearly 8 inches in length—is one such new invasive that has taken up residence in Galapagos. Known to consume at least 500 different types of plants, scientists consider the GALS to be
15 one of the most destructive snail species in the world. It now poses a serious threat to the native snails and plants of Galapagos.

Invasive Giant African Land Snails were first detected on Santa Cruz Island
20 in 2010, and currently less than 20 hectares (50 acres) are infested—but the snails are expanding their range every wet season. Experience has shown that once an invasive species becomes established, it is
25 almost impossible to remove. At this point in time, it is still possible to eradicate the GALS from Galapagos if additional management techniques are integrated into current activities.

CONTINUE

30　　Previously, staff from the Galapagos Agency for the Regulation and Control of Biosecurity and Quarantine (ABG) had to search for and collect GALS on rainy nights using headlamps—an extremely
35　challenging and unsustainable solution to the permanent eradication of the snails. Dogs, on the other hand, have an incredible sense of smell and can be trained to detect scents imperceptible to the human
40　nose, making them ideal for the detection of the GALS. Detection dogs have been used for finding contraband drugs and shark fins in Galapagos, but not for other purposes. This project entails uti-
45　lizing two scent detection dogs to detect GALS in order to help clear currently affected areas and search for previously undetected populations in the islands.

　　During the first phase of the project,
50　which took place in the fall of 2014, two detection dogs were trained by Dogs for Conservation (DFC) in the United States to specifically detect GALS. Darwin, a golden Labrador retriever, was rescued
55　after he was unable to successfully complete a service dog training program, and Neville, a black Labrador retriever, was saved from a shelter. Darwin and Neville were selected for this project based on
60　their detection abilities and temperament for working with multiple handlers, in preparation for work with new handlers in Galapagos. In December of 2014, the dogs were brought to Galapagos where
65　six ABG staff were trained as handlers for this and future detection projects. Many had never worked with dogs before and had to learn the basics of canine behavior, learning theory, scent theory, training
70　methods, and handling skills. New kennels were built by ABG personnel with materials funded through this project in order to house the dogs.

　　Both dogs required a period of ac-
75　climation to Galapagos and to their new roles. The dogs could only be trained on dead snails in the US due to biosecurity risks for this highly invasive species, so additional training was needed upon
80　their arrival in Galapagos to transition them to live snails and snail eggs. Darwin and Neville have now been fully trained to detect the invasive snails, and the dogs will be regularly assisting with
85　GALS eradication and monitoring on Santa Cruz.

　　DFC continues to provide guidance and support to the GALS K9 team, with whom they are in weekly communica-
90　tion. Future updates to the project will be posted … as they occur. This project is also serving as a pilot to establish a permanent canine detection program in the Galapagos. Expertly trained dogs
95　and experienced handlers will be a highly cost-effective detection tool for ongoing biosecurity programs aimed at eliminating targeted invasive species that threaten the unique and fragile ecosystems of
100　Galapagos.

22. The passage's primary purpose is to

　　A. increase tourism to the Galapagos.

　　B. raise funding for the organization from the general public and the government.

　　C. inform the public about the problems of invasive species and measures to reduce them.

　　D. persuade people that it is important to keep species of animals and plants from becoming extinct.

CONTINUE ▶

Practice Test 2

23. The main idea of the passage is best summarized by the statement that

    A. dogs can help reduce invasive species in the Galapagos.

    B. scientists have found no way to reduce invasive species in the Galapagos.

    C. Galapagos ecosystems include unique species.

    D. organizations are working together to rid the Galapagos of invasive species.

24. It can reasonably be inferred from the passage that the Galapagos have unique ecosystems because

    A. islands can only support certain kinds of species.

    B. there were no mammals there until humans brought them.

    C. only certain types of animals and plants can live there because of the climate.

    D. They were isolated for a long time, so little interference with the natural ecosystems occurred.

25. Which statement best describes the threat of GALS to the Galapagos Islands?

    A. GALS growth patterns would lead them to overrun the islands.

    B. GALS thrive in hot climates.

    C. GALS are difficult to detect.

    D. GALS eating habits present a problem for native plant-life and animal species.

26. According to the passage, the GALS problem on the Galapagos Islands

    A. has been solved by hunting dogs.

    B. has been exaggerated by the media.

    C. is steadily growing worse every year.

    D. is the biggest problem impacting the islands.

27. Which choice provides the best evidence for the answer to the previous question?

    A. Lines 12–16 ("Known to . . . the world.")

    B. Lines 21–23 ("the snails . . . season.")

    C. Lines 30–36 ("Previously, staff . . . the snails.")

    D. Lines 76–78 ("The dogs . . . biosecurity risks")

28. Why are dogs considered an invasive species to the Galapagos?

    A. The dogs' sense of smell helps them find native species and use them for food.

    B. The dogs required time to get acclimated to the environment.

    C. The dogs did not inhabit the Galapagos until brought by humans.

    D. The dogs once thrived on the Galapagos, but they had depleted their limited food sources.

29. Why did the scientists decide to try using dogs to find the GALS?

    A. Dogs are friendly animals that are easy to work with.

    B. Dogs can also be trained to find illicit drugs.

    C. Dogs are trainable and able to find GALS by smell.

    D. Dogs can go into the small spaces in which GALS hide.

30. Which choice provides the best evidence for the answer to the previous question?

    A. Lines 37–41 ("Dogs, on . . . GALS.")

    B. Lines 41–44 ("Detection . . . purposes.")

    C. Lines 44–48 ("This project . . . islands.")

    D. Lines 49–53 ("During the . . . detect GALS.")

CONTINUE ▶

31. As used in lines 74–75, "acclimation" is best defined as

    A. adjusting to changes in the environment.

    B. conforming to one's surroundings.

    C. adaptation of a species.

    D. modification of behavior.

32. As used in line 77, "biosecurity" most nearly means

    A. safe handling of animals.

    B. safety from dangerous animals and plants.

    C. protection to keep wildlife from extinction.

    D. protection of an ecosystem from invasive species.

Questions 33–42 are based on the following passages.

Passage 1 is an excerpt from a speech modeled on the Declaration of Independence, written and read by Elizabeth Cady Stanton at the Woman's Rights Convention, held in Seneca Falls, New York, July 19, 1848. About 300 people attended the event and about a third (68 women and 32 men) signed the declaration.

Passage 2 is excerpted from The Narrative of Sojourner Truth, *the memoir of a slave in pre-Civil War New York. Born into slavery as Isabella, after being freed in 1827, she took the name Sojourner Truth to express her strong faith. Because Truth was illiterate, she dictated her story to the writer Olive Gilbert, whom she had met in Massachusetts. The book was published in 1850 and was widely distributed by Abolitionists to help further their cause.*

PASSAGE 1

The history of mankind is a history of repeated injuries and usurpations on the part of man toward woman, having in
Line direct object the establishment of an ab-
5 solute tyranny over her. To prove this, let facts be submitted to a candid world.

He has never permitted her to exercise her inalienable right to the elective franchise.

10 He has compelled her to submit to laws, in the formation of which she had no voice.

He has withheld from her rights which are given to the most ignorant
15 and degraded men—both natives and foreigners.

Having deprived her of this first right of a citizen, the elective franchise, thereby

CONTINUE ➤

leaving her without representation in the
20 halls of legislation, he has oppressed her
on all sides.

He has made her, if married, in the
eye of the law, civilly dead.

He has taken from her all right in
25 property, even to the wages she earns.

He has made her, morally, an ir-
responsible being, as she can commit
many crimes with impunity, provided
they be done in the presence of her hus-
30 band. In the covenant of marriage, she is
compelled to promise obedience to her
husband, he becoming, to all intents and
purposes, her master—the law giving him
power to deprive her of her liberty, and to
35 administer chastisement.

He has so framed the laws of divorce, as to what shall be the proper
causes, and in the case of separation, to
whom the guardianship of the children
40 shall be given, as to be wholly regardless
of the happiness of women—the law, in
all cases, going upon a false supposition
of the supremacy of man, and giving all
power into his hands.

45 After depriving her of all rights as a
married woman, if single, and the owner
of property, he has taxed her to support
a government which recognizes her only
when her property can be made profit-
50 able to it. ...

He has endeavored, in every way that
he could, to destroy her confidence in her
own powers, to lessen her self-respect,
and to make her willing to lead a depen-
55 dent and abject life.

Now, in view of this entire disfran-
chisement of one-half the people of this
country, their social and religious degradation, in view of the unjust laws above
60 mentioned, and because women do feel
themselves aggrieved, oppressed, and
fraudulently deprived of their most sacred
rights, we insist that they have immediate

admission to all the rights and privileges
65 which belong to them as citizens of these
United States.

Passage 2

After emancipation had been decreed by
the State, some years before the time fixed
for its consummation, Isabella's master
70 told her if she would do well, and be faithful, he would give her "free papers," one
year before she was legally free by statute.
In the year 1826, she had a badly diseased
hand, which greatly diminished her use-
75 fulness; but on the arrival of July 4, 1827,
the time specified for her receiving her
"free papers," she claimed the fulfillment
of her master's promise; but he refused
granting it, on account (as he alleged) of
80 the loss he had sustained by her hand.
She plead that she had worked all the
time, and done many things she was not
wholly able to do, although she knew she
had been less useful than formerly; but
85 her master remained inflexible. Her very
faithfulness probably operated against
her now, and he found it less easy than
he thought to give up the profits of his
faithful Bell, who had so long done him
90 efficient service.

But Isabella inwardly determined
that she would remain quietly with him
only until she had spun his wool—about
one hundred pounds—and then she
95 would leave him, taking the rest of the
time to herself. "Ah!" she says, with emphasis that cannot be written, "the slaveholders are TERRIBLE for promising to
give you this or that, or such and such a
100 privilege, if you will do thus and so; and
when the time of fulfillment comes, and
one claims the promise, they, forsooth,
recollect nothing of the kind; and you are,
like as not, taunted with being a LIAR; or,
105 at best, the slave is accused of not having
performed *his* part or condition of the

CONTINUE ▶

contract." "Oh!" said she, "I have felt as if I could not live through the *operation sometimes.* Just think of us! *so* eager for
110 our pleasures, and just foolish enough to keep feeding and feeding ourselves up with the idea that we should get what had been thus fairly promised; and when we think it is almost in our hands, find
115 ourselves flatly denied! Just think! How *could* we bear it?"

33. Stanton presented the "Declaration of Sentiments" in order to

A. show that women could write important documents.

B. shock the audience in upstate New York.

C. explain why women needed rights.

D. gain support for equal protection of minorities.

34. Which choice provides the best evidence for the answer to the previous question?

A. Lines 5–6 ("To prove this . . . candid world.")

B. Lines 13–16 ("He has withheld . . . and foreigners.")

C. Lines 22–23 ("He has made . . . civilly dead.")

D. Lines 26–29 ("He has made her . . . of her husband.")

35. As it is used in line 18, "elective franchise" most nearly means

A. sports elections.

B. selection of a business.

C. an election's team.

D. the right to vote.

36. In Passage 1, Stanton supported her argument that women have been forced into obedience by

A. stating that women can't work outside the home.

B. expressing anger at the idea that women are not allowed to vote.

C. demonstrating dismay at how children can be taken from mothers in cases of divorce or separation.

D. explaining how marriage legally compels women to obey their husbands.

37. According to Passage 2, what set Isabella's master apart from other slaveholders?

A. He didn't mistreat her as much.

B. He allowed her to learn to read and write.

C. He would set her free before he had to.

D. He made promises he didn't keep.

38. Which choice provides the best evidence for the answer to the previous question?

A. Lines 67–72 ("After emancipation . . . by statute.")

B. Lines 73–75 ("In the year . . . usefulness")

C. Lines 85–90 ("Her very faithfulness . . . service.")

D. Lines 91–96 ("But Isabella . . . to herself.")

Practice Test 2

39. In lines 86–87, Truth uses the phrase "faith-fulness probably operated against her" in order to

 A. suggest Isabella's faith in God would help her through the difficulties operating against her.

 B. imply that Isabella's loyalty made her more important and valuable to her master.

 C. explain that Isabella needed to be faithful to her God so that her master would not break his promises.

 D. indicate that Isabella needed to be faithful in the face of her master's inflexibility.

40. As used in line 109, "operation" most nearly means

 A. surgery.

 B. military action.

 C. activity.

 D. math.

41. What do the two passages suggest as similarities between their subjects?

 A. Neither women nor slaves could get paid for their work.

 B. Both women and slaves had to take care of the children in a family.

 C. Both women and slaves had to obey the will of someone else.

 D. Men made and broke promises to both women and slaves.

42. Which of the following statements is true about the two passages?

 A. Both passages express anger at a lack of freedom.

 B. Stanton expresses deep sadness while Truth's passage is focused on regret.

 C. Truth's tone is bitter while Stanton expresses outrage.

 D. Both Stanton and Truth express frustration about their current situations and the state of their societies.

Questions 43–52 are based on the following passage.

The following passage has been adapted from "New Dinosaur's Keen Nose Made It a Formidable Predator, Penn Study Finds" by Katherine Unger Baillie, originally published by the University of Pennsylvania, May 11, 2015. (This passage was edited for length.)

A researcher from the University of Penn-sylvania has identified a species of dino-saur closely related to *Velociraptor*, the
Line group of creatures made infamous by the
5 movie *Jurassic Park*. The newly named species likely possessed a keen sense of smell that would have made it a formi-dable predator.

Steven Jasinski, a doctoral student
10 in the School of Arts & Science's Depart-ment of Earth and Environmental Science at Penn, and acting curator of paleontol-ogy and geology at the State Museum of Pennsylvania, discovered the new species
15 while investigating a specimen originally assigned to a previously known species. His analysis suggests the fossil—part of the dinosaur's skull—actually represents a brand new species, which Jasinski has
20 named *Saurornitholestes sullivani*. The creature's genus name Saurornitholestes, which means "lizard bird thief," gives a sense of what the prehistoric predator would have looked like. These animals
25 were lightly built with long legs and jaws lined with teeth, and they are believed to be very distant relatives of today's birds…

The specimen, roughly 75 million years old, was discovered by paleontolo-
30 gist Robert Sullivan in the Bisti/De-Na-Zin Wilderness Area of New Mexico in 1999. When first described, scientists believed it was a member of *Saurornit-holestes langstoni*, a species of theropod

CONTINUE ▶

35 dinosaurs in the Dromaeosauridae family that had been found in present-day Alberta, Canada.

But when Jasinski … began a comparative analysis of the specimen to other 40 *S. langstoni* specimens, he found subtle differences. Notably, he observed that the surface of the skull corresponding with the brain's olfactory bulb was unusually large. This finding implies a powerful 45 sense of smell.

"This feature means that *Saurornitholestes sullivani* had a relatively better sense of smell than other dromaeosaurid dinosaurs, including *Velociraptor, Drom-* 50 *aeosaurus*, and *Bambiraptor*," Jasinski said. "This keen olfaction may have made *S. sullivani* an intimidating predator as well."

S. sullivani comes from the end of the 55 time of dinosaurs, or the Late Cretaceous, and represents the only named dromaeosaur from this period in North America south of Montana.

At the time *S. sullivani* lived, North 60 America was split into two continents separated by an inland sea. This dinosaur lived on the western shores in an area called Laramidia. Numerous dromaeosaurs, which are commonly called 65 raptors, are known from more northern areas in Laramidia, including Alberta, Canada, and Montana. However, *S. sullivani* represents the only named dromaeosaur from the Late Cretaceous of 70 southern Laramidia.

S. sullivani shared its world with numerous other dinosaurs… Though a distinct species, *S. sullivani* appears to be closely related to *S. langstoni*. Finding the 75 two as distinct species further shows that differences existed between dinosaurs between the northern and southern parts of North America.

At less than 3 feet at its hip and 80 roughly 6 feet in length, *S. sullivani* was not a large dinosaur. However, previous findings of related species suggest the animal would have been agile and fast, perhaps hunting in packs and using its 85 acute sense of smell to track down prey.

"Although it was not large, this was not a dinosaur you would want to mess with," Jasinski said.

43. The main idea of the passage is that

   A. the *S. sullivani* was a predator aided by its keen sense of smell.

   B. the new species resembled today's birds.

   C. scientific discoveries make important contributions to our knowledge of prehistoric animals.

   D. recent fossil evidence identified a new species of dinosaur.

44. Based on how the *S. sullivani* was discovered, one can conclude that

   A. students can sometimes make amazing discoveries.

   B. scientific investigations can yield surprising results.

   C. students do important work with academics in their field of studies.

   D. some discoveries are attributable to chance.

45. As used in lines 7–8, "formidable" most nearly means

   A. frightened.

   B. inspiring.

   C. impressive.

   D. difficult.

CONTINUE

46. What does the name of the new species tell us about this dinosaur?

    A. Dinosaurs are named after real people.

    B. The name tells us where the dinosaur fossils were found.

    C. Dinosaurs are given names based on where they lived.

    D. The name suggests what the dinosaur might have looked like.

47. Which choice provides the best evidence for the answer to the previous question?

    A. Lines 17–20 ("His analysis . . . *sullivani.*")

    B. Lines 24–27 ("These animals . . . birds.")

    C. Lines 28–32 ("The specimen . . . in 1999.")

    D. Lines 32–37 ("When first . . . Alberta, Canada.")

48. Based on the passage, scientists recognized that the fossil they found was a new species by

    A. noticing the fossil was larger than others that they had found previously.

    B. seeing the fossil had different markings than other species.

    C. looking at its closest relatives, then realizing this was a different species.

    D. comparing it to other fossils, then noticing differences in the skull.

49. Which choice provides the best evidence for the answer to the previous question?

    A. Lines 9–16 ("Steven Jasinski . . . known species.")

    B. Lines 38–41 ("But when . . . differences.")

    C. Lines 44–45 ("This finding . . . smell.")

    D. Lines 54–58 ("*S. sullivani* . . . of Montana.")

50. As used in line 43, "olfactory" most nearly means

    A. bulb.

    B. unusually large.

    C. surface of the skull.

    D. sense of smell.

51. According to the passage, a strong sense of smell helps a predator because it

    A. would help a predator find food.

    B. could help a predator sense danger.

    C. would compensate for poor eyesight.

    D. could help a predator find an appropriate mate.

52. Based on the passage, *S. sullivani* had numerous predatory advantages, one of which was

    A. hunting in packs.

    B. bird-like features.

    C. a uniquely shaped skull.

    D. size greater than that of its prey.

STOP
If you finish before time is called, you may check your work on this section only.
Do not turn to any other section.

Section 2: Writing and Language Test

35 Minutes—44 Questions

TURN TO SECTION 2 OF YOUR ANSWER SHEET TO ANSWER THE QUESTIONS IN THIS SECTION.

DIRECTIONS: Each passage below is accompanied by a number of multiple-choice questions. For some questions, you will need to consider how the passage might be revised to improve the expression of ideas. Other questions will ask you to consider how the passage might be edited to correct errors in sentence structure, usage, or punctuation. A passage may be accompanied by one or more graphics—such as a chart, table, or graph—that you will need to refer to in order to best answer the question(s).

Some questions will direct you to an underlined portion of a passage—it could be one word, a portion of a sentence, or the full sentence itself. Other questions will direct you to a particular paragraph or to certain sentences within a paragraph, or you'll be asked to think about the passage as a whole. Each question number refers to the corresponding number in the passage.

After reading each passage, select the answer to each question that most effectively improves the quality of writing in the passage or that makes the passage follow the conventions of standard written English. Many questions include a "NO CHANGE" option. Select that option if you think the best choice is to leave that specific portion of the passage as it is.

Questions 1–11 are based on the following passage.

THE GLASS CEILING

"The Glass Ceiling" is a metaphor that refers to the imperceptible and subversive forms of discrimination women in the workforce encounter when pursuing upper-level management positions. A popular phrase in the 1980s, it has become less widely used over the ensuing years. **1** Other phrases from past decades are still in frequent use. **2** However as recent data make clear, "The Glass Ceiling" remains a solid barrier to women working in America.

1 The writer is considering deleting the underlined sentence. Should the writer do this?

A. No, because it provides a detail that supports the main topic of the paragraph.

B. No, because it acts as a transition to the next paragraph.

C. Yes, because it repeats information that has been provided.

D. Yes, because it is a detail that is irrelevant to the main topic of the paragraph.

2

A. NO CHANGE

B. However as recent data make clear

C. However, as recent data make clear,

D. However, as recent data, make clear

According to data from the U.S. Bureau of Labor Statistics and the Pew Research Center, women make up 57.2% of the nation's workforce **3** <u>but hold 5% of CEO only positions in Fortune 500 companies.</u> Women also account for only 17% of board membership at Fortune 500 companies. While these percentages note a minimal increase in female leadership over the **4** <u>passed</u> thirty years, barriers still seem to exist.

5 <u>In 1995, a bipartisan Federal Glass Ceiling Commission was: formed to determine the root of gender discrimination within corporate America.</u> The committee, headed by Secretary of Labor Robert Reich, noted that "At the highest levels of corporations the promise of reward for preparation and pursuit of excellence is not equally available to members of all groups." Two barriers that contributed most to "The Glass Ceiling" **6** <u>effect</u> were "supply barriers" and "internal business barriers."

3

A. NO CHANGE

B. but hold only 5% of CEO positions in Fortune 500 companies.

C. but hold 5% of only CEO positions in Fortune 500 companies.

D. but hold 5% of CEO positions only in Fortune 500 companies.

4

A. NO CHANGE

B. passing

C. passive

D. past

5

A. NO CHANGE

B. In 1995, a bipartisan Federal Glass Ceiling Commission was formed; to determine the root of gender discrimination within corporate America.

C. In 1995, a bipartisan Federal Glass Ceiling Commission was formed to determine the root of gender discrimination within corporate America.

D. In 1995 a bipartisan Federal Glass Ceiling Commission was formed, to determine the root of gender discrimination within corporate America.

6

A. NO CHANGE

B. affect

C. effective

D. affection

Practice Test 2

CONTINUE ➡

"Supply barriers" represent the lack of leadership, education, and experience women are given access to during high school and college. Corporations have viewed this lack of access as an educational reform issue, not a business issue, and they do not think it's **7** her responsibility to fix it. However, corporations are **8** equipped with both financial and educational resources to overcome this "supply barrier." If corporations are serious about ending discrimination in the workplace, they need to invest in educational programs that train women to be future leaders. This includes creating more mentoring programs and school-to-work initiatives and providing more educational scholarships.

9 The difference between what corporate executives say they want to do. In regard to discrimination, and efforts being made (or not made) to end discriminatory practices is another issue. Talking the talk and not walking the walk is what the "internal business barrier" is all about. The reason for this discrepancy is that many white males working in the highly competitive corporate America believe they are "losing the corporate game, losing control, and losing opportunity." In essence, white men in corporate leadership feel threatened by including women in their ranks.

7

A. NO CHANGE

B. their

C. his

D. your

8

A. NO CHANGE

B. implemented

C. furnished

D. supplied

9

A. NO CHANGE

B. The difference between what corporate executives say they want to do in regard to discrimination, and

C. The difference between what corporate executives say they want to do and in regard to discrimination and

D. The difference between what corporate executives say they want to do in regard to discrimination and

CONTINUE

10 While many efforts have been made to prevent overt discriminatory practices, 65% of women still see gender bias as a barrier they have to overcome. **11** <u>Until women can be as equals accepted in the corporate sphere, "The Glass Ceiling" will remain firmly intact.</u>

 10 Which of the following sentences would make an effective opening sentence for this paragraph?

A. Ending discrimination against women in the workforce is a relatively easy problem to fix.

B. Ending discrimination against women in the workforce is an involved, complicated process.

C. There are plenty of opportunities for women to find fulfillment and success.

D. Technology is helping modern societies overcome issues involving gender bias.

11

A. NO CHANGE

B. Until women can be accepted as equals in the corporate sphere, "The Glass Ceiling" will remain firmly intact.

C. Until women can be accepted as equally in the corporate sphere, "The Glass Ceiling" will remain firmly intact.

D. Until women can be accepted in the corporate sphere as equally, "The Glass Ceiling" will remain firmly intact.

Practice Test 2

Questions 12–22 are based on the following passage and supplementary material.

THE LIBRARY OF CONGRESS

The Library of Congress is the world's largest and most open library. **12** <u>With collections numbering</u> more than 158 million items on 838 miles of shelving, it includes materials in 470 languages; the basic manuscript collections of 23 presidents of the United States; maps and atlases that have aided explorers and navigators in charting both the world and outer space; and the earliest motion pictures and examples of recorded sound, as well as the latest databases and software packages. **13** <u>The Library's services extend, not only to members and committees of Congress, but also to the executive, and judicial branches of government, to libraries throughout the nation and the world, and to scholars, researchers, artists, and scientists</u> who use its resources.

14 <u>This was not always the case.</u> When President John Adams signed the bill that provided for the removal of the seat of government to the new capital city of Washington in 1800, he created a reference library for Congress only. The bill provided, among other items, $5,000 "for the purchase of such books as may be necessary for the use of Congress—and for putting up a suitable apartment for containing them therein...."

After this small congressional library was destroyed by fire along with the Capitol building in 1814, former President Thomas Jefferson offered as a **15** <u>substitute</u> his personal library, accumulated over a span of fifty years. It was considered to be one of the finest in the United States. Congress accepted Jefferson's offer. Thus the foundation was laid for a great national library.

12

A. NO CHANGE

B. It is difficult to maintain such a vast collection—

C. Among the collections of

D. Already collections number

13

A. NO CHANGE

B. The Library's services extend not only to members and committees of Congress but also to the executive and judicial branches of government; to libraries throughout the nation and the world; and to scholars researchers, artists, and scientists

C. The Library's services extend not only to members and committees of Congress but also to the executive and judicial branches, of government, to libraries throughout the nation, and the world and to scholars, researchers, artists, and scientists

D. The Library's services, extend not only to members and committees of Congress but also to the executive and judicial branches of government to libraries, throughout the nation and the world, and to scholars, researchers, artists, and scientists

14

A. NO CHANGE

B. A little history is in order here.

C. Nevertheless, John Adams signed a bill to create the library.

D. We're lucky we have this institution.

15

A. NO CHANGE

B. replacement

C. stand-in

D. copy

CONTINUE ➡

By the close of the Civil War, the collections of the Library of Congress had grown to 82,000 volumes and were still principally used by members of Congress and committees. In 1864, President Lincoln appointed as Librarian of Congress a man who was to transform the Library: Ainsworth Rand Spofford, who opened the Library to the public and greatly expanded **16** it's collections. Spofford successfully advocated a change in the copyright law so that the **17** Library would receive two, free copies of every book, map, chart, dramatic, or musical composition, engraving, cut, print, or photograph submitted for copyright. Predictably, Spofford soon filled all the Capitol's library rooms, attics, and hallways. In 1873, he then won another lobbying effort, for a new building to permanently house the nation's growing collection and reading rooms to serve scholars and the reading public. The result was the Thomas Jefferson Building, completed in 1897. Since then, two more buildings have been constructed to house the Library's **18** ever-expanding collection.

The first librarian in the new building was a newspaperman with no previous library experience, John Russell Young. He quickly realized that the Library had to get control of the collections that had been overflowing the rooms in the Capitol. Young set up organizational units and devised programs that changed the Library. **19** Instead of being essentially an acquisitions operation, it became an efficient processing factory that organized the materials and made them useful.

16

A. NO CHANGE
B. their
C. its
D. its'

17

A. NO CHANGE
B. Library would receive two free copies of every book, map, chart, dramatic or musical composition, engraving, cut, print, or photograph, submitted for copyright.
C. Library would receive two, free copies of every book, map, chart, dramatic or musical composition; engraving, cut, print, or photograph submitted for copyright
D. Library would receive two free copies of every book, map, chart, dramatic or musical composition, engraving, cut, print, or photograph submitted for copyright.

18

A. NO CHANGE
B. ever-existing
C. ever-expending
D. ever-expounding

19 Which choice most effectively sets up the information that follows?

A. NO CHANGE
B. In spite of being essentially an acquisitions operation,
C. Once it was essentially an acquisitions operation,
D. In addition to it being essentially an acquisitions operation,

CONTINUE ➤

20 <u>Formerly head of the Boston Public Library, Herbert Putnam succeeded Young.</u> Putnam served as Librarian of Congress for 40 years. While Librarian, Spofford had collected the materials, Young had organized them, and Putnam set out to ensure that they would be used. **21** <u>They</u> took the Library of Congress directly into the national library scene and made its holdings known and available to the smallest community library in the most distant part of the country.

In about 1912, both Librarian Putnam and members of Congress became concerned about the distance that was widening between the Library and its employer, the Congress. Various states had begun to set up "legislative reference bureaus," which brought together skilled teams of librarians, economists, and political scientists whose purpose was to respond quickly to questions that arose in the legislative process. Congress wanted the same kind of service for itself, so Putnam designed such a unit for the Library of Congress. Called the Legislative Reference Service, it went into operation in 1914 to prepare indexes, digests, and compilations of law that the Congress might need, but it quickly became a specialized reference unit for information transfer and research. This service was the forerunner of the Library's current Congressional Research Service. **22**

20

A. NO CHANGE

B. Young was succeeded. Herbert Putnam had formerly been head of the Boston Public Library.

C. Young was succeeded by someone else— Herbert Putnam, former head of the Boston Public Library.

D. Young was succeeded after only two years by Herbert Putnam, formerly the head of the Boston Public Library.

21

A. NO CHANGE

B. Them

C. He

D. We

22 Which choice best describes a conclusion that can be drawn from the chart on the following page?

A. There are more public university than private university libraries that are similar in scope and scale to the Library of Congress.

B. University libraries of the same scope and scale as the Library of Congress are more common than one would expect.

C. When it comes to university libraries of the same scope and scale as the Library of Congress, the private sector is doing more to create them than the public sector.

D. As the years go on, university libraries of the same scope and scale as the Library of Congress are rapidly increasing.

Practice Test 2

CONTINUE ➡

Number of Libraries in Volume Category*

Institutional characteristic	Less than 5,000	5,000–9,999	10,000–19,999	20,000–29,999	30,000–49,999	50,000–99,999	100,000–249,999	250,000–499,999	500,000–999,999	1,000,000 or more
All higher education institutions	320	158	241	450	450	691	747	275	153	160
Control										
Public	43	57	77	145	297	362	231	146	106	109
Private	277	101	136	96	153	329	516	129	47	51
Level										
Total 4-year and above	115	48	90	89	155	361	673	273	151	160
Doctor's	12	6	8	5	14	35	131	83	93	151
Master's	35	19	24	22	39	177	378	151	51	9
Bachelor's	68	23	58	61	102	148	164	39	7	0
Less than 4-year	205	110	123	152	295	330	74	2	2	0
Size (FTE enrollment)										
Less than 1,500	309	138	186	193	257	352	363	36	4	1
1,500 to 4,999	9	20	26	47	185	249	297	135	36	7
5,000 or more	2	0	1	1	8	90	87	104	113	152
Carnegie classification (1994)										
Research I and II	0	0	0	0	0	0	1	1	10	113
Doctoral I and II	1	0	0	0	0	0	10	20	44	35
Master's I and II	1	0	3	4	3	47	211	164	76	9
Baccalaureate I and II	1	5	5	6	26	178	292	66	17	3
Associate of Arts	150	75	85	150	317	328	74	2	1	0
Specialized	50	33	67	60	82	116	126	21	3	0
Not classified	117	45	53	21	2	22	33	1	2	0

*Source: US Department of Education, National Center for Education Statistics, 1996 Integrated Postsecondary Education Data System, "Academic Libraries Survey" (IPEDS-L: 1996).

CONTINUE ➤

Practice Test 2

Questions 23–33 are based on the following passage.

LAVINIA & EMILY

The Homestcad was quiet and still, a pre-ternatural quiet Lavinia Dickinson had become all too accustomed to. Looking around her sister **23** Emily's now forever empty bedroom that contained nothing, Lavinia recalled some verses penned by Emily many years ago:

> The bustle in a house
> The morning after death
> Is solemnest of industries
> Enacted upon earth, —
> The sweeping up the heart,
> And putting love away
> We shall not want to use again
> Until eternity.

Some people wondered at Emily's seeming **24** preoccupation with death. But Lavinia found it natural for her **25** sisters inquisitive mind to be drawn to exploring this final journey in the cycle of life, especially since Emily had seen so many loved ones pass into eternal slumber. Emily had always had a curious mind, and a voracious appetite for learning. She also greatly enjoyed being in nature. Faith was something she refused to accept blindly, without thought, much to the chagrin of the Calvinist community around her. For Emily, faith was more than rote belief.

> Faith is a fine invention
> For gentlemen who see;
> But microscopes are prudent
> In an emergency!

23

A. NO CHANGE

B. Emily's now forever empty bedroom, Lavinia recalled some verses

C. Emily's bedroom, Lavinia recalled some verses

D. Emily's now forever empty bedroom, Lavinia recalled some verses and poetry

24

A. NO CHANGE

B. predisposition

C. predilection

D. predetermination

25

A. NO CHANGE

B. sister's

C. sisters'

D. sister

CONTINUE

26 Emily had felt very fully her isolation as one "standing alone in rebellion" of faith. Reading **27** through her letters and the poems Emily had hidden away, Lavinia realized just how isolated her beloved sister had felt. Perhaps that was why the self-professed "belle of Amherst" had withdrawn so much from the public sphere.

Emily felt, quite keenly, the limitations of womanhood. Lavinia still remembered the indignation Emily had expressed during the Whig Convention of 1852 when women were not allowed to be delegates. "Why can't *I* be a Delegate? ...don't I know all about Daniel Webster, and the Tariff and the Law?" **28**

26 Which of the following sentences would make an effective addition to this paragraph?

A. One reason for Emily's sense of isolation was her resistance to common ideas of her time.

B. One reason for Emily's sense of isolation was her refusal to take part in social events.

C. One reason for Emily's sense of isolation was her need to be alone to write poetry.

D. One reason for Emily's sense of isolation was her house's remote location.

27

A. NO CHANGE

B. tough

C. though

D. thought

28 At this point, the writer is considering adding the following sentence:

But Lavinia also knew that her sister was not cut out for politics and all the socializing and public display it would entail.

Should the writer make this addition here?

A. Yes, because it adds more information about Emily's personality.

B. Yes, because it explains the contrast between Emily's words and actions.

C. No, because it detracts from the point about women's issues.

D. No, because it is not relevant to Emily's life.

CONTINUE ➤

Yes, it seemed to Lavinia that her sister had most decidedly felt the trappings of being a woman. And, as much as ㉙ they tried to eschew them ㉚ by not becoming a wife or mother, she still felt trapped by society's strict bonds.

I never hear the word "escape"
Without a quicker blood,
A sudden expectation,
A flying attitude.

I never hear of prisons broad
By soldiers battered down,
But I tug childish at my bars, —
Only to fail again!

Emily never understood the power of the gift she ㉛ is given.

The Duel
I took my power in my hand.
And went against the world;
'T was not so much as David had,
But I was twice as bold.

I aimed my pebble, but myself
Was all the one that fell.
Was it Goliath was too large,
Or only I too small?

Sitting in the stillness of Emily's room, surrounded by her internal monologue expressed through thousands of poems, ㉜ it was deciding by Lavinia that it was time the world knew the full treasure her sister was. ㉝

㉙

A. NO CHANGE

B. we

C. she

D. her

㉚ Which choice best fits with the style and tone of the passage?

A. NO CHANGE

B. by never being a wife or mother

C. by postponing choosing to be a wife or mother

D. by refusing the role of wife or mother

㉛

A. NO CHANGE

B. was giving.

C. had been given.

D. had been giving.

㉜

A. NO CHANGE

B. decides

C. was decided

D. had been decided

㉝ Which of the following would make an effective concluding sentence for this paragraph and passage?

A. The world will never know this unique treasure.

B. The world was about to receive a gift it would long cherish.

C. The world already had enough special voices.

D. The world is approximately 4.5 billion years old.

CONTINUE

Questions 34–44 are based on the following passage.

WHAT IS SLEEP?

Scientists have known for some years that sleep is important to human health. In fact, cases of long-term sleep deprivation have even led to death. **34** Yet, scientists are still studying this unique state in which humans spend a third of their lives.

35 [1] It isn't only current scientists who are intrigued with sleep. [2] Throughout history, people have attempted to understand this remarkable experience. [3] Many centuries ago, for example, sleep was regarded as a type of anemia of the brain. [4] Alcmaeon, a Greek scientist, believed that blood retreated into the blood vessels, and the partially starved brain went to sleep. [5] Plato supported the idea that the soul left the body during sleep, wandered through the world, and woke up the body when it returned. [6] During the twentieth century, great strides were made in the study of sleep.

Recently, more scientific explanations of sleep have been proposed. Looking at them, we see a variety of ideas about the nature of sleep. **36** Research may be able to help people who have sleep disorders. According to one theory, the brain is put to sleep by a chemical agent that accumulates in the body when it is awake. Another theory is that weary branches of certain nerve cells break connections with neighboring cells. The flow of impulses required for staying awake is then disrupted. These more recent theories have to be subjected to laboratory research.

34

A. NO CHANGE

B. Scientists are yet studying

C. Scientists are studying yet

D. Yet, scientists study still

35 Which sentence in this paragraph is the best choice to move to the fourth paragraph to create a more logical sequence?

A. Sentence 1

B. Sentence 2

C. Sentence 4

D. Sentence 6

36 Which choice most effectively sets up the information that follows?

A. NO CHANGE

B. Some of the newer ideas may yield important data about the science of sleep.

C. Although science has not yet solved the mysteries of sleep, breakthroughs are imminent.

D. However, some of the old ideas may prove to be correct.

CONTINUE ▶

Why do we sleep? Why do we dream? Modern sleep research is said to have begun in the 1920s with the **37** discovery of a machine that could measure brain waves, the electroencephalograph (EEG). The study of sleep was further enhanced in the 1950s **38** and Eugene Aserinsky, a graduate student at the University of Chicago, and Nathaniel Kleitman, his professor, observed periods of rapid eye movements (REMs) in sleeping subjects. When awakened during these REM periods, subjects almost always remembered dreaming. **39** Nevertheless, when awakened during non-REM phases of sleep, the subjects rarely could recall their dreams. Aserinsky and Kleitman used EEGs and other machines in an attempt to learn more about REMs and sleep patterns.

40 Guided by REMs, it became possible for investigators to "spot" dreaming from outside and then **41** view the sleeper to collect dream stories. They could also alter the **42** dreamers' experiences with noises, drugs, or other stimuli before or during sleep. Thankfully, it appears the body takes care of itself by temporarily paralyzing muscles during REM sleep, preventing the dreamer from "acting out" dream activities.

37

A. NO CHANGE

B. invention

C. idea

D. suggestion

38

A. NO CHANGE

B. when

C. or

D. so

39

A. NO CHANGE

B. Even so,

C. As predicted,

D. On the other hand,

40 Which choice sets up the most logical introduction to the sentence?

A. NO CHANGE

B. Regardless of REMs,

C. No longer hampered by REMs,

D. Nevertheless, with REMs,

41

A. NO CHANGE

B. wake up

C. awaken

D. study

42

A. NO CHANGE

B. dreamer's experiences

C. dreamers experiences

D. dreamers experiences'

CONTINUE

Since the mid-1950s researchers **43** <u>has been drawn</u> into sleep laboratories. There, bedrooms adjoin other rooms that contain EEGs and other equipment. The EEG amplifies signals from sensors on the face, head, and other parts of the body, which together yield tracings of respiration, pulse, muscle tension, and changes of electrical potential in the brain that are sometimes called brain waves. These recordings supply clues to the changes of the sleeping person's activities. These sleep studies have changed long-held beliefs that sleep was an inactive, or passive, state only used for rest and recuperation. As scientists have learned more about the purpose of sleep and dreams during REM **44** <u>sleep. They</u> are now turning to the study of sleep disorders to learn more about problems during sleep.

43

A. NO CHANGE

B. were been drawn

C. have been drawn

D. was drawn

44

A. NO CHANGE

B. sleep—they

C. sleep; they

D. sleep, they

STOP
If you finish before time is called, you may check your work on this section only.
Do not turn to any other section.

Part VII

SECTION 3: Math Test—NO CALCULATOR

25 Minutes—20 Questions

TURN TO SECTION 3 OF YOUR ANSWER SHEET TO ANSWER THE QUESTIONS IN THIS SECTION.

DIRECTIONS: For **Questions 1–15**, solve each problem, select the best answer from the choices provided, and fill in the corresponding circle on your answer sheet. For **Questions 16–20**, solve the problem and enter your answer in the grid on the answer sheet. The directions **before Question 16** will provide information on how to enter your answers in the grid.

ADDITIONAL INFORMATION:

1. The use of a calculator in this section is **not permitted**.

2. All variables and expressions used represent real numbers unless otherwise indicated.

3. Figures provided in this test are drawn to scale unless otherwise indicated.

4. All figures lie in a plane unless otherwise indicated.

5. Unless otherwise specified, the domain of a given function f is the set of all real numbers x for which $f(x)$ is a real number.

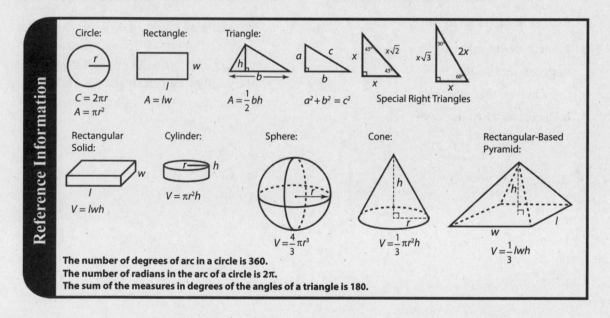

Circle:
$C = 2\pi r$
$A = \pi r^2$

Rectangle:
$A = lw$

Triangle:
$A = \frac{1}{2}bh$

$a^2 + b^2 = c^2$

Special Right Triangles

Rectangular Solid:
$V = lwh$

Cylinder:
$V = \pi r^2 h$

Sphere:
$V = \frac{4}{3}\pi r^3$

Cone:
$V = \frac{1}{3}\pi r^2 h$

Rectangular-Based Pyramid:
$V = \frac{1}{3}lwh$

The number of degrees of arc in a circle is 360.
The number of radians in the arc of a circle is 2π.
The sum of the measures in degrees of the angles of a triangle is 180.

Reference Information

Practice Test 2

CONTINUE ➤

NO CALCULATOR

1. If $\dfrac{x+2}{5} = m$ and $m = -3$, what is the value of x?

    A. −17
    B. −15
    C. −5
    D. −1

2. If $d = m - \dfrac{50}{m}$, and m is a positive number, then as m increases in value, d

    A. increases in value.
    B. decreases in value.
    C. increases, then decreases.
    D. decreases, then increases.

3. Pieces of wire are soldered together so as to form the edges of a cube whose volume is 64 cubic inches. The number of inches of wire used is

    A. 24.
    B. 48.
    C. 64.
    D. 96.

4. Myra baked 6 sheets of cookies with r cookies on each sheet. Neil baked 7 sheets of cookies with p cookies on each sheet. Which of the following represents the total number t of cookies baked by Myra and Neil?

    A. $t = 13pr$
    B. $t = 42pr$
    C. $t = 6r + 7p$
    D. $t = 7r + 6p$

CONTINUE

5. If $b = a + 3$ and $c = -a^2 + 3a + 10$, then what is $b^2 - 2c$ in terms of a?

A. $2(a + 3)^2(-a + 5)(a + 2)$

B. $3a^2 - 6a - 2$

C. $-a^2 + 6a + 29$

D. $3a^2 - 11$

6.
$$y = \frac{(x - 3)^3}{4}$$

Which expression is equivalent to x?

A. $\sqrt{4y} + 3$

B. $\sqrt{4y + 3}$

C. $\sqrt[3]{4y} + 3$

D. $\sqrt[3]{4y + 3}$

7. Hannah recently purchased a plant that grows 4.5 centimeters each week. The height of Hannah's plant can be found using the equation $h = 4.5w + 6$, where h is the height of the plant in centimeters, and w is the number of weeks. What is the meaning of the 6 in the equation?

A. Hannah's plant will be 6 centimeters tall after 4.5 weeks.

B. Hannah's plant grows 6 centimeters each week.

C. Hannah's plant will grow for 6 weeks.

D. Hannah's plant was initially 6 centimeters tall.

8. $(x)^6 + (2x^2)^3 + (3x^3)^2 =$

A. $5x^5 + x^6$

B. $17x^5 + x^6$

C. $6x^6$

D. $18x^6$

Practice Test 2

CONTINUE

727

■ NO CALCULATOR

Question 9 refers to the following graph.

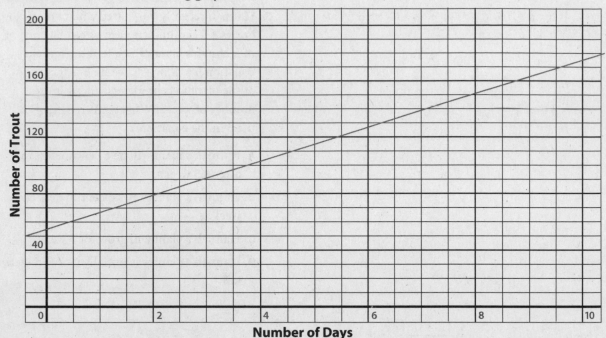

9. Stephen was studying the population of a certain trout pond. When he started his study, there were 55 trout in the pond. He observed the pond each day for 10 days and observed that there were 12 new trout each day. The graph above represents the relationship between the number of trout in the pond and the number of days. Which of the following is an equation for the graph?

   A. $y = 12x + 55$

   B. $y = 10x + 12$

   C. $y = 55x + 12$

   D. $y = 12x + 10$

10. Which of the following is equal to $\left(-\dfrac{27}{8}\right)^{-\frac{1}{3}}$?

    A. $-\dfrac{3}{2}$

    B. $-\dfrac{2}{3}$

    C. $\dfrac{2}{3}$

    D. $\dfrac{3}{2}$

CONTINUE ▶

11. The area of a square is $49x^2$. What is the length of a diagonal of the square?

A. $7x$

B. $7x\sqrt{2}$

C. $14x$

D. $\dfrac{7x}{\sqrt{2}}$

12. The distance, s, in feet that an object falls in t seconds when dropped from a height is obtained by use of the formula $s = 16t^2$. When graphed, what is the meaning of the slope between any two points in the graph?

A. The height in feet from where the object falls

B. The average speed, in feet per second, of the object as it falls

C. The time in seconds it takes for the object to fall to the ground

D. The acceleration, in feet per second squared, of the object as it falls

13.
$$D + B = 24$$
$$4D + 2B = 84$$

In this system of equations, the first equation represents the total number of dogs, D, and birds, B, in a pet store. The second equation represents the number of legs a dog has, $4D$, and the number of legs a bird has, $2B$. How many dogs and birds are in the pet store?

A. $D = 6$; $B = 18$

B. $D = 18$; $B = 6$

C. $D = 24$; $B = 84$

D. $D = 60$; $B = 24$

14.
$$f(x) = x^2 - 4x - 21$$

Which of the following is an equivalent equation that shows the zeros of the function as coefficients or constants?

A. $f(x) = (x - (-7))(x - 3)$

B. $f(x) = (x - 7)(x - (-3))$

C. $f(x) = (x - 2)^2 - 21$

D. $f(x) = (x - 2)^2 - 25$

Practice Test 2

CONTINUE ➤

729

NO CALCULATOR

15. Which equation represents the equation of a line perpendicular to $y = 3x - 2$ that goes through the point $(1, 3)$?

A. $y = -3x + 6$

B. $y = -\dfrac{1}{3}x + \dfrac{10}{3}$

C. $y = -\dfrac{1}{3}x + \dfrac{9}{3}$

D. $y = 3x$

CONTINUE

NO CALCULATOR 📱

DIRECTIONS: For **Questions 16–20**, solve the problem and enter your answer in the grid, as described below, on the answer sheet.

1. Although not required, it is suggested that you write your answer in the boxes at the top of the columns to help you fill in the circles accurately. You will receive credit only if the circles are filled in correctly.

2. Mark no more than one circle in any column.

3. No question has a negative answer.

4. Some problems may have more than one correct answer. In such cases, enter only one answer.

5. **Mixed numbers** such as $3\frac{1}{2}$ must be entered as 3.5 or $\frac{7}{2}$.

   If $3\frac{1}{2}$ is entered into the grid as 3 1 / 2, it will be interpreted as $\frac{31}{2}$, not $3\frac{1}{2}$.

6. **Decimal answers:** If you obtain a decimal answer with more digits than the grid can accommodate, it may be either rounded or truncated, but it must fill the entire grid.

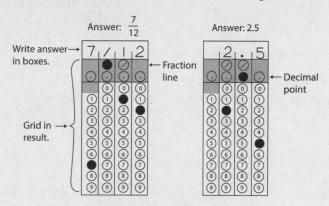

Practice Test 2

16.

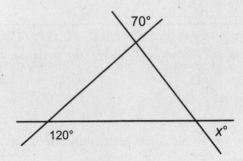

In the figure above, $x =$

17. The only factors of the function f are $(x + 3)^2$ and $(3x - 2)$. What is the product of its three zeroes?

18.

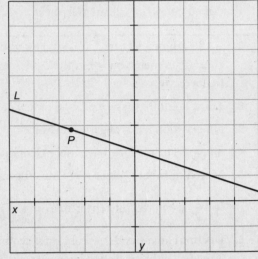

A line drawn through point p perpendicular to line L will have what slope?

19.
$$\sqrt{4 - x^2} = \sqrt{3x}$$

What is one solution to the equation?

20.
$$2x + 3y = 7$$
$$ax - 12y = b$$

According to the system of equations above, what is the value of ab that will make the system of equations have an infinite number of solutions?

STOP
If you finish before time is called, you may check your work on this section only.
Do not turn to any other section.

SECTION 4: Math Test—CALCULATOR ▨

55 Minutes—38 Questions

TURN TO SECTION 4 OF YOUR ANSWER SHEET TO ANSWER THE QUESTIONS IN THIS SECTION.

DIRECTIONS: For **Questions 1–30,** solve each problem, select the best answer from the choices provided, and fill in the corresponding circle on your answer sheet. For **Questions 31–38,** solve the problem and enter your answer in the grid on the answer sheet. The directions **before Question 31** will provide information on how to enter your answers in the grid..

ADDITIONAL INFORMATION:

1. The use of a calculator in this section is **permitted**.

2. All variables and expressions used represent real numbers unless otherwise indicated.

3. Figures provided in this test are drawn to scale unless otherwise indicated.

4. All figures lie in a plane unless otherwise indicated.

5. Unless otherwise specified, the domain of a given function f is the set of all real numbers x for which $f(x)$ is a real number.

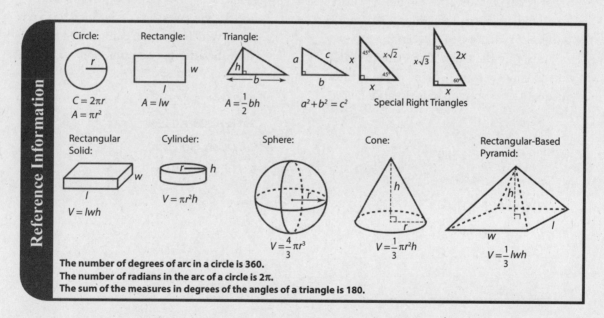

The number of degrees of arc in a circle is 360.
The number of radians in the arc of a circle is 2π.
The sum of the measures in degrees of the angles of a triangle is 180.

CONTINUE ▶

Practice Test 2

📊 CALCULATOR

1. If $9x + 5 = 23$, what is the numerical value of $18x + 5$?

A. 46

B. 41

C. 36

D. 32

3. If 15 cans of food are needed for 7 adults for two days, how many cans are needed to feed 4 adults for seven days?

A. 15

B. 20

C. 25

D. 30

2. A pickup truck has maximum load capacity of 1,500 pounds. Bruce is going to load small radiators, each weighing 150 pounds, and large radiators, each weighing 250 pounds, into the truck. There are 15 radiators to choose from. Which system of linear inequalities represents this situation?

A.
$$x + y < 15$$
$$150x + 250y < 1,500$$

B.
$$x + y \geq 15$$
$$150x + 250y \geq 1,500$$

C.
$$x + y > 15$$
$$150x + 250y > 1,500$$

D.
$$x + y \leq 15$$
$$150x + 250y \leq 1,500$$

4. Fiona earns $28 per hour working for herself. She saves 25% of her income to pay taxes. Which function can be used to determine the after-tax amount Fiona earns for working x hours?

A. $f(x) = 28(0.25x)$

B. $f(x) = 28 + 0.25x$

C. $f(x) = 28(0.75x)$

D. $f(x) = 28 + 0.75x$

Questions 5 and 6 refer to the following information.

Total Annual Sales

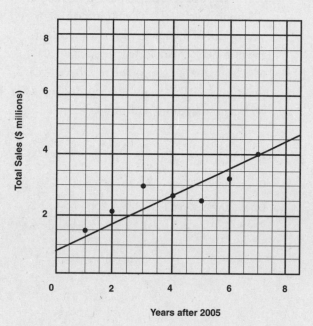

The graph above represents the sales for a company after 2005.

5. Which phrase best describes the correlation between the years after 2005 and the total sales?

   A. Weak negative

   B. Strong negative

   C. Weak positive

   D. Strong positive

6. Which equation best models the data shown in the graph?

   A. $y - 0.4x + 1$

   B. $y = x + 0.5$

   C. $y = 1.5^x$

   D. $y = 0.5^x$

7. If a box of notepaper costs $4.20 after a 40% discount, what was its original price?

   A. $2.52

   B. $5.88

   C. $7.00

   D. $10.50

CONTINUE ▶

📱 **CALCULATOR**

8. The average attendance at basketball games at a local university over the last 10 years can be modeled by the equation $y = 329x + 6,489$, where y represents the average attendance at basketball games x years after 2004. Which of the following describes the meaning of 329 in the equation?

A. The average attendance at basketball games in 2004.

B. The total attendance at basketball games in 2004.

C. The annual increase in average attendance at basketball games.

D. The total increase in average attendance at basketball games for the last 10 years.

9. One supercomputer can process a job 1.5 times faster than another supercomputer. When both supercomputers are used simultaneously to complete a job, the job is completed in 3 hours. How long would it take the slower supercomputer to complete the job alone?

A. $\frac{2}{3}$ hour

B. 4.5 hours

C. 6 hours

D. 7.5 hours

10. A local library had 25,825 books at the beginning of 2010. Since then, it has added 375 books each year. The library can fit a maximum of 35,000 books. If x represents the number of years after the start of 2010, which inequality shows the number of years that the library can continue adding books at this pace without adding space?

A. $35,000 - 375 \leq x$

B. $35,000 \leq 375x$

C. $35,000 \geq 375x - 25,825$

D. $35,000 \geq 375x + 25,825$

11.

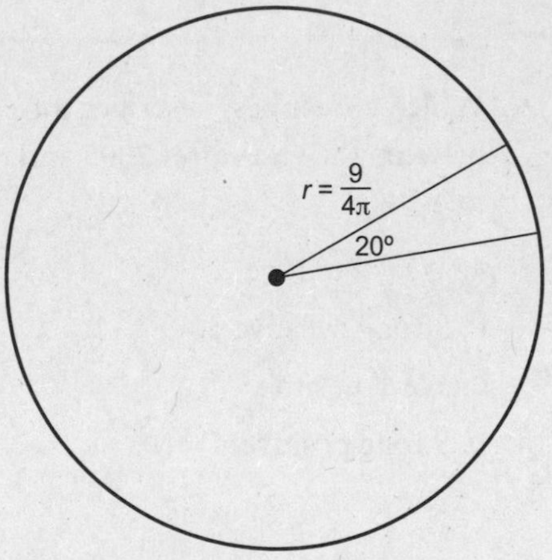

$r = \dfrac{9}{4\pi}$

20°

Note: Figure not drawn to scale.

Given the circle shown above, what is the length of the arc formed by the 20° angle?

A. $\dfrac{45}{\pi}$

B. $\dfrac{\pi}{4}$

C. $\dfrac{1}{2}$

D. $\dfrac{1}{4}$

CONTINUE ➡

Practice Test 2

12. A study was performed to determine if a new medication, Z, helps people who suffer from a certain affliction. A group of 500 randomly selected people who have the affliction were included in the study. Of the group, 200 people were given Z, 200 people were given an old medication, Y, and another 100 people received no treatment. The data showed that people who received Z had significantly decreased effects of the affliction, more than people who received no treatment or who were given medicine Y. Based on the design and results of the study, which of the following is an appropriate conclusion?

A. Z is likely to lessen the effects of the affliction in people who suffer from the affliction.

B. Z is likely to lessen the effects of the affliction better than any other medication.

C. Z is likely to lessen the effects of the affliction for anyone who takes the medication.

D. Z is likely to lessen the effects of the affliction for those who received no treatment.

13. One model for the growth of atmospheric carbon dioxide based on data from Mauna Loa observatory in Hawaii uses the quadratic equation, $C = 0.013t^2 + 0.518t + 310.44$, where C is the concentration in parts per million (PPM) and t is the number of years since 1950. Suppose we want to compare the concentrations predicted by that quadratic model to a model predicting linear—constant year-to-year—growth. Base the linear growth model on the data from 2000 and 2010 shown below. Which statement best describes the difference predicted by the two models for the year 2100?

Year	CO_2 concentration (PPM)
2000	370
2010	390

A. The quadratic model predicts a concentration in the year 2100 that is about 90 PPM less than the linear model predicts.

B. The quadratic model predicts a concentration in the year 2100 that is about 10 PPM greater than the linear model predicts.

C. The quadratic model predicts a concentration in the year 2100 that is about 90 PPM greater than the linear model predicts.

D. The quadratic model predicts a concentration in the year 2100 that is about 110 PPM greater than the linear model predicts.

CONTINUE ▶

🖩**CALCULATOR**

14. After installing a circular pond with diameter 12 feet, Kosi decided to install an 18-inch walkway around the entire pond. The stone costs $7.25 per square foot. What is the total cost of the stone for the walkway?

   A. $130.50
   B. $461.23
   C. $819.96
   D. $1,281.18

15. If $a^2 + 12a = 45$ and $a < 0$, what is the value of $a + 6$?

   A. −15
   B. −9
   C. −3
   D. 3

CONTINUE ▶

Practice Test 2

CALCULATOR 🖩

Questions 16 and 17 refer to the following information.

The graph provided shows the population of California, in millions, from the years 1860 to 1980. Each point represents the population at a particular year. The best fit relation between the points is drawn to connect them.

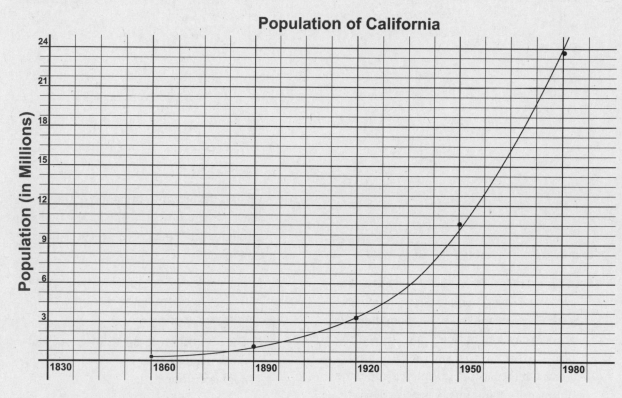

Population of California

16. Which phrase describes the relationship between the population and the number of years?

   A. Linear increasing

   B. Linear decreasing

   C. Exponential growth

   D. Exponential decay

17. Based on the graph, which of the following would be the best prediction of the population of California in 1990?

   A. 20 million

   B. 23 million

   C. 25 million

   D. 30 million

CONTINUE ▶

CALCULATOR

18. A rectangular sign is cut down by 10% of its height and 30% of its width. What percent of the original area remains?

    A. 37%

    B. 57%

    C. 63%

    D. 70%

19. A recent report states that if you were to eat each meal in a different restaurant in New York City, it would take you more than 19 years to cover all of New York City's eating places, assuming that you eat three meals a day. On the basis of this information, the number of restaurants in New York City

    A. exceeds 20,500.

    B. is fewer than 20,000.

    C. exceeds 21,000 but does not exceed 21,500.

    D. exceeds 21,500.

20.

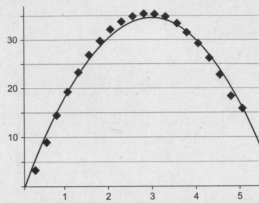

What is the best interpretation of the graph above, which shows the line of best fit drawn through a set of data points recorded in an experiment?

A. The distance from the thrower of a ball thrown horizontally, versus time, fitting a quadratic model

B. The distance from the thrower of a ball thrown horizontally, versus time, fitting a nonlinear model

C. The distance from the thrower of a ball thrown vertically, versus time, fitting a quadratic model

D. The distance from the thrower of a ball thrown vertically, versus time, fitting an exponential model

CONTINUE

21.

$$\frac{3x-1}{2x+3} - \frac{2x+3}{3x-1}$$

Which of the following is equivalent to the expression above?

A. $\dfrac{5x^2 - 18x - 8}{6x^2 + 7x - 3}$

B. $\dfrac{x - 4}{6x^2 + 7x - 3}$

C. $\dfrac{5x^2 + 10}{6x^2 + 7x - 3}$

D. $\dfrac{5x^2 - 12x - 8}{6x^2 + 7x - 3}$

22. Lines A and B shown in the graph have equal slope. If lines A and B represent a system of two equations with two variables, then how many solutions does the system have?

A. 1 solution

B. Infinitely many solutions

C. No solution

D. Not enough information is provided to determine the number of solutions.

Questions 22 and 23 refer to the following graph.

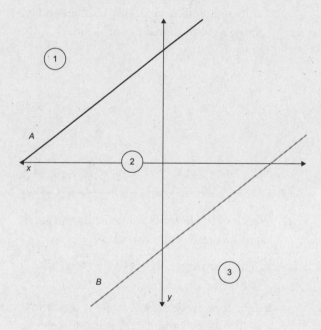

23. We convert the equation for line A, $y = mx + a$, to an inequality by replacing "=" with "<". We convert the equation for B, $y = mx + b$, by changing "=" to ">". Which statement is true?

A. A point, (x, y), satisfying both inequalities, would lie in Region 1 of the graph.

B. A point, (x, y), satisfying both inequalities, would lie in Region 2 of the graph.

C. A point, (x, y), satisfying both inequalities, would lie in Region 3 of the graph.

D. There is no point, (x, y), that would satisfy both inequalities.

CONTINUE ▶

CALCULATOR

24. The number of people living in a certain city has been growing at a constant rate of about 3.8% each year since 1980. The population in 2000 was 38,500. If y is the population of the city x years after 1980, which equation best represents this situation?

   A. $y = 18,260(1.038)^x$

   B. $y = 38,500(1.38)^x$

   C. $y = 38,500(1.038)^x$

   D. $y = 81,172(1.38)^x$

25. If $f(x) = |x|$ and $g(x) = -\dfrac{1}{x}$, then for $x < 0$, $g(f(x)) =$

   A. $-\dfrac{1}{x}$

   B. 0

   C. $\left|\dfrac{1}{x}\right|$

   D. $\dfrac{1}{x}$

Questions 26 and 27 refer to the following information.

A recent poll surveyed a random selection of 850 likely voters in a state election. Of the sample, 31% say that they favor candidate A, and 18% say that they favor candidate B. The margin of error reported for this was ±3.4% with 95% confidence.

26. Which of the following statements can accurately be drawn from this data?

   A. The margin of error is too large to make any conclusions.

   B. The sample of likely voters doesn't represent all voters.

   C. The sample size is too small to represent the voters across the entire state.

   D. The sample was randomly selected and is large enough to make conclusions.

27. Which of the following statements can accurately be drawn from this data?

   A. The true percentage of likely voters who will vote for candidate A is 31%.

   B. The true percentage of likely voters who will vote for candidate A is most likely between 27.6% and 34.4%.

   C. The true percentage of likely voters who will vote for candidate B is 18%.

   D. The true percentage of likely voters who will vote for someone other than candidate A or candidate B is most likely between 45.6% and 52.4%.

CONTINUE ➡

Part VII

28. In a certain course, a student takes eight tests, all of which count equally. When figuring out the final grade, the instructor drops the best and the worst grades and averages the other six. The student calculates that his average for all eight tests is 84%. After dropping the best and the worst grades, the student averages 86%. What was the average of the best and the worst grades?

A. 68

B. 73

C. 78

D. 88

29. $x^2 + y^2 - 8x + 12y = 144$

What is the length of the radius of the circle with the equation above?

A. 6

B. 12

C. 14

D. 24

30. If a represents a real number, what condition must a satisfy so that the graph of $f(x) = 2(3a - x) - (5 + ax)$ does not intersect Quadrant III?

A. $a < \dfrac{5}{6}$

B. $-2 \leq a < \dfrac{5}{6}$

C. $a > \dfrac{5}{6}$

D. $a \leq -2$

Practice Test 2

CONTINUE ▶

📟 CALCULATOR

DIRECTIONS: For **Questions 31–38,** solve the problem and enter your answer in the grid, as described below, on the answer sheet.

1. Although not required, it is suggested that you write your answer in the boxes at the top of the columns to help you fill in the circles accurately. You will receive credit only if the circles are filled in correctly.

2. Mark no more than one circle in any column.

3. No question has a negative answer.

4. Some problems may have more than one correct answer. In such cases, enter only one answer.

5. **Mixed numbers** such as $3\frac{1}{2}$ must be entered as 3.5 or $\frac{7}{2}$.

   If $3\frac{1}{2}$ is entered into the grid as [3 1 / 2], it will be interpreted as $\frac{31}{2}$, not $3\frac{1}{2}$.

6. **Decimal answers:** If you obtain a decimal answer with more digits than the grid can accommodate, it may be either rounded or truncated, but it must fill the entire grid.

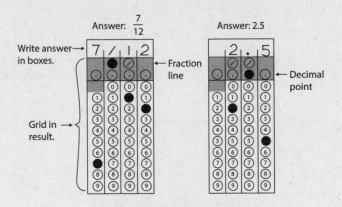

Answer: $\frac{7}{12}$ Answer: 2.5

Write answer in boxes. ← Fraction line ← Decimal point

Grid in result.

Answer: 201
Either position is correct.

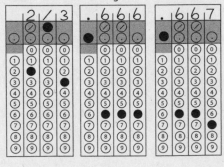

Acceptable ways to grid $\frac{2}{3}$ are:

Part VII

CONTINUE ▶

31. The 50 members of a governing body of an organization have held office for the following number of complete terms. (Note that a zero means that the member is currently in the process of serving his or her first term.)

Number of Complete Terms Served	Number of Members
0	6
1	13
2	21
3	4
4	5
5	1

What is the mean number of terms served by the members of this governing body?

32. If $\dfrac{x}{12} + \dfrac{x}{18} = 1$, what is the value of x?

33. An African elephant can lift a total of approximately 660 pounds with its trunk. A small bundle of twigs weighs 12 pounds. If an African elephant lifts a small log that weighs 50 pounds, what is the greatest number of small twig bundles that it could theoretically lift in addition to the log?

Practice Test 2

CONTINUE ▶

■ CALCULATOR

Questions 34 and 35 refer to the following information.

The table below shows the party affiliations of the 45 US presidents, whose terms began in the eighteenth, nineteenth, twentieth, or twenty-first centuries.

Party	Century				
	18th	**19th**	**20th**	**21st**	**Total**
Federalist	2	0	0	0	2
Demo-cratic-Republican	0	4	0	0	4
Democrat	0	8	7	1	16
Whig	0	4	0	0	4
Republican	0	7	10	2	19
Total	2	23	17	3	45

34. In what century did the highest percentage of Democrats serve as president? Enter your answer as a two-digit number (for example, enter "18" for the eighteenth century).

35. To the nearest percentage point, what percentage of US presidents have *not* been Democrats or Republicans? Members of the "Democratic-Republican" party were neither Democrats nor Republicans. Enter your answer as a two-digit number.

36.
$$5x + 4y = 11$$
$$6x - 8y = 10$$

In the system of equations above, what is the value of *y*?

CALCULATOR 🖩

37. A car travels from town A to town B, a distance of 360 miles, in 9 hours. How many hours would the same trip have taken had the car traveled 5 mph faster?

38.

$$\frac{2}{x+2} + \frac{3}{x-5} = \frac{4x+7}{x^2-3x-10}$$

What is the solution to the equation shown above?

STOP
If you finish before time is called, you may check your work on this section only.
Do not turn to any other section.

Practice Test 2

Section 5: Essay

50 Minutes—1 Essay

DIRECTIONS: The essay gives you an opportunity to show how effectively you can read and comprehend a passage and write an essay analyzing the passage. In your essay, you should demonstrate that you have read the passage carefully, present a clear and logical analysis, and use language precisely.

Your essay will need to be written on the lines provided in your answer booklet. You will have enough space if you write on every line and keep your handwriting to an average size. Try to print or write clearly so that your writing will be legible to the readers scoring your essay.

As you read the passage below, consider how the writers, Alex Jensen and Susan M. McHale, use the following:

- Evidence, such as facts, statistics, or examples, to support claims.
- Reasoning to develop ideas and to connect claims and evidence.
- Stylistic or persuasive elements, such as word choice or appeals to emotion, to add power to the ideas expressed.

Adapted from "What makes siblings from the same family so different? Parents" by Alex Jensen and Susan M. McHale, originally published in The Conversation, July 6, 2015. Alex Jensen is an Assistant Professor of Human Development at Brigham Young University. Susan M. McHale is a Professor of Human Development and Family Studies at Pennsylvania State University.

WHAT MAKES SIBLINGS FROM THE SAME FAMILY SO DIFFERENT? PARENTS

1   A colleague related the following story: while running errands with her 11- and 7-year-old daughters, a back seat battle began to rage. My colleague's attempts to defuse the situation only led to a shouting match about who was to blame for the skirmish. Finally the 11-year-old proclaimed to her sister, "You started it the day you were born and took away Mom's love!"

2   This pair of sisters fight frequently, and from their mother's perspective, part of the reason is that the two have little in common. As it turns out, their situation is not unique.

3   Despite the fact that siblings are, on average, 50% genetically similar, are often raised in the same home by the same parents, attend the same schools and have many other shared experiences, siblings are often only as similar to each other as they are to children who are growing up across town or even across the country.

4   So, what is it that makes two siblings from the same family so different?

WHAT MAKES THE DIFFERENCE?

5   As researchers of sibling and family relationships, we knew that at least one answer to this question comes from theory and data showing that, at least in some families, siblings try to be different from one another and seek to establish a unique identity and position in their family.

6   From a child's perspective, if an older brother excels at school, it may be easier to attract her parents' attention and praise by becoming a star athlete than by competing with her brother to get the best grades. In this way, even small differences between siblings can become substantial differences over time.

7   But parents may also play a role. For instance, when parents notice differences between their children, children may pick up on parents' perceptions and beliefs about those differences. This, in turn, can increase sibling differences.

8   We wanted to test these ideas to see what makes siblings different. So, we used data from first- and second-born teenage siblings from 388 two-parent families to examine sibling differences in school performance.

9   We asked mothers and fathers to report on whether they thought the two siblings differed in their academic abilities, and if so, which sibling was more capable. We also collected school grades from both siblings' report cards.

PREFERENCE FOR THE FIRSTBORN

10 Our analyses showed some interesting results: parents tended to believe that the older sibling was better in school. This was even when older siblings did not actually receive better grades, on average.

11 This may be a product of parents having greater expectations for firstborns or that, at any given time, the older sibling is undertaking more advanced school work.

12 There was, however, an exception to this pattern: in families with older brothers and younger sisters, parents rated the younger sibling as being more capable. In fact, in those families, younger sisters received better grades than their older brothers.

13 Our findings also showed that it was not sibling differences in school grades that predicted parents' ratings of their children's abilities. Rather, parents' beliefs about differences in their children's abilities predicted later sibling differences in school grades.

14 In other words, when parents believed one child was more capable than the other, that child's school grades improved more over time than their sibling's.

SUSTAINING BELIEFS

15 Although we expected that children's school grades and parents' beliefs about their children's relative abilities would be mutually influential, it turned out that parents' beliefs did not change much over their children's teenage years.

16 Instead, sibling differences in school grades did change and were predicted by parents' beliefs. In this way, parents' beliefs about differences between their children may encourage the development of actual sibling difference.

17 The above comment by an 11-year-old highlights that children are sensitive to their place and value in the family—relative to those of their siblings. Parents may strive to show their love for their children, but they also should be aware that small differences in how they treat their children can have large effects—including on their children's development and adjustment and also on the sibling relationship.

18 Indeed, some research suggests that sibling conflict arises when children try to be different from their siblings.

19 My colleague may be correct that her daughters fight frequently because they have nothing in common. But their conflicts may also be motivated by her daughter's perception that their differences started on the day her sister was born "and took away Mom's love."

Write an essay in which you explain how the writers build an argument to persuade their audience that parents are the reason why siblings from the same family behave differently. In your essay, analyze how Alex Jensen and Susan M. McHale use one or more of the features previously listed (or features of your own choice) to strengthen the logic and persuasiveness of their argument. Be sure that your analysis focuses on the most relevant aspects of the passage.

Your essay should not explain whether you agree with the writers' claims but rather explain how they build an argument to persuade their audience.

ANSWER KEYS AND EXPLANATIONS

Section 1: Reading Test

1. D	12. B	23. A	33. C	43. D
2. B	13. A	24. D	34. B	44. C
3. A	14. B	25. D	35. D	45. C
4. A	15. C	26. C	36. D	46. D
5. C	16. B	27. B	37. C	47. B
6. B	17. C	28. C	38. A	48. D
7. A	18. B	29. C	39. B	49. B
8. B	19. D	30. A	40. C	50. D
9. A	20. B	31. A	41. C	51. A
10. D	21. D	32. D	42. D	52. A
11. B	22. C			

READING TEST RAW SCORE ☐
(Number of correct answers)

1. **The correct answer is D.** The narrator's attention to detail frequently shows how ridiculous Golightly looks (lines 20–23). The descriptions show the character to be helpless in the face of a normal event—a rainstorm (lines 36–39). Contrasted with his vanity, the picture the narrator paints is mocking. While some of the narrator's statements border on the ironic ("it was looking like 'an Officer and a gentleman'" and "It was a sad thing that happened"), such statements are not pervasive. Surrealness and pride are not shown, so choices A, B, and C are incorrect.

2. **The correct answer is B.** Lines 7–11 offer Golightly's ability to recognize a horse as one of his virtues; since this is something almost anyone can do, it is hardly a virtue of any significance and can be interpreted as an instance of the narrator mocking Golightly. Choice A (lines 1–3) makes a statement about Golightly's pride in "looking like" an officer, but that alone is not ridiculous enough to reveal the passage's overall mocking tone. Choice C (lines 19–23) provides an in-depth description of Golightly's dress, but without

additional context, it lacks the proper tone. Choice D (lines 33–35) describes the "monsoonish" rainfall but does not provide commentary on Golightly.

3. **The correct answer is A.** Golightly is described as an officer (lines 1–3) dressing in "honor of the Service." We are told he was returning to his post from a period of leave, which would indicate a military post (lines 15–16). There is no indication that he was trying to escape capture by the Indian government (choice B). Golightly was not an outlaw (choice C), nor was he a businessman on an overseas trip (choice D).

4. **The correct answer is A.** The previous correct answer classifies Golightly as a proper military man returning to his post from a period of leave. In lines 11–13, "nobody ever dreamed of seeing him handcuffed" because he was so proper, and the description of him as a "deserter" shows that it is believed he has abandoned his post, because that is the crime of which deserters are guilty. Choice B suggests that he was alarmingly close to the end

of his leave and was thus rushing. Choice C describes what Golightly was wearing; it does not say what he does. Choice D describes the incident with his second horse and is thus unrelated.

5. **The correct answer is C.** Kipling piles on the missteps Golightly makes, each one adding to the other, making Golightly look silly and inept throughout the passage. For a person whose title is "officer," Golightly does not show professionalism or skill at handling a relatively minor problem. The rainstorm (choice B) is a backdrop for the setting in which he falters and is not in itself a way to make fun of the character. There is no satire shown, so choice A is incorrect. Golightly's trouble with the horse (choice D) went beyond "difficulty."

6. **The correct answer is B.** Lines 16–17 present an idiomatic way of saying that Golightly was using his leave time to the greatest extent possible without incurring wrath from his superiors. His capture by the authorities was a result of misidentification because he was so unrecognizable from being out in the rainstorm and falling off the horse. He was doing what was expected, so there was nothing to get caught doing (choice D), except that he looked suspicious to others in his disheveled state. Choice A is contrary to the meaning of the text; he *had* told his superiors. The sentence is about how much leave he could take, not about leaving without permission (choice C).

7. **The correct answer is A.** It is the detail of the descriptions that give the story its mocking tone and attitude. Kipling sets up the character by describing his intense vanity, which contrasts with the way he looks when caught in the rainstorm (lines 61–84). The passage's purpose is focused on conveying the comedy of Golightly's misadventure. No commentary is provided on the setting or state of the military affairs in India. As such,

these details are not relevant to any of the other choices.

8. **The correct answer is B.** Lines 37–39 explain that the pony was walking through mud, which would logically slow down its pace, so choice B is the best answer and *sped* (choice A) can be eliminated. A mire is a muddy pool, but it makes no sense to say that a pony "pooled," (choice C). Indicating that the pony started eating at this point in line 38 would not flow naturally from the previous statement about how the path had turned into mud, so choice D is not the best answer.

9. **The correct answer is A.** In the passage, the narrator states that Golightly's focus on his appearance led him to not take enough money with him (lines 27–29). This results in him negotiating with the Station Master for a first-class ticket and his subsequent arrest. His pride, lack of an umbrella, and fall from his horse may have been contributing factors to his arrest, but none of those are the best answer. It was not pride alone that led to the arrest as, even with an umbrella, Golightly would still have had no money for a ticket, and Golightly was not responsible for the fall, as it was an accident.

10. **The correct answer is D.** Throughout the excerpt, the narrator uses an omniscient perspective to tell the story. But in this line, the narrator editorializes and injects his own opinion. Instead of describing the character's response, the narrator judges it as unworthy of recording and then continues to describe Golightly's behavior. The narrator does not report the character's verbal response (choice A), thoughts (choice B), or add dialogue (choice C).

11. **The correct answer is B.** Throughout the passage, the author is primarily concerned with historical details about how English towns developed. The author does not spend much time comparing towns to manors (choice A) or proving that English towns

evolved from marks (choice C). While the author does describe some of the qualities that define a town (choice D), this is mostly limited to the first paragraph, and the best answer should capture the purpose of the entire passage.

12. **The correct answer is B.** In the fourth paragraph, the author writes that "London was of course a great port and trading center …," and the use of the phrase "of course" implies that this is something well known, so choice B is the best answer. At the end of the second paragraph, the author writes, "But all the English towns were far less flourishing before the arrival of the Normans than they afterwards became," and since London was one such town, choice A is not the best answer. Choice C seems to refer to the quotation about how a town is "one part of the district where men lived closer together than elsewhere," but this is a statement made by Professor Freeman, not the author. While the author refers to the privileges of town life several times in the passage, the author implies that such privileges make *him* prefer town life. Nowhere does the passage state that this was true in general, so choice D lacks sufficient support.

13. **The correct answer is A.** The first paragraph of the passage establishes the many traits of manors, one of which is that it could also be referred to as a rural township. According to the first paragraph, a town, not a manor, is a group of townships, so choice D is incorrect. The paragraph also states that manors were not as easily defended as towns, making choice B a distortion of the details. Choice C inverts the details of the passage; a manor was a Saxon settlement called as such by the Normans.

14. **The correct answer is B.** The author refers to a mound in terms of a town being defensible, so it must be something that protects, which makes choice B the best answer. Choice A

describes a moat, which is also mentioned in line 10, rather than a mound, so this definition is both incorrect and redundant. Choices C and D could both be definitions of *mound* in another context, but they fail to imply something used to defend or protect a town.

15. **The correct answer is C.** The answer to this question can be found in the second paragraph, which states that some towns "grew silently in the shadow of a great abbey or monastery." While towns did spring from the camps of the invaders; the invaders referenced were Normans, not Saxons (choice A). Neither shops nor stores are mentioned as contributing to town growth (choice B). And Bristol, Southhampton, and Norwhich (choice D) are mentioned as port towns, and thus, being towns themselves, they could not be a place that towns arose.

16. **The correct answer is B.** The author calls William the Norman's survey, "our great authority" before referring to details within it. No records are referenced from the "sacked and deserted" Roman towns (choice A). The work of Professor Freeman is referenced once (choice C). The town charters, while described, are not identified as the source of significant historical detail (choice D).

17. **The correct answer is C.** The answer to this question can be found in the third paragraph, which explains that *in demesne* means "in default of a lord," and later indicates that the towns that are "in demesne" *belong* to lords. This eliminates choices A and B, which both suggest that towns that are "in demesne" belong to someone other than their lords. While some towns that are "in demesne" may be shared, the passage shows that this is not true of all such towns, so choice D is not the best answer.

18. **The correct answer is B.** The best evidence for the previous question is found in the

third paragraph as it identifies the meaning of *in demesne*, and establishes the lord as the owner of the town, even as the town may fall within the king's demesne. Choice A identifies a detail of where towns grew. Choice C supports an incorrect answer to the previous question (that towns were shared with other lords). Choice D identifies details related to the *firma burgi*, a form of taxation.

19. **The correct answer is D.** In the fourth paragraph, the author states that London "had many foreign merchants in it" and that it was ". . . the centre of English national life, and the voice of its citizens counted for something in national affairs." This supports the conclusion in choice D. While London was a successful trading center (choice A), the author does not imply that this alone made London influential in national affairs, as other ports mentioned were important trading hubs but had no explicit input into national matters. London also had a civic constitution (choice C), but this is not described as influential in the town's role in national affairs either, nor is the town's ability to distinguish itself from other towns (choice B).

20. **The correct answer is B.** According to the passage, London's distinguishing trait was its many foreign merchants, information that is included in the lines in choice B. Choice A provides support for what made it a unique location in Norman England, but it does not provide key support for why it played a role in national matters. Choice C identifies other great ports but does not explain London's role on the national stage. Choice D may suggest that London's size would qualify it for greater status and privilege, but that information is not explicit in the passage.

21. **The correct answer is D.** The surrounding sentences are focused on taxation of town and the securing of the *firma burgi*, which allowed towns to determine how much they

would pay in taxes, rather than the determination being made by a third party, such as a sheriff. *Estimated* provides a valid option related to the determination, evaluation, or estimation of the amount of taxes to be collected. *Tested* (choice A) infers a common meaning of *assessed* as related to testing, but this would be inappropriate for the context of the passage. *Examine* (choice B) implies that the Sheriff is making observations but not making decisions related to the levied tax. *Arrested* (choice C) distorts the context as attached to the sheriff.

22. **The correct answer is C.** The article emphasizes the problem of GALS, an invasive species that threatens the ecosystems of the islands. The article is informational and does not attempt to persuade readers (choice D), encourage them to visit (choice A), or raise money (choice B).

23. **The correct answer is A.** The main discussion of the article is about how scientists are trying to contain and eliminate GALS by using trained dogs to detect them. Choice B states the opposite of the correct answer. Choice C is a true statement, but it is not the main idea of the article. Choice D is also true, but the article does not focus on how organizations are collaborating; rather its emphasis is on training dogs to help solve the specific problem of one invasive species.

24. **The correct answer is D.** The first four lines of the introductory paragraph before the article mention the location of the islands, which are quite a distance from any mainland. This fact of geography likely kept people from settling there for a long time. This meant that the natural ecosystems were in balance. Choices A and C may be true, but they do not explain why the Galapagos have unique ecosystems. Choice B is not supported by the passage.

25. **The correct answer is D.** The article explains that the GALS is very destructive because it

eats so many different types of plants (lines 12–16). Once this snail enters a population, it takes over by eating plant species that keep the ecosystems in balance. While their ability to hide (choice C) makes them difficult to find, the threat comes from their eating habits. Choices A and B are unsupported by the passage.

26. **The correct answer is C.** According to the passage, GALS only affected 50 acres of land as of its writing (lines 20–21), but they are covering more ground every year, and since they will destroy much needed plant life on that ground, choice C is the best answer. Although dogs are being used in an effort to solve the GALS problem, that problem has not been solved yet, so choice A is not the best answer. There is no discussion of media treatment of the problem in this passage, so choice B is incorrect, nor is the GALS problem compared to other invasive species problems on the island, so choice D cannot be determined.

27. **The correct answer is B.** Lines 21–23 explain how GALS are covering more ground "every wet season," and since they will destroy the plant life on that ground, this proves that the problem is getting worse with each passing season or year. Choice A (lines 12–16) introduces the problem; it does not explain how it is getting worse, which is what the correct answer to the previous question states. Choice C (lines 30–36) and choice D (lines 76–78) only explain efforts to solve the problem; they are not evidence that shows how the problem is steadily growing worse every year.

28. **The correct answer is C.** Dogs are not native to the Galapagos, which are islands far from any mainland, inhabited mostly by species unique to the islands, such as giant tortoises and iguanas. Dogs were brought to the islands (lines 63–66) by people to help them find the invasive species that are upsetting

the balance found on the islands. The dogs' sense of smell makes them good hunters for the invasive species on the islands, but that does not explain why they are invasive, so choice A is incorrect. The text explains that the dogs had to be acclimated both to the islands and their trainers, but their adjustment was so that they could be trained properly for their role as hunters. This acclimation does not explain why they would be considered invasive, so choice B is incorrect. Choice D is incorrect because the text does not say that dogs ever thrived on the islands or were predators of any native species; it only stated that the dogs brought by the project helped in finding a particular invasive species so that it could be eradicated.

29. **The correct answer is C.** Dogs have a very highly developed sense of smell and can be trained to follow a scent that humans cannot detect (lines 37–40), so choice C is the best answer. Dogs were not chosen based on their ease of interaction with people or for their ability to find drugs, so choice A and choice B are incorrect. The passage never indicates that GALS hide in small spaces or that dogs track them in such spaces, so choice D is incorrect.

30. **The correct answer is A.** Lines 37–41 reveal that dogs "have an incredible sense of smell and can be trained to detect scents," which is basically a rewording of the correct answer to the previous question. Choice B (lines 41–44) seems to have mistaken choice B for the correct answer to the previous question, since it references how dogs can detect drugs. Choice C (lines 44–48) describes how dogs are used in the project, not why they are ideal for the project. Choice D (lines 49–53) just explains when the first phase of the project began.

31. **The correct answer is A.** *Acclimation*, as used in the context provided, describes how the dogs had to adjust to the Galapagos, which was not their native environment.

Conforming (choice B) suggests blending in rather than adjusting. *Adaptation* (choice C) is a process that takes many years, not a few days or weeks. Training is a type of behavior modification (choice D), but it is unrelated to acclimation.

32. **The correct answer is D.** *Biosecurity* is a combined form of the prefix *bio-* (meaning life) and *security*. As used in the passage, the word refers to security from harmful biological species, and is therefore protection of the ecosystems. *Biosecurity* is not related to handling of animals (choice A) or plants (choice B). The article does not mention extinction (choice C).

33. **The correct answer is C.** The content of the speech shows Stanton's concern about how women were treated unfairly, with few rights. Although some people at the time may have been shocked by her speech, her purpose was not shock value (choice B), but to inform and persuade. Although she was sympathetic to the plight of minorities/African Americans, this speech was focused on women's issues, so choice D is incorrect. Choice A is unsupported by the passage.

34. **The correct answer is B.** The best evidence for the answer to previous question can be found in lines 13–16 ("He has withheld from her rights which are given to the most ignorant and degraded men—both natives and foreigners."). These lines succinctly address Stanton's primary concern. Choice A acts as an introduction for the following statements, not indicating the precise claim. Choices C and D provide a critique of a woman's rights when married.

35. **The correct answer is D.** *Franchise* is another word for the right to vote. By pairing the word with *elective* in line 18, the focus is on the right to vote in elections. Stanton emphasizes how women are deprived of this basic right. A more modern meaning of franchise is in sports, indicating a team that is a member of a larger group or league. At the time of the speech, there were no such sports leagues, and the word was commonly used to refer to the right to vote, thus making choices A, B, and C incorrect.

36. **The correct answer is D.** In lines 29–35, Stanton shows how women have been enslaved by the legal system and by men, who are considered superior. Some women did have jobs outside the home, as is implied by lines 24–25 (choice A), but Stanton explains that they were not allowed to keep their wages. Women were not allowed to vote (choice B), and Stanton includes this in her list of grievances, but voting rights is not directly related to obedience. Choice C is implied by lines 36–41, but this issue is not directly related to obedience.

37. **The correct answer is C.** Isabella's master was willing to give her freedom before he had to, and the introduction tells us that she was granted her freedom in 1827, before it was legally mandated. Forcing her to work longer than he had originally said was a form of mistreatment, making choice A incorrect. He did not allow her to learn to read and write, which was why her narrative is told through someone else's voice (choice B). Although he did make promises that he didn't keep (choice D), Truth suggests that all slaveholders used this tactic to get more work out of their slaves.

38. **The correct answer is A.** Lines 67–72 convey the relatively good treatment of Isabella's master as he set her free before she was legally required to go free. Choice B (lines 73–75) makes a statement about Isabella's physical condition; it does not reveal anything about her master, so it cannot serve as evidence to support the previous correct answer. Choice C (lines 85–90) speaks to how Isabella's faithfulness may have contributed to her master refusing to keep his previous promise. Choice D (lines 91–96) makes a

statement about the work Isabella would do, and if anything, it shows that her master was inconsiderate by making her do work "she was not wholly able to do."

39. **The correct answer is B.** Although Truth had great religious faith, the faithfulness referred to here is about loyalty, not religion, which eliminates choices A and C. Truth reminisces here about her service to her master. He had asked that she be a faithful servant (lines 69–72), which she was, but then she recognizes that, ironically, this is exactly why she has become so valuable to her master (lines 85–90). Choice D contradicts the passage in that continued faithfulness is unlikely to affect the master's inflexibility if it was the cause of his broken promise initially.

40. **The correct answer is C.** The word operation often refers to an organized activity, either medical, military, mathematical, etc.; in this case, the operation refers to the continued enslavement or the process of trying to appease her master to earn her just due. While the context of the passage may suggest some sort of medical operation in relation to Truth's injured hand, nothing explicitly is mentioned (choice A). The same is true of choices B and D.

41. **The correct answer is C.** The commonality is in the necessity for obedience. For women, obedience to their husbands was the rule of law (lines 29–55); for slaves, it was a given that they had to obey their masters. In some cases, women did get paid for their work (choice A), and women, whether or not they were slaves, were generally in charge of children, whether their own or others' (choice B). While some men may break promises, only the Sojourner text discusses how her master continually broke his promises to her, so choice D is incorrect.

42. **The correct answer is D.** Stanton's list of grievances shows her frustration and resulting anger at the system that has denied women basic rights. Truth's narrative expresses her feelings of frustration at being promised her freedom only to have it denied. Truth doesn't show anger (choice A), regret (choice B), or bitterness (choice C). She shows resolve and determination to get her freedom.

43. **The correct answer is D.** The overall main idea encompasses the discovery and its meaning (a new species). Choices A and B are details that support the main idea. Choice C is a general statement that could be a conclusion, but it is not the main idea.

44. **The correct answer is C.** The article describes how the discovery was made by a student and other researchers (lines 9–16). The discovery was important because it identified a new species (lines 17–20) and will help scientists and researchers continue to add to our body of knowledge about prehistoric animals. The discovery wasn't totally by chance because Jasinski was conducting related research (choice D). Choices A and B are general statements that could have general application, but they are not conclusions based on facts in the article.

45. **The correct answer is C.** *Formidable* can mean "impressive" in the sense of its size or power, and in this context, the predator—the newly discovered species—would have been threatening to other species. The predator might have even been frightened at times, but this is not a defining characteristic of predators, which are generally thought to inspire fear more than feel it, so choice A is not the best answer. Choice B would be an odd description of the effectiveness of a predator, so it is not a very good answer either. While *difficult* can be used as a synonym for *formidable*, it would be better used to describe an opponent in a contest, not a predator that presents more of a danger

than a challenge, so choice D is not the best answer choice.

46. **The correct answer is D.** The meaning of the genus name *Saurornitholestes* provides clues about the dinosaur's appearance (lines 20–24). None of the Latin names indicate where the fossils were found (choice B) or where the dinosaurs lived (choice C). The discovered species was named after a human, as are others on occasion, but the name does not reveal anything about the dinosaur.

47. **The correct answer is B.** The first part of the dinosaur's name, *Saurornitholestes*, means "lizard bird thief" (line 22), and lines 24–27 reveal that it had physical characteristics similar to those of birds (it was "lightly built with long legs") and lizards (it had "jaws lined with teeth"). Choice A merely states the Latin name without explaining what it means, so unless the reader speaks Latin, there is little way to use this information to learn anything about how the dinosaur looked. The fact that Robert Sullivan discovered the dinosaur explains why the second part of its name is *sullivani*, but it says nothing about the dinosaur's traits. Choice D merely mentions a mistake in classifying the dinosaur; it provides no clue to what its name says about its appearance.

48. **The correct answer is D.** The passage explains the process by which Jasinski noticed that the species he was examining differed from the description of what was expected (lines 38–45). He didn't recognize this because of either the size of the fossil (choice A) or its markings (choice B). Scientists did not know what its closest relatives were because they had not yet realized that it was a different species, so choice C is incorrect.

49. **The correct answer is B.** The author states that Jasinski realized that the fossil actually had "subtle differences" (lines 40–41)

from the one to which he compared it and was, therefore, a different species. Choice A merely introduces Jasinski; it says nothing about how he figured out he had found a new species. Choice C explains one of the things Jasinski discovered about the dinosaur; it does not suggest that the dinosaur's sense of smell is how he knew he was dealing with a new species. Choice D only explains when the dinosaur lived.

50. **The correct answer is D.** Lines 41–45 provide context clues that the olfactory bulb is related to the sense of smell. The organs that are used for smell are contained in that part of the skull, which was unusually large, but the clue is in the next sentence that defines *olfactory*. These clues eliminate *bulb* (choice A), *unusually large* (choice B), and *surface of the skull* (choice C), which are not supported by the passage.

51. **The correct answer is A.** Lines 84–85 explicitly state how its sense of smell made the *S. sullivani* an effective predator as it used "its acute sense of smell to track down prey." Choices B, C, and D could all be correct in another context, but this question specifies that the answer must be determined "according to the passage," which does not provide evidence for any answer except for choice A.

52. **The correct answer is A.** In the ninth paragraph, the author lists several traits that speak to predatory success, one of which is pack behavior. While the dinosaur does have bird-like features (choice B), these did not necessarily contribute to hunting success. While *S. sullivani* did have a unique skull, what distinguished it from *S. langstoni* and harbored its large olfactory bulb, the skull itself did not necessarily contribute to success (choice C). Lines 79–81 and line 86 state the *S. sullivani* was not a large dinosaur; therefore, it did not have size on its side (choice D).

Section 2: Writing and Language Test

1. D	10. B	19. A	28. C	37. B
2. C	11. B	20. D	29. C	38. B
3. B	12. A	21. C	30. D	39. D
4. D	13. B	22. A	31. C	40. A
5. C	14. A	23. B	32. C	41. C
6. A	15. B	24. A	33. B	42. B
7. B	16. C	25. B	34. A	43. C
8. A	17. D	26. A	35. D	44. D
9. D	18. A	27. A	36. B	

WRITING AND LANGUAGE TEST RAW SCORE

(Number of correct answers)

1. **The correct answer is D.** The underlined sentence should be deleted because other phrases from the 1980s are not related to the Glass Ceiling. Choices A and B are incorrect because the sentence should not be kept, as it does not support the main topic, nor does it act as a transition. Choice C is incorrect because the underlined sentence is does not repeat information that has already been provided.

2. **The correct answer is C.** The phrase "as recent data make clear" is nonessential information and should thus be separated from the rest of the clause with a form of punctuation—a comma, an em dash, or even a set of parentheses. Choice A lacks the comma before "as," which is necessary both to separate the nonessential information and the transition "However" from the rest of the sentence. Choice B removes the commas and thus complicates the meaning of the sentence. Choice D inappropriately divides the phrase "as recent data make clear" in half, seemingly making the phrase "make clear" a command that does not relate to the rest of the sentence.

3. **The correct answer is B.** As written, the text has a syntax error. The intention of the writer is to say that the number of women

in CEO positions in Fortune 500 companies is just 5% of the total. To convey this, the modifier *only* has to be placed correctly in the sentence—before 5%. Choices A and C are incorrect because they say women hold 5% of CEO positions (but may or may not hold that percentage of any other positions), and they take the emphasis off the low figure of 5% and place it on CEO positions; this is not what the writer means to say. Choice D is incorrect because it says women hold 5% of CEO positions in Fortune 500 companies (but may or may not hold that percentage in other kinds of companies), and it takes the emphasis off the low figure of 5% and places it on Fortune 500 companies; this is not what the writer means to say.

4. **The correct answer is D.** This sentence requires a word that means "having existed or taken place in a period before the present," which is what *past* means. *Passed* (choice A) is the past tense of *pass*. (*Past* and *passed* are commonly confused words.) *Passing* (choice B) doesn't have the right meaning for this sentence. While it refers to time going by, it changes the sense of the sentence by referring to passing years rather than events that have taken place. *Passive* (choice C) doesn't make sense in this sentence.

5. **The correct answer is C.** The only internal punctuation this sentence requires is a comma after the introductory phrase "In 1995," as shown in choice C. Choice A includes a colon after *was*, which creates a sentence fragment before the colon. Choice B is incorrect because, while it removes the incorrect colon, it introduces a new error by including a semicolon after *formed*, which creates a sentence fragment after the semicolon. While choice D removes the incorrect colon, it introduces two new errors by removing the comma after 1995 and by placing a comma after *formed*, which interrupts the flow of the sentence's idea.

6. **The correct answer is A.** This sentence requires a word that means "result," or "something caused by something else," which is the meaning of *effect*—a noun that means "the result of something." *Affect* (choice B) is the wrong word for this sentence. It is a verb that means "to bring about a result." (*Effect* and *affect* are commonly confused words. One way to know the difference between them is to remember that after you *affect* something, there is an *effect*.) The words *effective* (choice C) and *affection* (choice D) do not make sense in this sentence.

7. **The correct answer is B.** The sentence uses the plural pronoun form *they* earlier in the sentence, which provides a clue that another plural pronoun is needed here to replace the plural noun *corporations*, in this case the pronoun *their*. The pronouns *her* (choice A), *his* (choice C), and *your* (choice D) are singular and are thus incorrect.

8. **The correct answer is A.** The corporations have the financial and educational resources to overcome this "supply barrier"; therefore, they are "equipped" with them. *Implemented* (choice B) is incorrect because the corporations are not implementing the resources; this word choice is contradictory to the point

of the passage. Both *furnished* (choice C) and *supplied* (choice D) imply someone or something had given the corporations these resources, which is not supported in the passage. The source of the resources is never mentioned. The point of the sentence is simply that the corporations are equipped with the necessary resources to solve this issue but are not using them.

9. **The correct answer is D.** The original punctuation creates a sentence fragment; combining the text eliminates the fragment. Choice A is incorrect because the period after *do* creates a sentence fragment. While choice B eliminates the incorrect period, it introduces a new error by adding a comma after *discrimination*, which, with the accompanying coordinating conjunction *and* implies that the following information is an independent clause—which it is not. Choice C is not correct because, although it removes the incorrect period, it introduces a new error by including and additional conjunction *(and)*. With this addition, the sentence no longer makes sense.

10. **The correct answer is B.** This paragraph discusses some of the obstacles and challenges that persist regarding gender discrimination and bias that have proven difficult to overcome. A good opening sentence would support this notion, which choice B does. Choices A and C provide direct opposition to this point of view. Choice D is out of context and unsupported by this paragraph and passage.

11. **The correct answer is B.** The writer is saying that women must be accepted "as equals" in the corporate sphere. Only choice B places this modifier after *accepted*, the correct position in the sentence. Choice A is incorrect because the modifying phrase "as equals" is not placed in the right part of the sentence, creating a syntax error. While choice C repositions the modifying phrase, it introduces

a new error by using the adverb form of *equally*. Choice D repositions the modifying phrase (which could be correct in this part of the sentence); however, it, too, incorrectly uses the adverb form of *equally*.

12. **The correct answer is A.** The sentence as written introduces details that describe the entire collection. Choice B adds information not supported by the passage. Choice C implies the examples are not inclusive. Choice D is incorrect because *Already* has no meaning in the context of the sentence.

13. **The correct answer is B.** Semicolons are needed when items in a series already contain commas; additionally, no comma is necessary between the correlative conjunctions *not only* and *but also*. Only choice B correctly shows the proper separation of items in a series with semicolons and commas. Choice A incorrectly places commas after *extend* and *executive*. Choice C incorrectly places a comma after *branches* and incorrectly eliminates the comma after *world*. Choice D incorrectly places a comma after *services* and incorrectly eliminates the comma after *government*.

14. **The correct answer is A.** The author is introducing a new topic (going from an overview of the modern Library of Congress to its beginnings) and pointing out that the Library did not start out as large as it is today. The sentence in the original text is the best transition phrase for cohesion. Choice B might sound correct, but it changes the tone of the passage from formal to informal, so it is not the best answer. Choice C changes the sense and meaning of the text and creates a sentence that does not support the main idea of the paragraph. Choice D might appear to be correct, but like choice B, it changes the tone of the passage from formal to informal, so it is not the best answer.

15. **The correct answer is B.** After the original Library of Congress was destroyed, the nation needed a new, similar institution. In other words, the library had to be replaced. *Substitute* (choice A) is incorrect because it suggests a new library as well as the continued presence of the original library, which was not the case. *Replacement* is the better word choice because it is a more precise word in this context. *Stand-in* (choice C) also indicates a new library, but like choice A, it suggests the continued presence of the original library. Choice D is incorrect because the new library was a replacement as opposed to a copy of the old library.

16. **The correct answer is C.** The sentence specifies that the collections of the library were expanded. Because the collections belong to the library, the sentence requires a corresponding possessive pronoun. The correct choice is the possessive determiner *its*, which does not require an apostrophe. Choice A is incorrect because *it's* is a contraction of "it is." *Their* (choice B) is incorrect because it is a plural possessive pronoun, which does not agree with the antecedent *library*. Choice D is incorrect because *its'* is not a word.

17. **The correct answer is D.** This text requires seven commas, and only choice D has all the necessary commas in the right places. Choice A incorrectly places commas after *two* and *dramatic*. Choice B incorrectly places a comma after *photograph*. Choice C incorrectly places a comma after *two* and a semicolon after *composition*.

18. **The correct answer is A.** The library's collection keeps growing—in other words, it is ever-expanding. *Ever-existing* (choice B) changes the meaning of the sentence to say that the library's collection always exists. This is not what the author means. *Ever-expending* (choice C) and *ever-expounding* (choice D) make no sense.

19. The correct answer is A. Choice A best expresses the idea that Young instigated the change. Choice B incorrectly implies that there was opposition to the change. Choice C implies that it had to be an acquisitions library first before making the change. Choice D is incorrect because the introductory phrase implies that there was an addition to the operation rather than a replacement of one system for another.

20. The correct answer is D. In this paragraph the author is shifting from John Russell Young to Herbert Putnam. Choice D adds the phrase "after only two years," a detail with additional information that gives the reader a fuller sense of this story and creates a smoother transition. Choices A, B, and C make the shift from Young to Putnam, but none of the answer choices has the additional information or makes as smooth a transition as choice D.

21. The correct answer is C. This paragraph is mainly about Herbert Putnam, and Putnam (in the previous sentence) is the antecedent of the pronoun that starts this sentence. Putnam is one person, so the singular pronoun *he* is required. Choice A is incorrect because if *they* is used, the meaning of the sentence changes—it means Spofford, Young, and Putnam "took the Library of Congress directly into the national library scene." *Them* (choice B) is the objective case, and this sentence requires a pronoun in the subjective case. *We* (choice D) is incorrect because the antecedent of the pronoun that starts this sentence is *Putnam*, so a singular pronoun is required.

22. The correct answer is A. The last column of the chart shows information for the largest libraries (the category of the Library of Congress). According to the chart, there are 109 of these in the private sector and 51 in the private sector. Therefore, there are more public than private libraries similar in scope

and scale to the Library of Congress, making choice A correct. The chart does not support the conclusions in choices B, C, and D.

23. The correct answer is B. As written, this sentence contains a redundancy—*empty* and *contained nothing* mean the same thing. Choice B eliminates this redundancy. While choice C eliminates the redundancy, it is not the best answer because it changes the sense and intent of the sentence, taking away the weight and urgency of the bedroom being "forever empty." Choice D is incorrect because, although it eliminates the original issue, it adds a new redundancy: verses and poetry are the same thing.

24. The correct answer is A. Emily Dickinson had a seeming obsession with death, which was a common theme in many of her poems. *Predisposition* (choice B) is a tendency to act or think in a particular way, *predilection* (choice C) is a preference for something, and *predetermination* (choice D) is the doctrine (usually associated with Calvinism) that God has foreordained every event throughout eternity. None of these words express Dickinson's attitude toward death.

25. The correct answer is B. Emily is the sister in question, so this sentence calls for a singular possessive pronoun. *Sister's* is the possessive pronoun for *sister*. Sisters (choice A) is the plural of *sister*, not the possessive pronoun for the word. *Sisters'* (choice C) is a plural possessive pronoun (for *sisters*), not a singular possessive pronoun (for *sister*). *Sister* (choice D) is not a possessive pronoun.

26. The correct answer is A. The paragraph is mainly about Emily's isolation and the reason for it. In Emily's own words, she was "one 'standing alone in rebellion' of faith" as she resisted ideas common to her time. Only choice A refers to this. Choice B might seem like a good answer, but Emily's refusal to take part in social events stemmed from her sense of isolation rather than acting as the cause of it. The passage does not say she became isolated after refusing to participate in social events; it implies her refusal to be social was a decision she made because she felt so isolated. Choices C and D are not supported by the passage. The author does not say either of these reasons caused Emily's sense of isolation.

27. **The correct answer is A.** Choice A is the only choice that supplies the correct word *through* for this sentence. The words *tough* (choice B), *though* (choice C), and *thought* (choice D) do not make sense in the sentence.

28. **The correct answer is C.** The writer should not add the sentence because it detracts from the point about women's issues. The added sentence focuses on the idea of Emily being involved in politics, which is not the point Lavinia is making. Choices A and B are incorrect because the information is not directly related to the point being made by Lavinia. Choice D is incorrect because, although the statement is about Emily's life, it is misplaced in the midst of Lavinia's thoughts about how Emily viewed the limitations society imposed on women.

29. **The correct answer is C.** Because it is clear that it was Emily who felt "the trappings of being a woman," the required word is the singular subjective pronoun *she*. Choice A is incorrect because *they* is plural. If *they* is used, the sentence appears to be saying that both Emily and Lavinia "tried to eschew" the trappings of being a woman, which is not supported by the passage; in addition, the rest of the sentence will make no sense because *her* is used toward the end of the sentence. Choice B is incorrect because there is no antecedent for *we*. Choice D is incorrect because the sentence calls for a subjective pronoun; *her* is a possessive or an objective pronoun.

30. **The correct answer is D.** The passage is written in a formal style and has a literary tone. Instead of saying Emily did not accept the role of women, the author writes she "eschewed" "the trappings of being a woman." Only choice D matches this style and tone. Choices A, B, and C are incorrect because while each conveys this same thought, the uninspired word choice in each answer does not match the style or tone of the passage. In addition, choice C is also unnecessarily wordy.

31. **The correct answer is C.** A past tense verb is required to indicate that Emily received her gift in the past before this moment. In this situation, the simple past tense would also be acceptable, but it is not among the available answer choices. Choice A incorrectly has the present tense *is*, which is inappropriate because these events occurred in the past. Choices B and D use proper past tense helping verbs but change the participle *given* to *giving*, thus changing the meaning of the sentence—implying that Emily was sharing her gift, which does not fully align with later information in the passage.

32. **The correct answer is C.** The correct form of the verb "to decide" in this situation is the past tense *decided*—the preceding word *was* provides a helpful context clue to make this determination. Choices A and B feature incorrect verb tenses for this sentence. Choices C and D both possess proper past tense verbs, but choice C better aligns with the presence of the other simple past tense verbs *surrounded*, *was*, and *knew* while also being more concise than choice D.

33. **The correct answer is B.** This passage chronicles the early years of the famous writer Emily Dickinson, whom the world would eventually get to know and cherish, and the preceding sentence provides an important context clue to answer this question: "…it was time the world knew the full treasure her sister was." Choice B makes the best sense to follow and build upon this

notion. Choices A, C, and D don't make sense given the context of the passage.

34. **The correct answer is A.** The point of this opening paragraph is to establish the fact that even though scientists have long known that sleep is important to human health, they continue to study sleep. The "even though" part of this idea is conveyed by the word *yet*, which must be placed in the right part of the sentence if the sentence is to make sense. Only choice A does this. Choices B and C change the meaning of the sentence by eliminating the "even though" element that the writer wants to convey, and they demonstrate clumsy syntax. Choice D is incorrect because while it places *yet* correctly in the sentence, the rest of this answer demonstrates clumsy syntax.

35. **The correct answer is D.** This passage is mainly concerned with past theories about sleep. The fourth paragraph addresses sleep study in the twentieth century. Sentence 6 refers to advances in the study of sleep that were made during the twentieth century, so the passage would have a more logical sequence if this sentence were moved to the fourth paragraph. Sentences 1 and 2 (choices A and B) serve as transitions to the topic of past theories about sleep and should remain in this paragraph. Sentence 4 (choice C) describes one of these past theories about sleep. Therefore, it, too, should remain in this paragraph.

36. **The correct answer is B.** The sentence in choice B leads to the introduction of the theories that follow. Choice A is irrelevant to this part of the passage. Choices C and D are incorrect because the text does not imply either statement.

37. **The correct answer is B.** This sentence tells the reader that modern sleep research began with a machine. Machines are created, or invented, and only choice B conveys this idea. The words in the other answer choices each convey a different idea. A machine isn't discovered (choice A), though a new use for a machine may be discovered. The passage makes it clear that a sleep study went beyond the idea (choice C) or suggestion (choice D) of a machine.

38. **The correct answer is B.** The second part of the sentence is a subordinate clause, and a subordinating conjunction is necessary to establish the clause's connection to the beginning of the sentence: The study of sleep was enhanced *as a result of* Aserinsky and Kleitman's work. Choice B is the only answer with a subordinating conjunction. The other answer choices are all coordinating conjunctions that, if used, change the meaning of the sentence and would be incorrect with the absence of a comma before the revision point. *And* (choice A) makes the enhancement of sleep study and Aserinsky and Kleitman's work separate and equal things rather than one being the result of the other. *Or* (choice C) creates an illogical sentence for the context. *So* (choice D) changes the cause and effect of the situation: it means that Aserinsky and Kleitman did their work *because* the study of sleep was enhanced, as opposed to acting as a driving force behind improved sleep studies.

39. **The correct answer is D.** The link between the ideas in this sentence and the previous sentence is contradiction. Subjects awakened during REM sleep almost always remembered dreaming, *but* subjects awakened during non-REM sleep could rarely recall dreams. To convey this idea, a contradictory transition word or phrase is required, and the phrase "On the other hand," is the best answer among the choices given. While the phrases "Nevertheless," (choice A) and "Even so," (choice B) can indicate contradiction, in this case each creates a sentence that does not make sense. "As predicted," (choice C) is incorrect because the passage does not say

any predictions were made about what would happen during this study.

40. **The correct answer is A.** The underlined phrase leads directly to the idea presented in the second part of the sentence. Choice B is incorrect because this part of the passage links to REMs; it is not regardless of them. Choice C contains an erroneous implication. Choice D is incorrect because the adverb used implies that there is contradictory text preceding it, which there is not.

41. **The correct answer is C.** Stories cannot be acquired simply by viewing a sleeping person, so a change must be made. *Awaken* is more concise and active than the phrase "wake up" (choice B). In order to "collect dream stories" (the purpose stated in the second half of the sentence), it is necessary for the dreamer to wake up and share his or her stories verbally. Also, stories cannot be shared by studying a sleeping person, so choice D is incorrect.

42. **The correct answer is B.** The intent of this sentence is to talk about changing the experiences of a dreamer, thus requiring singular possession. This is signified by *'s* at the end of the possessing noun. Choice A implies that the sentence is discussing the experiences of multiple dreamers, but the surrounding context (*sleeper, dreamer*) requires use of the singular for consistency. Choice C provides no apostrophe to indicate possession. Choice

D incorrectly attaches the apostrophe to the possessed object rather than the owner of the experiences, the dreamer.

43. **The correct answer is C.** The subject and verb in a sentence must agree in number. The subject of this sentence (*researchers*) is plural, so a plural verb in the right tense is required. Only choice C reflects agreement between the subject and verb, as well as appropriate verb tense. Choice A is incorrect because the subject of the sentence (*researchers*) is plural, and "has been drawn" is singular. Choice B is plural but there is no such verb as "were been drawn." Choice D is incorrect because "was drawn" is singular.

44. **The correct answer is D.** The original punctuation creates a sentence fragment. Combining the text in a grammatically correct way eliminates the fragment, and only choice D does this. Choice A is incorrect because the period after *sleep* creates the sentence fragment. While choice B eliminates the incorrect period after *sleep*, replacing the period with a dash creates a sentence that does not make sense. Choice C removes the incorrect period, but then introduces a different error by replacing it with a semicolon. Remember, semicolons are used with complete thoughts. The first part of this sentence is not a complete thought, so choice C does not correct the original fragment.

Section 3: Math Test—NO CALCULATOR

1. A	**5.** D	**9.** A	**13.** B	**17.** 6
2. A	**6.** C	**10.** B	**14.** B	**18.** 3
3. B	**7.** D	**11.** B	**15.** B	**19.** 1
4. C	**8.** D	**12.** B	**16.** 50	**20.** 224

MATH TEST—NO CALCULATOR RAW SCORE
(Number of correct answers)

1. **The correct answer is A.** Substitute the value for m and solve for x:

$$\frac{x+2}{5} = m$$
$$\frac{x+2}{5} = -3$$
$$x + 2 = -15$$
$$x = -17$$

2. **The correct answer is A.** If h is any positive quantity, then letting $d_h = (m+h) - \dfrac{50}{m+h}$, we can see that dh is greater than d, since h is greater than zero, and $\dfrac{50}{m}$ is greater than $\dfrac{50}{m+h}$. Therefore, d increases as m does.

3. **The correct answer is B.** The volume of a cube is $V = s^3$. A side of this cube is $\sqrt[3]{64}$ in. Since there are 12 edges to a cube, the amount of wire needed is 12×4 in., or 48 inches.

4. **The correct answer is C.** The total number of cookies is equal to the sum of the cookies that Myra baked plus the cookies Neil baked. Myra baked 6 sheets of r cookies, or $6r$ cookies, and Neil baked 7 sheets of p cookies, or $7p$ cookies. The total number of cookies must be $6r + 7p$.

5. **The correct answer is D.** Substitute $a + 3$ for b, and $-a^2 + 3a + 10$ for c, into the expression $b^2 - 2c$ and combine terms.

$$(a+3)^3 - 2(-a^2 + 3a + 10)$$
$$= a^2 + 6a + 9 + 2a^2 - 6a - 20$$
$$= a^2 + 2a^2 + 6a - 6a + 9 - 20$$
$$= 3a^2 - 11$$

6. **The correct answer is C.**

$$y = \frac{(x-3)^3}{4}$$
$$4y = (x-3)^3$$
$$\sqrt[3]{4y} = x - 3$$
$$\sqrt[3]{4y} + 3 = x$$

7. **The correct answer is D.** The plant grows 4.5 centimeters a week, and that is represented by the $4.5w$ in the equation. Since the 6 is a constant in the equation, this represents the initial height of the plant. Therefore, the plant must have been 6 centimeters tall when Hannah bought it.

8. **The correct answer is D.**

$$x^6 + (2x^2)^3 + (3x^3)^2 = x^6 + 8x^6 + 9x^6 = 18x^6$$

9. **The correct answer is A.** The graph shows that the y-intercept is approximately at the point (0, 55). The equation that shows a y-intercept of 55 is in choice A. To further verify, substitute points in for the number of days to find the corresponding number of trout. For example, substitute 10 in for x: $y = 12(10) + 55 = 120 + 55 = 175$. The point (10,175) is on the graph.

10. **The correct answer is B.**

$$\left(-\frac{27}{8}\right)^{-\frac{1}{3}} = \left(-\frac{8}{27}\right)^{\frac{1}{3}} = -\frac{2}{3}$$

11. **The correct answer is B.** If the area is $49x^2$, the side of the square is $7x$. Therefore, the diagonal of the square must be the hypotenuse of a right isosceles triangle of leg $7x$.

Using the Pythagorean theorem, calculate the length of the hypotenuse, h:

$$h^2 = (7x)^2 + (7x)^2$$
$$h = \sqrt{2(7x)^2}$$
$$h = \sqrt{2}\,(7x)$$

12. The correct answer is B. The slope of the graph between any two points (t_1, s_1) and (t_2, s_2) is:

$$\frac{s_1 - s_2}{t_1 - t_2} = \frac{\text{change in height of the object}}{\text{elapsed time}}$$

Distance divided by time is speed, so choice B is correct.

13. The correct answer is B. Solve the system of equations by solving for one of the variables in the first equation, and then substitute that expression into the second equation:

$$D = 24 - B$$
$$4(24 - B) + 2B = 84$$
$$96 - 4B + 2B = 84$$
$$96 - 2B = 84$$
$$-2B = -12$$
$$B = 6$$

Then, substitute $B = 6$ into the other equation, and solve for D:

$$D + 6 = 24$$
$$D = 18$$

Therefore, the number of dogs in the pet store is 18, and the number of birds in the pet store is 6.

14. The correct answer is B. Both choices B and D are equivalent to the original function. This can be shown by multiplying the binomial factors and simplifying the product. The form of the equation in choice D gives coordinates of the vertex as its coefficients. Choice B is in intercept form, showing that

7 and –3 are the zeros of the function, the values of x for which $f(x) = 0$.

15. The correct answer is B. The slope of a line perpendicular to another line will be the negative reciprocal of the slope of the first line. So the slope of the new line must be $-\frac{1}{3}$. The only equations with that slope are choices B and C. Check which equation is correct by substituting the given point. Using choice B, you will see that it is correct:

$$y = -\frac{1}{3}x + \frac{10}{3}$$
$$3 = -\frac{1}{3}(1) + \frac{10}{3}$$
$$3 = \frac{9}{3}$$

16. The correct answer is 50. Use the facts that opposite angles are congruent, that supplementary angles add up to 180°, and that the sum of the measures of the angles in a triangle is 180°.

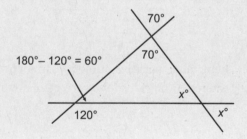

$$60 + 70 + x = 180$$
$$x = 180 - 60 - 70$$
$$= 50$$

17. The correct answer is 6. The factor $(x + 3)$ occurs twice. So the zero –3 should be counted twice. Also, $(3x - 2)$ is a factor, making $\frac{2}{3}$ a zero. Therefore, the product of the three zeros is $(-3)(-3)\left(\frac{2}{3}\right) = 6$.

18. The correct answer is 3. The slope of line L is $-\frac{1}{3}$, as can be determined by selecting any two points on the line and calculating the ratio of the difference in the y-values to the difference in the corresponding *x*-values. Using the points (−3, 3) and (0, 2), we can represent the slope as:

$$m = \frac{2-3}{0-(-3)} = -\frac{1}{3}$$

The slope of *any* line perpendicular to the line *L* will be the negative reciprocal of the slope of *L*. The negative reciprocal of $-\frac{1}{3}$ is 3.

So the slope of a line perpendicular to the graphed line will have a slope of 3.

19. **The correct answer is 1.**

$$\sqrt{4-x^2} = \sqrt{3x}$$
$$4 - x^2 = 3x$$
$$0 = x^2 + 3x - 4$$
$$0 = (x+4)(x-1)$$
$$x = -4, x = 1$$

$x = -4$ produces a negative solution:

$$\sqrt{4-(-4)^2} = \sqrt{3(-4)}$$
$$\sqrt{-12} = \sqrt{-12}$$

Remember, negative numbers cannot be entered on a grid, so the correct answer is $x = 1$.

20. **The correct answer is 224.** The system will have an infinite number of solutions when the two equations are equivalent. In order to make the *y* coefficients the same in the two equations, we can multiply the first one by −4. So multiply each term in the first equation by −4 to find the values for *a* and *b*, then find their product:

$$-4(2x + 3y) = -4(7)$$
$$-8x - 12y = -28$$

For the two equations to be equivalent, *a* must be −8 and *b* must be −28.

$$-8x - 12y = -28$$
$$ax - 12y = b$$
$$a = -8$$
$$b = -28$$
$$ab = -8(-28) = 224$$

Section 4: Math Test—CALCULATOR

1. B	9. D	17. D	25. D	33. 50
2. D	10. D	18. C	26. D	34. 20
3. D	11. D	19. A	27. B	35. 22
4. C	12. A	20. C	28. C	36. 1/4 or .025
5. D	13. D	21. A	29. C	
6. A	14. B	22. C	30. C	37. 8
7. C	15. B	23. B	31. 1.84	38. 11
8. C	16. C	24. A	32. 36/5 or 7.2	

MATH TEST—CALCULATOR RAW SCORE
(Number of correct answers) [ ]

1. **The correct answer is B.** If $9x + 5 = 23$, $9x = 18$, and $x = 2$. Thus, $18x + 5 = 36 + 5 = 41$.

2. **The correct answer is D.** There can be at most 15 radiators, so $x + y \le 15$. Each small radiator weighs 150 pounds, so the combined weight of all the small radiators is represented by $150x$. Each large radiator weighs 250 pounds, represented by $250y$. The maximum load can be equal to but not exceed 1,500 pounds: $150x + 250y \le 1,500$.

3. **The correct answer is D.** Each adult needs 15 cans/7 adults $= \frac{15}{7}$ cans in two days, or $\left(\frac{1}{2}\right)\left(\frac{15}{7}\right) = \frac{15}{14}$ cans per adult per day. Multiply this by the number of adults and by the number of days:

$$\frac{15}{14} (4 \text{ adults})(7 \text{days}) = 30 \text{ cans of food}$$

4. **The correct answer is C.** Fiona's non-taxed amount is 75% of what she earns each hour, or $0.75x$. This is multiplied by the hourly rate, which in this case is $28, leading to the expression $28(0.75x)$.

5. **The correct answer is D.** The data are increasing and stay relatively close to a line of best fit that would pass through the center of the points. This means that there is a strong positive correlation between the years after 2005 and the total sales.

6. **The correct answer is A.** Using a line that passes through (2, 1.9) and (6, 3.5), the slope is

$$\frac{3.5 - 1.9}{6 - 2} = \frac{1.6}{4} = 0.4$$

The line passes through (0, 1), making the equation $y = 0.4x + 1$.

7. **The correct answer is C.** Let x = original price. Then:
$$0.60x = \$4.20$$
$$\text{or} \quad 6x = \$42.00$$
$$x = \$7.00$$

8. **The correct answer is C.** The number 329 represents the slope of the graph of the equation, which is the rate of increase in attendance.

9. **The correct answer is D.** When they work together, the faster supercomputer will complete 1.5, or $\frac{3}{2}$, times the work of the slower supercomputer. That means the slower supercomputer does $\frac{2}{5}$ of the work, and the faster computer does $\frac{3}{5}\left(\frac{2}{5} \times \frac{3}{2} = \frac{3}{5}\right)$. If the

slower supercomputer completes $\frac{2}{5}$ of the job in 3 hours, then it would take 7.5 hours to complete the entire job alone:

$$\frac{2}{5}t = 3 \text{ hours}$$
$$2t = 15 \text{ hours}$$
$$t = 7.5 \text{ hours}$$

10. **The correct answer is D.** The number of books that the library adds is 375x, or 375 times the number of years. The total number of books must be the sum of 375x and 25,825 (the number they already have), not to exceed 35,000.

11. **The correct answer is D.** First, we convert 20° to radians:

$$\frac{\pi \text{ radians}}{180°} \text{ x } 20° = \frac{\pi}{9} \text{ radians.}$$

Then, we use the formula for the length of an arc, s, formed by an angle of θ radians on a circle of radius, $r : s = r\,\theta$. Evaluating this formula for the given radius and central angle measure, in radians, gives $\frac{9}{4\pi} \cdot \frac{\pi}{9} = \frac{1}{4}$. So, the length of the arc that intercepts the given central angle is $\frac{1}{4}$.

12. **The correct answer is A.** Choice C is incorrect because we cannot say with certainty that a medication will help all people who need it. Choice D doesn't make sense; the medication cannot help people who don't take it. Choice B is incorrect because we only compared Z against one other medication, Y. The inference can be applied only to the given medications and populations.

13. **The correct answer is D.** To use the quadratic model, substitute $t = 150$ into the given equation:

$$C = 0.013(150)^2 + 0.518 \times 150 + 310.44 = 680.64$$

For the linear model, note that the constant rate of change of carbon dioxide concentration based on the data in the table is

$$\frac{390 - 370}{2010 - 2000} = \frac{20}{10} = 2 \text{ PPM} \text{ increase per}$$

year. So the increase from 2000 to 2100 would be 200 PPM, meaning that the concentration in 2100 would be 370 + 200 = 570 PPM. The quadratic model predicts a higher concentration in 2100, by about 110 PPM.

14. **The correct answer is B.** Draw the following diagram:

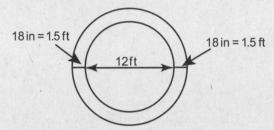

The area of the pond plus the walkway:
The diameter is 15 feet, so the area is:

$$\pi\left(\frac{15}{2}\right)^2 = \frac{225\pi}{4} \text{ square feet}$$

The area of the pond only:
The diameter is 12 feet, so the area is:

$$\pi\left(\frac{12}{2}\right)^2 = 36\pi \text{ square feet}$$

So the area of the walkway is the difference of these two areas:

$$\frac{225\pi}{4} - 36\pi = \frac{81}{4}\pi \text{ square feet}$$

Therefore, the cost is:

$$(\$7.25)\left(\frac{81}{4}\pi\right) \approx \$461.23$$

15. **The correct answer is B.** We can rewrite the equation as a quadratic set equal to zero and factor or apply the quadratic formula. Here we factor:

$$a^2 + 12a - 45 = 0$$
$$(a + 15)(a - 3) = 0$$
$$a = -15 \text{ or } a = 3$$

We are given $a < 0$, so it must be that $a = -15$, and $a + 6 = -9$.

16. **The correct answer is C.** The graph shows points connected by a curve with an increasing positive slope that approximates an exponential graph, so this is exponential growth.

17. **The correct answer is D.** The graph shows an exponential growth curve, and the population of California in 1980 is approximately 24 million. Therefore, choices A and B can be eliminated because, based on the exponential growth, the population in 1990 would be more than the population in 1980. It appears on the graph that 25 million was reached before 1980. So, 30 million would be the best prediction.

18. **The correct answer is C.** Let the original sign be 10 by 10.

Then, the new sign is 7 by 9.

$$\frac{63}{100} = 63\%$$

19. **The correct answer is A.** Three meals a day times 365 days per year means there are $3 \times 365 = 1,095$ meals in one year. Over 19 years, there are $1,095 \times 19 = 20,805$ meals. Therefore, the number of restaurants in New York City exceeds 20,500.

20. **The correct answer is C.** The graph shows the distance decreasing after about three units of time, which is what a ball thrown vertically upward does, but not a ball thrown horizontally. The shape of the graph is roughly a parabola, which is the graph of a quadratic equation.

21. **The correct answer is A.** Subtract by using a common denominator, and then simplify:

$$\frac{3x-1}{2x+3} - \frac{2x+3}{3x-1} = \frac{(3x-1)(3x-1)}{(2x+3)(3x-1)} - \frac{(2x+3)(2x+3)}{(3x-1)(2x+3)}$$

$$= \frac{(3x-1)^2 - (2x+3)^2}{(2x+3)(3x-1)}$$

$$= \frac{5x^2 - 18x - 8}{6x^2 + 7x - 3}$$

22. **The correct answer is C.** A solution to the system would be a pair of values, (x, y), satisfying both equations. Such a solution would be represented on the graph as a point (or a set of points) that lies on both lines. Because lines A and B are parallel, they do not intersect, so no point lies on both lines. There is no solution to the system of equations represented by lines A and B.

23. **The correct answer is B.** The coordinates of any point (x, y) lying below line A satisfy the inequality $y < mx + a$. On the graph, Regions 2 and 3 lie below line A. Any point lying above line B satisfies $y > mx + b$; these points are in regions 1 and 2. To satisfy both point inequalities, (x, y) must lie in region 2.

24. **The correct answer is A.** To write an exponential equation for this situation, you need to find P, the population in 1980. Use the formula for exponential growth and the known population 20 years after 1980.

$$38,500 = P(1 + 0.038)^{20}$$
$$\frac{38,500}{(1.038)^{20}} = P$$
$$18,260 \approx P$$

25. **The correct answer is D.**

If $x < 0$, then $f(x) = |x| = -x$.

Then, $g(f(x)) = g(-x)$.

Finally, $g(-x) = \left(\frac{1}{-x}\right) = \frac{1}{x}$.

For instance, assume $x = -3$:

So $f(-3) = 3$ and $g(f(-3)) = g(3) = -\frac{1}{3}$.

26. **The correct answer is D.** The sample size leads to the margin of error that is given with the data. As long as the margin of error is considered when making conclusions, those conclusions are reasonable.

27. **The correct answer is B.** The 95% confidence that the margin of error is ±3.4% is important, and choices A and C ignore the confidence interval. Choice D is incorrect because this interval is centered on 49%, instead of 51%, which is the number of people who support a different candidate or no candidate at this time. Only choice B accurately uses the confidence interval and the data given in the problem.

28. **The correct answer is C.** If the average for the eight tests is 84%, then the sum of the eight tests must be 8 times 84, or 672. For the six tests, the sum must be 6 times 86, or 516. The two dropped tests must have accounted for 156 points. 156 divided by 2 is 78.

29. **The correct answer is C.** Complete the square to write the equation in standard form for a circle:

$$x^2 + y^2 - 8x + 12y = 144$$
$$x^2 - 8x + y^2 + 12y = 144$$
$$(x^2 - 8x + 16) + (y^2 + 12y + 36) = 144 + 16 + 36$$
$$(x - 4)^2 + (y + 6)^2 = 196$$

Since 196 is 14^2, the radius is 14.

30. **The correct answer is C.** First, put the function into slope-intercept form:

$$f(x) = 2(3a - x) - (5 + ax)$$
$$= 6a - 2x - 5 - ax$$
$$= -(2 + a)x + (6a - 5)$$

In order for the graph to not intersect Quadrant III, $(2 + a)$ must be nonnegative so that the slope of the line is negative or zero AND the y-intercept $(6a - 5)$ must be positive. This gives two conditions:

$$-(2 + a) \leq 0 \text{ AND } 6a - 5 > 0.$$

Solving these inequalities yields:

$$a \geq -2 \text{ AND } a > \frac{5}{6}$$

Both conditions must hold. So it must be the case that $a > \frac{5}{6}$.

31. **The correct answer is 1.84.** Compute the mean as follows:

$$\frac{0(6) + 1(13) + 2(21) + 3(4) + 4(5) + 5(1)}{50} = 1.84$$

32. **The correct answer is 36/5 or 7.2.** Begin by multiplying all terms of the equation by the LCD of 36:

$$36\left(\frac{x}{12}\right) + 36\left(\frac{x}{18}\right) = 1(36)$$
$$3x + 2x = 36$$
$$5x = 36$$
$$x = \frac{36}{5} \text{ or}$$
$$x = 7\frac{1}{5} = 7\frac{2}{10} = 7.2$$

33. **The correct answer is 50.** Write and solve an inequality that represents the situation. Then interpret the solution:

$$50 + 12x \leq 660$$
$$12x \leq 610$$
$$x \leq 50.8$$

Since the elephant cannot lift part of a bundle, the greatest number of bundles it can lift is 50.

34. **The correct answer is 20.** In the twentieth century, 7 of the 17 presidents were Democrats.

$\frac{7}{17} = 41\%$ rounded to the nearest percentage point.

The percentages for the nineteenth and twenty-first centuries are 35% and 33%, respectively.

35. **The correct answer is 22.** Presidents from the Federalist, Democratic-Republican, and Whig parties total $2 + 4 + 4 = 10$. The total number of presidents is 45.

$$\frac{10}{45} \approx 0.222.$$

Rounding to the nearest whole percent gives 22%.

36. **The correct answer is 1/4 or 0.25.** Solve using elimination so that the x-terms are eliminated:

$$-6(5x + 4y) = -6(11)$$
$$5(6x - 8y) = 5(10)$$

$$-30x - 24y = -66$$
$$+ 30x - 40y = 50$$
$$\overline{\quad\quad -64y = -16}$$
$$y = \frac{16}{64}$$
$$= \frac{1}{4}$$

37. **The correct answer is 8.**
Distance = rate × time:

$$360 = r(9)$$
$$40 = r$$

If r were $40 + 5 = 45$

$$d = rt$$
$$360 = 45t$$
$$t = 8$$

38. **The correct answer is 11.** Solve using a common denominator:

$$\frac{2}{x+2} + \frac{3}{x-5} = \frac{4x+7}{x^2 - 3x - 10}$$

$$\frac{2(x-5)}{(x+2)(x-5)} + \frac{3(x+2)}{(x-5)(x+2)} = \frac{4x+7}{x^2 - 3x - 10}$$

$$\frac{2x - 10 + 3x + 6}{x^2 - 3x - 10} = \frac{4x+7}{x^2 - 3x - 10}$$

$$5x - 4 = 4x + 7$$

$$x = 11$$

Check your answer:

$$\frac{2}{11+2} + \frac{3}{11-5} = \frac{4(11)+7}{(11)^2 - 3(11) - 10}$$

$$\frac{2}{13} + \frac{3}{6} = \frac{51}{78}$$

$$\frac{2(6)}{13(6)} + \frac{3(13)}{6(13)} = \frac{51}{78}$$

$$\frac{51}{78} = \frac{51}{78}$$

Section 5: Essay

Analysis of Passage

The following is an analysis of the passage by Alex Jensen and Susan M. McHale, noting how the writers used evidence, reasoning, and stylistic or persuasive elements to support their claims, connect the claims and evidence, and add power to the ideas the writers expressed. Check to see if you evaluated the passage in a similar way.

WHAT MAKES SIBLINGS FROM THE SAME FAMILY SO DIFFERENT? PARENTS

1 A colleague related the following story: while running errands with her 11- and 7-year-old daughters, a back seat battle began to rage. My colleague's attempts to defuse the situation only led to a shouting match about who was to blame for the skirmish. Finally the 11-year-old proclaimed to her sister, "You started it the day you were born and took away Mom's love!"

1 *The writers begin the essay with an anecdote drawn from personal experience. This story (which includes the evocative statement "You... took away Mom's love!") immediately makes the essay more personal and prepares the reader to engage with the writers' argument.*

2 This pair of sisters fight frequently, and from their mother's perspective, part of the reason is that the two have little in common. As it turns out, their situation is not unique.

2 *The writers broaden their point of view from the personal to the objective and give the reader more perspective on the topic.*

3 Despite the fact that siblings are, on average, 50% genetically similar, are often raised in the same home by the same parents, attend the same schools and have many other shared experiences,

3 *The writers use statistics and factual information to provide context for and lay the foundation of their argument.*

4 siblings are often only as similar to each other as they are to children who are growing up across town or even across the country.

4 *Jensen and McHale clearly state a key premise of their argument — siblings are rarely similar. Having said this, they now have to support the rest of their argument: parents are the reason for these differences.*

5 So, what is it that makes two siblings from the same family so different?

5 *The writers pose a rhetorical question to introduce support for their argument.*

WHAT MAKES THE DIFFERENCE?

6 As researchers of sibling and family relationships, we knew that at least one answer to this question comes from

6 *The writers provide their backgrounds, which show why they're qualified to be making this argument: they are researchers of sibling and family relationships.*

7 theory and data showing that, at least in some families, siblings try to be different from one another and seek to establish a unique identity and position in their family.

7 *The writers refer to theory and data that support their argument: "some siblings try to be different from one another, and seek to establish a unique identity and position in their family."*

8 From a child's perspective, if an older brother excels at school, it may be easier to attract her parents' attention and praise by becoming a star athlete than by competing with her brother to get the best grades. In this way, even small differences between siblings can become substantial differences over time.

8 *The writers go into more detail about this information, presenting a concrete example that is easily understood by the reader.*

9 But parents may also play a role. For instance, when parents notice differences between their children, children may pick up on parents' perceptions and beliefs about those differences. This, in turn, can increase sibling differences.

9 *The writers now discuss the role of parents in sibling differences, paving the way to support the central point in their argument: parents are a major force in sibling differences.*

10 We wanted to test these ideas to see what makes siblings different. So, we used data from first- and second-born teenage siblings from 388 two-parent families to examine sibling differences in school performance.

10 *The writers explain how they tested the validity of their argument.*

11 We asked mothers and fathers to report on whether they thought the two siblings differed in their academic abilities, and if so, which sibling was more capable. We also collected school grades from both siblings' report cards.

11 *The writers provide more detailed information about the study they conducted to test the validity of their argument.*

PREFERENCE FOR THE FIRSTBORN

12 Our analyses showed some interesting results: parents tended to believe that the older sibling was better in school. This was even when older siblings did not actually receive better grades, on average.

12 *The writers provide results of their study that revealed parents' perceptions of and ideas about older siblings. Specifically, parents tended to believe that the older sibling was better in school (whether this was true or not).*

13 This may be a product of parents having greater expectations for firstborns or that, at any given time, the older sibling is undertaking more advanced school work.

13 *The writers go into more detail about parents' perceptions of and ideas about older siblings.*

14 There was, however, an exception to this pattern: in families with older brothers and younger sisters, parents rated the younger sibling as being more capable. In fact, in those families, younger sisters received better grades than their older brothers.

14 *The writers go into further detail about results of their study. This detail shows a difference in how parents regarded their children, apparently favoring girls over boys in the area of academic capability.*

15 Our findings also showed that it was not sibling differences in school grades that predicted parents' ratings of their children's abilities. Rather, parents' beliefs about differences in their children's abilities predicted later sibling differences in school grades.

15 *The writers provide additional details from their study, showing parental beliefs and attitudes toward their children's abilities greatly affected sibling differences regarding academic performance.*

16 In other words, when parents believed one child was more capable than the other, that child's school grades improved more over time than their sibling's.

16 *Jensen and McHale explain these details and show how they support their argument: When parents believed one child was more academically capable than the other, that child's school grades improved more over time than their sibling's.*

Sustaining beliefs

17 Although we expected that children's school grades and parents' beliefs about their children's relative abilities would be mutually influential, it turned out that parents' beliefs did not change much over their children's teenage years.

17 *The writers provide information showing that once parents form perceptions and beliefs about their children's academic abilities, these attitudes and ideas do not greatly change.*

18 Instead, sibling differences in school grades did change and were predicted by parents' beliefs. In this way, parents' beliefs about differences between their children may encourage the development of actual sibling difference.

18 *Jensen and McHale use the information revealed by their study to prove their argument: While parents' beliefs about their children's academic abilities did not change, sibling differences in school grades did. Thus, "parents' beliefs about differences between their children may encourage the development of actual sibling difference."*

19 The above comment by an 11-year-old highlights that children are sensitive to their place and value in the family—relative to those of their siblings. Parents may strive to show their love for their children, but they also should be aware that small differences in how they treat their children can have large effects—including on their children's development and adjustment and also on the sibling relationship.

19 *The writers strengthen their argument by returning to their introductory anecdote and summing up what their study revealed: "Children are sensitive to their place and value in the family," and differences in how parents treat their children can have "large effects" on them.*

20 Indeed, some research suggests that sibling conflict arises when children try to be different from their siblings.

21 My colleague may be correct that her daughters fight frequently because they have nothing in common.

22 But their conflicts may also be motivated by her daughter's perception that their differences started on the day her sister was born "and took away Mom's love."

20 *The writers conclude the essay by referring to research that supports the mother's statement in the introductory anecdote: sibling conflict can be created "when children try to be different from their siblings."*

21 *While this may seem like the writers are giving up on their argument, acknowledging their colleague might be right about the cause of her daughters' conflicts demonstrates the writers' honesty and objectivity.*

22 *Jensen and McHale then end the essay by offering additional insight about their colleague's daughters. Here, they provide an alternative explanation for the girls' differences, restating their argument and repeating the 11-year-old girl's evocative remark: the conflict between these two siblings may also be motivated by the girl's belief that the birth of her younger sister changed their mother's behavior toward the older girl because the younger sister "took away Mom's love."*

Answers | Practice Test 2

Scoring Rubric

Use the following scoring rubric as a guide to help you evaluate the sample essays that follow. Then, read and evaluate your own essay for each scoring category. Assign your essay a score between 1 and 4 for each category (Reading, Analysis, and Writing). Next, double each score to simulate that the essay was scored twice. You will now have three scores ranging from 2 to 8 for each category. These are not combined.

Score Point	Reading	Analysis	Writing
4 (Advanced)	The essay shows a comprehensive understanding of the source text, including the author's key claims, use of details and evidence, and the relationship between the two.	The essay offers an "insightful" and in-depth evaluation of the author's use of evidence and stylistic or persuasive features in building an argument. Supporting details and evidence are relevant and focus on those details that address the task.	The essay includes all of the features of a strong essay, including a precise central claim, body paragraphs, and a strong conclusion. There is a variety of sentence structures used in the essay, and it is virtually free of all convention errors.
3 (Proficient)	The essay shows an appropriate understanding of the source text, including the author's key claims and use of details in developing an argument.	The essay offers an "effective" evaluation of the author's use of evidence and stylistic or persuasive features in building an argument. Supporting details and evidence are appropriate and focus on those details that address the task.	The essay includes all of the features of an effective essay, including a precise central claim, body paragraphs, and a strong conclusion. There is a variety of sentence structures used in the essay, and it is free of significant convention errors.
2 (Partial)	The essay shows some understanding of the source text, including the author's key claims, but uses limited textual evidence and/or unimportant details.	The essay offers limited evaluation of the author's use of evidence and stylistic or persuasive features in building an argument. Supporting details and evidence are lacking and/or are not relevant to the task.	The essay does not provide a precise central claim, nor does it provide an effective introduction, body paragraphs, and conclusion. There is little variety of sentence structure used in the essay, and there are numerous errors in grammar and conventions.
1 (Inadequate)	The essay demonstrates little or no understanding of the source text or the author's use of key claims.	The essay offers no clear evaluation of the author's use of evidence and stylistic or persuasive features in building an argument. Supporting details and evidence are nonexistent or irrelevant to the task.	The essay lacks any form of cohesion or structure. There is little variety of sentence structures, and significant errors in convention make it difficult to read.

Practice Test 2

Sample Essays

The following are examples of a high-scoring and low-scoring essay, based on the passage by Alex Jenson and Susan M. McHale.

High-Scoring Essay

No two siblings are alike. Alex Jensen and Susan M. McHale are two university professors who investigated the reasons for the differences between siblings. They concluded that parents cause the differences. To explain their conclusion, they use professional authority, personal experience, statistics, results of a study they conducted, and references to other research.

Professional authority is established immediately—both authors are identified as university professors in the area of human development. In the second section, they reinforce their authority by stating that they are researchers of sibling and family relationships. This demonstrates their knowledge specifically in the area of siblings. Readers can trust their conclusions.

The article begins with a personal story of two young siblings who constantly fight. During a particular fight, the 11-year-old girl accuses her 7-year-old sister of starting the fight when she was born and "took away mom's love." This harsh accusation hooks readers into wondering about the real cause of sibling differences.

A quick look at statistics provided by the authors reveals many reasons for siblings to be similar rather that different. Siblings are 50% genetically similar and share the same parents, schools, and other experiences. Again, this makes the reader wonder about the cause of sibling differences.

The answer comes from theory and data, reinforcing their role as authorities in the subject. One cause, the authors state, is that siblings try to be different from each other to be unique in the family. They support this with an example of how one sibling can choose to excel at athletic pursuits because an older sibling already excels in academics. Over time, one small choice made to be different, such as joining a soccer team, causes other, bigger differences. One sibling becomes an athlete while the other becomes a scholar.

Finally, the authors address the role of parents in sibling differences. They theorize that parents notice small differences between children and children react to their parents' perceptions by becoming even more different. To confirm their theory, the authors conducted a study of the first and second siblings in 388 two-parent homes. Readers can easily see the study as a reasonable approach to determining the cause of the differences. The authors asked parents about their perceptions of their children's academic abilities and compared the perceptions to the children's report cards. In effect, they compared parents' perceptions to actual performance.

The authors present the analysis of the study results. Parents seem to expect the oldest sibling to perform better than the younger child, even though it wasn't always true. They describe an exception: If the older sibling is male and the younger sibling is female, the parents expect the girl to perform better academically, and the girl does get better grades than her brother.

The authors present their findings. Overall, the authors determined that parents' perception caused siblings' academic performance. If the parents believed that Suzy would perform better that Sally, Suzy's grades would improve until they were better than Sally's. Over time, parents' perceptions caused behaviors to change; behaviors did not cause parents' perceptions to change.

Parents have a large role in shaping their children and the relationship between their children. The authors briefly cite other research that points to differences between siblings as the cause of conflict between siblings.

At the end of the article, the authors return to the personal story told at the beginning of the article. The authors' colleague says that the conflict between her daughters is caused by the differences between the daughters. After reading the authors' findings though, readers can conclude that the differences are caused by the parents. Hence, the conflict between the siblings is actually caused by the parents. The authors have successfully presented their theory and their results to convince readers that parents should be more aware of the effect they have on their children.

Low-Scoring Essay

Alex Jensen and Susan M. McHale are two professors who researched the cause of sibling rivalry. They start the article with a story about two sisters having a fight in the backseat of a car. One of the girls accuses the other of stealing Mom's love. It refers to the age-old argument that "Mom loves you best."

The researchers look at some of the reasons that siblings fight even though they share so many of the same things, including genes, parents, schools, and probably clothes. They conclude that siblings try to be different on purpose so they can have a unique place in the family. The differences might start as things their parents notice like, "You're better at math than Mike," or "You run faster than Jake." Eventually, the small differences that parents notice become big things. Jake becomes an accountant because he's better at math. Mike becomes a gym teacher and coaches at the local high school because he's a better athlete.

The authors talk about a study they did about sibling rivalry. The differences between the siblings are caused by the way that parents expect the children to act. Children act the way they do to get attention.

The authors tell us that parents should be careful about the characteristics they encourage in their children and the perceptions they talk about. The "Mom loves you best" argument can shape children's lives. Parents should be careful to say good things about their children and interact evenly with both children. Then, no one will win the "Mom loves you best" argument and siblings will fight less.

COMPUTING YOUR SCORES

Now that you've completed this practice test, it's time to compute your scores. Simply follow the instructions on the following pages and use the conversion tables provided to calculate your scores. The formulas provided will give you as close an approximation as possible of how you might score on the actual SAT exam.

To Determine Your Practice Test Scores

1. After you go through each of the test sections (Reading, Writing and Language, Math—No Calculator, and Math—Calculator) and determine which answers you got right, be sure to enter the number of correct answers in the box below the answer key for each of the sections.

2. Your total score on the practice test is the sum of your Evidence-Based Reading and Writing Section score and your Math Section score. To get your total score, convert the raw score—the number of questions you got right in a particular section—into the "scaled score" for that section, and then you'll calculate the total score. It sounds a little confusing, but we'll take you through the steps.

To Calculate Your Evidence-Based Reading and Writing Section Score

Your Evidence-Based Reading and Writing Section score is on a scale of 200–800. First determine your Reading Test score, and then determine your score on the Writing and Language Test.

1. Count the number of correct answers you got on the **Section 1: Reading Test.** Remember that there is no penalty for wrong answers. **The number of correct answers is your raw score.**

2. Go to **Raw Score Conversion Table 1: Section and Test Scores** on page 785. Look in the "Raw Score" column for your raw score and match it to the number in the "Reading Test Score" column.

3. Do the same with **Section 2: Writing and Language Test** to determine that score.

4. Add your Reading Test score to your Writing and Language Test score.

5. Multiply that number by 10. This is your Evidence-Based Reading and Writing Section score.

To Calculate Your Math Section Score

Your Math score is also on a scale of 200–800.

1. Count the number of correct answers you got on the **Section 3: Math Test—No Calculator** and the **Section 4: Math Test—No Calculator**. Again, there is no penalty for wrong answers. **The number of correct answers is your raw score.**

2. Add the number of correct answers on the Section 3: Math Test—No Calculator and the Section 4: Math Test—Calculator.

3. Use the **Raw Score Conversion Table 1: Section and Test Scores** on page 785 and convert your raw score into your Math Section score.

To Obtain Your Total Score

Add your score on the Evidence-Based Reading and Writing Section to the Math Section score. This is your total score on this Practice Test, on a scale of 400–1600.

Subscores Provide Additional Information

Subscores offer you greater details about your strengths in certain areas within literacy and math. The subscores are reported on a scale of 1–15 and include Heart of Algebra, Problem Solving and Data Analysis, Passport to Advanced Math, Expression of Ideas, Standard English Conventions, Words in Context, and Command of Evidence.

Heart of Algebra

The **Heart of Algebra subscore** is based on questions from the **Math Test** that focus on linear equations and inequalities.

- Add up your total correct answers from these sections:
  - Math Test—No Calculator: Questions 1, 4, 7, 9, 13, 15, 18, 20
  - Math Test—Calculator: Questions 1, 2, 4, 8–10, 13, 21, 32, 33, 36
- Your Raw Score = the total number of correct answers from all of these questions.
- Use the **Raw Score Conversion Table 2: Subscores** on page 787 to determine your **Heart of Algebra** subscore.

Problem Solving and Data Analysis

The **Problem Solving and Data Analysis subscore** is based on questions from the **Math Test** that focus on quantitative reasoning, interpretation and synthesis of data, and solving problems in rich and varied contexts.

- Add up your total correct answers from these questions:
  - Math Test—No Calculator: None
  - Math Test—Calculator: Questions 3, 5–7, 12, 16–20, 26–28, 31, 34, 35, 37
- Your Raw Score = the total number of correct answers from all of these questions.
- Use the **Raw Score Conversion Table 2: Subscores** on page 787 to determine your **Problem Solving and Data Analysis** subscore.

Passport to Advanced Math

The **Passport to Advanced Math subscore** is based on questions from the **Math Test** that focus on topics central to your ability to progress to more advanced math, such as understanding the structure of expressions, reasoning with more complex equations, and interpreting and building functions.

- Add up your total correct answers from these questions:
  - Math Test—No Calculator: Questions 2, 5, 6, 8, 10, 12, 14, 17, 19
  - Math Test—Calculator: Questions 15, 22–25, 30, 38
- Your Raw Score = the total number of correct answers from all of these questions.
- Use the **Raw Score Conversion Table 2: Subscores** on page 787 to determine your **Passport to Advanced Math** subscore.

Expression of Ideas

The **Expression of Ideas subscore** is based on questions from the **Writing and Language Test** that focus on topic development, organization, and rhetorically effective use of language.

- Add up your total correct answers from these questions in Section 2: Writing and Language Test:
  - Questions 1, 3, 6, 8, 10, 12, 14, 15, 18–20, 22, 24, 26–28, 30, 33, 35–37, 39–41
- Your Raw Score = the total number of correct answers from all of these questions.
- Use the **Raw Score Conversion Table 2: Subscores** on page 787 to determine your **Expression of Ideas** subscore.

Standard English Conventions

The **Standard English Conventions subscore** is based on questions from the **Writing and Language Test** that focus on sentence structure, usage, and punctuation.

- Add up your total correct answers from these questions in Section 2: Writing and Language Test:
  - Questions 2, 4, 5, 7, 9, 11, 13, 16, 17, 21, 23, 25, 29, 31, 32, 34, 38, 42–44
- Your Raw Score = the total number of correct answers from all of these questions.
- Use the **Raw Score Conversion Table 2: Subscores** on page 787 to determine your **Standard English Conventions** subscore.

Words in Context

The **Words in Context subscore** is based on questions from the **Reading Test** and the **Writing and Language Test** that address word/phrase meaning in context and rhetorical word choice.

- Add up your total correct answers from these questions in Sections 1 and 2:
  - Reading Test: Questions 6, 8, 14, 21, 31, 32, 35, 40, 45, 50
  - Writing and Language Test: Questions 6, 8, 15, 18, 24, 27, 37, 41
- Your Raw Score = the total number of correct answers from all of these questions.
- Use the **Raw Score Conversion Table 2: Subscores** on page 787 to determine your **Words in Context** subscore.

Command of Evidence

The **Command of Evidence subscore** is based on questions from the **Reading Test** and the **Writing and Language Test** that ask you to interpret and use evidence found in a wide range of passages and informational graphics, such as graphs, tables, and charts.

- Add up your total correct answers from Sections 1 and 2:
  - Reading Test: Questions 2, 4, 18, 20, 27, 30, 34, 38, 47, 49
  - Writing and Language Test: Questions 1, 10, 12, 19, 26, 28, 36, 40
- Your Raw Score = the total number of correct answers from all of these questions.
- Use the **Raw Score Conversion Table 2: Subscores** on page 787 to determine your **Command of Evidence** subscore.

Cross-Test Scores

The SAT exam also reports two cross-test scores: Analysis in History/Social Studies and Analysis in Science. These scores are based on questions in the Reading Test, Writing and Language Test, and both Math Tests that ask you to think analytically about texts and questions in these subject areas. Cross-test scores are reported on a scale of 10–40.

Analysis in History/Social Studies

- Add up your total correct answers from these questions:

  - Reading Test: Questions 11–21, 33–42
  - Writing and Language Test: Questions 12, 14, 15, 18–20
  - Math Test—No Calculator: None
  - Math Test—Calculator: Questions 16, 17, 24, 26, 27, 31, 34, 35

- Your Raw Score = the total number of correct answers from all of these questions.

- Use the **Raw Score Conversion Table 3: Cross-Test Scores** on page 789 to determine your **Analysis in History/Social Studies** cross-test score.

Analysis in Science

- Add up your total correct answers from these questions:

  - Reading Test: Questions 22–32, 43–52
  - Writing and Language Test: Questions 35–37, 39, 40
  - Math Test—No Calculator: Questions 7, 9, 12, 13
  - Math Test—Calculator: Questions 12, 13, 20, 33

- Your Raw Score = the total number of correct answers from all of these questions.

- Use the **Raw Score Conversion Table 3: Cross-Test Scores** on page 789 to determine your **Analysis in Science** cross-test score.

Practice Test 2

Raw Score Conversion Table 1: Section and Test Scores

Raw Score	Math Section Score	Reading Test Score	Writing and Language Test Score
0	200	10	10
1	200	10	10
2	210	10	10
3	230	11	10
4	240	12	11
5	260	13	12
6	280	14	13
7	290	15	13
8	310	15	14
9	320	16	15
10	330	17	16
11	340	17	16
12	360	18	17
13	370	19	18
14	380	19	19
15	390	20	19
16	410	20	20
17	420	21	21
18	430	21	21
19	440	22	22

Raw Score	Math Section Score	Reading Test Score	Writing and Language Test Score
20	450	22	23
21	460	23	23
22	470	23	24
23	480	24	25
24	480	24	25
25	490	25	26
26	500	25	26
27	510	26	27
28	520	26	28
29	520	27	28
30	530	28	29
31	540	28	30
32	550	29	30
33	560	29	31
34	560	30	32
35	570	30	32
36	580	31	33
37	590	31	34
38	600	32	34
39	600	32	35

Raw Score	Math Section Score	Reading Test Score	Writing and Language Test Score
40	610	33	36
41	620	33	37
42	630	34	38
43	640	35	39
44	650	35	40
45	660	36	
46	670	37	
47	670	37	
48	680	38	
49	690	38	
50	700	39	
51	710	40	
52	730	40	
53	740		
54	750		
55	760		
56	780		
57	790		
58	800		

Conversion Equation 1: Section and Test Scores

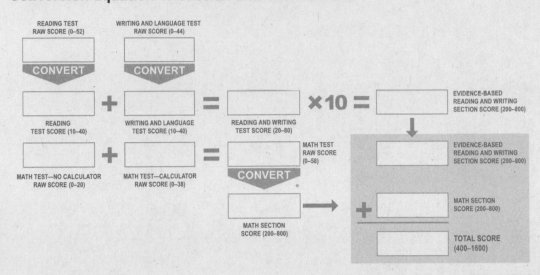

Practice Test 2

Raw Score Conversion Table 2: Subscores

Raw Score (# of correct answers)	Expression of Ideas	Standard English Conventions	Heart of Algebra	Problem Solving and Data Analysis	Passport to Advanced Math	Words in Context	Command of Evidence
0	1	1	1	1	1	1	1
1	1	1	1	1	3	1	1
2	1	1	2	2	5	2	2
3	2	2	3	3	6	3	3
4	3	2	4	4	7	4	4
5	4	3	5	5	8	5	5
6	5	4	6	6	9	6	6
7	6	5	6	7	10	6	7
8	6	6	7	8	11	7	8
9	7	6	8	8	11	8	8
10	7	7	8	9	12	8	9
11	8	7	9	10	12	9	10
12	8	8	9	10	13	9	10
13	9	8	9	11	13	10	11
14	9	9	10	12	14	11	12
15	10	10	10	13	14	12	13
16	10	10	11	14	15	13	14
17	11	11	12	15		14	15
18	11	12	13			15	15
19	12	13	15				
20	12	15					
21	13						
22	14						
23	14						
24	15						

Conversion Equation 2: Subscores

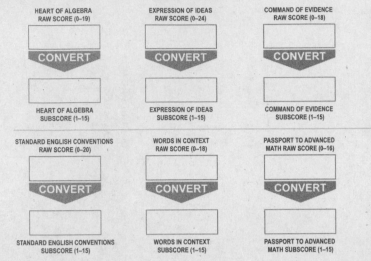

Practice Test 2

Conversion Equation 3: Cross-Test Scores

Raw Score (# of correct answers)	Analysis in History/ Social Studies Cross-Test Score	Analysis in Science Cross-Test Score	Raw Score (# of correct answers)	Analysis in History/ Social Studies Cross-Test Score	Analysis in Science Cross-Test Score
0	10	10	24	32	30
1	10	11	25	33	31
2	11	12	26	34	32
3	12	13	27	35	33
4	14	14	28	35	33
5	15	15	29	36	34
6	16	16	30	37	35
7	17	17	31	38	36
8	18	18	32	38	37
9	20	19	33	39	38
10	21	20	34	40	39
11	22	20	35	40	40
12	23	21			
13	24	22			
14	25	23			
15	26	24			
16	27	24			
17	28	25			
18	28	26			
19	29	27			
20	30	27			
21	30	28			
22	31	29			
23	32	30			

Conversion Equation 3: Cross-Test Scores

TEST	Analysis in History/Social Studies		Analysis in Science	
	QUESTIONS	RAW SCORE	QUESTIONS	RAW SCORE
Reading Test	11–21, 33–42		22–32, 43–52	
Writing and Language Test	12, 14, 15, 18–20		35–37, 39, 40	
Math Test— No Calculator			7, 9, 12, 13	
Math Test— Calculator	16, 17, 24, 26, 27, 31, 34, 35		12, 13, 20, 33	
TOTAL				

ANALYSIS IN HISTORY/
SOCIAL STUDIES
RAW SCORE (0–35)

CONVERT

ANALYSIS IN HISTORY/
SOCIAL STUDIES
CROSS-TEST SCORE (10–40)

ANALYSIS IN SCIENCE
RAW SCORE (0–35)

CONVERT

ANALYSIS IN SCIENCE
CROSS-TEST SCORE (10–40)

Practice Test 2

PART VIII:
APPENDICES

Parents' Guide to College Admission Testing

GETTING INVOLVED

The first step in creating a plan to help your teen prepare for college admissions tests is to define your role. As a parent, you already play a variety of roles in raising your children, wearing different hats at different times. You may find yourself acting as mentor, chauffeur, cook, coach, mediator, or even prison warden. All of these roles require different time commitments and often even require you to acquire new skills.

When it comes to helping your teen tackle the SAT exam, you might feel confused about which role to take. Many parents find becoming involved with their teen's education a bit challenging. Teenagers can have a hard time accepting their parents as teachers. Sometimes, when parents try to teach their teen, their efforts lead to the three "F's": *failure*, *friction*, and *frustration*. When these experiences arise, parents may conclude that they have no role to play in their child's education.

Of course, nothing could be further from the truth. In fact, there are many roles parents should choose to play in helping their teens prepare for college admissions tests.

ROLES FOR PARENTS

You can play a variety of roles in helping your teen prepare for college admissions tests. In guiding your teen, you may choose to be one, or any combination, of the following:

- Buyer
- Advocate
- Supporter
- Helper
- Organizer
- Manager
- Tutor

A

The Buyer

> *"Here's the money for the SAT test-prep books you want to buy."*

This parent feels that it is the teenager's job to prepare for college admissions tests, and the parent's job is to offer financial support. The teenager is the main decision maker and is responsible for obtaining the necessary materials and services. This parental role is supportive and not too time-consuming, although it may present problems for parents who are on a tight budget.

The Advocate

> *"How does your school help juniors prepare for the SAT exam?"*

This parent believes that it is the school's job to prepare students for the test. The parent starts the ball rolling and requests information from school personnel about what services are available. The teenager may or may not be involved in this information-gathering process. Most parents feel comfortable in this role, as it requires little time and is accepted by both school personnel and teachers.

The Supporter

> *"I know it's a tough test. I see you're working hard and spending a lot of time studying for it."*

This parent believes that the teenager has the major responsibility in preparing for the test. The teenager is the decision maker, and the parent offers suggestions and support. The parent is understanding, empathetic, and non-critical. This can be a comfortable parental role since it is non-threatening to the teenager, is positive, and requires a minimal amount of time.

The Helper

> *"I picked up this SAT practice book and made a list of some tutoring courses for you."*

This parent believes that it is the parent's job to help the teenager with his plans, but that it is up to the teenager to make the final decisions. This parent helps only when asked and follows the teen's timetable when possible. This is a comfortable role since it is supportive, non-threatening, and not time-consuming. However, this role might pose problems for working parents who do not have flexible schedules.

The Organizer

> *"I've signed you up to take a test-prep course."*

This parent feels that the teenager should not be responsible for the arrangements involved in test preparation. The parent assumes a major role in establishing a timetable, finding out about resources, arranging for services, and purchasing materials. The teenager's responsibility is to follow the parent's game plan. In short, the parent provides the framework so that the teenager can spend her time preparing effectively. This role is time-consuming and parent-directed.

NOTE

Educators and legislators recognize the importance of having parents involved in their children's education. Research shows that, when they have been taught how to do it, parents can successfully teach their teens.

TIP

Remember, no single role is superior to the other. Find roles that are best suited to you and your teenager's needs.

A

The Manager

"After you study your English conventions for 30 minutes, you can use the car."

This parent believes that good intentions are not enough to make her child perform well on the SAT exam. She believes in the rule "work first, play later." Firm guidelines and consequences are established to keep the ball rolling. The degree to which the teenager is involved in planning and implementing this approach depends on a number of factors, such as the teenager's maturity and motivation.

Your comfort with this role is related to the extent to which you believe in the "work first, play later" philosophy. If you already ascribe to this rule in raising your children, extending it to SAT exam preparation will be an easy task. Patience and willingness to check on study behavior are also important factors to consider when thinking about the role of manager.

The Tutor

"I'll explain the algebra problem to you."

Parents who take on the role of tutor believe that they can work effectively with their teenager on academic subjects. These parents offer direct instruction in one or more of the test areas, such as grammar, reading comprehension, geometry, or algebra.

WHICH ROLE IS FOR YOU?

Defining your role requires two steps:

1. Collecting information about yourself
2. Using this information systematically, as you decide which role you want to take on and when

To collect information about yourself, take the following "Parent Survey."

PARENT SURVEY

	Low	Medium	High
1. How much money is available for test preparation, tutoring books, etc.?	Up to $25 for books	$25–$150 for books and tutoring	More than $150 for courses, books, etc.
2. Do you question school personnel?	Never. I feel uncomfortable.	Sometimes, if it is important.	Usually. It's my right.
3. Do you make supportive statements about academic achievements?	Not usually. I don't want to spoil my child.	Sometimes, if grades are good.	Frequently, especially about trying hard.

		Low	Medium	High
4.	What resources are available in your school or community?	I don't have the faintest idea!	I thought I saw an advertisement for an SAT course.	I know a tutor and saw an SAT book in the store.
5.	How involved do you feel?	I don't know if I should be involved.	I'll do what I can if I'm asked.	This is important! I'll help whenever I can.
6.	How much time are you willing to devote to SAT exam preparation?	1–3 hours total	1–2 hours per week	3 or more hours per week
7.	How efficient is your decision making?	It's either too slow or too hasty.	Sometimes good, but it's a tiresome process.	Usually good. I consider options and select one.
8.	Who should be the primary decision maker?	Not me. It's not my job!	I'll make decisions sometimes.	Me. I have more experience.
9.	How organized are you?	I lose papers, forget dates, and am often late.	I write schedules but forget to follow them.	A place for everything and everything in its place!
10.	How comfortable are you with your teenager?	It's tough being around my child.	Some days are good, others aren't.	Minor problems, but we get along.
11.	How firm or consistent are your limits?	No one listens to me. I nag and yell.	My children know the rules, but I forget to enforce them.	My children follow the rules.
12.	Do you have reading and math skills?	Minimal skills; low confidence.	Some skills; average confidence.	Strong skills; high confidence.
13.	How effective are you as your teen-ager's teacher?	We always end up fighting.	Sometimes it works, sometimes it doesn't.	It's not easy, but we work together.

Choosing Your Role by Interpreting Your Survey Responses

While there are no hard and fast rules to use in choosing a role, your answers to the survey questions will help you select your role in a systematic way. Using your survey responses, you can use the following guidelines to identify which roles to try first. Remember that any combination of roles is good. To help clarify:

- **The roles of buyer, advocate, and supporter** are appropriate if a majority of your answers fall in the LOW or MEDIUM columns. These roles demand the least amount of direct parent-as-teacher involvement, yet they are an important part of test preparation. Most parents can assume these roles.

- **The roles of helper, organizer, and manager** require that the majority of your answers fall in the MEDIUM or HIGH columns. These roles involve more constant and direct interaction with your teen. Some parents can assume these roles.

- **The role of tutor** is the most demanding role and requires that at least 11 out of 13 responses fall in the MEDIUM or HIGH columns. There are few parents who can comfortably and successfully assume this role.

Depending on your time and resources, you may, for example, want to begin in the advocate and supporter roles, followed by that of a buyer. If necessary, you could find someone else to act as a manager and tutor. Or, alternatively, you might find yourself best suited to being an organizer, manager, helper, and supporter right away.

BECOMING ACTIVE

Parents entrust their most valuable assets—their children—to the schools. As an investor in your child's education, you have the same concerns as any other person investing in the future. Unfortunately, sometimes parents are made to feel that the school is the "expert." In some schools, parents are viewed as meddlers if they ask for, or insist upon, information about their children's progress. As a parent, you can, and should, be involved in your teen's education, even at the secondary level. Don't be afraid to pursue information on your teen's behalf—you need to be informed, ask questions, offer suggestions, and reject suggestions if they aren't the right solutions to the problems!

HOW TO APPROACH YOUR TEENAGER

For the first time, your teen may be striving for independence and questioning himself or herself and the future. These changes may make your role as a parent additionally tough, and you may find it hard to help your teen prepare for college admissions tests. The key to reaching your teen is to focus on where he or she is academically and personally.

GETTING INFORMATION FROM DIFFERENT SOURCES

To design your SAT exam preparation plan, you'll need to get up-to-date information about your teenager from several sources, including yourself, your teenager, and the school. Your child's guidance counselor is a primary source of information, since he or she can provide information from classroom teachers and across various subject areas.

You and Your Teen

The first source of information is you. Parents must neither overestimate nor underestimate the importance of their own information about their teenager. You can be most effective if you know which questions to ask and whom to ask. You need to know about your teenager's concerns, goals, attitudes, academics, work habits, general behavior, and special strengths and weaknesses.

To initiate this step, ask your teen to meet with you for an hour to discuss college plans and how he or she feels about preparing for the SAT exam. You can begin by asking your teen for his or her opinions on matters concerning his or her education and future goals. In this first conversation, you can ask about colleges he or she is considering. Because many colleges suggest that its applicants' test scores fall within a certain range, information about the college's requirements is important. The required scores may affect the amount of time and the kind of commitment required for the test preparation.

You may also want to ask your teen to evaluate his or her study skills and the kind of study skills needed to prepare for the SAT exam. Some teenagers work effectively in groups. Others are uncomfortable or distracted when studying in a group. Students' work habits and interactions with other people also influence their attitudes toward college admissions tests and their scores. Your teenager's reaction to tests in general is an important factor to take into consideration.

Don't feel rejected if your teen says, "I don't want to meet. I know what to do." Don't push it; just try again later. The timing may be right on the second go-around.

The School

Another important source of information is the school. Guidance counselors, teachers, and others, such as coaches or band directors, can tell you about your teenager's attitudes and interactions with peers and adults outside the home. These attitudes may influence your teen's college selection and in turn lead you to the most appropriate type of preparation for the college admissions tests.

Your teen's guidance counselor can review previous standardized test scores with you and discuss differences in performance between tests and grades. Reviewing standardized test scores and grades can help you establish realistic guidelines for SAT exam preparation.

Teachers and counselors can also describe specific weaknesses that might block an otherwise solid test performance. In addition, they can offer information about your child's work habits, such as whether homework is submitted on time or how well-organized his or her papers are.

Additional Options

Independent school counselors, or educational consultants, are another alternative to consider. These types of counselors are not affiliated with a school and work as private consultants. If you lack confidence in your teen's counselor or feel that the counselor is too busy to provide the extensive work necessary for appropriate college planning, you may want to work with an educational consultant.

A private consultant may work with students from all over the United States and foreign countries. This broader perspective can provide more diverse options for your child. Many independent counselors also have firsthand experience as college admissions officers and therefore are aware of the kind of information that should be collected and ways of presenting such information to colleges.

WHAT TO ASK

The following is a list of questions you'll want to ask yourself, your teen, and school personnel or educational consultants.

Goals

- What career choices is your teen considering?
- Are there specific colleges your teen wants to attend?
- What range of SAT exam scores do those colleges require? (Or are these scores optional?)

Attitudes

- How confident is your teen about his or her ability to succeed?
- What attitude does your teen have toward school and school personnel?
- Are your teen's friends a good influence in terms of future plans?
- How helpful is the family in terms of school success?
- What is your teen's attitude toward college admissions tests?

Academics

- How has your teen done on other standardized tests?
- Do standardized test scores accurately reflect your teen's skills or abilities?
- Do your teen's grades accurately reflect his or her skills or abilities?
- What are your teen's areas of strength?
- What are your teen's areas of weakness?

Work Habits

- How effective are your teen's organizational and study skills?
- Does your teen do better with certain study procedures (e.g., in a group or listening to recorded lectures)?
- How effective are your teen's test-taking skills?
- Are there obstacles that might interfere with effective test preparation (e.g., a job or extracurricular activities)?
- Are there barriers to effective test-taking (e.g., struggles with long reading passages or not liking multiple-choice tests)?

Behavior

- To what degree does your teen need or accept help?
- To what degree is your teen a good decision maker?
- How good is your teen at self-managing or being a self-starter?
- To what degree does your teen test limits or rules?
- How well does your teen cope with stress or adversity?

NOTE

Taking the SAT exam can create a lot of stress. Excessive anxiety interferes with test performance. Collecting information from your teenager will help identify his or her problems and concerns, so you can help reduce test-prep stress.

- How well does your teen relate to school personnel and teachers?
- How well does your teen relate to peers and classmates?
- How well does your teen relate to family members?
- With whom will your teen talk about problems (e.g., a sibling or a neighbor)?

Special Issues

- Does your teen have special talents or abilities?
- Does your teen have special challenges or obstacles?
- Have special challenges or obstacles been addressed previously?
- In what way will any of these issues affect preparation for the college admissions tests?

SAT Exam

- How do students in your teen's school perform on the test?
- How did your teen perform on other college admissions tests?
- How do your teen's test scores compare with others in the class?
- What services do school personnel provide for SAT exam preparation?

By asking these questions, you can really focus on your teenager. By answering these questions now, you'll reveal information gaps, identify consistencies or inconsistencies in opinions or behaviors, highlight strengths and weaknesses, and begin your systematic plan for helping your teen.

HOW TO USE THE INFORMATION

To get the most out of the information you have collected, pay particular attention to the following issues:

- **Consistency of answers provided by each of the sources**—for example, whether the counselor's answers conflict with your teenager's answers
- **Trends that emerge**—such as better work this year or more anxiety than last year
- **Gaps in information**—such as no previous standardized test scores available
- **Strengths and weaknesses**—such as being well organized or having poor reading comprehension

YOUR TEEN'S STRENGTHS

All teenagers have strengths. However, some teenagers' strengths are more obvious than others. As a parent, your job includes the following:

- Identifying, highlighting, maintaining, and increasing existing strengths
- Providing opportunities for new strengths to develop

Strengths may be grouped into several broad categories—knowledge, work habits, attitude, behavior, and special. To help clarify:

- **Strengths in the knowledge area** include mastering basic skills, achieving good grades, and having a potential for learning.
- **Strengths in the area of work habits** include applying skills and knowledge in an organized and effective way and achieving desired goals.

- **Strengths in the area of attitude** include having clear goals, optimism, motivation, and self-confidence.
- **Strengths in the behavior category** refer to the teenager's ability to cope, follow rules, and get along with peers and adults.
- **Special strengths** may include talents in areas such as music, art, writing, or science.

Too frequently, both parents and teachers forget to focus on the positive. They zero in on the weaknesses rather than on the strengths. To avoid this common mistake, review the information you have collected and list your teen's strengths and special talents in the following chart. We'll come back to filling in the problem areas later.

Source		Knowledge	Work Habits	Attitude	Behavior	Special
Parent	Strength					
	Problem					
Teenager	Strength					
	Problem					
School	Strength					
	Problem					

Remember to discuss these strengths with your teenager, especially if he or she does not recognize his or her own strengths or talents. Building your teen's confidence is important and will pay off enormously.

IDENTIFYING SPECIFIC PROBLEM AREAS

Several kinds of problems may become obvious as you collect information about your teenager. These problem areas may be grouped into the same five categories we used to identify strengths.

Knowledge Problems

Students with knowledge problems may make statements such as "I'm not even sure about getting all the ratio and proportion problems right," or "I hate reading," or "I never do those grammar parts—I skip most of them."

Knowledge problems include the following:

- Lack of mastery of basic skills, such as arithmetic
- Lack of understanding of rules and concepts in more advanced areas, such as geometry
- Lack of experience, which leaves gaps in some areas covered on the SAT exam
- Difficulties in one or more of the following: remembering previously learned material, analyzing material, or putting information together (e.g., as in a report)

Your teenager may have a knowledge problem in only one area, which may or may not have an effect on any other area. For example, Marcus, a 10th-grader, had a reading problem, and testing showed that he read two years below his present grade level. His computation skills were good, and he did well in algebra.

A

However, word problems were his downfall. In this case, a knowledge problem in one area had an effect on another area.

Work-Habits Problems

Statements such as "I can't find my notes," "I think I left my books at school," or "I'll study later, after my favorite TV show" signal work-habits problems.

Here are a few examples of work-habits problems:

- Poor study habits
- Test anxiety
- Ineffective test-taking skills
- Lack of organization
- Difficulty estimating how long a task will take

Teenagers with work-habit problems lack the skills necessary to study effectively or to apply the knowledge they have during a testing situation. These teenagers may work too slowly and be unable to complete portions of the test, or they may work too quickly and inadvertently skip questions and make careless errors.

Attitude Problems

Students with attitude problems may make statements such as "It doesn't matter how much I study, I'll never be able to do it," or "I don't care—the SAT doesn't matter anyway."

Attitude problems involve the following:

- Unrealistic self-image and academic goals
- Over- or underestimation of the importance of the SAT exam

On the one hand, teenagers may be overly optimistic in thinking that they are smart, do not need to prepare for the SAT exam, and can get into any college on the basis of grades alone. On the other hand, teenagers may have an overly negative view of their ability and therefore avoid school, worry about grades, panic on tests, and can be difficult or quarrelsome.

Attitude problems can influence the degree to which teenagers are willing to spend time and energy preparing for the SAT exam.

Behavior Problems

Teenagers with behavior problems are likely to make statements such as "I don't have to study just because you say so," or "I know I should study, but I just can't make myself do it," or "I keep getting headaches when I think about the SAT."

The following are a few behavior problems you may encounter with your teen:

- Poor self-control
- Lack of responsible behavior
- Inability to get along with peers, adults, or family

- Drug and/or alcohol abuse
- Inability or unwillingness to follow rules and maintain commitments in school and in the community

Teenagers with behavior problems usually use ineffective ways of coping with stress, are overly dependent or rebellious, are unable to control anger, and are unwilling to face or discuss problems with adults.

Special Problems

Teenagers with special problems may make statements such as "I've always had trouble with spelling and reading," or "I know I have physical problems, but I want to try to go to college," or "I can do those questions; I just need more time."

Special problems include these conditions:

- Specific learning disabilities
- Severe physical, sensory, or emotional limitations
- Language barriers
- Disadvantaged backgrounds that may result in a lack of culturally enriching experiences

Special problems may prevent or affect your teen's ability to take the test. If your teenager is eligible, he or she may be able to take the SAT exam with certain accommodations, such as extended time. Be sure to review the options and eligibility requirements and submit an accommodations request well in advance, as it can take several weeks to be approved.

To begin designing an SAT plan, you need to review your teenager's problems. List these problems on the same chart where you have already listed the teenager's strengths. When discussing these problems with your teenager, remember to talk about his or her strengths as well.

HOW TO USE THE INFORMATION ABOUT YOUR TEEN

After collecting information about your teenager, you should summarize the information by reviewing the chart you completed. Remember that strengths, along with weaknesses, may exist in each area. Keep the following in mind as you evaluate and summarize the information you have gathered:

- The number of sources that agree or disagree
- The number of objective measures that agree or disagree, such as tests, grades, or reports
- The number of times you are aware of the strength or problem—for example, if your teenager always seems to be studying or is always complaining

WORKING WITH YOUR TEEN'S GUIDANCE COUNSELOR

Relative to college admissions tests, the counselor's role is to help students understand the nature of these tests, the benefits of study and coaching, what test to take and when, and whether to retake a test in order to achieve a higher score.

The counselor can help you and your teen summarize information about how prepared your teen is for the SAT exam and can discuss strengths and weaknesses in light of current and past test results and grades. Making an appointment with your teen's guidance counselor now will enable you to make reasonable decisions about a course of action.

A

DEVELOPING EFFECTIVE WORK HABITS

In addition to assessing knowledge of English, math, and other content areas, the SAT exam tests how well your teen takes standardized tests. Part of becoming a successful test-taker involves developing effective work habits. Developing these habits now will save your teen lots of frustration, time, and energy and will inevitably improve his or her test scores.

MANAGING TIME

Consider the following example. John is a fairly good student and earns *B*'s and *C*'s in his high school courses. He is concerned about the SAT exam and wants to do well. During a practice test, he plods through each section and spends extra time on some of the more difficult questions. He doesn't finish parts of the test. His practice SAT test scores are unnecessarily low because he didn't have time to answer all of the questions he could have easily handled. John's test behavior indicates that he needs help in work habits, especially in learning to manage his time and pace himself during the test.

When people work in factories or offices, they are usually told how much time should be spent on different tasks. This process ensures productivity, allowing workers to know what is expected of them and helping them pace themselves so that they get the most done in the least amount of time. Similarly, your teen will also benefit from learning how to manage the time he has to take the SAT exam. Before taking the tests, he or she should know the following:

- How many questions are on each section of the test
- How much time is provided for each section
- Approximately how much time can be given to each question if he or she is to complete the test and if all of the questions are of equal difficulty
- The kinds of questions that he or she can't do and should skip until completing those questions he or she can definitely answer correctly

With test-taking, managing time means that your teen can predict what he or she has to do, how long it should take, how to pace himself or herself to get the job done, and how to leave time to check his or her work. Although most testing centers have clocks, your teen should wear an approved watch during the test (and practice tests) to keep track of time and check his or her pacing.

GETTING ORGANIZED AND STICKING TO TASKS

Now consider the case of another test-taker, Emma. The following takes place in her parents' kitchen after dinner:

7:05 p.m.	"Mom, did you see my SAT practice book?"
7:10 p.m.	"Mom, I found some paper. Where are some pencils?"
7:15 p.m.	"Oh, I'd better text Liam to see if I have a ride tomorrow!"
7:20 p.m.	"What time is it?"
7:22 p.m.	"I need to get on the computer."
7:25 p.m.	"That's enough math! I think I'll do some English."
7:40 p.m.	"I hate grammar! I'll go back to math."

Emma displays several work-habits problems. One problem is that she hasn't recognized what she can't do during study time—for example, disrupting herself by sending a text message. Another problem is that Emma jumps from task to task, breaking her own concentration.

Good work habits entail being organized. Teenagers need to learn how to organize materials, list what has to be done, and specify how much time might be needed to complete each job. Study styles may differ, but teenagers must find the most effective ways to use their time and follow their own plans.

Students like Emma benefit from guidelines to follow during study time, such as the following:

- Spend at least 20–30 minutes on each activity, maintaining concentration, and building up skills.
- Stick to some basic study rules, including not avoiding work because it is too difficult or boring.
- Invoke the rule: "Work first, play later." For example, text, go online, or make phone calls only after work is completed.

Sticking to a task is an essential work habit. Unless she changes her habits, Emma will not reach the critical test-related goal: accurately completing the greatest number of problems she can within specific time limits. Emma is also operating under some misconceptions. She really believes that she is working hard and that her fatigue is a result of studying. She may also begin to think that she is not as bright as her friends because they are getting better results on practice tests. All of these potential problems can be resolved by changing her work habits.

IF IT WORKS, DON'T CHANGE IT

Another 10th-grader, Caleb, likes his comforts. He loads up on soda and chips before he settles down to work. The radio is an essential part of his lifestyle. When his mother and sisters pass by his room, they see him sprawled on his bed with a small light turned on and papers and books all over the floor. Sometimes he's sound asleep. Because he seems so casual, everybody stops by and talks to him.

Some parents might assume that the manner in which Caleb goes about studying is totally ineffective. It doesn't appear that any teenager could concentrate and maintain attention curled up in bed with music blaring, people walking in and out, poor lighting, and a nap now and then. Most parents would be right. Caleb's parents had been concerned and were annoyed by his work habits. However, Caleb earns high grades in school, and on the first SAT exam he took, he scored more than 600 on the reading and writing sections. He has also shown his parents how his speed is increasing on certain practice SAT exercises. In this case, the parents have specific information and assurance that their son's work habits work for him, despite appearing inefficient.

Your objective here is to check the effectiveness of your teenager's work habits. Consider what effect these habits have on classroom or college admissions test performance. Remember to have your teen take a practice test under actual SAT exam conditions to see how his or her work habits hold up.

A

TAMING THE PROCRASTINATOR

Procrastination is a common problem for teens. Leslie is an 11th-grader having a conversation with her father, Mr. Rand.

Mr. Rand: "Did you start to study for the SAT?"

Leslie: "No, it's in two months."

Mr. Rand: "Shouldn't you start now?"

Leslie: "I wish you would stop nagging me. I can take care of myself."

Here's another scenario, between Mrs. Sanchez and her 11th-grader, Ricky:

Mrs. Sanchez: "I haven't seen that SAT book around. Are you studying in school?"

Ricky: "I started looking at it, but it's so long I'll never get through it."

Putting off work occurs when people feel overwhelmed, don't know where to begin, feel pressured to get other things done, or are distracted by other things they would rather do. Parents who recognize this work-habit problem in their teenagers may have similar habits themselves.

Procrastination becomes a particular problem for the following reasons:

- Time is limited; when time is limited, people feel pressure.
- There can be a penalty for delay—for example, you might miss the SAT because your payment was not received on time.
- Avoiding work increases the load, rather than decreases it.

By taking into account the time available before the SAT exam and the preparation that has to be done, you can help your teenager create a sensible plan that divides one seemingly overwhelming task into smaller and more manageable ones. Predicting what has to be done, and doing those tasks one by one, gives teenagers control over feelings of being swamped and unable to cope.

A WORK-HABITS CHECKLIST

To help your teenager develop effective work habits, ask him or her questions regarding time management, materials, atmosphere, and space. You may want to use the following checklist.

Time Management

- [ ] Are there signals to others that this is a study time (e.g., a "Do Not Disturb" sign)?
- [ ] Are there rules set up for the study time (e.g., no phone calls or no visitors)?
- [ ] As a time schedule agreed upon and posted?
- [ ] Are study breaks scheduled?

Materials

- ☐ Is a clock or kitchen timer available?
- ☐ Are supplies handy (e.g., pencils, eraser, computer)?
- ☐ Does the seating encourage attention and alert behavior (e.g., a chair and a desk rather than a bed)?

Atmosphere

- ☐ Is the lighting adequate?
- ☐ Is the noise level low?
- ☐ Is the area visually nondistracting?
- ☐ Is the area well-ventilated and does it have a moderate temperature?

Space

- ☐ Is there a special place designated (e.g., desk, room, or area) for studying?
- ☐ Is this space away from the main traffic of the home?
- ☐ Is the space large enough to allow for writing?
- ☐ Is there space available for storing or filing materials?

HOW TO HELP YOUR TEEN WITH WORK HABITS

Teenagers have difficulty finding time to do homework or household chores, but they usually seem to have a lot of time to text or talk on the phone, go online, or hang out with friends. Managing time comes down to establishing priorities. Here are some guidelines that you can use to help your teenager use his or her time more effectively:

- Set a realistic study schedule that doesn't interfere too much with normal activities.
- Divide tasks into small and manageable parts.
- Use what has just been learned whenever possible—for example, open a discussion about what your teen just learned and find a real-life example.
- Find times that are best for concentration and, if possible, have your teen avoid studying at times when he or she is tired, hungry, or irritable.
- Plan a variety of study breaks, such as music or jogging, to revive concentration.
- Encourage your teenager to get a group of friends together to practice taking the exam, review test items, compare answers, and/or discuss the ways they used to solve the problems. Such a group can range in size from two to six students.

A

WHY CREATE A PLAN?

It takes more than good intentions to do well on a college admissions test. It takes time, organization, and hard work. A test-prep plan provides the means for converting good intentions into meaningful test preparation. Take note of the specifics needed for an effective plan:

- Goals
- Responsibilities of parent and teenager
- Available resources
- Schedules
- Budgets
- Instruction
- Possible problems or concerns

By clearly establishing who is responsible for what, a test-prep plan removes many sources of conflict between parent and teenager and allows each person to channel all of his or her efforts toward the goal of improving test scores.

CREATING TEST-PREP PLANS

Let's look at some step-by-step ways of creating test-prep plans and what to expect as you create a plan for your teen.

Make Time to Plan

Family life is hectic. Finding time to sit down and talk together is frequently a problem. Like a well-managed business, families with educational concerns and goals also need to have planning meetings. They need to find the time and place that will allow for discussion and working together.

Setting up a time to talk about a plan with your teen will work best if you approach him or her when he or she is most apt to be receptive. How you proceed is as important as what you do. A first step in developing a plan is to set goals.

List Goals

Goals help identify in a concrete way what you want to happen, such as your teen raising his or her verbal score by 40 to 60 points. Sometimes teenagers choose goals that are too general, such as doing geometry problems more accurately or completing the reading section more rapidly. Goals should be specific to the SAT even when they include study skills. For example, just having a goal of studying for 30 minutes a night does not guarantee improvement. The following table contains some sample goals.

TIP

Some teenagers need to review a specific skill or subject; others have problems that require intensive instruction and practice. Since each teenager is unique, each test-prep plan must be individually tailored to fit specific needs.

A

Focal Point	Goal
Accuracy	Increase the number of correct math and English test answers.
Speed	Decrease the time needed to read comprehension exercises while maintaining an understanding of what is read.
Speed and accuracy	Decrease the time needed to read comprehension exercises and increase understanding of what is read.
Quantity	Increase the number of problems tried or completed.
Frequency	Study grammar rules and do essay writing practice exercises for about 30 minutes at least three times per week.
Duration	Increase study sessions to 1 hour, adding additional practice math problems.

After outlining the goals, the next step in planning is to prepare a schedule.

Make a Schedule

A test-preparation schedule should include a timetable and weekly or daily activity lists. First make the timetable. You can use a regular calendar that covers the time between the current date and the date of the SAT exam. To make your timetable, write down all activities related to preparing for the test and the test date on the calendar.

You should also keep weekly and/or daily lists to identify specific tasks, such as the type or number of practice exercises to be completed. Such scheduling spells out the tasks ahead of time, reduces unnecessary worrying, and allows for more realistic planning. Often, teenagers become overwhelmed by the thought of all that has to be done and end up doing nothing. Writing a list and assigning times to each task tends to make these jobs more doable and more realistic.

Talk About Costs

Although you want to do everything possible for your teen's college admissions test preparation, cost is an important consideration. Most families' budgets are already strained without adding the expenses of materials, tutors, or commercial courses—especially since test preparation comes at a time when parents are trying to save money for college tuition.

Regardless of who pays the bill—the parent, the teenager, or both—budgets should be discussed. The estimated costs of various alternatives should also be outlined. Any budget limits and expected responsibilities should be proposed. By discussing these issues up front, you clarify problems and provide a realistic basis for decision making.

Find Out About Resources

Your community may have a variety of resources to help teenagers prepare for college admissions tests. However, it may take a little detective work to find them. For example, many religious groups and local organizations, such as your department of recreation,

TIP
Remember to take action in a way that is sensitive to your teen's needs and schedules.

A

senior center, or the town library, sponsor young-adult activities. These groups usually know skilled people within the community who would be willing to help teenagers study for the SAT exam. In addition, parent or community groups may also be willing to sponsor special activities if they are aware of teenagers' needs.

Match Materials to Your Teen's Goals

You and your teen should now select which books, equipment, and/or specialized materials will be used. You should match these materials to your teenager's goals. Consider drawing on information from teachers or counselors, previous standardized tests, and test-prep books that analyze the SAT exam. Material can be purchased, borrowed, or shared by several teenagers.

Locate a Tutor

In finding a tutor, you should consider someone who has experience with the college admissions tests. You may actually hire more than one tutor, since instruction may be provided by volunteers, peers, schoolteachers, or professional tutors. Discuss various tutoring options with your teen.

Find a Place to Practice and Study

Regardless of your plan's specifics, your teen needs a suitable place in which to study. Teenagers who register for courses or who receive tutoring have to practice test-taking at home, too. It is important to select a quiet study place at home or at school for SAT homework assignments or for sessions with the tutor. It is also smart to turn off phones, the TV, computers, and mobile devices to reduce interruptions and distractions while your teen is preparing for the test. Some students do well working in a library or another area set aside for quiet study.

ANTICIPATE POSSIBLE HURDLES

Some common problems that arise during the test-prep process include:

- The teenager doesn't work well with the tutor.
- The instructor gets sick.
- The study group falls apart.
- One of the parents loses a job, so money is no longer available for a commercial course.

More subtle problems can occur when:

- Teenagers set unrealistic goals and then feel tired, frustrated, and angry.
- Parents become worried that their teenager isn't making enough progress.
- Parents feel angry and disappointed when things don't work out exactly as planned.

When managing a plan, you must assume that problems will arise and that plans have to be changed to deal with these problems. Helping your teenager shift gears and learn how to make adjustments is vital preparation for the real world and a valuable skill for him or her to learn now.

WAYS TO TRACK PROGRESS

Here are some ways you can check on your teen's performance progress:

- Keep records for each study session.
- Keep track of the number of problems completed correctly.
- Keep track of how much time it takes to complete the work.
- Review the records to see if changes to the plan need to be made.
- Make sure your teen is focused on the specific test sections or questions that need special attention.

Teenagers can check on their progress in several ways. These methods include calendars, checklists, charts, and graphs. The best method is the one that your teen will regularly use.

Timing Your Comments

You should comment on performance when the progress has occurred, not a week or two later. Teenagers usually do not want anyone to know that they are studying for the tests, so it's best to comment when no one else is around. You should also be especially sensitive to how your teenager will receive any comments about his or her work. Teenagers often view these helpful hints as criticism, even when they are offered in a positive way. You may find it easier to use notes or humor as a way of making a point that can be accepted by your teen. For example, Anne's father wrote her the following note:

> Dear Anne:
>
> I see that you're keeping track of the number of problems you complete for the SAT. Looks as if you're doing at least 2–3 more problems each time—HOORAY!

FIXING PROBLEMS

When teenagers are not progressing as anticipated, parents frequently jump to conclusions and think that the teenager has done something wrong. It may appear that the teenager is lazy. In fact, he or she may just be feeling overwhelmed, confused, and exhausted. When you become aware of problems, you may need to take a second look at the situation, looking for specific performance obstacles.

Rather than blaming your teenager, or labeling his or her behavior as right or wrong, you might consider behavior in terms of its being efficient or inefficient. To help you pinpoint what's going on, you may want to ask your teenager two questions:

- How is your study schedule working?
- Are you learning what you thought you would?

Your teen can give you the information to zero in on the specific problem. Some common problems teenagers face stem from unrealistic goals, unsuitable materials, and inefficient organization.

TIP
Research suggests that tracking progress can positively influence a student's performance. Remember the days when you hung your children's drawings on the refrigerator? Recognition still goes a long way. Post progress charts where they can be seen and acknowledged.

Applying Solutions

Usually there is more than one solution for every identified problem. Here are some common SAT test-prep problems and a variety of possible solutions.

Problem:

The teen seems to give up because it appears to him or her that the material is too complicated.

Solution:

Remind the teen that habits are like muscles. The first time someone goes for a run, it may seem very difficult, but it gets easier each time the person does it. Incorporating regular study time for the SAT into the day will become easier the more the teen does it. If necessary, have the teen start small so she or he will be energized by successes.

Problem:

Progress is slower than anticipated and there isn't enough time left to reach the original goal.

Solutions:

- Lower the expectations about the scores.
- Rearrange the study schedule.
- Provide more intensive instruction.
- Schedule the test at a later date.
- Shoot for a later college admissions date.

Problem:

The teen is studying, but he or she does not remember anything the next day.

Solutions:

- Change from group to individual tutoring.
- Change from reading the information to listening to some of the information.
- Practice aloud before doing the test exercises.
- Study in a different place.
- Check that the teaching materials match the required skills. Also try to determine how the teen learns best and use the information to leverage those strengths. For example, some students remember better if they write things down by hand rather than if they type them. Other students benefit from talking out loud as they work through the steps of a difficult concept.

NOTE
Keep in mind that the idea is to study more effectively, not necessarily longer.

Problem:

The teenager is studying, but he or she seems to lose things and waste time.

Solution:

Give him or her information and techniques that will help him or her to become better organized.

Problem:

The teenager seems frantic and appears to be spending too much time studying.

Solution:

- Provide some written material that will help him or her rank what has to be done in order of importance.
- Review the goals, costs, and benefits, but keep in mind that the test is part of a larger picture.

MOTIVATING YOUR TEENAGER

Studying for the test usually isn't fun. It is hard work and teenagers need encouragement to keep going.

Sometimes teenagers are motivated because they immediately taste success. For example, Rico studied for a chemistry test and received an A. It is highly likely that he will study for the next test because he saw that his work paid off.

Checking on progress on the SAT practice tests is important. Doing so gives your teenager the opportunity to realize that his or her work does pay off and progress is being made.

Sometimes parents need to boost motivation when they see signs of fatigue or signals that their teenager is being turned off to studying. If you are trying to find ways to encourage your teenager, consider the following:

- Make positive statements, such as "I know you're working hard."
- Provide extra treats, such as a special dinner or extra use of the car.
- Leave a small, humorous gift in their room, such as a giant pencil or a silly figurine.
- Organize some special event, such as going to the movies, a concert, or out to eat with another family whose teenager is also taking the test.
- Do some chore for your teenager so that your teen has more time to study.

Setting Up Rewards

Like everyone else, not all teenagers are motivated the same way. This is why it's helpful to know as much as possible about your teen's personality. Some teens feel very comfortable with a lot of structure and being held accountable by a tutor, parent, or teacher.

TIP

Regardless of the system of rewards, remember to be positive, low-key, and avoid negative or punishing situations. The goal is to encourage and support effective studying, not to control your teenager. By establishing realistic goals and rewards, you help your teenager do his or her best and show him or her that you really care.

A

Others are fine with a lot of structure as long as the purpose behind it makes sense to them. Highly independent teens may perceive it as "being told what to do," however. Challenge teens for whom choice is essential to come up with their own plan for test preparation. These teens can be very good at "thinking outside the box" and may be more motivated by proving they can succeed doing things their way than by any other reward.

Sometimes, you need to put into practice methodical and consistent ways to make sure that plans are followed. In other words, you may need to make sure that certain events occur after, and only after, a task is completed. The following examples show how you can build in rewards for work accomplished.

- Ron tends to be forgetful. For a month, he had not done the grammar exercises he agreed to do. He and his parents worked out a plan so that if a certain number of exercises were completed on Tuesday and Thursday nights, he could have the car on Fridays.

- Diana, on the other hand, did not want the car—she loved talking on the phone. Her family devised a plan that required her to work on her writing exercises for 30 minutes, three nights a week, before she could talk on the phone.

- You can also set up a tracking system using counters such as paper clips, to record short blocks of study time—a half hour, for example. Each counter can represent something the student can use as he or she wishes. For example, each paper clip might represent a half hour that can be spent with friends or playing sports.

Research also shows that linking habits—also called anchoring or stacking habits—makes a person more likely to accomplish them. Have the student choose an activity he or she performs every day, then link a desired new habit to an existing one. For example, if Rose takes 5 minutes every night before she brushes her teeth to be sure that she's written out her study plan for the next day and gathered all the materials she will need, she's more likely to do so. The new habit, writing the study plan, is linked to an established habit, brushing her teeth.

This final list of questions is provided to help you check on your teen's progress and iron out problems. When plans are well-managed, trouble spots are easily identified and changes can usually be made without anyone feeling that he or she has failed, especially the teenager.

MANAGING YOUR PLAN: A CHECKLIST

- Is progress being checked using charts, checklists, graphs, or other means?
- Do charts or graphs show any problems?
- What adjustments are necessary?
- Have alternative solutions been considered?
- Are any additional resources or checklists necessary?
- Has progress been made toward the goals?

Originally published in a slightly different form in Parent's Guide to the SAT & ACT® (Lawrenceville, NJ: Peterson's, 2005), 27–133. Reprinted by permission of the authors.

Appendix B

Math Formulas for Memorization

NUMBERS AND OPERATIONS

Imaginary Unit, i	$i = \sqrt{-1};\ i^2 = -1;\ i^3 = -i;\ i^4 = 1$
Adding Complex Numbers	$(a + bi)(c + di) = (a + c)(b + d)i$
Subtracting Complex Numbers	$(a + bi) - (c + di) = (a - c) + (b - d)i$
Multiplying Complex Numbers	$(a + bi)(c + di) = (ac) + (adi) + (bci) + (bd)i^2$
Complex Conjugates	$(a + bi)$ and $(a - bi)$
Product of Complex Conjugates	$(a + bi)(a - bi) = a^2 + b^2$
Direct Variation	$y = ax$, where a is the constant of variation
Inverse Variation	$y = \dfrac{a}{x}$, where a is the constant of variation and a $\neq$ 0. where a is the constant of variation and $a \neq 0$.
Percent Increase	$\text{Percent Increase} = \dfrac{\text{Amount of Increase}}{\text{Original Amount}} \times 100$
Percent Decrease	$\text{Percent Decrease} = \dfrac{\text{Amount of Decrease}}{\text{Original Amount}} \times 100$

B

BASIC ALGEBRA

Rules of Exponents	$x^m \cdot x^n = x^{m+n}$
	$\dfrac{x^m}{x^n} = x^{m-n}$
	$x^{-n} = \dfrac{1}{x^n}$
	$\left(x^m\right)^n = x^{m \cdot n}$
	$x^{\frac{m}{n}} = \sqrt[n]{x^m}$
Standard Form of a Quadratic Equation	$ax^2 + bx + c = 0$
Quadratic Formula	$x = \dfrac{-b \pm \sqrt{b^2 - 4ac}}{2a}$

GEOMETRY

Convert Degrees to Radians	Multiply degree measure by
Convert Radians to Degrees	Multiply radian measure by
Area of a Rectangle	$A = bh$
Area of a Parallelogram	$A = bh$
Area of a Square	$A = s^2$
Area of a Triangle	
Area of a Trapezoid	

B

Part VIII

GEOMETRY (CONTINUED)

Length of an Arc on a Circle	Length of
Area of a Circle	
Circumference of a Circle	
Area of a Sector of a Circle	Area of sector
Length of a Chord of a Circle	Length of chord = where r represents the radius
Volume of a Right Rectangular Prism	$V = lwh$
Volume of a Cube	$V = s^3$
Volume of a Right Circular Cylinder	$V = \pi r^2 h$
Volume of a Sphere	
Volume of a Right Circular Cone	
Pythagorean Theorem	$a^2 + b^2 = c^2$, where a and b are legs of a right triangle and c is its hypotenuse
30-60-90 Right Triangle	Side length opposite the 30° angle: x Side length opposite the 60° angle: Side length opposite the right angle: $2x$
45-45-90 Right Triangle	Side lengths opposite both 45° angles: x Side length opposite the right angle:

GEOMETRY (CONTINUED)

Trigonometric Ratios	$\sin a° = \dfrac{\text{opposite}}{\text{hypotenuse}}$ $\cos a° = \dfrac{\text{adjacent}}{\text{hypotenuse}}$ $\tan a° = \dfrac{\text{opposite}}{\text{adjacent}}$
Slope of a Line	$m = \dfrac{y_2 - y_1}{x_2 - x_1}$
Standard Form of the Equation of a Circle with Center at (h, k)	$(x - h)^2 + (y - k)^2 = r^2$

FUNCTIONS AND INTERMEDIATE ALGEBRA

Vertex of a Parabola	$\left(\dfrac{-b}{2a}, f\left(\dfrac{-b}{2a} \right) \right)$
Exponential Growth Function	$f(x) = ab^x$, where $a > 0$ and $b > 1$
Exponential Decay Function	$f(x) = ab^x$, where $a > 0$ and $0 < b < 1$
Translate Parent Quadratic Function b Units Up	$y = x^2 + b$
Translate Parent Quadratic Function b Units Down	$y = x^2 - b$
Translate Parent Quadratic Function b Units Right	$y = (x - b)^2$
Translate Parent Quadratic Function b Units Left	$y = (x + b)^2$
Arithmetic Sequence	$a_n = a_1 + (n - 1)d$
Geometric Sequence	$a_n = a_1 \cdot r^{n-1}$

B

DATA ANALYSIS, STATISTICS, AND PROBABILITY

Average (Arithmetic Mean)	$\bar{x} = \dfrac{\Sigma x}{n}$
Median	Median = the middle data value in a data set listed in ascending order Arrange numbers in order from least to greatest. If n is even, the median will be the average of the two middle values. If n is odd, the median will be the middle value.
Mode	Mode = the number that occurs most frequently
Range	Range = greatest data value − least data value
Weighted Average	$\bar{x} = \dfrac{\Sigma(w \cdot x)}{\Sigma w}$, where w is the weight and x is the data value
Multiplication Rule for Independent Events	$P(A \text{ and } B) = P(A) \cdot P(B)$
Multiplication Rule for Dependent Events	$P(A \text{ and } B) = P(A) \cdot P(B \mid A)$ or $P(A \text{ and } B) = P(B) \cdot P(A \mid B)$
Conditional Probability for Independent Events	$P(A \mid B) = P(A)$ or $P(B \mid A) = P(B)$
Conditional Probability for Dependent Events	$P(A \mid B) = \dfrac{P(A \text{ and } B)}{P(B)}$ or $P(B \mid A) = \dfrac{P(A \text{ and } B)}{P(A)}$
Empirical Rule	Approximately 68% of data values fall within 1 standard deviation. Approximately 95% of data values fall within 2 standard deviations. Approximately 99.7% of data values fall within 3 standard deviations.

B